Moonbeams of Mahāmudrā

The Tsadra Foundation Series

published by Snow Lion, an imprint of Shambhala Publications

Tsadra Foundation is a U.S.-based nonprofit organization that contributes to the ongoing development of wisdom and compassion in Western minds by advancing the combined study and practice of Tibetan Buddhism.

Taking its inspiration from the nineteenth-century nonsectarian Tibetan scholar and meditation master Jamgön Kongtrül Lodrö Tayé, Tsadra Foundation is named after his hermitage in eastern Tibet, Tsadra Rinchen Drak. The foundation's various program areas reflect his values of excellence in both scholarship and contemplative practice, and the recognition of their mutual complementarity.

Tsadra Foundation envisions a flourishing community of Western contemplatives and scholar-practitioners who are fully trained in the traditions of Tibetan Buddhism. It is our conviction that, grounded in wisdom and compassion, these individuals will actively enrich the world through their openness and excellence.

This publication is a part of the Tsadra Foundation's Translation Program, which aims to make authentic and authoritative texts from the Tibetan traditions available in English. The Foundation is honored to present the work of its fellows and grantees, individuals of confirmed contemplative and intellectual integrity; however, their views do not necessarily reflect those of the Foundation.

Tsadra Foundation is delighted to collaborate with Shambhala Publications in making these important texts available in the English language.

Moonbeams of Mahāmudrā

Dakpo Tashi Namgyal

With Dispelling the Darkness of Ignorance *by*
Wangchuk Dorje, the Ninth Karmapa

TRANSLATED, ANNOTATED, AND INTRODUCED BY
Elizabeth M. Callahan

FOREWORDS BY
His Holiness the Seventeenth Karmapa
AND
Khenchen Thrangu Rinpoche

SNOW LION
BOULDER
2019

Snow Lion
An imprint of Shambhala Publications, Inc.
2129 13th Street
Boulder, Colorado 80302
www.shambhala.com

9 8 7 6 5 4 3

Printed in the United States of America

Shambhala Publications makes every effort to print on acid-free, recycled paper.

Snow Lion is distributed worldwide by Penguin Random House, Inc., and its subsidiaries.

Library of Congress Cataloging-in-Publication Data
Names: Bkra-śis-rnam-rgyal, Dwags-po Paṇ-chen, 1512 or 1513–1587, author. | Callahan, Elizabeth M., author. | Dbaṅ-phyug-rdo-rje, Karma-pa IX, 1556–approximately 1603. Phyag chen zla ba'i 'od zer. English.
Title: Moonbeams of Mahāmudrā / Dakpo Tashi Namgyal; with Dispelling the Darkness of Ignorance by Wangchuk Dorje, the Ninth Karmapa; translated, annotated, and introduced by Elizabeth M. Callahan.
Other titles: Phyag chen zla ba'i 'od zer. English
Description: First edition. | Boulder, Colorado: Snow Lion, an imprint of Shambhala Publications, Inc., 2018. | Series: The Tsadra foundation series | Includes bibliographical references and index.
Identifiers: LCCN 2017058949 | ISBN 9781559394802 (hardcover: alk. paper)
Subjects: LCSH: Meditation—Buddhism. | Śamatha (Buddhism) | Vipaśyanā (Buddhism) | Mahāmudrā (Tantric rite) | Bkra-śis-rnam-rgyal, Dwags-po Paṇ-chen, 1512 or 1513–1587. Phyag chen zla ba'i 'od zer. | Dbaṅ-phyug-rdo-rje, Karma-pa IX, 1556–approximately 1603. Phyag chen zla ba'i 'od zer.
Classification: LCC BQ5612 .B57 2018 | DDC 294.3/420423—dc23
LC record available at https://lccn.loc.gov/2017058949

The authorized representative in the EU for product safety and compliance is eucomply OÜ, Pärnu mnt 139b-14, 11317 Tallinn, Estonia, hello@eucompliancepartner.com.

For Khenchen Tsültrim Gyamtso Rinpoche:
the guru of the profound view and sublime yogic manifestation,
with gratitude

Contents

Outlines of Texts

Foreword

His Holiness the Seventeenth Karmapa

Mahāmudrā is the practice at the heart of all Kagyu traditions. Brought to Tibet directly from India by the great Kagyu forefather Marpa the Translator and practiced by his disciple Jetsun Milarepa, it then flourished under Lord Gampopa.

This practice very much emphasizes working with the mind. The stages of the mahāmudrā path in this tradition are known as the four yogas: one-pointedness, freedom from elaborations, one taste, and nonmeditation. All of the stages of the paths and bhūmis are explained through the condition of your mind. Ultimately, this brings about a direct connection between you and the nature of your mind.

This book contains fresh translations of two of the most important texts in the Kagyu mahāmudrā tradition. Although the first text, *Moonbeams of Mahāmudrā* by Dakpo Tashi Namgyal, was composed in the sixteenth century, it is still regarded as the definitive guide to mahāmudrā, providing the blueprint for the practice itself and also clearly explaining the scriptural authority and logical reasonings that support the practice.

The second text, *Dispelling the Darkness of Ignorance*, is the medium-length part of the Ninth Karmapa Wangchuk Dorje's mahāmudrā trilogy, a comprehensive text full of practical instructions which complements Tashi Namgyal's.

I should like to thank the translator, Elizabeth Callahan, who has invested so much time and effort in this work. She has researched the material extensively and has been able to draw on many years of practice under the guidance of Khenchen Tsultrim Gyamtso and Khenchen Thrangu Rinpoche.

Finally, it is important that anyone reading this text bears in mind that it is a highly regarded practice book, through which many people have attained direct realization, and, as such, is not to be treated lightly. It is my aspiration that all who read it will be inspired to follow the mahāmudrā path practiced by these great masters diligently.

Seventeenth Karmapa, Ogyen Trinley Dorje
New York
August 5, 2018

Foreword

Khenchen Thrangu Rinpoche

These days the special short path of Secret Mantra, Vajrayāna, with its unbroken continuum of instructions, is famous for mahāmudrā and dzogchen. Of those, the sacred dharma of mahāmudrā has come down through a long lineage and a short lineage.

The teacher Vajradhara taught, in general, an infinite number of *niruttara tantras and, in particular, the tantras of the ultimate essence: the *Mahāmudrā-tilaka*, the glorious *Tantra on the Unsullied*, and others. Vajradhara transmitted these teachings to the bodhisattva Ratnamati, who taught the Great Brahman Saraha, the forefather of all the mahāsiddhas in the Noble Land [India]. Saraha instructed the supreme, glorious Nāgārjuna, and the transmission continued. That is the long lineage.

The mahāsiddha Tilopa, who was beyond being an ordinary human being, went to Akaniṣṭha where he heard all the vast and profound dharma from Vajradhara himself. He proclaimed, "I, Tilopa, have no human gurus. My guru is the Omniscient One." Subsequently, Tilopa went to the great kingdom of Sahor in the east, where he taught the dharma in the middle of the city. It is said that as a result many hundreds of thousands of people went to celestial realms, leaving the city empty. There lived at that time the great ācārya Nāropa, who was learned in Sūtra, Mantra, and the sciences, who had attained the Mantra siddhis. In keeping with prophesies from the ḍākinīs, he went to the region of Sahor [to meet Tilopa]. Having pleased Tilopa with the service of twelve austerities, he received all the instructions in the manner of one vase being poured into another. That is the short lineage.

In order to bring those special esoteric instructions to Tibet, the master Marpa Lotsāwa traveled to India on three occasions where he spent a long time studying with siddha-gurus—the exalted Nāropa, Maitrīpa, and others—and practicing all their profound instructions. On his return to Tibet, he trained many students who became siddhas, such as May

[Tsönpo], Ngok [Chödor], and Ram. His most exalted student was Mila Shepa Dorje of Gungtang, who pleased the Great Lotsāwa by enthusiastically undertaking physical hardships. Milarepa received the mahāmudrā esoteric instructions on the ultimate essence and the special instructions of the profound hearing lineage. Planting the victory banner of practice, he became renowned as a great lord of yogins in the Snowy Land [Tibet].

Milarepa's numerous students who became siddhas included his sunlike heart son, the exalted Gampopa. Gampopa was an exceptional being prophesized by the Teacher, the true, perfect Buddha, in the *King of Samādhi Sūtra*, the *White Lotus of [Great] Compassion*, and elsewhere. Exhorted by an emanated form of the Exalted One [Milarepa], he went to meet Milarepa and received all his instructions. He practiced the intended meaning of the *King of Samādhi Sūtra*, which is the instructions on the ultimate essence, the sacred dharma of mahāmudrā. His disciples included both his students and the students of his students, who formed what became known as the four senior and eight junior Kagyu schools. The lord of victors, the glorious Seventh Karmapa, Chödrak Gyatso, assembled the collection called the Indian Mahāmudrā Texts, which contains the Seven Siddhi [Texts], the Sixfold Essence Cycle, and others. The Eighth Karmapa, Mikyö Dorje, wrote *Mahāmudrā: Pointing Out the Three Kāyas*. The Ninth Karmapa, Wangchuk Dorje, composed three texts—extensive, intermediate, and abbreviated—that clearly present the experiential and esoteric instructions: the *Ocean of Definitive Meaning* and the others. Among these exceptional texts of instructions, *Moonbeams of Eloquence: Clarifying the Way to Cultivate Mahāmudrā, the Definitive Meaning*, by Dakpo Rabjampa Tashi Namgyal, is of immense benefit, as his *Clarifying the Suchness of the Innate State* states:

> For great meditators within whom realization has dawned,
> this composition is an offering that inspires clarity and confidence.
>
> For lesser meditators within whom the sprouts of experiences and realizations are growing,
> this composition is a feast of certainty that severs doubts.
>
> For diligent meditation students who cling to experience,
> this composition is a gift dispelling wrong views and faulty meditation.

For renunciates who are devoid of experiences and have piled up
years of study,
this composition is a bequest for achieving virtues and the abiding
state.

Thus, this text will be very beneficial to those with meditation experiences and those without.

When the supreme victor, the Sixteenth Karmapa, Rangjung Rigpe Dorje, was turning the dharma wheel in foreign lands, his devoted students asked him what instructions should be emphasized in the present times and in their countries. His advice was that it would be excellent to translate *Moonbeams* into other languages. Accordingly, the devoted, diligent, and well-qualified lotsāwa, Elizabeth Callahan, has translated *Moonbeams of Mahāmudrā* (part of the Light Rays Trilogy) and, among the three mahāmudrā texts by the Ninth Karmapa, the middle-length *Dispelling the Darkness of Ignorance.* I am certain that the English translations of these two texts will be of immense benefit to all practitioners. May all keep them in mind.

Written by the one called Thrangu Tulku. May virtue flourish.
May 14, 2017

Translator's Introduction

Mahāmudrā is at once the nectar and fruit of the Buddhist path. It is our mind's own nature with its empty yet vivid presence. Mahāmudrā meditation instructions show us how we find that vivid empty awareness within each moment, each thought, each experience, every breath. Throughout the centuries that these instructions have been passed down from generation to generation, both orally and in written form, some written works stand out. Contained in this volume are two such texts from the Marpa Kagyu tradition. *Moonbeams of Mahāmudrā*[1] is the sixteenth-century meditation master and scholar Dakpo Tashi Namgyal's compendium on the way to realize mahāmudrā, and *Dispelling the Darkness of Ignorance*[2] is the Ninth Karmapa's middle-length meditation manual within his renowned Mahāmudrā Trilogy. Traleg Kyabgon Rinpoche captures the cherished spot these texts occupy in this tradition:

> *Moonbeams of Mahāmudrā* is one of the three most important meditation manuals of the Kagyu tradition. Together with the ninth Karmapa, Wangchuk Dorje's *Ocean of Certainty* [*Ocean of Definitive Meaning*] and *Illuminating [Dispelling] the Darkness of Ignorance*, it tells us everything we need to know about Mahāmudrā practice. This is a specific type of practice inherited from our forefathers, the mahāsiddhas of India. The mahāsiddhas were not monks and nuns but lay practitioners and very serious ones at that.[3]

All the instructions, aphorisms, advice, and techniques in these texts have but one aim: to point out mahāmudrā and show us how to see through the clouds of unknowing, nothing more, nothing less.

The term "mahāmudrā" (*phyag rgya chen po*, great seal) is used to refer both to the nature of mind and the meditation techniques for its realization. The word first appeared in the Indian tantras as part of a four-fold schema of mudrās, with mahāmudrā being the culmination of the Vajrayāna, or

Secret Mantra, path. It is also used in the tantras to mean a hand gesture or a yogic consort.[4]

As the ground, path, and result of awakening, mahāmudrā features prominently in the teachings of the yogins and yoginīs of India, starting with Saraha (circa ninth century) and followed by Tilopa, Nāropa, Śavaripa, Maitrīpa, and their students in the tenth and eleventh centuries. These were charismatic, iconoclastic individuals, who often began their paths of study and meditation in monastic centers, later setting out to meet genuine masters embodying the true import of the buddhadharma, mahāsiddhas living outside of conventional society, Buddhist or otherwise. The mahāsiddhas taught their students in ways that were sometimes provocative, sometimes subversive, controversial, and indeed often in direct contradiction to the norms of established scholastic Buddhism. Their teachings varied depending on the personalities and backgrounds of both the student and the teacher but they were always direct and tactical, challenging their students to wake up and discover their own nature. The teachings of the mahāsiddhas have been preserved primarily in shorter texts, many of which are in the form of pithy verses, songs, or *dohās,* in Sanskrit or sometimes Apabhraṃśa. Some are scholastic expositions, particularly in the case of Maitrīpa and his students.

During the second wave of the introduction of the dharma from India to Tibet in the eleventh and twelfth centuries, the Secret Mantra tantras and the mahāsiddhas' instructions were both popular, prized teachings; however, with their simplicity and literally memorable qualities, it's been the mahāsiddhas' words that have pierced the hearts and lit up the minds of each generation of mahāmudrā practitioners. The Tibetan translations of their songs, texts, and life stories[5] are found in the Tengyur and other collections, the most well-known being Saraha's Dohā Trilogy, the Eightfold Treasury of Shorter Dohās, the Seven Siddhi Texts, the Sixfold Essence Cycle, and the Dharma Cycle on Amanasikāra (Nonattention).[6] While mahāmudrā is not mentioned explicitly in all those texts, they are regarded as scriptural authorities in the indigenous Tibetan writings on mahāmudrā. This is evidenced by the frequent citation of the songs and writings of these masters—Saraha, Virūpa, Ḍombi Heruka, Tilopa, Nāropa, Śavaripa, Maitrīpa, Indrabhūti, Lakṣmīṃkarā, and others—in mahāmudrā meditation manuals as well as their inclusion in the anthology called Indian Mahāmudrā Texts compiled by the Seventh Karmapa, Chödrak Gyatso.[7]

Among the many instructions on mahāmudrā, the ones relevant here are those that Saraha[8] gave to Śavaripa, who taught Maitrīpa,[9] who then instructed Marpa Lotsāwa, the great translator and founder of the Marpa Kagyu lineage, and those that Tilopa[10] transmitted to his student Nāropa,[11] who then taught Marpa Lotsāwa.[12] An interesting side note is that Maitrīpa had other students who played significant roles in the introduction of mahāmudrā in Tibet, Atīśa being the first and Vajrapāṇi being the foremost. Atīśa was part of the early transmission of mahāmudrā in Tibet, and Vajrapāṇi, who was a major figure in the transmission of Saraha's dohās, belonged to the intermediate phase. Vajrapāṇi's lineage of mahāmudrā teachings is called the "upper translation [tradition]" (*stod 'gyur*), as distinct from the "lower translation [tradition]" (*smad 'gyur*) of his student Asu, who taught Milarepa's student Rechungpa. In this classification of transmissions, the one coming from Marpa Lotsāwa is called the "subsidiary translation [tradition]" (*zur 'gyur*), signifying that the other transmissions were more important in their day.[13]

Continuing the Kagyu Mahāmudrā narrative, Marpa's most famous student was the hermit-yogin Milarepa and the one to whom he entrusted his practice instructions.[14] Milarepa's student Gampopa[15] (1079–1153) was one of the greatest, if not the greatest, promulgators of mahāmudrā in Tibet and, in a number of ways, the forefather of *Moonbeams of Mahāmudrā*. Gampopa is credited with blending the teachings of the Kadam tradition with those he received from Milarepa, and he is said to be the first in Tibet to clearly teach mahāmudrā as a stand-alone path free of tantric underpinnings.[16] The Kadam-Kagyu syncretism came about because, before meeting Milarepa, Gampopa had trained for about five years with Kadam teachers. The Kadam teachings originated in Tibet with Atīśa, whose most influential writing, the *Lamp for the Path of Awakening*,[17] the prototype "stages of the path" (*lam rim*) text, served as a model for many similar Tibetan works. The Kadampas emphasized monasticism and the gradual Mahāyāna path, which included the cultivation of bodhicitta, Madhyamaka philosophical studies, and Vajrayāna deity yoga.

Having heard of Milarepa, Gampopa was deeply moved and drawn to train with him. During the year he spent with Milarepa, Gampopa received his key instructions on both the Vajrayāna and mahāmudrā. After practicing these under Milarepa's careful guidance, he continued to meditate in retreat for many years before he started instructing students. Gampopa settled in his later years under the mountain called Daklha Gampo in the Dakpo region of Central Tibet, where for over thirty years he taught the numerous hermit-monks and yogins who gathered around him. He appointed his elder nephew, Gomtsul, as his successor and throne-holder of Daklha Gampo, starting a hereditary abbatial succession that passed from uncle to nephew for about fifteen generations.[18] Gampopa had many gifted students who, as they began teaching, initiated the branches of what at this point may either be called the Marpa Kagyu or Dakpo Kagyu tradition.

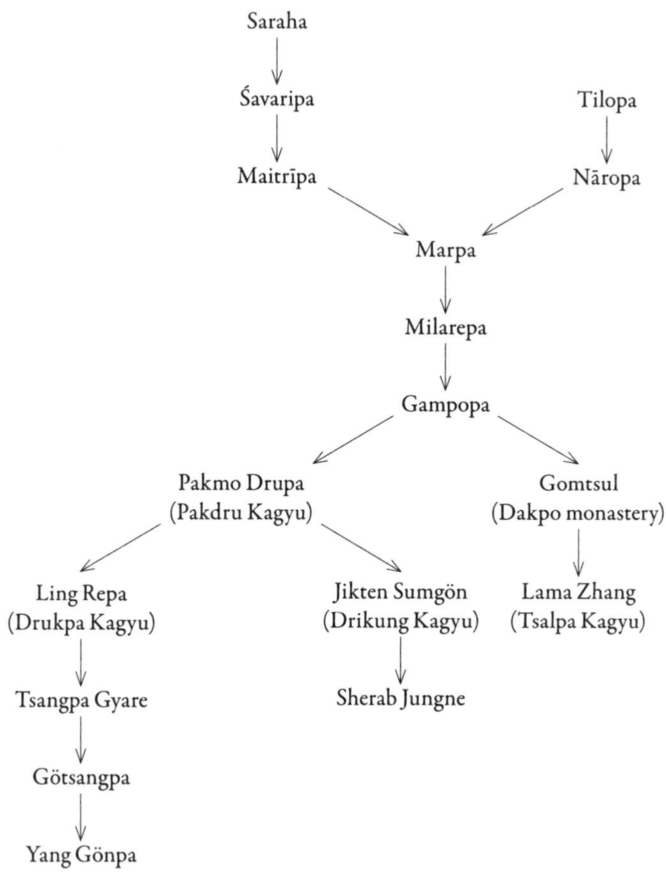

Four of Gampopa's students became the starting points of the four "senior" Kagyu sub-schools: Dusum Khyenpa began the Karma Kagyu, from Pakmo Drupa came the Pakdru Kagyu, Gomtsul and his student Lama Zhang were the originators of the Tsalpa Kagyu, and Darma Wangchuk launched the Barom Kagyu. Pakmo Drupa's eight main students established the eight "junior" sub-schools: Drikung, Drukpa, Taklung, Martsang, Yelpa, Yasang,

Tropu, and Shukseb. Of these four senior and eight junior schools, the Karma Kagyu, Drikung Kagyu, and Drukpa Kagyu have continued as independent major schools of the Dakpo Kagyu tradition. In the context of the mahāmudrā instructions contained in *Moonbeams,* the following teachers and lineages in the chart opposite are important.

Gampopa and Mahāmudrā As Path

Gampopa taught somewhat differently from his Kadam teachers and Milarepa. Marpa and Milarepa guided their students to the realization of mahāmudrā by first teaching them caṇḍālī and then mahāmudrā. Once their students had experienced the wisdom of caṇḍālī, the force of that brought forth the realization of mahāmudrā. While Gampopa did teach the same Vajrayāna path of method to certain disciples, he also taught other students mahāmudrā as a path distinct from the Mantra path and its methodology. An account of Gampopa's pedagogy is given by the fifteenth-century author of the *Blue Annals,* Gö Lotsāwa:

> The exalted Milarepa did not separate the path of method and mahāmudrā. However, [Gampopa only] gave the instructions on the path of method to those who were suitable recipients for the Mantra [path]. He gave instructions on mahāmudrā to those who were suitable recipients for the Pāramitā [approach] without bestowing abhiṣekas.
>
> He composed stages of instruction (*khrid rim*) on what is called "connate union" (*lhan cig skyes sbyor*). That is known as the dharma of realization of Dakpo [Gampopa]. Although the scriptures discuss many qualifications for gurus and students, [Gampopa] said that students don't need many: devotion alone is enough. He produced the realization of mahāmudrā without delay even in some who were dull-witted, impoverished, or evildoers.
>
> He also composed a treatise on the stages of the teachings (*bstan rim*) of the Kadam and gave many oral instructions. From then on, he was renowned for blending the two rivers of Kadam and Mahāmudrā.[19]

Gö Lotsāwa called Gampopa's second way of teaching mahāmudrā the "Pāramitā tradition,"[20] even though that doesn't exactly accord with Gampopa's own depictions. Gampopa's view of mahāmudrā as a path is summed up in his own delineations of three paths:

1. The Pāramitā path is for those of lesser abilities, who have faith and engage the path of accumulation.
2. Secret Mantra is for those of intermediate abilities, who have concepts and mental afflictions, and who engage the path of method.
3. Mahāmudrā is for those of sharpest abilities, who have prajñā and engage suchness.

And:

1. The path that utilizes inferential cognition involves analyzing phenomena in terms of being a single unit or a plurality, determining that they lack any nature, recognizing there is no other destination [or conclusion], and then meditating upon that.
2. The path that utilizes blessings purifies the channels, winds, and so forth, relying on the process of generating the deity's form.
3. The path that utilizes direct cognition is that of intrinsic mahāmudrā.[21]

Saying that mahāmudrā is for those of the highest abilities and yet teaching it to students of various capacities is not necessarily a contradiction. It indicates, as Trungram Gyaltrul Rinpoche Sherpa observes, the use of mahāmudrā in two senses:

> Mahāmudrā, [taught] without prerequisites such as initiation, thereupon became accessible to general audiences. There is a striking, paradoxical contradiction between the view that *mahāmudrā* is a insight meant for the few, and the claim that Mahāmudrā teaching is made available to the masses. This contradiction may be resolved by recognizing that the term *mahāmudrā* is here used in two distinct senses. The *mahāmudrā* of the third column [or element in Gampopa's list] has the older sense of this term: it is the realization of essence that is superior to the sutric and mantric paths. In its second sense, it consists in practical advice towards realization; it is a pedagogical system that includes many conventional Mahāyāna teachings and only culminates in the traditional *mahāmudrā*.[22]

Gampopa's dual approach to mahāmudrā gave a wider range of practitioners access to a direct, incisive, and simple path, one that Saraha calls the "path of the essence" (*snying po'i lam*). As was said, Gampopa's blend of Kagyu mahāmudrā instructions with the graduated Kadam path was a non-tantric approach to mahāmudrā, meaning that no abhiṣekas or preliminary Vajrayāna meditations were required to practice mahāmudrā. Gampopa also introduced a framework of progression: the four yogas of mahāmudrā (one-pointedness, freedom from elaborations, one taste, and nonmeditation); but he did not lay out the systematic training in śamatha and vipaśyanā that is seen in later mahāmudrā manuals, such as *Moonbeams* and *Dispelling the Darkness of Ignorance*.

By teaching mahāmudrā separate from the Vajrayāna path, it may seem that Gampopa had done something radical, something innovative with no precedence. But did he? This question does not seem to have been an issue during his lifetime or for his disciples and their students. It became one, however, when, about eighty years after Gampopa passed away, Sakya Paṇḍita famously stated that the mahāmudrā of Gampopa was not the mahāmudrā taught by Nāropa and Maitrīpa and linked it to what he called "the Dzogchen of the Chinese tradition."[23] In other words, he maintained that Gampopa's mahāmudrā was the discredited and censored "instantaneous," or "simultaneous," doctrine said to have been taught in Tibet during the eighth century by the Chinese master, Heshang Moheyan. Sakya Paṇḍita objected to mahāmudrā being taught outside of what he regarded as its only proper context: the tantric path. His perspective was that mahāmudrā is not found in the sūtras, only in Secret Mantra, and therefore it can *only* be practiced within the context of that path. By calling into question the authenticity of Gampopa's approach, he naturally provoked many responses from Kagyu scholars over the centuries, including Dakpo Tashi Namgyal in *Moonbeams*.[24]

The Repudiation of Heshang Moheyan

Some of Sakya Paṇḍita's critical remarks about Gampopa's mahāmudrā teachings hark back to the legend of the eighth-century Sino-Indian Debate at Samye monastery. The outcome of this seminal moment in the early spread of Buddhism in Tibet was to determine the direction Tibetans would follow in their adoption of Buddhism.

Briefly, according to the Tibetan accounts, during the time of King Trisong De-tsen, there was a disagreement over approach: is the path to awakening an instantaneous one or is it a gradual one? This polarity was said to be represented by the teachings of Chinese Ch'an Buddhist teachers and Indian Buddhist teachers respectively. The Chinese monk, Heshang Moheyan, had been teaching in Tibet, and it was alleged that he was promoting an instantaneous path that dispensed with the need to cultivate virtues, disregarded the principles of karmic cause and result, and only required not engaging mentally (*yid la mi byed pa*). The Indian Buddhist approach, which had been clearly laid out for Tibetans by the master Śāntarakṣita, emphasized the progressive path of the pāramitās, scholastic study and meditation, and monasticism, all leading to and culminating in the realization of wisdom. To determine which path was the authentic one, the Indian teacher Kamalaśīla was invited to Tibet to debate with Heshang Moheyan. King Trisong De-tsen served as arbiter and, in the end, when Heshang Moheyan admitted defeat, Kamalaśīla was declared the winner, the Indian gradualist approach became the royally sanctioned Buddhism of Tibet, and Heshang Moheyan was expelled from Tibet.[25]

This story has been repeated throughout the centuries in Tibetan histories, all of which can be, more or less, traced back to the *Testimony of the Ba [Clan]*,[26] the first narrative of the debate in Tibetan sources. While that purports to be an eyewitness-account, it did not actually appear until sometime in the eleventh or twelfth century. It's worth mentioning that earlier documents do not substantiate the *Testimony*'s version of events. For example, the ninth-to-tenth-century Nyingma author Nubchen Sangye Yeshe's *Lamp for the Eyes of Meditative Concentration* includes the instantaneous approach as the second of four stages of the path.[27] And, according to a manuscript found at Dunhuang written by Moheyan's student Wangxi, the debate was conducted through an exchange of letters, and Heshang Moheyan's teachings were declared genuine by the king.[28]

Despite those differing accounts, the *Testimony*'s portrayal of the outcome of the debate has been used to substantiate the claim that India was (and is) the *only* valid source of Buddhism for Tibetans and that anything other than a gradualist approach may very well involve straying into "Heshang-style meditation"—regardless of whether the instructions originated with authentic Indian teachers or not. The *Testimony* set the stage for subsequent polemical writings, as we see when Sakya Paṇḍita criticizes Gampopa's Mahāmudrā approach by saying, "The present-day Mahāmudrā is for the most part a Chinese dharma tradition."[29] Then, about three hundred years later, in *Moonbeams* Tashi Namgyal rebukes Sakya Paṇḍita and defends the Dakpo Kagyu Mahāmudrā system by listing how it differs from the Heshang system, point by point.[30]

Non-tantric Mahāmudrā: Who Started It?

Gampopa himself did not use the term "Sūtra Mahāmudrā" (*mdo lugs phyag rgya chen po*) or say that he taught "Sūtra Mahāmudrā," even though he *is* said to have taught a Sūtra- or Pāramitā-based mahāmudrā in addition to mahāmudrā as part of a Vajrayāna path, as we have seen above. Regardless of whether the non-Vajrayāna mahāmudrā that Gampopa taught to certain students consists of a third path (neither Sūtra nor Mantra) or is Sūtra Mahāmudrā, was Sakya Paṇḍita right that it was not the mahāmudrā taught by Nāropa and Maitrīpa? For answers, we can look briefly at what may have been part of the mahāmudrā transmission that Gampopa relied upon. Besides the teachings he received from Kadam masters and Milarepa, Gampopa is said to have named specific texts as relevant for his mahāmudrā teachings. In *Replies to the Exalted Pakmo Drupa's Questions,* when asked which mahāmudrā texts conclusively explain dharmatā and mind-itself, Gampopa says:

> The texts that teach mahāmudrā are the dohās, the three new cycles, and so forth.[31]

The dohās referred to are most likely Saraha's dohās, though they could certainly include those by Tilopa and others. The three new cycles (*gsar ma skor gsum*) are the Seven Siddhi Texts, the Sixfold Essence Cycle, and the Dharma Cycle on Amanasikāra (Nonattention), the latter being a collection of texts by Maitrīpa. In that reply Gampopa identifies one textual link between his mahāmudrā teachings and the transmission of mahāmudrā from Saraha through Śavaripa, Maitrīpa, Marpa, and Milarepa. Another link between Gampopa's mahāmudrā teachings and Maitrīpa is the statement attributed to Gampopa in Gö Lotsāwa's *Blue Annals* reportedly made to Pakmo Drupa: that the basis for his mahāmudrā was the *Highest Continuum* (*Uttaratantra*). Gö Lotsāwa also cites a text by Maitrīpa's student Sahajavajra and another by Jñānakīrti as evidence that mahāmudrā was taught within a Sūtra (or Pāramitā) context in India.[32] Klaus-Dieter Mathes, who has done extensive research into this question of an Indian precedence for Sūtra Mahāmudrā, concludes:

> It could be shown that both Sahajavajra's *Tattvadaśakaṭīkā* and Jñānakīrti's *Tattvāvatāra* contain not-specifically-Tantric *mahāmudrā* teachings which are a synthesis of the Tantric element of directly realising emptiness or reality in a non-analytical way with general Mahāyāna or Pāramitāyāna. Our study of the *Tattvadaśakaṭīkā* has shown that no Tantric empowerment or such skillful means as great bliss are required by this type of *mahāmudrā*, which merely depends on the pith-instructions of one's guru. . . .
>
> By arguing that *mahāmudrā* is just another name for Prajñāpāramitā and for what is intended by the word 'Mahāyāna' in *Laṅkāvatārasūtra* X.257d, Jñānakīrti tried to link non-Tantric *mahāmudrā* meditation with the Sūtras, wherefore it should no longer be maintained that not-specifically-Tantric *mahāmudrā* is a later Tibetan invention. The label '*sūtra mahāmudrā*' (Tib. *mdo lugs phyag rgya chen po*) came into use only later in Tibet, however. Even though it cannot be ruled out that the *mahāmudrā* practices of the Kagyupas inherited Ch'an elements from early Sino-Tibetan traditions, it should be noted that *sūtra*-based *mahāmudrā* teachings have Indian roots which can be clearly identified. To sum up, the blending of the Sūtras with the Tantras is something that definitely started in India and not in Tibet.[33]

Although more study needs to be done of Gampopa's Collected Works, his life and times, and other transmissions of mahāmudrā in India and Tibet, it is becoming clear that, while he may have done some things differently than his teachers, Gampopa did not teach in an unprecedented way and did not teach a mahāmudrā that was different from that taught by Maitrīpa and his students. Gampopa, therefore, did not teach a mahāmudrā that "is for the most part a Chinese dharma tradition."[34]

Dakpo Tashi Namgyal: Times and Sources

Dakpo Tashi Namgyal (1513–1587) composed and compiled his instructions for the cultivation of mahāmudrā, *Moonbeams of Mahāmudrā*, in an Ox Year, either 1565 or 1577, a little over four hundred years after Gampopa passed away.

Tashi Namgyal lived during a period when, broadly speaking, the Kagyu, Nyingma, Sakya, and Geluk monasteries coexisted on more or less equal terms with varying degrees of uneasiness, rivalry, political flare-ups, and wars between them, alongside dialogue, debate, and intellectual cross-fertilization. There had been and would be greater turmoil and changing fortunes for certain monasteries depending on who dominated the political sphere but, during Tashi Namgyal's lifetime, the Geluk school, founded by Tsongkhapa (1357–1419), did not yet control the religious-political world of central Tibet. Its control of secular and religious affairs would not happen until the 1640s when, aided by Mongolian troops, the Fifth Dalai Lama was installed as both the spiritual and political ruler. The period following that saw the suppression, and in some cases conversions and destruction, of non-Geluk monasteries in central Tibet.[35]

Overall, the fifteenth and sixteenth centuries were a time when the individual lineages were consolidating their teachings, setting them out in relation to each other, and situating them within their transmitted doctrine. Major commentarial literature was being written: tomes were composed on philosophy, epistemology, abhidharma, vinaya, tantra, history, stages of the path, and, of course, stages of meditation. Although many conditions facilitated this, there were two important developments related to books. First, during the fourteenth and fifteenth centuries, the Tibetan translations of the sūtras and tantras were organized into the collection called the Kangyur (bKa' 'gyur, "Translated Word") and the Tibetan translations of the Indian commentarial literature into the collection called the Tengyur (bsTan 'gyur, "Translated Treatises"). The second development was the introduction of xylograph (woodblock) printing.

Xylograph printing developed in China during the seventh century and made its way slowly across central Asia. It was widely used in China by the eleventh century, but it was not until the early part of the fifteenth century that it became a more commonly adopted method for printing Tibetan texts.[36] This new technology enabled monasteries to print large collections of texts, such as the Kangyur and Tengyur and multivolume collected works of individual authors, and make them available in an unprecedented way. Prior to that, the only option was to copy books by hand.

Thus, at the same time that the great scholars and lineage holders were writing to define, clarify, and elaborate their approaches to the view and the path, they had greater access to the works of previous masters of their own and other lineages. This presumably enabled them to draw on the earlier texts with more ease and weave them into new compositions, as we will see in looking at the possible sources for Tashi Namgyal's *Moonbeams*.

Tashi Namgyal was heir to Gampopa's teachings—as the first recognized incarnation of Gampopa, as his distant relative, and as the seventeenth throne-holder of his monastery. He grew up and trained under the guidance of his uncle, Gampo Chöje Sönam Lhundrup (1488–1552), the sixteenth throne-holder of Dakpo monastery.[37] As his biography recounts, Tashi Namgyal studied and read widely when he was young. His primary teachers were Karma Tinle, Khenchen Shākya Zangpo of Daklha Gampo monastery, and his uncle, Sönam Lhundrup. His uncle is cited as the main one who transmitted mahāmudrā instructions to him, and it was under his tutelage that Tashi Namgyal came to realize the teachings of Gampopa. During his early twenties, Tashi Namgyal practiced meditation in retreat for about six years, which culminated in his realization of the nature of ordinary mind and the equal taste of all phenomena. After that he said he had "no attainment or loss, no fluctuations in his spiritual practice."[38] During his retreat period he also studied all the books contained in the monastery's library, which included the Collected Works of Gampopa, Indian Mahāmudrā Texts, and the Book of Kadam. From then on, he spent much of his life in retreat, interspersed with periods of teaching and creating the circumstances for others to practice dharma.

These days, Dakpo Tashi Namgyal is best known for his Light Rays Trilogy: *Sunrays*[39] (a commentary on the *Hevajra Tantra*), *Jewel-Light Rays*[40] (a commentary on Vajrayāna), and *Moonbeams of Mahāmudrā*. Two of his shorter works are also well known: *Clarifying the Suchness of the Innate State*[41] (an abbreviated version of *Moonbeams*) and *Clarifying the Suchness of the Great Secret*[42] (an abbreviated version of *Jewel-Light Rays*), both of which have been translated into English. Because Tashi Namgyal does not provide the element associated with the year for his compositions, his writings cannot be precisely dated (we can only assign them to two or three possible dates in the twelve-year Tibetan cycles) and, therefore, a chronology cannot be established at this point. However, since it is only within the last fifteen years that we have had access to a biography for Dakpo Tashi Namgyal, it is possible that more historical records will appear that will enable us to date and order his writings.

In recent times, this Dakpo Tashi Namgyal, the author of *Moonbeams*, has been confused with Dakpo Paṇchen Tashi Namgyal of Nālendra monastery.[43] Since almost nothing has been written in English about this Tashi Namgyal's life, and his biography seems little known even among Tibetans, a translation of his biography follows this introduction.[44]

Moonbeams of Mahāmudrā

Dakpo Tashi Namgyal combined numerous sources and instructions on mahāmudrā and śamatha and vipaśyanā meditation to create this comprehensive guidebook to the cultivation of mahāmudrā. Although it hasn't been possible to identify all the sources he used, at the moment it seems we can say that the following are relevant to the composition of *Moonbeams*:

- Collected Works of Gampopa.[45] The texts included in this collection are for the most part not authored by Gampopa but are records of his oral teachings written down by his students and, in some instances, by students of subsequent generations. The first xylograph printing was made in 1520 under the direction of Tashi Namgyal's uncle, Sönam Lhundrup, and includes his biography of Gampopa, *The Flag of Renown*.[46]
- Indian Mahāmudrā Texts.[47] Compiled by the Seventh Karmapa, Chödrak Gyatso, (1454–1506). This collection contains the Seven Siddhi Texts, the Sixfold Essence Cycle, and the twenty-four texts in the Dharma Cycle on Amanasikāra (Nonattention).
- Collected Works of Pakmo Drupa and Jikten Sumgön. These may have been available to Dakpo Tashi Namgyal in the Drikung Kagyu Treasury of Dharma,[48] compiled by the sixteenth Drikung throne-holder, Kunga Rinchen (1475–1527).
- Collected Works of the Drukpa Kagyu masters Tsangpa Gyare, Götsangpa, and Yang Gönpa.
- Gö Lotsāwa's *Mirror Illuminating Suchness: A Commentary on the "Highest Continuum."*[49]
- Tsongkhapa's *Great Treatise on the Stages of the Path to Awakening*.[50]

Moonbeams of Mahāmudrā is called a *gom rim* (*sgom rim*), "stages of meditation" or "approach to meditation" text, which makes it part of the genre of "stages" texts, the others being *lam rim*, "stages of the path," and *ten rim* (*bstan rim*), "stages of the doctrine."[51] These works discuss a graduated series of topics that lead the practitioner towards the goal of awakening. In the case of this *gom rim*, since Dakpo Tashi Namgyal's stated aim is to guide us towards realizing mahāmudrā, the nature of mind (*sems don*), he begins by discussing why we should meditate on the nature of mind. This is followed by the presentation of the process of meditation, divided into two main sections: the common samādhis and the uncommon mahāmudrā.[52]

Part 1, Common Samādhis, provides the basis for the following section (part 2), Uncommon Mahāmudrā. The Sūtra-based śamatha and vipaśyanā presented in part 1 are not actual Mahāmudrā śamatha and vipaśyanā; they serve as what might be called the preliminaries or general training for mahāmudrā meditation. Many of the topics covered in part 1—mindfulness (*dran pa*) and alertness (*shes bzhin*), the identification of flaws in meditation, and the remedies for those flaws—are found in part 2, and the reader is often referred back to part 1. Overall, there is a fugue-like interplay between the two parts and the various chapters. While it may be tempting to skip to the parts we find most inviting, the later sections presume familiarity with the earlier ones.

Part 1 has been divided into four chapters. Chapter 1 is on śamatha and vipaśyanā together; chapter 2, śamatha; chapter 3, vipaśyanā; and chapter 4, removing doubts. They all include extensive citations from texts found in the Kangyur and Tengyur; however, based on the textual variations between the *Moonbeams* citations and the Tibetan translations preserved in the Kangyur and Tengyur, it seems that Tashi Namgyal turned not to the Kangyur and Tengyur for his citations but to the works of previous Tibetan authors. The two likely sources are Gampopa's Collected Works—particularly his *Sunrays of Scriptural Citations*[53] and *Ornament of Precious Liberation*[54]—and Tsongkhapa's *Great Treatise*.

Of the approximately 237 canonical citations in part 1, 110 are found in the *Great Treatise* (and not in Gampopa's Collected Works), 41 are found in Gampopa's Collected Works (and not in the *Great Treatise*), 12 are found in both, and 70 are not found in either.[55] While it is possible that Dakpo Tashi Namgyal drew directly from canonical literature or from authors other than Tsongkhapa, a close reading of the *Great Treatise* reveals similarities to part 1 of *Moonbeams* that go beyond shared citations: they range from topics to outline headings to whole sentences or paragraphs. Some details of these similarities are found in the endnotes.

Another thread running throughout *Moonbeams* is that, sporadically, Tashi Namgyal frames uncertainties we may have in the form of questions or addresses misunderstandings held by others. Some of the latter are identifiable as being positions held by Tsongkhapa and his followers, though Tashi Namgyal always refers to Tsongkhapa as a "certain person" or "certain scholar." He quotes Sakya Paṇḍita directly (but never identifies him by name), and then refutes him systematically. All of this gives the impression that he is at times in a dialogue with Tsongkhapa and Sakya Paṇḍita—and also with us, his target audience.

Chapter 1, "Śamatha and Vipaśyanā," opens with a brief discussion about how śamatha and vipaśyanā contain all forms of samādhi, from those practiced in the Hīnayāna and Mahāyāna through Secret Mantra and Mahāmudrā. Then, the question is asked, How is it that śamatha and vipaśyanā include all those samādhis? The reply contains definitions of śamatha and vipaśyanā that are used throughout the text. Simply put, śamatha is when the mind engages one-pointedly with its object of meditation, and vipaśyanā is when prajñā is aware of the nature of that object. The chapter continues with a list of the causes for śamatha, which are related to location, state of mind, and conduct; and the causes of vipaśyanā, which are related to the qualities necessary in teachers and the need for study. It identifies the five obscurations and five faults we experience in samādhi and their remedies, focusing particularly on the primary obscurations: dullness and agitation. Of the remedies, the most important mental skill to develop is that of mindfulness. While there are many uses and understandings of mindfulness (particularly recently), one of the most common definitions in Buddhist texts is the one Asaṅga provides in his *Compendium of Abhidharma*:

> [Mindfulness] is not forgetting a familiar object. Its function is to be undistracted.[56]

Mindfulness is paired with alertness, which is the quality of mind that recognizes dullness or agitation. It is also said that when mindfulness is fully present, alertness is as well. In the section called "The Analysis of the Order of Śamatha and Vipaśyanā," Tashi Namgyal refutes the idea that vipaśyanā can only be undertaken when meditation practitioners have achieved suppleness in śamatha. In "The Way to Unify Śamatha and Vipaśyanā," he explains why śamatha is not only a nonconceptual meditation and vipaśyanā is not only a conceptual meditation.

Chapter 2, "Śamatha," presents four objects of meditation: universal objects of meditation, objects of meditation for purifying previous behavior, objects of meditation for expertise, and the objects of meditation for purifying mental afflictions. It discusses the initial objects of meditation, the role of mindfulness and alertness, the well-known nine stages for achieving mental stillness, and how those are cultivated with the eight applications, the six strengths, and four types of attention.[57]

Chapter 3, "Vipaśyanā," starts by providing various characterizations of vipaśyanā. These are followed by a discussion of the view, or understanding, we need for practicing vipaśyanā: that there is no truly existent self of persons or self-entity of phenomena. The chapter guides us in identifying the correct view and how to apply that during both meditative equipoise and postmeditative attainment.

Chapter 4, "Removing Doubts," begins with descriptions of analytical meditation and resting meditation, then discusses their roles in śamatha and vipaśyanā and in the context of the view. Having possibly drawn from Tsongkhapa's *Great Treatise* during chapters 1 through 3, in this chapter, Tashi Namgyal sets out how the Dakpo Kagyu approach differs from that of Tsongkhapa and his followers. In "Analyzing Other Systems," he starts with brief dismissals of some views purportedly held by earlier and later Tibetan scholars, and then turns to four assertions that Tsongkhapa lists and refutes in the *Great Treatise*, giving his own assessment of Tsongkhapa's refutations. Next he gives a long rebuttal to what he says is the position of Tsongkhapa and his followers: that once we have identified the view, we must then generate strong certainty about the emptiness that is the emptiness of inherent nature, the emptiness of any reality. In a nutshell, Tashi Namgyal considers this approach flawed because it involves clinging to the absence of reality or emptiness. He again disputes that śamatha is only nonconceptual and vipaśyanā only conceptual, and does not accept that all forms of meditation on nonconceptuality stray into being the repudiated Heshang-style meditation. The chapter and part 1 close with "Establishing Our Own System." This is presented in terms of what ordinary practitioners can do, not from the perspective of those who directly realize emptiness, something only possible for those dwelling on the bhūmis. Tashi Namgyal says, "The most important thing is to discover the view of emptiness, regardless of how we do that, whether it be by using analytical meditation or through resting meditation."[58] Discerning prajñā must be employed to discover the view yet, in the end, that very prajñā disappears and mind rests without elaborations.

Part 2, "Uncommon Mahāmudrā," is the longer section of the book and has been divided into eleven chapters.

Chapter 5, "Generating Confidence," focuses on developing confidence in the dharma, or topic, of mahāmudrā and in the transmitters of that dharma. It begins by discussing the term "mahāmudrā" and its divisions (ground, path, and fruition), and then looks at how it is presented in the sūtras and tantras. In "The Way the Expositions of Three and Four Mudrās Are Taught," Tashi Namgyal addresses one of Sakya Paṇḍita's critical remarks about the mahāmudrā taught by Gampopa and his followers. After "The Way the Uncommon Mahāmudrā Is Taught," he again turns to rebutting any notion that meditation on abiding-state mahāmudrā is similar to a Heshang-style meditation, doing so in a thorough way.

In "How [Mahāmudrā] Is the Profound Point of the Sūtras and Tantras," Tashi Namgyal presents different ways the path of Mahāmudrā is viewed: When the path is only divided into Sūtra and Mantra, it is considered to be Mantra. In the Secret Conduct Collection's[59] three-yāna system of the Philosophical Pāramitāyāna, Secret Mantra Vajrayāna, and the Yāna of the Unsurpassed Essence, the path of Mahāmudrā is the latter. He mentions Saraha's reference to a "path of the essence" as being a short path and outlines Gampopa's categorizations of three types of paths, where the Mahāmudrā path is the one that utilizes direct cognition, recognizes the bases, and is for those of sharpest abilities. The chapter closes with an account of how the mahāmudrā instructions were transmitted in India through the actual lineage and in Tibet through the practice lineage.

Chapter 6, "Preliminaries," looks at what we need as a basis. This is first considered from the perspective of the general approach to the path (turning our mind from saṃsāra, seeking liberation, and so on). Then Tashi Namgyal talks about Gampopa's presentation of mahāmudrā as a short path that does not incorporate elements of Secret Mantra practice. If that is the path we practice, he says:

> Those of highest abilities, who are instantaneous types, first investigate the view and then are given the esoteric instructions on the methods for resting evenly right within the view. This is similar to the guidance given these days according to the Four Syllables of Mahāmudrā. Those of lesser abilities, who are gradual types, are guided through śamatha, then gradually through vipaśyanā. This is similar to the guidance given nowadays according to the Instructions on Connate Union.[60]

After Gampopa, Tashi Namgyal says, teachers in the Kagyu traditions combined mahāmudrā instructions with aspects of Secret Mantra and, if that is the path we follow, it is necessary to receive abhiṣeka as part of our preliminaries. Probably following what had become common practice, the fourfold preliminary practices are presented as the contemplation of impermanence, taking refuge and arousing bodhicitta, offering maṇḍalas, Vajrasattva meditation, and guru yoga. Chapter 4 closes with advice applicable to all of our spiritual practices: training in the five qualities conducive to liberation, how to begin and end meditation sessions, and how to conduct ourselves between sessions. It offers a much-repeated gem of advice: keep meditation sessions short and repeat them often.

Chapter 7, "Mahāmudrā Approaches," is a short introduction to how the Mahāmudrā path is practiced by the instantaneous and the gradual types. After giving a brief historical overview of which teachers taught for which type, Tashi Namgyal addresses those who maintain that meditation on the true nature must be based only on the explanations found in the Sūtra-oriented texts, something asserted by those who are critics of the esoteric instructions of the mahāsiddhas. He concludes by describing the approach he takes in *Moonbeams*:

> This Dakpo practice lineage contains both instructional traditions: One is taught for the instantaneous type, who first eliminate their misinterpretations concerning the ground and root and are then taught the techniques for resting in that [ground]. The other is provided for the gradual type, who first pursue mental stillness and then are led to vipaśyanā gradually. Although these days most people, being of the type that has a very clear and active mind, would at this point be more appropriately guided according to the first approach, here I will give the explanation according to the latter approach in consideration of what is better known at the moment.[61]

Chapter 8, "Śamatha," begins with topics already discussed in chapters 1 and 6, and continues with an explanation of the seven-point posture for meditation. The objects of meditation used for the practice of śamatha here are categorized under the headings "The Objects of Meditation Involving Characteristics" and "Śamatha without Characteristics."[62] The first are further divided into those with supports and those without supports.

Objects of meditation involving characteristics and supports include using ordinary, or impure, objects (a pebble, a twig, and the like) and pure objects, such as the image of the Buddha. Tashi Namgyal explains that either is suitable since both can help us develop mental stillness. Objects of meditation involving characteristics without supports are either the breath or not using any reference point at all. In "Śamatha without Characteristics," Tashi Namgyal discusses the key techniques of tightening and relaxing and the roles of mindfulness and alertness, along with much practical advice. The last sections of this chapter describe the way to achieve mental stillness through the nine stages in conjunction with the six strengths and four types of attention. Tashi Namgyal explains that, in this practice tradition, mental stillness is the foundation for vipaśyanā meditation. Therefore, simply being able to maintain stillness either effortlessly or with just a small amount of effort is sufficient for the purposes of this context (in other words, achieving śamatha suppleness is not a requirement for vipaśyanā). Throughout the śamatha section, we are reminded to keep our sessions short, how to use the techniques to achieve mental stillness, and how to identify its development.

Chapter 9, "Vipaśyanā," states that the Mahāmudrā vipaśyanā of the Kagyu follows the instructions of Saraha, Śavaripa, and Tilopa, as well as such Sūtra-oriented texts as Ratnākaraśānti's *Instructions on Prajñāpāramitā,* Kamalaśīla's three *Stages of Meditation*, and Atīśa's *Instructions on Madhyamaka*. In brief: Mahāmudrā vipaśyanā is meditation on the essence of mind, the means by which the nature of percepts and perceivers is seen and direct perception is taken as the path. Throughout this chapter, Tashi Namgyal situates this system within the larger context of the Mahāyāna by quoting from the aforementioned texts and from sūtras and tantras.

Here, the vipaśyanā instructions are divided into two main sections: "Determining the Essence of Mind and Its Various Appearances" and "Eliminating Misinterpretations About a Root or Basis." In the first section, mind, thoughts, and appearances are analyzed to determine their shape and color, abode and support, and then their identity and manifestation. This leads us to the recognition that mind and its radiance lack any nature. Although thoughts are mental appearances, and all manifestations of mind are considered appearances, here thoughts and appearances are examined separately. Appearances, what appear to the six modes of consciousness, are not broken down into increasingly smaller particles and then determined to lack any nature. Instead, it is the mind perceiving those appearances that is analyzed because, once the nature of mind is determined, "the fetters of perceived objects are self-liberated." He also makes a point here that sums up the view of the Dakpo Kagyu approach to mahāmudrā meditation:

> In some instructional traditions the various ways to investigate the mind are only methods that lead to a nonconceptual mind with its clarity-awareness. They do not examine and analyze [mind] right with its movements and appearances. These can be seen as somewhat rudimentary because their practice causes most types of minds to be comfortable meditating when the mind is still but to be uncomfortable meditating with its movements and appearances.[63]

In "Eliminating Misinterpretations About a Root or Basis," the origin, abiding, and departure of mind, thoughts, and appearances are analyzed, leading us to the recognition that thoughts and appearances are inseparable from the essence of mind. Then, the stillness and movement of mind-itself are examined so that we see they are identical in essence and just discrete isolates or facets. Finally, we are led to conclude that everything that seems to arise is unborn. Tashi Namgyal says, "Through such analysis you will experience the abiding state of mind, which is beyond conception and description. In the end, even discernment, which is what does the analyzing, will be self-pacified, dissolving into itself. Nonconceptual wisdom will dawn."[64] Towards the end of the chapter, Tashi Namgyal discusses what we should expect of our vipaśyanā practice, which includes the following:

> What are the criteria for determining whether vipaśyanā has developed or not? Genuine vipaśyanā, which directly realizes the truth of dharmatā, does not arise before the level of greater freedom from elaborations. Here [we are discussing] only the vipaśyanā that occurs within the sphere of ordinary beings' minds . . . Therefore, in this context what must be considered vipaśyanā is an awareness of the key point that our own mind, and thoughts and appearances, which arise as its expressive power (as discussed above)—in brief, all phenomena, what are perceived and are perceivers—are ultimately without arising, cessation, or abiding. It is also to discover from within experience, and with certainty, that all such phenomena lack any essence or nature.[65]

He also distinguishes this vipaśyanā approach from that of the Sūtra approach:

> The sequence of how [the nature of] objects and perceiving subjects are determined is different. In the Sūtra context, it is taught that without first determining [the nature of] objects (what are perceived), [the nature of] the mind (the perceiving subject) will not be determined... Here it is thought that approaching it that way makes determining [the nature of] the perceiving mind later on much harder, whereas determining the perceiving mind first makes it easy to determine perceived objects—it will be as if they are self-liberating.[66]

Chapter 10, "Pointing-Out Instructions," starts with a presentation of what we are to ascertain: the abiding state of mind and connateness. The description of the abiding state of mind is based on the records of Gampopa's teachings on the essence, nature, and characteristic of mind. While all three are simply different terms used for the same intrinsic essence of mind, they point to its different facets, as Gampopa says:

> ... The essence [of mind] is that it is clear yet nonconceptual. Its nature is that it is free from arising, abiding, and ceasing. Its characteristic is that it appears as both saṃsāra and nirvāṇa.[67]

In "Ascertaining Connateness," it is said that the essence of connateness is natural luminosity. "Connate" (*sahaja, lhan cig skyes pa*) means that all phenomena and their nature are "present simultaneously from the beginning with neither preceding or following the other."[68] Connateness is typically classified as ground, path, and fruition but, in this context, the divisions used are those made by Gampopa: the connateness of mind-itself and the connateness of appearances. These are augmented by Gomchung's split of the latter into the connateness of appearances and the connateness of thoughts. A short mention is made of "connate union," a term used by Gampopa to refer to the practice of uniting mind-itself (dharmatā or emptiness) with its display (awareness, clarity, thoughts, or appearances). Since Gampopa says that this is what he practiced, the term seems to have originated with him, and it is used later in the Dakpo Kagyu traditions to refer to his style of mahāmudrā instruction.[69]

Next, this chapter provides the actual pointing out of connateness in three sections: pointing out the connateness of mind-itself, of thoughts, and of appearances. In each instance, it provides instructions that combine śamatha and vipaśyanā. In "Pointing Out the Connateness of Thoughts," Tashi Namgyal corrects misunderstandings about the meaning of "thoughts are dharmakāya" and takes issue with Sakya Paṇḍita's adherence to "the tenet of the inseparability of saṃsāra and nirvāṇa while being an adversary of the expressions 'thoughts are dharmakāya' and 'delusion arises as wisdom.'"[70]

The last part of chapter 10 is devoted to how to eliminate problems in meditation and identify flawless meditation. The first subsection contains advice relating to various types of śamatha and vipaśyanā experiences we may have, and includes the following observations from Gampopa:

> During stillness, nonconceptuality is prolonged. If you prolong nonconceptuality as the essence [of mind], you do not understand the key point of the dharma.[71]

And:

> Some regard blocking every thought as it arises and resting with the mind wrapped up in nonconceptuality as a positive thing. That cannot serve as the path. It will cripple wisdom.[72]

Chapter 10's "The Identification of Flawless Meditation" is a three-part discussion of ordinary mind. It states first that ordinary mind means the natural mind, the naturally luminous mind; second, that it is uncontrived; and third, that recognizing ordinary mind and sustaining that in meditation is mahāmudrā meditation.

Chapter 11, "Sustaining Mahāmudrā," again focuses on the role of mindfulness and alertness, and includes conscientiousness (*bag yod*) this time, but, as always, the greatest emphasis is placed on mindfulness. Up to this point the discussions of mindfulness have emphasized its function of not forgetting the object of meditation and maintaining an undistracted mind. Now the understanding of mindfulness is expanded, starting with it being the state of mind that takes up virtue. The *Sūtra of the Teaching of Akṣayamati* describes the mindfulness that is part of the path to awakening:

> What is true mindfulness on the path to awakening? It is the mindfulness that realizes phenomena. It is what discerns phenomena. It is that which analyzes phenomena. It accompanies phenomena. It reflects upon phenomena. It considers phenomena. That mindfulness realizes the characteristics belonging to each and every phenomenon.[73]

The *Compendium of Dharma Sūtra* presents the bodhisattvas' foundation of mindfulness:

> Child of good family, what is the bodhisattvas' foundation of mindfulness? What is mindfulness? What is the abode of mindfulness? I will answer those questions. Child of good family, mindfulness is the bodhisattvas' recognition that phenomena are unborn. Bodhisattvas have the aspiration to know the unborn. Their mindfulness is fully trained through their recognition of the unborn. Always imperturbable, their mindfulness is unwavering. Its depth and limits are unfathomable.[74]

Tashi Namgyal next outlines four types of mindfulness, which progress from the mindfulness involving effort to effortless mindfulness. He then takes up the question of the meaning of nonmindfulness (*dran pa med pa*) and nonattention, or lack of mental engagement (*yid byed med pa*), and gives a brief synopsis: "nonmindfulness and nonattention refer to sustaining the stream of nonconceptual wisdom that is discovered through first analyzing with prajñā."[75]

Next, meditative equipoise and postmeditative attainment are identified based on the words of Zhang Rinpoche:

> Resting in unceasing empty clarity,
> vibrant and crisp without center or edge,
> like the middle of clear open space,
> is the meditative equipoise of the first yoga.
>
> When a thought appears within that,
> even if you are meditating on your cushion, that is postmeditative attainment.
> If you remain in vibrant, crisp clarity-emptiness

> while talking, moving, or sitting around,
> you remain in a state of meditative equipoise.[76]

This is followed by some famous pithy advice on the ways to sustain mahāmudrā meditation, including Gampopa's three skills, Tilopa's six ways to rest, and Gampopa's four methods: remain relaxed, rest in freshness, rest freely, and rest loosely. Tashi Namgyal sums these up saying, "no matter how long we are able to sustain meditative equipoise, the point is that we need to bring out clarity-awareness right within the essence of mind and have the quality of stillness that is not distracted from that."[77] The next instructions are not to meditate with mental formulations—in other words, not meditate on anything—and to sustain that without being distracted. Nonmeditation and nondistraction sum up all the previous methods and contain both śamatha and vipaśyanā. As Tashi Namgyal says:

> Leaving the mind in its natural condition without meditating is śamatha. Not being distracted from the nature [of mind] is vipaśyanā. Nonmeditation and nondistraction becoming of equal taste contains all the points related to unifying śamatha and vipaśyanā.[78]

Chapter 11's "The Methods for Sustaining Postmeditative Attainment" begins by discussing (once again) mindfulness and alertness. Here the emphasis is primarily on the experience of the connateness of mind-itself but with a slightly different orientation. Now "it's not that the manifestations of thoughts or appearances are rounded up and then stopped or made to vanish as if we are narrowing in on the essence [of mind] . . . Be mindful [aware], without grasping, that all thoughts are empty movements and all appearances are empty appearances." This section also contains instructions for taking thoughts as the path and experiencing the postmeditative state as illusionlike. The first are instructions Gampopa received from his Kadampa teacher Geshe Chakri on three ways to incorporate thoughts into the path: as the impact of meeting, as the aftereffect, and as nonexistent fantasies. In "The Way Postmeditative Attainment Manifests as Illusionlike," Tashi Namgyal clarifies the meaning of "illusionlike" and of the sayings "sustain the mind naturally settled without contrivance" and "sustain the mind experiencing unsettling circumstances without altering it," by both pointing out wrong understandings and correct ones. He explains the way to mix meditative equipoise with postmeditative attainment and how that occurs on all levels of the four yogas (one-pointedness and the others).

Chapter 12, "Eliminating Deviations and Strayings," addresses how to eliminate deviations, strayings, and hindrances in meditation. There are four deviations in relation to emptiness, which have two modes each: a fundamental deviation and a temporary deviation. The four are deviating from emptiness as the basic nature of knowable objects, as the path, as the remedy, and as the seal. Straying occurs in relation to the three types of experiences—bliss (or pleasure), clarity, and nonconceptuality—if we fixate on them. As Tashi Namgyal says:

> Most experiences, which are part of bliss, clarity, and nonconceptuality, become strayings due to the following circumstances. When we aren't certain that all those experiences are free from an essence that arises or ceases, that they have no nature that can be identified, and that they are unborn emptiness, we go astray by reifying, or taking to be real, those meditative experiences that, born of latent tendencies, arise as mere conventionalities through the interdependence of the channels, winds, and bindus in the body. Therefore, we should sustain [our meditation] with the continuous mindfulness that ascertains everything to be unborn, without the clinging that reifies. By doing so we will keep from straying.[79]

Chapter 12 concludes with brief sections on clearing away the general hindrances for samādhi (dullness and agitation)—referring us back to chapter 1's more extensive discussion—and on clearing away outer and inner hindrances.

Chapter 13, "Enhancement," has two parts: "Breaking Through to the Unborn Transparency [of Mind]" and "Refinement through the Conducts for Path Integration." "Breakthrough" (*la bzla*) is a term defined in a Mahāyāna context as "reaching a conclusion"; however, here it means "to have cut through conceptual elaborations about your own mind (such as that it arises, abides, or ceases, or that it has three periods of time) and to have reached the conclusion that it is a great unborn transparency (*zang thal chen po*)."[80] This discussion and the accompanying instructions follow the previous chapters because of the timing of breakthroughs, as Tashi Namgyal says:

> [Breakthroughs are] when, as practitioners, we have purified stagnate experiences of bliss, clarity, or nonconceptuality, and we arouse brilliant clarity in our awareness. Then, meditation on spacelike clarity-emptiness is an unbroken flow. Or, that experience [of spacelike clarity-emptiness] is an unbroken flow even with the allure of daytime appearances . . . . In brief, when all thoughts are empty clarity and appearances are empty appearances, and we experience all as illusionlike with decisive certainty, that is a breakthrough.[81]

In this context, direct yogic perception is needed and misinterpretations are to be cut through experientially. Thoughts, appearances, the object of meditation, and the meditator are examined in ways that are similar to what was presented in the previous sections on vipaśyanā and pointing out the connateness of thoughts and appearances. We are urged to not only have conclusive certainty about the essence of each, but also to destroy any clinging we might have to that certainty. Specific instructions are given on how to cultivate a breakthrough in "The Actual Breakthrough to the Unborn Transparency [of Mind]," the achievement of which is described by Tashi Namgyal as follows:

> Your attachments to good experiences or grasping at joyful sensations will unravel. Your clinging to negative, confused thoughts as problems and your annoyance with them will subside. Whatever ordinary state of mind you have, or arises, or manifests, it is of the nature of meditation, an expression of emptiness . . . [W]hen all the appearances of the world arise as objects for the mind, they are self-arising, self-occurring. When they subside, they are self-pacifying, self-liberating. This is the unrivaled, single transparent state. Everything is of the nature of meditation. Meditation is a constant flow; meditation never goes away.[82]

This is followed by a series of quotations, which begins with Saraha:

> Mind in its essence is free from faults and virtues.
> That state needs no actions at all.
> The mind that's let go of actions is sublime great bliss.[83]

And ends with several quotations from Gampopa, such as these:

> First, since mind-itself does not exist,
> who recognizes the wisdom of stillness and movement?
> Thus, all that has been done and is being done
> is merely the difficult task of farming in space.[84]

And:

> When you realize there is no mind, appearances are set free.
> When you don't evaluate, thoughts arise and release.
> When you don't have ambitions, everything is equal.
> When you realize that, your meditation is continuous.[85]

"Refinement through the Conducts that Integrate [All Experiences] into the Path" begins with an explanation of the timing, necessity, and purpose of using different types of conduct, or behavior, as a way to refine our experience of mahāmudrā. Instructions are given for how to integrate our normal, deluded thoughts into the path instead of allowing them to pull us into confusion. Specifically, there are six contexts for applying the instructions: with thoughts, mental afflictions, god-demons, suffering, illness, and death.

Chapter 14, "Realization and the Four Yogas," describes how realizations of mahāmudrā will develop using the framework of the four yogas: one-pointedness, freedom from elaborations, one taste, and nonmeditation. It outlines this according to whether we are the instantaneous, bypassing, or gradual type, and then explains the differences between understanding, experience, and realization. Tashi Namgyal provides citations from the *Descent into Laṅkā Sūtra* and elsewhere to demonstrate that descriptions of the four yogas are found in the sūtras and tantras, while also saying that they are a dharma of realization (*rtogs chos*) of Gampopa. He credits Gampopa with "categorizing precisely the experiences and realizations of each of the four yogas and their gradations, and . . . laying these out in a way that is easy to understand even for practitioners these days."[86] Gampopa's explanations of the four yogas are preserved in the writings of his students, such as Gomtsul, Gomchung, and Pakmo Drupa, and their students, Tsangpa Gyare, Zhang Rinpoche, and others. Tashi Namgyal draws on their works to look at the four yogas in terms of their distinctive realizations, range of experiences, meditative equipoise, postmeditative attainment, time, and other features.

Chapter 15, "The Four Yogas in Detail," is drawn from, or resembles, texts by Pakmo Drupa, Jikten Sumgön, Tsangpa Gyare, and Yang Gönpa.[87] Each of the four yogas can be divided into lesser, intermediate, and greater levels, making twelve. Tashi Namgyal comments that they are not, however, like rungs of a ladder: we may find that even when we haven't perfected the greater level of a particular yoga, we may develop the lesser or intermediate level of the next yoga. Each of the four yogas is discussed in terms of its divisions, the way experiences arise, and the methods for sustaining those.

In the sections on their divisions, Tashi Namgyal defines each one, describes its subdivisions, and applies six criteria used by Tsangpa Gyare to determine whether the realization of the respective yoga has developed or not: whether the essence has been seen, mastery has been achieved, thoughts arise as meditation, excellent qualities have developed, there is proficiency with the conventional, and the seeds for the rūpakāyas have been planted. The sections on how experiences arise and the methods for sustaining those offer close-up descriptions and practical instructions.

The conclusion of *Moonbeams*, "How the Bhūmis and Paths Are Traversed through Those [Four Yogas]," comes under the heading "The Way Realization Develops through Sustaining Meditation," which began in chapter 14. Tashi Namgyal notes that Gampopa and his nephews, Gomtsul and Gomchung, did not explicitly teach a correspondence between the four yogas of meditation and the bhūmis and paths; therefore, he refers to correlations provided by Zhang Rinpoche, Tsangpa Gyare, and Götsangpa, and then gives his own "rough correlation." Tashi Namgyal sums this up by saying that "the excellent qualities of the bhūmis taught in the philosophical yānas are intentionally ambiguous" and are not clear indicators of a particular stage of the path.[88] Therefore, it isn't possible to identify the attainment of a meditator solely based on externally evident signs. With that, the presentation of the stages of meditation on mahāmudrā, the abiding state, is completed.

Moonbeams is a tapestry woven with the threads of the instructions of the Indian mahāsiddhas and early Dakpo Kagyu masters, especially Gampopa. The rich display of the resulting work has also provided the starting threads for other compositions and teachings. Sections of *Moonbeams* are incorporated into the Third Khamtrul Rinpoche's *Unsurpassable Complete Path,*[89] Karma Tashi Chöpel's catalog (*dkar chag*) to the Palpung edition of Indian Mahāmudrā Texts,[90] and Jamgön Kongtrul's *Treasury of Knowledge: Foundations of Study and Practice*,[91] to name a few. Smaller parts have been incorporated into many texts, both within the Kagyu tradition and without, for example, Jigme Lingpa's *Lion's Roar* and *White Lotus*.[92] Undoubtedly, more will be identified as we have greater access to Tibetan texts in searchable digitized forms or in translation. The tapestry continues to supply threads of instruction for contemporary Kagyu masters' teachings, some of which have been published as books.[93] Lhalungpa's translation of *Moonbeams* aided Western scholars' knowledge of Tashi Namgyal's mahāmudrā presentation and his rebuttal of Sakya Paṇḍita's criticisms of Kagyu Mahāmudrā.[94] *Moonbeams* is also part of the curriculum in contemporary Karma Kagyu and Drikung Kagyu monastic colleges. But primarily it is a text for meditators: its instructions are to be internalized through practice. And so it is hoped that this new translation will allow the brilliance of *Moonbeams* to reach English readers, and that they will pair its breadth and depth with the more concise, session-based approach of the Ninth Karmapa's *Dispelling the Darkness of Ignorance*.

The Ninth Karmapa's *Dispelling the Darkness of Ignorance*

Wangchuk Dorje, the Ninth Karmapa, (1556–1601/1603) is renowned for his Mahāmudrā Trilogy: *Ocean of Definitive Meaning*,[95] *Dispelling the Darkness of Ignorance*, and *Pointing Out the Dharmakāya*.[96] He also made an important contribution to Karma Kagyu scholarship by arranging abbreviated versions of the Eighth Karmapa's lengthy commentaries on the *Entrance to the Middle Way*[97] and the *Treasury of Abhidharma*,[98] as well as composing other works on Vajrayāna practice and philosophical topics.

The texts in Wangchuk Dorje's Mahāmudrā Trilogy are called extensive, middle-length, and abbreviated, even though the middle-length one, *Dispelling the Darkness of Ignorance*, is only slightly longer than the one designated as abbreviated, *Pointing Out the Dharmakāya*. (In the edition used for preparing this English translation of *Dispelling the Darkness of Ignorance*, this middle-length text is only five pages longer than the abbreviated one.) Since Wangchuk Dorje did not provide dates for his mahāmudrā compositions, we do not know the order in which they were written. They are very similar topically and structurally and can be used as complimentary instruction manuals. All three texts are divided into numbered sections designed to be progressive meditation sessions (*dmigs pa*), and all three include remarks specifically aimed at teachers. Additionally, the *Ocean of Definitive Meaning* contains teaching sessions (*chos thun*), some of which contain questions that teachers should ask their students. Overall, they are extremely useful texts for those giving mahāmudrā instructions and for those practicing mahāmudrā meditation. It should be mentioned that in the Karma Kagyu Mahāmudrā tradition, a text is never considered a sufficient starting place—practitioners are always introduced to mahāmudrā by a qualified teacher, someone who can transmit the experiences and realizations of mahāmudrā, the nature of mind. Texts provide supports and guides to the both the teacher and the practitioner. Then, as a practitioner matures, texts serve as "the guru in the form of the words of the Sugata," one of four gurus described by Wangchuk Dorje.[99]

Dispelling the Darkness of Ignorance begins with the four preliminaries: taking refuge and arousing bodhicitta, Vajrasattva meditation, maṇḍala offering, and guru yoga; and the four contemplations: on death and impermanence, karma, the deficiencies of saṃsāra, and the opportunities of a human life. It is followed by brief sections on the four conditions for mahāmudrā practice: weariness with saṃsāra as the causal condition, reliance on a genuine spiritual mentor as the dominant condition, certainty in the natural state of dharmatā as the object condition, and being free from hopes and fears as the immediate condition.

The main practice is divided into eight sessions on śamatha and eight sessions on vipaśyanā. The śamatha instructions include a description of the posture for meditation and ways to cultivate śamatha using a variety of focal supports, using no supports, or relying on the breath. This is followed by the techniques for counteracting dullness and agitation, and the section closes with a description of authentic śamatha.

The instructions for vipaśyanā are grouped into two sets of four ways to develop recognition. First there are four instructions for looking: at stillness, movement, appearances and the body, and stillness and movement. Then there are four pointing-out instructions: in relation to stillness, nonconceptuality and conceptuality, appearances and the body, and stillness and movement.

The final section of the text, the Conclusion, covers enhancement; the five mistaken ideas, three skills, and three kāyas; three strayings and four deviations; five difficult passages and three hindrances; and the development of virtues and progression on the path.

Stylistically, *Dispelling the Darkness of Ignorance* is somewhat less formally written than *Moonbeams* and has almost no citations or general observations. It speaks more directly to how we implement mahāmudrā instructions during meditation sessions. *Moonbeams* addresses aspects of practice that are either not mentioned at all in Wangchuk Dorje's Mahāmudrā Trilogy or it discusses them in more detail. Taken together, the two texts compliment each other well.

A Word to the Readers

Mahāmudrā instructions are meant to be given gradually in accordance with a practitioner's development. In the case of texts, they are meant to be read slowly, preferably with the guidance of an experienced teacher. Those who have received a lot of mahāmudrā instruction may not find much that is new here but this massive amount of magnificent instruction and advice is best digested slowly and experientially. Those who are new to mahāmudrā practice should also proceed slowly, gradually absorbing the advice and approach. And we should all probably circle around again, reread and reabsorb.

This translation is dedicated to all who amble along the Mahāmudrā path: may it be the right companion.

Acknowledgments

My profound thanks to my teachers: Khenchen Tsültrim Gyamtso Rinpoche and Khenchen Thrangu Rinpoche. Thrangu Rinpoche, who set me on my way as a Buddhist practitioner many decades ago, kindly suggested that translating *Moonbeams* would be a good project for me to undertake. I have benefited enormously and I thank him for that. Whatever I have understood of mahāmudrā instructions that has enabled me to undertake this translation is primarily due to the impeccable guidance and teachings I received from Khenchen Tsültrim Gyamtso Rinpoche over many decades. Along the way I have received instructions and assistance from other great masters and friends: Khenchen Thrangu Rinpoche, the late Kalu Rinpoche, the late Tenga Rinpoche, Ringu Tulku Rinpoche, Dzogchen Ponlop Rinpoche, Sangye Nyenpa Rinpoche, Ācārya Lama Tenpa Gyaltsen, Druppön Khenpo Lodro Namgyal, and Khenpo Ugyen Tenzin, all of whom contributed, directly or indirectly, to this translation. Ringu Tulku Rinpoche and

Ācārya Lama Tenpa Gyaltsen were especially helpful and generous with their time in answering the seemingly endless questions of a translator.

I am grateful for the prior publications of translations of *Moonbeams* by Traleg Kyabgon Rinpoche and Lobsang Lhalungpa, and Alexander Berzin's translation of *Dispelling the Darkness of Ignorance*, entitled *The Mahāmudrā: Eliminating the Darkness of Ignorance*. The pioneering translations by Lobsang Lhalungpa and Alexander Berzin have provided us with access to these two mahāmudrā texts in English for decades, and Traleg Kyabgon Rinpoche's book is an insightful, illuminating presentation of *Moonbeams*, a record of a mahāmudrā master's teachings through translation.

It would not have been possible to complete this translation in the manner that I did without the Buddhist Digital Resource Center (BDRC, previously known as Tibetan Buddhist Resource Center) or the Buddhist Canons Research Database, a project of the American Institute of Buddhist Studies (AIBS) and the Columbia University Center for Buddhist Studies (CCBS). A special thanks to Paul Hackett and his team for their Research Database—an amazing resource, which came online just in time for this translation to benefit.

Many thanks to Karma Lekshey Ling for its digital downloads, and to Khenpo Namgyal and Khenpo Tengye for sharing digital inputs of the Tibetan text of *Moonbeams*. Another special thanks to Sean Price of Tsadra Foundation and Khenpo Shedup Tenzin for making available various digital inputs of collected works at just the right moment. I'm very grateful for all the support that Tsadra Foundation provides for our translation work: thank you Drupgyu (Tony) Chapman and Christiane Buchet for friendship and advice; and thank you Marcus Perman, Jeremi Plazas, Laura Goetz, and Aric Parker, the Digital Research Center team, for all kinds of timely help. My thanks to Christian Charrier, Karl Brunnhölzl, Thupten Jinpa, Yeshe Gyamtso (Peter O'Hearn), Klaus-Dieter Mathes, Sarah Harding, Peter Roberts, and Gerardo Abboud for assisting me in various ways. To all the translators and scholars, Tibetan and English-speaking, who have gone before, whose skill and erudition I've relied on, knowingly and unknowingly, I thank you. More thanks to my Ocean friends who beta-tested sections of the translation in a weekly discussion group—any lack of improvements to the translation are my fault alone. Thank you to Steve Tibbetts for his editorial skills, rhythm, encouragement, and carrying on the exacting tradition of Olive Colón; and to Casey Kemp of Shambhala Publications for her care, precision, and perseverance in editing this manuscript.

And most of all my deepest thanks to Eric Colombel of Tsadra Foundation for vision, friendship, and support. This work could not happen without such commitment.

TECHNICAL NOTES

The preparation of the translations contained in this volume relied upon the following editions of texts:

Moonbeams of Mahāmudrā (*Phyag chen zla ba'i 'od zer*)

Primary edition: Varanasi: Vajra Vidya Institute Library, 2005.[100]
Consulted editions:

- Bir, India: D. Tsondu Senghe, The Bir Tibetan Society, 1978. Reproduced Dvags lha sgam po blocks, from the library of rTogs ldan Rin po che of sGang sngon Monastery, Ladakh. BDRC W4CZ15298.
- In the rTsibs ri'i par ma (dKar rnying gi skyes chen du ma'i phyag rdzogs kyi gdams ngag gnad bsdus nyer mkho rin po che'i gter mdzod), vol. 3. Darjeeling: Kargyu Sungrab Nyamso Khang, 1978–1985. BDRC W20749.
- Rigpe Dorje Practice Series, vol. 13. Kalimpong, India: Rigpe Dorje Publications, 2010.[101]
- Delhi: Drikung Kagyu Publications, 2004. BDRC W29341.
- Karma Lekshey Ling. Digital edition.[102]
- mDo khams sde dge: dPal spungs dgon pa, n.d. BDRC W3CN631.

Dispelling the Darkness of Ignorance (*Ma rig mun sel*)

Primary edition: Rigpe Dorje Practice Series, vol. 10, 303–40. Kalimpong: Rigpe Dorje Publications. 2010.
Consulted editions:

- In Nges don phyag rgya chen po'i khrid mdzod, vol. 10, 39–83. New Delhi: rNam par rgyal ba dpal zhwa dmar ba'i chos sde, 1997. BDRC W23447.
- In Collection of Commentaries from Newly Printed Old Text at Palpung (dPal spungs dpe rnying gsar bskrun las khrid yig phyogs

bsgrigs), vol. 4, 375–420. Upper Bhattu, India: dPal spungs gsung rab nyams gso khang, 2006. BDRC W1KG4336.

- In *Phyag chen rgyas pa/ nges don rgya mtsho/ phyag chen 'bring po/ ma rig mun sel/ phyag chen bsdus pa/ chos sku mdzub tshugs*, 215–50. Varanasi: Vajra Vidya Institute Library, 2006.
- Karma Lekshey Ling. Digital edition.[103]

An Abbreviated Biography of Dakpo Tashi Namgyal (*Dvags po bkra shis rnam par rgyal ba'i rnam thar mdor bsdus*)

Primary edition: With *Phyag rgya chen po'i sgom rim gsal bar byed pa legs bshad zla ba'i 'od zer*, iii–xxxiv. Delhi: Drikung Kagyu Publications, 2004. BDRC W29341.

Consulted editions:

- A probable Daklha Gampo edition (date and publication information unknown). BDRC W00EGS1016800.
- In the Drikung Kagyu Great Treasury of Dharma, vol. 76, 341–585. Lhasa: n.a., 2004. BDRC W00JW501203.

An Abbreviated Biography of Dakpo Tashi Namgyal is extracted from the *Garland of Vaiḍūrya: An Account of the Holy Hereditary Throne-Holders [of the Seat] of the Glorious Gampopa, Regent of the Teacher in This Snowy Land*.[104]

In each translation the small numbers embedded in square brackets are references to the page numbers of the primary editions used.[105]

The endnotes primarily contain textual variants between the primary and consulted editions, textual variants between the source Tibetan texts and citations, and citation references. An attempt has been made to note all obvious or important textual variants but some may have escaped notice. To identify the sources of Kangyur and Tengyur citations, the Buddhist Canons Research Database has been used along with its linked Asian Classics Inputs Project (ACIP) e-texts (hence the use of the Lhasa Kangyur and the Derge Tengyur for page referents). When citations are noted as not found, there is still the possibility that they are in the cited text but were not located due to textual variants or the shortcomings of the searcher.

For citations and references to the Collected Works of Gampopa,

Karma Lekshey Ling's digital edition was used.[106] This edition is based on the 2000 Kathmandu publication by Khenpo Shedup Tenzin and Lama Thinley Namgyal, which in turn seems to be based on the Derge xylograph edition (BDRC W22393).[107] Since the Lekshey Ling edition is a digital file and its pagination is changeable, the folio numbers that are included in the electronic text are provided, which correspond to the Derge edition. For citations and references to the Collected Works of Pakmo Drupa and the Collected Works of Götsangpa, I primarily relied on searchable digital files and, except for the few instances when I referred to BDRC files, was not able to give page and line references.

In the main body of the translations, a Tibetan phonetic system is used; see "Table of Tibetan Transliterations" for the correlation between the phonetic spelling and Wylie transliteration. Also, Sanskrit diacritics are used (readers should note that ṛ is pronounced *ree*, c is similar to *ch* in *chill*, and ś and ṣ are similar to the English unvoiced *sh*). In the endnotes, bibliographies, and glossaries, Wylie transliteration is used for Tibetan, with the modification that the head letter is capitalized in proper nouns and text titles. Any hypothetically reconstructed Sanskrit from Tibetan is preceded by an asterisk. Throughout the translations, any text in brackets has been added by the translator.

The "Glossary," "Glossary of Enumerations," and "Translation Equivalents" are provided to allow the translations of the mahāmudrā texts to be unencumbered with notations and yet give readers with less familiarity with these topics some additional information and those who read Tibetan access to some of the choices made in these translations. Given the sophistication of these texts and their instructions, it is not possible to clarify all points in glossaries or provide biographical information for all the Indian and Tibetan masters cited. Some informative notes have been given for the translation of Dakpo Tashi Namgyal's biography but a full annotation of his biography, identifying all persons, places, practices, and objects, is beyond the scope of this work.

An Abbreviated Biography of Dakpo Tashi Namgyal

Dharma King of the Three Realms, an Emanation of the Great, Incomparable Gampopa

[1b] Here is a brief account of the story of the incomparable Dakpo [Gampopa's] manifestation, the one who performed singularly great deeds at the [Daklha Gampo] monastic seat, the dharma king of the three realms: Tashi Namgyal.

In the *Proclamation of Samaya*, a treasure of prophesies revealed to Dechen Lingpa,[108] Padmasambhava, omniscient one of the three times, declares:

> An emanation of Candraprabha Kumāra
> will appear in the actual location.
> His name will be Tashi and Gyal ["Auspiciousness" and "Victory"]
> and he will bestow happiness.[109]

Tashi Namgyal was also prophesized in many treasure [texts], such as those of Rigdzin Gödem, Sangye Lingpa, and Zhigpo Lingpa.[110] When the omniscient, exalted Gampopa, who was repeatedly praised in prophesies by the Victor, sang his song called "*Sho mo*! Come back up!" to the three men of Kham, he also predicted, "When a tree bearing fruit grows from under this boulder, my emanation will appear here."[111] [2a]

The activities of this holy being will be presented in six parts.

Part 1: Birth in a Family Lineage of Siddhas

Tashi Namgyal's father, Dedak Chenmo Chöwang,[112] belonged to the family lineage of the nephews of the exalted Dakpo [Gampopa]. Due to the ripening of the results of previously accumulated [merit], he was someone with grace and good fortune. He benefited the teachings with the estate lands and harvests of Zhol-teng Sarma. He practiced the instructions "joining lion and tiger face-to-face,"[113] and devoted himself to [the practice of] Object Severance on a Single Seat[114] for a long time. He performed many acts of a siddha, such as extracting a large quantity of gold from a boulder near the bank of the Jorpu river. [2b] Tashi Namgyal's mother, Rigdzin Drolma, had all the signs of a ḍākinī. She was the sister of the famous Daktong Gyalpo, who belonged to the filial lineage of Lama Sangye Drumpa, a descendant of Datong Chewa. She spent her time doing virtuous deeds; in particular, she observed the lay precepts[115] during the holy days and took White Tārā and Green Tārā as her yidams.

Tashi Namgyal was born to these parents on the eighth day of the third Tibetan lunar month in the Female Water Bird Year [1513], called "Śrīmukha,"[116] in the garden of Len-me Gyalwa, the source of all pleasures, amidst a rain of flowers and the thunder of dragons. He was given the name Dönyö Gyatso. At that time, an apricot [appeared on a tree] growing near a rock with the footprints [left by Gampopa and his disciples]. His mother then bathed and nurtured him.

Part 2: Nonsectarian Studies [3a]

First, as he heard his mother reciting refuge prayers, Praises of Gampopa, the Ten Deeds [of the Buddha], and other chants, he learned them spontaneously and would recite with her. Until the age of five or six, he stayed in his parents' home, learning to read at the same time as playing children's games.

At the age of seven, he went to Gampo monastery to stay with his uncle [Gampo Chöje Sönam Lhundrup].[117] He memorized the *Name-Chanting of Mañjuśrī*,[118] Vajravidāraṇā, Vajravārāhī, Hevajra, and reparation and restoration [liturgies]. He also mastered the ability to write the different scripts without being formally taught them. Under the tutelage of Loppön Chöpel Tashi, he began his studies with the ritual of the Eleven-Faced [Avalokiteśvara] and the Sixteen Suchnesses. He rose to the head of the ranks of those practicing dhāraṇīs and brought such conviction to his rituals, dedications, and prayers of auspiciousness that he established everyone on the bhūmi of faith.[119]

With the approval of his uncle, he enthusiastically practiced the virtuous ritual of *nyung-ne*[120] for long periods. [3b] Through that, signs of the purification of obscurations appeared in his dreams and his determination to be released [from saṃsāra], his disenchantment [with saṃsāra], and his love and compassion increased.

Then, he studied the rituals, procedures, drawings, measurements, consecrations, and the four-activities burnt offerings of Kālacakra and Sarvavid [Vairocana]. He also studied astronomy consisting of the five components of both siddhanta and karaṇa, plus the others: eclipses, ascendants, the five planets, along with the foundations of astrology.[121] He memorized the *Ornament of Precious Liberation*[122] and *Entrance to the Bodhisattva's Way of Life*.[123] Under the tutelage of Khenpo Jang Rampa, he studied reading mantras, the great Kālacakra commentary [*Stainless Light*], and [the Third Karmapa's] *Profound Inner Principles* with its commentaries.[124] Through those, he developed a clear understanding of the presentations of outer, inner, and "other." He mainly resided at Segul. At that time, he gave rise to the samādhi in which [all things are experienced as] illusionlike. He was able to pass through rocks unhindered and, specifically, when he wished to visit his uncle, he went right through the walls of Gomde unobstructed. [4a] Some people said he was possessed by a nonhuman but most considered him a source of wonder. His uncle was also amazed, but to cut through his pride, he reprimanded him.

At the age of fourteen [1527], in the presence of his uncle, khenpos, and loppöns, he took [novice] monastic ordination, receiving the name Tashi Namgyal Chökyi Palzangpo.

At that time, the khenpos, loppöns, his elder brother Chöje Rabjampa, and others advised him to go to U and Tsang, so with a small group of disciples he went to Nyukla Lekshe Ling.[125] He made lavish offerings of tea and alms [to the monastic community]. There, with the help of Chuzang Loppön, he easily created the compilations and calculations [for calendars].[126] Under the tutelage of Sherab Namgyal of the [Nyukla Lekshe Ling] monastic seat, he studied in detail the *[Eight] Concordant Topics of the Major [Prajñā]pāramitā Scriptures*[127] and [Vasubandhu's] *Treasury of Abhidharma* treatise with its [auto]commentary.[128] [4b] He also received explanations on the higher abhidharma [Asaṅga's *Compendium of Abhidharma*]. He studied all the general topics of the vinaya and, in particular, the texts of the *Three Hundred Stanzas* and the *Fifty Kārika* with its word commentary.[129] He received extensive teachings on the three vows and the general topics of madhyamaka, and also studied some of the associated reasonings in the [system of] pramāṇa [valid cognition]. The teachings he received from Je Rinpoche Karma Tinle—on sūtras, tantras, śāstras, esoteric instructions, abhiṣekas, commentaries, critiques, and more—are too numerous to list here. We should consult [Tashi Namgyal's] longer biography and his record of received teachings.[130]

With Tana Gelong,[131] he studied additional dharma [subjects], such as grammar, poetics,[132] and the Lañtsa and Vartu scripts. He did not let his studies remain as just hearsay—he applied his intelligence and analyzed well, thereby truly internalizing the meaning of the thought of the Victor. [5a] By this point in his stay at this monastery it was evident that he had become [an eloquent] lecturer and teacher, and the fame of his erudition spread far and wide. He then wished to go to a large monastery in the Tsang area to complete his nonsectarian studies, and later engage in perfect [meditation] practice—with no concern for food, clothing, or conversation—in the practice places of the Jetsun [Milarepa].

However, because Dakpo [monastery] sent an invitation for him to return, which included a mule [for him to ride], he returned to Gampo. For all the guests assembled at Gampo, common and special, who organized his welcoming reception, he gave detailed explanations on the sūtras and tantras, as appropriate. In particular, with his uncle Chöje, his elder brother Chöje Rabjampa, Khenchen Shākya Zangpo, and other great geshes, he discoursed extensively and provided critiques on many major treatises, all in the form of question and answer. [5b] This caused them to have great confidence in him and declare that the earlier [news] they had received of his fame as a scholar was correct. Then, from Khenchen Rinpoche he received the reading transmission of the Collection of Secret Mantra Tantras.[133] He requested his uncle for permission to return to U and Tsang but his uncle strongly urged [him to stay] while [his uncle] moved [from] the monastic seat, and he could not refuse.

At the age of twenty, just after the new year of the Water Dragon Year [1532], Tashi Namgyal was installed as the precious one [abbot] of the monastic seat on its ornate lion's throne, [the seat of Gampopa,] the one renowned throughout Jambudvīpa as the second buddha. There were many days of festivities that combined the celebration [of his enthronement] and the consecration of statues of Nāropa and Marpa, which was assisted by Chöje Rupa Samten Gyatso and Tulku Sönam Rinchen. Great lamas of the area—Drikung, Taklung, Karma Kagyu, and others—and high-ranking local officials vied with each other to make offerings. [6a] On that occasion, the numerous wondrous [signs], music in the sky and a shower of flowers, transported everyone to a glorious experience of joy.

In keeping with the wishes of his uncle, he received from Khenchen Shākya Zangpo many abhiṣekas and reading transmissions, including *Mahāmudrā: Connate Union*,[134] *Molten Gold of the Six Dharmas*,[135] the deity instructions for Vajravārāhī, the completion-phase commentaries on *Nondual Wind-Mind*,[136] *Vajramālā*,[137] and Mitra's One Hundred.[138]

From his uncle, Chöje Rinpoche, he received the abhiṣekas of the five deities of the yidam Cakrasaṃvara and the five deities of Vajravārāhī, and also many abhiṣekas and ritual permissions, such as those for Amitāyus according to Siddharājñī's tradition, the Eleven-Faced [Avalokiteśvara], Ucaryā Vajrapāṇi, Caṇḍa [Vajrapāṇi], White Tārā, and Vajravidāraṇā. He also received the reading transmissions for the Collected Works of Gampopa, Indian Mahāmudrā Texts, the root text and commentaries of the Four Dharmas of Gampopa,[139] and the Book of Kadam[140]—in brief, he received the reading transmissions for whatever the library contained. [6b] In particular, his uncle gave him, by means of questions and answers, instructions on the ways to sustain the view and meditation of mahāmudrā, through which Tashi Namgyal received the transference of the actual lineage. This enabled him to realize the teachings of the unequaled Dakpo [Gampopa], in general, and the meaning of *Revealing the Hidden Characteristics of Mind*[141] specifically. Thus, his uncle's kindness was unmatched.

In that year, on the holy fifteenth day of Saga Dawa,[142] in the shrine hall of Gomde Tse, he took full ordination[143] with his uncle, Chöje Rinpoche, a manifestation of the virtues of stability and scholarship, as upādhyāya; with Khen Shākya Zangpo as ācārya; and his elder brother, Chöje Rabjampa, as secret preceptor and time keeper. The ceremony took place within an assembly of ten saṅgha [monks]. Lacking the stains of even the smallest wrongdoing, be it natural or proscribed, he became a source for many to become holders of the vinaya.

For the next three years, he was only required to be present as the throne occupant, and his uncle continued the management of the two "traditions" [that is, the secular and religious affairs] of the monastic seat. [7a] He did retreat at Gomde Tse, where he read and studied in detail all the books in the library. He became one who could speak unhindered about all the teachings. He also achieved the signs related to the approach and accomplishment of numerous yidam practices, including Cakrasaṃvara, Hevajra, and Vajravārāhī.

Part 3: Bringing the Meaning of Study and Reflection into Experience through Meditation

One summer he had a house with a surrounding [fence] constructed at Dre-drang Chumik Nakpo. Except for when his attendance was required during major ceremonies, he stayed there for more than three years in a strictly sealed retreat, devoting himself to meditative equipoise. Whenever he had slight difficulties sustaining [his meditation], he practiced caṇḍālī yoga, in general, and supreme caṇḍālī specifically. Also by doing trulkhor[144] consistently, many signs of the winds entering the avadhūti arouse. [7b] During the periods between sessions, he read whatever core teachings of the previous Kagyu masters were available, such as those of the incomparable Dakpo.

Sometimes he went to visit the precious reliquary[145] [of Gampopa] at Zang-lung where he made aspiration prayers and supplications with great faith and devotion. On one occasion, near the Zhal-kor Bumpa, he actually met the incomparable [Dakpo] Rinpoche and received his blessings and prophesies that he would be of vast benefit to beings. That encounter was seen by Lama Nyima Drakpa as the meeting of the Exalted One in two forms: older and younger. [Tashi Namgyal] also left many footprints in front of his house. Furthermore, he saw the faces of yidams and dharma protectors and had vast visions of purity, but since writing about those would be excessive, I will not do so.

He also sometimes went to the caves of upper and lower Guru Teng and Pang Melong. By putting a great deal of energy into his practice, he freed himself from feeling any unease with appearances and thoughts in meditation. [8a] He knew unerringly the abiding mode of his intrinsic ordinary mind and actualized the view and meditation expounded by the incomparable Dakpo. All phenomena of ground, path, and fruition—all appearances of the world, good and bad circumstances and so forth—became of equal taste, and he gave rise to unshakable faith in the incomparable Dakpo. He said that after that he had no attainment or loss, no fluctuations in his spiritual practice. Then he applied himself one-pointedly to meditation practice in many sacred places, such as the isolated places of greater and lesser Drö and northern Bab-rom. He sang many songs of experience that are peerless in both word and meaning. Even while at the monastic seat, he primarily remained in retreat and, in that way, he served as a holder of the teachings.

Part 4: Benefitting the Teachings and Beings

In the tradition of the previous dharma lords [of Daklha Gampo], he decided to continue the succession of the great [lineage] representations [statues] that so far went up to exalted Marpa by adding one of the Jetsun [Milarepa]. [8b] When he consulted his parents and younger brother, they said that would be difficult to achieve at present. Nevertheless, the Exalted One [Tashi Namgyal], thinking that nothing is impossible if one supplicates the three jewels, was determined to construct [the statue].

At that time, many great sons [disciples], such as Chöje Cham Gönpa, Chö Gowa, and Lhodrak Ku-kye, gathered, and he brought them to [spiritual] maturity with abhiṣekas and instructions. He also conferred full ordination on many, including Chö Gowa. They vied with each other to offer gold and copper, and his parents offered him much gold.[146] Thus, the great representation [statue] was constructed immediately. The Exalted One rolled the dhāraṇīs, placed [the sacred objects inside the statue], and performed the consecration himself, making [the statue] a powerful source of blessings. He caused [all who were involved] to rejoice by providing a grand almsgiving ceremony for the many monastics and laity and by giving much material compensation to the Nepali [artisans]. [9a]

On the invitation of Gyatönpa, he traveled through Nyedo to visit Deteng, Dagön and elsewhere. He continued through Ngu-gang Khyungpo and other places, visiting Gomde Nang, its two branches,[147] and also the region of Kar [and] Zur[mang]. In all those places, the lamas, officials, and monastic leaders paid him great respect, placing their heads at his feet. He established all the monastics and laity in [spiritual] maturity and liberation. Since each offered whatever they could, much wealth resulted. There he met Serdok Chöje Drakpa, who requested many abhiṣekas and dharma teachings, and pressed him to go to Markham. However, the Exalted One, caring nothing for crowds, honor, or fame, and being [only] intent on practice, declined his request. Turning his mount around, he headed back to Gampo.

During the two years he had been in the Kham area, his father had passed away at the age of fifty-two. [9b] [When Tashi Namgyal returned] the memorial services for his father were concluding. As part of a grand almsgiving ceremony, in the manner of giving presents, he offered gifts in "sets of hundreds" to his uncle, articles appropriate to their rank to the head lamas and administrators, and tea and silk scarves to the monks and laity of Ritil.

At the age of thirty-one, in the Rabbit Year [1544], he installed his younger brother Tup-wang Tenzin [as the throne-holder] at the monastic seat and made an offering of all his revenue. He intended to depart for Lay-tö[148] to devote himself to practice. However, at that point, his uncle gathered the three brothers and told them, "In keeping with the tradition of the previous exalted ones, I erected a statue of Tilopa in honor of the exalted Sönam Gyatso.[149] Now, in keeping with whatever merit [or wealth] you have, you brothers should construct a large statue of the incomparable Rinpoche [Gampopa] to honor your father." [10a] With that guidance, they began the construction of a magnificent statue, "Glory of Jambudvīpa,"[150] with a back relief and much ornamentation. During this period, grand arrangements and offerings were prepared to be able to receive Karmapa Mikyö Dorje at Gampo.

With a small group of disciples, Tashi Namgyal traveled to Uru to see the sacred sites in that region. Led by the monastic heads of Drikung and Taklung, the lamas and officials all welcomed him with great respect. He bestowed upon them abhiṣekas, teachings, and instructions according to their individual wishes and made offerings of tea and alms to the monastic communities. Thus, with abhiṣekas, dharma teachings, and more, he fulfilled their hopes in terms of the two traditions [that is, the secular and religious affairs].

The lamas and officials of Hor, such as the Barom Ka-zhi-druk Lama, collectively came to invite him, and so he went to Drum Tsa-nyin Sibwa in the north, where the offerings [he received] during three months seemed to cover the ground. He turned the wheel of the sacred dharma by giving abhiṣekas, reading transmissions, and explanations, thereby establishing many beings on the path to liberation. [10b]

With the assistance of the Barompa hermits, he returned to Gampo. He gave gifts to each as appropriate [to their rank]. The lavish offerings of gold given by Gyatön Namkha Lekpa, Zhab-de Önpo, and others from Kham were used to increase the splendor of the great representation [the Gampopa statue]. Based mostly on the revenue [received] from the north, he created an estate for a new retreat center, complete with a retreat building [called] Dzi-go Chö-yak, assembly hall, the three representations, and retreatants.

The Exalted One primarily resided at Chumik Nakpo, where many people committed to [meditation] practice gathered. He bestowed upon them the instructions suitable for their individual circumstances, such as those of mahāmudrā or the six dharmas. Through certainty in their own [meditation] experiences, most of them became "those who have begun [their journey on] the path," and many achieved the state where all phenomena are liberated within the expanse of ordinary mind. [11a]

At this point, the statue "Glory of Jambudvīpa" was completed, and his uncle, Chöje, was invited to the consecration celebration, where elaborate offerings were made and the monastics and laity of Ri-zhol were treated to a grand alms-giving ceremony.[151] The artisans were pleased by the excellent material compensation they received.

Being dissatisfied with the ritual, procedures, and performance during the major ceremonies, Tashi Namgyal gathered recruits, [boys from each family] among his followers, and set up a new monastic community.[152] He appointed Lama Nyima Drakpa as the ācārya and directed his younger brother, as the throne occupant, to establish a monastic residence and a temple called Palace of Secret Mantra.[153] The Exalted One spent three years sealed in the retreat center but continued to give dharma teachings through a small window. During that period, his younger brother (as the throne occupant) completed the shrine hall and the huts. [11b] Tashi Namgyal then visited and performed the blessings. He took the students of the monastic community with him and went to the region on Drak-long. He urged the monks to focus on their studies. He also visited the hermitages offered to his uncle and arranged support for the retreatants at Nam-tser Kha. At Kyol Zam Dong he left a footprint [in a rock]. When a benefactor requested him to bless their turquoises, he left the imprint of his thumb with even its nail clearly on three beautiful turquoises.

During this period, Chöje Rabjampa returned from the Kham area with a large amount of offerings. The brothers conferred and decided to construct a statue of Vajradhara about twenty-four spans high in the Palace of Secret Mantra in honor of their mother. They organized a huge almsgiving ceremony in celebration [of the dedication of] the representation [statue]. Then, with silk cloths and mud, they had fashioned many statues of Mantra [deities]—including Cakrasaṃvara, Hevajra, Kālacakra, Guhyasamāja, and Bhairava—and, in the protector chapel, [statues of] the three Principal Ones and Retinue,[154] the Four-Armed One, Six-Armed One, Daṇḍa [Mahakala], Śankhapālo, Vaiśravaṇa, and others, all exceeding one story in height. [12a] Wall murals [painted] with resins and offerings were also created. The consecration was masterfully performed by the Exalted One.

At Gomde there was a previously established custom of the dhāraṇī practice of Bhaiṣajyaguru [Medicine Buddha] and Sixteen Suchnesses. In addition, during the holy days of Saga Dawa, he initiated the performance of the rituals and dances, and the creation of the drawn [maṇḍalas] of Cakrasaṃvara, Hevajra, Guhyasamāja, the five yidam deities of Cakrasaṃvara, and protectors. He arranged the necessary conditions, [future] income, and material goods [for this to continue].

Feeling that these [concerns with] material needs and busyness were creating obstacles for the paths and bhūmis, he longed to pursue the true practice [of meditation]. With two disciples, he made plans to leave, intending to go to Namtso'i Donang. Having set out, he was recognized by those of Drikung Yangri [when he reached] Pö-sang Sum-do and invited [to their monastery]. [12b] He bestowed upon them all the offerings received from those of Nyi Triru. Although he proceeded to Barom Dza De'u, since there was too much busyness there, he went into a very strict retreat. During that period, he received a request urging him to come to [perform the ritual] "leading to the higher states" for the deceased Hor-pön Tarpa Bum, but he turned it down. Again, many lay people arrived with the [same] invitation and request for him to come to the north, and so he acquiesced.

He met Taklung Zim-jilpa. He taught him the Four Dharmas of Gampopa, gave him its reading transmission, and, by exchanging questions and answers, cut through his doubts about the view and meditation of mahāmudrā. He also fulfilled many specific wishes by teaching the head lamas, such as those of Barom and Dzare, the dharma they desired and by conferring on others, such as Pön Karma Pal, the one hundred longevity abhiṣekas.[155]

Despite the matchless offerings and honors, he left [everything] right there and went on to Namtso. [13a] Since the lake was separated from the shore, [that is, the ice had melted], he was unable to reach Nangdo. He resided as he pleased in the ravines around Tashi Do and elsewhere. The local rulers, Tro-gyal Bum, Lhasung, and others, made many requests for abhiṣekas and dharma teachings and offered copious amounts of material goods. He bestowed on the many head lamas and monastics of Taklung, Wolwawa, and elsewhere abhiṣekas, reading transmissions, and explanations in keeping with their wishes.

Again, he went to Barom and, while staying there, received an invitation from Dakpo and a letter from both Drikung Khang-tok to perform the consecration of the silver reliquary of the exalted Rinchen Puntsok.[156] Having arranged a date [to return] with the emissary from Dakpo, he went to Drikung. He made offerings to the monastic leaders and presented, in the manner of gifts, tea and alms to those of Tel and Yangri. He performed the consecration for the silver reliquary and bestowed abhiṣekas and reading transmissions, such as those of Hevajra, on the precious descendants of the family line and those of Yangri. [13b] He was invited by Chöje Machen from Tsewa[157] and the mother and sons from Pakmo, upon whom he bestowed the one hundred longevity abhiṣekas and more.

Then, with immeasurable goods and wealth, he returned to the great seat [of Daklha Gampo], where he was greeted with much joy by all those in the community, led by his younger brother, the throne occupant. He distributed gifts lavishly. Shortly thereafter, his younger brother, the throne occupant, passed away [1563]. He performed all the funeral services for his brother. In his honor, as the inner representation, he erected a statute of the exalted Gomchung with a back relief made from gilded copper, more than a story tall, and [filled] it with magnificent [sacred] objects.[158]

Furthermore, in the upper gallery, he commissioned back reliefs and golden hats to be made for [the statues of Gampopa's] two nephews [Gomtsul and Gomchung]. In the guru temple,[159] a "statue of the Exalted One himself"[160] was made from medicinal herbs and clay, and [statues] of the Sage and sixteen arhats,[161] the succession of [Dakpo] abbots,[162] and the multitude of Kagyu [masters] were constructed from gilded copper. [14a]

At Gomde Tse, he also erected gilded copper statues of the succession of [Dakpo] abbots. At Zang-lung, he had the roof of the reliquary[163] covered in gold and given gold ornaments. The two precious statues, "Meaningful to Behold"[164] and "Glory of Jambudvīpa," were given exceptionally beautiful cloaks, and the other "Great Deities" [statues] received brocade coverings and silk scarves. In each of the temples, special offering substances were arranged and presented, including pendants and canopies, gold and silver maṇḍalas, offering bowls, and silk coverings [for the tangkas].

As for his dharma compositions: His [major] expositions include *Sunrays*, the great commentary on the *Two-Part [Hevajra Tantra]*; *Moonbeams*, the eloquent explanation that clarifies the way to cultivate mahāmudrā; and *Jewel-Light Rays*, a summation of the general points of Secret Mantra. He also wrote instruction manuals on such topics as mahāmudrā and the six dharmas,[165] many maṇḍala rituals (such as those of Cakrasaṃvara, Hevajra, Guhyasamāja, Vajravārāhī, the five deities of Cakrasaṃvara, Sarvavid [Vairocana], and Sixteen Suchnesses), and numerous [liturgies for] consecrations, burnt offerings, and reparation and restoration. In brief, most of the daily rituals and liturgies that are currently recited at this seat [of Daklha

Gampo] today were composed by this holy being.[166] [14b] Additionally, his many aphorisms, eloquently expressing vast meaning in a few words, are often found in colophons. He also re-edited and printed the text and commentaries of the Four Dharmas [of Gampopa] and the *Ornament of Precious Liberation.*

On the main temple, he repaired the rotten woodwork and ornamentation on the western side and the carvings on the southeastern side. He also restored the roof and gold ornaments on the great Tik hall.[167] He arranged the [future] income and material goods for fifteen practitioners to reside continuously at Zang-lung. In the main temples in Lhasa, Samye, and elsewhere, he offered vast numbers of lamps and silk scarves. Without sectarianism, he offered meals and provisions at the major monastic centers in U and Tsang. [15a] For the monastics and laity of Gampo Ritil, he arranged great almsgiving ceremonies along with [distributing] provisions. [Altogether] he completely gave away everything he owned eight or nine times.

He arranged for five hundred million [recitations] of the *maṇi* mantra; two thousand [recitations] each of Cakrasaṃvara, Hevajra, and Guhyasamāja; eight thousand [recitations] of Sarvavid [Vairocana]; one hundred thousand [recitations] of the confession of downfalls;[168] twenty thousand [recitations] of Bhaiṣajyaguru [Medicine Buddha]; and more. In brief, during the summer and winter, he used all his material goods for beneficial purposes through great festivals of offerings and generosity that concluded with feasts for the poor.

He also demonstrated many miraculous powers as signs of accomplishment, such as revealing sources of water, leaving imprints of his hands and feet, and being able to ride around the rear circumambulation route.

The omniscient Pema Karpo and Tulku Sönam Gyatso visited Gampo. They both greeted Tashi Namgyal in an elegant and respectful manner by bowing and paying homage first. [15b]

Primarily, he [spent his time] remaining in the cultivation [of meditative equipoise] while also uninterruptedly turning the dharma wheel of the provisional and definitive meanings, thereby establishing all disciples in the fruition of separation and maturation.

Part Five: His Activity of Nirvāṇa [Passing Away]

In the year 1587, when he had reached the age of seventy-five, he said that the offering festivals should be held earlier in the year since he would have other engagements in the later months. He gave instructions regarding the construction of the "Great Deities" [statues] and prepared the material for the statues with his own hands. Furthermore, he gave advice on training until his last days and also his assurance that his tulku would appear just as the rising of the sun can't be held back with a stick.

At dawn on the fourteenth day of full moon of Puṣya,[169] he demonstrated the way to dissolve into the expanse. At that time, many inconceivable portents and miracles appeared: the earth trembled and rainbows filled his room. His corpse remained intact for a time. All his funeral services were performed by Tri Rinpoche Tashi Kundrak[170] assisted by Ka-chen Tashi Lekpa. They opened the door of immeasurable offerings and generosity. [16a]

Part Six: His Students

Within Gampo [monastery, his students included] Chen-nga Tup-wang Tenzin, Trichen Tashi Kundrak, Chöje Tashi Tinle, Tulku Tinle Namgyal, the exalted Drung Rabjampa Tashi Palzang, the vajra holder Nyima Drakpa, Yong-dzin Sönam Chöpal, the exalted Pang Karwa Tashi Chöjor, Zhal-nga Önpo Gendün Seng-ge, Tulku Tashi Tinle, Deteng Tulku Tashi Gyatso, and Drupwang Mipam Tashi Lodrö.

From other areas, they included the precious Drikung uncles, nephews, and brothers, Taklung Zim-jilpa, Wolwawa uncle and nephews, Barom Ka-zhi-drug Chöje, Gyatön Namkha Lekpa, Drungpa Namkha Dorje, Nang-chen Seng-ge Gyaltsen, Tsang-sar Go Shri, [16b] Zurmang Chöje Padma Gyalpo, Serdok Chöje Drakpa, Mar-yulway Gyalse Chöje, Chöje Ngokpa, Lodrak Ku-kye, Chöje Chö Gowa, Chöje Cham Gönpa, Chöje Khyung-tsangpa, Ka-zhipa, La-dingwa, and others. All were great beings who served the teachings and possessed the ability to benefit beings.

This [account] summarizes the essential points of [Dakpo Tashi Namgyal's] biography and draws slightly from the *Glorious Treasure of Devotion*.[171]

This [biography of Dakpo Tashi Namgyal] has been extracted in its entirety from the Daklha Gampo printing of the *Garland of Vaiḍūrya: An Account of the Holy Hereditary Throne-Holders [of the Seat] of the Glorious Gampopa, Regent of the Teacher in This Snowy Land*, starting from folio 49a.1. The

Garland of Vaiḍūrya—a presentation of the succession of dharma expounders on the lion throne of the great Gampo [monastery]—was composed by the one with the name Shākya Gelong Zangpo in the Water Tiger Year [1662].

Moonbeams of Mahāmudrā

Moonbeams of Eloquence: Clarifying the Way to Cultivate Mahāmudrā, the Definitive Meaning

Dakpo Tashi Namgyal

Introduction

Devoted homage to the guru and the vajra of mind.

Homage to Vajradhara, the lord pervading all entities and nonentities.
His nature is free from elaborations, and yet he displays all sorts of elaborations as rūpakāyas.
He is free from expression and beyond the sounds of words, and yet his melodic voice of indestructible self-sounds arises.
He has purified characteristics related to dualistic appearances of self and others, and nevertheless has the characteristics of compassion, the ground for benefit and happiness.

I bow to the unequaled Teacher, the sole friend for all with fortune, the one endowed with the three secrets.
Emanating variously throughout the realms, his body demonstrates the play of illusion.
From the view of his disciples, his speech proclaims the dharma of the three yānas to each in their own language.
With nonreferential vast love—equally for everyone—his mind embraces all beings.[172]

Receiving even a bit of Caṇḍa's compassion reveals the meaning of hundreds of definitive and provisional treatises.
During exposition, debate, or composition, he bestows fearless, unobstructed intelligence.
He enables us to realize easily and directly profound suchness, what's hidden for the ordinary.
I bow to the supreme deity, exalted Caṇḍa: please bestow the supreme gift of confidence.

I bow respectfully to Saraha with a body of space, Nāgārjuna,
Śavaripa, Tilopa, Nāropa, Maitrīpa, Marpa, and Milarepa.
Having actualized the suchness of the profound and clear intrinsic state, they see all misinterpreted phenomena as false.
They perfected ground, path, and result within inseparable expanse-awareness, the essence of space. [22]

I bow to the second Teacher, famous throughout the three planes as "Gampopa."
Though previously awakened in the presence of the Victor, he took the guise of the Victor's son Candraprabha Kumāra.
The Victor prophesized that as the bhikṣu Jīvaka he would appear out of his love for the beings of the Snowy Land of Tibet
and proclaim the definitive and provisional dharma widely during these degenerate times.

In this Snowy Land, ordinary scholar-monks and arrogant Secret Mantra practitioners
analyze with their dialectics or practice with their experiences yet achieve almost nothing.
I bow with respect to those of the glorious Dakpo Kagyu,
who, having seen the very face of mind's abiding state, are skilled
in revealing it to others effortlessly: please grant your blessings.

This dharma approach is called "mahāmudrā."
Its path—which pacifies the machinery of false conventionalities
and uproots the various intellectually fabricated experiences—
is the definitive meaning of the sūtras and tantras.

Others chase the mirages of conventionalities.
Some gaze at the physical expressions of their imagination.
A few cling to the rainbows of experience.
Those are not ways for anyone seeking swift liberation.

You may have heard many discourses on the definitive and provisional, [23]
and reflected upon and analyzed their meaning well,
but if you have not meditated upon the true nature,
the attainment of liberation is a long way off.

Some say that nowadays is not a time for meditation.
Such remarks are perverse speech that discourages oneself and others.
Fortunate ones who close their ears and banish [such ideas]
will find they can exert themselves in meditation.

Containing all the points in the treatises of sūtra and tantra,
the moon of the abiding state appears,
and the moonlight of eloquent elucidation radiates here and now.
May it delight the minds of those who wander in the darkness of unknowing.

Those of excellent fortune and discernment
who wish to practice meditation on the true nature—
who have not turned their backs on achieving a great purpose
and are not tangled up in tenet systems with wrong views—
please listen with respect.

Once we have entered the door of the precious doctrine of our Teacher, the true, perfect Buddha, we turn to practicing the genuine dharma he taught. The most well-known approach is through the ten dharma activities. Of those ten, it is said that the primary one and the ultimate object of engagement is meditation upon the true nature. Here I will explain the stages for meditating upon that. [24]

Nowadays I observe that most who listen to and reflect on the dharma do not undertake the approach of practice and even the few who do practice seem to have a rudimentary understanding of the essential points of the stages of meditation. I will explain [meditation upon the true nature] out of my sincere wish to benefit those who have confidence in me. Since I fear that emphasizing technical terminology and a formal compositional style would make this somewhat harder for the ordinary person to understand, the presentation will be done in a way that is easy to comprehend.

[The explanation of the stages of meditation for cultivating the true nature] has two parts:[173]

I. The Reasons It Is Necessary to Meditate on the Nature of Mind
II. The Explanation of the Ways to Cultivate Samādhi

I. The Reasons It Is Necessary to Meditate on the Nature of Mind

This has three sections:

A. All Phenomena Are Taught to Be Mind
B. The Problems of Not Meditating on the Nature of Mind
C. The Virtues of Such Meditation

A. All Phenomena Are Taught to Be Mind

Generally speaking, all phenomena contained within saṃsāra and nirvāṇa—all possible appearances—are our own mind. The *Sūtra on the Ten Bhūmis* says:

> O sons and daughters of the victors, these three realms are simply mind.[174]

The *Vajra Pañjarā* states:

> Outside of the precious mind
> there are no buddhas or sentient beings.[175]

The *Samputa* proclaims:

> Every external and internal thing [25]
> is imagined by mind.
> Something other than mind
> does not exist.[176]

The Lord of Hermits [the Śavara, Saraha] explains:

> All phenomena are your own mind.
> Apart from mind, there's not even an atom of some phenomenon.[177]

In that case we may ask, What is it that appears as the things we perceive to be external objects, such as forms and sounds? Mind-itself, being itself unaware of its own abiding state, has appeared as self and other without beginning. By conceptualizing those perceptions, we have amassed latent tendencies and external referents appear to our mistaken perspective. The *Descent into Laṅkā Sūtra* teaches:

The mind disturbed by latent tendencies
appears as referents.
There are no existent referents, just mind.
Seeing external referents is mistaken.[178]

The *Sampuṭa* observes:

All phenomena are mind's delusion.
There are no phenomena not mind.
What appear as phenomena are the deluded mind.[179] [26]

In the same way that water can create earthen and stone forms when it is whipped up and stirred by wind, external entities (which are solid, hard, and so forth) appear from the full-blown latent tendencies of the deluded mind. As Saraha says:

When wind hits water and whips it up,
even soft water can turn to stone.
When whipped up by thoughts,
formless confusion can become solid and hard.[180]

Nevertheless, we still may wonder, How does mind-itself become saṃsāra and nirvāṇa? When mind is deluded, it does not know the nature of percepts and perceivers. Confused, there is saṃsāra. When that is reversed, there is nirvāṇa. The *Two-Part [Hevajra Tantra]* explains:

When there is confusion, there are the forms of saṃsāra.
When there is no confusion, saṃsāra is pure.
Thus, saṃsāra is nirvāṇa.[181]

The *Sampuṭa* says:

Those crazed and electrified by the overwhelming
pervasiveness of the darkness of their many imaginations
have minds that the Vajra Holder described as "saṃsāra,"
tainted by the stains of desire and the like, so difficult to stop.

Natural luminosity is free from concepts.
The supreme, powerful mind, devoid of percepts and perceivers,

> is untainted by the stains of desire and the like. [27]
> That is said to be sublime nirvāṇa.[182]

Nāgārjuna observes:

> What serves as the cause for saṃsāra
> is itself, once purified,
> the very purity that is nirvāṇa.[183]

That being the case, mind creates the roots of all failings and all virtues. They arise from causes that are mental. They arise from mind. The *Descent into Laṅkā Sūtra* remarks:

> Forms appearing in a mirror
> are visible although they do not exist.
> Likewise, when the appearances of mind are not recognized,
> they arise as dualistic conceptuality.
>
> Linked to the latent tendencies of concepts,
> myriad things arise from mind.
> The external appearances [manifesting] to people
> are merely the mind of worldly ones.
>
> Those nonexistent external appearances—
> the body, possessions, places, and all—
> are mind arising as various things.
> I declare all to be simply mind.[184]

The *Avataṃsaka* states:

> Mind is like a painter.
> Mind creates the skandhas.
> All worldly realms,
> each and every one, are drawn by the mind.[185] [28]

The *Jewel Cloud Sūtra* says:

> Mind leads the world
> yet mind doesn't even see itself.

Actions, virtuous or unvirtuous,
are amassed by mind.

Mind circles like a firebrand.
Mind undulates like waves.
Mind burns like fire in a forest.
Mind swells like a great river.[186]

The *Vajra Pañjarā* states:

Throughout beginningless existence,
external referents have been imagined.
All are projections of mind
and are always mind-itself.[187]

It also says:

There is nothing outside of mind.
All that appears individually—forms and so forth—
are only appearances of this mind.[188]

B. The Problems of Not Meditating on the Nature of Mind

If we do not meditate upon the true nature, we may engage with the Buddha's teachings, but no matter how much we listen to and reflect upon the words of the genuine dharma, we will only be able to attain a temporary type of result. We will not be able to achieve final liberation. This has been taught using many analogies, such as those found in the *Gaṇḍavyūha*:

The teachings of the true Buddha
are not realized by simply listening to them. [29]

For example, someone may be helplessly
carried away by a river
but still die of thirst.
To not meditate on the dharma is like that.

Some provide food and drink
for many people

> yet die of hunger themselves.
> To not meditate on the dharma is like that.
>
> A doctor may be in possession of
> every kind of medicine
> but die of an intestinal ailment.
> To not meditate on the dharma is like that.
>
> Those guarding a vault of treasures
> may count up the riches
> but not get anything for themselves.
> To not meditate on the dharma is like that.
>
> Someone born as a servant
> in a royal palace full of many delights
> may have neither food nor drink.
> To not meditate on the dharma is like that.
>
> In the midst of a marketplace,
> a blind artist can create drawings
> but not see them.
> To not meditate on the dharma is like that.
>
> Ferrymen on a great ocean
> may rescue many people
> and yet die in the ocean themselves.
> To not meditate on the dharma is like that.
>
> Some may stand in the crossroads
> and wish everyone prosperity
> but they won't receive any of it themselves.
> To not meditate on the dharma is like that.[189]

If we do not meditate, we will succumb to our mental afflictions and fall into the negative states.[190] [30] The *Play [of Mañjuśrī] Sūtra* observes:

> If you do not realize the nature of mind, you will come under the control of your thoughts. Thus you will cycle through the three realms and wander in the six modes.[191]

The *Entrance to the Bodhisattva's Way of Life* points out:

> A distracted person's mind
> is caught between the fangs of the afflictions.[192]

It also says:

> Those who don't know the secret of mind,
> what is of sublime importance in the dharma,
> will wander futilely for a long time—
> despite their desire to attain happiness and destroy suffering.[193]

If we do not cultivate meditative concentration, we will not develop prajñā. Without prajñā we cannot achieve awakening. The *Letter to a Friend* states:

> When there is no meditative concentration, there is no prajñā.[194]

Therefore, those who abide in ethical conduct and engage in listening to and reflecting on the dharma, in the end, must practice meditation, as the *Treasury [of Abhidharma]* confirms:

> Those who abide in ethical conduct, who have listened and reflected,
> will practice meditation.[195]

C. The Virtues of Such Meditation

The merit of meditating on the true nature is immeasurable. The *Sūtra Revealing Suchness* says:

> Śāriputra, someone who cultivates the samādhi of suchness for just [the amount of time it takes] to snap their fingers increases their merit more than someone who listens [to the dharma] for even as long as an eon. [31] Śāriputra, it is for this reason that I strenuously recommend this samādhi of suchness to others.[196]

The *Sūtra of the Great Uṣṇīṣa* states:

> The merit of meditating on the meaning of dharmatā for one day is greater than that of listening to and reflecting on [the dharma]

for many eons. Why? Because that [meditation] takes you far away from the path of birth and death.[197]

The *Sūtra of Expanding Realization* observes:

Resting in a moment of meditative concentration
is more meaningful than saving the lives
of all the people in the three realms.[198]

The cultivation of samādhi is taught to have many excellent qualities. It reverses fixating on the sense pleasures, it cuts through the sources of doubts, it gives rise to supercognitive abilities and samādhis, arouses great compassion, causes us to see the true nature, and gives us the ability to bring disciples to awakening.[199] The *Verses That Summarize the Prajñāpāramitā Sūtras* says:

Meditative concentration dispenses with inferior sense pleasures
and makes awareness, supercognitive abilities, and samādhis manifest.[200]

The *Sūtra of the Ten Wheels of Kṣitigarbha* teaches:

Cultivating samādhi severs doubts.
Without that realization nothing else can be effective.
Thus samādhi meditation is supreme.
The wise should exert themselves in that.[201]

The *Compendium of Dharma Sūtra* comments:

By resting the mind evenly, what is true will be seen just as it is. [32] By seeing what is true just as it is, bodhisattvas engage with great compassion for the sake of all sentient beings.[202]

The *Ornament for the Mahāyāna Sūtras* adds:

Through meditative concentration, [bodhisattvas] establish all beings in the three levels of awakening.[203] [33]

PART ONE

Common Samādhis

I

Śamatha and Vipaśyanā

II. The Explanation of the Ways to Cultivate Samādhi

This has two parts:

A. The Presentation That Summarizes the Exposition of the Common Samādhis

B. The Explanation That Elaborates upon the Way to Cultivate the Uncommon Mahāmudrā

A. The Presentation That Summarizes the Exposition of the Common Samādhis

This has two sections:

1. The Summary Identification of Samādhi and Dispelling of Doubts
2. The Systematic Presentation of Śamatha and Vipaśyanā

1. The Summary Identification of Samādhi and Dispelling of Doubts

No matter which of the various approaches to practicing the samādhis of the Hīnayāna and Mahāyāna is being discussed, these days the most well-known divisions and presentations of samādhi are the ones elucidated in Sūtra-oriented treatises. Since what appears in numerous sūtras of the Bhagavān (such as *Unraveling the Intent*),[204] the Dharma Treatises of Maitreya,[205] Asaṅga's Five Divisions of the *Yogācāryābhūmi*[206] and *Compendium of Abhidharma*,[207] Ratnākaraśānti's *Instructions on Prajñāpāramitā*[208] (which summarizes those texts), and Kamalaśīla's Stages of Madhyamaka-Meditation Trilogy[209] are the most well known and the most clear explications, I will explain the general principles of samādhi according to the teachings found in those texts.

A summary of samādhi. It is said in *Unraveling the Intent*:

> Know that all the many aspects of samādhi, which I have presented for śrāvakas, bodhisattvas, and tathāgatas, are included within śamatha and vipaśyanā.[210]

The middle *Stages of Meditation* comments: [34]

> Because these two contain all samādhis, yogins and yoginīs should definitely practice śamatha and vipaśyanā at all times.[211]

Thus it is explained that all the samādhis of the Hīnayāna and Mahāyāna are included within śamatha and vipaśyanā, like the way that every part of a tree (its leaves, branches, and the rest) is connected to its main trunk.

Nevertheless, we may wonder, How is it that śamatha and vipaśyanā include the many different types of Hīnayāna and Mahāyāna samādhis (those with objects of meditation and those without), the various ones associated with the Mantra approach (those with characteristics and those without characteristics), and the numerous samādhis of bliss, clarity, and nonconceptuality that are found in the Mahāmudrā system? Regardless of whether samādhi has an object or not, characteristics or not, when the mind is engaged one-pointedly with a virtuous object of meditation it is in accord with śamatha. All virtuous states of prajñā that differentiate the nature of that object are in keeping with vipaśyanā. Similarly, in Mahāmudrā, all states of mind, high or low, that are concentrated undistractedly on their particular object of meditation are in keeping with śamatha. Differentiation and awareness of the nature of that object are in keeping with vipaśyanā.

In that way, all forms of samādhi are included within śamatha and vipaśyanā. The *Sūtra on Cultivating Faith in the Mahāyāna* comments:

> Child of good family, this list will inform you that faith in the Mahāyāna of bodhisattvas and everything that develops from the Mahāyāna comes from correctly contemplating reality and the dharma with an undistracted mind.[212]

"An undistracted mind" is a mind that is one-pointedly concentrated on an object of meditation. [35] "Correct contemplation of the dharma" is the discernment and differentiation of reality.

Therefore, all the excellent qualities of the Hīnayāna and Mahāyāna must be achieved by uniting one-pointed concentration on an object of meditation with the prajñā that analyzes reality. The final *Stages of Meditation* begins:

> The Bhagavān taught immeasurable and limitless types of samādhis for bodhisattvas. Nevertheless, since śamatha and vipaśyanā cover all samādhis, I will explain the path that unites śamatha and vipaśyanā.[213] [36/37]

2. The Systematic Presentation of Śamatha and Vipaśyanā

This has two parts:

a. The Common Exposition of Śamatha and Vipaśyanā
b. The Ways to Cultivate Śamatha and Vipaśyanā Individually

a. The Common Exposition of Śamatha and Vipaśyanā

This has seven sections:

i. The Presentation of the Causes of Śamatha and Vipaśyanā
ii. The Elimination of the Obscurations of Śamatha and Vipaśyanā
iii. The Identification of the Essences of Śamatha and Vipaśyanā
iv. The Presentation of the Divisions of Śamatha and Vipaśyanā
v. The Analysis of the Order of Śamatha and Vipaśyanā
vi. The Way to Cultivate the Unification of Śamatha and Vipaśyanā
vii. The Explanation of the Results of Śamatha and Vipaśyanā

i. The Presentation of the Causes of Śamatha and Vipaśyanā

It is said in *Unraveling the Intent*:

> "Bhagavān, from what causes do śamatha and vipaśyanā arise?"
>
> "Maitreya, they develop from the cause of pure ethical conduct and the cause of the pure view that is [known through] listening and reflecting."[214]

The exalted Gampopa explains the causes that way and teaches that śamatha develops from the gurus' blessings, dependent origination, amassing the accumulations [of merit and wisdom], and purifying obscurations.[215] Those also serve as causes for vipaśyanā.

The middle *Stages of Meditation* lists six causes of śamatha: to reside in a conducive place, have few desires, be content, reduce activities, have pure ethical conduct, and relinquish thoughts [involving desire and so forth]; and three causes of vipaśyanā: to rely upon holy beings, pursue much listening [that is, study], and reflect properly.[216]

Six Causes of Śamatha

Reside in a conducive place. The place should have good resources, meaning that food, clothing, and other necessities can be acquired with few difficulties. [38] It should be a safe location, one where dangerous beings, such as enemies or predatory animals, are not found. It should be in a good area, one where epidemics do not occur. There should be good companions, meaning friends with similar ethical conduct and views. It should be mentally comfortable, somewhere without too many people during the day and little noise at night. This is stated in the *Ornament for the Mahāyāna Sūtras*:

> The place where the wise practice
> is one with good resources, is a safe location,
> in a good area, has good companions,
> and has the requisite things for comfortable yoga.[217]

Have few desires. Do not crave more or better food, clothing, and so forth.

Be content. Always feel satisfied with simple food, clothing, and the like.

Reduce activities. Refrain from negative activities (including business ventures), excessive socializing with lay people or monastics, as well as practicing medicine and astrology.

Have pure ethical conduct. Protect the foundations of your training just as they are taught, be they the vows of the prātimokṣa, of bodhisattvas, and so forth. If you happen to damage a vow due to a lack of conscientiousness, feel remorse and repair it according to the dharma.

Relinquish thoughts involving desire and so forth. Abandon thoughts involving desire by contemplating the deficiencies of all desires, both in this lifetime and the next, or by contemplating that all things in saṃsāra—beautiful or ugly—are impermanent, quickly separated from, and so forth. [39]

Three Causes of Vipaśyanā

Rely upon holy beings. Rely upon spiritual mentors who have unerring knowledge of the key points of listening, reflection, and meditation, and who have śamatha and vipaśyanā realizations.

Pursue much listening. Engender the prajñā of listening by hearing the stainless teachings on the definitive meaning. This is not developed through listening to [the dharma of] conventional expressions and the provisional meaning.

Reflect properly. Contemplate the meaning of what you have heard about the definitive meaning and, by means of inference, generate the unerring view in the form of an abstract idea [or general understanding].

ii. The Elimination of the Obscurations of Śamatha and Vipaśyanā

This has two parts:

A) The Identification of Obscurations
B) The Explanation of the Remedies That Remove Those [Obscurations]

A) The Identification of Obscurations

It is said in *Unraveling the Intent*:

> "Bhagavān, among those five obscurations, which are the obscurations for śamatha? Which are the obscurations for vipaśyanā? Which obscure both?"
>
> "Maitreya, agitation and remorse obscure śamatha. Sluggishness, drowsiness, and doubts obscure vipaśyanā. Pleasure-seeking and malice obscure both."[218]

Agitation. The *Compendium of Abhidharma* explains:

> What is agitation? It is an unpeaceful mental state that is a type of desire in that it pursues attractive characteristics. Its activity is to interrupt śamatha.[219]

Once something pleasurable and lovely is focused upon, craving for that object projects outwards and disrupts mental stillness. [40]

Remorse. The same text says:

> A mind that regrets intentional or unintentional activities and things not done—be they virtuous, unvirtuous, or unspecified [neutral], timely or untimely, appropriate or inappropriate—is a type of bewilderment. It works to interrupt śamatha.[220]

When our mind repeatedly and continuously regrets activities it has done or not done, appropriately or not, that prevents mental stillness.

Sluggishness. The same text states:

> What is sluggishness? Being a type of bewilderment, it makes the mind unworkable. Its function is to assist all the mental afflictions and the secondary mental afflictions.[221]

The *Explanation of the "Treasury of Abhidharma"* says:

> What is sluggishness? It is physical heaviness and mental heaviness. It is the unworkability of body and the unworkability of mind.[222]

When there is sluggishness, both body and mind are heavy and useless. Here dullness and sluggishness are considered to be concordant types and dullness is not mentioned separately; however, the middle *Stages of Meditation* says:

> Know that whenever your mind cannot see its object clearly—feeling as if it is blind, is immersed in darkness, or your eyes are shut—that is dullness.[223]

Therefore, dullness is slightly different from sluggishness since dullness is when physical or mental lethargy cause the clarity of the object to become lax.

Drowsiness. The same text [*Compendium of Abhidharma*] states: [41]

> What is drowsiness? It is the dissolution of mental activities that occurs based on the causes for sleep—be they virtuous, unvirtuous, or unspecified [neutral], timely or untimely, appropriate or inappropriate. It is a type of bewilderment. It works to create a basis for activities to lapse.[224]

On the basis of the causes for drowsiness, the operative [sense] consciousnesses, regardless of their objects, withdraw and lose their objects.

Doubt. The same text explains:

> What is doubt? It is to be uncertain about the truth. Its activity is to create a basis for not undertaking something virtuous.[225]

[Generally] we entertain doubts about the two truths (the conventional and [the ultimate]) and the four truths (suffering and the others). In this context, having hesitations about what is to be practiced—doubts about what it is or is not, or whether it can be achieved or not—cause us to be reluctant about undertaking the practice.

Pleasure-seeking. This is a mental activity that comes from craving to obtain an object of desire.

Malice. This is a mind that sets out to harm others due to anger or jealousy.

Other interruptions to śamatha are the five distractions explained in *Unraveling the Intent*:

> "Bhagavān, when bodhisattvas are engaged in śamatha and vipaśyanā, how many mental distractions do they find?"
>
> [The Bhagavān] replied: "Maitreya, there are five: distractions of attention, external mental distractions, internal distractions, distractions related to characteristics, and distractions related to negative propensities."[226] [42]

Those are identified in the same text as follows:

> Maitreya, if bodhisattvas set aside attention to the Mahāyāna and lower themselves to the attentions of the śrāvakas and pratyekabuddhas, that is the distraction of attention. If they let their mind pursue the five external sense pleasures, busyness, characterizations, thoughts, [mental afflictions,] secondary mental afflictions, or outer objects, that is external mental distraction.
>
> If they become afflicted by dullness caused by sluggishness or drowsiness, afflicted by savoring meditative absorption, or afflicted by any of the secondary mental afflictions during meditative absorption, that is internal mental distraction. If, on the basis of external characteristics, their minds engage with characteristics that are within the domain of internal samādhi, that is the distraction related to characteristics.
>
> If, on the basis of internal attention, they become conceited because of their accumulation of negative propensities—thinking, "[That is] me," in relation to feelings that have arisen—that is the distraction related to negative propensities.[227]

The *Differentiation of the Middle and the Extremes* states:

> Laziness, forgetting the instructions,
> dullness and agitation,
> lack of application, and [excessive] application
> are said to be the five faults.[228]

Laziness, forgetfulness, dullness and agitation, nonexertion, and [excessive] application are the five faults. Alternatively, if dullness and agitation are counted separately, there are six. Those are taught to be the hindrances for śamatha and, similarly, they are faults for vipaśyanā.

Laziness. Whether it is [laziness that comes from] pessimism, idleness, or discouragement, laziness causes the mind to fall into bad habits and lose its exertion for cultivating samādhi. [43]

Forgetfulness. This is to lapse into not remembering the object of your practice and to become distracted by something else.

Dullness and agitation. They are as described above.

Nonexertion. This is when the mind does not actively apply itself to abandoning dullness or agitation and leaves them be.

[Excessive] application. This is when dullness and agitation are pacified and yet the mind does not settle naturally but keeps applying itself to the object.

B) The Explanation of the Remedies That Remove Those [Obscurations]

This has two parts:

1) The General Explanation of the Remedies for Obscurations
2) The Specific Explanation of the Ways to Prevent Dullness and Agitation

1) The General Explanation of the Remedies for Obscurations

It may seem that specific remedies for the aforementioned obscurations are not clearly taught. However, since for the most part [those obscurations] are included within dullness and agitation, an understanding [of how to remedy the aforementioned obscurations] follows automatically from [knowing] how to prevent [dullness and agitation]. Nevertheless, we should be aware of the following key points.

- For agitation, bring your mind down by meditating on impermanence.
- When feeling remorseful, do not pay attention to its object.
- For dullness, rouse your mind.
- When drowsy, generate a sense of illumination.
- Doubts [are quelled] by settling the mind on one point.
- Pleasure-seeking [is overcome] by reflecting on the problems with the sense pleasures and by feeling content.
- For a malicious mind, arouse kindness and altruism.

Similarly, by applying those principles we will understand [the remedies for] the five distractions.

The *Differentiation of the Middle and the Extremes* says:

> Eight applications eliminate five faults.[229]

It explains that there are eight applications that eliminate the aforementioned five faults.*

- The remedies for laziness are four: faith, motivation, exertion, and suppleness.
- The remedy for forgetfulness is mindfulness.
- The antidote for dullness and agitation is the alertness that recognizes them.
- The remedy for nonexertion is applied intention. [44]
- The antidote for [excessive] application is the equanimity of remaining in the natural state.

The first three are easy to understand.

Suppleness. The *Compendium of Abhidharma* says:

> What is suppleness? It is physical and mental flexibility that [comes about] because the negative propensities of body and mind have been eliminated. Its function is to eliminate all obscurations.[230]

The negative propensities of body and mind prevent the cultivation of physical and mental virtues. The force of suppleness brings physical flexibility: the attainment of physical buoyancy and ease, free from problems, such as feeling heaviness in the body. And it brings mental flexibility: the joy and happiness attained once the mind can focus on an object without any trouble. Ācārya Sthiramati explains:

> Physical flexibility is what allows the activities of the body to take place readily and with buoyancy. Mental flexibility is the specific quality of the mental factor that is the cause for creating

*See also "The Way the Eight Applications Produce Mental Stillness," pp. 56–57, and "The Way Those Modes Sustain Mental Stillness," pp. 204–7.

> buoyancy and pleasure in the mind engaging in correct attention. It is called "mental flexibility" because when the mind possesses that [mental factor] it is able to engage its object unhindered.[231]

Suppleness cannot be perfected right from the beginning of our practice of samādhi; however, a modicum can be achieved through effort. When we have refined [our abilities] through gradual training, we will achieve suppleness. Furthermore, through the force of achieving mental suppleness, the winds that serve as the causes for achieving physical suppleness will circulate in our body. Once they have pervaded our body, we achieve physical suppleness. This is explained in the *Śrāvakabhūmi*.[232]

Mindfulness. The *Compendium of Abhidharma* says:

> What is mindfulness? [45] It is not forgetting a familiar object. Its function is to be undistracted.[233]

When we don't forget an object of meditation that is something with which we are previously familiar, our mind engages it continuously and is not distracted to anything else. That is like, for example, if we are afraid of forgetting something we value, we will make sure we don't forget it by repeatedly recollecting it. In the beginning we must arouse mindfulness repeatedly.

Alertness. The *Subcommentary on the "Differentiation of the Middle and the Extremes"* explains:

> As for alertness, the statement, "when mindfulness has become nonforgetfulness, there is recognition of dullness and agitation," indicates that when mindfulness is fully present it possesses alertness.[234]

Within the sustained stream of the aforementioned mindfulness, alertness examines what is present or not and continuously stands guard. The *Entrance to the Bodhisattva's Way of Life* observes:

> When mindfulness sits at the mind's door
> for the sake of guarding it,
> alertness will appear.[235]

It also says:

> Repeatedly examine
> the condition of your body and mind.
> That alone sums up the definition
> of what it means to protect alertness.[236]

Applied intention. The *Compendium of Abhidharma* states:

> What is intention? It is the mental activity that activates the mind. Its function is to cause the mind to engage with what is virtuous, unvirtuous, or unspecified [neutral].[237]

This is the mental factor that stirs and rouses the mind towards what is virtuous, unvirtuous, or unspecified [neutral]. In this context, it is the applied, or deliberate, intention to abandon any dullness or agitation. It arises once alertness recognizes the presence of either one. [46]

The equanimity of remaining in a natural state. The *Śrāvakabhūmi* says:

> What is equanimity? It is the evenness of a mind free from any afflictive phenomena when it is focused in śamatha or vipaśyanā. It is [characterized by the ability] to remain in a natural state, to enter [that] automatically, to focus with effortless activities following [the development of] mental flexibility, and by mental ease.[238]

When, free from dullness and agitation, śamatha and vipaśyanā are balanced, we can settle in those states naturally. Having relaxed strenuous effort, we are skilled in resting in mental flexibility. The same text continues:

> What are the signs of equanimity? They are that the object of meditation creates equanimity in your mind and that excessive exertion towards that object is not required.[239]

It concludes:

> When is there equanimity? When, during śamatha and vipaśyanā, your mind is free from dullness and agitation.[240]

2) The Specific Explanation of the Ways to Prevent Dullness and Agitation

This has two parts:

a) The Elimination of the Causes of Dullness and Agitation
b) The Ways to Prevent Dullness and Agitation

a) The Elimination of the Causes of Dullness and Agitation

Most of what obscures samādhi is included within the categories of dullness and agitation. The causes of dullness and agitation are said to lie in the various kinds of impure conduct of the three doors. The *Yogācāryābhūmi* states:

> What are the signs of dullness? Not restraining your sense faculties. Being inattentive of your food consumption. Not applying yourself to the practice of not lying down [that is, staying awake] during the first and last periods of the night. Remaining without alertness. Acting out of stupidity. Sleeping too much. Being unaware of the methods. [47] Being lazy about your motivation, diligence, intention, and analysis. Being habituated to śamatha. Bringing to mind a one-dimensional śamatha that is not a completely refined śamatha. Having a foggy mind. Not enjoying focusing on an object of meditation.[241]

The text continues:

> What are the signs of agitation? As before, there are the four: not restraining your sense faculties and the others [up to remaining without alertness]. Acting out of desire. Having an unpeaceful manner. Not being disillusioned [with saṃsāra]. Being unaware of the methods. Being overly keen about your motivation and the other aforementioned [qualities]. Not being habituated to diligence. Meditating in a one dimensional [way], meaning that your concentration has not been refined. Being distracted by any type of phenomena that is conducive to agitation, such as thoughts of relatives.[242]

"The signs of dullness and agitation" are the causes of dullness and agitation. "Being lazy" applies to diligence, intention, and analysis [as well as motivation]. "Being habituated to śamatha" means to be habituated only to experiences of it. "Being overly keen" means to concentrate too much on pleasurable objects. "Motivation and the others" refers to the four: [motivation,] diligence, [intention, and analysis].

That being so, we should apply ourselves to the ways to eliminate those causes of dullness and agitation.

b) The Ways to Prevent Dullness and Agitation

To stop the coarse dullness, just described, once it has arisen, it is taught that we should bring to mind things characterized by illumination and the excellent qualities of the buddhas, analyze with our discerning prajñā, increase the scope of our focus, uplift our mind by rejoicing, and the like. The first *Stages of Meditation* says:

> Whenever you are overcome by sluggishness or drowsiness, your apprehension of the object of meditation will be unclear and your mind dull. When that happens, cultivate a sense of illumination or bring to mind things that inspire you, such as the excellent qualities of the buddhas. [48] Those will clear away sluggishness and you will be able to focus firmly on the object of meditation.[243]

The *Synopsis of the Pāramitās* states:

> The force of persevering in vipaśyanā
> uplifts and stimulates your mind when it is slack.[244]

The *Heart of the Middle Way* instructs:

> When your mind is slack, expand it
> by meditating with a vast focus.[245]

Things characterized by illumination. The *Śrāvakabhūmi* says:

> Concentrate on the quality of illumination coming from the light of a butter lamp, the light of a bonfire, or the orb of the sun.[246]

We should focus our mind on those light rays lighting up and illuminating everything.

As for the actions we should take in the case of dullness, the *Śrāvaka-bhūmi* explains that we should bring to mind things with illuminating characteristics, uplift our mind by focusing on what inspires us (such as the sixfold recollection), contemplate the disadvantages of sluggishness and drowsiness (the causes of dullness) and then abandon those, move about, gaze in all directions and at the moon and stars, splash water on our face, and so forth.[247]

Coarse agitation is averted by contemplating impermanence and being disillusioned [with saṃsāra], by reflecting on the problems of distractions and rejecting them, and by resting in śamatha, letting the mind settle into its natural state. The first *Stages of Meditation* explains:

> When you observe mental agitation on occasion as you recall previous agitations and amusements, pacify those agitations by bringing to mind things that cause your mind to be disillusioned [with saṃsāra], such as impermanence. Then apply yourself to engaging the object of meditation without allowing your mind to become [overly] active.[248] [49]

The *Heart of the Middle Way* states:

> When distracted, see the problems inherent in distraction
> and draw [your mind inward].[249]

The *Synopsis of the Pāramitās* says:

> When your mind becomes agitated,
> reverse that with śamatha.[250]

As for the actions we should take in the case of agitation, we should restrain our sense faculties, give up strenuous [activities] as if we were invalids, not bring to mind objects that cause agitation, do many prostrations, and so forth.

For subtle dullness and agitation, we should use well-known instructions such as:

- When your mind is dull, rouse it and tighten [your concentration].
- When agitated, settle your mind down and relax.

iii. The Identification of the Essences of Śamatha and Vipaśyanā

Unraveling the Intent states:

> Staying alone in isolation and having correctly settled [their mind] internally, [bodhisattvas] bring to mind those dharma topics upon which they have reflected carefully. They are attentive because their mind continuously engages internally with the mental state that is being brought to mind. The physical and mental suppleness that arises while abiding that way and resting in that repeatedly is called śamatha.[251]

It continues:

> Having achieved physical and mental suppleness, they abide there and relinquish mental images. They discern, and have conviction about, the dharma topics being reflected upon as the representations for the sphere of internal samādhi. [50] With regard to those representations for the sphere of samādhi, any differentiation of the meaning of the knowable objects, thorough differentiation, complete discernment, complete analysis, forbearance, interest, differentiation of particulars, view, or thought is called vipaśyanā.[252]

The *Jewel Cloud Sūtra* observes:

> Śamatha is the one-pointed mind. Vipaśyanā is discernment of what is true.[253]

The *Ornament for the Mahāyāna Sūtras* says:

> Know the path of śamatha
> to be the summary of the names of the dharma.
> Know the path of vipaśyanā
> to be the analysis of their meaning.[254]

It also says:

> Because, on the basis of correct stillness,
> mind rests in mind,

> and because phenomena are thoroughly differentiated,
> those are śamatha and vipaśyanā.[255]

In his commentary on that text, Ācārya Vasubandhu remarks:

> Because, on the basis of correct samādhi, mind rests in mind and because phenomena are thoroughly differentiated, we should know that those are, respectively, śamatha and vipaśyanā. They are not an absence of samādhi. Those are the characteristics of śamatha and vipaśyanā.[256]

Generally speaking, it is clearly taught that concentrating on any object of meditation and resting the mind one-pointedly without distractions is śamatha. And it is taught that the mind that differentiates and analyzes by discerning the nature of knowable objects is vipaśyanā.[257] Furthermore, everything from the first stages of settling the mind on its object and resetting up through the final stages of creating a single continuum and equipoise is said to be śamatha.* [51] Everything from attention and differentiating the characteristics of the nature of knowable objects up through the final stages, the full development of the spontaneous engagement of expertise and prajñā, is said to be vipaśyanā. The *Bodhisattvabhūmi* states:

> Focusing the mind with certainty on just an inexpressible entity or an object that is a mere referent brings to mind perceptions that are free from elaborations and mental distractions. With dedication to all objects of meditation, settling the mind on the characteristics of internal samādhi, resetting, and up through the full development of creating a single continuum and the engagement in samādhi are called śamatha.
>
> What is vipaśyanā? The same mental attention cultivated during śamatha that brings to mind the characteristics of those dharma topics being reflected upon, that differentiates, that thoroughly differentiates, that thoroughly differentiates dharma topics, up through that which fully develops expertise and that which engages with prajñā are considered vipaśyanā.[258]

*These are the nine mental states of resting. For details, see "The Presentation of the Divisions of Śamatha and Vipaśyanā," pp. 34–36 and "The Way to Achieve Mental Stillness through Nine Stages," pp. 57–59.

The objects of meditation for śamatha and vipaśyanā. The objects of meditation for śamatha are, among knowable objects, nonconceptual images, and for vipaśyanā they are, among knowable objects, conceptual images. It is said in *Unraveling the Intent*:

> "Bhagavān, how many types of objects are there for śamatha?"
> He replied: "One: nonconceptual representations."
> "How many kinds of objects are there for vipaśyanā?"
> He replied: "Only one: conceptual representations." [52]
> "How many types of objects are there for both?"
> He replied: "Two: the limits of existence and the accomplishment of purpose."*[259]

The *Instructions on Prajñāpāramitā* comments:

> All nonconceptual representations—qualitative and quantitative—are the objects of śamatha. All conceptual representations—qualitative and quantitative—are the objects of vipaśyanā.[260]

According to the Sūtra-oriented approach, authentic śamatha and vipaśyanā must be posited as the attainment of suppleness and the attainment of samādhi that engages continuously and naturally. The first *Stages of Meditation* teaches:

> Once distractions related to external objects are pacified, resting in the mind that is supple and takes delight in engaging an internal object continuously and naturally is called śamatha. While resting in śamatha, any analysis of just that is called vipaśyanā.[261]

Nevertheless we may ask, How are the śamatha and vipaśyanā in which suppleness has not been achieved described? It is in this context that the term "an approximation of śamatha and vipaśyanā" is used. *Unraveling the Intent* explains:

> "Bhagavān, during the period that bodhisattvas have not attained

*See "Universal Objects of Meditation," pp. 48–49.

> physical and mental suppleness when they inwardly attend to mind observing mind, what is that attention called?"
>
> "Maitreya, that is not śamatha. It can be said to be similar to a conviction that approximates śamatha."[262]

It continues:

> "Bhagavān, during the period that bodhisattvas have not achieved physical and mental suppleness when their mind inwardly attends to those dharma topics (that have been properly reflected upon) as the representations for the sphere of samādhi, what is that attention called?" [53]
>
> "Maitreya, that is not vipaśyanā. It can be said to be similar to a conviction that approximates vipaśyanā."[263]

In keeping with that, the *Instructions on Prajñāpāramitā* comments:

> Bodhisattvas, dwelling alone in isolation, bring to mind the topic upon which they have reflected. Casting aside mental conversation, they frequently direct attention to mind, however it appears. During the period that physical and mental suppleness has not developed, that attention is an approximation of śamatha. When suppleness has developed, it is śamatha.[264]

It continues:

> Then [bodhisattvas] rest in that very attainment of physical and mental suppleness. With strong conviction about the topic being reflected upon as the sphere of activity that is the representation for internal samādhi, they bring discernment to bear. During the period that physical and mental suppleness has not developed, that attention is an approximation of vipaśyanā. When suppleness has developed, it is vipaśyanā.[265]

We may now ask, At what point do the paths of śamatha and vipaśyanā become fully pure? It is taught that when sluggishness and drowsiness are overcome, śamatha is pure, and when agitation and remorse are destroyed, vipaśyanā is pure, as is stated in *Unraveling the Intent*:

> "Bhagavān, at what point is the path of śamatha pure?"
> "Maitreya, when sluggishness and drowsiness are completely conquered, śamatha is pure.
> "Bhagavān, at what point is the path of vipaśyanā pure?"
> "Maitreya, when agitation and remorse are fully overcome."[266]
> [54]

iv. The Presentation of the Divisions of Śamatha and Vipaśyanā

When śamatha is categorized in terms of its nature, there are the two types: mundane śamatha and transmundane śamatha. When it is categorized by its functions, there are three: the śamatha of resting at ease in the present life and the others. The most well-known categorization is by means of method: the nine mental states. The *Ornament for the Mahāyāna Sūtras* states:

> After you have directed your mind to an object of meditation,
> do not be distracted from the continuity of that.[267]

In his explanation of that text, Vasubandhu lists the nine mental states:

> [Beginning with, "After you have directed your mind to an object of meditation,"]* these four verses describe the methods for settling the mind through the nine mental states of resting. They are called settling, constant settling, definite settling, increased settling, taming, pacification, thorough pacification, creating a single continuum, and equipoise.[268]

The *Compendium of Abhidharma* also lists them:

> What is śamatha? It is settling the mind on what is internal, continuous settling, renewed settling, increased settling, taming, pacification, full pacification, one-pointedness, and equipoise.[269]

They will be described in the section on śamatha.†

*The four verses are cited on pp. 57–59.
†See "The Way to Achieve Mental Stillness Through Nine Stages," pp. 57–59.

The categorizations of vipaśyanā.* There are the three types, vipaśyanā arising from characteristics and the others, taught in *Unraveling the Intent*:

> "Bhagavān, how many types of vipaśyanā are there?"
>
> "Maitreya, there are three: that which arises from characteristics, that which arises from thorough investigation, and that which arises from discernment."[270] [55]

That text identifies them as follows:

> What is the vipaśyanā that arises from characteristics? It is that which only brings to mind a conceptual representation for its sphere of samādhi.
>
> What is the vipaśyanā that arises from thorough investigation? It is that which brings to mind dharma topics that were not well understood by the prajñā [that was directed] at them, in order that such [topics] be understood.
>
> What is the vipaśyanā that arises from discernment? It is that which brings to mind dharma topics that were well understood by the prajñā [that was directed] at them, in order that [bodhisattvas] may feel bliss through liberation.[271]

There are also the four types of vipaśyanā—the vipaśyanā that differentiates phenomena, that differentiates thoroughly, discerns completely, and analyzes completely—taught in the *Compendium of Abhidharma*:

> What is vipaśyanā? It is the differentiation, thorough differentiation, complete discernment, and complete analysis of phenomena because it is the remedy for negative propensities and characteristics, overturns what is fallacious, and is the settling of the mind in what is not fallacious.[272]

They are identified in the *Śrāvakabhūmi* as follows:

> What are the four types of vipaśyanā? Bhikṣus, based on the

*For additional explanation, see "Correlating This Vipaśyanā with Other Approaches," pp. 255–58.

> internal mind's śamatha, they are the differentiation, thorough differentiation, complete discernment, and complete analysis of phenomena. [56]
>
> How is differentiation done? Differentiation is conducted with the quantitative aspects of the objects of meditation for purifying behavior, the objects of meditation for expertise, and the objects of meditation for purifying mental afflictions. Thorough differentiation is conducted with the qualitative aspect [of those three objects].
>
> When attention endowed with prajñā joins with discernment to apprehend the characteristics [of those three objects], that is complete discernment. When there is correct discernment, that is complete analysis.[273]

Furthermore, the *Śrāvakabhūmi* says:

> Those are the three doors of vipaśyanā and the focuses on the six categories of the basis. In brief, these encompass all forms of vipaśyanā.[274]

Although it uses the term "six categories," those are six modes of inquiry undertaken with the vipaśyanā of thorough investigation. Since they are explained as the investigation of meaning, entities, characteristics, qualities, time, and reasonings, they are called "the vipaśyanā that investigates meaning" and so forth.

v. The Analysis of the Order of Śamatha and Vipaśyanā

Most Sūtra-oriented treatises contain numerous references to practicing śamatha first, then vipaśyanā. The *Ornament for the Mahāyāna Sūtras* says:

> On the basis of what is earlier, the later develop.
> Because they are inferior and superior,
> coarse and subtle,
> they are given in that order.[275] [57]

In the case of the six pāramitās, it is taught that the later ones depend on the earlier ones and, consequently, the earlier ones are considered inferior and the later superior and, similarly, coarse and subtle. The *Letter to a Friend* observes:

> There is no prajñā without meditative concentration.[276]

The *Entrance to the Bodhisattva's Way of Life* instructs:

> By being aware that vipaśyanā imbued with śamatha
> can conquer your mental afflictions,
> begin by pursuing śamatha.[277]

Similar explanations are found in the *Śrāvakabhūmi*, *Stages of Meditation*, and *Instructions on Prajñāpāramitā*.

On the basis of such statements, some claim with conviction that it is always the case that vipaśyanā meditation can only be undertaken once śamatha has been practiced and mastered. As their reason, they say, "Śamatha is not achieved without achieving suppleness. Without achieving those two, vipaśyanā and its suppleness will not be achieved."[278] That is not correct because there are those who achieve both śamatha and vipaśyanā without having achieved suppleness.

We may ask, How is that so? It is because the *Bodhisattvabhūmi*, *Compendium of Abhidharma*, and *Instructions on Prajñāpāramitā* explain clearly that śamatha is the nine mental states (beginning with settling the mind) and vipaśyanā is the four, the differentiation of phenomena and the others.[279] And it is very difficult for beginners to achieve suppleness in the early phases of achieving śamatha and vipaśyanā. [58]

Furthermore, according to those [who make such assertions], whatever is śamatha must be consummate śamatha and whatever is vipaśyanā must be consummate vipaśyanā because they say that whatever is śamatha or vipaśyanā must be the achievement of its respective suppleness. If they accept that, then, for the same reason, whatever is a path must be a consummate path.

We may now ask, Why do *Unraveling the Intent* and *Instructions on Prajñāpāramitā* teach that meditations in which suppleness has not been achieved are not śamatha or vipaśyanā?* Such statements have in mind the criteria for the achievement of consummate śamatha and vipaśyanā

*See citations on pp. 32–33.

because, were that not the case, there would be many internal contradictions according to the above explanations and disagreements with scriptures and reasonings.

Therefore, explanations that vipaśyanā meditation depends on śamatha are intended for the gradual type of individual because there are those who achieve vipaśyanā even though they have not achieved śamatha. The *Compendium of Abhidharma* states:

> Some achieve vipaśyanā but do not achieve śamatha. They will strive for śamatha on the basis of vipaśyanā.[280]

The *Yogācāryābhūmi* explains:

> You may know [the truths] from suffering to the path—accurately, just as they are—without having attained the first meditative concentration or beyond. As soon as you have such [knowledge], rest your mind and do not engage in differentiating phenomena. On the basis of that superior prajñā, you can pursue the practice of superior states of mind.[281]

Those are indisputable statements. Also, throughout the tantras and the treatises on the generation and perfection phases, there are instructions for meditating with characteristics at the beginning of the session and meditating without characteristics at the end of the session. Those [indicate that] it is not the case that the approach is that [only] when śamatha has been practiced and mastered can we meditate on vipaśyanā. There are many instructions by numerous mahāsiddhas to cultivate vipaśyanā right from the beginning without pursuing śamatha separately. [59] In particular, since this practice lineage teaches two approaches—pursuing meditation within the view and pursuing the view within meditation—it is not certain that there is one definite [order].

vi. The Way to Cultivate the Unification of Śamatha and Vipaśyanā

This has two parts:

A) The Reason Both Śamatha and Vipaśyanā Are Necessary
B) The Way to Unify Śamatha and Vipaśyanā

A) The Reason Both Śamatha and Vipaśyanā Are Necessary

Since a mind without śamatha moves about like water, it lacks equipoise. A mind that cannot rest in equipoise will not achieve what is true and correct. Vipaśyanā that has no śamatha is unstable, like a candle flame in a windy place. Since it cannot give rise to the brilliant light of wisdom, śamatha is necessary. The first *Stages of Meditation* says:

> Because the mind is fluid like water, it will not be still without the foundation of śamatha. The mind that does not rest in equipoise cannot know what is true just as it is. The Bhagavān said, "By resting in equipoise you will know what is true just as it is."[282]

The middle *Stages of Meditation* states:

> With a vipaśyanā that has no śamatha, yogins' and yoginīs' minds are distracted by objects. Like a candle flame in a windy spot, they are unstable. In that case, the light of wisdom will not shine brilliantly. Thus it is that you should practice both.[283]

It is taught that no matter how much we cultivate a śamatha that lacks vipaśyanā we won't be able to eliminate our obscurations, even though we may suppress our mental afflictions for a time.[284] We won't be able to destroy the dormant tendencies of our mental afflictions and won't be liberated from the problems of saṃsāra: birth, aging, sickness, death, and so forth. [60] The middle *Stages of Meditation* explains:

> Becoming familiar with just śamatha alone does not remove obscurations for yogins and yoginīs—it simply suppresses their mental afflictions for a while. Without the light of prajñā, dormant tendencies cannot be destroyed. Therefore, *Unraveling the Intent* says:
>
> Meditative concentration suppresses the mental afflictions. Prajñā destroys their dormant tendencies.[285]

It continues:

> The *Bodhisattva's Piṭaka* states:

> Those who have not heard the teachings of the *Bodhisattva's Piṭaka*, who have not heard the noble dharma of the vinaya, and who take samādhi alone to be supreme succumb to overt pride through the force of their arrogance. They will not be free from birth, aging, sickness, death, sorrow, lamentation, suffering, unhappiness, or distress. They will not escape from the saṃsāra of the six kinds of beings. They will not be liberated from the heaps of suffering. With that in mind, the Tathāgata said, "Those who listen to [or learn from] others about what is suitable will escape aging and death."[286]

Śamatha is necessary so that mind does not move from its object. Vipaśyanā is necessary for the realization of suchness that prevents being swayed by bad views; it makes [the mind] like a mountain. We need both śamatha and vipaśyanā, as the *Moon Lamp Sūtra* says:

> The force of śamatha makes [your mind] unwavering.
> Vipaśyanā makes it like a mountain.[287] [61]

B) The Way to Unify Śamatha and Vipaśyanā

We may wonder, How exactly are śamatha and vipaśyanā unified? In the context of meditating on vipaśyanā without having achieved the ninth mental state of resting, there are ways of unifying [vipaśyanā with] each [stage of śamatha]. However, here the approach is to unify the consummate śamatha and vipaśyanā. Once you have achieved the ninth mental state of resting—the śamatha of equipoise, free from the faults of dullness or agitation—when you exert yourself in the vipaśyanā of the differentiation of phenomena, that vipaśyanā engages naturally.[288] Like the ninth mental state of resting, it proceeds effortlessly without needing [excessive] application. Vipaśyanā becomes pure and cleansed. When it mixes with mental stillness and they become balanced, that is the unification of śamatha and vipaśyanā. The *Śrāvakabhūmi* says:

> How do you mix śamatha and vipaśyanā and unify them in a balanced way? Why is that called a path of unification? It is said that [it develops] from the nine mental states of resting. Based on hav-

> ing achieved the ninth state (equipoise) and mastering samādhi, you exert yourself in the superior prajñā of differentiating phenomena. At that time, you naturally and effortlessly engage that path of differentiating phenomena. Since the path of śamatha is the appropriate absence of active application, vipaśyanā is pure, cleansed, follows śamatha, and is infused with a delightful feeling. Such śamatha and vipaśyanā mix and become balanced. That is called the path that unites śamatha and vipaśyanā.[289] [62]

The final *Stages of Meditation* comments:

> Because [your mind] is isolated from dullness and agitation, it rests evenly and engages naturally. When this brings suchness clearly to mind, you have equanimity because you have relaxed your efforts. Know that at that point you have mastered the path that unites śamatha and vipaśyanā.[290]

The *Instructions on Prajñāpāramitā* says:

> Next, focus on a conceptual representation. When your mind experiences both [śamatha and vipaśyanā] in an uninterrupted and continuous stream of attention, that is called the path that connects the pair, śamatha and vipaśyanā. Śamatha and vipaśyanā are the pair. "Connects" means to possess [each other]: they operate bound together.[291]

"Conceptual representations" are the objects of vipaśyanā.

Generally, it is taught that nonconceptuality is the object of meditation for śamatha and conceptuality is the object of meditation for vipaśyanā. Based on that, some assert that śamatha is only the mind not attending to any phenomenon and not conceptualizing anything at all and that vipaśyanā is only the mind conceptualizing all phenomena. That is illogical. Were that the case, it would be impossible to have śamatha with characteristics, such as the generation process. What does that mean? It means that when they cultivate the śamatha that focuses on the Tathāgata's form, they would have to accept that the image of the [Tathāgata's] form is not conceived of and is not observed because they have asserted that during śamatha the mind does not engage any phenomenon and is nonconceptual. [63] The unification of śamatha and vipaśyanā would also be impossible because, if śamatha does not conceive of any phenomenon and vipaśyanā is conceptual, there can be no common locus for nonconceptuality and conceptuality. If [a common locus] were possible, it would be the source of ridicule for dialecticians.

We might ask, Is it that the image of the [Tathāgata's] form is merely appearing to the mental [consciousness] but it is not conceptual? If it is not designated by thought, there is no object appearing in that way. An appearance is what appears to thought because everything with characteristics (such as the generation process) is said to be conceptually imputed.[292]

It is also illogical to say that all vipaśyanā involves conceptuality because the *Stages of Meditation* speaks of an unmoving vipaśyanā, because nonconceptual wisdom is the object seen by vipaśyanā, and because that [wisdom] is the true vipaśyanā.

Furthermore, śamatha involving discerning prajñā would be impossible because they say that śamatha involving conceptuality is impossible and that śamatha is only not thinking about anything at all. Also [their assertion] would mean that the teachings that śamatha is attentiveness and that it has four types of attention are wrong, and that mindfulness and alertness during śamatha meditation would have to be the mind not being attentive because they have asserted that śamatha is the mind not attending to any phenomenon.

Now we may ask, Why are the objects of śamatha and vipaśyanā taught in that way? Those are said to be the usual objects of śamatha and vipaśyanā. [64] However, if we take one locus, such as śamatha and vipaśyanā observing a deity's form, there will be two aspects: śamatha's vivid image of the form that is the focus for, and what appears to, the mental [consciousness], and the nature of that [form] that vipaśyanā differentiates and analyzes. As that shows, śamatha is not thinking about any phenomenon other than the object of meditation and settling the mind right on that object. Vipaśyanā is differentiating and conceptualizing the nature of that object or having the certainty that knows it to be without any essence. On that basis, the two mix and become inseparable. Being of one essence but discrete isolates, śamatha and vipaśyanā are unified.

vii. The Explanation of the Results of Śamatha and Vipaśyanā

Unraveling the Intent states:

> What are the results of those [śamatha and vipaśyanā]? Pure mind is the result. Pure prajñā is the result.[293]

In that statement, pure mind is [the result] of śamatha and pure prajñā is that of vipaśyanā. Pure mind means that thoughts involving mental afflictions have been purified. Pure prajñā means that the latent tendencies of ignorance have been purified. The same text teaches that śamatha and vipaśyanā liberate us from two forms of bondage:

> "Bhagavān, what are the functions of śamatha and vipaśyanā?"
> "Maitreya, they liberate you from two forms of bondage: the bondage of characterizations and the bondage of negative propensities."[294]

It is also explained that, during this life, śamatha reverses our attachment to sense pleasures, gives rise to supercognitive abilities and samādhis, and, in future lives, it [results in] the attainment of a god's form that is free from desire. [65] The *Verses That Summarize the Prajñāpāramitā Sūtras* explains:

> Meditative concentration dispenses with inferior sense pleasures
> and makes awareness, supercognitive abilities, and samādhis
> manifest.[295]

The *Letter to a Friend* says:

> The four meditative concentrations that reject
> pleasure[-seeking] conduct, joy, bliss, and suffering
> bring the attainment of fortune equaling that of the gods
> in [Great] Brahmā, Clear Light, Flourishing Virtue, and Great
> Result.[296]

The *Lamp for the Path of Awakening* observes:

> Once the yoga of śamatha is perfected,
> supercognitive abilities are achieved.[297]

It is said that, on the temporal level, vipaśyanā brings happiness to all beings and, when it recognizes the nature of phenomena, it liberates us from the three realms. The *Verses That Summarize the Prajñāpāramitā Sūtras* states:

> All the enjoyments of the buddhas,
> their offspring, śrāvakas,
> pratyekabuddhas, and gods
> spring from supreme prajñāpāramitā.[298]

It also says:

> When prajñā recognizes the nature of phenomena
> it takes us beyond all three realms.[299] [66]

The ultimate result of śamatha and vipaśyanā is the attainment of complete awakening. The *Bodhisattvabhūmi* teaches:

> Once bodhisattvas perfect the pāramitā of meditative concentration, they have awakened completely to unsurpassable true, perfect buddhahood, they will awaken completely, and they are currently awakening completely.[300]

The *Prajñāpāramitā in Seven Hundred Lines* states:

> Mañjuśrī, if they cultivate prajñāpāramitā, great bodhisattvas will quickly and fully awaken to unsurpassable true, perfect buddhahood.[301]

In the general context of śamatha and vipaśyanā, the exalted Gampopa teaches:

> It is said:
>
> > Śamatha and vipaśyanā are the doors to all the dharma teachings.
>
> Each has five points: cause, function, hindrances, obscurations, and pure path. The cause of śamatha is pure ethical conduct, and the cause of vipaśyanā is the prajñā derived from listening and reflecting. The function of śamatha is to free us from the bondage

of characterizations. Vipaśyanā's function is to liberate us from the bondage of negative propensities.

What hinders śamatha is our concern for our body and possessions. What hinders vipaśyanā is not being satisfied with the words of the noble ones. Busyness and being content with just a little [meditation experience] hinder both.

Obscurations: Agitation, remorse, and doubts obscure śamatha. Drowsiness and sluggishness obscure vipaśyanā. Pleasure-seeking and malice obscure both. To have subdued sluggishness and drowsiness is the pure path of śamatha. To have subdued agitation and remorse is the pure path of vipaśyanā. When those two have fully subdued the two obscurations, you achieve the resultant pure dharmakāya.[302]

That completes the common exposition of śamatha and vipaśyanā. [67]

2

Śamatha

b. The Ways to Cultivate Śamatha and Vipaśyanā Individually

This has three parts:

i. The Way to Cultivate Śamatha
ii. The Way to Cultivate Vipaśyanā
iii. Removing Doubts About How to Sustain Meditation on the View

i. The Way to Cultivate Śamatha

This has three sections:

A) The Preparation for Śamatha Practice
B) The Exposition of the Objects of Meditation
C) The Way to Practice Śamatha

A) The Preparation for Śamatha Practice

As explained before, develop the causes for śamatha and avoid the causes of dullness and agitation: not restraining your sense faculties, being inattentive of your food consumption, and so forth.* On a comfortable seat, sit in the seven-point posture of meditative concentration.† Let your breath settle. As you inhale and exhale, do not make noises, pant, or breath heavily. Breath slowly, without effort. You must also practice with a willingness to tolerate difficulties. The *Lamp for the Path of Awakening* states:

> When śamatha and its branches are impaired,

*See "The Presentation of the Causes of Śamatha and Vipaśyanā," pp. 17–19, and "The Elimination of the Causes of Dullness and Agitation," pp. 27–28.

†See pp. 180–81 for a description of the seven-point posture.

> you may meditate with intense exertion
> for a thousand years
> but you will not produce any samādhi.[303]

The first *Stages of Meditation* says:

> You can master śamatha quickly when you disregard the desire for possessions and the like, properly maintain ethical conduct, have a disposition that readily tolerates difficulties, and apply yourself with diligence.[304]

B) The Exposition of the Objects of Meditation

This has four parts:

1) The General Exposition of the Objects of Meditation
2) Who Should Observe What
3) The Explanation of the Initial Objects of Meditation
4) The Way Mindfulness and Alertness Sustain the Object of Meditation [68]

1) The General Exposition of the Objects of Meditation

This has four sections:

a) Universal Objects of Meditation
b) Objects of Meditation for Purifying Behavior
c) Objects of Meditation for Expertise
d) Objects of Meditation for Purifying Mental Afflictions

a) Universal Objects of Meditation

These are specific ways to focus on the latter three objects. They are categorized as four:

1. The focus on conceptual representations is primarily done during vipaśyanā, however, here [in śamatha] it is a quality of meditation with characteristics.
2. The focus on nonconceptual representations is to concentrate on the object of meditation and rest without analytical thinking.

It is explained that "representations" means that the objects upon which we focus are not actual specifically characterized ones, but rather are images of those [actual objects] appearing to our mind.[305]

3. The focus on the limits of existence [is twofold]. It is to have the mental certainty that thinks, "This is the only way that things are; they do not exist in any other way," in relation to the qualitative. It is also to have the mental certainty that thinks, "There is just this much and nothing more," in relation to the quantitative. Of these, the former is an object of meditation during vipaśyanā.
4. The focus to accomplish the purpose is to repeatedly familiarize yourself with an object of meditation. Once you have separated from your negative propensities, you will achieve your aim.

b) Objects of Meditation for Purifying Behavior

These are specific objects of meditation that purify previous behavior involving the mental afflictions (desire and so forth) and prevent their subsequent arising.[306] There are five:

1. The focus on ugliness is to focus on internal ugliness (such as hair, feces, and urine) and external ugliness (such as the blue appearance [of a corpse] and its decomposition). [69]
2. The focus on kindness is to arouse the wish to benefit and bring happiness equally to enemies, friends, and people towards whom you have neutral feelings.
3. The focus on dependent origination is to contemplate the twelve links of dependent origination (ignorance and the rest) and the dependent origination of causes and their results.
4. The focus on the categories of dhātus is done while differentiating the six dhātus: earth, water, fire, wind, space, and consciousness.
5. The focus on the inhalation and exhalation of breath is to count or watch your breath moving in and out, keeping your mind undistracted.

c) Objects of Meditation for Expertise

These are specific objects of meditation that enable us to refute a self of persons that is not part of [that is, is thought of as being outside of] the skandhas, dhātus, and so forth. They are the following five:

1. Expertise in the skandhas is to know that a self and what belongs to a self do not exist apart from the five skandhas (forms and the others).
2. Expertise in the dhātus is to know the causal conditions by which the eighteen dhātus (the eyes and the others) arise from their own seeds.
3. Expertise in the āyatanas is to know that the six internal āyatanas are the dominant conditions for the six sense consciousnesses, that the six external āyatanas are their object conditions, and that the mentation that has just ceased is their immediate condition.
4. Expertise in dependent origination is to know that the twelve links of dependent origination are impermanent, involve suffering, and lack a self-entity.
5. Expertise in what is the case and what is not the case is to know that it is the case that the maturation of virtue is pleasing situations and that it is not the case that the maturation of unvirtue is pleasing situations.[307] This is similar to expertise in dependent origination. [70]

d) Objects of Meditation for Purifying Mental Afflictions

These are the objects of meditation that serve as general antidotes for the mental afflictions. There are two:

1. The focus on calmness and coarseness is to focus on the desire, form, and formless realms, up to the sphere of Nothingness, where the lower ones are comparatively coarse and the higher ones are comparatively calm.
2. The focus on the four truths is to focus on the sixteen aspects (impermanence and the others) of the truths of suffering, the origins of suffering, cessation, and the path.

It is explained that, of these two, the first reduces the strength of the seeds of the mental afflictions and the latter eradicates them completely.

Although these objects of meditation are shared by śamatha and vipaśyanā, for the most part the majority [of commentators] discuss them in the context of śamatha. To take these as objects of meditation during śamatha, first focus on those objects. Concentrate your mind on the image of the object that arises with whatever recognition you have, without doing any analysis.

2) Who Should Observe What

As for which individuals should focus on which objects of meditation for purifying behavior, the *Śrāvakabhūmi* quotes the *Sūtra of the Questions of Revata*:[308]

> If bhikṣu-yogins who are practitioners of yoga find they are dominated by attachment, they should focus their mind on ugliness as the object of their meditation. If their behavior is dominated by aggression, they should focus on kindness. [71] If their behavior is dominated by bewilderment, they should focus on the dependent origination of this condition. If pride is what they entertain, they should focus their mind on differentiating the dhātus.[309]

It continues:

> If their behavior is dominated by thoughts, they should concentrate on being aware of the inhalations and exhalations of their breath. In that way, they concentrate on the appropriate object of meditation.[310]

As for which individuals should focus on which objects of meditation for expertise, the same sūtra [cited in the *Śrāvakabhūmi*] says:

> If bhikṣu-yogins who are practitioners of yoga are confused about the characteristics of formative forces or if they are confused about the entity of a self, the sentient being, the life-force, the one reborn, the one nourished, or the person, they should focus their mind on the objects for expertise in the skandhas. If they are confused about causes, they should concentrate on the objects for expertise in the dhātus. If they are confused about conditions, they should concentrate on the objects for expertise in the āyatanas. If they are confused about impermanence, suffering, or the absence of self, they should focus their mind on the

> objects for expertise in dependent origination and on what is and is not the case.[311]

As for which individuals should focus on which objects of meditation for purifying the mental afflictions, the same sūtra [cited in the *Śrāvakabhūmi*] states:

> Those who wish to be free from the attachments of the desire realm should concentrate on the coarseness of the desire realm and the calmness of the form realm. Those who wish to be free from the attachments of the form realm should focus on the coarseness of the form realm and the calmness of the formless realm. [72]
>
> Those who wish to become disenchanted with and freed from everything related to the perishing collection [that is, the skandhas] should focus their mind on the truth of suffering, the truth of its origins, the truth of cessation, and the truth of the path.[312]

If you are an individual whose behavior balances the mental afflictions, or are someone with few mental afflictions, it is fine to concentrate on whichever one of the previously explained objects you like. The *Śrāvakabhūmi* comments:

> Those whose behavior is balanced should apply themselves to whatever they like in order to rest their mind for a time. That is not done for the sake of purifying behavior. Know that those with few mental afflictions should do the same as those with balanced behavior.[313]

3) The Explanation of the Initial Objects of Meditation

We may wonder, Among all those varieties of aforementioned objects, which one should we focus on first? Although we should train with the objects that are [suitable] for each one of us as individuals, it is important for those of us with a preponderance of thoughts to meditate on our breath. It is also necessary to rely upon just one branch of [or technique for] mental concentration in the beginning. As the *Lamp for the Path of Awakening* states:

> Rest your mind in virtue
> [using] any one object of meditation.[314]

Āryaśūra makes a similar remark:

> Stabilize mental concentration
> by relying on one object of meditation.
> Letting your mind pursue many objects of meditation
> will agitate it with mental afflictions.[315] [73]

It is explained that the initial focal supports are of many types, there is not [just one] prescribed [object of meditation]. Ācārya Bodhibhadra says:

> Here, śamatha is twofold: one that is attained through looking inward and the other by focusing on something seen externally.
>
> Looking inward takes two forms: focusing on the body and focusing on what is based on the body. Focusing on the body is threefold: focusing on the body as a deity, focusing on the body as ugly (such as being a skeleton), and focusing on the body as a special symbol (such as a khaṭvāṅga). Focusing on what is based on the body is fivefold: focusing on the breath, on subtle symbols, on bindus, on light rays, and on joy and bliss.
>
> Focusing on something seen externally is of two kinds: special and ordinary. Focusing on something special is twofold: focusing on the body and on speech.[316]

That being so, those who reject concentrating the mind on a pebble, twig, or bindu have simply not seen such comprehensive presentations.*

Nevertheless, most texts on the stages of meditation explain that we should concentrate on the image of the Tathāgata's form. Since that involves many great purposes—such as giving rise to merit, amassing the accumulations, and purifying obscurations—it is truly excellent. The *King of Samādhi Sūtra* states:

> The Protector of the World is beautiful in all ways,
> with a body like the color of gold.

*For a more detailed refutation of this point, see pp. 185–86.

> Those who rest their mind upon this object
> are said to be bodhisattvas in meditative equipoise.[317] [74]

The final *Stages of Meditation* teaches:

> First, yogins and yoginīs should practice śamatha by placing their attention on whatever they have seen and heard about the Tathāgata's form.[318]

Thus, we should practice resting our mind on that one type of focal support. When our concentration has improved and become more stable, then we can practice with any of the previously mentioned objects of meditation. The first *Stages of Meditation* comments:

> When your concentration has improved, then you should focus in detail with specific objects such as the skandhas and dhātus.[319]

4) The Way Mindfulness and Alertness Sustain the Object of Meditation

The proper practice of samādhi is crucial. First, we should be certain about the identification of mindfulness and alertness, and dullness and agitation, according to the previous explanations.* Here, mindfulness properly maintains the stream of awareness in which our mind is not distracted from its object of meditation. Alertness recognizes whether our mind has strayed from that or not. The *Explanation of the "Ornament for the Mahāyāna Sūtras"* states:

> Mindfulness and alertness create a close focus because the first prevents the mind from straying from its object and the second recognizes when it has strayed.[320]

Our mind is like an untamed elephant. The tether of mindfulness binds it to its object of meditation, which is like a sturdy post. If it doesn't stay there,

*For the definitions of mindfulness and alertness, see pp. 25–26; for the identification of dullness and agitation, see "The Elimination of the Causes of Dullness and Agitation," pp. 27–28.

alertness, like an iron hook, catches it and gradually brings it under control. This analogy is explained in the *Heart of the Middle Way*: [75]

> The wayward elephant of our mind
> is fastened securely
> to the sturdy post of the object
> with the tether of mindfulness
> and gradually tamed by the iron hook of prajñā.[321]

If we become too tight [or concentrated] by being overly diligent, agitation will arise. If we are too relaxed, our mind will become slack and dull. Seek flawless samādhi on the edge where tightness and looseness are balanced, and sustain that. Candragomin laments:

> If I apply exertion, agitation arises.
> If I abandon that, slackness occurs.
> If it is so hard to find the right balance between those,
> what should I do with my disturbed mind?[322]

His *Praise of Confession* continues:

> If I engage with effort, agitation is the result.
> If I loosen up, slackness ensues.
> If it is so hard to find a practice in their middle,
> what should I do with my disturbed mind?[323]

C) The Way to Practice Śamatha

This has four parts:

1) The Way the Eight Applications Produce Mental Stillness
2) The Way to Achieve Mental Stillness through Nine Stages
3) The Way Those [Nine] Mental States Are Achieved through the Six Strengths
4) The Way the Four Types of Attention Are Involved in This [Process][324]

1) The Way the Eight Applications Produce Mental Stillness

The *Differentiation of the Middle and the Extremes* states:

> Focusing on that [diligence] and developing flexibility
> bring the achievement of all aims. [76]
> This occurs from the cause of relying on
> the eight applications that eliminate five faults.
>
> Laziness, forgetting the instructions,
> dullness and agitation,
> lack of application, and [excessive] application
> are said to be the five faults.
>
> There are the basis, what is based on that,
> causes and results,
> not forgetting the object of meditation,
> recognition of dullness and agitation,
> active application to rejecting those,
> and remaining naturally once there is pacification.[325]

The identification of the five faults and the eight applications was presented above.* We may now ask, How is meditative concentration practiced through abandoning those [faults] with those [applications]?

- First, if the three types of laziness arise—which involve being disinterested in cultivating samādhi and delighting in what is not conducive to it—you should arouse the three types of faith, which entail seeing the excellent qualities of samādhi and being enraptured by them.
- You must have a strong, firm motivation that is highly focused and intent upon samādhi.
- Having considered the excellent qualities of samādhi, exert yourself in adopting and rejecting [its causes and impediments respectively]. Arouse great diligence.
- By being willing to tolerate hardships when physical or men-

*See "The General Explanation of the Remedies for Obscurations," pp. 23–26.

tal weariness arise, you gradually develop physical and mental suppleness.

- When placing your mind on an object of meditation, if you become distracted because you forget the instructions, arouse a strong stream of mindfulness. Again bring your mind back to the object of meditation and rest.
- At that time, if the faults of dullness or agitation arise, or you are afraid they will, activate the watchfulness of alertness and recognize them.
- When you are distracted by dullness and agitation, and are unable to apply yourself to the object of meditation or lack the energy to do so, arouse your exertion and diligence to clear away dullness and agitation by either tightening or relaxing, then meditate. [77]
- As the force of dullness and agitation diminishes, over-applying your mind will cause it to move. When that occurs, remain in the equanimity of not applying your mind to anything. Be skillful in nurturing and sustaining that samādhi.

This way of practicing śamatha is well known in most treatises on the stages of meditation and in the esoteric instructions.*

2) The Way to Achieve Mental Stillness through Nine Stages

The *Ornament for the Mahāyāna Sūtras* says:

> After you have directed your mind to an object of meditation,
> do not be distracted from the continuity of that.[326]

That begins its description of the nine mental states of resting.

1. Settling. Completely draw in the mind that is not resting—when it strays to, and is distracted by, externally appearing objects and so forth—and direct it inwardly to the object of meditation.[327] As the text says:

> After you have directed your mind to an object of meditation, . . .[328]

*See also "The Way to Sustain Mental Stillness with These Approaches" pp. 204–7.

2. Continuous settling. Without letting the mind that was initially directed towards an object of meditation be distracted to anything else, settle in prolonging the continuity of that [concentration].[329] As it says:

> . . . do not be distracted from the continuity of that.[330]

3. Renewed settling. If you are distracted by forgetfulness, recognize that and again apply your mind to its object of meditation. [78] The text continues:

> Recognize distraction immediately,
> and renew [your focus] on that [object] once again.[331]

4. Increased settling. Repeatedly withdraw your mind from broader diversions. As you refine [your concentration,] you settle more and more fluidly.[332] It continues:

> More and more, the wise
> draw their mind inward.[333]

5. Taming. By contemplating the excellent qualities of samādhi and dedicating yourself to [achieving] those, your mind is tamed. It continues:

> Then, seeing the virtues in this,
> your mind is tamed within samādhi.[334]

6. Pacification. Contemplating the disadvantages of distractions, any dislike of samādhi is pacified. The text continues:

> Because you see the faults of distraction
> disinclination towards [samādhi] is pacified.[335]

7. Full pacification. When faults in samādhi arise (such as attachment, unhappiness, sluggishness, or drowsiness), pacify them with the appropriate methods. It continues:

> When attachment, unhappiness, and so forth arise,
> pacify them accordingly.[336] [79]

8. One-pointedness. By actively applying yourself to samādhi, you familiarize yourself with it so that later it arises continuously and without effort. The same text says:

> Then, those committed to their vows
> achieve a natural flow in their mind
> with active application.[337]

9. Equipoise. After familiarizing yourself with the eighth mental state, your mind settles effortlessly, spontaneously, and naturally. You attain mastery. It concludes:

> Familiarity with that yields a lack of application.[338]

3) The Way Those [Nine] Mental States Are Achieved through the Six Strengths

According to the teachings in the *Śrāvakabhūmi*[339] on cultivating śamatha by means of the six strengths, the six are the strengths of hearing, reflection, mindfulness, alertness, diligence, and familiarization:

1. The strength of hearing produces the [first] mental state of settling because it enables you to settle your mind on an object of meditation simply by having heard from someone else about how to settle the mind on an object of meditation.
2. The strength of reflection ensures the [second] mental state of continuous settling. It enables you to settle a bit more by extending the continuity [of your concentration] since you repeatedly reflect upon, and sustain, your initial examination of the object of meditation. [80]
3. The strength of mindfulness yields the two mental states of renewed settling and increased settling. If you are distracted from the object of meditation, mindfulness will cause you to recollect the previous object of meditation and draw [your attention] back. From the start, the force created by the strength of mindfulness prevents the mind from wandering from its object of meditation.
4. The strength of alertness brings the achievement of the two mental states of taming and pacification. Alertness is aware of thoughts

and secondary mental afflictions as they arise and the mind pursues them. Alertness also sees their disadvantages and does not allow the mind to scatter.

5. The strength of diligence produces the two mental states of full pacification and one-pointedness because, not tolerating even the smallest thought or secondary mental affliction, it energetically eliminates them and because it creates a continuous samādhi not interrupted by dullness or agitation.
6. The strength of familiarization results in the mental state of equipoise because the strength of familiarization with, and habituation to, all of the above causes your mind to settle in samādhi naturally and effortlessly.

4) The Way the Four Types of Attention Are Involved in This [Process]

It is explained that four types of attention work with the above nine mental states of resting. They are attention that is tightly focused, attention that engages intermittently, attention that engages uninterruptedly, and attention that engages spontaneously.

- During the first two mental states, there is attention that is tightly focused since it is necessary to strenuously tighten [your concentration].
- Then, during the next five mental states, there is attention that engages intermittently since you are unable to sustain [śamatha] for a long time due to interruptions by dullness, agitation, and so forth.
- During the eighth mental state, there is attention that engages uninterruptedly since you are able to sustain [śamatha] for a long time without being interrupted by dullness, agitation, and so forth. [81]
- During the ninth mental state, there is attention that engages spontaneously because samādhi flows naturally without the need for intense continuous effort.

The *Śrāvakabhūmi* explains:

> Be aware that the nine mental states of resting involve four types of attention: attention that is tightly focused, attention that

> engages intermittently, attention that engages uninterruptedly, and attention that engages spontaneously.
>
> Settling and correct settling involve the attention that is tightly focused. Resetting, increased settling, taming, pacification, and thorough pacification involve the attention that engages intermittently. Creating a single continuum involves the attention that engages uninterruptedly. Engagement in samādhi involves the attention that engages effortlessly.[340]

Here, some of the names for the nine mental states of resting are different from the ones used above, however, their essence is the same.

We may wonder, Since the first two mental states have attention that engages intermittently and the middle five need attention that is tightly focused, why are the processes described as they are above? Even though that is the case, it is taught that the term "attention that is tightly focused" is used for the first two since they are predominantly when the mind is not inclined towards samādhi. The term "attention that engages intermittently" is used for the middle five because they are when the mind is mostly inclined towards samādhi.

When undertaking such śamatha, if you practice settling too often with a mixture of negative distractions, it will be difficult for you to achieve anything—even though you may practice for thousands of years. [82] It is explained that the opposite of that [is true]: you will produce samādhi before very long if you rely on the aforementioned collection of causes and, without being interrupted by negative distractions, arouse continuous diligence. The *Lamp for the Path of Awakening* observes:

> When śamatha and its branches are impaired,
> you may meditate with intense exertion
> for a thousand years
> but you will not produce any samādhi.[341]

The *Synopsis of the Pāramitās* says:

> With uninterrupted yoga,
> strive to produce meditative concentration.
> If you repeatedly slack off,
> fire will not appear from friction.

> The process of yoga is the same:
> do not stop until you reach what is exceptional.[342]

That completes the explanation of the way to cultivate śamatha. [83]

3

Vipaśyanā

ii. The Way to Cultivate Vipaśyanā

This has two parts:

A) The General Way of Cultivating Vipaśyanā
B) The Way to Generate the View for Vipaśyanā

A) The General Way of Cultivating Vipaśyanā

Broadly speaking, there are three types of vipaśyanā: mundane vipaśyanā, a lesser type of supramundane vipaśyanā, and Mahāyāna vipaśyanā. The first is vipaśyanā that focuses on the aspects of calmness and coarseness. The middle is the vipaśyanā that focuses on the four truths with an emphasis on refuting a self of persons. The latter is the vipaśyanā that is to be cultivated here.

Unraveling the Intent explains three types of vipaśyanā:

1. The vipaśyanā that arises from characteristics is the prajñā that engages the characteristics of the objects, which is a preparatory phase of vipaśyanā.
2. The vipaśyanā that arises from thorough investigation is the prajñā that understands what was not understood about the abiding state of the view.
3. The vipaśyanā that arises from discernment is the prajñā that is [capable of] liberation and is [directed towards] dharma topics that were well understood.*

*For the relevant citations from *Unraveling the Intent*, see p. 35.

The latter is cultivated once we have discovered the view of the definitive meaning.

Unraveling the Intent and the *Compendium of Abhidharma* describe four types of vipaśyanā:

1. The vipaśyanā that differentiates phenomena is the prajñā that focuses on quantitative phenomena by means of the objects of meditation for purifying behavior and the others [that is, the objects of meditation for expertise and for purifying mental afflictions].
2. The vipaśyanā that differentiates thoroughly is the prajñā that focuses on qualitative phenomena.
3. The vipaśyanā that discerns completely is the prajñā that differentiates coarse qualitative and quantitative objects by means of apprehending characteristics conceptually. [84]
4. The vipaśyanā that analyzes completely is the prajñā that correctly differentiates subtle qualitative and quantitative objects.*

The *Śrāvakabhūmi* teaches the vipaśyanā of six categories. Those six categories, which it says contain all forms of vipaśyanā, are the investigation of meaning, entities, characteristics, qualities, time, and reasonings. The point is that they are modes of inquiry for the vipaśyanā that arises from thorough investigation.†

Also, the *Ornament for the Mahāyāna Sūtras* states:

> Using mental expressions,
> continuously investigate and examine.
> Without the expressions of attention,
> analyze with one taste.[343]

Vasubandhu's *Explanation of the "Ornament for the Mahāyāna Sūtras"* discusses eleven modes of vipaśyanā:

> Those four verses [beginning with "Using mental expres-

*For the relevant citation from *Unraveling the Intent*, see p. 30, and for the relevant citation from the *Compendium of Abhidharma*, see pp. 35–36.

†For the relevant citation from the *Śrāvakabhūmi*, see p. 36.

> sions, . . ."]* present eleven types of attentiveness: that which involves conceptuality and analysis, that which is only analysis without conceptuality, that which involves neither conceptuality nor analysis, attentiveness to śamatha, attentiveness to vipaśyanā, attentiveness to their unification, attentiveness with the characteristics of concentration, attentiveness with the characteristics of śamatha, attentiveness with the characteristics of equanimity, constant attentiveness, and devoted attentiveness.[344]

Those eleven modes of vipaśyanā are a comprehensive presentation of vipaśyanā: the first are concerned with the investigation of the view, the middle with meditation on the view, and the latter with the vipaśyanā that is directed towards the view. [85]

To summarize, the sūtras and texts on the stages of meditation use the analogy of fire arising from the friction of two sticks to demonstrate the necessity of the prajñā of discernment and analysis during the preparatory phase of vipaśyanā and the analogy of the fire and the sticks burning up and disappearing in the end to show that there is no object of meditation for discernment, analysis, and so forth during the actual practice of vipaśyanā. That is also explained in the *Instructions on Madhyamaka* by the Great Lord [Atīśa].†[345] Thus, giving rise to the view is essential to the process of cultivating vipaśyanā.

*The remaining three verses that Vasubandhu quotes (verses 5–7 of chapter 15) are:

> Know the path of śamatha
> to be the summary of the names of the dharma.
> Know the path of vipaśyanā
> to be analysis of their meaning.
>
> Know the path of unification
> to be their combination.
> A slack mind must be concentrated,
> and an agitated one pacified.
>
> Then, when your mind is balanced on the object of meditation,
> remain in equanimity.
> With those, apply constancy
> and devotion.

†For the relevant citations from the *Instructions on Madhyamaka*, see p. 107.

B) The Way to Generate the View for Vipaśyanā

This has two parts:

1) Various Ways to Determine the View
2) The Way to Determine the View in This Context

1) Various Ways to Determine the View

According to [the teachings of] Maitreya's Dharma Treatises and Asaṅga and his brother [Vasubandhu], when we explore the view there are two types of reasonings to use to determine [the nature of] percepts and perceivers: Cittamātra reasonings, such as that one thing can arise as many and the ascertainment of simultaneous observation, which demonstrate that perceived objects do not exist; and Madhyamaka reasonings or the reasoning that if one [of a pair] is absent the other does not arise, which demonstrate that if there are no perceived objects, the perceiving mind does not exist. Their approach explains that the actual view is the wisdom in which the duality of percepts and perceiver is absent.

In keeping with [the teachings of] Nāgārjuna and his son [Āryadeva], when Svātantrika-Mādhyamikas investigate the view, they dissect and analyze the phenomena of percepts and perceivers using the reasoning of those being neither a single unit nor a plurality. In doing so they do not find or discover anything else. Asserting that the perceiving subject is nonconceptual wisdom, they posit that objects are not observable as anything. They explain that the actual view is designated with the term "the wisdom of intuitive reflexive awareness." [86]

In keeping with the Prāsaṅgika-Mādhyamika [approach], when we pursue the view, we analyze the nature, causes, and results of all entities that are objects and perceiving subjects, since these are primarily what are focused on by connate ignorance, which, with its belief in a self and "mine," forms the root of saṃsāra. Using reasonings, such as being neither a single unit nor a plurality, we determine emptiness and thereby avoid the extreme of existence. Using the reasoning of dependent origination, we determine appearances and thereby avoid the extreme of nonexistence. This approach asserts that the actual view is the unification of emptiness and appearances, free from the extremes of existence or nonexistence.

In the many Indian and Tibetan esoteric instructions we can find a variety of explanations, such as that the phenomena of percepts and perceivers are ascertained to be mind, and mind is determined to be empty of inherent nature, free from being something that can be identified as having an essence that exists, does not exist, arises, ceases, or the like. In the end, the view posited is that the dharmatā of phenomena is the expanse free from conceptual elaborations. At this point, however, I will explain a little bit about the way to cultivate vipaśyanā that is well known in the general scriptural tradition.

2) The Way to Determine the View in This Context

This has two parts:

a) The General Presentation of the Ways to Meditate on the Absence of Self
b) The Specific Explanation of the Ways to Meditate on the View

a) The General Presentation of the Ways to Meditate on the Absence of Self

This has three sections:

i) The Reasons for Meditating on the Absence of Self
ii) The Ways to Meditate on the Twofold Absence of Self
iii) The Way Those [Meditations] Generate the View

i) The Reasons for Meditating on the Absence of Self

To begin with, we must identify the self [or self-entity] and our belief in a self. It is explained that on the basis of connate ignorance (the root of saṃsāra), we superimpose existence onto phenomena despite their being inherently nonexistent. The two types of self-entities are that of phenomena and that of persons, which are believed to have, and fixated upon as having, their own natures. [87] Their absence of inherent nature is said to be the two types of absence of self-entity [or self]. In his *Commentary on the "Four Hundred Verses,"* Candrakīrti says:

> A "self" is that essence, or nature, of entities that does not depend on anything other [than itself]. The absence of that is [termed] the absence of self. When categorized as phenomena and persons, it is understood to be twofold: the absence

> of a self-entity of phenomena and the absence of a self of persons.[346]

It is taught that phenomena are what hold their own characteristics and are what compose percepts and perceivers, and persons are what hold the continuity of the compulsive skandhas and are endowed with awareness. The *Sūtra of Fragments* says:

> What hold characteristics are called "phenomena."[347]

And:

> The continuity is called "person."[348]

A personal self is what a person takes to be permanent and single, and then fixates on and believes in, thinking, "Me, I." A self-entity of phenomena is what we fixate on and believe in with phenomena (which are the skandhas of that [person] and the like): being real other entities. [Our beliefs in] those two self-entities create all faults and flaws, such as the mental afflictions, as Dharmakīrti says:

> If there is self, other is cognized.
> From the pair of self and other come clinging and anger.
> The connections with these two
> produce all faults.[349]

The *Precious Garland* observes:

> As long as you cling to the skandhas,
> you will take them to be an "I."
> If you believe in an "I," you create karma.
> From karma there will be birth.[350] [88]

To abandon saṃsāra, which is produced by our belief in a self, it is crucial that we meditate on the absence of self. Dharmakīrti states:

> Without invalidating the object
> it is impossible to eliminate it.[351]

The *Four Hundred Verses* says:

> When you see that the object has no self-entity,
> the seed of existence is destroyed.[352]

The *Entrance to the Middle Way* explains:

> Seeing that all afflictions and flaws
> arise from the view of the perishing collection
> and knowing that its object is a self,
> yogins and yoginīs refute a self.[353]

Furthermore, by meditating on the absence of self-entity, the view of [or belief in] the perishing [collection, that is, the skandhas,] as being a self or "mine" is reversed. Overturning that extinguishes the conditions—craving, grasping, existence, and so forth—that lead to the skandhas taking rebirth. Thus liberation is achieved. The *Fundamental Treatise on the Middle Way* states:

> Because the sense of self and "mine" has been pacified
> there is no belief in a self or belief in "mine."[354]

It also says:

> When notions of "I" and "mine" are extinguished
> in relation to inner and outer,
> the appropriated [skandhas] cease.
> Since those are extinguished, birth is extinguished.
> Since karma and afflictions are extinguished, there is liberation.[355]
> [89]

ii) The Ways to Meditate on the Twofold Absence of Self

This has two parts:

(A) The Refutation of a Self of Persons

(B) The Refutation of a Self-Entity of Phenomena

(A) The Refutation of a Self of Persons

In keeping with the Madhyamaka scriptural tradition, the *Precious Garland* observes:

> It is said that a self and "mine" exist.
> In terms of the ultimate that is wrong.[356]

In the context of its explanation of the absence of a personal self, this system's [approach to understanding] the absence of self is as follows. If [a self] exists, it would have to arise from itself, from other, from both, or during the three times. However, because it does not arise in any of those ways, there is no self. The same text says:

> Because it is not obtained from itself, other, both,
> or in the three times,
> belief in an "I" is extinguished.[357]

Alternatively, if a personal self exists, it must exist as the same as or different from its skandhas. However, neither is reasonable. The *Fundamental Treatise on the Middle Way* refutes that [a self] is the same as skandhas as follows:

> When it is agreed that no self exists
> apart from the appropriated [skandhas],
> if [you conclude that] a self is the appropriated [skandhas],
> your self does not exist.[358]

And:

> If the self is the skandhas,
> it is subject to birth and destruction.[359]

Assertions that a self can be something subject to birth and destruction are refuted by the reasonings that it would mean that recollection of [previous] rebirths would not be possible, actions done would be wasted [that is, they would not produce results], and [the results of] what is not done could be encountered.

The refutation of a self and skandhas being different from each other is stated in the same text: [90]

If it is something other than the skandhas,
it would have none of the characteristics of the skandhas.[360]

It also says:

It is not possible that the self is something
other than the appropriated [skandhas].
If it were something other, it would be perceived
without the appropriated [skandhas], but it is not.[361]

The *Entrance to the Middle Way* remarks:

Therefore, no self exists apart from the skandhas
because there is no perception of it without the skandhas.[362]

The implication of refuting a personal self is the negation of what belongs to a self, such as its eyes and ears. The *Fundamental Treatise on the Middle Way* states:

If no self exists,
how can what belongs to it exist?[363]

The *Entrance to the Middle Way* explains:

Objects do not exist without an agent.
Therefore, what is mine does not exist since a self does not exist.
Thus, by seeing the emptiness of a self and "mine"
yogins and yoginīs are liberated.[364]

A brief summation of the meditation on the lack of a personal self is found in the first *Stages of Meditation*:

A person is not observed separately from skandhas, dhātus, or āyatanas. A person is not of the nature of skandhas and the rest because skandhas and the rest are of the nature of something impermanent and multiple, and a person is imagined by others to be of the nature of something permanent and single. [91] A person that cannot be said to be either identical with or other than [skandhas and so on] cannot be an existent thing because

> there are no other forms for existent things [that is, they must either be identical or different]. That being so, our analysis will show that what are called "I" and "mine" in the world are simply mistaken.[365]

(B) The Refutation of a Self-Entity of Phenomena

The bases to which a person is imputed are phenomena: skandhas, dhātus, āyatanas, and so forth. The way their nature is refuted is as follows. The *Fundamental Treatise on the Middle Way* opens with a general refutation of arising from the four possibilities:

> Not from self, not from other,
> not from both, not without cause:
> there is never an existent thing
> that comes into being in any way.[366]

The same text refutes arising from self by stating:

> If cause and result are the same,
> producer and product will be the same.[367]

It refutes arising from other by reasoning:

> If cause and result are separate,
> cause and noncause will be equivalent.[368]

The *Entrance to the Middle Way* refutes the other two possibilities as well:

> Since things do not arise from self, other, or both
> and not without relying on causes, they are devoid of nature.[369] [92]

Although all phenomena, such as skandhas, are dependent upon causes and conditions, that does not imply an inherent nature. The *Fundamental Treatise on the Middle Way* says:

> An inherent nature arising from causes and conditions
> would be a product.

An inherent nature that is a product—
how is that possible?[370]

When we examine and analyze, we see that percepts and perceivers do not exist as real entities. If they did, they would have to be either a single unit or a plurality, and neither of those two exist. Dharmakīrti states:

If you analyze entities,
there is no entity as such.
Therefore, they lack
the nature of being a single unit or a plurality.[371]

Singularity does not exist, as stated in the *Commentary on Bodhicitta*:

The particles of form do not produce the sense consciousnesses:
those [particles] are not the sense [consciousnesses].
When those produce by aggregation,
their collection cannot be accepted [as an ultimate substance].

When dissected in terms of spatial divisions [or parts],
even a particle is seen to be divisible.
How can that which is analyzed in terms of parts
logically be a [partless] particle?[372]

Plurality does not exist, as the same text says:

A single external referent
can be cognized differently.
A form that is pleasing to one
may be different for another.

One person's body
may be thought of in three different ways:
as a corpse, an object of desire, or as food
by ascetics, the lustful, or dogs.[373] [93]

However, we may wonder, How is it that the various percepts and perceivers appear? They are simply the mistaken consciousness appearing as external referents due to its impure latent tendencies. The *Descent into Laṅkā Sūtra* explains:

> The mind disturbed by latent tendencies
> appears as referents.
> There are no existent referents, just mind.
> Seeing external referents is mistaken.[374]

Mere appearances do not truly exist: they are like illusory creations. The *King of Samādhi Sūtra* says:

> Illusionists conjure up forms,
> creating various horses, elephants, and chariots.
> Those appear despite not existing at all.
> Know all phenomena are this way.[375]

A brief summation of this meditation is found in the first *Stages of Meditation*:

> The absence of a self-entity of phenomena is meditated upon by analyzing as follows. "Phenomena" can be summed up as being the five skandhas, twelve āyatanas, and the eighteen dhātus. Anything that is a skandha, āyatana, or dhātu is, ultimately speaking, not outside of being a manifestation of mind because, when it is broken down into minute particles and the minute particles are scrutinized as to the nature of their parts, no essence is perceived.
>
> That being so, from beginningless time forms and so forth have not been real. However, for immature beings, due to the force of their excessive fixations, mind-itself appears as forms that seem to be external and separate, like the way the appearances of forms and so forth seem to be in dreams. [94] Ultimately, forms and so forth are nothing other than manifestations of mind.[376]

iii) The Way Those [Meditations] Generate the View

As stated, there are two types of self-entity to be negated. They are negated in order to reverse our fixation on, and belief in, the entities of percepts and perceivers as objectively real things. However, if ultimately we grasp at the entities of percepts and perceivers as empty or cling to them as nonexistent, that too is wrong. The *Fundamental Treatise on the Middle Way* observes:

> The victors teach emptiness
> as what brings definite release from all views.
> Those for whom emptiness is a view
> are said to be unable to accomplish anything.[377]

[The *Discourse for Kāśyapa* in] the Heap of Jewels says:

> Kāśyapa, those who hold the person as their view, even if it's as big as Mount Meru, are superior, unlike arrogant ones for whom emptiness is a view. Why? Kāśyapa, even though emptiness is the source of all views, those for whom emptiness itself is a view are incurable.[378]

The *Commentary on Bodhicitta* states:

> Nonarising, emptiness [as a nonaffirming negation],
> "absence of self-entity," or emptiness [as the absence of reality]
> are what inferior beings meditate upon.
> That is not the way to meditate on that [emptiness].[379]

The Exalted Lord [Atīśa] remarks:

> Those who cultivate prajñā [95]
> through the force of meditating with method
> will achieve awakening quickly,
> unlike those who only meditate on the nonexistence of self.[380]

We may wonder, Why is that? Because all phenomena, what are perceived and are perceivers, do appear simply as dependently originated—they are not only empty or just nonexistent. When they are dissected and analyzed, no individual nature or essence [is found]. Therefore, they have no identifiable substance and are not truly existent. The *Fundamental Treatise on the Middle Way* teaches:

> There is no existent phenomena
> that is not dependently originated.
> There is, therefore, no existent phenomena
> that is not empty.[381]

And:

> Do not say, "It is empty,"
> and do not proclaim, "It is not empty."
> Also do not say that it is both or not both.
> [Such expressions] should only be used as [conventional]
> designations.[382]

It also states:

> To say something exists is to hold it to be permanent.
> To say it does not exist is to view it nihilistically.
> Thus, the wise do not abide
> in either existence or nonexistence.[383]

The *Autocommentary on the "Two Truths"* explains:

> Therefore, the Bhagavān said
> things are not empty,
> not nonempty, not existent-and-nonexistent,
> not nonarising, and do not arise.[384]

People are accustomed to engaging with their various mental constructs and are frightened by the nonexistence of bases that provide their minds with grounds with which to engage, such as perceived characteristics or reference points. [96] By taking comfort in sources of perceived characteristics and so forth, they cling to existence, nonexistence, emptiness, nonemptiness, and so forth, and bring ruin to the world. The *Precious Garland* observes:

> People who are afraid of this baseless dharma
> take comfort in bases.
> Since they cling to existence and nonexistence,
> the unwise are ruined.[385]

We may now ask, Since the entities that are percepts and perceivers do not exist at all—as entities, nonentities, or anything else—is this the Cittamātra's view of reflexive awareness, reflexive clarity? [It is not.] Although that [reflexive awareness] may occur during some meditative experiences, generated by circumstances, actually it does not exist. The *Descent into Laṅkā Sūtra* explains:

> External entities are neither existent nor nonexistent.
> Mind is ungraspable.
> All views are relinquished.
> That is the characteristic of nonarising.[386]

Entrance to the Bodhisattva's Way of Life says:

> If [cognition] is never seen by anyone,
> it is pointless to speculate
> about whether it is illuminating or not,
> just as it would be [to speculate] about the beauty of a barren woman's child.[387]

It also says:

> Once neither entities nor nonentities
> remain before the mind,
> since there is no other form,
> there is peace, free from reference point.[388]

A summary of those points is found in the first *Stages of Meditation*:

> Thus it is that you should consider: these three realms are only mind. Therefore, all imagined phenomena are understood to be simply mind. If you discern that, you discern the nature of all phenomena. And thus you discern the essential nature of the mind. [97]
>
> Analyze that [mind] as follows. Mind cannot possibly be real in an ultimate sense. How can the mind that apprehends forms and so forth—things which are of a false nature—and that itself appears as various images be real? Just as forms and so forth are

> false, so too is the mind false since it does not exist apart from those [forms and so forth].
>
> Just as forms and so forth are neither of the nature of a single unit nor of the nature of a plurality since they have various manifestations, mind is neither of the nature of a single unit nor of the nature of a plurality since it does not exist apart from those [forms and so forth].
>
> That being so, mind simply seems to be of the nature of illusions and so forth. And, just like the mind, all phenomena simply seem to be of the nature of illusions and so forth. Thus you analyze.
>
> Therefore, when you discern the nature of mind with prajñā, ultimately you neither observe the mind to be internal nor do you observe it to be external. You do not observe it to be neither of those two. You do not observe a past mind, a future mind, and not even a present one. When the mind arises, it does not come from anywhere. When it ceases, it does not go anywhere. The mind is not graspable. It cannot be shown, and it does not have form.
>
> What is the nature of that which cannot be shown, cannot be grasped, and is not physical? [The *Discourse for Kāśyapa*] in the Heap of Jewels comments:
>
> Kāśyapa, when you look for mind it is not found. What cannot be found cannot be observed. What cannot be observed is neither past, nor future, nor present.[389]

This way of determining that phenomena are mind and recognizing experientially that mind is spacelike dharmatā, beyond identification, is far superior to the common ways of meditating on an analytical emptiness or an intellectually fabricated emptiness. [98] It accords with the following explanations. The *Ornament for the Mahāyāna Sūtras* teaches:

> Aware that there is nothing other than mind,
> they then recognize that mind also does not exist.
> These intelligent ones are aware that both are nonexistent
> and abide in the dharmadhātu devoid of those.[390]

Vasubandhu's *Explanation [of the "Ornament for the Mahāyāna Sūtras"]* comments:

> It says, "There is no object observed that is other than mind." By recognizing that, [bodhisattvas] comprehend deeply that mere mind is also not existent since there is no perceiving subject if there is no perceived object.
> Aware that those two do not exist, [bodhisattvas] abide in the dharmadhātu, which has neither of those and is free from the characteristics of percepts and perceivers. In that way, [bodhisattvas] directly realize the dharmadhātu.[391]

b) The Specific Explanation of the Ways to Meditate on the View

This has three parts:

i) Identifying the Correct View
ii) The Way That [View] Is Cultivated in Meditative Equipoise
iii) The Way [the View] Is Experienced During Postmeditative Attainment

i) Identifying the Correct View

As explained above, intellectually meditating upon anything—entities, nonentities, both of those, neither of those, and so forth—causes us to cling to the extremes of permanence or nihilism. Even meditating on emptiness, nonarising, the absence of reference points, and the like in an intellectual way involves a conceived object or misdirected arrogance. None of those are [the way to meditate on] the actual view. [99]

In that case, we may ask, What is? It is possible that we can [identify the actual view] through analytical resting using the reasonings explained in the scriptural traditions. It is also possible to do this by cutting through misinterpretations [superimpositions] and denial using the meditation techniques explained in the esoteric instructions. In actuality, however, we must be certain that all phenomena, what are perceived and are perceivers, are simply appearances of our own mind. And the ultimate abiding mode of our mind has never inherently existed in any way. It is not veiled by entities or characteristics. It is free from arising, ceasing, or abiding. It remains beyond being an object for the analytical mind. It is free from identification and is uninterrupted. The analogy is space.

However, as beginners, the correct view is to recognize and determine both our illusionlike experiences and our discernments with subtle mindfulness-awareness *within* our [meditative] experience—not letting those remain simply as objects of theoretical understanding. The *Sūtra on Not Moving from Dharmatā* observes:

> Phenomena inherently do not arise, innately do not abide, are free from the extremes of actions and deeds, and are beyond being conceptual and nonconceptual objects.[392]

The *Verses That Summarize the Prajñāpāramitā Sūtras* states:

> Knowing that phenomena lack any nature
> is the practice of the sublime prajñāpāramitā.[393]

The same text says:

> Not conceiving of either nonarising or arising
> is the practice of the sublime prajñāpāramitā.[394]

The *Sūtra Presenting the Undifferentiable Nature of the Dharmadhātu* comments:

> Mind is not physical, it cannot be demonstrated, it does not appear, it is unobstructed, and is not cognizable. It does not dwell internally, externally, or in between those two. Thus, it is pure and nonexistent. [100] It has nothing to free. It is of the nature of the dharmadhātu.[395]

The *Praises to the Mother* says:

> Prajñāpāramitā, inexpressible through speech or thought . . .[396]

The *Fundamental Treatise on the Middle Way* states:

> Not relinquished, not attained,
> not annihilated, not permanent,
> not ceased, not arisen:
> that is nirvāṇa.[397]

The Exalted Lord [Atīśa] explains:

It is profound and free from elaborations.
What is luminous and unconditioned
is unborn, unceasing primordial purity.
The dharmadhātu, natural nirvāṇa,
is without center or end.

It is seen by the sharp eyes of the intellect, free from concepts,
not blurred by dullness or agitation.[398]

He also says:

It is explained that prajñā
is knowing the emptiness of nature
in the context of realizing the nonarising of
the skandhas, dhātus, and āyatanas.[399]

ii) The Way That [View] Is Cultivated in Meditative Equipoise

Generally speaking, meditation is to be undistracted from the view. Rest naturally settled in the view (that was just explained) with mindfulness and alertness, simply not straying from that view. All other objects of meditation and states of attention should be given up. Without altering or manipulating, diminishing or augmenting, examining or analyzing, remain naturally settled in a nonmeditating mode. The *Spacelike Samādhi Sūtra* says: [101]

With the amṛta from the genuine guru
you will know your mind to be like space.
To not waver from that state
is taught to be samādhi.[400]

The *Sūtra of Genuine Samādhi* states:

In dharmatā, just as it is,
so rests mind that is just like it.
Experience unhindered by words dawns.
That is called samādhi.

In the inexpressible dharmatā
so rests mind that is just like it.
Experience without limitations dawns.
That is called samādhi.[401]

The *Prajñāpāramitā in Seven Hundred Lines* explains:

> Not adopting, not holding, and not rejecting any phenomenon is prajñāpāramitā meditation. Not contemplating and not observing anything is prajñāpāramitā meditation.[402]

The *Prajñāpāramitā in Eight Thousand Lines* says:

> To meditate on prajñāpāramitā means not meditating on any phenomenon.[403]

It also says:

> To meditate on prajñāpāramitā is to meditate upon space.[404]

It concludes:

> Space is nonconceptual and prajñāpāramitā is nonconceptual.[405]

The *Sūtra of Precious Space* and Maitreya remark:

From this there is nothing to remove.
To this nothing need be added.
Look truly at what is true.
Those who see truly will be free.[406]

The *Avataṃsaka* says:

Those who wish to enter the domain of the victorious ones [102]
should train with a spacelike attitude,
abandon clinging to concepts, thoughts, and discriminations,
and engage this [domain] with a spacelike mind.[407]

The *Ornament for the Mahāyāna Sūtras* demonstrates:

> Intelligent ones rest in the dharmadhātu, the root
> [of the excellent presentations of the genuine dharma taught by the sages].
> Those steadfast in their recognition that all instances of mindfulness are mere conceptuality
> quickly perfect the ocean of virtues.[408]

The *Commentary on Bodhicitta* states:

> The mind free from reference point
> rests with the characteristics of space.
> Meditating on space
> is described as meditating on emptiness.[409]

The Exalted Lord [Atīśa] explains:

> In the dharmadhātu, free from elaborations,
> rest your mind free from elaborations.[410]

These and many other sayings of the mahāsiddhas that contain similar explanations will be presented in the section on mahāmudrā.

iii) The Way [the View] Is Experienced During Postmeditative Attainment

When you experience postmeditative appearances (which are outside of meditative equipoise), embrace them with the energy or light touch of the mindfulness cultivated during the spacelike equipoise described above. [103] In truth, appearances do not inherently exist, and yet they manifest vividly in their own mode of appearance as if they exist. That is [why] postmeditative attainment is called "illusionlike." This is referred to in many statements, such as the following. The *Verses That Summarize the Prajñāpāramitā Sūtras* explains:

> Those who know the five skandhas to be like illusions
> and don't take illusions to be one thing and skandhas to be another
> are free from the myriad discriminations and experience peace.
> That is the practice of the sublime prajñāpāramitā.[411]

The *King of Samādhi Sūtra* says:

> Like mirages and cities of gandharvas,
> illusions and dreams,
> all characteristics you entertain are empty of any essence.
> Know all phenomena are this way.[412]

The meaning of "illusionlike" is as follows. The conceptualization of the appearances that arise to the postmeditative mind with the thought, "They are not real, they are illusionlike," is called "intellectually fabricated illusions" and is just a presumption that [things] are illusionlike. While that may be useful in some phases, since it involves conceptualization, it is not the point of meditating [on all phenomena] as being illusionlike.

In that case, we may wonder, How is it [done]? The horses and elephants that illusionists conjure up can serve as an analogy. Although they have never had the nature, or essence, of horses and elephants, they undeniably appear as horses and elephants. [104] [The perception of] the way they appear is the same for both the audience and the illusionist, but in terms of [the understanding of] the way they actually are there is a difference: one group believes those to be real horses and elephants while the other does not. Similarly, in relation to persons and phenomena, it is logical that ordinary beings believe things to be as they appear. Yogins and yoginīs, however, know from within that whatever appears is simply an appearance and does not have the nature, or essence, of that entity.

Therefore, in the same way that illusionists regard their illusory creations, yogins and yoginīs know that ultimately all phenomena lack any nature and yet conventional appearances simply occur unceasingly. That is said to be the meaning of illusionlike. As the *King of Samādhi Sūtra* explains:

> Illusionists conjure up forms,
> creating various horses, elephants, and chariots.
> Those appear despite not existing at all.
> Know all phenomena are this way.[413]

Once you are habituated to yoga, you can mix your meditative equipoise that does not move from dharmatā and your postmeditative attainment [of seeing things] as illusionlike. Then everything manifests as the play of dharmatā. Freed from dualistic perception, you attain the realization of unification. The *Verses That Summarize the Prajñāpāramitā Sūtras* states:

> There is no manipulation of thinking, "I am resting evenly," or "I am getting up."
> Why? Because you understand the nature of phenomena.[414] [105]

Having discovered the view for vipaśyanā, when you are sustaining it, do the following. Cultivate a stream of mindfulness that is not distracted from that very view. Be watchful with the alertness that dispels dullness and agitation. Arouse applied intention right within the view, free from dullness and agitation. Rely on equanimity such that your mind does not apply itself to anything other than that [view]. With all of those, employ the four types of attention (the attention that is tightly focused and the rest), being aware that they apply equally to śamatha and vipaśyanā, as the *Śrāvakabhūmi* explains.[415]

That completes the explanation of the way to cultivate vipaśyanā. [106/107]

4

Removing Doubts

iii. Removing Doubts About How to Sustain Meditation on the View

This has four parts:

A) The Distinctions between Analytical Meditation and Resting Meditation
B) The Roles of Analytical and Resting Meditations in Śamatha and Vipaśyanā
C) The Roles of Analysis and Resting in Meditating on the View
D) The Explanations That Remove Doubts Concerning the Actual View

A) The Distinctions between Analytical Meditation and Resting Meditation

Some think that the meditation of paṇḍitas is only analytical meditation and that the meditation of kusalis is only resting meditation. Similarly, others think that the only thing scholars do is analyze in the context of study and reflection based on the scriptural systems and all kusalis do is rest in equipoise referring to esoteric instructions. That is not how it is. Scholars need the resting meditation of remaining in equipoise with the object of meditation, and kusalis need the analytical meditation that cuts through misinterpretations [superimpositions] and denials in the context of the view. Those who don't use both analysis and resting will have difficulty discovering the true object of meditation because the view that is sought through critical investigation alone is an intellectually created view and the view that only involves resting stays at the level of a mental experience.

We may wonder, How are analytical meditation and resting meditation defined? What are their differences? The terms "analytical" and "resting" are designated from the perspective of what they emphasize. "Analytical meditation" refers to the meditative process that uses inferential cognition as its path and primarily determines the view by relying on critical investigation using scriptures and reasonings. "Resting meditation" refers to the meditative process that uses direct cognition as its path and primarily determines the view through remaining in equipoise with suchness. [108] The former is the meditation process that is based on the texts of the noble Asaṅga and the protector Nāgārjuna in which analysis using scriptures and reasonings is emphasized. The latter is the meditation process transmitted from the Great Brahman [Saraha], the lord Śavaripa, and others in which remaining in equipoise with the actual abiding state is emphasized. The view that is discovered through either approach must be the same in terms of the abiding state, emptiness, as Götsangpa teaches:

> The analytical meditation of paṇḍitas and the resting meditation of kusalis have the same final destination, but the kusali approach is faster.[416]

It is only just possible to realize the correct view by relying on the critical investigation of scriptures and reasonings because such critical investigation is conceptual analysis that involves terms and referents, and Dharmakīrti has explained that that cannot determine [the view] as a direct cognition. There are numerous accounts about how the majority of great paṇḍitas and siddhas belonging to the two great chariot-systems were liberated through relying on esoteric instructions such as those found in Secret Mantra. In particular, there are stories of many great paṇḍitas, including Nāropa and Maitrīpa, who were unable to achieve liberation through listening and reflection that relied upon scriptures and reasonings but were liberated through the esoteric instructions on the ultimate essence. It seems that most mahāsiddhas of India and Tibet have been liberated solely by relying upon esoteric instructions.

That being so, those who say that, generally, the view cannot be realized without relying on scriptures and reasonings and that, specifically, the true view cannot be realized without relying on the Madhyamaka reasonings of the father Nāgārjuna and his son [Āryadeva] are simply espousing their own idiosyncratic [ideas]. They are quite wrong. [109] Were they right, it would mean that the true view was not realized prior to Nāgārjuna's and his son [Āryadeva's] composition of their treatises included in the Collection of Reasonings and that most buddhas, bodhisattvas, and Indian and Tibetan siddhas did not realize the true view.

Furthermore, broadly speaking, if [we look at this] from the perspective of the use of the terms "analysis" and "resting," meditations that involve critical investigation must be considered analytical meditation, and meditations during which we settle into the natural state and rest must be resting meditation. Other meanings of the words "analysis" and "resting" would be difficult to explain [or justify]. That being so, all meditations involving intelligent critical investigation—beginning with the meditation on the difficulties of acquiring the leisures and opportunities [of a precious human life] and the meditation on impermanence up through determining the two absences of self-entity—must be analytical meditation. All types of resting evenly on the object of meditation that is the subject of analysis, with one-pointed mindfulness and alertness, must be resting meditation.

On the other hand, some think that when they analyze they are unable to rest because they must analyze conceptually, and when they rest they cannot analyze because they must settle nonconceptually. They regard analysis and resting as incompatible. They are wrong for many reasons. The first *Stages of Meditation* explains that prajñā examines within a state of śamatha and that the prajñā of equipoise analyzes.[417] Vasubandhu's *Explanation of the "Ornament for the Mahāyāna Sūtras"* says that there is vipaśyanā with both conceptuality and analysis, vipaśyanā with no conceptuality but with analysis, and vipaśyanā with neither of those two.[418] Also, vipaśyanā analysis is often used to ensure that the state of resting does not slip away. For example, during śamatha, the arousing of alertness is examination occurring within a resting state. [110]

B) The Roles of Analytical and Resting Meditations in Śamatha and Vipaśyanā

Certain people assert that only resting meditation is done in śamatha practice because alternating between analysis and resting makes it impossible to perfect śamatha. And they say that if vipaśyanā practice does not include analysis with discerning prajñā it vanishes. Such ideas are very wrong. If the former were the case, some of the objects of meditation in śamatha—such as those for purifying behavior and purifying the mental afflictions—would be unsuitable, and it would be inappropriate to arouse discerning prajñā and forceful alertness during śamatha practice.[419] If the latter were the case, the vipaśyanā described as the pacification of discernments at the end of the analysis done by discerning prajñā would be illogical, and the teachings on nonconceptual vipaśyanā and unmoving vipaśyanā, found in the texts on the stages of meditation, would be invalid.

Furthermore, those who advocate such [positions] then have to say that there is no śamatha during analysis and no vipaśyanā during resting, because they assert that analysis is exclusively conceptual analysis and śamatha is solely nonconceptual, and because they assert that during resting meditation vipaśyanā vanishes and there is no discerning prajñā. If they say those things, there are huge [absurd] consequences: the unification of śamatha and vipaśyanā would be impossible, and there can be no common locus for direct nonconceptual cognition and vipaśyanā. [111]

Then we may ask, What are the roles [of analysis and resting in śamatha and vipaśyanā]? In the context of śamatha, resting meditation predominates, in keeping with the practice tradition of the nine ways of resting the mind. It is taught, however, that it is necessary to do analytical meditation once samādhi has improved, as the first *Stages of Meditation* explains:

> When your concentration has improved, then you should focus in detail with specific objects such as the skandhas and dhātus.[420]

There are also many types of analytical meditations recommended in the context of śamatha, such as meditating on ugliness as the antidote for desire, on kindness as the antidote for anger, and dependent origination as the remedy for bewilderment.

In the context of vipaśyanā, analytical meditation predominates in keeping with the three or four stages of vipaśyanā. However, at the end of the analysis done by discerning prajñā, discernments are pacified and nothing is seen.[421] Since vipaśyanā does not vanish and that is the true object seen in vipaśyanā, at that point we must use resting meditation. The *Sūtra of the Questions of Kāśyapa* states:

> Fire springs up from the rubbing of two sticks,
> and its presence then consumes those two.
> Similarly, once the faculty of prajñā arises [from discernment]
> its presence consumes those two [prajñā and discernment].[422]

The *Entrance to the Middle Way* says:

> Ordinary beings are bound by their concepts.
> Yogins and yoginīs without concepts are free. [112]

> Thus, the wise teach the reversing of concepts
> to be the result of analysis.[423]

Once we have achieved the unification of śamatha and vipaśyanā, we should primarily do resting meditation, though on occasion it will be necessary to alternate that with analytical meditation. The relevant scriptural sources will be provided below.

Nevertheless, it is explained that, as beginners, when we experience agitation from an excess of analytical meditation and vipaśyanā, we should cultivate śamatha and, when we feel sluggishness from too much resting meditation and śamatha, we should cultivate vipaśyanā. When we can rest with equal amounts of śamatha and vipaśyanā, we should cultivate equanimity without active application. The first *Stages of Meditation* explains:

> If you do not dispel mental dullness, extreme dullness will prevent vipaśyanā and cause your mind to be like a blind person. Since that is the case, when dullness occurs you must dispel it.
>
> When cultivating vipaśyanā, prajñā may become dominant. At that point, because that is all there is [meaning your śamatha is weak], your mind will waver like a candle flame in a windy location and, consequently, you will be unable to see suchness clearly. Since that is the case, when it happens, cultivate śamatha. When śamatha becomes dominate, cultivate prajñā.[424]

It also says:

> When you are able to rest equally in both, remain without any active application as long as that does not strain your body or mind.[425]

Once śamatha and vipaśyanā mix and are unified, it's not necessary to repeatedly alternate between analysis and resting while the one-pointed mind remains in equipoise. [113] It is said in *Unraveling the Intent*:

> "At what point do śamatha and vipaśyanā mix and become evenly unified?"
>
> [The Bhagavān] replied: "When there is attentiveness to the one-pointed mind."[426]

It also says:

> What is the one-pointed mind? It understands that representations for the sphere of samādhi are simply cognition. Having understood that, it is attentive to thusness.[427]

Ācārya Jñānagarbha's commentary on that text explains:

> The path of śamatha is not different from the path of vipaśyanā because [śamatha] observes the mind that is the object of vipaśyanā. On the path of śamatha, since only the mind that is the object of vipaśyanā is observed, the object observed and the observer are [identical] in being of the nature of the mind. Therefore, [śamatha and vipaśyanā] are not different.[428]

C) The Roles of Analysis and Resting in Meditating on the View

Certain people explain that when we are sustaining the view, first we must forcefully generate an apprehension of the emptiness of reality by analyzing with scriptures and reasonings, and then practice a little bit of resting meditation on that. If we were to practice resting meditation for a long time, it would simply become śamatha and any vipaśyanā would vanish. Therefore, they say that we must analyze as before and meditate while alternating analysis and resting in that way.

That is very illogical. Later I will explain the reasons why, if we have any kind of apprehension of the emptiness of reality that arises based on analysis using scriptures and reasonings, we won't get beyond grasping at emptiness and, consequently, will not develop the correct view for vipaśyanā.* That being the case, practicing resting meditation on that [apprehension of emptiness] is not correct meditation. [114]

If, in their approach, analysis and resting are [always] alternated, then even those who rest evenly in the view will be unable to master it because they say that it is impossible to perfect śamatha when analysis and resting are alternated, and those reasonings that apply to resting evenly in śamatha are equally applicable to resting evenly in the view.

It would become illogical to do resting meditation at the end of analysis

*See pp. 99–101.

because, since they say that vipaśyanā vanishes when we rest, resting meditation on a view in which vipaśyanā has disappeared would not be a correct meditation.

It is also illogical that once we give rise to the view in which śamatha and vipaśyanā are unified, if we do not repeatedly analyze it, it reverts to being just śamatha. When the view in which śamatha and vipaśyanā are unified has arisen, one-pointed resting meditation on just that [view] contains both śamatha and vipaśyanā completely. That is the unification of śamatha and vipaśyanā.

It is not feasible that after having done resting meditation on the view we must again repeatedly analyze. Analysis using scriptures and reasonings does not go beyond being a conceptual process involving terms and referents and, since that is ignorant conceptuality, it is explained as being an object to be abandoned for nonconceptual wisdom. Although the *Sūtra of the Questions of Kāśyapa* and the *Stages of Meditation* teach that nonconceptual wisdom arises from discerning prajñā, they only say that such prajñā is essential at first when determining the view—they do not say that we must repeatedly examine and analyze to sustain the view. For the most part, certainty that [results from] rational analysis does not go beyond being inferential rational cognition arising from reflection, and it is not nonconceptual unmistaken cognition. [115]

It is also untenable to equate the meditation of resting in the view with śamatha because the two are significantly different. Śamatha is simply to sustain the stream of mindfulness that does not consider anything other than its object of meditation. Resting right within the view is to ascertain the emptiness of inherent nature and then sustain the stream of freedom from elaborations that is concordant with that [emptiness].

Then, we may ask, What are the roles of analysis and resting in sustaining the view? First, while investigating the view, the prajñā arising from listening and reflection cuts through misinterpretations concerning specifically and generally characterized [phenomena]. For inducing certainty this is crucial, like showing a horse the racetrack. However, for investigating the correct view, the discerning prajñā arisen from meditation is of the utmost importance. When we look and analyze with that [prajñā], without relying on inference, we are able to directly comprehend that all phenomena lack any nature or essence, and that very discernment will be experienced as disappearing and not existing with any essence. That is the actual view.

Looking and analyzing in that way is analysis with the prajñā of equipoise in which the stream of mindfulness during resting meditation is not lost. It is not analysis involving a conceptual process of terms and referents, as is explained in the first *Stages of Meditation*:

> Once you have stabilized your mind on an object of meditation with śamatha, if you examine with prajñā, the light of true wisdom will manifest. At that time, the dawning [of wisdom's] light will be like that which dispels darkness.
>
> Those two [śamatha and prajñā], like eyes and light, are mutually compatible [conditions] for the dawning of true wisdom. They are not internally incompatible as light and darkness are.
>
> Samādhi is not of the nature of darkness. What is it? It is characterized as being the one-pointed mind. [116] Since it is said, "When you rest evenly in that, you know what is true just as it is," [samādhi] is completely compatible with prajñā, not incompatible.
>
> That being so, when the prajñā of equipoise examines, its nonobservance of phenomena is the genuine nonobservation. Such characteristics of a yogin's or yoginī's śamatha phase are spontaneously existent because there is nothing to be seen outside of that.[429]

After discernment is self-pacified, there is naturally an absence of seeing any phenomenon whatsoever. That is seeing the true nature. The same text states:

> [It is said in the sūtras:]
>
> > What does seeing the ultimate [mean]? It is the absence of seeing any phenomenon.
>
> With that absence of seeing in mind, [the Buddha] said, "There is no seeing." That is not the no seeing that is the result of not being attentive or the incompleteness of conditions, such as is the case with someone who has their eyes shut or who is blind.[430]

And:

> When the prajñā of equipoise examines, its nonobservance of phenomena is the genuine nonobservation.[431]

For those reasons, when we are investigating the view, at first we definitely must engage in analytical meditation using our discerning prajñā within meditative equipoise. Once we have discovered the view, if at any point our intellectual process of apprehending characteristics makes our state of mind unworkable, we should then do whatever analytical meditation is appropriate. When we have incontrovertible certainty in the view, we should do resting meditation right within the view on all occasions that create familiarization with the view. There is no need to alternate with analytical meditation. The relevant scriptural sources will be provided below.

D) The Explanations That Remove Doubts Concerning the Actual View

This has two parts:

1) Analyzing Other Systems
2) Establishing Our Own System [117]

1) Analyzing Other Systems

Some earlier Tibetans assert the view of not engaging the mind with any positive phenomena after having negated the apprehension of characteristics. That is illogical. Someone else says that is in keeping with the system of Heshang [Moheyan].[432] Regardless of his statement, it is illogical because, lacking the certainty that is aware of suchness, [their view] will only promote a confused or unspecified [neutral] state of mind.

Certain later [Tibetan] scholars assert that the view is the stream of certainty in not finding the phenomena of percepts and perceivers having analyzed with scriptures and reasonings that employ reasons having the three modes. That position is not feasible because it is what the exalted Gampopa refers to as negated nonarisings.[433] And because it is a partial emptiness conceptually fabricated on the basis of inference. As the *Compendium of Valid Cognition* states:

> Those who are led to dharmatā through the path of logic
> corrupt the Sage's teachings in terms of both the dharma and the world.[434]

And the Exalted Lord [Atīśa] teaches:

> To say that emptiness is seen
> by means of the two cognitions—
> direct and inferential—
> is said to be confusion that just sees a short distance.[435]

Other earlier [Tibetans] assert that the view, based on Madhyamaka reasons, is a nonimplicative negation, the emptiness that is the exclusion of a self and skandhas. That is wrong because the *Kālacakra Tantra* regards that as falling slightly to the side of annihilation, and it does not accord with emptiness endowed with the most sublime of manifestations.[436]

There are some who assert that, having discovered the unerring view, free from elaborations—using scriptures, reasonings, or esoteric instructions—resting the mind free from elaborations within that [view] is meditating on the view. [118] When the mind rests evenly in that, there will be experiences of the unification of awareness and emptiness, which is clear and brilliant, free from turbidity. They assert that to be nonconceptual wisdom, dharmatā. Someone else refutes them saying that it is illogical that they disparage the meditations of Heshang and yet do the same thing when they are practicing. Be that as it may, this view and method of resting is in keeping with the texts of paṇḍitas and siddhas. However, experiences [generated by] the brilliance of the channels and dhātus are not to be considered nonconceptual wisdom, dharmatā, because a consciousness not separated from the dankness of experiences—despite any excellence—does not transcend the appearances of percepts and perceivers arising from conditions.

Certain scholars refute all other views and then assert that their own system is to make absolutely no assertions at all. That is not positive. It has been described as a treacherous view. Although they hold Madhyamaka positions, they do not assert the meaning of those texts. That seems to be merely a subterfuge devoid of any certainty in suchness.

(1) Some say the view of the absence of a self is not discovered by ascertaining with scriptures and reasonings but they meditate on the actual abiding state when they rest their mind, without conceiving of anything, on an object, which does not exist in any way. They say that since emptiness, the abiding state, is without any type of identification, that is the way to rest.[437] Someone else refutes them saying that is Heshang-style meditation and amounts to the position of a nihilistic view.[438]

Nevertheless, as a practice, that is not wrong, though the mode of explanation may be clumsy. [119] If we analyze this approach, we see that if there is awareness of the key point of objects not existing in any way and an understanding of the vital point that emptiness, the abiding state, is without any identification, that is *not* not discovering the view. Without such understanding and awareness, however, it is just remaining suspended in ordinary nonconceptuality.[439] When the mind resting in that manner has alertness that differentiates and analyzes with discerning prajñā and has mindfulness that keeps it from wandering elsewhere—while that may not be the way to sustain the view that cuts through misinterpretations about the abiding state—it is concordant with the way to sustain the view since it is how beginners nurture śamatha and vipaśyanā. Even when that [sustaining of the view] is absent, if both mindfulness and alertness are present, it will become the way to nurture nonconceptual śamatha. If there is a stagnate experience of dullness and sluggishness, a lack of clear mindfulness and alertness, that is a faulty state called "stagnant nonconceptuality."

(2) Some assert that although it is necessary to discover the view that is ascertained through scriptures and reasonings, once discovered, all instances of resting without conceiving of anything at all are meditation on the view.[440] Someone else refutes that saying that were it the case, all instances of nonconceptuality, such as deep sleep and śamatha meditation alone, would be meditation on the view.[441]

If we analyze this, it seems that whether a particular mode of resting without conceptuality is meditation on the view or not depends on whether both mindfulness and alertness that involve certainty in the view are present or not. Any remaining [considerations] are as stated above.

(3) Some assert that once the view has been discovered, if analysis with discerning prajñā is done first [each time], all subsequent instances of resting in nonconceptuality are meditation on the view.[442] [120] Someone else refutes this with objections similar to those stated above, such as saying that if a period of analysis with discerning prajñā is done first, then [even the nonconceptuality of] deep sleep [would be meditation on the view].[443] If we analyze this, [our conclusions] are as before: whether that type of resting [is meditation on the view or not] depends on whether mindfulness and alertness that involve certainty in the view are present or not.

(4) Some do not agree with the three previous approaches. They assert that the true meditation on the view is to [first] develop certainty in the meaning of emptiness and then, holding the mind unwaveringly in that state, to rest without analyzing anything else. They say this is unlike the first

approach in that it is not that their mind is not directed towards emptiness. It is unlike the second approach since it is not the case that they are not mindful of the view while resting in nonconceptuality. And this is unlike the third approach because it is not that they analyze the view first but then do not rest right within the view.[444]

Someone else refutes their approach, saying such [meditation on the view] involves simply being mindful of the view and then doing resting meditation within the view. Since it contains śamatha that is a resting meditation on emptiness but is missing the cultivation of vipaśyanā that is analytical meditation, it is one-sided [meditation] in which śamatha and vipaśyanā are not connected.[445]

That refutation is unreasonable because if that [meditation on the view] is resting meditation that is undistracted from the view—the view which is discovered and established [through] vipaśyanā that is analytical meditation—there is no need to again analyze it in each moment with conceptuality involving terms and referents. The issue [in this case] will be simply whether there is fixation on the experience of the fundamental view or not. Otherwise, the mode of explanation is fine.

A certain scholar [Tsongkhapa] explains that when we have identified the view, we must, by means of eradicating the cognitive process of misinterpretation [or superimposition, created] by our own ignorance, strenuously generate the opposite: strong certainty about the emptiness that is the emptiness of inherent nature. Then we must meditate on emptiness. [121] Being mindful of the view and habituated to just resting in it is only a way to nurture śamatha. Therefore, we must forcefully generate certainty through repeated analysis. He explains that all apprehensions of the meaning of dharmatā do not involve the apprehension of characteristics that are taken to be real, that all types of nonconceptuality free from discernment are Heshang[-style] meditation, and so forth.

Some of his followers when analyzing and investigating all phenomena, what are perceived and are perceivers, using Madhyamaka reasonings, [conclude that] everything being empty of reality [is] the meaning of the absence of self-entity. Turning their minds to that, they generate a powerful apprehension of the emptiness of reality or the absence of self. They consider that certainty in the view and resting evenly, astride the horse of śamatha, to be meditation on the correct view. Their statements regarding the other aspects of the approach are the same as the previous ones [put forth by Tsongkhapa].

These should be analyzed. According to the first [person, Tsongkhapa,] certainty about the emptiness that is the emptiness of inherent nature should be strenuously generated. Since that certainty does not go beyond the fixations of thinking, "There is no nature," or, "Nothing exists inherently," his assertions are clearly like the latter [his followers]. With the latter, their apprehension that all phenomena lack a self-entity or are empty of reality does not go beyond grasping at the absence of self-entity or the lack of reality. The strong force of their certainty creates a correspondingly strong degree of grasping. Thus, although they have negated clinging to a self, they seem to cling to the absence of a self or [adhere to] that view. And even though they have negated clinging to reality, it seems they cling to the lack of reality or [adhere to] that view. Such an approach is said to be very flawed because it directly contradicts the explanation found in the *Stages of Meditation*, which begins:

> Understand that all phenomena lack any nature. The thought, "There is no nature at all," is abandoned by correct prajñā.*[446] [122]

It is also flawed because it is the opponent [or object of refutation] in the following citations. The *Fundamental Treatise on the Middle Way* says:

> Those for whom emptiness is a view
> are said to be unable to accomplish anything.[447]

And:

> Do not say, "It is empty,"
> and do not proclaim, "It is not empty."[448]

And:

> Those who [hold] a view of a nature and extrinsic entities,
> entities and nonentities,
> do not see the suchness
> within the Buddha's teachings.[449]

*See p. 108 for the full citation.

And finally:

> To say something exists is to hold it to be permanent.
> To say it does not exist is to view it nihilistically.[450]

The *Commentary on Bodhicitta* states:

> Nonarising, emptiness [as a nonaffirming negation],
> "absence of self-entity," or emptiness [as the absence of reality]
> are what inferior beings meditate upon.
> That is not the way to meditate on that [emptiness].[451]

Furthermore, they are approaching what is [warned against] by the *Fundamental Treatise on the Middle Way* when it says:

> If emptiness is seen incorrectly,
> those of little intelligence are ruined.[452]

And by its commentary, *Lucid Words*:

> The moment you think that everything is empty and say, "Everything does not exist," you have developed a wrong view.[453]

Also, if we are to fixate on something, it is slightly better [to lean towards] the side of existence, as the *Fundamental Treatise on the Middle Way* says: [123]

> Those who assert existence go to the happy states.
> Those who assert nonexistence proceed to the negative ones.[454]

Moreover, it is not feasible that being mindful of the view and then resting within that is simply śamatha because, if both śamatha and vipaśyanā are not present, the view is not the correct view and, if both are present, resting within that [view] contains vipaśyanā. For those who assert that all types of vipaśyanā are conceptual and all types of śamatha are nonconceptual, a one-pointed state of mind in which śamatha and vipaśyanā are unified is an impossibility since it is impossible for there to be a common locus for conceptuality and nonconceptuality. And that assertion is also wrong because, in the context of discussing the unification of śamatha and vipaśyanā, Ācārya Jñānagarbha states in his commentary on *Unraveling the Intent*:

> On the path of śamatha, since only the mind that is the object of vipaśyanā is observed, the object observed and the observer are [identical] in being of the nature of the mind. Therefore, [śamatha and vipaśyanā] are not different.[455]

Grasping at emptiness or grasping at nonexistence generated by repeated analysis while resting in suchness is not something asserted in any statements on the definitive meaning, Indian or Tibetan. It is untenable because it is contradicted by numerous citations, such as the following. The *Praises of the Dharmadhātu* says:

> Once we abandon conceptions and what is conceptualized
> in the mind, the principal phenomenon,
> we should meditate on phenomena's lack of nature
> as the dharmadhātu.[456]

The Great Brahman [Saraha] declares:

> The unstained essence, untainted by extremes,
> is not an object of analysis: its nature is primordially pure.
> Analyze and a poisonous snake bites, that's all.[457] [124]

Such an approach is also illogical because conceptual analysis involving terms and referents is a mistaken consciousness, the conventional intellect. The genuine definitive meaning resists analysis. As Nāgārjuna says:

> The ultimate is not the province of the intellect.
> The intellect is said to be conventional.[458]

It is unjustifiable [to assert, as Tsongkhapa does,] that the apprehension of the meaning of dharmatā does not involve the apprehension of characteristics because in the prajñāpāramitā [teachings] everything experienced—from forms up to and including omniscience—is said to involve preoccupation with characteristics, as the *Verses That Summarize the Prajñāpāramitā Sūtras* teaches:

> Bodhisattvas who think, "This skandha is empty,"
> are preoccupied with characteristics and do not have faith in the unborn state.[459]

It is also unjustifiable because of many statements such as these by the Great Brahman [Saraha]:

> If the mind that thinks, "This is attractive,"
> takes that to heart and cherishes it,
> even pain the size of a sesame seed husk
> will cause constant affliction.[460]

And:

> If you have an attachment, let it go.[461]

It is also quite wrong to state [as Tsongkhapa does] that all types of nonconceptuality that are free from discernments are Heshang[-style] meditation because that would mean all explanations of resting nonconceptually would be a Heshang[-style] meditation, including those described in the following quotations. The *Commentary on Bodhicitta* states:

> The absence of conceptualization is emptiness.
> Where there is conceptualization, [125]
> how can there be emptiness?[462]

The *Entrance to the Middle Way* says:

> The wise teach the reversing of concepts
> to be the result of analysis.[463]

In the context of the methods for resting, the *Instructions on Madhyamaka* by the Exalted Lord [Atīśa] explains:

> At this point, mind does not think about anything, it does not grasp at anything.[464]

Furthermore, the prajñā that takes everything to be empty of reality is what the Dharma Treatises of Maitreya say is conceptuality apprehending permanence and what nonconceptual wisdom abandons. Thus it is not suitable as the correct view. Even though it may be mounted on the horse of śamatha, it is not meditation on the correct view. According to them, when there is śamatha, it must be nonconceptual and, when there is nonconceptuality, vipaśyanā vanishes, therefore the horse and its rider are incompatible. Since it is explained that at the end of analyzing with discernment, discernments themselves are pacified, at that point—according to them—vipaśyanā would vanish and *that* would be Heshang[-style] meditation. Although we could apply many more analyses with scriptures and reasonings [to counter such ideas], I will not elaborate further out of a concern for being excessive. [126]

2) Establishing Our Own System

We can understand [our own system] from the previous explanations in the vipaśyanā section on identifying the view and the ways to sustain it* and from the scriptures and reasonings presented throughout [this] section on removing doubts. Nevertheless, I will discuss it a little bit more now. Since it is taught that the direct realization of the true view of emptiness occurs when the bhūmi of the noble ones is attained, at this juncture I will present the view that is within the sphere of experience of ordinary beings.

The most important thing is to discover the view of emptiness, regardless of how we do that, whether it be by using analytical meditation or through resting meditation, both of which were presented above. The sūtras teach that no matter how good our view and meditation are, if they lack that [view of emptiness], we will not be able to sever the roots of cyclic existence. Accordingly, the *Commentary on Bodhicitta* remarks:

> Those who don't know emptiness
> are not receptive vehicles for liberation.
> Those confused beings will circle
> in the prison of existence as one of six kinds of beings.[465]

It is absolutely not acceptable for us not to discover the unerring view, as Nāropa's *Summary of the View* explains:

*See "The Specific Explanation of the Ways to Meditate on the View," pp. 79–85.

> When the view is not mistaken,
> meditation and conduct are in harmony with things
> and awakening is attained.
> It's like a horse who has been shown the race course.
>
> If the view does not accord with things,
> meditation and conduct will be confused,
> and no result will be achieved.
> It's like a blind person without a guide.[466]

When seeking the view, it is not enough to end up with simply an intellectual understanding of it through relying on the prajñā arising from listening and reflecting. [127] It is essential that we experience and know the view right within our own mind by relying primarily on the prajñā arising from meditation. The sūtras, Secret Mantra, and esoteric instructions all teach that the culmination of the meditative process is achieved by observing the mind. The *Guhyasamāja* says:

> When you examine your mind,
> all phenomena reside within your mind.
> These phenomena reside in the vajra of space.
> There are neither phenomena nor dharmatā.[467]

The *Vajra Pañjarā* proclaims:

> Inspired by the precious mind
> and meditating on mind-itself, there is buddhahood.[468]

The *Descent into Laṅkā Sūtra* teaches:

> By relying on mind alone,
> you do not conceive of outer referents.
> Resting with thusness as your object,
> you transcend mind alone as well.
>
> Once you transcend mind alone,
> go beyond the absence of appearances.
> Yogins and yoginīs who abide in the absence of appearances
> see the Mahāyāna.[469]

The *Ornament for the Mahāyāna Sūtras* observes:

> Aware that there is nothing other than mind,
> they then recognize that mind also does not exist.[470]

The Great Brahman [Saraha] says:

> When mind is fettered you are bound. [128]
> It can be liberated—have no doubts.[471]

For those reasons, both [Kamalaśīla's] Stages of Madhyamaka-Meditation and [Ratnākaraśānti's] *Instructions on Prajñāpāramitā*—which [expound] the paths of the two great chariot-systems—expand the meaning of what is taught in the *Descent into Laṅkā Sūtra* and explain the yogas of focusing on the mind alone, focusing on thusness, and focusing on the absence of appearances.

Thus, all texts on the stages of meditation, regardless of whether they belong to the sūtras, Secret Mantra, or esoteric instructions, explain that initially when we are investigating the view it is impossible not to employ discerning prajñā. There are many reasons for this, such as what is taught in the final *Stages of Meditation*:

> Although all phenomena are already simply empty of any inherent nature, if we lack discernment, we will not realize their emptiness.[472]

Nevertheless, when we analyze with discernment, in the end discernment itself must be pacified and lead into nonconceptuality. The *Sūtra of the Questions of Kāśyapa* states:

> Kāśyapa, it is like this: For example, fire arises when wind causes two trees to rub together. Once fire appears, it consumes those two trees. Similarly, Kāśyapa, when there is discernment of what is true, the noble ones' faculty of prajñā arises. Once that arises, it will consume the discernment of what is true.[473]

The middle *Stages of Meditation* teaches:

> The Buddha taught that when the fire of understanding what

> is true, just as it is, arises from discernment of what is true, the wood of conceptuality is consumed, just like the fire [produced from] rubbing kindling [consumes the kindling itself].[474] [129]

Analysis is not confined to examination and analysis involving terms and their referents—it is also necessary to analyze during meditative equipoise. The sūtras say:

> When you rest evenly, you know what is true just as it is.[475]

The [first] *Stages of Meditation* teaches:

> Once you have stabilized your mind on an object of meditation with śamatha, if you examine with prajñā, the light of true wisdom will manifest.[476]

Through analysis, discernments (which are the analyzer) are pacified in and of themselves and become a nonconceptual state that has no essence at all. That is the actual view in this context. A sūtra states:

> The absence of seeing phenomena is true seeing.[477]

The [first] *Stages of Meditation* adds:

> [It is said:]
>
> > What does seeing the ultimate [mean]? It is the absence of seeing any phenomenon.[478]

At this point, the mind, free from dullness or agitation, does not conceive of anything and does not grasp at anything. Free from mindfulness and attention involving percepts and perceiver, mind rests free from elaborations. It is said in a sūtra:

> In dharmatā, just as it is,
> so rests mind that is just like it.
> Experience unhindered by words dawns.
> That is called samādhi.[479]

The Exalted Lord [Atīśa] teaches:

> In the dharmadhātu, free from elaborations,
> rest your mind free from elaborations.[480]

He also says:

> The dharmadhātu is without center or end. [130]
> It is seen by the sharp eyes of the intellect, free from concepts,
> not blurred by dullness or agitation.[481]

The Exalted Lord [Atīśa's] *Instructions on Madhyamaka* explain:

> The past mind has ceased and disappeared. The future mind has not arisen or appeared. The present mind is very hard to examine. If you analyze and investigate what can be shown through reasonings—that [the present mind] has no color or shape; that, like space, it does not exist; that it is neither singular nor a plurality; that it does not arise; or that it is naturally luminous—you will realize it does not exist.
>
> If both those two [that is, material and nonmaterial entities]* are things that have no essence at all and are simply nonexistent, discerning prajñā also does not exist. An analogy is fire: the fire that arises from rubbing two sticks together will burn up the sticks and, when they no longer exist, the fire that consumed them will go out on its own. Similarly, when prajñā has proven that all phenomena—both specifically characterized and generally characterized—do not exist, that prajñā disappears and is luminosity, which has no essence at all. Thus, everything that could be a flaw (such as dullness or agitation) is cleared away.
>
> At this point, mind does not think about anything, it does not grasp at anything. Mindfulness and attentiveness are cast aside. As long as the enemy, or thief, of characterizing or conceptualizing does not arise, rest mind that way.[482]

I will put that explanation in a way that may be slightly easier to understand. First, when investigating the view, you should understand that all

*This section of the *Instructions on Madhyamaka* describes how to examine the two kinds of entities, material and nonmaterial. *Moonbeams* only quotes the second part on how to examine the nonmaterial, that is, mind.

phenomena (percepts and perceivers) are mind. Then, you should examine and dissect the mind using various rational means, such as [investigating the mind] in the three times, applying the reasonings that it is neither singular nor a plurality, that it does not arise, cease, or abide, and that it is naturally luminous. Using that approach, you will understand that it does not exist innately. [131] When you see that percepts and perceivers do not exist as any kind of entities, are simply nonexistent, the discerning [prajñā] that understands that also does not exist. The analogy is the fire [produced from] rubbing wood consumes the wood and then goes out itself. In the same way, discerning prajñā disappears, is luminosity, and does not exist at all. When you discover that type of view, the faults of dullness and agitation are dispelled. At this point, your mind does not think about anything and does not grasp at anything. The mindfulness of the intellect involved with percepts and perceivers and all attentiveness are cast aside. It says unambiguously that as long as the faults of apprehending characteristics or conceptualizing do not arise, you should rest your mind like that. The *Stages of Meditation* teaches:

> Understand that all phenomena lack any nature. The thought, "There is no nature at all," is abandoned by correct prajñā. With objects, which are beyond existing or not existing, meditate with no reference point in your mind, which is free from existing or not existing.[483]

As discussed above,* those who assert that sustaining the view should be based on śamatha along with forceful certainty in an analytical emptiness, certainty in the lack of any nature, or certainty in the absence of self should contemplate well the meaning of those quotations. Then they will find certainty in the view.

Moreover, there are many explanations that, having discovered the view, we should meditate without conceptuality. The *King of Samādhi Sūtra* says:

> The wise who understand conditioned and unconditioned phenomena
> destroy their discrimination of characteristics.
> Resting in that absence of characteristics,
> they always know that phenomena are empty.[484] [132]

*See pp. 98–103.

The [middle and final] *Stages of Meditation* quote the *Jewel Cloud Sūtra*:

> If they fully investigate the essence of what is understood by the mind, they will know it to be empty. Through such understanding, they enter the yoga of the absence of characteristics.[485]

The [final] *Stages of Meditation* also says:

> Having examined with vipaśyanā, we recognize the absence of any essence. That is the entrance to the absence of characteristics.[486]

The middle *Stages of Meditation* explains:

> Thus, when yogins and yoginīs do not take the nature of a thing to be ultimate, having analyzed it with their prajñā, they enter nonconceptual samādhi.[487]

Kamalaśīla's *Commentary on the "Dhāraṇī of Entering Nonconceptuality"*[488] explains that at the end of analysis, we should only rest in nonconceptuality. The *Lamp for the Path of Awakening* teaches:

> When, through scriptures and reasonings,
> you have ascertained the absence of any nature,
> which is that all phenomena are without arising,
> you should meditate without any conceptuality.[489]

That completes the explanation on removing doubts about the view and meditation. Up to this point I have provided what is essential [to know] about the approach to practicing samādhi as it is taught in the sūtras, tantras, and esoteric instructions. This has been a cursory presentation given in a generalized way. [133]

PART TWO

Uncommon Mahāmudrā

5

Generating Confidence

B. The Explanation That Elaborates upon the Way to Cultivate the Uncommon Mahāmudrā

This has three parts:

1. The Particulars That Generate Confidence in the Beginning
2. The Exposition of the Preliminaries for the Meditation Process
3. The Actual Explanation of the Way to Cultivate Mahāmudrā

1. The Particulars That Generate Confidence in the Beginning

This has two sections:

a. The Explanation of the Greatness of the Dharma, What Is Practiced
b. The Explanation of the Greatness of the Individuals, the Practitioners

a. The Explanation of the Greatness of the Dharma, What Is Practiced

This has four divisions:

i. The Particulars of Mahāmudrā
ii. How [Mahāmudrā] is Presented in the Sūtras and Tantras
iii. Specifically How [Mahāmudrā] Is Taught in the *Niruttara Tantras
iv. How [Mahāmudrā] Is the Profound Point of All Sūtras and Tantras

i. The Particulars of Mahāmudrā

This has three parts:

A) The Meaning of Its Name and Its Enumerations
B) Its Essence and Divisions
C) The Benefits of Knowing Mahāmudrā and the Problems of Not Knowing It

A) The Meaning of Its Name and Its Enumerations

The name for this dharma is mahāmudrā, which is rendered [into Tibetan] as *chak-gya chenpo* (*phyag rgya chen po*). As for "mudrā" (*phyag rgya*): Generally speaking, mudrā ("seal"), mark, sign, and characteristic are synonyms.[490] Something is called a mudrā in the sense that it will be, or has been, imprinted on something else. For example, in the world, when a stamp is, or has been, imprinted on something else, that is called a seal. Similarly, since this [dharma] is, or has been, imprinted on all phenomena of saṃsāra and nirvāṇa, it is called mudrā. Something that signifies is referred to as mudrā. In the same way that the marks and signs on armor and the like signify specific traits, since this [dharma] signifies [or shows] the nature, or abiding state, of saṃsāra and nirvāṇa, it is called mudrā. Something that cannot be superseded is called a mudrā. For example, a king's decree that is imprinted with his seal cannot be superseded [or overturned] by his subjects. Correspondingly, since the phenomena of saṃsāra and nirvāṇa do not supersede this [dharma], it is called mudrā. [134] A similar description is found in the *Sūtra of the Questions of Gaganagañja*:

> "Being imprinted with the mudrā of the tathāgatas" means that mudrā is what is inseparable from thusness. It is without divisions, without engagement, and without adherence. It does not move nor is it something that is moved. It cannot be swayed by the world with its gods, humans, and asuras.
>
> Why? Because that mudrā is imprinted upon the world with its gods, humans, and asuras.
>
> That mudrā of the tathāgatas is the mudrā of nonarising. It is the mudrā of emptiness. It is the mudrā of the absence of characteristics. It is the mudrā of the absence of expectancy. It is the mudrā of unconditionality. It is the mudrā of separation from desire. It is the mudrā of thusness. It is the mudrā of the true end. It is the mudrā of space.[491]

"Mahā" (*chen po*) signifies that there is nothing higher than this dharma, as the *Secret Siddhis* states:

> The fourth is the highest cause.
> It is what brings actual awakening:

it is the meditation on mahāmudrā.
There's nothing higher than that.[492]

Alternatively, [the term mahāmudrā] is explained in the *Mahāmudrā-tilaka*:

This is mahāmudrā.
"Mudrā" (*phyag*) is the wisdom of emptiness.
"Mudrā" (*rgya*) is free from the phenomena of saṃsāra.
"Mahā" is unification.[493]

As it states, "mudrā" (*phyag*) signifies wisdom that is reflexively aware of emptiness. The *Five Stages* adds: [135]

What is seen: wisdom aware of itself by itself,
here is "mudrā" (*phyag*).[494]

"Mudrā" (*rgya*) indicates being free from saṃsāra's phenomena of percepts and perceivers and that that has been, or is, imprinted on all phenomena. The *Guhyasamāja Tantra* proclaims:

Free from all entities,
devoid of skandhas, dhātus, and āyatanas,
percepts and perceivers,
it is equality in which a self-entity of phenomena is absent.[495]

"Mahā" signifies unifying, or uniting, method and prajñā and the like. And it means that this is the most sublime of all meditations. Maitrīpa's *Ten Verses on Suchness* states:

Uniting method and prajñā
is the meditation for the best yogins and yoginīs.
It is to unite with mahāmudrā.[496]

Other explanations of the meaning of this name include the following. Kālacakramahāpāda's *Padmani: Commentary on the Difficult Points* explains:

"Mahāmudrā" is prajñāpāramitā, which gives birth to all tathāgatas, past, present, and future. It is "mudrā" (*phyag rgya*)

> because nonabiding nirvāṇa, or unreleased bliss, imprints its seal on bliss. It is "mahā" because it is superior to karmamudrā and jñānamudrā and because it is free from the latent tendencies of saṃsāra.[497] [136]

The exalted Gampopa says:

> "Mudrā" (*phyag*) is the realization that all that appears and exists, all of saṃsāra and nirvāṇa, does not pass beyond unborn dharmatā. "Mudrā" (*rgya*) means that whatever appears and whatever exists does not transcend the intrinsic state. "Mahā" is the realization that dharmatā is free in itself.[498]

Serdingpa's *Lamp for the Yānas* states:

> The etymology of mahāmudrā is as follows.
> Because karma, mental afflictions, and obscurations
> are linked with the dharmakāya—your own mind, free in itself—
> it is called "mudrā" (*phyag*).
>
> Because concepts of characteristics
> cannot go beyond it, it is "mudrā" (*rgya*).
>
> Since it's greater than all the yānas—
> the philosophical yāna, kriyā, caryā, and so forth—
> it is "mahā."[499]

The enumerations of this name. It is taught that ultimate suchness, unsurpassable wisdom, universal excellence, mahāmudrā, and dharmakāya are equivalents. Indrabhūti in his *Sādhana for the Siddhi of Wisdom* observes:

> This is the ultimate.
> It is the unsurpassable wisdom vajra,
> called "universal excellence"
> and "mahāmudrā."
> Know this to be the dharmakāya.[500]

Enumerations of names are explained in the *Seven Yogas*:

> Enumerations, such as the lack of nature, thusness,
> dharmatā, the equality of phenomena,
> and the ultimate,
> are only about this very lack of nature—
> they do not point to anything else.[501] [137]

B) Its Essence and Divisions

The essence of mahāmudrā. It is explained as not abiding anywhere, being free from all characteristics, and pervading everything, like space. Indrabhūti teaches:

> Just as nonabiding space
> is omnipresent and free from characteristics,
> so too is the ultimate.[502]

Maitrīpa says:

> Mahāmudrā—unification transcending the intellect—
> is clear yet nonconceptual.
> Like space, it's pervasive and vast.
> Great compassion appears though without nature,
> like the moon in water.
>
> Being clarity, it's free from labels, center, or edge.
> Not veiled by anything, it's unstained, beyond hopes or fears.
> Like the dream of a mute, it's inexpressible.[503]

Its divisions. There are three: ground, path, and fruition mahāmudrā. Generally speaking, ground mahāmudrā is the dharmatā of all phenomena, naturally luminous emptiness, which is primordially free from elaborations and is the governing principle of saṃsāra and nirvāṇa. Specifically, it is the basic nature, the primordial abiding state, of our own mind—clear, brilliant, unidentifiable—which is beyond being an object of thought or expression. [138] Path mahāmudrā relies on the paths of listening, reflecting, and meditating. It is the realization that all phenomena (which include all that appears and exists, all of saṃsāra and nirvāṇa) are luminous emptiness, primordially without any nature that arises, abides, or ceases. It is the special meditation on the view that is recognized right within our own experience. Having become familiar with that ground mahāmudrā through path mahāmudrā and having purified all the most subtle dualistic appearances, wisdom endowed with twofold purity, free from obscuration, manifests like the sky free from haze. That is fruition mahāmudrā.

Those are also subdivided. We should be aware that the threefold classification of thusness, such as is found in the *Highest Continuum*, is a categorization of ground mahāmudrā. That text states:

> Impure, impure-pure,
> and completely pure
> are the phases of sentient beings,
> bodhisattvas, and tathāgatas.[504]

Classifications of path mahāmudrā include the divisions of śamatha and vipaśyanā, which are referred to in the *Saṃvarodaya*:

> Because emptiness is discerned,
> meditative concentration also becomes prajñā.[505]

Path mahāmudrā also includes the divisions into the four mudrās, as the *Heart of Wisdom Tantra* teaches:

> Here mahāmudrā is divided into four: karmamudrā, samayamudrā, jñānamudrā, and dharmamudrā.[506]

We should be aware that the classifications of the five wisdoms, three kāyas, and so forth, such as those described by Indrabhūti in his *Sādhana for the Siddhi of Wisdom*, are divisions of fruition mahāmudrā. He says:

> In the same way that your own image
> appears clearly in a mirror, [139]
> wisdom appears as the dharmakāya
> and is thus called "mirror[like]."[507]

C) The Benefits of Knowing Mahāmudrā and the Problems of Not Knowing It

If we do not understand and realize the abiding state of mahāmudrā, even if we know hundreds of thousands of other yogas, we will not attain the supreme result of liberation. It is said that if we do understand and realize it, we will know all dharmas and be Vajrasattva. The *Mahāmudrā-tilaka* says:

> Whoever does not know mahāmudrā
> may be a buddha but they're not a yogin or yoginī.
>
> Those who do not know this purity,
> the bindu of mahāmudrā,
> may be a yogin or yoginī knowing
> a hundred thousand yoga and yoginī tantras
> but the sublime result will elude them.
>
> When all dharmas are known
> that is certainly buddhahood.
> When mahāmudrā is known
> you are the glorious Vajrasattva.
>
> His wisdom nature
> is the definition of mahāmudrā.[508]

The *Commentary on Bodhicitta* observes: [140]

> Those who don't know emptiness
> are not receptive vehicles for liberation.
> Those confused beings will circle
> in the prison of existence as one of six kinds of beings.[509]

Maitrīpa states:

> Once this is realized,
> all that can possibly appear is mahāmudrā:
> the great pervasive infinite dharmakāya.[510]

He also says:

> Those who do not realize that
> will not be free, apart from some temporary moments.
> When that's realized, what can bind?[511]

ii. How [Mahāmudrā] Is Presented in the Sūtras and Tantras

The sūtras teach the meaning of mahāmudrā using a variety of names of other mudrās. The *Sūtra of the Questions of Sāgaramati* says:

> Sāgaramati, all phenomena are imprinted with the mudrā of liberation: they are nondual and pure.[512]

It also says:

> Because all phenomena are undifferentiated, like the center of space, they are imprinted with the mudrā of equality.[513]

It presents twenty types of mudrās, [beginning with]:

> There is the mudrā that is stainless and internally pure by virtue of having purified belief in a self.[514]

It concludes [that list with this summarizing verse]:

> This dharma is stainless, pure, virtuous, natural luminosity, [141]
> equal to and the same as space, primordially unborn,
> not arising, not occurring, nonabiding, and unceasing.
> It is the unwavering and stainless mudrā of the victors.[515]

The *Sūtra on Maitreya's Setting Forth* presents fifteen mudrās [beginning with]:

> Child of good family, all phenomena are of the mudrā of emptiness.[516]

The *Sūtra of the Questions of Gaganagañja*[517] lists ten mudrās, which were already stated.* There are many other references to mudrās, such as that found in the *Sūtra of the Questions of the Girl Ratna* [that is, the *Instructions on the Mahāyāna*]:

> The characteristic of all phenomena
> is the characteristic that is equivalent to space.
> This characteristic is similar to a mudrā:
> the imprint of a mudrā can't be undone.[518]

The numerous [other uses of mudrā in the sūtras] include the terms "jñānamudrā" and "dharmamudrā" in the *Sūtra of the Good Eon*[519] and the term "dharmamudrā" in the *Teaching of the Armor Array.*[520]

In the lower tantras [there are the following uses of mudrā]: the *Mañjuśrī Root Tantra*[521] uses mahāmudrā for the way hand mudrās bind, and the *Vairocanābhisambodhi*[522] uses mahāmudrā to designate the deities' emblems. In the yoga tantras there are many occurrences, such as using the four mudrās for the way hand mudrās bind.

To summarize, the teachings in the sūtras and tantras on the ground abiding state—such as that tathāgatagarbha [buddha nature] abides primordially in the mindstreams of sentient beings and that the nature of mind is luminosity—are presentations of ground mahāmudrā. [142] Teachings on the development of the dhātu of [tathāgata]garbha, on freedom from elaborations, instances of emptiness, the unreality of phenomena, their absence of a self-entity, their equality, and their unification are all considered path mahāmudrā. Teachings on the awakening of the wisdom of complete omniscience (such as the four kāyas and five wisdoms) are presentations of fruition mahāmudrā.

iii. Specifically How [Mahāmudrā] Is Taught in the *Niruttara Tantras

This has three parts:

A) The Way the Expositions of Three and Four Mudrās Are Taught
B) The Way the Uncommon Mahāmudrā Is Taught
C) The Ancillary Topic: Dispelling the Wrong Views of Others

*See p. 114. Note that the "mudrā of the tathāgatas" is counted as the first of the ten.

A) The Way the Expositions of Three and Four Mudrās Are Taught

The *Kālacakra Root Tantra* states:

> Having given up the karmamudrā
> and the imputed jñānamudrā entirely,
> meditate on mahāmudrā
> through uniting with the immutable.[523]

It also says:

> Union with a karmamudrā,
> the passion of a jñānamudrā,
> and the single union with mahāmudrā
> increase immutability.[524]

Padmavajra advises in his *Secret Siddhis*:

> Abandon all your ideas about
> karmamudrās with their wrathful displays
> and do the same with jñānamudrās.
> Meditate on mahāmudrā.[525]

The *Synopsis of Our View Asserted by Mañjuśrī* teaches:

> Cast aside your many notions about
> the left-handed and malicious karmamudrās
> and the similar jñānamudrās.
> Rely on mahāmudrā.[526] [143]

Those depictions of three mudrās (karmamudrās, jñānamudrās, and mahāmudrā) are followed by some mahāsiddhas. There are other presentations of three mudrās, such as the one in the fourth chapter of the *Illuminating Lamp*:

> As for mudrās, there are the three: dharmamudrās, mudrās of characteristics, and mahāmudrā.[527]

There are also presentations of four mudrās. The *Vajramālā*, an explanatory tantra, states:

> Next the Vajra Bhagavān said:
> "The highest divisions of mudrās
> are correctly said to be
> dharma, karma, samaya, and mahāmudrā."[528]

The *Secret Tilaka of the Moon* explains:

> The first is dharmamudrā.
> The second is samayamudrā.
> The third is mahāmudrā.
> The fourth is karmamudrā.[529]

The *Heart of Wisdom Tantra* discusses mahāmudrā by categorizing it as the four: karmamudrā, samayamudrā, jñānamudrā, and dharmamudrā.* *Pramuditāvajra's *Commentary on the "Sarvabuddha-samayoga"*[530] looks at four mudrās: mahāmudrā, samayamudrā, dharmamudrā, and karmamudrā. Ācārya Abhayākaragupta in his *Commentary on the "Buddha-kapāla"*[531] categorizes the four mudrās in terms of the perfection phase, the fruition period, and the generation phase, with each having the four: karmamudrā, dharmamudrā, mahāmudrā, and samayamudrā. Nāropa's commentary on the *Hevajra Tantra* explains karmamudrā, jñānamudrā, mahāmudrā, and samayamudrā:

> The luminosities called "karma, jñāna,
> mahāmudrā, and samaya"
> are the cause, the object of meditation,
> the attainment, and the indestructible.[532] [144]

Maitrīpa in his *Determining the Four Mudrās*[533] explains the four as karmamudrā, dharmamudrā, mahāmudrā, and samayamudrā. The order of the four mudrās is presented variously in the many texts and commentaries by mahāsiddhas, and there are many different explanations about their identi-

*See the citation on p. 118.

fication. I have not included all the permutations, however, because it would become too much.

About this approach, a certain person [Sakya Paṇḍita] comments:

> Whatever is the mahāmudrā of
> Nāropa and Maitrīpa
> is exactly what is taught
> in the Secret Mantra tantras:
> it consists of the karma, dharma,
> and samaya [mudrās], and mahāmudrā.[534]

That indicates he has not registered that the compositions by those two mahāsiddhas, in which they explain the four mudrās according to the Mantra texts, contain different sequences and identifications. His remark seems to be the guesswork of someone who has never looked at any of their texts where they expound the abiding-state mahāmudrā because their works contain many different sequences and identifications of the four mudrās, and their sequencing and what he "repeats" do not match.

If we analyze his statement just a bit, it implies that those two mahāsiddhas only gave presentations of the four mudrās in accordance with the Mantra texts, that there are no texts by them in which they expound the abiding-state mahāmudrā. That is plain wrong. Although Nāropa had traversed the ocean-like sūtras and tantras, he remained unsatisfied and apprenticed himself to the mahāsiddha Tilopa, undergoing twelve great austerities. Through being taught the ultimate-essence mahāmudrā, which does not rely on the Secret Mantra path, he was liberated. [145] [If Sakya Paṇḍita's statement is correct,] it means that the many texts on that type of mahāmudrā—such as Tilopa's various dohās including the one renowned as the *Ganges [Mahāmudrā]*,[535] and Nāropa's *Summary Verses on Mahāmudrā*,[536] *Clarifying Wisdom*,[537] and *Summary of the View*—are not Nāropa's viewpoint. Maitrīpa also perfected his knowledge and realization of the Sūtra and Mantra systems yet, feeling dissatisfied, he apprenticed himself to the glorious lord Śavaripa. Having received from him the instructions on the ultimate essence, which are not based on Secret Mantra, he was liberated. [If Sakya Paṇḍita is right,] it means that the texts in his dharma cycle—the dohās of Saraha senior and junior, Maitrīpa's own dohās, and his *Summary Verses on Mahāmudrā*—are not Maitrīpa's viewpoint.

If [Sakya Paṇḍita] accepts those texts as the viewpoints of Nāropa and

Maitrīpa, then the force of "whatever is" in his statement, "Whatever is the mahāmudrā of Nāropa and Maitrīpa," overturns his rejection of any of their compositions that expound a mahāmudrā that is not part of the four mudrās.

B) The Way the Uncommon Mahāmudrā Is Taught

The mahāmudrā found within the aforementioned explanations of three or four mudrās is taught by some to be the uncommon mahāmudrā. Among the many such instances, the mahāmudrā presented in the Kālacakra [system] is the uncommon mahāmudrā. It says that emptiness endowed with the most sublime of manifestations, unchanging bliss, and one taste are mahāmudrā. [146] When [the *Stainless Light*] says, "mahāmudrā is unchanging bliss,"[538] it is abundantly clear that that unchanging bliss is not a nominal wisdom based on experiences involving karmamudrās, jñānamudrās, and the like. It is natural connate bliss.

The forty-sixth chapter of the *Vajramālā* begins by describing the mahāmudrā that is the abiding state of the ground:

> Next I will explain
> the characteristics and meaning of mahāmudrā.
> It is peace, the result of great yoga,
> the summation of the meaning of great wisdom.
>
> It is the excellent fortune of great bliss,
> the epitome of the supreme great taste,
> the great illusion, what is most subtle,
> the greatness of the great, great space.
>
> The mudrā that is the wisdom of the tathāgatas
> is the citadel of nonconceptuality,
> the abode of the indivisible Vajrasattva,
> nonconceptual great bliss,
> unblemished, like space.[539]

It continues with a description of the mahāmudrā that is the path:

> Devoid of any nature and groundless,
> it is nondual, without self, and inexpressible.
> Yogins and yoginīs with their reflexive awareness

abandon all the imagined phenomena
of skandhas, dhātus, and āyatanas.

They abandon meditation, an object of meditation,
equipoise, and the twofold process.
They separate consciousness from wisdom
and give up mantras, recitations, and approach [practices].[540]

It concludes by describing the mahāmudrā that is the result:

Crossing over from the abodes of entities,
they request great wisdom.
Know that the great siddhi is here.
It is unsurpassable mahāmudrā.[541] [147]

The commentary on this tantra by the paṇḍita Alaṃkakalaśa provides clear explanation of those scriptural passages.[542]

The *Mahāmudrā-tilaka* says:

[Sūrateśvarī said:]
"Bhagavān Jñānaḍākārka, you have taught
the secrets that destroy the fog of ignorance
but you have not taught mahāmudrā.
Lord of Victors, please teach
mahāmudrā just as it is."[543]

In response to that supplication, the text continues:

The Bhagavān replied:
"Listen Goddess Mahāmudrā,
sublime bliss.
Mahāmudrā is the great secret.
It is inexpressible, inexhaustible, unborn.
It has the form of all and yet has no form.

"Formless, its form is the sublime principle.
Beyond subtle or grand,

its nature is immeasurable.
Truly stainless, it is luminous.

"Not abiding anywhere,
it does not arise and does not subside.
Always arising, its manifestation is supreme.
Liberated from time and circumstances,
it creates birth and destruction."[544]

That passage begins with a description of the abiding state of the ground, and continues with an explanation of the methods for realizing it, the benefits of knowing it and the problems of not knowing it, the result, and the identification of its characteristics.[545] The meaning of those topics are also clearly presented in Ācārya Gambhīravajra's commentary.[546] [148]

The *Wisdom Tilaka* observes:

Vastly beyond the realm of Brahmā,
you, Sūrateśvarī, imprint with a mudrā.
Because you imprint a mudrā on infinity
you are known as mahāmudrā.[547]

Its commentary, *Secret Suchness*, explains:

On the basis of wisdom's radiance—the caṇḍālī of mahāmudrā, free from elaborations—there is, in the progression of joys, natural joy. Through that, we discover the nature of mahāmudrā, natural joy devoid of elaborations.[548]

It also says:

Since all sentient beings possess the nature of a buddha, mahāmudrā is the mother of the bhagavān, and the nature of the cause and result is the same. For that reason and because of the etymology of sealing, you are known as mahāmudrā.[549]

Thus, nonelaboration, natural joy, and ground dharmatā are explained as mahāmudrā.

The *Commentary on the Difficult Points of the "Buddha-kapāla Tantra"* composed by Saraha explains that great emptiness, the seal endowed with the most sublime of manifestations, is mahāmudrā:

> "Mahāmudrā, intelligent lady" [means that the bhagavatī-goddess] is mahāmudrā because the nature of great emptiness seals all tathāgatas.[550]

Kālacakramahāpāda's *Padmani: Commentary on the Difficult Points* explains that the prajñāpāramitā view is mahāmudrā:

> "Mahāmudrā" is prajñāpāramitā, which gives birth to all tathāgatas, past, present, and future.[551]

The *Commentary on the Difficult Points of "Ascertaining Abhiṣekas"* written by Rāmapāla pinpoints the etymology of mahāmudrā and its essence:

> Because it imprints its mudrā on the [other] three mudrās, it is mahā and a mudrā. It is not reached by analysis; it's the very essence of what does not abide. It is actualized by reverence for and continuous cultivation of path wisdom. [149] It is nonexistent, free from cognitive obscurations and the rest. It is the ground for all excellence. It is the one essence of existence and nirvāṇa. It embodies great, nonreferential compassion and is the one mahāsukhakāya. That is mahāmudrā.[552]

All those citations identify ground, path, and fruition mahāmudrā. Similarly, there are many ways that [mahāmudrā] is discussed in the tantras—in the *Buddhasamāyoga*,[553] *Saṃvarodaya*, *Vajra Pañjarā*, *Two-Part [Hevajra Tantra]*, *Samputa*, and elsewhere—and in the texts by mahāsiddhas (such as the Seven Siddhi Texts), but I will not elaborate more here because it would be too much.

In brief, we should know that all the presentations on the ground abiding state of phenomena, natural emptiness, natural connateness, equality, unchanging bliss, great bliss, being free from arising, abiding, and ceasing, profound peace, and freedom from elaborations in the tantras and texts of the mahāsiddhas are presentations of mahāmudrā.

In that case, when a certain person [Sakya Paṇḍita] makes the oblique criticism aimed at others, "Therefore, I do not maintain a mahāmudrā that is not taught in the tantras,"[554] it is simply the talk of someone who has not used their intelligence to examine the intended meaning of the sūtras and tantras. The approach in those [sūtras and tantras] does not operate on the level of exclusions or [positive] inclusions [that is, negations or affirmations].

C) The Ancillary Topic: Dispelling the Wrong Views of Others

A certain person [Sakya Paṇḍita] says:

> Actually there is no difference between
> the present-day Mahāmudrā
> and the Dzog-chen of the Chinese tradition, [150]
> except for changing the terms
> "descending from above" and "climbing from below"
> to "instantaneous" and "gradualist."[555]

That statement reflects nothing more than his desire to say something [critical]. Dzog-chen is called "atiyoga" and is regarded as the culmination of Secret Mantra, whereas the meditation of Heshang is asserted to be part of *Drawn from Eighty Sūtras*.[556] Therefore, not only are there many differences in their meditation systems, the sources of their teachings are different. There is no one who explains a dzog-chen of the Chinese tradition as authentic. To say that dzog-chen is the meditation of Heshang is to reduce the dharma to nondharma. It also shows a complete lack of understanding that the meaning of mahāmudrā lies in the thought expressed in the Dohā Trilogy, the Eightfold Treasury of Shorter Dohās, [Seven] Siddhi [Texts, the Sixfold] Essence [Cycle], the Dharma Cycle on Amanasikāra [Nonattention], and other similar texts.

Likewise, [Sakya Paṇḍita's] account that begins, "The appearance of this dharma tradition . . ."*[557] is not trustworthy because it contains many

*The section referred to in the *Analysis of the Three Vows* reads:

> The appearance of this dharma tradition
> came about just as foretold
> by the bodhisattva Śāntarakṣita
> to King Trisong De-tsen.

inventions that are not in keeping with respected sources of the account, such as that given by Kamalaśīla's students at the beginning of the *Stages of Meditation*.[558]

[Sakya Paṇḍita] continues:

> Relying only on the texts
> of the Chinese scholar's scriptural tradition,
> some secretly changed the name of his [system]
> to Mahāmudrā.
> The present-day Mahāmudrā
> is for the most part a Chinese dharma tradition.[559]

That is just his conjecture and actually complete fiction. There are absolutely no sources or references for saying that [present-day Mahāmudrā] is based on the texts of the Chinese scholar and that the name [of his teachings] was later changed to Mahāmudrā. [151] The name "Mahāmudrā" was already well known in the tantras and their commentaries and to all paṇḍitas and siddhas. By concealing his own faults of not comprehending most of the tantra texts that teach that [subject, Sakya Paṇḍita] makes the mistake of deciding that the dharma is nondharma.[560] To make such accusations while being uncertain is not the conduct of those with sound modes of discourse.

Again, someone casts aspersions:

Listen, I will relate that prophesy:
"King, here in your Tibetan country,
tīrthikas will not appear
because Ācārya Padmasambhava
placed Tibet under the care of the twelve guardians.

Nevertheless, due to several interrelated causes,
the dharma tradition will split into two.
At first, after I have passed away,
a Chinese bhikṣu will appear
and teach an instantaneous path,
called the "self-sufficient white [remedy]."

At that time, invite my student,
the great scholar Kamalaśīla, from India
and he will refute that.

Then, instruct the faithful to practice
according to his dharma system."
Later, everything came to be
just as he said it would.

> Heshang of China did not advocate [the observance of] causes and their results in the context of conduct. In the context of the view and meditation, citing *Drawn from Eighty Sūtras*, he [taught] not engaging mentally in any concepts, good or bad. In the context of the result, he did not accept that buddhahood is anything other than the realization of mind. Therefore, present-day mahāmudrā meditators seem to belong to his tradition.[561]

Subsequent conceited scholars have not used their intelligence to examine [such statements] and instead repeat that explanation despite it being unfounded. They just spout nonsense with their highly exaggerated accusations while not having understood the vital points of their opponents' philosophical tenet system, view, and meditation. The final *Stages of Meditation* sets out Heshang's positions and refutes them:

> Some think that sentient beings experience results (including the higher realms) and circle in saṃsāra due to the power of virtuous and unvirtuous actions, which are created by mental concepts. Thus, those who think nothing and do nothing are fully liberated from saṃsāra. Therefore, we should not think anything and should not engage in virtuous conduct, such as generosity. The practice of generosity and so forth is only taught from the perspective of foolish people.
>
> Those who think and speak in that way have rejected the entire Mahāyāna. Since the Mahāyāna is the root of all yānas, to reject it is to reject all yānas. Thus, to say, "Do not think anything," causes the rejection of the prajñā whose nature is the discernment of what is true. [152] Since discernment of what is true is the root of true wisdom, to reject that [discernment] is to reject transcendent prajñā by cutting its root.
>
> To say, "Do not practice generosity and so forth," is to utterly renounce methods, such as generosity.[562]

While it is the case that discerning prajñā is abandoned in the context of view and meditation, and that virtues, such as generosity, are downplayed in that same context, it is one's own misunderstanding to say that [Heshang] does not advocate [the observance of] causes and their results.[563] At the start of its presentation of [Heshang's] assertions, [the *Stages of Meditation*] gives [his] statement regarding virtuous and unvirtuous actions and their results. If [Heshang] adhered to *Drawn from Eighty Sūtras*, he understood causes and their results. Furthermore, the detailed account of the debate between Heshang and Kamalaśīla that [Sakya Paṇḍita] gives in his treatise is completely unreliable since it contains many instances of disjointed statements, exaggerated accusations, internal contradictions, and corruptions of Kamalaśīla's refutations.[564]

Therefore, to say that meditation on the abiding-state mahāmudrā is similar to that [Heshang system] is simply an exaggerated conjecture but I will not go into a refutation of that right now out of a fear of becoming too wordy. However, to put to rest wrong notions, I will present now some of the ways that Mahāmudrā differs from the Heshang system.

In the context of conduct:

- Heshang asserts that the actions of amassing [merit] and purifying [negative deeds] are taught for the foolish because they do not understand suchness and, in fact, he downplays amassing [merit] and purifying [negative actions]. [153] Here [in our Mahāmudrā system] it is said, "Emptiness arises in causes and their results." Once we realize emptiness, it is necessary to be very assiduous about the interdependent connections between causes and their results. Similarly, [our Mahāmudrā system] contains very subtle distinctions, such as whether one taste manifests as the interdependence of the many or not, whether there is proficiency with the conventional or not, and whether there is an understanding of how to plant the seeds of the rūpakāyas or not.

In the context of meditation:

- Heshang asserts not thinking about anything and not engaging mentally. Here, in the beginning when developing stillness, we need to cultivate mindfulness that is not distracted from its object and the vivid alertness that recognizes dullness and agitation.
- Heshang advocates only remaining suspended in nonconceptuality and not considering whether there are faults or virtues. Here, that is called "stagnant nonconceptuality" and is considered a flaw.
- Heshang does not engage in any examination or analysis during meditation. Here, discerning prajñā must examine and analyze the object of the meditation, as appropriate.

- Heshang rests in a state in which the mind is unengaged, one that is [karmically] unspecified [or neutral], free from mindfulness and awareness. Here, we must not be distracted for even a moment from mindfulness and awareness of the specific object of the meditation.
- Heshang considers not thinking about anything to be sufficient. Here, such things are strayings and deviations, and their flaws must be cleared up.

In the context of the view:

- Heshang does not advocate prajñā that arises from reflection or from meditation. Here, we must use those two types of prajñā to discover and realize the view of the abiding state.
- Heshang lacks the view for realizing suchness. [154] Here, once we have cut through a root, or basis, of percepts and perceivers, we must sustain the view in which we are aware of the abiding state of those [percepts and perceivers].

In the context of the result:

- Heshang asserts that liberation is attained only by habituating ourselves to the continuity of simply not thinking about anything. Here, it is explained that having realized suchness and, having habituated ourselves to that by not wandering from it, we must purify all of even the most subtle of dualistic appearances.

For all those reasons, it is unseemly [for someone] to make statements out of jealousy that are misinterpretations and denials of the true nature because they cause those who trust him to create the karma for abandoning the dharma.

[Sakya Paṇḍita] makes this statement about his own system:

> Our mahāmudrā
> is the wisdom arisen from abhiṣeka
> and is the self-arisen wisdom
> manifesting from the samādhis of the two processes.[565]

If we examine that assertion, we can say that there is no doubt that the realization of the four mudrās in general and the uncommon abiding-state mahāmudrā in particular can arise on the basis of cultivating the samādhis of the two processes. Nevertheless, it is highly illogical to assert that mahāmudrā is the experience in which emptiness seals the bliss that is the satisfying sensation accompanying the physical and mental released bliss occurring during the third abhiṣeka. Such assertions are refuted by many, such as Indrabhūti:

> Evil persons say,
> "The bliss arising from the two organs is suchness."
> The supreme victors did not teach
> that such [bliss] is great bliss.
>
> What arises through interdependence
> cannot be the recognition of suchness [155]
> because that is a bliss
> not inherently present on all occasions.
>
> The wisdom of the sugatas
> knows its own nature.
> It is said to be great bliss
> since it is the foremost of all types of bliss.
>
> Great bliss is not impermanent.
> Great bliss is always permanent.[566]

[Sakya Paṇḍita's assertion is also illogical] because it contradicts the Kālacakra teaching that mahāmudrā is unchanging bliss and because that [mahāmudrā he asserts] is the sensation of released bliss, which is changeable.[567]

It is even more illogical to assert that that [released bliss] is sealed with analytical emptiness because the emptiness [that is the result of] analyzing the skandhas is said to be a nihilistic emptiness, as is explained in the following citations. The *Kālacakra Tantra* says:

> Emptiness [that is the result of] analyzing the skandhas
> has no essence, like a banana tree.
> Emptiness endowed with the most sublime of manifestations
> is not like that.[568]

The "Achievement of Unchanging Wisdom" [section of the *Stainless Light*'s commentary on] the Wisdom Chapter of the *Kālacakra Tantra* says:

> Keep far away from a nihilistic emptiness, the emptiness [that is the result of] analyzing phenomena, which are of the nature of an aggregation of minute particles.[569]

Furthermore, in [Sakya Paṇḍita's] system it is very illogical that the illustrative wisdom of the third abhiṣeka is pointed out to be released bliss, which is changeable, and that the actual wisdom of the fourth abhiṣeka is pointed out to be a nihilistic emptiness, which is given the name freedom from elaborations, because that means he accepts the positions of the opponents refuted by both the *Kālacakra Tantra* and the *Siddhi of Wisdom.* It also means that although the illustrative and actual wisdoms must necessarily be causes and results that are of similar types and connected, they are pointed out as two things that are unconnected and of dissimilar types. [156]

The logical entailment of the position he takes in *Clarifying the Sage's Intent*[570] that mahāmudrā must arise from abhiṣeka is unreasonable because it requires him to explain how ground mahāmudrā, the primordial abiding state of all phenomena, arises from the bestowal of an abhiṣeka. If he does not accept ground mahāmudrā is that way, then he must say that there is no path mahāmudrā and no resultant mahāmudrā since the result becomes manifest through the process of habituating oneself during the path to what is present as the ground. [His position that mahāmudrā must arise from abhiṣeka is also unreasonable] because it necessitates the karma of abandoning the dharma found in many texts, such as the previously mentioned mahāmudrā texts by Saraha senior and junior, Tilopa, Nāropa, Maitrīpa, and others, and many related texts, such as the Seven Siddhi Texts. And finally it is unreasonable because it would mean that the mahāsiddhas who composed those texts must be refuted for their wrong views.

iv. How [Mahāmudrā] Is the Profound Point of All Sūtras and Tantras

This has two parts:

A) Precisely Identifying the Essence of This Path
B) The Way This Path Includes the Profound Points of the Sūtras and Tantras

A) Precisely Identifying the Essence of This Path

It is explained in the Dohā Collections and some of the Symbolic Transmission of Mahāmudrā Cycle[571] that this path system is, within the two categories of Sūtra and Mantra, the Secret Mantrayāna. Within that, it is the third of its divisions into a path of blessings, a path of reviving, and a path of direct cognition. It is taught that it requires the ripening abhiṣekas, extensive or abbreviated. It is also said that since the preceding yānas are like steps on the path, they should not be ignored and should be cultivated as suitable. [157]

Within the Secret Conduct Collection,[572] [this Mahāmudrā path system] is said to be the latter of the three classifications of the Philosophical Pāramitāyāna, Secret Mantra Vajrayāna, and the Yāna of the Unsurpassed Essence, which are designated from the perspective of those to be trained being of lesser, intermediate, or supreme intelligence. [This Mahāmudrā path] is explained in four ways: it is not directly concordant with the preceding two yānas, it does not contradict them, it has some concordant aspects, and it is superior. Nevertheless, some abhiṣekas and blessings, elaborate or concise, are required and deity meditation is taught according to the circumstances. In which case, [this Mahāmudrā path] must be considered to be a division of Secret Mantrayāna.

Looking at the texts of the Great Brahman [Saraha], we see that he speaks of a "path of the essence" as a short path. The *Dohā [for the Queen]* states:

> On this path, the essence of the unsurpassed Mahāyāna,
> results are integrated into the path, results are present
> primordially.[573]

It also proclaims:

> Devoid of maṇḍalas and burnt offerings,
> without mantras, mudrās, or consecrations,
> it can't be produced through tantras or śāstras:
> this vajra wisdom is lovely in its natural state.[574]

[The *Dohā for the People*] says:

> No tantra, no mantra, no object of contemplation or contemplation itself.
> Those just create confusion in our mind.[575]

It also observes:

> Why do we need candles? Why offering cakes?
> What will such things do? What's the use of teaching Secret
> Mantra?[576] [158]

Through those statements and others, [Saraha] teaches that the essence of this path does not rely on Secret Mantra. He asserts it to be without the three conditions, beyond the four joys, and superior to luminosity. However, since the *Dohā for the Queen* describes how to rely upon karmamudrās, mature them through abhiṣekas, and engage in the conduct of discipline, if [mahāmudrā practice] is combined with Secret Mantra, that is fine.[577]

The teachings of the incomparable Dakpo [Gampopa] say:

> Generally speaking, there are three types of paths:
>
> 1. The path that utilizes inferential cognition involves analyzing phenomena in terms of being a single unit or a plurality, determining that they lack any nature, recognizing there is no other destination [or conclusion], and then meditating upon that.
> 2. The path that utilizes blessings purifies the channels, winds, and so forth, relying on the process of generating the deity's form.
> 3. The path that utilizes direct cognition is that of intrinsic mahāmudrā.
>
> Alternatively, the three paths are the following:
>
> 1. The path that abandons the bases is that of the Pāramitā[yāna]. Its relinquishment is one where what is relinquished and the remedies are taken to be separate.
> 2. The path that transforms the bases is that of Secret Mantra. The transformation of the support is to generate the body as the deity. The transformation of the supported is to regard the faculties as a vajra and lotus. The transformation of phenomena is to take mental afflictions as the path. Thoughts are regarded

as wisdom, stains cleanse stains, and thoughts sever thoughts.

3. The path that recognizes the bases is that of Mahāmudrā. It has nothing to abandon, no remedy, nothing to transform, and no transformer. All is the magical display of mind. Awakening occurs by recognizing that the primordially unborn nature, the dharmakāya, is present innately within mind-itself and becoming familiar with seeing that.

Or the three paths are as follows:

1. The Pāramitā path is for those of lesser abilities, [who have faith,] and engage the path of accumulation.
2. Secret Mantra is for those of intermediate abilities, who have concepts and mental afflictions, and who engage the path of method. [159]
3. Mahāmudrā is for those of sharpest abilities, who have prajñā, and engage suchness.[578]

Those demonstrate that Gampopa considers Mahāmudrā to be a short path separate from both Sūtra and Mantra. On some occasions he uses the term "path of blessings" to refer to when realized gurus guide worthy students who have forsaken the activities of this life and they are liberated through the single-stride path of Mahāmudrā, which does not rely upon the main paths of Sūtra or Mantra.[579] Later on, those of the practice lineage incorporated many practices of Sūtra and Mantra—the requisite maturing abhiṣekas, sets of preliminaries, and enhancement techniques related to specific circumstances—[into the Mahāmudrā path] to conform with Sūtra and Mantra. That being so, to consider [Mahāmudrā] a profound path that is shared with Sūtra and Mantra is useful for many levels of intellect and does not involve contradictions.

B) The Way This Path Includes the Profound Points of the Sūtras and Tantras

All the Victor's teachings, be they sūtras or tantras, teach the methods for realizing suchness, the abiding state of phenomena. The intention of his teachings is to lead us to suchness. The culmination of practice ends up being suchness. All his instructions, no matter what mode they are, profound or vast, are directed towards suchness. It is said in the sūtras:

> All the teachings of the Tathāgata lead to suchness, end up at suchness, are directed towards suchness.[580]

The middle *Stages of Meditation* explains:

> The words of the Bhagavān are excellently presented. Either directly or indirectly, they elucidate suchness and lead us to suchness.[581] [160]

The Exalted Lord [Atīśa] teaches:

> All the teachings within
> the eighty-four thousand collections of dharma
> lead to and end up at this: dharmatā.[582]

No sūtra or tantra taught does not contain the methods for realizing emptiness, the abiding state. The *Five Stages* states:

> The suchness presented
> in the various sūtras and tantras
> does not describe anything other than
> this total emptiness.[583]

The *Nīvaraṇaviṣkambhin's Praise of the Bhagavān* says:

> You taught the dharma:
> primordial peace and the absence of arising.
> You turned the dharma wheel
> of natural nirvāṇa.[584]

Thus, the two paths of Sūtra and Tantra are presented as methods for realizing emptiness. Among those, the core of the Sūtra path is listening, reflection, and meditation in general and the practices of the six pāramitās in particular. The point of all those is explained as being contained within meditation on the abiding state. The *Vajra Samādhi Sūtra* states:

When you do not move from emptiness
the six pāramitās are present.[585] [161]

The *Sūtra of the Questions of Brahmaviśeṣacintin* says:

> Not deliberating is generosity. Not differentiating is ethical conduct. Not separating is patience. The absence of adopting or rejecting is diligence. Nonattachment is meditative concentration. Nonconceptuality is prajñā.[586]

The Great Brahman [Saraha] comments:

Reading is it, retaining and meditating are it too.
Explaining the śāstras and purāṇas is it as well.[587]

The *Tantra of Nonabiding* states:

Having eaten the food of the uncontrived natural state,
you'll be satisfied with all the philosophical tenets.
The childish, lacking understanding, rely on terms and words.
Everything is of the characteristic of your own mind.[588]

The core of the Mantra path is said to be the two processes [of generation and perfection], where all such elaborations are taught in order to unite us with the realization of nonelaborate wisdom. The ultimate intended meaning is nonelaboration. The *Vajra Ḍāka* says:

To realize the natural yoga
use contrived meditations
and contrived recitations.

Once you realize the natural yoga
on the other side of contrived yogas,
don't do anything contrived.

Just as someone who has clung to a raft
to cross a river
will discard it on the other side,
so should we treat contrivances.[589] [162]

Vajragarbha's *Commentary* observes:

> Those who are bound by the latent tendencies of concepts
> should rely on conceptual rituals at first.
> Once they've recognized the nature of concepts,
> they will enter nonconceptuality.[590]

It is taught, therefore, that nonelaborate suchness contains completely the meaning of all the yogas of Secret Mantra. The *Two-Part [Hevajra Tantra]* remarks:

> Mantras and deities are truly present
> within the nature of nonelaboration.[591]

It also says:

> It is mantra recitation, asceticism, and burnt offerings.
> It is those belonging to the maṇḍala and the maṇḍala itself.
> In sum, mind is the [all-]inclusive form.[592]

The *King of the Tantras of Secret Amṛta* states:

> When you discover that all activities and actions—
> making offerings, tormas, and the like—
> are the suchness of mind,
> you'll be certain that contains everything.[593]

Nevertheless, in terms of bringing about the realization of true wisdom, it is said that if we do not have these mahāmudrā instructions we will find it difficult to realize luminosity-mahāmudrā, the ultimate abiding state, through just the main paths of Sūtra or Mantra. [163] The Great Brahman [Saraha] proclaims:

> Those priests, called bhikṣus,
> śrāmaṇeras, or sthaviras, are monastics.
> Some set out to teach the sūtras.
> Some regard one taste as a way to hold the mind.
>
> Others rush into the Mahāyāna.
> They [encounter] the authentic śāstras of the scriptural traditions.

Others meditate on maṇḍala cakras.
A few expound the meaning of the fourth.

Some conceptualize the dhātu of space.
Still others make emptiness into a view.
Mostly they engage the opposite [of what they seek].

Those who are divorced from the connate state
separate nirvāṇa from the meditator.
The ultimate is not achieved in isolation.[594]

Tilopa observes:

The specific texts and philosophies
of those who expound Mantra, of the pāramitās,
vinaya, sūtras, and the various piṭakas [164]
will not bring you to see luminosity-mahāmudrā.[595]

If we rely on these instructions of mahāmudrā, the definitive meaning, it is said to be easy to realize the ultimate abiding state. The *Abhidhāna Tantra* states:

Those who definitely enjoy mahāmudrā
will perfect meditation.
They will achieve in this lifetime
both freedom and buddhahood.[596]

The *Sun and Moon Sādhana* says:

Yogins and yoginīs of superior abilities
cultivate the samādhi of bliss-emptiness, the natural outflow,
by relying on ultimate mahāmudrā
and training in unwavering meditative concentration.
It is taught that after three years and three half months
they will achieve the supreme siddhi.[597]

b. The Explanation of the Greatness of the Individuals, the Practitioners

This has two parts:

i. The Greatness of This Actual Lineage in India
ii. The Greatness of This Practice Lineage in Tibet

i. The Greatness of This Actual Lineage in India

The teacher Vajradhara taught an infinite number of *niruttara tantras and, in particular, he taught the tantras of the ultimate essence—*Mahāmudrā-tilaka,* the glorious *[Tantra on] the Unsullied,*[598] *Tantra of Nonabiding,* and others—which he entrusted to Guhyapati. [165] In the land of Oḍḍiyāna, [Guhyapati] instructed wisdom ḍākinīs. The incarnate king called Visukalpa went to Oḍḍiyāna[599] where he received all the instructions and teachings from the wisdom ḍākinīs, and he brought forth many Secret Mantra [teachings]. He examined [potential] recipients and saw that the Great Brahman Saraha was one of the very highest abilities, a gifted individual who was karmically destined as an instantaneous type. Visukalpa gave him the instructions and Saraha was freed. Saraha put all the instructions on the ultimate into songs and set many fortunate beings free. This is the well-known origin of the actual lineage.

According to the accounts in the dohās, Root Symbols, and Indian Secret Conduct, once the true, perfect Buddha had turned the dharma wheel three times for the three types of disciples and was about to show the way to pass into nirvāṇa, he saw that it was time to teach the wondrous ultimate essence of his dharma. He went to the southern regions where, in the city of Vedalī,[600] at the request of Mañjuśrī and Avalokiteśvara, he bestowed this dharma of the ultimate essence on the immeasurable number of bodhisattvas gathered there. He prophesized that later the two bodhisattvas, the Brahman Saraha, Nāgārjuna, Śavaripa, and others would appear to teach the ultimate essence. Subsequently, Mañjuśrī took the illusory emanation of the divine son Ratnamati and Avalokiteśvara took that of the divine son Sukhanātha, and they both taught the Great Brahman. It is said that Saraha was instantly free.

Other accounts agree on most of those points except for a few details such as that Ratnamati was an emanation of the Buddha and Sukhanātha was an emanation of Guhyapati. [166] Such variances do not create contradictions because ultimately everything—the five excellences and so forth—are said to be the display of the Teacher.

Thus, there are accounts that the Teacher, Vajradhara, taught the two emanated bodhisattvas. They taught and liberated the Great Brahman Saraha, the forefather of all the mahāsiddhas in the Noble Land [India]. Saraha taught the protector Nāgārjuna, who was renowned as being like a second victor. These two were gurus for most of the early mahāsiddhas in the Noble Land. In particular, Nāgārjuna liberated the glorious lord Śavaripa, who was a gifted person of the dancer caste, one karmically destined as an instantaneous type. Later, Śavaripa directly received the instructions on the ultimate essence from the two bodhisattvas and Saraha himself. It is well known that they all attained illusory kāyas, or space kāyas, and that since then worthy beings can encounter them on Śrī Parvata[601] in the south.

The transmission of their teachings spread in the Noble Land in the form of numerous instructions on the essence, such as the Seven Mahāmudrā Siddhi Texts, the Sixfold Essence Cycle, the twenty-four texts in the Dharma Cycle on Amanasikāra [Nonattention], as well as the longer and shorter dohā texts. Those inspired such great awe towards the instructions on the ultimate essence in the wise paṇḍitas and siddhas of later times that most set out to find the gurus and instructions of this lineage.

The scholar-siddha Maitrīpa was one who heard of the greatness of the lineage and the dharma of the ultimate essence. With tremendous difficulty, he traveled to Śrī Parvata in the south looking for the lord Śavaripa.[602] [167] At first, when he was unable to find him, he began to feel suicidal. Finally he met Śavaripa and gradually received the instructions on the essence. Then he went to Madhyadeśa [Central India]. Later on, due to those [instructions], he became known as the master Maitrīpa in Vajrāsana [Bodh Gaya] itself, someone more outstanding than others. He promulgated many texts and commentaries on the esoteric instructions of the ultimate essence. In particular, the lineage from [his student] Bhārata-pāṇi [Indian Vajrapāṇi] expanded the instructions on the ultimate essence, such the dohās, Root Symbols, and Secret Conduct.[603]

According to what is well known in this practice lineage, the renowned mahāsiddha Tilopa, who was beyond being an [ordinary] human being, is regarded by some as an emanation of the bhagavān Cakrasaṃvara and by others as an emanation of the bodhisattva Cittavajra.[604] In his illusory kāya he went to Akaniṣṭha where he heard all the vast and profound dharma from Vajradhara himself. Having mastered the Secret Mantra, he became like [the bodhisattva] Vajrapāṇi. Tilopa combined the Mantra generation processes into the four and six branches, the perfection process of the father tantras into the five stages, and the perfection processes of the mother tantras into the four mudrās and six branches. His statement, "I, Tilopa, have no human gurus," caused others to doubt him. To ease their concerns, as an externalized mode of appearance, he again studied with human gurus. His gurus for the four transmissions were the ācārya Nāgārjuna, Kṛṣṇācārya, the mahāsiddha Kambala, and the ḍākinī Subhaginī.[605] He took as his gurus many mahāsiddhas—including Luyipa's disciples, the "brothers" Ṭeṅgipa and Dārikapa, Indrabhūti, and Vajraghaṇṭā—and numerous yoginīs, and then demonstrated liberation.[606] [168]

Subsequently, Tilopa went to the great kingdom of Sahor[607] in the east, where he taught the dharma in the middle of the city. It is said that as a result many hundreds of thousands of people went to celestial realms, leaving the city empty. He is also known for subjugating eight siddhas through his miraculous powers.[608] Thus there are accounts of his liberating innumerable beings. It is also said that as long as the Buddha's teachings endure Tilopa himself remains and continues to practice his yogic conduct in his illusory kāya.

There lived at that time the great ācārya Nāropa, who was learned in Sūtra, Mantra, and the sciences, who had attained the Mantra siddhis. On the basis of prophesies from the bhagavān Cakrasaṃvara and ḍākinīs, he went to the region of Sahor to find the great lord of yogins [Tilopa]. Having met him there, Nāropa pleased him with the service of twelve austerities and received all the instructions in the manner of one vase being poured into another. Afterwards, he went to Madhyadeśa, where he benefited many disciples, who included the seven like himself (such as Maitrīpa),[609] one hundred and eight siddhas (Paiṇḍapātika and others), fifty-four yogins practicing [yogic] discipline, one thousand one hundred qualified yoginīs, the Nepalese Pamtingpa, and the Tibetan Marpa Lotsāwa. [Nāropa] is renowned for having attained an immortal rainbow-like body. [169]

ii. The Greatness of This Practice Lineage in Tibet

The master Marpa Lotsāwa traveled to India on three occasions where he spent a long time studying with siddha-gurus, the exalted Nāropa, Maitrīpa, and others. Through his practice of their profound instructions, he severed his misinterpretations. Of all the lotsāwas who went to India, this master

Marpa was famous for the profound and vast instructions [he received]. He was a leader among those who spoke two languages, and his fame for being a siddha spread. He had many students who became siddhas, such as the three—May [Tsönpo], Ngok [Chödor], and Ram—as well as Tshur-tön, Go-lek, and others.[610]

In particular, Mila Shepa Dorje of Gungtang pleased that great master by enthusiastically undertaking physical hardships. He then received the general instructions and, specifically, the mahāmudrā esoteric instructions on the ultimate essence and the special instructions of the profound hearing lineage. Having undergone difficulties that fill all who hear of them with amazement and sadness, Milarepa planted the victory banner of practice and became renowned as a great lord of yogins in the Snowy Land [Tibet]. He had many students who became siddhas, led by the four great repas, the eight minor repas, and the six teachers.

The practice lineage up through the Great Exalted One [Milarepa] primarily focused its meditation on the esoteric instructions of Secret Mantra. During practices such as caṇḍālī and luminosity, mahāmudrā instructions would be given as appropriate. Following that time, the exalted, great Gampopa, out of his limitless compassion and in order to facilitate realization in all his disciples—superior and inferior—skillfully extracted the mahāmudrā instructions on the ultimate essence and taught them widely, thereby spreading and expanding them. [170] They became the single path traversed by all those of good fortune.

There is a special connection established previously that is worth discussing briefly. In an earlier time, the exalted Gampopa was the bodhisattva Candraprabha Kumāra in the retinue of the bhagavān Munīndra. When the Teacher was presenting the *King of Samādhi Sūtra,* he asked the large assembly of bodhisattvas, "In future hard times when the genuine dharma is declining, who will explain the meaning of this sūtra and spread it?" Candraprabha Kumāra rose and promised that he would do so. The Teacher placed his hand on his head and, calling on the assembly of bodhisattvas, such as Ajita [Maitreya], and the world with its gods as witnesses, prophesized that in the future when there are great terrors, Candraprabha Kumāra would always adhere to pure conduct, promulgate genuine samādhi, reveal the dharma treasures of the sugatas, have a retinue of no fewer than five hundred, and finally awaken as the victor Vimalaprabhā. The Teacher gave his blessings to prevent obstacles occurring. In the same spirit, eight hundred dharma teachers stood up and promised to preserve the meaning of the *King of Samādhi Sūtra* as [Candraprabha Kumāra] had done. Eight hundred million gods, nāgas, yakṣas, and others pledged to protect those holy beings. All of this is explained in the *King of Samādhi Sūtra*.[611] [171]

The *White Lotus of [Great] Compassion* teaches that [the Buddha] reassured Ananda that after he passed into nirvāṇa a bhikṣu named Jīvaka would appear in the north, who would receive much praise, and increase and spread the Teacher's doctrine. Upon his death Jīvaka would go immediately to the worldly realm known as Guṇālaṃkāra within Amitābha's land of Sukhāvatī, where he would awaken as the tathāgata Vimalaprabhā.[612]

There are many other prophesies, such as that to the north of Vajrāsana [Bodh Gaya] in the Snowy Land, on the banks of the great Lohit river,[613] in dense forests and rocky mountains, a dharma teacher and bhikṣu named Jīvaka with a retinue of not less than five hundred would enjoy the tathāgatas' wisdom. Since such accounts are numerous, I will not write about them here for fear of being too wordy. Those who wish for more should refer to those sūtras.

In keeping with those prophesies, to the north of Vajrāsana, in the dense forests and rocky mountain region of the glorious Daklha Gampo there appeared the one known as the exalted Gampopa, the bhikṣu Jīvaka[614] [Physician], with a retinue of disciples not less than five hundred. They practiced the intended meaning of the *King of Samādhi Sūtra*, the instructions on the ultimate essence known as mahāmudrā, and spread that widely among their disciples.

Similarly, in keeping with the scriptural passage in which the previous eight hundred dharma-teacher bodhisattvas promised [to preserve the meaning of the *King of Samādhi Sūtra*], there appeared in the land of Tibet many famous mahāsiddhas who were either students of Gampopa or students of his students. They held, preserved, and spread the teachings on the essence. [172] The great roar of their fame in the regions of Snowy Tibet reverberated throughout the world. The glorious Dakpo Kagyu became renowned in neighboring lands, India, Nepal, China, Mongolia, and beyond. Even now, which is the most degenerate time in a very degenerate period, individuals cast aside their concerns for this life and plant the victory banner of practice in terrifying charnel grounds, under rocky outcroppings, in deserted, empty valleys, in isolated seclusion. Everyone can clearly see that they are beings superior to those of other lineages.

That completes the brief explanation of the particulars that generate confidence. [173]

6

Preliminaries

2. The Exposition of the Preliminaries for the Meditation Process

This has three parts:

a. The Sequence of the Path of the General Teachings
b. The Description of the Preliminaries for This System's Path
c. The Explanation of the Preliminaries in This Context

a. The Sequence of the Path of the General Teachings

Broadly speaking, as individuals who are tired of the sufferings of saṃsāra and who have set their sights on liberation, we engage the precious teachings of the Buddha. The sequence for the practice of the genuine dharma is as follows. First, as the root of the path, we should seek out and study with a qualified spiritual mentor, having examined them thoroughly. Then we should take up the appropriate training in ethical conduct as the ground from which virtues spring forth and maintain that correctly. We should listen closely to the teachings of the Victor generally and, particularly, to the dharma that is the graduated path for the three kinds of beings, as that is the undeceiving path that brings irreversibility and will unite our mind with the genuine dharma. Having a single moment of theoretical understanding of what we have heard does not yield much: we must repeatedly reflect well on the meaning. Then, from deep within, we should turn away from our attachments to the alluring appearances of this life and arouse an exceptional state of mind directed towards definite goodness in future lives.[615] By scrutinizing whatever we might arrogantly do for the sake of the dharma, we will recognize that anything that looks like casual dharma, dharma for a livelihood, dharma for erudition, or ostentatious dharma will not benefit our future lives and will be of some harm. We will delight in undertaking the cultivation of the proper practice of the dharma to whatever degree we can. [174] Nāgārjuna says:

> Listening increases prajñā.
> Once you have both listened and reflected,
> cultivate meditation fully.
> Unsurpassable siddhis will result.[616]

The *Treasury [of Abhidharma]* states:

> Those who are ethical, who listen and reflect,
> can practice meditation well.[617]

The [first] *Stages of Meditation* teaches:

> First generate the prajñā arising from listening. That brings retention of the meaning of the scriptures. Then, using the prajñā arising from reflection, differentiate between the definitive and provisional meanings. Next, relying on the meaning that has been distinguished, meditate on the true nature, not on what is not true.
>
> If you don't do that, because you will be meditating incorrectly and won't have removed your doubts, correct cognition will not arise. Consequently, your meditation will be pointless, similar to the meditations of tīrthikas.[618]

That being the case, it is best right from the start that those with less capacity to practice the profound meaning are guided through the gradual path for the three types of beings, a process that is likened to climbing stairs. The *Lamp That Summarizes Conduct* says:

> So that sentient beings with beginners' karma
> may enter the genuine reality, [175]
> the perfect buddhas presented
> this method, which is like a set of stairs.[619]

The *Two-Part [Hevajra Tantra]* states:

> "How are unfortunate sentient beings,
> the recalcitrant, to be trained?"
>
> The Bhagavān replied:

"First give them the poṣadha,
then the ten points for training.
Next give them Vaibhāṣika teachings,
then those of the Sautrāntika,
and then the Yogācāra.

"Following that, teach them Madhyamaka.
Once they understand the stages of Mantra,
they may then be taught Hevajra.
Students who take this up with devotion
will become accomplished—have no doubt."[620]

Thus it is taught that first beings should be trained in the stages of the yānas, then gradually in the Mantra path.

b. The Description of the Preliminaries for This System's Path

It is necessary to know the differences between the two types of individuals who practice the profound meaning. Fortunate ones with training [in previous lives] are gifted because they can be taught the profound path immediately. Those with beginners' karma should be taught the profound path gradually. This is stated in both the *Earlier Authoritative Text* and the *Latter Authoritative Text*: [176]

Given the differences in individuals' intellectual capacities,
there are gradual types and instantaneous types.

A powerful medicine for the gradual type
is a strong poison for the instantaneous type.
A powerful medicine for the instantaneous type
is poison for the gradual type.

Those possessing the continuity of training
should be taught as the instantaneous type.
Sentient beings with beginners' karma
should be taught as the gradual type.[621]

Accordingly, the way to teach this profound path is as follows. The exalted Gampopa presents this as a short path that does not depend on Secret Mantra and, therefore, he does not say that the maturing abhiṣekas are required as preliminaries. He teaches the way to lead [students] to the nature of mind that relies only on taking refuge in the three jewels and the gurus, cultivating kindness, compassion, and bodhicitta, offering maṇḍalas to those [sources of refuge], confessing negative actions, and supplicating with fervent devotion.

Furthermore, those of highest abilities, who are instantaneous types, first investigate the view and then are given the esoteric instructions on the methods for resting evenly right within the view. This is similar to the guidance given these days according to the Four Syllables of Mahāmudrā. Those of lesser abilities who are gradual types, are guided through śamatha, then gradually through vipaśyanā. This is similar to the guidance given nowadays according to the Instructions on Connate Union. The reason for stating that there are these [two approaches] can be understood from the instruction manuals, advice, and questions and answers in [Gampopa's] precious Collected Works and from the Exalted One's advice preserved in the Collected Works of the glorious Pakmo Drupa and the exalted Dusum Khyenpa.[622] [177]

Then, later ones in the practice lineage [incorporated elements] to conform with the practices of Secret Mantra creating the renowned Fivefold Mahāmudrā, a systematization of bodhicitta, yidam deities, guru yoga, sequential meditations on mahāmudrā, and concluding dedications.[623] The Instructions on Connate Union and the Four Syllables also were joined with a fourfold preliminary practice that gives rise to meditation: reflections on impermanence, meditations and recitations of Vajrasattva, maṇḍala offerings, and guru yoga. If that is the approach we undertake, since it is one that is mixed with Secret Mantra, it is definitely necessary to receive either an extensive or abbreviated ripening abhiṣeka first. The *Mahāmudrā-tilaka* observes:

> If there is no abhiṣeka, there will be no siddhi,
> just as pressing sand will not yield butter.[624]

The *Buddha-kapāla* comments:

> When a veena has no strings
> it cannot be strummed.
> Analogously, when you lack abhiṣeka
> you cannot practice mantras or meditative concentration.[625]

Thus, to engage with the main instructions of mahāmudrā alone according to the system of the exalted Gampopa does not require receiving the ripening abhiṣekas. We can practice according to the preliminaries taught by the exalted Gampopa himself without doing the meditations and recitations of Vajrasattva, generating ourself as a deity, generating the guru as Vajradhara and requesting abhiṣeka, and so forth.

However, we may wonder, Are not the counting and retention of breath found in the śamatha instructions a yoga of Secret Mantra? [178] They are not because Sūtra-oriented śamatha practices include numerous explanations on counting the breath, following it, and so on.

Nevertheless, nowadays it appears that practitioners meditate on mahāmudrā and Secret Mantra by blending them, and that enhances their realization. The preliminary practices also incorporate many Mantra practices. If we engage in that manner, it is definitely necessary to receive the ripening abhiṣekas first. Furthermore, in the case of a yidam such as Cakrasaṃvara with consort, it is necessary to receive either an extensive or abbreviated abhiṣeka that has a pure source in the tantras and contains the flow of blessings of the lineage.

c. The Explanation of the Preliminaries in This Context

This has two parts:

i. The Explanation of the Uncommon Preliminaries
ii. What Is to Be Done Prior to the Meditation Processes Themselves

i. The Explanation of the Uncommon Preliminaries

This has five sections:

A) The Contemplations on Impermanence and the Like to Overcome Laziness
B) The Taking of Refuge and Arousing of Bodhicitta to Dispel Obstacles
C) The Offering of Maṇḍalas to Amass the Accumulations
D) The Meditation and Recitations of Vajrasattva to Cleanse Obscurations
E) The Meditation of Guru Yoga to Receive Blessings

A) The Contemplations on Impermanence and the Like to Overcome Laziness

Through carefully contemplating the difficulties of acquiring the leisures and opportunities [of a precious human existence], the way to make it meaningful once acquired, the way it can quickly change due to its impermanence, the way our karma takes control once we die, the way karma will mature without losing its potency, how we will experience actions and their results in three ways, the attendant sufferings of the six classes of beings, and the problems of the seeming happiness within existence, we will arouse a strong motivation to strive for liberation. Since that is the root of dharma, it is most important at all times. It is well known that revulsion is the foot of meditation and that revulsion is the master of meditation. If we leave those contemplations as a one-time theoretical understanding, at first our meditation may develop, but afterwards, not only will we be unable to suppress our attachment, aversion, and confusion, we will be under the sway of the sense pleasures, such as food and clothing, and the seduction of fame and desires.[626] [179] The reason it is so rare that practice is brought to fruition comes down to just this.

That being so, we should do as Tilopa instructs:

> KYE MA. Contemplate worldly phenomena well.
> They do not endure, being like dreams and illusions.
> Dreams and illusions in fact don't exist.
> Become disenchanted and cast aside worldly activities.
>
> Sever your love-hate ties with those around you.
> Meditate alone in the wilderness, in forests or mountains.[627]

B) The Taking of Refuge and Arousing of Bodhicitta to Dispel Obstacles

Those of us who seek liberation out of fear and anxiety about the sufferings of saṃsāra place ourselves under the protection of the three precious jewels no matter what. Taking refuge is most important since it is the root of the dharma. The sūtras teach:

> Whenever someone takes refuge
> in the buddha, dharma, and saṅgha,

> they will see with prajñā
> the four truths for noble ones:
> suffering, the origins of suffering,
> the true transcendence of suffering,
> the happiness of the eightfold path of nobles ones,
> the way to nirvāṇa. [180]
>
> That refuge is primary.
> That refuge is the best.
> Relying on that refuge
> they will be freed from all sufferings.[628]

The benefits of taking refuge. The benefits are unimaginable, as the *Synopsis of the Pāramitās* explains:

> If the merit of taking refuge had a form
> these three realms would be too small a container.
> The great ocean is a treasury of water
> that can't be fathomed by incremental measurements.[629]

Specifically, the eight benefits of taking refuge are that we become Buddhists, we have a support for all other vows, our karmic obscurations from previous actions are exhausted, we amass vast merit, we do not fall into the negative states, we are unaffected by the obstacles of humans and nonhumans, we achieve our intentions, and we will quickly awaken. In addition to those benefits, it is explained that the Mahāyāna refuge protects us from falling onto paths that do not contain correct methods or into the Hīnayāna.

Therefore, we should take refuge with clear certainty about the objects of refuge, the timing, intention, ceremony, and so forth. Nowadays some regard the process of taking refuge simply as a gateway for beginners. Considering it insignificant for future [practices], they dismiss it and don't train in the precepts of the refuge vows. That is very unwise since it is difficult for them to be regarded as Buddhists.

Arousing bodhicitta. Bodhicitta is the entryway and root of the path for all who have entered the Mahāyāna and wish to achieve unsurpassable awakening. [181] Nāgārjuna says:

> If you and others in this world
> wish to attain unsurpassable awakening,
> you need its root, bodhicitta,
> firm as the mighty king of mountains.[630]

The *Gaṇḍavyūha* states:

> Child of good family, bodhicitta is like the seed of all the Buddha's dharma.[631]

Bodhicitta necessarily arises from kindness and compassion for sentient beings. Kindness and compassion come from recognizing that all sentient beings have been our mother, that all mothers have been kind, and that we wish to repay their kindness. Since bodhicitta depends on having an altruistic attitude, we must think well about those points and cultivate that attitude.

The benefits of cultivating kindness, compassion, and bodhicitta. The benefits are described in numerous texts, such as the following. The *Precious Garland* teaches:

> Even giving away three times a day
> food in three hundred cooking pots
> does not match a portion of the merit
> of just one instant of kindness.
>
> Even though you may not be liberated,
> you will attain the eight virtues of kindness:
> Gods and humans will feel kindly towards you
> and will offer their protection.
> You will have much happiness and mental ease
> and be unharmed by poison and weapons.
> Effortlessly you will achieve your aims
> and be born in the world of Brahmā.[632] [182]

The *Account of the Noble Deeds of Avalokiteśvara* says:

> If having one quality is like having all the Buddha's qualities in the palm of your hand, what is that one? It is great compassion.[633]

Candrakīrti states:

> Since kindness is said to be the seed for the Victor's abundant harvest,
> to be like water that causes growth,
> and what ripens into a state enjoyed for a long time,
> I begin with a praise of compassion.[634]

The *Sūtra of the Questions of Vīradatta* says:

> If bodicitta's merit
> were to take a form,
> it would be grander than
> something filling the whole of space.[635]

It continues:

> One person may fill buddha fields
> equaling the number of grains of sand in the Ganges river
> with precious substances and offer them to the sugatas.
> Another who joins their palms together
> and bows to bodhicitta
> makes a superior offering,
> one without limit.[636]

Furthermore, it is explained that aspirational bodhicitta has eight benefits: it brings us into the Mahāyāna, it is the support for all the trainings in bodhicitta, it annihilates all our negative actions, it sets down the roots of awakening, it confers immeasurable merit, it pleases all the buddhas, it benefits all sentient beings, and it brings awakening quickly. [183] Additionally, engaged bodhicitta has many benefits including being the source of a stream of benefit for oneself and of a variety of benefits for others.

Having developed certainty about the objects of meditation for, and natures of, kindness, compassion, and bodhicitta, we must earnestly cultivate them because it is explained that roots of virtue, in general, and meditation on emptiness, specifically, that lack bodhicitta are not the path of the Mahāyāna or causes of perfect awakening.

C) The Offering of Maṇḍalas to Amass the Accumulations

Broadly speaking, if we do not amass a collection of causal merit, we will not achieve either temporal or lasting happiness. Particularly, if we do not gather a stock of merit as the means for amassing a collection of resultant wisdom, we will not realize the view of emptiness. Therefore, it is important to gather a collection of merit in the beginning. The sūtras state:

> Because merit brings happiness,
> human beings should amass merit.
> They should do so again and again.
> They should do so this very day.[637]

The *Verses That Summarize the Prajñāpāramitā Sūtras* observes:

> As long as the roots of virtue are not complete, [184]
> genuine emptiness is not achieved [or realized].[638]

The benefits or purpose of accruing the accumulations. The *Sūtra on the Inconceivable Secret Teachings of the Tathāgatas* explains:

> The accumulation of wisdom eliminates the mental afflictions. The accumulation of merit sustains sentient beings. Bhagavān, this being so, bodhisattva mahāsattvas should apply themselves to [amassing] the accumulations of merit and wisdom.[639]

The *Precious Garland* remarks:

> To summarize the form kāya:
> King, it arises from the collection of merit.
> To summarize the dharmakāya:
> King, it arises from the collection of wisdom.[640]

In brief, all the benefits of the six pāramitās are the benefits of the two accumulations.

Although, generally speaking, the methods for accruing merit are to train in the ten dharma activities and the four ways of gathering [students], in this context it is explained that the accumulations are amassed through the sevenfold service with an emphasis on the branch of offerings in the form of maṇḍalas. The way to offer maṇḍalas is as follows. Those of us belonging to the practice lineage should create or visualize a practice maṇḍala (however we can) as the field for amassing the accumulations and then present offering maṇḍalas to that. As is said, "Without any reservations, present what you can imagine, things you own, whatever you can set out."

We also gather the accumulations by means of the sevenfold service. Homage, offerings, requesting [teachings], and supplicating [not to pass into nirvāṇa] amass the accumulations. [185] Confession purifies obscurations. Rejoicing increases virtue. Dedication vastly increases the virtue of that amassing, purifying, and increasing, and it ensures [the accumulations] do not lose their potency. Since it is taught that these are the ways to achieve immeasurable heaps of merit, we should greatly exert ourselves towards them.

D) The Meditation and Recitations of Vajrasattva to Cleanse Obscurations

Throughout our beginningless sequence of lives until the present time, the maturation of the negativity of our bad actions has been a powerful force obscuring liberation, realizations on the path towards omniscience, and actualization of the result. While those have not been purified, we have experienced suffering wandering endlessly in saṃsāra. And we will continue to experience the sufferings of saṃsāra no matter what, like a stream flowing through a waterwheel. Therefore, we should apply ourselves to purifying our negative actions and obscurations. The *Collection of Meaningful Expressions* warns:

> Even a small negative action
> can cause great fear and massive destruction
> in the next world,
> like what happens when we swallow poison.[641]

It also says:

> The maturation of negative actions—
> wild and evil actions done
> for the sake of your own happiness—
> result in experiences that'll make you weep.[642]

There are many such sayings.

The methods for purifying negative actions are typically said to be the four powers, which are listed in the *Sūtra Teaching Four Qualities*: [186]

> Maitreya, if bodhisattva mahāsattvas have four qualities, they will overpower the negative actions they have done and amassed. What are the four? They are thus: the practice of repudiation, the application of remedies, turning away from wrong doing, and the power of reliance.[643]

The first power is to confess previous negative actions with remorse. The second power includes memorizing or reading the sūtras, having conviction about emptiness, performing recitations, creating statues or stūpas, making offerings to those, and reciting the names of buddhas and bodhisattvas. The third power is to vow to refrain from committing the ten unvirtuous actions from this time on. The fourth power includes taking refuge, cultivating bodhicitta, and the like. Even though [those are the usual means for purifying negative actions,] in this context, we make confessions on the basis of meditation and recitation. If we have remorse for negative actions and the resolve to refrain from them, from now on, all four powers are actually present.

Specifically, [the methods for] purifying negative actions are taught to be verbal recitations, as the *[Tantra] of the Questions of Subāhu* says:

> Just as the flames of a fire spreading through the woods in early
> summer
> will consume the wilderness without impediment,
> the fire of verbal recitations, flamed by exertion
> and fanned by the winds of ethical conduct,
> will consume negative actions.
>
> Just as snow when struck by sunlight
> cannot withstand the intensity and melts,
> the snow of negative actions vanishes
> when the sunlight of verbal recitation and ethical conduct strikes. [187]
>
> Just as when a small candle is lit in a dark room
> the darkness vanishes,

> the candle flame of verbal recitations quickly vanquishes
> the darkness of negative actions amassed during thousands of lifetimes.[644]

Right from the first moment, wrongdoings and downfalls are committed, regardless of which one of the four causes is involved—ignorance, excessive mental afflictions, carelessness, or lack of respect—they should not be tolerated. We should repeatedly confess them. The *Collection of Meaningful Expressions* instructs:

> Do not scorn even a tiny negative action,
> thinking it won't cause any harm.
> By gathering small drops of water
> eventually you can fill a large container.[645]

The *Excellent Siddhi [Tantra]* states:

> Any careless things you have done during the day
> should be confessed one by one at night.
> Those done at night should be confessed in the day.
> Do that well and you will feel delight.[646]

The meditation and recitations of Vajrasattva. The *Ornament of the Heart* teaches:

> Visualize Vajrasattva
> on top of a white lotus and moon seat.
> Recite the hundred syllables according to the ritual,
> twenty times each.
>
> Giving his blessing [as you confess] downfalls,
> he says, "They will not increase."
> Thus do the supreme accomplished ones explain.
> Do this between sessions.
>
> If you perform this recitation one hundred thousand times,
> you will become a purified being.[647] [188]

E) The Meditation of Guru Yoga to Receive Blessings

Overall, the sūtras and tantras teach that studying with a guru is the root of the path that aims for liberation. They describe in detail gurus' qualifications, the way we should study with them, the purpose of such study, and the benefits. The Secret Mantra texts, in particular, explain that siddhis accompany ācāryas, and they teach extensively about how we must be attentive to the way we study with them. Since this practice lineage is called the path of blessings, it especially emphasizes that the development of meditation (when it has not yet developed) and the enhancement of it (once it has developed) depend upon the blessings of the guru. We should, therefore, apply ourselves to meditating upon guru yoga.

We may ask, What is the reason for that? Gurus are praiseworthy as the *Name-Chanting of Mañjuśrī* says:

> Worthy of offerings, worthy of honor,
> place of homage, always worthy of worship,
> worthy of veneration, supreme among those to be respected:
> the sublime guru is worthy of homage.[648]

It is also said:

> Homage to the guru:
> embodiment of the buddhas,
> essence of Vajradhara,
> root of the three jewels.[649]

The purpose of undertaking [study with a guru]. It is to be able to achieve both temporal and ultimate siddhis. Bhavideva [Aśvaghoṣa] states: [189]

> Vajradhara teaches that
> siddhis follow the ācāryas.[650]

He also says:

> I bow at the lotus feet of the guru,
> the cause for attaining the state of glorious Vajrasattva.[651]

The way to meditate on the guru. The *Ornament of the Vajra Heart* says:

The disciple with constant devotion to the guru
looks upon them in this way:
the guru is the same as the buddhas,
always Vajradhara.[652]

The *Vajra Pañjarā* teaches:

The one known as Vajrasattva
takes the form of an ācārya.
With the aim of helping sentient beings
he remains in an ordinary form.[653]

Bhavideva states:

Do not regard the guru
as separate from Vajradhara.[654]

The way to meditate upon the guru as the embodiment of all buddhas. The *Vajra Ḍāka* instructs:

[The gurus'] form is of the nature of all buddhas.
Their limbs are the bodhisattvas,
their body hairs are arhats,
the crown of their head is the buddhas of the five families,
worldly ones are the seats below their feet,
and their light rays are Secret Yakṣa and others.
Yogic practitioners should always see
[the gurus'] form as being of the nature of such excellent qualities.[655]
[190]

There are similar statements in the *Caturpīṭha* root text and its commentaries.[656] We should learn more about these modes.

The purpose of meditating in that way. Ācārya Ratnākaraśānti explains that we do this to equalize our faith in Vajradhara and the guru, stabilize the pride of Vajradhara, and quickly become accomplished by amassing the accumulations with little effort.[657]

The making of special offerings to and worship of the guru, along with the benefits of doing so. The *Five Stages* says:

Put aside all other forms of worship,
and concentrate on worshipping the guru.
By pleasing them,
you will attain supreme, omniscient wisdom.[658]

The *Guhyasamāja Tantra* states:

Worshipping a single hair of the guru's body
is of greater merit
than worshipping the buddhas of the three times.[659]

The *Sampuṭa* explains:

Offer each and every thing of beauty
to your guru
with no expectations.[660]

The *Ornament of the Vajra Heart* comments:

With all your energy,
worship your guru, Vajradhara.
Accordingly you will please them,
and that will please all buddhas.[661]

Bhavideva [Aśvaghoṣa] says:

Those who long for what is inexhaustible
should offer to the guru
whatever is pleasing,
regardless of whether it is exceptional or merely a trifle. [191]

To give in that way
is identical to continuously giving to the buddhas.
To give in that way collects merit.
That collection results in the supreme siddhi.[662]

The value of arousing the force of faith and devotion in the guru is explained by the *Ten Dharmas Sūtra*:

To have faith in guides with [the wish] for definite emergence
is the supreme of yānas.
Thus, intelligent people follow and study with those with faith.

Virtuous qualities will not be born
in humans with no faith,
just as a green sprout [will not arise]
from a seed burnt by fire.[663]

The *Precious Torch Dhāraṇī* also explains this:

Faith is a prerequisite: it engenders like a mother.
It protects all virtues and increases them.
It slays doubts and transports us across rivers.
Faith reveals a city of peace and goodness.

Faith is free from turbidity and clarifies the mind.
It replaces pride and is the root of respect.
Faith is a gem, a treasure, and the best of feet.
Like a hand, it is the basis for gathering up virtue.[664] [192]

Recalling the guru's kindness, our powerful longing brings us close to tears. The *Gaṇḍavyūha* says:

Sudhanakumāra, spiritual mentors protect you from the negative states. They enable you to realize the equality of phenomena. They show you which paths are good and which are not. They instruct you in the conduct of Samantabhadra. They show you the path to the city of omniscience. They escort you to the place of omniscience. They bring you to the ocean of the dharmadhātu. They explain the ocean of knowable objects in the three times. They reveal the maṇḍalas of the assembly of noble ones. Spiritual mentors increase your virtuous qualities. Bear this in mind and weep.[665]

There are many such sayings.

If we have devotion, we will receive blessings. If we receive blessings, realization of the mind will follow. The *Two-Part [Hevajra Tantra]* observes:

> The connate cannot be described by others,
> cannot be discovered anywhere.
> Follow your guru's timing and his methods:
> you will recognize it with your merit.[666]

Nāgārjuna says:

> Once you begin falling from the peak of Mount Meru,
> you will keep falling despite thinking, "I can't fall."
> Once you discover the beneficial path through the kindness of the guru
> you will be liberated despite thinking, "I can't be liberated."[667]

Gampopa teaches:

> Ours is a lineage of blessings. [193] If we do not receive our guru's blessings, it is impossible for us to experience the actual transmission of mahāmudrā. For those who receive their guru's blessings there are no difficulties. Those with devotion will receive them by supplicating.
>
> Those with the greatest degree of devotion will receive the greatest degree of blessings. Those with an intermediate degree of devotion will receive an intermediate degree of blessings. Those with a lesser degree of devotion will receive a lesser degree of blessings. Those with no devotion will receive absolutely no blessings. That is the way of things.[668]

He also says:

> The means of arousing realization in those for whom it has not yet arisen is to supplicate the guru with devotion and honor them—there is no other way. The means of stabilizing realization in those for whom it has arisen is to have devotion for the guru and habituate themselves to that.[669]

He concludes:

> As for how to supplicate: While walking here and there, supplicate. While sitting around, supplicate. When waking up, supplicate.[670]

That is what is well known in this practice lineage.

Nowadays, the custom of those who know the esoteric instructions is to do guru yoga meditation as follows. When confessing impaired or broken vows and strayings to your guru, meditate upon them as being in front of you or on your head, while you remain in your ordinary form. In all other contexts, since it is not appropriate to receive abhiṣekas in your ordinary form, meditate upon yourself as a yidam and meditate that your guru is Vajradhara, the embodiment of all buddhas, above your head. Present to them maṇḍalas and the like as the outer, inner, and secret offerings. With strong devotion, supplicate them for your desired aims. Request the samādhi abhiṣeka. In the end, meditate that your guru dissolves into you. This way of practicing guru yoga is excellent because it contains many key points of the paths of maturation and liberation. [194]

The locations for meditating on the gurus are explained in the *Abhidhāna*:

> When the guru possessing kindness
> is seated in the center of someone's heart,
> on the crown of their head, or the palm of their hand,
> that person holds
> the virtues of a thousand buddhas.[671]

The exalted Gampopa mostly taught that we should meditate on our guru as being in the space in front. The exalted Yang Gönpa says:

> During offerings and gaṇacakras, [the guru] is in the sky in front.
> When supplicating, they are above your head.
> At all times, the guru is in the center of your heart.[672]

The signs of having meditated intently on the preliminary practices are as follows:

- On the basis of having contemplated impermanence, we will turn away, in both our attitude and behavior, from attachment to sense pleasures and the seductions of this life. Contentment [the feeling of not needing anything] will arise in our mindstream. Our focus will become more immediate, our eight worldly values pacified, and our mindstream tamed.

- On the basis of taking refuge, we will experience serenity, inspiration, cheerfulness, and a sense of ease.
- On the basis of offering maṇḍalas, we will have a clear complexion, joy, no feelings of hunger even when we have not eaten, lucid awareness, and our prajñā will grow. As omens in dreams, we may dream of the sun or moon rising, seeing many flowers, walking upwards, and so on.
- On the basis of the meditation and recitations of Vajrasattva, our body will become light, we will sleep less, feel healthy and lighthearted. As omens in dreams, we may dream of pus and blood oozing from our body, vomiting or excreting, and bathing.
- On the basis of guru yoga meditation, we may feel that we wish to touch our guru when we are in their presence, our mind may become captivated by our guru and we yearn for them, we may wish to supplicate them day and night, experiences may blaze, and our perceptions fade. [195] As omens in dreams, we may dream of meeting our guru, that they explain the dharma or bestow abhiṣekas.

Such accounts are found in the teachings of all those of the practice lineage.

Anyone who considers these preliminaries to be only things beginners need to boost their meditation at first and to be of little significance after that are greatly ignorant of the vital points of the dharma because these teachings are the main support for the Mahāyāna path.

Since I am afraid of being too wordy here, I have presented only a tiny bit on this subject. Nevertheless, the preliminaries are the root of the dharma and central to the path, and, therefore, crucial. It is important that we listen to and reflect upon teachings about the extensive graduated path and the like, come to a definitive understanding in a thorough way, and apply ourselves to this over an extended period of time.

ii. What Is to Be Done Prior to the Meditation Processes Themselves

This has two parts:

A) The Particulars of What Is to Be Known First
B) The Way to Maintain Sessions

A) The Particulars of What Is to Be Known First

We should train in the five qualities conducive to liberation taught in the *Compendium of Abhidharma*.[673]

Ethical conduct for ordinary beings. Turning our mind from any attitude or behavior that involves a basis of harm to others and habituating ourselves to the mindset that renounces such [intentions or actions] is the practice of ethical conduct. The *Entrance to the Bodhisattva's Way of Life* says:

> There is nowhere fishes and the like
> can go that they will not be killed.
> The achievement of a mindset that renounces [such actions]
> is explained as the pāramitā of ethical conduct.[674]

We preserve our ethical conduct by having mindfulness and alertness, by being conscientious about whatever precepts we have (such as the vows of an *upāsaka*), and by avoiding all unwholesome conduct involving misdeeds. [196] The *Letter to a Friend* observes:

> Just as the earth supports all that moves and is still,
> ethical conduct is said to be the basis for all virtues.[675]

The *Sūtra on Ethical Conduct* states:

> Just as the blind cannot see forms,
> so it is that those without ethics cannot see the dharma.[676]

Restraining the sense faculties. Following the arising of any of the six sense consciousnesses—which are based on the six objects (such as forms) and the six sense faculties (such as the visual one)—we should control our mental consciousness and not be attached to any of the six attractive objects or feel aversion for any of the six unattractive ones that may arise. Without grasping at characteristics or signs, we keep our mind away from desire and aggression, and rest it on something virtuous or neutral, as the sūtras say:

> The eyes see forms [but] do not grasp at characteristics or signs.[677]

Alert behavior. Whenever we do something, such as a physical activity, we should engage conscientiously, being mindful of and alert to adopting what is appropriate and avoiding what is inappropriate. The *Entrance to the Bodhisattva's Way of Life* says:

> Repeatedly examine
> the condition of your body and mind. [197]
> That alone sums up the definition
> of what it means to protect alertness.[678]

The *Verses That Summarize the Prajñāpāramitā Sūtras* advises:

> Walk, move, sleep, and sit with alertness.[679]

The sūtras say:

> When you engage in an activity, recognize that and think, "I am active." When you stand, notice that, thinking, "I am standing." When you sit, be aware of that and think, "I am sitting."[680]

There are many similar statements. The purpose of this is explained in the Heap of Jewels:

> If you always turn to mindfulness and alertness,
> you will not be affected by mistaken notions.[681]

Moderation of food. If we eat only a very small amount of food, we will feel hungry and weak. If we consume too much, our body will feel heavy and our drowsiness and dullness will increase. Indigestible or unwholesome food provokes new or old illnesses. All of those will make our body unsuitable for spiritual practices. Food involving the mental afflictions of attachment, aversion, and so forth causes us to commit misdeeds and makes our mind unsuitable [for spiritual practices]. We should consume food that does not fall into those categories, relying on it as we do medicine, and eat moderately just what we need to sustain our body. The *Letter to a Friend* states:

> Take food appropriately, like medicine,
> without desire or aversion.
> Do not eat out of pride or arrogance,
> or for the sake of satiation—eat only to sustain your body.[682]

This point rests on contemplating the disadvantages of craving food. We should consider that no matter what kind of food it is, as soon as we eat it, it becomes something unpleasant, like vomit. It also can cause physical disease, and it creates unclean substances, which in the end must be excreted. [198] We undergo many difficulties and sufferings for the sake of food and the causes of food. Food arouses our attachment, aversion, and confusion. It causes us to engage in negative actions and the like, such that in the end we will fall to the lower realms. We should reflect upon how enjoying moderation benefits our patrons, nourishes the microorganisms in our body, and enables us to work for the welfare of sentient beings. These points are discussed by the noble Asaṅga.[683]

Exertion in yoga during the first and last periods [of the night] instead of sleeping. We should be diligent in practicing yoga meditation with mindfulness and alertness throughout the day and during two-thirds of the night, the first and last periods. The *Verses That Summarize the Prajñāpāramitā Sūtras* teach:

> Diligence will not obscure virtuous qualities.
> It uncovers the victors' treasure: infinite wisdom.[684]

The *Letter to a Friend* says:

> Wise one, recite all day
> and also during the first and last periods of the night.
> Then in the interim, sleep with mindfulness
> so that your time asleep is not wasted.[685]

We may wonder, What do those statements imply about how we should conduct ourself during sleep? There are four aspects.

Our physical deportment [or posture]. During the middle third of the night we should lie on our right side with our left leg resting on top of our right, and sleep like a slumbering lion. It is explained that that posture is a key technique that naturally prevents our body becoming [overly] relaxed, our sleep becoming heavy, our mindfulness lapsing while we are sleeping, and our dreams being bad ones or involving negative actions.[686] [199]

Mindfulness. Until we fall asleep we should maintain mindfulness of whatever is our specific object of meditation during the day. It is explained that such mindfulness will lead us to spiritual practice also during our sleep.

Alertness. While we are practicing mindfulness, we must recognize when mental afflictions or the like arise and abandon them. It is said that alertness will diminish our delusion during sleep and dreams.

The mental orientation for waking up. Since sleep increases the regenerative elements in our body, we should sleep for a small amount of time in order to strengthen it. We should set the stage by thinking, "I will rise early and exert myself in spiritual practices." Then we should visualize shining light and go to sleep concentrating on that. It is taught that this prevents our mind from sinking into darkness, keeps our sleep light, wakes us up on time, and increases our diligence for spiritual practices during the early morning.

B) The Way to Maintain Sessions

Generally speaking, it is explained that we should engage in our spiritual practices in two or three sessions each day. There are, however, also many instructions to do four sessions, and that is the custom in this practice lineage. They are specified as being at dawn, in the morning, afternoon, and evening. We should know that each session has preparatory practices, main practices, and concluding practices.

Preparatory practices. If you have the three representations [of awakened body, speech, and mind], arrange them [on a shrine] and place whatever offerings you may have before them. Sit on a comfortable seat, and let your body and mind settle naturally. [200] Cut off the flow of extraneous wishful thinking. If you do not cut the flow of such thoughts at this point, the reverberations of that will definitely show up as problems when you try to maintain the main spiritual practices.[687]

Next, you must have bodhicitta to begin your spiritual practices. It ensures that whatever you do as a main practice will be a cause for awakening.

Main practices. Keep clearly in your mind the number of objects of meditation that are to be cultivated and their sequence, whether they are objects of meditation discussed already (such as contemplating impermanence) or objects of meditation involving characteristics or the lack of characteristics, which have yet to be explained. Arouse a strong resolve, thinking, "I will not let my mind stray into jumbling up the various meditation objects, taking one thing from the beginning and another from the end." Then, with mindfulness and alertness, practice correctly according to the number and sequence of the objects for meditation.

If you don't do that and instead practice with some meditation objects and not others [of a particular sequence], with some mindfulness, some distraction, it is said that you will fall into the bad habit of doing that and will have problems in your spiritual practice throughout your life. Therefore, from the outset, it is essential to guide your mind in a straightforward and sequential manner.

As a beginner, if you try to sustain [your concentration] on an object of meditation for a long time right from the start, your mind will come under the sway of dullness and agitation. If you fall into that bad habit, it will be hard to correct later on. Thus, [as a beginner you should meditate] for short sessions frequently. It is said:

> Short sessions are without problems.
> Repeating them increases your excellent qualities.

Given this, it is taught that if you stop when the object of meditation is clear and then meditate again, you will have less fatigue and be enthusiastic about resuming your meditation. [201] On the other hand, if you let yourself get weary with meditation, you will not want to meditate later on. Once you have a bit of stability, increase the length of your sessions. Later, having some familiarization, your endurance in meditation will increase and it will become your natural way. If you always keep your sessions short, you will get stuck in that routine and spiritual practice will not become your natural mode at any point in your lifetime.

Concluding practices. When you have suspended your session, share the virtue of your spiritual practice with all sentient beings. Dedicate it as a cause for unsurpassable awakening and make pure aspiration prayers because it is explained that those will ensure that the roots of virtue are not lost, not wasted, and will increase.

Between sessions. With the appropriate [qualities conducive to liberation] that were explained above (preserving ethical conduct, restraining your sense faculties, and so on), you should apply yourself to activities that amass [merit and wisdom] and purify [negative karma], such as the ten dharma activities, prostrations, and circumambulations. However, if upon leaving your sessions you do not bother with any of that—meaning you do not make any effort towards being mindful and aware of the object of meditation you are training with, and you let your mind go wherever it wants—you will not make much progress in your spiritual practice. Therefore, strive to sustain the view of and reflections upon your [object of meditation] and related dharma practices, and repeatedly cultivate flashes of mindful awareness of them.

We should know that for the most part those instructions are the way to practice beginning with the meditations on impermanence up through the final accomplishment of the view and meditation of mahāmudrā (with some exceptions when certain focuses have their own way of being maintained).

That completes the concise explanation of the exposition of the preliminaries for the meditation process. [202/203]

7
Mahāmudrā Approaches

3. The Actual Explanation of the Way to Cultivate Mahāmudrā

This has two parts:

a. The Presentation of the Divisions of the Meditation Process
b. The Explanation of the Meditation Process in This Context

a. The Presentation of the Divisions of the Meditation Process

Broadly speaking, there are two approaches to meditating on the definitive meaning. The instantaneous types, who are of the highest abilities, begin by cutting through their misinterpretations about the view and then cultivate the methods for resting their mind right within that view. The gradual types, who are either of intermediate or lesser abilities, begin by investigating the view from within their cultivation of the still mind and the like, and then they familiarize themselves with the view. Among these two approaches, the glorious Saraha, Śavaripa, Indrabhūti, Tilopa, Maitrīpa, and others teach the first approach from the perspective of those of highest abilities. The Dharma Treatises of Maitreya, the [Five] Divisions of the Yogāchāryābhūmi, Kamalaśīla's *Stages of Meditation,* and Ratnākaraśānti's *Instructions on Prajñāpāramitā* present the latter approach from the perspective of those of intermediate abilities on down.

In Tibet, the approach of meditating on the ultimate essence is found in the teachings of some early Kadampas. It is present in the esoteric instructions of mahāmudrā that the Exalted Lord [Atīśa] received from Ḍombīpa as transmitted by Indrabhūti and in the transmission from Naljorpa and Gönpawa, students of the Exalted Lord [Atīśa]. Nevertheless, most of what Drom Tönpa transmitted to the three brothers [Potowa, Puchungwa, and Chen-ngawa] is Sūtra-orientated stages of meditation that are based on the stages of the path. [204]

The exalted Gampopa's instructional tradition contains both styles mentioned above, many esoteric instructions based on Secret Mantra perfection processes, and more. Nevertheless, his approach emphasizes the stages of meditation of mahāmudrā, where first misinterpretations about the view are eliminated and then that [view] is brought into experience using the techniques for resting. The esoteric instructions on the dohās, Root Symbols, and Secret Conduct, which were transmitted by Maitrīpa's student Bhārata-pāṇi [Indian Vajrapāṇi] and others and spread later in Tibet, are in keeping with the exalted Gampopa's instructional tradition, [confirming] the very pure sources [and authenticity of Gampopa's instructions].[688]

Some assert that meditation on the true nature must be based on the explanations found in the Sūtra-oriented texts. They criticize the esoteric instructions of the mahāsiddhas which, by emphasizing vipaśyanā right from the start, are not in accordance with those [Sūtra-oriented texts]. That amounts to having contempt for the mahāsiddhas, including authors of the treatises in the Seven Siddhi Texts, the Sixfold Essence Cycle, and authors of esoteric instructions of the Great Secret [Mantra]. It also shows they simply do not understand the meaning expressed in the *Earlier Authoritative Text* and the *Latter Authoritative Text*:

> A powerful medicine for the gradual type
> is a strong poison for the instantaneous type.
> A powerful medicine for the instantaneous type
> is poison for the gradual type.[689]

By overly believing in the explanations found in the Sūtra-oriented texts that without physical and mental suppleness śamatha will not be attained, without which vipaśyanā will not be achieved, and without those two there will be no realization of suchness, they conclude that achievement of that approach cannot and will not occur these days. [205] Saying, "Now is not a time for meditation," they cause themselves and others to turn their backs on meditation. That is quite absurd. [If it were true,] it would mean that the various kinds of dharma the Buddha taught in relation to different levels of abilities are incorrect. It also causes them to amass the karma of abandoning the dharma of the Great Secret's esoteric instructions (which involve little effort but great benefit) and the dharma of the many short paths that arose from the mahāsiddhas' own practices.

This Dakpo practice lineage contains both instructional traditions: One is taught for the instantaneous type, who first eliminate their misinterpretations concerning the ground and root and are then taught the techniques for resting in that [ground]. The other is provided for the gradual type, who first pursue mental stillness and then are led to vipaśyanā gradually. Although these days most people, being of the type that has a very clear and active mind, would at this point be more appropriately guided according to the first approach, here I will give the explanation according to the latter approach in consideration of what is better known at the moment. [206/207]

8

Śamatha

b. The Explanation of the Meditation Process in This Context

This has four parts:

i. First: The Process of Instruction
ii. The Process of the Pointing-Out [Instructions] in Spiritual Practice
iii. The Way to Sustain the Practice of Meditation
iv. The Way Realization Develops Through Sustaining Meditation

i. First: The Process of Instruction

This has two sections:

A) The Instructions in Śamatha
B) The Instructions in Vipaśyanā

A) The Instructions in Śamatha

This has seven divisions:

1) The Preparations Necessary for Śamatha
2) The Physical Pose for Practicing Meditative Concentration
3) The Way to Focus the Mind on an Object of Meditation
4) The Actual Objects for Practicing Mental Stillness
5) The Way to Sustain Mental Stillness with These Approaches
6) The Process of Achieving Mental Stillness
7) The Purpose of Practicing Mental Stillness

1) The Preparations Necessary for Śamatha

Your practice must include an understanding of what was presented above in the general explanation of śamatha and vipaśyanā, such as the reliance on the causes for achieving śamatha and, especially, the identification and elimination of the causes for dullness and agitation.* Moreover, at this point, in a very secluded place—one unfrequented by other people during the day, with little noise at night, and where all the necessary conditions of water, wood [fuel], and so forth are available—you should cast aside anything that causes you physical or mental distraction. Establish the boundaries [for your retreat] and be slow and gentle, mimicking the behavior of a sick person. Your practice should certainly include the elements that were laid out above: restraining your sense faculties, alert behavior, moderation of food, and so forth† because without those it is difficult to achieve mental stillness. As the Exalted Lord [Atīśa] explains: [208]

> When śamatha and its branches are impaired,
> you may meditate with intense exertion
> for a thousand years
> but you will not produce any samādhi.[690]

2) The Physical Posture for Practicing Meditative Concentration

Nāropa says:

> The way to rest the body is the key to meditation.[691]

There is a saying in the practice lineage:

> If you want your mind to rest, keep your body in the meditation posture.[692]

It is also said that by arranging the interdependent connections within the body, realization will arise in the mind. All of those attest to the importance of the essential points for the body.

The generally well-known seven-point posture of meditative concentration is as follows:

1. On a soft and comfortable cushion, sit in the vajra position or, if that is not possible, in the bodhisattva position.

*See pp. 17–29.
†See pp. 169–71.

2. Hold your hands in the mudrā of equipoise (meaning your right palm rests on top [of your left] with the tips of your thumbs touching) four fingerwidths below your navel.
3. Straighten your spine and keep your entire body taut.
4. Keep your upper arms and elbows straight, not bent, and your shoulders raised.
5. Bend your neck slightly so that your chin presses lightly towards your Adam's apple.
6. Rest the tip of your tongue on your palate, leave a bit of space between your upper and lower teeth, and barely close your lips.
7. Your eyes should be in a peaceful gaze, looking into the space beyond the tip of your nose, neither moving nor closed.

Since this position resembles the way the buddha Vairocana is seated, it is called the seven-point posture of Vairocana. [209] Some include the explanation to leave your lips and teeth just as they are, but this presentation is better.[693]

Two of Kamalaśīla's *Stages of Meditation* state that, in addition to those [seven] points, you should inhale and exhale without making a sound, panting, or breathing heavily, and let your breath flow in and out without any sense of its movement, gently and effortlessly.[694] Their explanation of an eight-point physical posture is most excellent.

Furthermore, the *Vajramālā* states:

> Your shoulders should be even, tongue and palate joined,
> teeth and lips at ease,
> and your gaze directed towards the tip of your nose.[695]

Ācārya Amītavajra instructs:

> Sit on a comfortable seat in the vajra position
> with your hands in the mudrā of equipoise.
> Straighten your body and bend your neck.[696]

Nāropa teaches:

> Now I will explain the key points for the body.
> Like jewels strung on a reed,
> be very straight and [then] bend.

Tighten internally like ḷ and ṛ,
and sit in the knot-like position.
Pull up to your full potential.
Press with the mudrā of equipoise.
Be crossed like lattice.[697]

"Be crossed like lattice" is specific to another context. The other lines describe straightening the spine, bending the neck, keeping the body taut, raising the shoulders, and holding the mudrā of equipoise. [210]

The purpose or benefits of using those essential points for the body are as follows. The leg position controls the downward-expelling wind. Pressing with the mudrā of equipoise below the navel retains the fire-coinciding wind. Straightening the spine and holding the body taut controls the pervading wind. Not bending the elbows and upper arms and stretching up the shoulders holds the life-force wind. Bending the neck and resting the tongue on the palate controls the upward-moving wind. By controlling those root winds, the secondary winds are naturally controlled and, specifically, an unwavering gaze controls the secondary winds.

It is explained that those [points of the physical posture] cause the channels, winds, and bodhicittas [bindus] to abide in their own places and be stable. Those in turn balance your body's elements and enhance your complexion. Since the operative [sense] consciousnesses are not engaging their objects, samādhi naturally arises. Mind's dullness and agitation lessen, and awareness becomes clear and lucid.

The problems associated with an incorrect posture are described by those aware of the esoteric instructions of this practice lineage. If you lean to the right, at first you will experience clarity but that will be followed by many thoughts related to perceived objects. If you drift towards the left, at first there will be bliss but later you will have many thoughts related to the perceiving subject. If you lean forward, initially you will have sharp clarity but later on your mind will be turbulent. If you lean backwards, to begin with there will be brilliance and spaciousness but it will be followed by much distraction. If you change your gaze, your operative consciousnesses will engage and you will have many thoughts.

The *Śrāvakabhūmi* explains that this physical posture quickly brings suppleness, enables us to sit in it for a long time, and does not cause physical exhaustion. This posture is superior to that of the tīrthikas and our adversaries. When [others] see us in this posture, they are inspired. Since the Buddha and his śrāvaka disciples used this posture, we should too.[698] [211]

3) The Way to Focus the Mind on an Object of Meditation

We should engage the object of meditation with enthusiasm for cultivating samādhi. Since that enthusiasm comes from seeing the excellent qualities of samādhi, the sūtras present those in terms of the broad reasons that we should meditate on the dharma, as it is said:

> If you do not meditate on this dharma,
> you will not see dharmatā.
> Just seeing and hearing about water,
> but not drinking, it doesn't alleviate thirst.[699]

The common excellent qualities of meditative concentration are described in the *Verses That Summarize the Prajñāpāramitā Sūtras*:

> Meditative concentration dispenses with inferior sense pleasures
> and makes awareness, supercognitive abilities, and samādhis
> manifest.[700]

Specifically, when we achieve śamatha, our physical and mental joy and happiness increase and our mind is able to focus on its object. Mental distractions, which are distortions, are automatically pacified, thus preventing much negative conduct. Excellent qualities, such as the supercognitive abilities and miraculous powers, are achieved, on the basis of which the realizations of vipaśyanā develop. Once those arise and are sustained, we see the temporal and ultimate excellent qualities, such as swift liberation from cyclic existence. Keeping those in mind, we should engage the object of meditation.

The *Differentiation of the Middle and the Extremes* explains:

> There are the basis, what is based on that,
> causes and results . . .[*701] [212]

"The basis" is the basis of effort: having the strong motivation to pursue samādhi. "What is based on that" is strong effort: the ability to be diligent consistently. "Causes" are the causes of our motivation: the faith that entails

*For a full citation of this verse, see p. 56.

seeing the excellent qualities of samādhi and being enraptured by them. "Results" are the results of efforts: achieving physical and mental suppleness.

We should understand those points and then concentrate our mind on the object of meditation.

4) The Actual Objects for Practicing Mental Stillness

This has two parts:

a) The Objects of Meditation Involving Characteristics
b) Śamatha Without Characteristics[702]

a) The Objects of Meditation Involving Characteristics

This has two sections:

i) [The Objects of Meditation Involving Characteristics] With Supports
ii) [The Objects of Meditation Involving Characteristics] Without Supports

i) [The Objects of Meditation Involving Characteristics] With Supports

This has two divisions:

(A) The Actual Objects of Meditation
(B) The Identification of Mental Stillness

(A) The Actual Objects of Meditation

Individuals of lesser intelligence at the beginning of their pursuit of mental stillness may use any appropriate method for concentration. As Tilopa says:

> Using various kinds of methods—gazes and ways of concentrating—hold [your mind] in awareness until it is still.[703]

The sūtras and Kamalaśīla's *Stages of Meditation* explain that we will achieve mental stillness by focusing on the form of the Tathāgata as the first object of meditation.* Those of the practice lineage, however, consider it easier to give rise to mental stillness by concentrating on an ordinary object because

*See citations on pp. 73–74.

[meditators of] lesser intelligence can find it difficult to generate an image of the Tathāgata's form as a mental object right from the start. Therefore, they provide two ways to concentrate the mind: focusing on something impure, a pebble or twig, and focusing on something pure, the Tathāgata's form. [213] They explain that during the day we can concentrate on such things as a pebble or twig or, if that is not comfortable, sometimes on a small object in the shade. During the night, we can concentrate on white or black bindus [spheres of light] of various sizes at the point between our eyebrows or sometimes above ourself.

Direct your mind loosely to those focal supports, not letting it wander to anything else, just remaining without distraction. Concentrate closely on the focal support but don't entertain thoughts that study or analyze its color, shape, or the like. In brief, in a nonconceptual mode—not thinking anything at all—pursue a resting state that is intense and quiet. Once you have achieved a moment of such stillness, suspend [your meditation] while in that state of stillness. After a short break, again apply yourself to resting. It is said that you should train in short sessions often. By parting on good terms with your meditation you'll look forward to meditating again. If you become overly tired in the beginning you'll reach a point of exhaustion and won't enjoy returning to meditation.

Some say that since other texts do not teach pursuing stillness through relying on pebbles, twigs, and bindus, [this kind of presentation] simply demonstrates ignorance of the objects for cultivating mental stillness.[704] Such criticisms are most unreasonable because the purpose [of these methods] is to allow those of lesser intelligence to develop mental stillness easily. These are profound key points that confer great benefit with little effort. It is also not the case that other texts do not present them. Ācārya Bodhibhadra states:

> Here, śamatha is twofold: one that is attained through looking inwards and the other by focusing on something seen externally.[705]

He continues with more explanation as quoted above,* concluding with: [214]

*See p. 73.

> Focusing on something seen externally is of two kinds: special and ordinary.[706]

Thus it is permissible to use ordinary things such as pebbles and twigs. [Bodhibhadra also] mentions mental concentration that is based on bindus:

> Focusing on what is based on the body is fivefold: focusing on the breath, on subtle symbols, on bindus, on light rays, and on joy and bliss.[707]

Nevertheless, we may wonder, Is it wrong to cultivate mental stillness on the basis of a sense consciousness looking at an external substance (such as a pebble or twig) when mental stillness must be cultivated with the mental consciousness? There is nothing wrong with that. The visual consciousness serves as the primary initiator of movement towards objects for the sense consciousnesses. The key point is that most movements of the mental consciousness are related to the sense consciousnesses. By holding a gaze where the visual faculty does not move, that sense consciousness does not move and the movements of the other sense consciousnesses are minimized. When those do not move, the mental consciousness' movements decrease. This technique makes developing stillness easy. Directing the mental and visual consciousnesses towards something like a pebble or a twig is merely a symbol [reminding] the mind to not wander somewhere else. It is analogous to remembering a point on the basis of a mnemonic.

The symbols used for settling the mind are not [just one] prescribed [object of meditation] because even in the descriptions of the symbols of unpleasantness, such as a rotting image, there are many different kinds of symbols. There are many other presentations, including settling the mind on the form of a letter, a sound, light, or a name. Also the *Stages of Meditation* explains that the objects for śamatha are not [just one] prescribed [object of meditation].[708]

That said, among these approaches, concentrating on the Tathāgata's form is laudable. The *Sūtra of the Questions of Bhadrapāla* states: [215]

> Bhadrapāla, it is like this: Just as I am now seated before you and teaching the dharma, bodhisattvas should bring to mind the tathāgatas, seated on buddhas' thrones and expounding the dharma. They should bring to mind the tathāgatas, who have all

> the most sublime attributes, have a perfect form, are beautiful and lovely to behold, and are endowed with the most excellent body.
>
> They should meditate on the major marks of the tathāgatas, each one of which is generated by a hundred merits.[709]

There are many such statements. As cited above,* the *King of Samādhi* observes:

> [The Protector of the World is beautiful in all ways,]
> with a body like the color of gold.[710]

The final *Stages of Meditation* also states that.[711]

Āryaśūra and the Exalted Lord [Atīśa] explain that when first seeking mental stillness, among the many objects of meditation, it is best to practice with whatever object we find suitable.† The first *Stages of Meditation* teaches that once we have developed mental stillness we can train with any object.[712] For example, within the Sūtra-oriented approaches, there are numerous explanations of the objects of meditation for purifying previous behavior, purifying mental afflictions, and so on, which were described earlier.‡

In the practice lineage, these approaches are referred to using the term "with support" because the mind rests either on something actual as its support for concentration, such as a pebble or twig, or on a support that is visualized by the mind, such as a bindu. [216]

(B) The Identification of Mental Stillness

Although broadly speaking there are many instances of mental stillness, in this context we are cultivating the aspect of resting in nonconceptuality. Tilopa explains:

> Give up physical activities: be at ease.
> Don't talk a lot, it's just echoes.
> Don't think: behold the phenomenon of the breakthrough.[713]

*See pp. 53–54.
†See citations on pp. 52–53.
‡See pp. 48–51.

Ācārya Dignāga teaches:

> Always reject the multitude of concepts:
> objects, subjects, duality, nonduality,
> self, others, nirvāṇa, saṃsāra.
> Remain in equipoise.[714]

At this point in training in mental stillness, most will find it difficult to give rise to flawless śamatha samādhi. Therefore, you should use focal supports to reverse your previous habit of letting your mind ramble. When—within nonwandering mindfulness, without any thoughts popping up—your mind relaxes and is tranquil for any length of time, you have achieved a small degree of stillness. While in a state of stillness, interrupt that: take a break for a short period. Then continue as before. If nonconceptuality becomes something stagnant, having trailed off into a lack of mindfulness, that is a problem. Energize yourself and increase the intensity of your mindfulness. Continue to do this repeatedly for short periods. [217] If your mindfulness does not completely fade away but stillness seems dull, sometimes you can continue with that for brief periods since it is a problem that will automatically correct itself.

While you remain in a state of mindfulness, if there is a small degree of stillness along with a seeming increase in thoughts, it is that previously you did not notice that your thoughts came in a line [like] lambs linked together. Now you notice that they arise one after another. You have achieved a small degree of stillness so do not regard this as a problem. Relax your sense of expectation as much as you can and simply be undistracted in a state with little suppression or promotion, not inhibiting thoughts or pursuing them.

Alternatively, if you are not sure whether your mind is still or is moving, that indicates a somewhat weaker intelligence. In which case, after a sudden loud noise, in between the cessation of one thought and before the next one arises, [notice that] an open, crisp state of mind occurs. Since you can understand that to be a sign of the mind's nonconceptuality, extending that [experience] just a bit will produce stillness.

We should know that these techniques are also appropriate for objects of meditation that use the breath, which will be explained next.

ii) [The Objects of Meditation Involving Characteristics] Without Supports

This has two parts:

(A) Those That Use the Breath
(B) Those That Do Not Use the Breath

(A) Those That Use the Breath

This has two sections:

(1) Concentrating on Counting Breaths
(2) Concentrating on Filling [with Breath]

(1) Concentrating on Counting Breaths

In general, both the sūtras and tantras teach using the breath as a means for developing mental stillness. In this regard Tilopa says:

> If those of lesser intelligence can't rest in that state,
> they should use the technique of the breath and extract awareness.[715]

The Sūtra-oriented texts on the stages of meditation teach that those with a predominance of thoughts should meditate on the breath. [218] The *Explanation of the "Treasury of Abhidharma"* explains this approach:

> There are six ways [to practice mindfulness of the breath]:
> counting, following, settling,
> examining, changing, and purifying.[716]

1. *Counting.* Concentrate by focusing on counting the inhalations and exhalations of the breath from twenty-one times to a pāṇīpala, [then] a ghaṭikā, counting flawlessly.
2. *Following.* After that, asking whether the breath goes everywhere in the body or just to one place, focus on following and reversing it throughout your entire body.
3. *Settling.* Place your mind on [your breath pervading] everywhere and on nonconceptuality specifically.
4. *Examining.* Examine the nonreferential essence of breath.

5. *Changing.* Move the mind that is focused on the breath to another object of meditation for śamatha.
6. *Purifying.* Meditate within nonconceptuality, where thoughts of percepts and perceivers have been purified.

In the Mantra-oriented approaches, there are many variations on the ways to meditate with the breath but I will not go into them out of a concern of it becoming too much. At this point I will explain the teachings found in the esoteric instructions of the practice lineage on the ways to cultivate mental stillness based on counting the breath and filling with it.

Counting the breath. This is commended in the *Sūtra of the Ten Wheels of Kṣitigarbha*:

> How do we examine the internal and external movements of the breath in a precise way using mindfulness? By counting them precisely.[717]

It continues:

> Those who remain in meditative concentration while being mindful of the comings and goings [of the breath] are said to be sentient beings who abide in the true dharma, the ultimate. [219] They are said to be cultivating true meditative concentration precisely.[718]

The *Saṃvarodaya* states:

> Yogins and yoginīs resting in equipoise
> should count the breaths that enter,
> up to one hundred thousand and more,
> always doing the repetitions without a sound.
>
> The practitioner who silently
> completes one hundred thousand repetitions
> will, without a doubt, live for five more years
> even though their life should be over.[719]

Now, using the previously described essential points for the body and the gazes, settle your mind naturally. The breath through your nostrils should not be forced, noisy, or rough. Inhale and exhale gently. When exhaling, do so with mindfulness. When inhaling, concentrate with mindfulness. Do not be distracted to anything else. You should train by first simply concentrating for three rounds, then just for five, later seven, as you can. In between take short breaks. Finally, your training should build up to concentrating with uninterrupted mindfulness for one hundred rounds of breath.

For those who have achieved mental stillness in the context of previous mental concentrations, this approach will bring proficiency. For those who have not achieved that, these are wonderful instructions for pursuing stillness. Therefore, it is important to apply yourself to them. [220]

(2) Concentrating on Filling [with Breath]

Overall there are two ways filling with the breath [can be used as a technique for cultivating mental stillness]: by stopping it naturally and using vase-breathing. The *Vajra Ḍāka* explains:

> When filling makes your body full,
> poisons and the fevers of flu are vanquished.
> When vase-breathing binds your doors,
> the pathways of your [sense] doors are purified.[720]

The *Saṃvarodaya* says:

> Those who practice vase-breathing
> are always victorious over death.
> With awareness of your nature,
> fill everywhere with breath as far as your soles.
> Stabilize vase-breathing.[721]

It is taught that vase-breathing involves uniting the upper and lower winds. As the *Saṃvarodaya* states:

> With the mind, unite
> the winds that move above and below.
> Familiarity with that yoga
> brings the attainment of a stable state.[722]

The *Kālacakra Tantra* also explains:

> The mouth is closed; through both nostrils all the external winds
> are drawn in by the force of the life-force [wind] and united with the
> downward expelling wind, which is like pure lightning.
> In time, through the yoga of being familiar with this, they become of
> equal taste in the middle of the moon, sun, and fire.
> This eliminates physical thirst, hunger for food, and the like, and
> confers immortality.[723] [221]

It is important to know the key points of the four yogic techniques for this practice. As Nāropa says:

> If you do not know the four yogic techniques—
> inhaling, filling, dispersing,
> and releasing like an arrow—
> there is the danger that good qualities will become problems.[724]

Nevertheless, since in this context the instruction manuals do not provide detailed explanations of the esoteric instructions on breath yoga, filling with breath is simply an ancillary practice for concentrating the mind. Fill your body with breath, hold it as much as you can, and within that seek a nonconceptual resting state. This is done as follows. Do the preliminaries of letting your breath settle gently, expelling the stale breath, and so forth. Use the gazes and the essential points for the body as before. Inhale a breath fully and slowly through both nostrils without making a noise, panting, or breathing unevenly. Press it down slightly to the lower part of your abdomen. Keep your upper body area spacious and light. Hold your breath as long as it is not uncomfortable. When it becomes uncomfortable and you want to exhale, do so immediately and smoothly, without any sound or unevenness. All the phases—from inhaling a breath, holding it internally, to releasing it—should be done within a state of undistracted mindfulness as before. Particularly, as long as you hold [the breath] internally, there should be a continuous flow of resting that is open, crisp, awake.

Do that for three rounds to begin with, then increase to five, seven, and so on as possible. Then take a break. When you are accustomed to this you can lengthen your sessions. During this practice, if your mind becomes agitated, just be aware of the distraction and keep your mind internally relaxed. If you feel more disturbed, you are exhausted and need to remedy this as much as you can. If you become dizzy or light-headed, you should eat nourishing food and get massages since your winds have become somewhat unsettled. [222] The technique of holding the breath itself will not increase dullness.[725] However, should that happen, direct your gaze upwards with intensity. As long as you are not swept away by the undercurrents of thoughts, do not regard the arising of small thoughts within a state of mindfulness as problematic or cause for alarm. Again arouse the force of mindfulness. Your state of mind should be like something that is taut [or firm] at the bottom but relaxed at the top.

Those are ancillary practices for concentrating the mind. Since they are said to be esoteric instructions for settling the mind that has not settled, by the end you will certainly discover nonconceptual stillness.

(B) Those That Do Not Use the Breath

Whatever stillness has been achieved through those ancillary practices for concentrating the mind is refined by using the following practices that do not involve a support or a reference point.[726] Adopt the essential points for the body as before. Do not do any practice that involves focusing or concentrating the mind on anything, such as on an external focal support or the internal comings and goings of the breath. Your mind should have no support at all and not be disturbed by any concepts about attention. Leave your mind in its own state. Do not think about the past, about what you have done before or things that have happened. Do not speculate about the future, what you may do, or how you may do it. Do not engage in analysis of the present, what is around you now, or what appears to be the case. Leave your mind to be free, loose, and unconstrained. The *Guhyasamāja* describes this way to rest as follows: [223]

> Make mind be not mind,
> then do not think about anything.[727]

The *Dohā [for the People]* says:

> Cast away thoughts and their objects,
> and you'll rest like a small child.[728]

When, not attending to anything, you leave mind to be like space, the winds of thoughts are bound and an unmoving stillness of mind arises. The *Dohā [for the People]* says:

> When [mind] is taken to be like space, the winds are bound.
> Recognizing their equality, they dissolve.
> Saraha says: when you have this ability,
> you can quickly abandon the impermanent and the moving.[729]

It is explained that when we stabilize our mind as unmoving and nonconceptual, immediately some signs of the external and internal winds dissolving will arise, and in the end we will be liberated from the things of saṃsāra. The *Kālacakra Tantra* teaches:

> Once you leave all thoughts behind,
> look closely for one day.
> If no signs arise,
> I am a liar.[730]

The *Dohā [for the People]* states:

> When your mind is unmoving, stable in its own place,
> it is self-liberated from the things of saṃsāra.[731]

With this approach to pursuing mental stillness, you should train by doing many short sessions. [224] As before, if your mind is dull, energize it. If it is agitated, relax your expectations. If your mind is sluggish and you are unable to arouse clarity and lucidity or if your mind seems unworkable, the esoteric instructions recommend doing many prostrations and confessions of negative actions in front of special objects [of worship] and making strong supplications for samādhi to arise.

If, in this context of not using a support or reference point, it isn't easy to apply whatever slight degree of stillness you may have achieved previously, you won't be able to make progress with practices that are without characteristics.[732] Therefore, it is important to train [with these methods first].

These approaches of pursuing mental stillness with the breath or without the breath do not involve using an object with a shape and color (such as a pebble or twig) as a support for the mind. Therefore, the practice lineage uses the term "without support" [for these techniques] and calls them "instructions for stabilizing the settled mind."

b) Śamatha Without Characteristics

This has two parts:

i) The Way to Pursue Flawless Śamatha
ii) Identifying That [Flawless Śamatha] Samādhi

i) The Way to Pursue Flawless Śamatha

This has three sections:

(A) The Importance of Knowing the Vital Points of Tightening and Relaxing
(B) The Techniques for Tightening
(C) The Techniques for Relaxing

(A) The Importance of Knowing the Vital Points of Tightening and Relaxing

At this point, texts on the stages of mahāmudrā meditation teach the techniques for tightening and relaxing in keeping with the Sūtra-oriented explanations on how to dispel the faults of dullness and agitation in samādhi. When we have developed some degree of mental stillness using the above ancillary practices for concentrating the mind, if the fault of dullness arises, it is dispelled by the techniques of tightening and, if the fault of agitation arises, it is cleared up by the techniques of relaxing.

Generally speaking, there are many descriptions of what obscures samādhi, such as the list of agitation, remorse, sluggishness, drowsiness, doubt, pleasure-seeking, and malice found in *Unraveling the Intent.** [225] However, for the most part, they are all included in the categories of dullness and agitation. Although sluggishness, drowsiness, and dullness do have their specific differences, since that sūtra [*Unraveling the Intent*] does not list dullness, the implication is that dullness and sluggishness are concordant types. Similarly, although there are specific remedies for each of those obscurations, since the texts on the stages of meditation consider that

*See p. 19 for the relevant citation.

removing the faults of dullness and agitation alleviates most other problems, they explain only the ways to dispel the faults of dullness and agitation.

Therefore, we should know how to identify and eliminate the causes of dullness and agitation, how to recognize their characteristics, and how to dispel them as explained in the section of the common exposition of śamatha and vipaśyanā.* In brief, flawless śamatha samādhi requires both the presence of sharp clarity, which is the mind's lucidity, and the quality of stillness, which is to rest one-pointedly in nonconceptuality. The problems that afflict the former are created by dullness, and the problems that impede the latter are created by agitation. Since that is the case, dullness and agitation create the primary hindrances for sustaining samādhi and the methods for dispelling them are critical.

The Sūtra-oriented texts on the stages of meditation explain that when we have dullness, we should uplift our mind , bring joyful things to mind, concentrate on things characterized by illumination, and so forth. When we experience agitation, we should contemplate impermanence, reflect on the disadvantages of distraction, cultivate śamatha, and so on.† Here, however, we primarily banish dullness and agitation and pursue the key points of samādhi by tightening our mind or relaxing it.[733] We must understand that the technique [lies in being aware of balance], thinking, "Is just this much tightening and relaxation without the fault of dullness?" and, "Is just this much without the problem of agitation?" [226]

(B) The Techniques for Tightening

Tightening is predominantly used for all types of dullness, but it may also be applied to certain types of agitation.

Dullness is described as follows. When we are practicing with nonconceptual stillness, the force of the mindfulness perceiving that may gradually relax to the point where finally we lose our object of meditation or it becomes unclear, and our mind becomes lethargic. That is strong, or coarse, dullness. Alternatively, we may not lose our object of meditation but our perception of that object may lack clarity, and we may be resting in a fuzzy way in just a nonconceptual state.[734] That is subtle dullness, a blemished, unbroken dullness.[735] The uneducated may consider the latter to be flawless śamatha. If we sustain such subtle dullness and do not dispel it, sharp

*See pp. 19–29.

†See "The Ways to Prevent Dullness and Agitation," pp. 28–29.

clarity will not emerge in our mind, our mindfulness will become weak, our forgetfulness stronger, and so forth. As long as we do that, we create serious problems.

The way to dispel that flaw is as follows. With the essential points for the body as before, raise your gaze and look straight ahead. Reverse any slackness or feeling of being dazed that may have come about by withdrawing your mind before. Expand your mind's vision. Make it spacious and vibrant. Those are explained as being capable of dispelling dullness, as the *Synopsis of the Pāramitās* says:

> Uplift and stimulate your mind when it is slack.[736]

The *Heart of the Middle Way* also says:

> When your mind is slack, expand it
> by meditating with a vast focus.[737]

If those [techniques] banish coarse dullness but not subtle, you should train as follows.[738] Arouse sharp clarity and tighten that so you are not distracted for even an instant. [227] Without a reference point for ambitions, remain in a vibrant, crisp, awake one-pointed mind. Do that for a short time and then interrupt it. Again tighten up and rest your mind fully, not distracted for even a moment.

Having trained in that way, once your previous lethargic or fuzzy stillness has become a wakeful state, recognize [the still mind] to be vibrant, crisp, sharp, naked. To sum up, post the lookout of a vivid, sharp mind that detects whether dullness or agitation has arisen or is arising within a nonconceptual state. The *Differentiation of the Middle and the Extremes* says:

> [Abandon] dullness, agitation, or concepts.[739]

The last two *Stages of Meditation* advise:

> Look for dullness or the possibility of laxity.[740]

And they continue:

> Look for agitation or the possibility of agitation.[741]

This approach can arouse sharp mental clarity in some agitated states of mind, but if that only lasts for a short period of resting in nonconceptuality, do not see that as a fault. By training in short sessions repeatedly flawless śamatha will arise. However, if you only [develop] a small degree of stillness no matter what you do, you need to know how to let go without losing sharp clarity and train in that.

(C) The Techniques for Relaxing

Generally speaking, there are many variations of relaxing but in this context it is directed at dispelling the flaw of agitation. Although agitation is described as a quality of craving that arises once something attractive is observed, here it includes everything belonging to the category of discursiveness when the mind is not peaceful, such as remorse, doubt, and malice. All such states of mind are what are to be pacified. [228]

It is taught that mindfulness pacifies all faults and flaws, including distractions in general and attachment in particular. The *Ornament for the Mahāyāna Sūtras* teaches:

> Because you see the faults of distraction
> disinclination towards [samādhi] is pacified.
> When attachment, unhappiness, and so forth arise,
> pacify them accordingly.[742]

The *Heart of the Middle Way* states:

> When distracted, see the problems inherent in distraction
> and draw [your mind inward].[743]

Agitation is pacified by not thinking about the objects of discursiveness and by remaining within a state where blocking and encouraging are relaxed, as the *Synopsis of the Pāramitās* says:

> When your mind becomes agitated,
> reverse that with śamatha.[744]

Hold the essential points for the body as before and lower your gaze slightly. Without any preoccupations—such as meditating on this, not meditating on that, delighting in stillness, being upset by scatteredness—let go and relax into a spacious, vibrant mind. Do not manipulate that with the contrivances of preventing or creating things. Quietly and loosely remain in a naturally settled state of your mind, however that may be. Arouse expansive, vivid mindfulness, thinking, "I will not be distracted elsewhere." Sustain that.[745]

While maintaining that, if a coarse thought appears suddenly and palpably, don't get caught up in distraction by carelessly letting it be or pursuing it.[746] [229] Don't create a rigid state of mind, one where all manifestations are blocked. Be skilled in refreshing your mindfulness and nurturing a stream of nondistraction.

Don't become alarmed about, block, or encourage hazy, subtle thoughts while you are being mindful. Continue in a state in which fresh, relaxed mindfulness is simply not lost. Then interrupt that quiet, vibrant stillness and take a short break. Resume your practice as before.

Previously when you were tightening, once all coarse and subtle thoughts seemed to stop, you would be slightly uncomfortable because you felt as if you needed to press your mind into being a one-pointed state of vibrant, crisp nonconceptuality.[747] Now when you are relaxing, it is enough to let your mind just be—however it is comfortable—in its own state, a state in which fresh, undistracted mindfulness is simply not lost. When coarse or subtle thoughts arise, if your mindfulness can be resilient and not let thoughts seize control, sooner or later they completely subside and [mindfulness] proceeds with ease right within stillness. Since you do not need any ambition other than to be mindful, your mind will be more spacious than before.[748] Knowing the key point of interrupting your ambitions and allowing your mind to let go and relax, to be unconstrained and loose, is the enhancement [technique] of relaxing. As Saraha says:

> If the mind twisted into knots
> is relaxed, it's free—there is no doubt.[749]

He continues:

> What is bound wants to run in the ten directions.
> When let go, it stays still and motionless.
> I understand these camel-like perversities.[750]

Maitrīpa observes:

> When a thought arises in the mind,
> yogins and yoginīs remain uncontrived, relaxed, like cotton wool.[751]
> [230]

At this point, some are confused about the saying in this practice lineage, "the most relaxed have the best meditation," and think that it pertains to this context. They criticize it, saying that when mindfulness and alertness become slack, the arising of dullness can be mistaken for the arising of meditation.[752] That reflects their desire to say something [critical] even when they are confused about the meaning. The meaning of the saying ["the most relaxed have the best meditation"] is the same as what Saraha said above and the following two citations. Tilopa says:

> Be relaxed in the uncontrived intrinsic state.
> Relax your bonds and there's no doubt: you will be liberated.[753]

Saraha advises:

> If you have an attachment, let it go.[754]

In the context of the main practice of meditation, that saying describes a method for destroying fixation to experiences. The mahāsiddha Zhang explains:

> When your mind lets go and relaxes,
> an experience of clarity free of conceptuality
> dawns like the center of clear open space.
> That's the dharmakāya, luminosity.[755]

Therefore, when we don't understand how to relax our mind, and our mindfulness and alertness deteriorate, the confused state created by thick dullness is called "stagnant resting." That is regarded as a fault. Who would take that to be what is meant by "the most relaxed have the best meditation"? Such falsehoods should not be uttered.

If, not understanding relaxing, you succumb to the undercurrents of thoughts and don't recognize that your mindfulness has become distracted or if you're unaware of whether you're thinking or not, you may slip into a vacant, unmindful state. That indicates that your mindfulness and alertness are very weak. If, within a state of mindfulness, thoughts seem to be free floating or swirling about, your ability to relax is inadequate or your ambitions are too rigid. Be aware of the timing for balancing tightening and relaxing. [231]

In brief, if your previous mindfulness and alertness create the energy for continued mindfulness and alertness, even as a beginner you should remain loose and unconstrained right within that and not repeatedly arouse mindfulness. When the energy of your mindfulness and alertness begins to diminish, tighten up a little bit until they return. Know the ways to cultivate [meditation] that dispels faults as they come up in the course of practice.

By practicing that way, if you rest unwaveringly in vibrant, clear mindfulness-awareness and if, within that state, visual or auditory appearances (forms, sounds, and so forth) arise unimpededly, unconstrained, naked—radiant, expansive, amorphous—śamatha has developed.[756]

ii) Identifying That [Flawless Śamatha] Samādhi

When, on the basis of the ways to pursue mental stillness that were explained in stages above, flawless śamatha samādhi finally arises, that samādhi must definitely combine both the quality of stillness (resting quietly and one-pointedly in nonconceptuality) and the sharp clarity in which mindfulness and alertness are unimpaired and are accompanied by certainty. Mind not resting one-pointedly on its object and getting involved in various kinds of thoughts, or mind not involved in thinking but being a stagnant state of impaired mindfulness, or the mind that hasn't lost all mindfulness but nevertheless rests lethargically without any sharp clarity are all considered to be faults in samādhi.

The absence of sharp clarity in mindfulness and alertness is the flaw of dullness. The mind not resting one-pointedly is the flaw of agitation. Therefore, the ways to dispel the flaws of dullness and agitation are critical. [232] They have been explained* and will again be discussed, so just to summarize here: When you have dullness, arouse mindfulness, alertness, and the mind's sharp clarity, and intensify those. When you sense agitation, as needed, relax your ambition to tighten your mind on the focus. When, through balancing tightening and relaxing, [samādhi] arises according to your wishes, do not

*See "The Ways to Prevent Dullness and Agitation," pp. 28–29.

apply any critical investigation: maintain and prolong that natural state, simply not letting its continuity vanish. Nāgārjuna's *Delineating the Four Empowerments* states:

> When feeling dull or heavy, rouse yourself.
> When scattered and unfocused, remain in a natural state.[757]

Of the two, mindfulness and alertness, mindfulness keeps the mind from wandering away from its object of meditation, and alertness detects whether it has become distracted or not, whether it is dull or agitated. Intensify your resolve, thinking, "I will not be distracted from the object of meditation for even an instant." Prolong that stream [of mindfulness] and make your commitment to being mindful, without forgetfulness, be heartfelt. Within that state, alertness—which recognizes distraction or its absence and the faults of dullness and agitation—should simply be a lookout watching fixedly without engaging in lots of extra critical investigation.

In the Sūtra context there are many explanations that differentiate between mindfulness and alertness, but the esoteric instructions of the practice lineage often reduce those to just mindfulness-awareness or even just mindfulness.[758] We may wonder, How can this be? There is no mistake, as the *Entrance to the Bodhisattva's Way of Life* explains:

> When mindfulness sits at the mind's door
> for the sake of guarding it, [233]
> alertness will appear.[759]

Since mindfulness and alertness are distinguished in terms of being broad and specific, basic and refined, alertness is contained within clear, strong mindfulness. The *Subcommentary on the "Differentiation of the Middle and the Extremes"* remarks:

> Those who abide in mindfulness possess alertness.[760]

At this point intelligent ones may wonder, What should we do? When concentrating one-pointedly on an object of meditation with mindfulness and alertness, if you give rise to subtle thinking that discerns whether you're resting on the object or not and whether dullness or agitation have arisen or not, that will not be a nonconceptual state. But without [such subtle thinking] there will be no alertness that recognizes dullness, agitation, and so forth. The uneducated regard that subtle thinking as a flaw and yet, even though they lack the sharp clarity of alertness, they seem to sustain a resting state that has some degree of mental lucidity. However, that kind of subtle thinking is not thought in the usual sense: it is alertness or awareness, which are congruent with vipaśyanā, and therefore must be generated. The middle *Stages of Meditation* teaches:

> Having placed your mind on the object of your choice, you should repeatedly and continuously rest your mind there. While doing that, analyze your mind. Examine it by thinking, "Is it properly focused on its object of meditation? Has it become dull? Or has it become distracted by getting involved with external objects?"[761]

The way to generate that kind of thinking is not to do so after you have let the continuity of undistracted mindfulness lapse. [234] It is done simply by being watchful right within a sustained state of samādhi. If you repeatedly generate this thinking in a very forceful way, you may produce problematic thinking in which mindfulness has been lost. Therefore, simply let the force of previous [moments of] certainty not evaporate and the subsequent moments will be watchful. In brief, be skilled in the ways of balancing tightening and relaxing. This is the most critical point for the approaches to cultivating meditative concentration.

To sum up, samādhi refers to a mental state possessed of continuous mindfulness recollecting its object, a mental state without the flaws of dullness and agitation, and a mental state that possesses the joy of settling naturally. In this context, the object of meditation is nonconceptuality and clarity-awareness, and the mindfulness and alertness of those are continuous.

The *Śrāvakabhūmi* says:

> What is a one-pointed mind? It is any continuum of mind that is repeatedly mindful, that focuses on a consistently similar object, is continuous, that is without flaws, and is possessed of joy. That is called "samādhi." It is also referred to as a "one-pointed virtuous mind."[762]

As for what is meant by being "repeatedly mindful": it is explained as bringing the occasional distractions [created by] listening and reflecting back to meditative equipoise. The *Śrāvakabhūmi* continues:

> What are you to be repeatedly mindful of? Take [as your object of meditation] the qualities of someone on the level of resting in equipoise from the vantage point of any dharma that you have memorized or heard, upon which you have received instructions and teachings from your guru. Engage and focus on that object of meditation with continuous mindfulness.[763] [235]

5) The Way to Sustain Mental Stillness with These Approaches

You should be aware of the following during each session of sustaining samādhi. When setting out to cultivate samādhi, begin by recollecting the excellent qualities of samādhi to arouse faith, the motivation to strive, diligence, and suppleness.* If you don't generate those four applications, you will lack enthusiasm for samādhi meditation and will succumb to laziness. After that, continuously rely upon vigorous mindfulness, which neither wanders from nor forgets the flawless samādhi explained above. If such mindfulness is weak, you will become forgetful and not concentrate on the object of meditation. Next, within that mindfulness, generate quick-witted alertness that detects dullness or agitation and, with that, keep a continuous watch for whether the faults of dullness or agitation arise or not. If you do not have clear or established alertness, you will not notice the faults that hinder samādhi.

Following that, if dullness or agitation occur, arouse exertion involving the mental applications that are the ways to dispel those faults (as explained before) because, if that type of exertion is minimal, you will come under the influence of dullness and agitation and flawless samādhi will not develop. Then, when the faults of dullness and agitation are pacified, put aside mental applications and settle into the equanimity of remaining in a natural state. If you do not rely upon that type of equanimity, your samādhi will break down and you will be unable to rest in equipoise. [236]

This approach is the topic described in the *Differentiation of the Middle and the Extremes*:

> There are the basis, what is based on that,
> causes and results,
> not forgetting the object,

*These are four of the eight applications. See "The Way the Eight Applications Produce Mental Stillness," pp. 56–57.

> recognition of dullness and agitation,
> active application to rejecting those,
> and remaining naturally once there is pacification.[764]

Some of us do not generate faith, motivation, and so forth towards samādhi in the beginning and just proceed in our own fashion. Since our mindfulness is weak, distractions dominate our mind. Since our alertness is not incisive, we do not recognize the faults of dullness and agitation. Even if we do notice them, we think that [recognition] is a thought and identify it as something to be rejected, thereby belittling the sharp clarity of our awareness. Not being able to recognize flawless samādhi, we presume that whatever we experience is samādhi. Sometimes we may have some kind of flawless samādhi but, because we don't settle naturally into just that, our many mental applications will again cause scatteredness and agitation. We are not skilled in the methods for practicing samādhi.

Therefore, as beginners, you should arouse vigorous mindfulness. Those whose minds are predominately active can develop the problem of agitation becoming a habit. If you dispel that flaw by recognizing it with alertness, you may quell coarse agitation but hazy, subtle thoughts involving scatteredness and agitation may persist. Don't be alarmed. By slightly relaxing your ambitions, subtle thoughts will subside on their own. When that happens, since the next concern is that subtle or coarse dullness will obscure your mind's sharp clarity, guard against dullness and tighten slightly. There will come a point when the force of both dullness and agitation will be reduced and flawless samādhi will emerge. [237]

In a similar way, those with predominately dull minds need to dispel coarse and subtle dullness. Then you must guard against agitation and cultivate samādhi. When flawless samādhi arises, if you have too much mental application or exertion, those may become major hindrances to settling naturally within samādhi. Rest in the equanimity of simply not deviating from samādhi.

Mindfulness. If your strong intention generates vigorous mindfulness and you hold that, as long as there is that vigor, your mind will not be distracted from its object of meditation. The onset of even a small degree of distraction indicates a slight weakening of the vigor of mindfulness, and distraction means mindfulness has lapsed. Therefore, simply don't let the energy of previous moments of mindfulness weaken or lapse, and again arouse the strength and vigor of mindfulness. In brief, the moments of mindfulness should follow one after another as if you are adding more mindfulness on top of mindfulness.

Alertness. Alertness arises from within vigorous mindfulness. It should simply act as the lookout in the sense of watching fixedly to see whether the faults of dullness or agitation have arisen or not. In this context it is not suitable [for alertness] to involve examination, analysis, investigation, and the like, which are extensions of that [mere watching], because they will hinder the one-pointed mind.

Exertion or application. If dullness or agitation occur, you should actively apply yourself to the methods that dispel those. However, once dullness or agitation have been dispelled, such [applications] are not suitable because arousing mental applications and keeping the mind unmoving are mutually exclusive and because the last two *Stages of Meditation* explain:

> If you exert yourself [while] your mind rests in equipoise, you will become distracted.[765] [238]

Equanimity. When you have pacified the flaws of dullness and agitation, and have balanced tightening and relaxing, your mind settles naturally. Dispensing with exertions and mental applications, you skillfully nurture samādhi, as the middle *Stages of Meditation* says:

> When you have no dullness or agitation and see that [your mind] naturally remains with its object, relax your effort and be equanimous. Then remain that way as long as you like.[766]

Now you may wonder, How long should my sessions be for such practices? As a beginner, if you attempt to do long sessions, the vigor of your mindfulness and alertness will naturally, automatically dissipate, and you'll become forgetful and distracted. You won't quickly notice the faults of dullness and agitation, and you will be engulfed by distractions, dullness, and agitation. Therefore, meditate repeatedly in short sessions. However, once you have become slightly familiar [with the practice], you will be skilled in the way to sustain mindfulness and alertness. When you settle naturally in flawless samādhi, extending your sessions slightly will not be problematic. To sum up, rest evenly as long as that does not cause obstacles to samādhi, either physically or mentally. If that happens, dispel the faults of those obstacles and meditate. Other than that, there are no explanations about the definite length of time for sessions.

Here I have explained certain key points for how to sustain mental stillness. However, since I already discussed what hinders or obscures śamatha, identified the applications that remove those, and presented all the relevant [scriptural] sources, I will not do so again.* [239]

6) The Process of Achieving Mental Stillness

The mahāsiddha Tilopa says:

> In the beginning, it feels like water cascading over a cliff.
> In the middle, it's the gentle flow of the Ganges river.
> At last all waters become like the reuniting of a mother with her children.[767]

That description can be applied to the phase of stillness although it is not necessarily only about that. While you are a beginner you are disturbed by many subtle and coarse thoughts, and so you must pursue and nurture nonconceptual stillness however you can. Your habitual state of mind is very unsettled and unstable, like water cascading over a cliff.[768]

Next, when you have become more habituated [to śamatha practice], coarse thoughts are mostly pacified or, even if they are not pacified, they disappear. Since [stillness] is not interrupted, it is somewhat easier to sustain. Like the gentle flow of the Ganges river, for the most part you are able to rest quietly right within the still mind. At other times, you won't be able to ground within your experience the strong movements of thoughts caused by various unsettling circumstances or objects.

Then, subtle and coarse thoughts do not manifest or, if a few subtle ones do, they are self-pacified, self-purified. Like the great ocean where all "mother and child" waters meet, once all impressions and sensations become of one taste in the expanse of mindfulness and alertness, the waves of thoughts do not roll.

*See also "The Elimination of the Obscurations of Śamatha and Vipaśyanā," pp. 19–29 and "The Way the Eight Applications Produce Mental Stillness," pp. 56–57.

Accordingly, the stages of mental stillness can be condensed into three. Or they can be correlated to the nine mental states, which are taught in the Sūtra-oriented approach, as follows: [240]

1. First, by drawing in the mind that is projecting and focusing it on the object of meditation, you achieve the mental state of settling.
2. By prolonging the continuity of that resting mind without distraction, you achieve continuous settling.
3. By reapplying your mind to that object when you are distracted, you achieve renewed settling.
4. By repeatedly drawing your mind in and refining [your concentration], you achieve increased settling.
5. Seeing the excellent qualities of samādhi and dedicating yourself to those, you achieve taming.
6. Seeing the disadvantages of distractions, you quell them and achieve pacification.
7. When faults arise in samādhi (such as thoughts involving attachments), by pacifying them you achieve full pacification.
8. Through familiarizing yourself with samādhi by applying your mind to it, you achieve one-pointedness.
9. After familiarizing yourself with that [eighth mental state], since your mind settles in samādhi spontaneously, naturally, and effortlessly, you achieve equipoise.

The *Ornament for the Mahāyāna Sūtras* teaches:

> After you have directed your mind to an object of meditation,
> do not be distracted from the continuity of that.[769]

These [stages for developing mental stillness] relate to the discussion of the six strengths as follows:

1. Listening to the esoteric instructions for samādhi are the strength of hearing.
2. Practicing them are the strength of reflection.
3. Undistracted mindfulness is the strength of mindfulness.
4. Awareness of dullness or agitation is the strength of alertness.
5. Applying yourself with great effort to samādhi is the strength of diligence.

6. Becoming very familiar [with samādhi] is the strength of familiarization.

They relate to the four types of attention as follows:

1. Since in the beginning it is necessary to use great effort to focus the mind tightly and one-pointedly in samādhi, attention is tightly focused.
2. Next, when there is interference from dullness or agitation, attention engages intermittently.
3. When there are no such intrusions, attention engages uninterruptedly. [241]
4. Finally, when [samādhi] occurs naturally without effort, attention engages spontaneously.

All these techniques have been explained above.*

[During the cultivation of the nine stages for] mental stillness, [from the first] up through the sixth, the strength of the diligence of exertion is aroused by faith towards and motivation for samādhi and by vigorous mindfulness and alertness. When the seventh and eighth stages have been achieved, the strength of familiarization obviates the need for great effort and gives rise to the ninth mental state where samādhi proceeds naturally, as a matter of course. When you have become very familiarized, if you rest evenly once at the beginning with mindfulness [or recollection] of your intention to meditate in samādhi, your samādhi will proceed comfortably without the need to be constantly mindful and alert. An analogy is that when you haven't learned to read or recite [from memory], you must generate some degree of effort that involves tightening your mindfulness and alertness. However, once you are familiar with them, those activities come naturally without the effort of continuous mindfulness and alertness—all you need to do is arouse an initial intention.

Such samādhi, along with its experiences of bliss, clarity, and nonconceptuality, may bring a mixing of meditative equipoise with postmeditative attainment. The uneducated presume that is excellent spiritual practice but

*See "The Way to Achieve Mental Stillness through Nine Stages," pp. 57–59, "The Way Those [Nine] Mental States Are Achieved through the Six Strengths," pp. 59–60, and "The Way the Four Types of Attention Are Involved in This [Process]," pp. 60–62.

it is said to be just an experience of mental stillness. It is not at all what this practice lineage describes as spiritual practice.

In that case we might wonder, What constitutes authentic śamatha? The Sūtra-oriented texts on the stages of meditation equate the achievement of suppleness with śamatha. They consider samādhi without that achievement, no matter how excellent, to be only the one-pointed mind that is part of the levels of the desire realm. It cannot possibly be the actual stage of meditative concentration that is part of the higher realms and is not even posited as the preparatory stage since the attainment of the preparatory stage requires the achievement of suppleness. [242] Therefore, the one-pointed mind of the desire realm is an approximation of śamatha and is referred to with the term "the level of not resting in equipoise." The meditative concentration of the higher realms is referred to with the term "the level of resting in equipoise."

The way the one-pointed mind of the desire realm gradually achieves suppleness and so forth is as follows. That [one-pointed mind] with the power of its bliss, clarity, and nonconceptuality nurtures samādhi and, being without any discomforts, its joy and delight increase. Thus, the suppleness of mental flexibility develops first. Through the force of that, the winds that serve as the causes for flexibility flow through the body.[770] Once they have pervaded the body, the suppleness of physical flexibility develops. This is explained in the *Śrāvakabhūmi*.[771] It also describes that when the six types of attention—that which cognizes meaning, that which comes from conviction, that which isolates, that which consolidates joy, that which analyzes, and that which completes the practice—are present, [the one-pointed mind of the desire realm] becomes the preparatory stage for the first meditative concentration that is part of the form realm. Then, gradually the absorptions of the meditative concentrations, the formless realm, and so forth are achieved.[772] The [first] *Stages of Meditation* explains:

> When [meditative concentration] involves a feeling of equanimity [or indifference] and also discernment and analysis, it is called "not ineffective." This is the mental state that is the preparation for the first meditative concentration.
>
> When that is separated from the craving for pleasure and the qualities of negative actions and involves discernment, analysis, joy, and ease, it is called the first meditative concentration. Within the first meditative concentration, the absence of discernment is called "the special meditative concentration."

> When [meditative concentration] does not involve discernment or analysis, it becomes free from the craving of the level of the first meditative concentration. When it involves joy, ease, and inner tranquility, it is called the second meditative concentration. [243]
>
> When [meditative concentration] is free from the craving of the level of the second meditative concentration and involves purified ease, equanimity, mindfulness, and alertness, it is called the third meditative concentration.
>
> When [meditative concentration] is free from the craving of the level of the third meditative concentration, is neither suffering nor happiness, and involves purified equanimity and mindfulness, it is called the fourth meditative concentration.[773]

There are many such explanations but I will not include more details for fear of being excessive.

When we have attained such suppleness, we are able to rest evenly in samādhi for many days. At that point, having severed the stream of both physical and mental negative propensities, we have physical ease and mental joy, and are able to enter samādhi. For instance, we may be able to emulate the exalted Dakpo [Gampopa], who could remain in samādhi for thirteen days with a butter lamp on his head.

On the other hand, since the gurus of this practice lineage consider mental stillness to be simply the foundation, or basis, for meditation, they regard being able to effortlessly sustain mental stillness or being comfortable sustaining it with just a slight amount of effort to be śamatha—even though suppleness may not have been achieved exactly. And they teach that [someone at that point] can be guided in vipaśyanā. Since one-pointedness meditation, which combines śamatha and vipaśyanā, is said to have three stages, here the emphasis is on developing a spiritual practice that combines śamatha and vipaśyanā, not on stressing śamatha alone. [244]

Putting aside the specifics of each samādhi (which are what are to be sustained), we train in becoming familiar with the object of meditation using mindfulness, alertness, and effort. In the end, the way the equipoise that effortlessly rests upon its object of meditation develops is the same in all cases. Therefore, in this context I see that it is best for the gradual type of individual to establish a firm basis in śamatha, as the *Entrance to the Bodhisattva's Way of Life* shows:

> [By being aware that] vipaśyanā imbued with śamatha
> [can conquer your mental afflictions,
> begin by pursuing śamatha].[774]

It is said in the practice lineage:

> Without śamatha, there is no vipaśyanā.*[775]

And:

> If you undertake vipaśyanā too soon, there will be no śamatha.[776]

7) The Purpose of Practicing Mental Stillness

In general, we definitely must practice śamatha as the root of all paths, mundane and transmundane, for the following reasons:[777]

- In terms of the mundane path, to relinquish the mental afflictions that are part of the levels of the desire realm, it is necessary to give rise to remedies that are antithetical to the mental afflictions and to practice the vipaśyanā that observes the coarseness of the desire realm and the calmness of the form realm. Śamatha is necessary as a support for that.
- To practice the eight preparatory states of meditative concentration and the eight actual states of meditative concentration that are part of the levels of the form and formless realms, it is necessary to practice the vipaśyanā that focuses on the coarseness of the lower levels and the calmness of the higher ones. Śamatha is necessary as a support for that.
- In terms of the transmundane path, śamatha is necessary as the support that produces the vipaśyanā of the Hīnayāna, which focuses on the four truths and refutes a self of persons. [245]
- Śamatha is also necessary as the support for the development of the vipaśyanā of the Mahāyāna, which focuses on both absences of self-entity and is nondual wisdom.

*To translate the terms śamatha and vipaśyanā:

> If you do not rest peacefully, you will not see clearly.

Moreover, śamatha is necessary as the support for producing such excellent qualities as the four feet of miraculous powers, the meditative concentrations, the absorptions of the formless realm, the eight liberations, supercognitive abilities, the totalities, and the overpowerings. The first *Stages of Meditation* teaches:

> If you have the eight applications that eliminate [faults], your samādhi improves. It produces excellent qualities, such as the miraculous powers. It is said, therefore, in the sūtras:
>
>> Meditate on the foot of the miraculous power of possessing the eight applications for relinquishment.
>
> Since the one-pointed mind eventually possesses flexibility and attains the distinctions of the excellent qualities of its focus and so forth, it receives names such as meditative concentration, formless absorptions, and liberations.[778]

Furthermore, śamatha has many other purposes, such as suppressing overt thoughts involving the mental afflictions and freeing us from the bonds of [conceptualizing] characteristics. Here, however, its primary purpose is to enable us to practice vipaśyanā. Of the two types of vipaśyanā—the mundane vipaśyanā with the qualities of calmness and coarseness, which takes us to the Pinnacle of Existence, and the vipaśyanā with the quality of [realizing] the absence of self-entity, which eradicates the seeds of existence—śamatha is practiced for the sake of generating the latter.

The reason such practice is necessary. Vipaśyanā that lacks śamatha is unable to rest in equipoise because it is ever-shifting, like a waterfall or candle flame in the wind. [246] Without resting in equipoise, what is true, just as it is, is not known and is not clear. As the first *Stages of Meditation* teaches:

> Because the mind is fluid like water, it won't be still without the foundation of śamatha. The mind that does not rest in equipoise cannot know what is true just as it is.[779]

The middle *Stages of Meditation* teaches:

> With a vipaśyanā that has no śamatha, yogins' and yoginīs' minds are distracted by objects. Like a candle flame in a windy spot, they are unstable. In that case, the light of wisdom will not shine brilliantly.[780]

We may still wonder, How much śamatha should we practice here? If you can achieve just the śamatha that is part of the preparatory stage of the first meditative concentration (discussed above) that is commendable. If you cannot achieve that, it seems that achieving just the one-pointed mind of the desire realm will be sufficient since Ācārya Śūra explains:

> Beings who oppose your dharma
> are blinded by stupidity.
> Even though they may reach the Pinnacle of Existence,
> again they suffer and create saṃsāra.
> Those who follow your teachings
> may not achieve the actual meditative concentration
> but they will reverse saṃsāra
> even as Māra watches.[781]

That completes the explanation of the instructions in śamatha. [247]

9

Vipaśyanā

B) The Instructions in Vipaśyanā

This has six parts:

1) The Reasons That Vipaśyanā Meditation Is Necessary
2) The Preparations Necessary for Vipaśyanā
3) The Classifications of the Ways to Cultivate Vipaśyanā
4) The Way to Cultivate Vipaśyanā in This Context
5) The Differences between Vipaśyanā Developing or Not Developing
6) Correlating This Vipaśyanā with Other Approaches

1) The Reasons That Vipaśyanā Meditation Is Necessary

We should not be content with only the samādhi of śamatha just described. Since we strive for liberation and omniscience, we definitely must cultivate the vipaśyanā that has the distinction of [seeing] the absence of self. If we do not, we will not be liberated from existence because, although śamatha suppresses the mental afflictions for a time, it does not vanquish their dormant tendencies. The middle *Stages of Meditation* teaches:

> Becoming familiar with just śamatha alone does not remove obscurations for yogins and yoginīs—it simply suppresses their mental afflictions for a while. Without the light of prajñā, dormant tendencies cannot be destroyed. Therefore, *Unraveling the Intent* says:
>
> > Meditative concentration suppresses the mental afflictions.
> > Prajñā destroys their dormant tendencies.[782]

It also says:

> Thus it is that those who wish for pure wisdom to arise after the relinquishment of all obscurations should cultivate prajñā while remaining within śamatha.[783] [248]

The *King of Samādhi* states:

> Even though the worldly cultivate samādhi,
> they do not destroy the notion of a self.
> Mental afflictions return to disturb them,
> as they did for Udraka, who meditated in samādhi.
>
> If you discern the lack of self-entity of phenomena
> and cultivate that discernment,
> it will be the cause for the result: attainment of nirvāṇa.
> No other cause brings peace.[784]

Although those in the world cultivate samādhis (such as the four meditative concentrations), those samādhis alone are unable to rid them of the belief in a self, the root of saṃsāra. The force of that belief will cause the root and secondary afflictions to return and those beings to circle in the negative states due to their bad karma. Examples can be found among the non-Buddhist ṛṣis, such as Udraka, who meditated in samādhi. On the other hand, examining phenomena, which have no self-entity, with discerning prajñā and meditating on that is the cause for attaining the result of nirvāṇa. No other cause pacifies suffering and mental afflictions completely. Thus the meaning [of that quotation] is explained.[785] [249]

2) The Preparations Necessary for Vipaśyanā

Unraveling the Intent states that the cause of vipaśyanā is the pure view that is [known through] listening and reflecting.*[786] The middle *Stages of Meditation* explains that the three causes for vipaśyanā are relying on holy persons, pursuing much listening, and reflecting properly.[787] "Holy persons" here refers to spiritual mentors with śamatha and vipaśyanā realizations because those without such realizations do not achieve the point even though they may be learned in the terminology of the provisional definitive

*See citation on p. 17.

meaning. "Pursuing much listening" means to pursue the stainless teachings on the definitive meaning since listening to the dharma of conventional expressions and the provisional meaning does not teach us the definitive meaning. "Reflecting properly" means we must practice with the instructions transmitted from siddhas because the ultimate is not an object that can be examined and analyzed by logicians.

We may ask, What are the differences between the teachings on the provisional meaning and those on the definitive meaning? It is explained that teachings where the primary subjects are the conventional, words, letters, and so on are on the provisional meaning. Teachings on the ultimate and the profound, which are difficult to understand, are on the definitive meaning. The *Sūtra of the Teaching of Akṣayamati* states:

> What are the sūtras of the definitive meaning? What are the sūtras of the provisional meaning? Sūtras that present the establishment of the conventional are called provisional. Sūtras that teach to establish the ultimate are called definitive. Those sūtras that present the various words and letters are referred to as provisional. Those sūtras that discuss what is profound, which is difficult to see and difficult to comprehend, are known as definitive.[788] [250]

Next we may wonder, What are the conventional and the ultimate? Teachings on what have the qualities of arising and ceasing—such as a self, life-force, nourished being—are about the conventional. Teachings on emptiness—the absence of a self, nonarising, and so forth—are about the definitive meaning. The same sūtra says:

> Sūtras are called provisional when they teach as though there is an owner despite no owner existing, and use various expressions such as self, sentient being, life-force, nourished being, being, individual, humankind, human, agent, and experiencer.
>
> Sūtras are called definitive when they teach the doors of liberation: emptiness, the absence of characteristics, the absence of expectancy, no composition, no birth, no arising, no sentient beings, no life-force, no individuals, no owners.[789]

The *King of Samādhi* teaches:

> Know what is in keeping with the emptiness explained by the Sugata
> to be instances of definitive sūtras.
> Know the dharma that discusses sentient beings,
> individuals, and beings to be of the provisional meaning.[790]

Regardless of how the teachings of the Buddha and the explanations by paṇḍitas and siddhas that elucidate the intention of those teachings [are classified], through listening to and reflecting upon the undisputed scriptural tradition that clearly presents the unerring definitive meaning, we develop an abstract idea of the view. Since that development is explained to be the cause of vipaśyanā, we must practice in that way. Furthermore, we must attend to the preparations for meditative concentration explained above: abandoning the causes of dullness and agitation, restraining our sense faculties, alert behavior, moderation of food, and so forth.* In particular, since this practice lineage asserts that realization of the view requires the gurus' blessings, it is critical that we practice guru yoga and make strong supplications. [251] The *Two-Part [Hevajra Tantra]* states:

> The connate cannot be described by others,
> it cannot be discovered anywhere.
> Follow your guru's timing and his methods:
> you will recognize it with your merit.[791]

It also says:

> This is wisdom, reflexively aware,
> an experiential domain beyond speech.
> It is [revealed through] the stages of blessings;
> thus the wisdom of the omniscient ones is the same.[792]

3) The Classifications of the Ways to Cultivate Vipaśyanā

Among the many types of vipaśyanā, there are mundane vipaśyanā, with its aspects of calmness and coarseness, and Hīnayāna vipaśyanā that is concerned with the four truths. Although it is excellent to practice those, they

*See "The Elimination of the Causes of Dullness and Agitation," pp. 27–28. For restraining the sense faculties, alert behavior, and moderation of food, see pp. 169–71.

are not essential. The vipaśyanā of meditating on the absence of self is the vipaśyanā to be practiced here because it is the necessary basis by which we ascertain the abiding mode of all phenomena (which are included within percepts and perceivers).

The way to give rise to such vipaśyanā is as follows. The extensive approach is the fourfold vipaśyanā taught in *Unraveling the Intent* and the *Compendium of Abhidharma*.* [252] The intermediate approach is the threefold vipaśyanā explained in *Unraveling the Intent*.† There is also the vipaśyanā of meditating on the twofold absence of self-entity, which summarizes those [other approaches]. Looking at this from the perspective of the latter, most who expound the scriptures and reasonings of the Indian masters explain many ways to meditate on the view of emptiness. Based on the treatises of the noble Nāgārjuna and Asaṅga, they analyze using the great reasonings, such as [demonstrating that a phenomenon] is neither a single unit nor a plurality, and thereby cultivate the view of emptiness in which all percepts and perceivers are determined to lack any reality. In this land of Tibet, while it is possible to realize the correct view on the basis of that approach, nowadays it seems that most rely on their inferential rational cognition and take an abstract idea of emptiness as their mental object. The way that leads to an intellectually fabricated, partial emptiness (an analytical emptiness, an emptiness of the inanimate, and so forth) was discussed already with references to scriptures and reasonings.‡

In this context, by relying on the major and minor texts, as well as shorter esoteric instructions, transmitted from the Great Brahman [Saraha], the glorious Śavaripa, and the lord of yogins Tilopa, we focus on just the mind to determine [the nature of] all percepts and perceivers—which is the instruction for taking direct perception as the path. This is the way to give rise to the view of the emptiness of nature. It has many distinctive profundities in that it involves little hardship and brings great benefit. It is, for the most part, identical with the key points of the Sūtra-oriented texts on the stages of meditation, the *Instructions on Prajñāpāramitā*, Kamalaśīla's three *Stages of Meditation*, and the Exalted [Lord Atīśa's] *Instructions on Madhyamaka*. It is most wonderful. This is the approach that I will explain as best I can.

*See citations on p. 30 and p. 35.

†See citation on p. 35.

‡See "Analyzing Other Systems," pp. 95–103.

4) The Way to Cultivate Vipaśyanā in This Context

This has two parts: [253]

a) Determining the Essence of Mind and Its Various Appearances
b) Eliminating Misinterpretations About a Root or Basis

a) Determining the Essence of Mind and Its Various Appearances

This has three sections:

i) The Reasons That Objectives Are Achieved by Observing Just the Mind
ii) Determining the Essence of Mind, the Root
iii) Determining the Essence of Thoughts and Appearances, [Mind's] Expressive Power

i) The Reasons That Objectives Are Achieved by Observing Just the Mind

In a general sense, the presentation that all phenomena are mind, the problems that ensue from not meditating on the nature of mind, and the benefits of doing so were already explained.* In brief, since the troubles of saṃsāra and the virtues of nirvāṇa depend on the mind, or arise from mind, it is crucial that we focus on our mind in meditation, as the *Compendium of Dharma Sūtra* explains:

> The bodhisattva Mativikrama supplicated, to which the Bhagavān responded: "Phenomena, what we refer to as 'things,' do not abide as objects and do not abide spatially. Furthermore, phenomena are simply dependent on your own mind. Thus it is that you should concentrate on your mind, take it to its limits, tame it, rest it in equipoise, and subjugate it."[793]

It is taught that if we understand mind, we understand all phenomena, and that if mind is liberated, everything is liberated. The *Jewel Cloud Sūtra* says:

> The mind comes before all phenomena. If you comprehend the mind, you know all phenomena.[794]

*See "The Reasons It Is Necessary to Meditate on the Nature of Mind," pp. 6–12.

The *Wisdom at the Moment of Death* states:

> When the mind is realized, there is wisdom. Therefore, meditate with the awareness that buddhahood is not to be sought anywhere else.[795]

The Great Brahman [Saraha] says:

> When mind is fettered you are bound. [254]
> It can be liberated—have no doubts.[796]

He also says:

> KYE HO. When the confused mind is realized to be mind,
> it is self-liberated from all evil views.
> Remaining in the sublime great bliss
> under its power is the genuine siddhi.[797]

Tilopa states:

> If you sever the one root of a tree with spreading branches full of leaves,
> all those many branches will wither.
> The same thing happens to saṃsāra when you sever the root of mind.[798]

Thus it is explained that cutting through the basis, or root, of mind cuts the continuum of saṃsāra.

Śāntideva teaches that when we do not understand mind, everything is a cause of suffering, and that recognizing the mind is the best protection and discipline. *Entrance to the Bodhisattva's Way of Life* says:

> Those who don't know the secret of mind,
> what is of sublime importance in the dharma,
> will wander futilely for a long time—
> despite their desire to attain happiness and destroy suffering.[799]

It continues:

> Therefore, I will hold my mind well
> and protect my mind well.
> If my mind is not protected and disciplined, [255]
> what use is discipline?[800]

Some expounders of conventionalities say that, although it is taught that liberation comes from meditating on emptiness, if mind-itself is asserted to be the primordial buddha and meditating on mind brings liberation, all sentient beings will be liberated effortlessly. Since it is their own idea that emptiness is something good and mind is something bad, it is their own fault that they do not understand the abiding modes of those [emptiness and mind]. This exposes their hidden flaw of not having looked at the scriptural tradition much. Since the way the fundamental state of emptiness and the abiding state of the mind are the same and the way meditating on those two are the same can be understood from the explanations that will be gradually given, I will not elaborate here, but I will show how mind-itself is taught to be the primordial buddha with the following citations. The *Descent into Laṅkā Sūtra* says:

> Mind-itself, devoid of conceptuality,
> is the opposite of the mental consciousness.
> Since it knows each and every phenomenon,
> [I] declare the mind to be the buddha.[801]

The *Kālacakra Root Tantra* explains:

> The mind-itself of sentient beings is luminosity,
> primordially free from arising, abiding, and ceasing.
> From the beginningless past,
> it is the supreme first buddha,
> causeless and unadulterated by conditions.[802]

The *[Kālacakra] Laghutantra* says:

> Sentient beings are buddhas. No other great buddhas exist in these worldly realms.[803]

The *Secret Vajra Ḍāka Tantra* states: [256]

> Because their mind realizes itself,
> sentient beings are primordially buddhas.[804]

The *Two-Part [Hevajra Tantra]* observes:

> Nowhere else in the world
> is the buddha to be found:
> the mind is the perfect buddha.
> Buddha is not taught to be anything else.[805]

The *Oral Teachings of Mañjuśrī* states:

> The principal substance of all entities
> is the essence of our own mind.
> When that's realized,
> it's the awakening of buddhas.[806]

There is an abundance of such citations. The practice of the ultimate method for actualizing that primordial buddha is referred to with the term "meditating on mind." The way liberation is attained by that meditation is described in many statements, such as the following. The *Sūtra of the Questions of Rāṣṭrapāla* says:

> On that basis, while meditating on mind
> you will know that everything is empty.
> Once phenomena are recognized to be empty
> even awakening is empty.[807]

The *Vajra Pañjarā* states:

> Inspired by the precious mind
> and meditating on mind-itself, there is buddhahood. [257]
> That holy being is buddha.[808]

It also says:

> Whenever the mind meditates
> on the inseparability of emptiness and compassion,

> that is the teaching of the buddha,
> dharma, and saṅgha.[809]

We should know that such statements are similar to those in the Sūtra-oriented texts that use the expressions "meditating on conventional bodhicitta" and "meditating on ultimate bodhicitta."

ii) Determining the Essence of Mind, the Root

This has four parts:
(A) Where This Is Taught
(B) The Actual Stages of This Meditation
(C) The Citation of Relevant Scriptural Sources
(D) The Way to Determine [the Essence] of Mind

(A) Where This Is Taught

We may ask, Generally speaking, where do we find teachings on the ways to meditate on the vipaśyanā view that cuts through misinterpretations by discerning that phenomena are mind and that mind lacks any essence? The *Ornament for the Mahāyāna Sūtras* explains:

> Aware that there is nothing other than mind,
> they then recognize that mind also does not exist.
> These intelligent ones are aware that both are nonexistent
> and abide in the dharmadhātu devoid of those.[810]

The *Commentary on Bodhicitta* states:

> Abiding in mind alone,
> the fortunate abandon even that [teaching].* [258]
>
> For the Vijñānavādins
> this manifold [world] is mind.

*The previous two lines of this verse (25) are:

> To overcome a belief in a self,
> [the Buddha] taught on the skandhas, dhātus, and so forth.

What is the nature of consciousness?
I will now explain just that.

"All this is merely mind,"
said the Muni
to alleviate the fears of the childish,
not as [a statement of] the way things are [ultimately].

The imagined, the dependent,
and the consummate
have but one nature: emptiness.
They are imputations in the mind.

For those who delight in the Mahāyāna
the Buddha taught in brief:
all phenomena lack self-entity and are equal,
mind is primordially unborn.[811]

The first *Stages of Meditation* teaches:

> Thus it is that you should consider: these three realms are only mind. Therefore, all imagined phenomena are understood to be simply mind. If you discern that, you discern the nature of all phenomena. And thus you discern the essential nature of the mind.
>
> Analyze that [mind] as follows. Mind cannot possibly be real in an ultimate sense. How can the mind that apprehends forms and so forth—things which are of a false nature—and that itself appears as various images be real? Just as forms and so forth are false, so too is the mind false since it does not exist apart from those [forms and so forth].
>
> Just as forms and so forth are neither of the nature of a single unit nor of the nature of a plurality since they have various manifestations, mind is neither of the nature of a single unit nor of the nature of a plurality since it does not exist apart from those [forms and so forth].
>
> That being so, mind simply seems to be of the nature of illusions and so forth. And, just like the mind, all phenomena sim-

> ply seem to be of the nature of illusions and so forth. Thus you analyze.[812] [259]

Similar explanations are found in the other *Stages of Meditation*.[813]

(B) The Actual Stages of This Meditation

Earlier, during the cultivation of śamatha samādhi, the emphasis was on resting meditation that relies mainly on a nonconceptual samādhi. In this context, to cultivate vipaśyanā the emphasis is on analytical meditation that examines and analyzes your own mind with discerning prajñā. To do this, arouse sharp mental clarity within a śamatha state that is simply mind not being distracted from its object of meditation.

At this point, determining the essence of mind-itself is similar to determining the lack of a self of persons in the Sūtra context. The approach involves adopting the essential points for the body as before and using the gaze of looking straight ahead with open eyes. The Great Brahman [Saraha] states:

> Yogins and yoginīs who do not close their eyes or meditate . . .[814]

He also says:

> Yogins and yoginīs with open eyes
> are superior to all other yogins and yoginīs.[815]

And:

> Tīrthikas and Brahmans look up.
> The peaceful śrāvakas look down.
> Vajra eyes stare straight ahead.[816] [260]

Next, let your mind rest evenly in a clear yet nonconceptual śamatha samādhi. In that state, your mind should look nakedly at itself, either in its externally oriented aspect or its internally oriented aspect, whichever is easier. Systematically examine and analyze what that mind's shape and color are like, what abode and support it rests upon, and what its identity and manifestation are as follows:

- Examine its shape: Does it have a shape that is round, square, or the like? Or does it have the shape of earth and stones, a rock mountain, or something like that? Or is its shape that of a human or a specific animal? Look at its color: is it white, or black, or red?
- Examine its abode and support: Is mind supported by, or resting upon, something external, something in the environment or its inhabitants? Or is it supported by, or resting upon, something internal, your own body? If you think it abides in your body, look to see whether it resides in a specific part or area—anywhere from the top of your head to the soles of your feet—or whether it resides pervasively throughout your body. If it is present throughout, look at that: is it present in the sense of [the body being] outer and [the mind being] inner, or is it present in the sense of being mixed [with the body]? If it seems to be mixed [with the body], look to see what happens when the mind projects to an object, such as a form.
- Examine its identity and manifestation: Is the mind something that can be identified as empty or is it a manifestation of that? Or is it identified as clarity and a manifestation of that? If it is empty, look to see how that is: is it an emptiness that is a nothingness or an emptiness that is like empty space? If it is clarity, is it clarity that is like light radiating from the sun, the moon, or a candle? Or is it reflexively clear without a color or light?

Examine and analyze your mind from those many points of view. If, having heard this and having developed some theoretical understanding, you don't examine [your mind], you won't gain assurance and reach a final conclusion about the abiding mode of mind. Mind must examine itself, like a rock pulverizing bones. [261]

By examining in that way, you become certain that [mind] does not exist substantially, like a specific external or internal thing, and yet you meditate by resting your mind quietly in its clarity-emptiness. Even though you may have had some previous experiences of resting, you may still lack assurance about the abiding mode of mind. Supplicate [your guru] with strong devotion. Then again, when there is clarity, examine and analyze its mode, and when there is emptiness, examine and analyze the mode of emptiness. You may be unable to state clearly the situation by describing a shape, color, abode, support, identity, or manifestation, such that you could say "it is like this." Nevertheless, you may at this point experience mind, not as radiant light, a color, or the like, but as reflexively aware, reflexively clear. Or you may experience it as reflexively empty, devoid of something that can be identified. Additionally, when mindful awareness is present, you may have the slight sense of something being experienced that is vibrant and crisp. But when your mindful awareness is distracted, that disappears and you feel convinced that you are helplessly ordinary. Those are experiences that may occur at this point. At that time, while not identifying mind as being "this," rely continuously on mindful awareness that does not stray from being reflexively aware and reflexively clear. Maintain that without a moment's distraction.

When you examine and analyze in that way, do so with discerning prajñā while remaining in a state of nondistraction. Once your mindful awareness wanders and ordinary thinking occurs, that is not analysis, as is explained by the following. The Great Brahman [Saraha] says:

> KYE MA. Look: [mind] itself reveals suchness to itself.
> If your undistracted mind's looking slips away,
> your distracted mind won't realize suchness.[817]

The [first] *Stages of Meditation* observes:

> Once you have stabilized your mind on an object of meditation with śamatha, if you examine with prajñā the light of true wisdom will manifest.[818] [262]

(C) The Citation of Relevant Scriptural Sources

The practice lineage refers to the meditation techniques just discussed with the term "investigating mind." Those who say that since the mind does not exist as an entity, there is nothing to investigate, and that when something does not exist, there's no point in searching for it, are ignorant of a key point related to the ultimate. The term "investigating mind" is found in many texts including the following. [The *Discourse for Kāśyapa* in] the Heap of Jewels says:

> Accordingly, the mind should be investigated.[819]

The *Sūtra of the Questions of Ratnacūḍa* states:

> That is the investigation of mind.[820]

The *Sūtra of the Chapter on the Thirty-Three* teaches:

> Those wise investigate the dharmatā of mind.
> When they investigate the dharmatā of mind
> and see mind and the dharmatā of mind,
> they do not see any nature to that mind
> and the mind performing its investigation.[821]

Although the mind is not an entity, investigating it through analysis is done deliberately so that we may realize that the mind is empty of any nature, as the [middle and final] *Stages of Meditation* explain by citing the *Jewel Cloud Sūtra*:

> If those who meditate repeatedly on emptiness thoroughly investigate those things and the natures of those things that the mind engages with and takes delight in, they will understand them to be empty. If they examine what the mind is, they will understand it to be empty. If they fully investigate the essence of what is understood by that mind, they will know it to be empty. Through such understandings, they enter the yoga of the absence of characteristics.[822] [263]

The way to analyze or investigate the mind is described in numerous texts found in both the sūtras and tantras. In the Heap of Jewels, the *Sūtra Teaching the Undifferentiatable Nature of the Dharmadhātu* states:

> [The emanated bhikṣu] said: "Venerable ones, examine your mind: Is it what is called 'blue'? Is it what is known as 'yellow'? Or is it a color such as red, white, maroon, or crystal? Is it real or not real? Is it permanent? Impermanent? Is it material? Or is it not material?"
>
> They replied: "Venerable one, mind is not material. It is not demonstrable and does not appear. It is without obstruction, without abode, and not something cognizable."
>
> Then that emanated bhikṣu said to those bhikṣus: "That is so. Venerable ones, do you think that that mind—which is not

material, not demonstrable, nonappearing, without obstruction, without abode, and not something cognizable—is observable, such that you could say, 'It abides internally,' or, 'It resides externally,' or, 'It rests between the two'?"

They replied: "No, it is not that way."

[The emanated bhikṣu] said: "Venerable ones, if that mind cannot be observed—in that it is not material, not demonstrable, nonappearing, without obstruction, without abode, not something cognizable, not internal, not external, and not between the two—do you think that it is truly and completely existent?"

They replied: "No, it is not that way."[823]

[The *Discourse for Kāśyapa*] in the Heap of Jewels teaches:

Accordingly, the mind should be investigated. Is the mind that feels desire, or becomes angry, or feels stupid something in the past? Is it something in the future? Or something in the present? You may think that past mental states are gone, future ones have not arisen, and what occurs in the present has no abode. [264]

Kāśyapa, since the mind does not exist internally, externally, or in both, it is not observed. Kāśyapa, mind cannot be analyzed, it cannot be demonstrated, it is not a support, it is without appearance, and is not something cognizable.[824]

It adds:

Kāśyapa, if you fully investigate the mind, it is not found. What is not found is not observed. What is not observed is not something in the past, is not something in the future, and not something in the present. Whatever is not in the past, future, or present is truly beyond the three times. Whatever is truly beyond the three times is not existent and is not nonexistent.[825]

The *Sūtra of the Questions of Ratnacūḍa* states:

When we investigate the mind, we do not truly see the mind as something internal. We do not truly see the mind as something external, as something external and internal, as the skandhas, dhātus, or āyatanas. Therefore, since we do not truly see the

> mind, we explore the mind's continuum, asking, "Where does mind originate?" Thinking, "It is this," we may think that mind arises from an existent object.
>
> Are that object, about which we think, "It is this," and that mind other than each other? Or is it that the object is the mind? If the mind and its object are other than each other, then that mind is two things. On the other hand, if the object and that mind are identical, how is it that mind sees mind? It is not possible that mind sees mind.[826]

The *Vairocanābhisambodhi* explains:

> Guhyapati, how should you know your mind? [265] It is thus: even though you may search for it as an image, a color, a shape, an object, a form, a feeling, a discrimination, a formation, a consciousness, a self, "mine," a percept, a perceiver, something pure, something impure, a dhātu, an āyatana, or as any type of aspect, you will not observe it.[827]

It also instructs:

> Guhyapati, awakening and omniscience should be sought in your own mind. Why? Mind is pure by nature. It is neither internal nor external. It is not observed between those two.
>
> Guhyapati, the mind has not been seen and will not be seen by the tathāgata, arhat, true, perfect buddhas. It is not blue, and is not yellow, red, white, purple, the color of a crystal, short, long, round, square, light, dark, female, male, or neuter.
>
> Guhyapati, mind is not of the nature of the desire realm, it is not of the nature of the form realm, and is not of the nature of the formless realm. It is not of the nature of any class of sentient being, be it gods, nāgas, yakṣas, gandharvas, asuras, garuḍas, kiṃnaras, mahoragas,[828] humans, or nonhumans.
>
> Guhyapati, mind does not reside in the eyes, in the body, or in mentation. Why? Mind has the characteristics of space and, therefore, it is free from thoughts and concepts.[829] [266]

In brief, it is taught that when we examine and analyze mind to see what its color and shape, its abode and support, its identity and manifestation are like, we analyze everything external and internal, which compose percepts and perceivers. At the conclusion of our analysis, we will have many distinctive [understandings], such as that the essence of mind is not material, not demonstrable, and so forth. It is taught that it is like space: not abiding anywhere external or internal and free from concepts. The *Commentary on Bodhicitta* summarizes this by explaining:

> Mind is simply a name.
> It is nothing but a name.
> View consciousness as just a name.
> A name is devoid of nature.
>
> The victors have not found [mind],
> not internally, externally,
> or between the two.
> Thus mind is of an illusory nature.
>
> Mind does not abide as something
> with the nature of a color or shape,
> as a percept or perceiver,
> as male, female, neuter or the like.
>
> In brief, the buddhas
> have never seen it and will not see it.
> How could they see something
> whose nature is to be devoid of any nature?[830]

The *Lamp That Summarizes Conduct* explains:

> The mind, about which you inquire—which is not the province of those who turn away from following the true esoteric instructions of the tathāgatas, which is difficult to really grasp, and is the province of the buddhas—is without root, without abode, without foundation, without characteristics, without color, without shape. It is beyond the sense faculties and is not an object for logicians.[831] [267]

It also says:

> In truth, mind has no color or shape, it is mere illumination, its essence is the same as space, and it is difficult to contact like ultimate truth.[832]

(D) The Way to Determine [the Essence of] Mind

It is taught that once we have investigated properly using the techniques for searching the mind (as explained above), finally we will see that mind is not something material (such that it has shape, color, and so on), that it is without abode and support, is beyond identity and manifestation, and is not veiled by conceptual elaborations. An analogy is space. There are numerous mentions of the mind being like space. The *Sūtra Teaching Great Compassion* explains:

> Mind is similar to space. It has the nature of space. It is equivalent to space.[833]

The *Sūtra of the Questions of Maitreya* says:

> "Bhagavān, how should the internal mind be viewed?"
> He replied: "Mind is devoid of shape. It is like space."[834]

The *Vairocanābhisambodhi* states:

> Mind has the characteristics of space and, therefore, it is free from thoughts and concepts.[835]

There are other similar statements, such as that by the Great Brahman [Saraha]:

> Regard the mind as being like space.
> Take the mind to be of the nature of space.[836]

The Śavara [Saraha] teaches:

> The mind whose root has been severed is just like space.[837] [268]

Although there are many ways mind resembles space, here it means that the pacification and purification into nonconceptuality of the examination process (which occurs at the end of analysis by discerning prajñā) is similar to the cessation of seeing that occurs by looking at space.[838] Tilopa teaches:

> For instance, when we look into the middle of space seeing stops.
> Similarly, when mind looks at mind,
> the masses of thoughts cease and unexcelled awakening is attained.
>
> For example, mist and clouds vanish into space.
> They go nowhere and reside nowhere.
> Similarly, when the masses of thoughts rising up in the mind
> are seen to be mind itself, the waves of thoughts vanish.[839]

He continues:

> For example, we use the term "empty" to refer to space,
> but space cannot be described as being "like this."
> Similarly, your mind is said to be luminous,
> yet there is no basis to which the expression "it exists like this" applies.
> In that way, the nature of mind is like space.[840]

The Śavara [Saraha] observes:

> Although we thoroughly investigate the realm of space,
> it has no edge and no center—and our seeing stops.
> Similarly, by thoroughly investigating mind and phenomena, [269]
> we do not find even a particle's worth of an essence.
> Since the thoroughly investigated mind is not observed,
> that not seeing of anything is seeing.[841]

The *Sūtra of the Questions of Kāśyapa* says:

> Fire springs up from the rubbing of two sticks,
> and its presence then consumes those two.
> Similarly, once the faculty of prajñā arises [from discernment]
> its presence consumes those two [prajñā and discernment].[842]

It is explained that first discerning prajñā analyzes, then, in the end, that examination process itself is pacified and nonconceptual wisdom arises.

We might now wonder, Is there any difference between mind and space? There is because it is taught that space is not reflexively aware cognition and that when mind is realized, it is reflexively aware wisdom. *Unraveling the Intent* explains:

> The sphere of intuitive reflexive awareness, beyond characteristics,
> is inexpressible and devoid of terms.
> Undisputed, it is the ultimate phenomena.
> Those are characteristics that lie beyond logicians.[843]

The *Tantra Prophesying the Intent* states:

> The definitive meaning of bodhicitta
> should be properly contemplated once again.
> It is not internal and not external.
> It is neither both nor is it changeable.
> It is not permanent and not momentary.
> It is intuitive reflexive awareness.[844] [270]

The *Two-Part [Hevajra Tantra]* remarks:

> This is wisdom, reflexively aware,
> an experiential domain beyond speech.[845]

And:

> Reflexive awareness is great bliss.
> Reflexive awareness becomes awakening.[846]

There are many more such statements.

Those teach that the nature of intuitive reflexive awareness is beyond characteristics, is inconceivable and inexpressible, unchanging bliss, the ultimate abiding state. Here, however, the meaning of "aware of itself by itself" is that once mind examines mind, it is aware of its own key point: that the primordial abiding state of that very mind is free from the elaborations of characteristics. That is simply referred to with the term "reflexive awareness," but it is not that something to be identified exists and then we are aware of it as an object of awareness, the way eyes are aware of a form. As Tilopa states:

> KYE HO. This is reflexively aware wisdom.
> Beyond the realm of speech, it's not the province of mentation.
> I, Tilo, have nothing to teach.
> Know that it reveals itself.[847]

At this point, the uneducated may assume that when their mind looks at mind and a previous śamatha samādhi arises that experience is one of seeing mind. [271] Others may take any of the forms appearing [in their meditation], which [arise from] their latent tendencies, to be solid and assume that is seeing the mind. Some deliberately recreate experiences of the mind's clarity or of its emptiness and presume that is seeing the mind. They are all quite wrong because, without any real certainty that the abiding mode of mind is free from the elaborations of characteristics, they cling to meditative experiences arising from various fleeting causes and conditions.

Thus the term "seeing mind" is used for being aware of the key point that mind-itself is primordially free from all conceptually elaborated extremes. There is, however, no seeing or observation of someone seeing or something seen that is identifiable—not even a hair tip's worth. Actually, this transcends the objects of speech or thought. It has a nature that is unchanging at all times, as the following quotations demonstrate. The *Verses That Summarize the Prajñāpāramitā Sūtras* states:

> Sentient beings say, "I see space."
> Yet how is space seen? Examine this matter.
> The Tathāgata taught that that is how to see phenomena.[848]

The Great Brahman [Saraha] says:

> Look and look at the primordially pure nature of space,
> and seeing ceases.[849]

The Śavara [Saraha] concurs:

> When we search for mind and what appear as phenomena,
> nothing is found—there isn't even a searcher. [272]

What is nonexistent neither arises nor ceases in the three times.
It doesn't become something else.
It's the abiding state of natural great bliss.[850]

He also says:

I see myself: I am alone.
When I look at aloneness, I do not see aloneness.
With nothing to see and no seer, there's nothing to describe.
With nothing to describe, who is there to understand?[851]

Nāropa declares:

The mind, natural luminosity,
hasn't even a hair tip's worth of existence.[852]

Nevertheless, for beginners such indescribable experiences may occur as mindful awareness accompanied by certainty, as it is explained. The *Sūtra of Genuine Samādhi* says:

In dharmatā, just as it is,
so rests mind that is just like it.
Experience unhindered by words dawns.[853]

Tilopa observes:

Dharmatā, free from elaborations,
is experienced as sudden mindful awareness.[854]

Maitrīpa explains:

Mind is simply the currents of mindful awareness,
the expressive power of wind without any nature.[855] [273]

iii) Determining the Essence of Thoughts and Appearances, [Mind's] Expressive Power

This has three parts:
(A) Appearances Are Shown to Be Mind

(B) The Way Appearances Are Realized Once Mind Is Realized
(C) The Explanation of the Objects for the Stages of Meditation

(A) Appearances Are Shown to Be Mind

Those of us who do not understand the suchness of mind mistake thoughts and appearances (such as forms and sounds)—which manifest as the expressive power of mind—to exist objectively as things other than mind. And yet ultimately they are only our own mind. The *Descent into Laṅkā* explains:

> Linked to the latent tendencies of concepts,
> myriad things arise from mind.
> The external appearances [manifesting] to people
> are merely the mind of worldly ones.
>
> Those nonexistent external appearances
> are mind arising as various things.[856]

The *Vajra Pañjarā* states:

> The entities that arise as forms, sounds,
> smells, tastes, and tangible objects
> are here said to be the precious mind.
> They are pacified in the dharmadhātu.
>
> Forms, feelings, discriminations,
> formative forces, and consciousnesses
> were not said by the Muni to be
> anything other than entities of mind.[857]

In that case, we may ask, How is it that external entities, forms and so forth, appear? When the mind itself is unaware of, and unable to fathom, its own abiding state, it perceives a duality of self and other. By conceptualizing those perceptions we amass latent tendencies and, from those, the seeming external referents appear to our mistaken perspective. [274] The *Descent into Laṅkā* teaches:

> The mind disturbed by latent tendencies
> appears as referents.

> There are no existent referents, just mind.
> Seeing external referents is mistaken.[858]

The *Vajra Pañjarā* concurs:

> Throughout beginningless existence
> external referents have been imagined.
> All are projections of mind
> and are always mind-itself.[859]

We may now ask, Why is it that things not only appear to be external, they also seem to exist objectively as entities that are solid, hard, and so forth? When we become habituated to massive amounts of mistaken latent tendencies and they become rigid, there seem to be external entities that are objectively solid, hard, and so forth. The Great Brahman [Saraha] explains this using an analogy:

> When wind hits water and whips it up,
> even soft water can turn to stone.
> When whipped up by thoughts,
> formless confusion can become solid and hard.[860]

It is not possible that what just appears for a mistaken perspective is real. This is like the case of the floaters and visual distortions perceived by those with eye ailments. Although floaters and the like seem to be direct [or actual] perceptions for those with eye ailments, they do not appear to those with healthy eyes.

Next we may ask, Do those who know the abiding state of mind not [experience] external appearances? No, that is not the case. [275] As long as they have not nullified their shared karma and latent tendencies, which are like eye ailments, simply knowing the mistaken state and the abiding state of mind, which is analogous to knowing the problems of eye ailments, cannot cancel appearances. Virūpa teaches:

> When we don't remain in a state of realization and are distracted by the process of characterizing,
> we can't cancel our latent tendencies for dualistic appearances and characteristics.

> Those with a visual impairment may know they have an eye disease but, until their eye disease is cured, they can't cancel the appearances of that visual impairment.[861]

Nevertheless, it is explained that once we correctly realize the abiding state of mind, all appearances arise indivisibly with the nature of mind while manifesting unimpededly in their own appearing mode. The *Vajra Pañjarā* says:

> There is nothing outside of mind.
> All that appears individually—forms and so forth—
> are only appearances of this mind.[862]

The *Commentary on Bodhicitta* explains:

> The imagined, the dependent,
> and the consummate
> have but one nature: emptiness.
> They are imputations in the mind.[863] [276]

(B) The Way Appearances Are Realized Once Mind Is Realized

The Great Brahman [Saraha] explains that the root of all existence and peace is mind-itself:

> Mind-itself alone is the seed of everything:
> it radiates existence and nirvāṇa.[864]

He also explains that everything that radiates, or arises, from the mind is of nature of mind:

> Whatever radiates from mind
> is necessarily of the nature of the protector.
> Are water and waves different?
> Existence and equality are of the nature of space.[865]

The [Prajñāpāramitā] sūtras teach that the nature of mind is luminosity-emptiness:

> The mind is not mind: the nature of mind is luminosity.[866]

Consequently, when the essence of mind is realized to be emptiness, the essence of appearances will automatically be realized to be emptiness, as the sūtras say:

> When you know the thusness of one phenomenon, you know the thusness of all phenomena.[867]

Āryadeva echoes this:

> Those who see the thusness of one entity
> see the thusness of all entities.[868] [277]

Another way of saying this is found in the *Four Hundred Verses*:

> Whoever sees one entity
> is said to see all.
> The emptiness of one
> is the emptiness of all.[869]

It is explained that someone who analyzes, or sees, the nature of one entity, such as forms, is the same as someone who analyzes, or sees, the nature of all other entities, such as sounds. Similarly, the emptiness that is one entity (such as a form) being empty of a nature is the emptiness that is all other entities (such as sounds) being empty of nature. The Lord [Atīśa] says in the *[Entrance to] the Two Truths*:

> In emptiness there is
> no differentiation at all.[870]

Therefore, we should understand that applying the aforementioned reasonings, which determine the essence of mind using examination and analysis, is a way to determine the essence of all appearances. The *King of Samādhi* teaches:

> In the same way that you understand perceptions of a self,
> apply your mind similarly to everything else.
> The essence of all phenomena
> is purity like space.
>
> Through one, all is known.
> Through one, all is seen.[871]

In keeping with the teaching that knowing and seeing the abiding mode of one thing is to know and see the abiding mode of all phenomena, this practice lineage uses the aphorism "knowing one liberates all." [278]

Nevertheless, at this point when we determine the essence of appearances, emptiness—which is that the essence, or nature, of appearances is they do not exist as anything at all—must arise inseparably with the appearing mode of appearances, their unceasing manifestation. The *Commentary on Bodhicitta* states:

> Just as sweetness is the nature of molasses
> and warmth is that of fire,
> so too is emptiness asserted to be
> the nature of all phenomena.[872]

It also says:

> The conventional is taught to be emptiness,
> and emptiness itself is the conventional
> because one does not occur without [the other],
> like being produced and impermanent.[873]

(C) The Explanation of the Objects for the Stages of Meditation

At this point, the determination of [the nature of] thoughts and appearances is similar to the determination of the lack of self-entity of phenomena found in the Sūtra context. Although thoughts, which are mental events, are mental appearances, to facilitate an ease of understanding they will be examined and analyzed separately [from appearances].

First: determining thoughts. Adopt the essential points for body and the gazes as explained above. For a short time, rest evenly in clarity and emptiness, free from identification, without being distracted for an instant. [279] Within that state, a strong, clearly evident, coarse thought, such as an angry thought, may arise or you should provoke one. As soon as it pops up, look directly at it. Examine and analyze that thought repeatedly and systematically as explained before: What is its color and shape? What is its abode and support? Is its essence something that can be identified or does it have a manifestation?

If thoughts do not arise, there are no objects to examine and analyze. Therefore, allow a little distraction. Think about the harm someone, such as an enemy, may have done to you, and give rise to angry thoughts. Examine them. Using that model, examine other kinds of coarse thoughts. For example, generate thoughts involving desire for objects of attraction and look at them. Similarly, examine any type of subtle conceptual manifestation that arises or that you cause to arise.

By doing that, it is easy to recognize that subtle and coarse thoughts do not have a specific color, shape, abode, support, and so forth. If that then leads to a nonconceptual mind, a state of clarity-emptiness, that very thought will be self-purified and your mind will be drawn into equipoise. However, since that won't really sever your misinterpretations about thoughts, you must examine the manifestations of thoughts while they are unceasing and clear.

When a thought (any thought) is not blocked or does not vanish, it is clear and at the same time no reification of an object of thought is aroused, which is somewhat unlike your previous normal thoughts.[874] It is hard to identify its essence, saying, "It's like this." You need to feel certainty right within your experience. When you do, the experience relevant to this phase has developed: you have determined [the nature of] thoughts. Then, no matter what thought arises, subtle or coarse, continue to meditate undistractedly on thoughts while they are clear and yet unidentifiable. [280]

Next: determining appearances. The exalted Dakpo [Gampopa] taught that all manifestations of mind—whatever thoughts and appearances involving percepts and perceivers arise—are all included with the category of appearances. Nevertheless, to make this easy to understand, in this context the term "appearances" is used for what appears to the six modes of consciousness, that is, forms and the like, which are perceived objects. Those are what are to be analyzed and examined.

Appearances—what arise when the five sense faculties (such as the eyes) connect with the five objects (such as forms), which consist of karma and latent tendencies—are known to ordinary people as direct [experiences]. Specifically, they are the inevitable shared appearances for the sense consciousnesses and seem to be objectively existent with their own features, such as color and shape. That being so, here we do not break down those appearances of external objects (such as forms) into particles, directions, and the like, and do not examine and analyze that they lack any nature. Since it is said that once we determine [the nature of] the perceiving mind, the fetters of perceived objects are self-liberated, now the object of analysis is primarily the mind that is the perceiver of appearances.

As before, with your mind in a state of clarity-emptiness, cause an appearance of a form to arise vividly. When it does, carefully examine the mind perceiving that in terms of its color and shape, abode and support, identity and manifestation, as previously explained. Using the analysis of forms as the pattern, examine the perceiver of sounds, smells, and so forth. Similarly, examine and analyze the perceiver of whatever occurs or whatever you cause to occur: specific beings or things that are part of your environment, mental afflictions (such as attachment or aggression), and any other kind of subtle or coarse manifestation, including happiness or sadness. [281]

During that examination, the appearing manifestations may cease or disappear, subsiding into mind's clarity-emptiness. Then mental manifestations and perceiving thoughts may also subside and become equipoise. However, since that won't create certainty about appearances and the perceiver of appearances, you must again examine and analyze the perceiver of appearances right within appearances, whatever they may be.

In brief, while an appearance (any appearance) manifests unceasingly, the mind perceiving it arises as emptiness without any nature or identity. When that happens and you experience appearances devoid of fixation as amorphous and difficult to describe, a small degree of experience relevant to this phase has developed. Then, continue to meditate on whatever subtle or coarse appearances occur as being empty appearances, appearing yet lacking any nature.

In some instructional traditions the various ways to investigate the mind are only methods that lead to a nonconceptual mind with its clarity-awareness. They do not examine and analyze [mind] right with its movements and appearances. These can be seen as somewhat rudimentary because their practice causes most types of minds to be comfortable meditating when the mind is still but to be uncomfortable meditating with its movements and appearances.

Similarly, it is the case that by looking [at mind] right with its movements and appearances a few beginners are able to do what is called "collapse that and arrive at clarity-emptiness." Others, however, simply draw thoughts and appearances into a state of meditative equipoise through mindfulness. That is not integrating thoughts and appearances into the path through having determined [their nature]. These are distinctions we must understand. [282]

b) Eliminating Misinterpretations About a Root or Basis

This has three parts:

i) Concluding That Thoughts and Appearances Are Mind-Itself
ii) Cutting Through the Roots of Stillness and Movement Within Mind-Itself
iii) Concluding That Everything That Arises Is Unborn

i) Concluding That Thoughts and Appearances Are Mind-Itself

We may wonder, What is the difference between the previous determination of thoughts and appearances and this section? The above examination was an analysis of the essence of thoughts and appearances in terms of color, shape, and so forth that [resulted in] understanding their lack of any nature. Here, by analyzing the origin, abiding, and departure of thoughts and appearances, we come to understand that they are inseparable from the essence of mind. Here, as before, the examination and analysis is done with precision and point by point.

First: concluding that thoughts are mind-itself. Rest your mind evenly in a state of clarity-emptiness. Once a thought, such as one of anger, arises from that state or is triggered, analyze its origin, abiding, and departure. First, look at whether that thought has a foundation or cause from which it arises. If you cannot find another place of origin and you think that it arises from mind-itself, look at that: Is it arising as something self-sustaining, like a child born from a mother? Does it arise as mind's own expressive power, like light radiating from the sun or moon? Or is it that mind-itself became the thought?

In the middle, looking at how a thought resides. If you cannot discover another mode of abiding but think there does appear to be a manifestation of anger, look at that. Does that anger appear with a strongly motivated sense of reification? Or does it seem to be just the plain thought: there is a manifestation that looks like anger but there's nothing that can be precisely identified as its essence? [283]

In the end, examine how it departs. If you think that even though you cannot locate a place where it goes, it does become nonexistent, does that thought become nonexistent upon being blocked or does it become so upon vanishing? If it is through being blocked, who blocked it or what conditions caused it to cease? If it is by vanishing, does it vanish due to conditions or by itself? Using that as the model, carefully examine and analyze all other thoughts, subtle and coarse.

Then, specifically give rise to two contradictory thoughts, such as a happy one and a sad one. By examining the manifestations and essences of each of those, in the end you should see whether they differ in terms of their essences, such as one being positive and the other negative.

Examining in that manner, you may not find anything consistent with an origin, abiding, or departure of thoughts. The intellect that takes thoughts and mind to be dual—as being separate, external and internal, or like a body and its limbs—collapses. No matter how thoughts manifest, experience them as empty clarity without an identifiable essence, and know that mind-itself and thoughts are inseparable like water and waves. Waves are nothing but water. Water itself arises as waves and yet, despite manifesting as waves, it is never anything other than the essence of water. Analogously, every thought is, at the very moment that it arises, nothing but mind-itself, empty clarity. Since mind-itself is unimpeded in its manifestations, it can arise as any type of thought.[875] However, even though it arises as those, mind-itself—which has no identifiable essence—is not other than empty clarity. This is what you must conclude.

Next: concluding that appearances are mind-itself. Rest as before in a state of equipoise. [284] Cause something, such as an appearance of a form, to manifest vividly. First examine its origin, abiding, and departure as you did above. Then look to see if the appearing form and the mind are different or are identical. If they are different, examine that difference: are they mutually related, such as one being external and the other internal, or one being above and the other below? If they are that way, look to see if they exist with two separate, independent essences, or if it is that the mind is simply manifesting as appearing forms. If it is that the mind is simply manifesting as physical appearances, since there is only one mind, examine how [mind and appearances] cannot be separate.

If appearing forms and mind are identical, carefully examine that sameness: is it that they are the same once mind goes to an appearing form, or is it that they are the same once a physical form goes to the mind? Using that as the model, examine other kinds of coarse or subtle appearances, such as those of sounds and smells. Particularly, provoke two opposing kinds of appearances, such as a beautiful one and an ugly one, or a pleasant sound and an unpleasant sound. Examine the manifestations and essences of those two. In the end, see whether there is any difference in terms of their essences, such as one being positive and the other negative.

Examining that way destroys any dualistic perception you may have about appearances and mind-itself, such as that they are discrete external and internal entities or separate mutually related things. No matter how appearances manifest, experience them as empty appearances with no identifiable essence, and know that mind-itself and appearances are inseparable like the dreaming mind and dream appearances. In a dream, various external appearances arise and yet they are nothing but the dreaming consciousness. Dream appearances and the dreaming consciousness are undifferentiable. Analogously, external appearances, regardless of how they appear, are at the very moment they appear nothing but the unimpeded manifestations of mind-itself. Know that all the myriad appearances are indivisible from your own mind-itself. [285] Thus, not intentionally severing appearances and not setting mind-itself apart as something internal, conclude that appearances and mind are not a duality.

Nevertheless, as long as we have shared karma and impure latent tendencies, we cannot counteract the arising of shared appearances from mere consciousness, occurring through the interdependence of objects, sense faculties, and consciousnesses (and which themselves are part of that [shared karma and impure latent tendencies]). It is explained that eradicating misinterpretations about appearances and mind, being free from hopes and fears in relation to appearances, and mixing appearances and mind occur during the level of greater one taste. Therefore, here I have simply presented what is relevant in this context.

ii) Cutting Through the Roots of Stillness and Movement Within Mind-Itself

As before, rest your mind evenly in clarity-emptiness. In that state, look with your discerning prajñā directly at that nonconceptual, quiet stillness. Examine its origin, abiding, and departure as you did previously. Next, cause a thought, any type of thought, to arise suddenly and examine that as before. You won't find that either the stillness or the thought have any origin, abiding, or departure, or something that can be identified as their essence. Nevertheless, there may be a difference between quiet stillness and rippling movements in your meditation experience. Again, examine those two to see what differences there may be in terms of whether they do or don't have an identifiable essence, they are empty or not empty, are positive or negative, and so forth.

When you don't find that they have any such differences, look at your understanding of their lack of difference: Is it that stillness and movement have no difference because they are identical? Or is that they are not different because their manifestations are similar despite being separate? [286] If they are identical, look to see if they are identical in the beginning, the middle, or the end. If they are similar manifestations, carefully examine how they are similar. This will overturn any belief that the continua of stillness and movement are separate.

This is not only [true] for stillness and movement: all that is experienced is the one mind-itself. If you look, you will experience one taste, what is called reflexive awareness in which any variation can occur while nothing is being identified. Know that [stillness and movement] are the natural expression of the mind-itself, like the relationship between water and waves or the sun and its light. Conclude that regardless which occurs, stillness or movement, neither needs to be blocked or encouraged, rejected or adopted. Be certain that when mind is still or when it moves, right within that stillness or that movement your mind is clarity-emptiness, reflexively aware, reflexively clear, self-arising, and self-liberating.

We may ask, While stillness and movement are identical in being of the essence of mind, how is it that causes and conditions give rise to the specific experiences of stillness and movement? On the basis of the latent tendencies of karma and mental afflictions or on the basis of our body that is [the result of] maturation and appropriation, various experiences occur due to the radiance of the moving winds in our body and the interdependent connections between objects, sense faculties, and consciousnesses. The Great Brahman [Saraha] states:

> Mentation is gathered, and the coursing of winds
> moves and surges, causing wildness.[876]

Maitrīpa comments:

> Mind is simply the currents of mindful awareness,
> the expressive power of wind without any nature.[877] [287]

It is explained that in the same way that insentient sticks floating on the ocean are moved by waves, when the ālaya consciousness is based on the body, it is moved by the coursing of winds and, when it is not based on the body, it is intuitive reflexive awareness. The *Commentary on Bodhicitta* teaches:

> Just as sticks move on the ocean
> though they have no mind,
> the ālaya consciousness moves
> in relation to the body.
>
> When it is thought that without a body
> there is no consciousness
> that [shows there is] intuitive reflexive awareness.[878]

At this point, [we will look at] the topic of the single essence of stillness and movement. Some assert that there is no movement during stillness and that there is no stillness during movement. Others maintain that by looking at movement it vanishes and becomes stillness. Most assert that the recognition of movement occurs within stillness and that stillness establishes itself within movement. The first position is incorrect because other than simply knowing that the single mind is sometimes still and sometimes moving, they do not seem to have conviction that [mind] is fundamentally singular. The second assertion is wrong because it seems that they just stop movements without having determined their essence. The third view is slightly wrong because they just leave it that recognition within stillness is movement and movement without identification is stillness, and they aren't clear about how [stillness and movement] are of one essence.

We may then ask, How are [we to understand the single essence of stillness and movement]? In this context, as determined above, the analogy of water and waves shows that it must be that stillness and movement are of one taste in being empty of any nature with no identifiable essence, and yet they appear as separate in terms of what we experience. [288] As the Great Brahman [Saraha] declares:

> Just as calm water whipped up by winds
> can become roiling waves,
> so the King regards Saraha
> in many ways even though he is just one [man].[879]

We should understand from later explanations how it is that right within awareness, stillness and movement are designated as being identical in essence but discrete isolates.*

iii) Concluding That Everything That Arises Is Unborn

As before, with your mind in a state of clarity-emptiness, examine mind using mind itself. The arising of thoughts or various appearances is simply the expressive power of this mind-itself. Now look directly at what is simply labeled "mind," thinking, "What is its basic state, its abiding state, like?"

First, examine and analyze the causes from which mind arises. Since there are no causes from which it arises, no conditions that produce it, no artisan or agent who creates it, you conclude that it does not arise from causes and conditions, that it is groundless, free from a root, primordially unborn.

In the middle, examine the way mind abides. Since it does not have even a hair tip's worth of existence—such as having a shape or color, abode or support, identity or manifestation—you conclude that it has no location at all, nothing about which you could say, "Its mode of abiding is like this." [289]

In the end, examine how mind departs. Since there is no place it goes or trail left behind and no one able to end it or stop its manifestations, you conclude that it does not perish or terminate.

Furthermore, if this mind-itself is something in the past, it has necessarily ceased or been destroyed. If it is something in the future, it has not yet arisen or emerged. If it is something in the present, it must be something that can be identified. Thus, since it cannot be analyzed as something present in one of the three times, it is free from the extreme of being existent. However, despite not existing as something, it can arise as anything, and it is the root of saṃsāra and nirvāṇa. Therefore it is free from the extreme of not existing. Since it does not exist as an entity or characteristics, no analogy can fully illustrate it, such that we could say, "It is this." Since in the beginning it is not produced by causes, it is unborn. Now it is free from all identification and, therefore, does not abide. In the end, because it does not go anywhere and its manifestations are unceasing, it does not end. Since it does not emerge from causes, it is not destroyed by conditions. Since it does not appear just randomly, it is constant. Since it is free from arising, abiding, and ceasing, it is continuous. Since—realized or not—it is neither good nor bad, it does not fluctuate. It is present in all who do not recognize it, and thus it is neither

*See "Looking at the Essence of Thoughts and Appearances," pp. 386–88.

attained nor lost. Always unchanging, it does not diminish. In that way, by examining and analyzing the unborn nature with discerning prajñā, you analyze [rigorously, like] pulverizing bones with a rock, your experience of cutting through a root or basis and of the basic nature of mind-itself.

It is explained that through such analysis you will experience the abiding state of mind, which is beyond conception and description. In the end, even discernment, which is what does the analyzing, will be self-pacified, dissolving into itself. Nonconceptual wisdom will dawn. The Great Brahman [Saraha] observes: [290]

> Look and look at the primordially pure nature of space,
> and seeing ceases.[880]

He also says:

> If mind reveals mind,
> thoughts do not stir, and it remains firm.
> Just as salt dissolves in water,
> so mind dissolves into its nature.[881]

This approach to examining how the mind is unborn is taught in many texts of both Sūtra and Mantra, such as the following. The middle *Stages of Meditation* explains:

> Therefore, when you discern the nature of mind with prajñā, ultimately you neither observe the mind to be internal nor do you observe it to be external. You do not observe it to be neither of those two. You do not observe a past mind, a future mind, and not even a present one. When the mind arises, it does not come from anywhere. When it ceases, it does not go anywhere. The mind is not graspable. It cannot be shown, and it does not have form.[882]

It continues with a quotation from [the *Discourse for Kāśyapa*] in the Heap of Jewels:

> Kāśyapa, when you look for mind it is not found. What cannot be found cannot be observed. What cannot be observed is neither past, nor future, nor present. What is not past, not future,

> and not present has no essence. What has no essence cannot emerge. What does not emerge cannot cease.[883]

The *Sūtra of the King of the Genuine Dharma* states:

> "Child of good family, if you desire freedom and liberation, cut off the sense pleasures. Do not contemplate mind as a duality—contemplate it as singular. [291] The mind that is thought to exist is empty. The essence of mind is emptiness. It has no departure, no letting go, and no attainment. Its name is awakening."
>
> [The Buddha] was asked: "If the discriminations of the mind are inconceivable, how is it that there is no departure, no letting go, and no attainment?"
>
> [The Buddha] replied: "When those who abide internally in unified meditative concentration look internally and examine internally, [they see] that the true essence is unborn."[884]

The *Sūtra on Holding the Genuine Dharma* teaches:

> Therefore, know the mind
> to be fallacious, hollow, and not existent.
> Do not take it to have a core.
> It is empty of any essence.
>
> Phenomena empty of an essence
> do not exist.
> Examining phenomena
> reveals their nature to be thus.
>
> Quashing the two extremes,
> the wise scrutinize the middle.
>
> That phenomena are empty of an essence
> is the path to awakening.
> This is what I teach.[885] [292]

5) The Differences between Vipaśyanā Developing or Not Developing

In all contexts of cultivating vipaśyanā, we analyze with discerning prajñā. Some who overemphasize the stillness of śamatha never gain confidence in the object of analysis no matter how much they analyze. Whenever they analyze, a śamatha samādhi arises. They become certain that the point of all analysis comes down to just that, and they mistake that to be seeing the essence [of mind]. Others who overemphasize emptiness during śamatha mistake experiences of the emptiness that is phenomena's lack of any essence to be seeing the essence [of mind]. Such meditators should from time to time use the methods for dispelling the experiences of śamatha and any clinging to them. Once they disperse the dankness of those experiences and again cultivate vipaśyanā, they will achieve their aim. Some of lower intelligence and strong karmic obscurations, however, will not see the essence [of mind] no matter how much they analyze. They should spend some time applying themselves to the methods for amassing [merit and wisdom] and purifying [obscurations]. Once they have aroused the sharp clarity of śamatha and practiced sustaining that, then at some point they [will be ready to] cultivate vipaśyanā.

On the other hand, some highly intelligent people may have an excellent understanding, which is an abstract idea, and presume they have developed [meditative] experience. Those who have heard [or studied] a lot may be eloquent but lack [meditative] experiences. Other types may not have the words to express themselves but, having developed experiences appropriate to their phase, they will give rise to conviction right within the essence [of mind].

It is very important to differentiate between such practitioners because meditation in which vipaśyanā has not developed, no matter how excellent it may be, is only a mundane meditation common to both tīrthikas and Buddhists. Since it will not even lead to Hīnayāna meditation, what need is there to mention [its chances of] becoming a Mahāyāna madhyamaka meditation or, more specifically, a mahāmudrā meditation? For those reasons, it is crucial that we apply ourselves to cultivating vipaśyanā. [293]

We might wonder, What are the criteria for determining whether vipaśyanā has developed or not? Genuine vipaśyanā, which directly realizes the truth of dharmatā, does not arise before the level of greater freedom from elaborations. Here [we are discussing] only the vipaśyanā that occurs within the sphere of ordinary beings' minds. This is analogous to referring to the moon on the first lunar day as the "moon" even though it does not possess all the features of the full moon.

Therefore, in this context what must be considered vipaśyanā is an awareness of the key point that our own mind, and thoughts and appearances, which arise as its expressive power (as discussed above)—in brief, all phenomena, what are perceived and are perceivers—are ultimately without arising, cessation, or abiding. It is also to discover from within experience, and with certainty, that all such phenomena lack any essence or nature. The relevant scriptural citations have been presented and more will follow.

Some may not develop even that [degree of vipaśyanā]. The gurus of this practice lineage teach that the vipaśyanā of a beginner is to develop the experience in which our own mind is confident that it is empty—its essence is free from identification—and that it is reflexively aware, reflexively clear. By cultivating just that to begin with, genuine vipaśyanā will gradually arise.

The criteria for achieving vipaśyanā. In the Sūtra context, it is taught that śamatha suppleness is achieved first and that when, on top of that, suppleness arises through the force of vipaśyanā meditation, that is authentic vipaśyanā. Any vipaśyanā prior to that is considered an approximation of vipaśyanā. Here, however, there is no such definitiveness because we find in most esoteric instruction traditions that the one-pointed mind that has not achieved suppleness is considered śamatha and that all types of analysis that are part of a vipaśyanā that has not achieved suppleness are considered to belong to vipaśyanā. [294] It is also relevant in this context to include the divisions of vipaśyanā within vipaśyanā since it is taught that its divisions are either as four types (such as the differentiation of phenomena) or three types (such as that which arises from characteristics).

The *Śrāvakabhūmi* explains that the four types of attention described in the context of śamatha are also present in vipaśyanā.[886] That being the case, there is no contradiction in considering the achievement of vipaśyanā to begin with the attention that engages uninterruptedly during vipaśyanā, because that is the attainment of engaging uninterruptedly in vipaśyanā.

Nevertheless, since there seem to be many different presentations in the sūtras, Mantra [texts], and esoteric instructions about the way śamatha and vipaśyanā are practiced, are identified, and are united, here the explanation emphasizes the approach of the esoteric instructions.

6) Correlating This Vipaśyanā with Other Approaches

A correlation [of the vipaśyanā presented here] with the explanation of the four types of vipaśyanā, such as the differentiation of phenomena, found in *Unraveling the Intent*[887] and elsewhere, is as follows:

- Here, our focus on the quantitative aspect of the phenomena of percepts and perceivers, which are included within the thoughts and appearances arising as the mind's expressive power, is the vipaśyanā that differentiates phenomena because, by focusing on all phenomena—that is, the quantitativeness of all knowable objects—they are differentiated.
- Our focus on all things that are perceived or are perceivers as lacking an essence of their own is the vipaśyanā that differentiates thoroughly because, by focusing on the qualitativeness of knowable objects, they are differentiated. [295]
- Our discernment of those two [the quantitative and the qualitative aspects] with an apprehension of their characteristics is the vipaśyanā that discerns completely because discerning coarse qualitativeness and quantitativeness along with an apprehension of their characteristics is discernment.
- Our careful analysis of those two [the quantitative and the qualitative aspects] is the vipaśyanā that analyzes completely because it is the correct analysis of the most subtle aspects of qualitativeness and quantitativeness.

The *Śrāvakabhūmi* teaches:

> How is differentiation done? Differentiation is conducted with the quantitative aspects of the objects of meditation for purifying behavior, the objects of meditation for expertise, and the objects of meditation for purifying mental afflictions. Thorough differentiation is conducted with the qualitative aspect [of those three objects].
>
> When attention endowed with prajñā joins with discernment to apprehend the characteristics [of those three objects], that is complete discernment. When there is correct discernment, that is complete analysis.[888]

A correlation [of the vipaśyanā presented here] with the explanation of the three types of vipaśyanā, such as that which arises from characteristics, found in *Unraveling the Intent,* is as follows:

- Here, the way we discern the objects of vipaśyanā is the vipaśyanā that arises from characteristics because that only brings to mind conceptual representations as the objects of vipaśyanā.
- The way we understand that all such [phenomena] lack an essence is the vipaśyanā that arises from thorough investigation because it is the attention comprehending an object of understanding that was not previously understood.
- The way we attain and become familiar with the liberation in which all phenomena lack an essence is the vipaśyanā that arises from discernment because, by realizing the abiding state of phenomena with our discerning prajñā, we feel true bliss through liberation and become familiar with that. [296]

Unraveling the Intent explains:

> What is the vipaśyanā that arises from characteristics? It is that which only brings to mind a conceptual representation for its sphere of samādhi.
>
> What is the vipaśyanā that arises from thorough investigation? It is that which brings to mind dharma topics that were not well understood by the prajñā [that was directed] at them, in order that such [topics] be understood.
>
> What is the vipaśyanā that arises from discernment? It is that which brings to mind dharma topics that were well understood by the prajñā [that was directed] at them, in order that [bodhisattvas] may feel bliss through liberation.[889]

Although those classifications of vipaśyanā are listed in the sūtras and *Unraveling the Intent,* the texts on the stages of meditation do not explain the way to determine each of them specifically. However, since their key points are contained within the determination of the two absences of self-entity and that approach is well known in the Sūtra context in both India and Tibet, those [two absences of self-entity] will be correlated with [the vipaśyanā presented here] as follows.

Here, the way the essence of mind is determined is similar to the way the absence of a self of persons is determined in the Sūtra context. In the Sūtra context, the person is considered to be what holds the continua of the skandhas with awareness. [Belief in] a self of persons is that that ["person"] takes itself to be permanent and singular, and believes itself to be "I" and "me." [Recognition of] the absence of a self of persons is to know that to be without any nature. [297] Here, what holds itself to be permanent and singular, and believes itself to be "I" and "me," is the mind itself. We determine that to be without any nature.

The way [the natures of] thoughts and appearances are determined is similar to the way that the absence of a self-entity of phenomena is determined in the Sūtra context. In the Sūtra context, phenomena [in this instance] refers to the skandhas, dhātus, and so forth that are imagined by the self of persons. [Belief in] a self-entity of phenomena is to believe those to be objectively existent things. [Recognition of] the absence of a self-entity of phenomena is to know those to be without any nature. Here we determine all objectively existent appearances—the mental events imagined by the mind itself and external forms, sounds, and so forth—to be without any nature.

Despite those similarities, the sequence of how [the nature of] objects and perceiving subjects are determined is different. In the Sūtra context, it is taught that without first determining [the nature of] objects (what are perceived), [the nature of] the mind (the perceiving subject) will not be determined. As Dharmakīrti observes:

> Without invalidating the object
> it is impossible to eliminate it.[890]

Āryadeva adds:

> When you see that the object has no self-entity,
> the seed of existence is destroyed.[891]

Here it is thought that approaching it that way makes determining [the nature of] the perceiving mind later on much harder, whereas determining the perceiving mind first makes it easy to determine perceived objects—it will be as if they are self-liberating. [298] It is analogous to the way that cutting the root of a tree causes its branches and leaves to wither, as taught by Tilopa.* This is what appears in all the instructions on the ultimate essence.

That completes the explanation of the instructions in vipaśyanā. [299]

*See the citation on p. 221.

10

Pointing-Out Instructions

ii. The Process of the Pointing-Out [Instructions] in Spiritual Practice

This has three parts:

A) First: The Presentation of What Is to Be Ascertained
B) The Actual Pointing Out of Connateness
C) Eliminating Flaws and Identifying the Point of the Meditation

A) First: The Presentation of What Is to Be Ascertained

This has two sections:

1) Determining the Abiding State of Mind
2) Ascertaining Connateness

1) Determining the Abiding State of Mind

This has three divisions:

a) The Essence of Mind
b) The Nature of Mind
c) The Characteristic of Mind

a) The Essence of Mind

Generally speaking, although the three terms "essence," "nature," and "characteristic," or "manifestation," are used for the abiding mode of mind, actually there is nothing other than the very essence of mind, as the *Kernels of Esoteric Instructions* states:

> The essence, which is the emptiness of all entities, is referred to as "nature" and "manifestation." It has no meaning other than that of "own essence."[892]

However, if [mind] is classified in terms of its isolates, it is divided into essence, nature, and characteristic, and those are individually identified. The exalted Gampopa explains:

> Among the essence, nature, and characteristic of mind, its essence is that it is clear yet nonconceptual. Its nature is that it is free from arising, abiding, and ceasing. Its characteristic is that it appears as both saṃsāra and nirvāṇa.[893]

He also states:

> There is an essence, nature, and characteristic of mind. What is called the nature of mind is its natural purity, what is unconditioned pervading saṃsāra and nirvāṇa. What is called the essence of mind is its unborn and unceasing awareness. What is known as the characteristic of mind is its appearances as the various representations of latent tendencies.[894]

The exalted Pakmo Drupa teaches: [300]

> Nondual mahāmudrā
> has three [aspects]: a characteristic, an essence, and a nature.
> Its nature is its clarity with unimpeded understanding.
> Its essence is its freedom from the elaborations of arising and cessation.
> Its characteristic is to appear as the many of saṃsāra and nirvāṇa.[895]

Thus, in actuality, mind's essence and nature are taught to have similar qualities.

Its manifestation is in keeping with its characteristic. As the exalted Rangjung Dorje says:

> It is empty in essence yet clear in nature,
> and its manifestations appear unimpededly as anything at all.[896]

The essence of mind. From the outset [the essence of mind] is free from all entities that arise, abide, and cease. It is not veiled by notions of percepts and perceivers, such as the skandhas, dhātus, and āyatanas. It abides as natural emptiness, which is a state of equality devoid of self: the essence of all phenomena. The *Guhyasamāja* says:

> Since it is free from all entities,
> devoid of skandhas, dhātus, āyatanas,
> percepts, and perceivers,
> it is equality in which a self-entity of phenomena is absent.
> Your own mind never arises:
> it is of the nature of emptiness.[897]

The *Commentary on Bodhicitta* explains:

> The buddhas maintain
> bodhicitta is not obscured
> by notions of self, skandhas, or consciousness.
> It is always characterized by emptiness.[898]

Therefore, as explained previously, when we analyze and investigate the essence of the mind in various ways, we do not find any existent instantiation, and the conceptual elaborations of the mind that is the searcher are also self-pacified, self-exhausted. [301] This is said to be the ultimate, the primordially present dharmatā—emptiness—as the *Entrance to the Two Truths* observes:

> If what appears as the conventional
> is examined with reasonings, nothing is found.
> That very not finding is the ultimate:
> primordially present dharmatā.[899]

The emptiness that is the essence of mind is also the emptiness that is the essence of all phenomena contained within saṃsāra and nirvāṇa (all possible appearances), as Āryadeva teaches:

> One entity has the essence of all entities.
> All entities have the essence of one entity.[900]

The *Four Hundred Verses* says:

> The emptiness of one
> is the emptiness of all.[901]

The *Entrance to the Two Truths* concludes:

> In emptiness there is
> no differentiation at all.[902]

b) The Nature of Mind

There are many statements that the nature of mind is luminosity, such as the observation by the *Prajñāpāramitā in Eight Thousand Lines*:

> The nature of mind is luminosity.[903]

And the statement in the *Descent into Laṅkā*:

> Mind is natural luminosity,
> tathāgatagarbha.[904] [302]

The meaning of luminosity. [Luminosity] is described as referring to what is not veiled and is purified of elaborations (such as those of arising and ceasing); what is stainless and devoid of particles (such as those of the skandhas or dhātus); what is always unchanging, like space; and what is nondual and of the nature of space. The *Sūtra of the Questions of Upāli* teaches:

> This mind's natural luminosity is taught to be purity,
> devoid of particles, free from particles, and stainless.[905]

The *Highest Continuum* explains:

> The luminosity that is the nature of mind
> is unchanging like space.[906]

The *Ornament of the Light of Wisdom* proclaims:

> Mañjuśrī, awakening is the natural luminosity that is the naturally luminous mind. Why is it called naturally luminous? Since its nature is to be without mental afflictions, to equal space, to be of the nature of space, to encompass space, and be like space, it is by nature very luminous.[907]

The *Vairocanābhisambodhi* states:

> Mind is pure by nature. It is neither internal nor external. It is not observed between those two.[908]

It also says:

> The nature of space is the nature of mind. The nature of mind is bodhicitta. Therefore mind, the expanse of space, and bodhicitta are nondual and cannot be made dual.[909] [303]

The *Guhyasamāja* teaches:

> Since all phenomena are natural luminosity,
> they are primordially pure, like space.[910]

The uneducated presume that the clarity aspect of any type of meditative experience is what is meant by natural luminosity and think that what is called luminosity is something that illuminates, like sunlight. They are very mistaken. As attested to by the above citations, the nature of mind—which is not covered by the stains of elaborations and is purified of such stains—is simply referred to with the term "naturally luminous." If the nature of mind was some luminous thing, such that it had color and radiance, the mind would be something with the nature of color and light. If that were the case, it would be unfeasible for the mind to be without nature and naturally pure.

We might, however, wonder, What about the mental states that are in and of themselves clear and reflexively aware due to the seemingly reflexive appearances, or self-illumination, of mind, which transcends being color or radiant light? What are these that arise in the experiences of yogins and yoginīs? They are simply experiences of clarity-awareness arising in the mind, as Nāropa's *Summary of the View* explains:

> These phenomena that appear and are possible
> are nothing apart from the reflexively aware mind
> because they appear and are clarity,
> like, for example, the experiences of reflexive awareness.[911]

It also says:

> This reflexive awareness, free from elaborations,
> appears yet is empty, is empty yet appears.

> Thus appearances and emptiness are indivisible,
> like, for example, the moon and its reflection in water.[912] [304]

Furthermore, even though nowadays it seems that the word "awareness" is used as an experiential term for such [experiences of clarity-awareness], because those [experiences] involve conceptuality, are not emptiness endowed with the most sublime of manifestations, and are not the governing principle of all, they are not true awareness, as the great commentary on the *Kālacakra Tantra* explains:

> What is awareness? What is called "awareness" is a nonconceptual, inner awareness: it is emptiness endowed with all manifestations. What is unchanging is awareness: it is without reference points, devoid of defilements, the embodiment of bliss. Awareness is the embodiment of causes and results: it is the inseparability of cause and result, the way that fire's light and its ability to burn are inseparable.[913]

The *Name-Chanting of Mañjuśrī* declares:

> Genuine all-knowing, awareness-of-all
> is beyond the reality (dharmatā) of consciousness.[914]

It also says:

> Awareness of self and awareness of other [are] everything.[915]

Therefore, the exalted Drikungpa [Jikten Sumgön] states:

> What is called "mahāmudrā"
> is this reflexive awareness.[916]

All awareness described as what is to be meditated upon should be understood according to those and other statements.

Similarly, whatever arises in the meditative experiences of yogins and yoginīs is definitely not considered to be the meaning of intuitive reflexive awareness and natural luminosity. *Unraveling the Intent* observes:

The sphere of intuitive reflexive awareness, beyond
characteristics,
[is inexpressible and devoid of terms.
Free from disputes, it is the ultimate phenomena.
Those are characteristics that lie beyond logicians.][917] [305]

The *Tantra of the Inconceivable Secrets* teaches:

Devoid of the extremes of permanence and annihilation,
birth and cessation, mind is reflexively aware
and primordially without elaborations.
Be certain that this point is inconceivable.[918]

As stated, reflexive awareness is the absence of characteristics and is inconceivable. Natural luminosity is as explained before.

c) The Characteristic of Mind

The essence of mind and its pure nature are obscured by adventitious stains. When [mind] itself is unaware of its own abiding state, on the basis of the interdependence of afflictions, the manifestations of saṃsāra appear: the six classes of beings with their happiness and suffering. Following the separation from adventitious stains and the awareness of [mind's] own abiding state, on the basis of the interdependence of purification, the kāya of ultimate dharmatā manifests and the manifestations of the rūpakāyas appear for others like illusions. The *Summary of the View* declares:

E MA HO. The mind-itself with stains
has projections of the six kinds of beings
throughout a limitless realm of space [306]
with unimaginable rounds of suffering.[919]

It also says:

E MA HO. The mind-itself without stains
has projections of the pure appearances
of the myriad displays of
[buddha] fields and maṇḍalas,

all encompassed by the rūpakāyas.
These marvelous projections
pervade the limitlessness of space.[920]

The Great Brahman [Saraha] states:

Mind-itself alone is the seed of everything:
it radiates existence and nirvāṇa.[921]

The *Sampuṭa* teaches:

Those tainted by the stains of desire and the like, so difficult to stop,
have minds that the Vajra Holder described as "saṃsāra."

Natural luminosity is free from concepts.
The supreme, powerful mind, devoid of percepts and perceivers,
is untainted by the stains of desire and the like.
That is said to be sublime nirvāṇa.[922]

We might think, If mind is naturally pure from the first, it doesn't make sense that it is veiled by adventitious stains. If that is possible, how can it be since, even when stains are removed, they would be able to return? [307] Such stains are referred to with the term "adventitious" due to their quality of being possible to remove. They are not called adventitious in the sense of being something previously nonexistent that suddenly emerges.[923] The way the stains to be abandoned reside with the mind-itself from the outset is taught through analogies, as the *Highest Continuum* says:

Just like a buddha in a decaying lotus, honey among bees,
grains in their husks, gold in filth,
a treasure in the earth, a shoot from a small fruit,
a statue of the Victor in rags,

a [future] ruler in the womb of a poor woman,
a golden image in clay,
the tathāgata dhātu abides in sentient beings
obscured by the stains of their adventitious mental afflictions.[924]

Therefore, although mind is naturally pure, when it has adventitious stains, its buddha qualities are not apparent. When it is free from stains, its buddha qualities manifest. The *Two-Part [Hevajra Tantra]* declares:

> Sentient beings are buddhas.
> But they are obscured by adventitious stains.
> When those are removed, they are buddhas.[925]

Nāgārjuna teaches:

> A vaiḍūrya [beryl] stone
> is always luminous, [308]
> but when confined within ore,
> its radiance is not apparent.
>
> Similarly, the dharmadhātu, itself stainless,
> when obscured by the mental afflictions
> doesn't make its light apparent in saṃsāra,
> but in nirvāṇa it is luminous.[926]

Thus it is that the [mind's] characteristic is described by the term "what appears as the multitude of saṃsāra and nirvāṇa."

These days, when yogins and yoginīs have experiences, although their manifestations of mind are not ascertained as anything and arise in a variety of ways without being blocked by anything, those manifestations arise as if they are external objects, even though they are not, due to the force of various latent tendencies. Furthermore, they appear in keeping with how they are imagined and influenced by the causes and conditions of karma and latent tendencies. Like woolen fabric changed by dye, the [mind's] essence does not change but its various manifestations do, as the *Descent into Laṅkā* explains:

> The mind is naturally pure and luminous. It appears just as it is conceptualized. This is analogous to white woolen fabric changing color when dyed.[927]

To determine the abiding and appearing modes of the mind in detail, we need to study the systematic presentations of the eight consciousnesses (the ālaya and the others) and mental events. Here the presentation is a cursory one providing what is relevant in this context.

2) Ascertaining Connateness

This has three parts:

a) The Essence of Connateness and the Meaning of the Term
b) Its Divisions and Their Identification
c) The Meaning of Connate Union

a) The Essence of Connateness and the Meaning of the Term

The essence of connateness. It is natural luminosity, which is like space and is the governing principle of everything animate and inanimate, saṃsāra and nirvāṇa. [309] This is stated often, such as in the *Two-Part [Hevajra Tantra]*:

> This is great wisdom,
> which abides in the bodies of all
> in a mode that is dual and yet nondual.
> It is the primary nature of entities and nonentities,
> pervading and abiding in the animate and inanimate.[928]

The experience of that is beyond speech, thought, cognition, and expression. It is the province of intuitive reflexive awareness. The *Praises to the Mother* says:

> Prajñāpāramitā, inexpressible through speech or thought,
> whose essence is unborn, unceasing space,
> the province of reflexively aware wisdom:
> I pay homage to the mother of the victors of the three times.[929]

Tilopa declares:

> KYE HO. This is reflexively aware wisdom.
> Beyond the realm of speech, it's not the province of mentation.[930]

The *Two-Part [Hevajra Tantra]* says:

> The connate cannot be described by others.[931]

The meaning of the term. "Connate" refers to all phenomena (all animate and inanimate entities) and the dharmatā of each of those (their thusness [tathātā]) being present simultaneously from the beginning with neither preceding nor following the other. [310] The *Two-Part [Hevajra Tantra]* observes:

> What arises from the connate state
> is called just that: connate.[932]

Ḍombi Heruka says in his *Accomplishment of the Connate*:

> Because it occurs connately,
> the inexpressible is said to be connate.[933]

The *Source Commentary on Indrabhūti's "Accomplishment of the Connate"* remarks:

> What arises concomitantly with something
> is thus called connate.
>
> As is said, connateness is that suchness is present connately with all entities, those that move and do not move. Thus it is referred to as such.[934]

b) Its Divisions and Their Identification

Generally speaking, connateness is classified as threefold: ground, path, and fruition connateness. Ground connateness is the naturally luminous mind, which is the ground, or essence, of saṃsāra and nirvāṇa. Path connateness is the view that, based on listening, reflecting, and meditating, realizes that the essence of all phenomena is emptiness. Fruition connateness is when, through familiarization with that [path connateness], ground connateness becomes connateness endowed with twofold purity.

The *Two-Part [Hevajra Tantra]* and other texts divide it into two: natural connateness and the connateness of melting bliss. The [Seven] Siddhi [Texts] and the [Sixfold] Essence Cycle add to those a third classification: the connateness of bliss-emptiness. [311] According to those classifications, natural connateness is the abiding-state mahāmudrā, the general-meaning luminosity. The connateness of melting bliss is the illustrative luminosity arising from melting conventional bodhicitta. The connateness of bliss-emptiness is the actual luminosity of the stage of unification.

What is relevant in this context. The exalted Dakpo [Gampopa] makes two divisions: the connateness of mind-itself and the connateness of appearances, and includes all types of thoughts (which are mental events) in appearances. The exalted Gomchung adds to those the connateness of thoughts, thereby distinguishing thoughts and appearances. His point is that the majority of people feel there is some difference between externally appearing objects, which arise as shared karmic appearances, and the appearing objects that are manifestations of thoughts.

They [Gampopa and Gomchung] teach that the connateness of mind-itself is the essence, or nature, of mind, which is clear yet nonconceptual, free from elaborations (as described above). [Mind's] own expressive power, or characteristic, appearing unceasingly as the various manifestations of saṃsāra and nirvāṇa is the connateness of appearances. Its proliferations as all kinds of thoughts (such as those related to the three poisons) is the connateness of thoughts. In fact, the latter two are both the connateness of appearances.

The reason for using the term "connateness" in relation to those [mind-itself and appearances] is as previously explained. Those phenomena, or dharmin, and their dharmatā, or emptiness, are present connately from the beginning, like molasses and its sweetness or fire and its heat. That is [what is meant by] "connateness." The connateness of mind-itself and the connateness of appearances are said to be inseparable, like the sun and its light or sandalwood and its scent. [312] Nāgārjuna comments:

> Just as sweetness is the nature of molasses
> and warmth is that of fire,
> so too is emptiness asserted to be
> the nature of all phenomena.[935]

He also says:

> The conventional is taught to be emptiness,
> and emptiness itself is the conventional
> because one does not occur without [the other],
> like being produced and impermanent.[936]

The exalted Gampopa says:

The connateness of mind-itself is the dharmakāya.
The connateness of appearances is the radiance of the dharmakāya.

The connateness of mind-itself is the essence of mind-itself or its way of being.
The connateness of appearances is the various recollections and thoughts that manifest in that [mind].
They are like the sun and sunlight or sandalwood and the scent of sandalwood.[937]

The exalted Gomchung remarks:

The connateness of mind-itself is the actual dharmakāya.
The connateness of appearances is the radiance of the dharmakāya.
The connateness of thoughts is the waves of the dharmakāya.
Inseparable connateness is the actuality of the dharmakāya.[938]

In this case, we might wonder, Since mind-itself and the arising of appearances are present within ordinary people, do they [experience their] connateness? Those on the path may or may not have recognized connateness but, regardless of whether they are able to recognize it or not, there is connateness. [Connateness] is unchanging and uninterrupted. [313] It is explained that this is like the way that a candle flame or sunlight [shine] without partiality and yet the blind experience darkness. The Great Brahman [Saraha] explains:

Though many candles may burn in a house,
the blind still remain in darkness.
Similarly, though connateness pervades everything,
it is still far away for the deluded.[939]

The Śavara [Saraha] instructs:

KYE MA. The sun free from clouds shines its light everywhere,
yet the blind always perceive darkness.
Connateness pervades all
but the deluded are far from it.[940]

Virūpa says:

> Thus all conventional phenomena, all possible appearances,
> have no essence: they're merely names, symbols, and imputations.
> There isn't the slightest difference between a name and its referent
> since from the beginning they are connate—there is nowhere else to look.[941] [314]

c) The Meaning of Connate Union

What is the meaning of calling mahāmudrā instructions "connate union"? The exalted Dakpo [Gampopa] taught that in a general sense thoughts are united with the four kāyas. As explained above, the mind-itself (dharmin), thoughts (which arise from mind), and emptiness (the dharmatā of those) are primordially connate and inseparable. However, not having realized that mode yet, we take those to be good or bad and to be separate things. Through the instructions on the ultimate essence and the pointing-out instructions, we recognize that those do arise and abide as connate from the beginning. Since [these instructions show us that] all those are united with the mind-itself alone, whose essence is inseparable, they are called "connate union," as the exalted Pakmo Drupa explains:

> Mind, thoughts, and the dharmakāya,
> from the first are connate.
> The instructions [that show us how] to unite them in mind
> are, therefore, called "connate union."[942]

There are [other instructions] such as those for uniting ordinary mind and appearances with connate wisdom or those for uniting the usual mind and appearances manifesting as characteristics with connate emptiness. In brief, everything that appears as dualistic phenomena—such as clarity and emptiness, appearance and emptiness, awareness and emptiness, or bliss and emptiness—is united within the state of connate unification. It would be possible to explain all these but I will not go into such elaborations.

B) The Actual Pointing Out of Connateness

This has three parts:

1) Pointing Out the Connateness of Mind-Itself
2) Pointing Out the Connateness of Thoughts
3) Pointing Out the Connateness of Appearances [315]

1) Pointing Out the Connateness of Mind-Itself

Let your mind be naturally settled in its intrinsic state, free from the faults of dullness or agitation, not distorted by positive or negative thoughts.[943] Then look with your mind at the abiding state, or abiding mode, of that mind. When you do so, all subtle and coarse manifestations of thoughts are not blocked—they are self-dissolving, self-purified, self-pacified. In a state in which nothing is identified, a naked or quiet stillness will occur. Since mind rests in the abiding state of mind, that is called śamatha. Within that state don't let your awareness become unclear, and don't slip into a neutral or indifferent state of confusion or lack of mindfulness. The essence of mind is clear yet unceasing; it is reflexively aware and reflexively clear. The way it is aware and the way it is clear are inexpressible. Its manifestation is that of vivid brilliance. When there is just that little bit of something experienced or something in which you have confidence, since that involves the thorough differentiation of observed phenomena, it is called vipaśyanā. This point is explained in the root text and commentary of the *Ornament for the Mahāyāna Sūtras*:

> Because, on the basis of correct stillness,
> mind rests in mind,
> and because phenomena are thoroughly differentiated,
> those are śamatha and vipaśyanā.*[944]

Śamatha and vipaśyanā can only be shown to be different as isolates. Actually, they are not different. Śamatha rests right within vipaśyanā: reflexive awareness and reflexive clarity. Vipaśyanā is reflexively aware of and clear about the qualities of śamatha: resting in the nature of mind with its essence not veiled by conceptual characteristics. [316] Thus they are the one-pointed mind in which śamatha and vipaśyanā are inseparable and unified, as *Unraveling the Intent* teaches:

*For Vasubandhu's commentary on this verse, see p. 31.

> "At what point do śamatha and vipaśyanā mix and become evenly unified?"
>
> [The Bhagavān] replied: "When there is attentiveness to the one-pointed mind."[945]

The identification of śamatha and vipaśyanā with scriptural citations and so forth has already been presented in the section on the general explanation of śamatha and vipaśyanā.* Combining such śamatha and vipaśyanā right within mind-itself explains [the line], "the connateness of mind-itself is the dharmakāya." There are numerous other synonymous terms that will be explained later.†

Accordingly, those who know the abiding state of mind are said to have recognized the mind and are called yogins and yoginīs. Sustaining that state is called meditation and samādhi. The *Sūtra on the Wisdom Mudrā* says:

> Phenomena are sealed by mind.
> Mind is sealed by nonexistence.
> Whoever recognizes mind
> is a practitioner of yoga.[946]

Unraveling the Intent states:

> "When is it said that bodhisattvas are meditating?"
>
> [The Bhagavān] replied: "When, through continuous attentiveness, they attend to the characteristics of mind."[947]

The *King of Samādhi* says:

> Kumara, "samādhi" is realization of the mind, that it is unborn.[948] [317]

It also explains:

> Without discernment and without conceptuality,
> not perceived and inexpressible,

*See "The Identification of the Essences of Śamatha and Vipaśyanā," pp. 30–34.

†See p. 276–77.

mind without reference point
is thus called samādhi.[949]

The *Spacelike Samādhi Sūtra* observes:

With the amṛta from the genuine guru
you will know your mind to be like space.
To not waver from that state
is taught to be samādhi.[950]

Cultivating nonconceptual wisdom is greatly praised. The *Avataṃsaka* states:

Those who wish to enter the domain of the victorious ones
should train with a spacelike attitude,
abandon clinging to discernments, thoughts, and discriminations,
and engage this [domain] with a spacelike mind.[951]

The *Play in Full* says:

Profound, peaceful, free from elaborations, luminous, and
unconditioned:
that is the nectar-like dharma I have discovered.[952]

The *Sampuṭa* observes:

When the nets of thoughts are cast off
the profound dharma spreads.
The path taught by the tathāgatas
is not to be conceptualized cognitively.

Thoughts, great ignorance,
are what plunge us into the ocean of saṃsāra.
Abiding in nonconceptual samādhi
brings stainlessness, like space.[953] [318]

The *Saṃvarodaya* teaches:

Meditate on mind, which is
one taste, equaling space.

It is free from forms and meditative concentrations.
It rejects the practices of logicians.
Mental events are stabilized as mind.
For beings, that is the natural mode.

With the form of space, it abides as space.[954]

Although there are a plethora of such statements in both the sūtras and tantras, since the sūtras, tantras, and esoteric instructions unanimously agree about this point, I will not elaborate with more scriptural citations. You can refer to those that have been presented and those that will follow.

Furthermore, there are numerous synonymous terms that occur in other [texts], all of which are identical in meaning. The *Summary of the View* states:

Reflexive awareness free from elaborations,
unstained by thoughts,
is nonabiding nirvāṇa.
It is also Vajrasattva.

It is the six buddhas.
It is the six classes [of beings].
It is Mañjuśrī-kumara.
It is Vairocana.

It is the dharmakāya and great bliss,
and unification too.
It is the fourth abhiṣeka.
It is connate joy.

It is the pure nature too.[955] [319]

It also says:

It is bodhicitta.
It is the buddha gotra.

It is sugatagarbha.
Since it experiences the taste of just what is,
it's great bliss too.[956]

And:

It is self-arisen wisdom.
Because it's awareness, it's clarity.
Because it's reflexive awareness, it's nonconceptual.[957]

It concludes:

Reflexive awareness free from elaborations
is the actual ground of saṃsāra.
This is nirvāṇa.
This is great madhyamaka.
This is what is to be seen.
This is what's to be cultivated.
This is what is to be attained.[958]

There are many such sayings. In brief, this [connateness of mind-itself] is the ground, or root, of all enumerations—dharmakāya, great bliss, connate wisdom, self-arisen wisdom, reflexively aware wisdom, ultimate bodhicitta, sugatagarbha, dharmatā, thusness, and so forth—as the *Tantra of Nonabiding Mahāmudrā* states:

This is mahāmudrā.
It is not covered by stains.
It has nothing to be blocked or produced.
It is not discovered through paths or remedies.

It is the kāya of all buddhas.
It is the ground of all virtues.
It is spontaneously existent.[959] [320]

2) Pointing Out the Connateness of Thoughts

While resting evenly in the connateness of mind-itself (that was just discussed), cause a pleasurable thought to arise with clarity and intensity. Or provoke a passionate or aggressive thought. When one arises, look directly at its appearing mode. As before, when you were determining [the essence of] thoughts, the manifestation of that thought itself is unceasingly clear and yet at the same time slightly different from the normal, distracted, deluded thoughts you ordinarily have.[960] It doesn't trigger the reification that solidifies the object of deluded thought. It is also empty: there is nothing to be identified as the essence or nature of a particular thought. In that way, clarity, the manifestation of a thought, and its emptiness, its lack of identification, are indivisible. When you experience emptiness as movement or movement as emptiness, you see the very connateness of thoughts themselves. The analogy is waves, which are never anything but water. Water arises as waves and, when it does, it is not something other than water. Similarly, with thoughts, their essence is never anything but emptiness. Since the display of emptiness is unceasing, the manifestations of thoughts simply arise due to the interdependence of causes and conditions. Though they arise, they are nothing other than emptiness because they have no identifiable essence.

At this point, śamatha is that any fixations you might have towards the unobstructed manifestations of thoughts are pure in their own ground. Vipaśyanā is your certainty in the recognition that those [thoughts] are the unborn dharmakāya or that they are of the nature of emptiness. Movements are of the nature of emptiness. Emptiness is of the nature of movement. In brief, the indivisibility of emptiness and movement, and of movement and emptiness, is the unification of śamatha and vipaśyanā.

This is thoughts arising as, or being free in, the dharmakāya. [321] On the basis of this, the followers of the Dakpo Kagyu present and use the expressions "thoughts are dharmakāya" and "delusion manifesting as wisdom" as dharma to be realized.

We may ask, Where is this taught in the sūtras and tantras? The *Sūtra of the Teaching of Akṣayamati* says:

> Because mental afflictions are realized, there is awakening. The essence of mental afflictions is the essence of awakening.[961]

The *Sūtra of the Questions of Sāgaramati* says:

> Sāgaramati said: "Bhagavān, this samādhi is difficult to discover."
>
> The Bhagavān replied: "That is because it realizes consciousness and wisdom to be equal."[962]

It also states:

> Realizing all phenomena to be equal is awakening. Therefore, bodhisattvas don't perceive awakening to be far away.[963]

The *Teaching on How All Phenomena Are Without Any Origin* remarks:

> It is taught that desire is nirvāṇa.
> Anger and stupidity are the same.
> Awakening is their abode.[964]

It also says:

> Awakening and desire are not dual.[965]

The Heap of Jewels teaches:

> Everything arises from the unborn.
> As soon as it is born, it is unborn.[966]

The *Two-Part [Hevajra Tantra]* states:

> There is not the slightest difference
> between the nature of pure wisdom
> and the thoughts of saṃsāra.[967] [322]

It continues:

> This is called "saṃsāra."
> This is called "nirvāṇa."[968]

It also says:

> Saṃsāra is anger and the rest.
> The dharma[tā] of those is nirvāṇa.[969]

The *Sampuṭa* declares:

> Saṃsāra and nirvāṇa
> do not exist as a duality.
> The recognition of the nature of saṃsāra
> is called nirvāṇa.[970]

The Great Brahman [Saraha] says:

> Wisdom, with its pure sunlike radiance,
> is the sublime wisdom turning unawareness into awareness.
> It turns all things into bliss as an elixir transforms [metals] into gold.[971]

Nāgārjuna states:

> Nirvāṇa is not even slightly
> different from saṃsāra.
> Saṃsāra is not even slightly
> different from nirvāṇa.[972]

Āryadeva's *Discussion of Nonconceptuality* explains:

> No nirvāṇa exists anywhere
> apart from the nature free from
> any type of thought.
> That is the essence of
> not contemplating any object at all.[973] [323]

Virūpa teaches:

> When you realize the intrinsic abiding state revealed by the guru,
> all recollections and thoughts self-destruct in the dharmadhātu.[974]

Tilopa states:

> Skandhas, dhātus, and āyatanas
> spring from and dissolve into
> the nature of mahāmudrā.[975]

The *Summary Verses* of Nāropa and Maitrīpa declare:

> Mental afflictions are great wisdom:
> like a forest feeds a fire, they aid yogins and yoginīs.[976]

And:

> Thoughts, free in themselves, are great wisdom.[977]

Maitrīpa adds:

> From the unborn, a thought suddenly appears.
> That very thought is the essence of the expanse.
> From the beginning, those two are not separate.
> Those two are of equal taste, I teach.[978]

Marpa sings:

> The movements of mind with its percepts and perceivers
> dissolve into the dharmakāya, free from elaborations.[979]

The Great Exalted One [Milarepa] sings:

> When this internal, moving mental consciousness
> has no realization, it is ignorance, [324]
> the basic root of karma and mental afflictions.
> When it is realized, it's reflexively aware wisdom
> from which all virtues spring.[980]

The exalted Gampopa sings:

> These thoughts manifesting with characteristics:
> know for sure they are the dharmakāya.[981]

There are numerous vajra statements in the precious Kagyu that are in keeping with this point but I will not elaborate more.

In this context, some take the meaning of thoughts being dharmakāya to be that looking at a thought purifies it and turns into being wholly nonconceptual. Some think that when there is realization, the nature of thoughts is dharmakāya but, when there is no realization, they are not the dharmakāya.

Both are incorrect. The first are wrong because, not knowing that the nature of thoughts themselves abides as the dharmakāya, they seem to think that thoughts must be purified and then become the primordial dharmakāya. That is not proof of thoughts being dharmakāya. The latter are wrong because, not knowing that the nature of thoughts abides continuously as the dharmakāya, they seem to think that [thoughts being dharmakāya or not] depends on whether an individual realizes that or not. If that were the case, the nature of those [thoughts] would be a dharmakāya that is subject to change.

We may ask, How [should they correct their understanding]? The point for the first is that the expression "thoughts are dharmakāya" is used in relation to the experience of, and certainty in, the unity of appearing thoughts and their nature, emptiness. The point for the second is that an individual having realization or not does not make the nature of thoughts be the dharmakāya or not be so. For example, someone having eyes or not does not determine whether the sun has light or not. [325] As long as the sun exists, it continuously has light. The scriptural sources [supporting this] are the same as those provided above.

A certain person [Sakya Paṇḍita] adheres to the tenet of the inseparability of saṃsāra and nirvāṇa while being an adversary of the expressions "thoughts are dharmakāya" and "delusion arises as wisdom." That simply reflects his desire to say something [critical]. [He is wrong for the following reasons.] Whatever proves his inseparability of saṃsāra and nirvāṇa also proves this, [that thoughts are dharmakāya]. Whatever invalidates his opponents also overturns his points. As for his fallacious statements, in that context, it is explained that actually there is no saṃsāra other than the mere manifestation of saṃsāra, and nirvāṇa is all there is. In which case, if the term "saṃsāra" isn't being used for the manifestation of saṃsāra, we cannot find a basis of imputation for the term "saṃsāra." If that is the case, there is no locus for the conventional term "saṃsāra" that is part of the inseparability of saṃsāra and nirvāṇa. Without that [saṃsāra], the unification of saṃsāra and nirvāṇa becomes only nirvāṇa. Congruent reasonings will create more damage [or contradictions] since all presentations of unification would become one-dimensional, such as the unification of method and prajñā being only prajñā.[982]

3) Pointing Out the Connateness of Appearances

Appearances are what manifest to just the mind, the objects that appear as if they are external referents without relying on conditions. They are simply the arising of appearing forms to thoughts based on previous latent tendencies. Thus they are not different from the connateness of thoughts. [326] Nevertheless, what is pointed out now is the connateness of the appearances (forms, sounds, and so forth) manifesting to the sense consciousnesses. These appearances are known to ordinary people as direct [experiences] based on shared karmic appearances.

Rest evenly in the connateness of mind-itself (that was explained before). Within that state, look directly at whatever external appearing form there is, such as a mountain, house, or pot. If that appearance ceases or is not vivid, mind-itself alone will not be a mere experience of empty clarity. As before when you were determining [the essence of] appearances, the characteristic of appearances, however they manifest, is clarity. And yet simultaneously, the essence or nature of their clarity is emptiness, which is the absence of anything to be identified. In brief, the manifestation of an appearance (however it appears) is its clarity. And that is indivisible from its emptiness, its lack of identification. When you experience appearances as empty or emptiness as appearances, the inseparability of appearances and the perceiver of appearances arises nakedly as appearance-emptiness. You see the very connateness of appearances themselves. The analogy is dreams: although various appearances of the environment and its inhabitants manifest in dreams, the very moment they arise they are not something other than the dreaming mind. Similarly, present appearances, whatever they may be, are the unceasing expressive power of your own mind, a display of emptiness. They will arise as such present appearances as long as your shared karma has not been purified.[983] At the very moment of arising, they are nothing other than your own mind's nature of emptiness. The exalted Ling Repa teaches:

> Mind-itself, without basis or root,
> that was dreaming last night
> is the ācārya who points out
> appearances to be mind—do you understand?[984]

The model used with appearing forms is to be applied to the other appearances of the six modes of consciousness, such as the appearances of sound, as Nāgārjuna says:

> Those who see the thusness of one entity [327]
> see the thusness of all entities.[985]

Since it is explained that the complete mixing of appearances and mind occurs during the meditation phase of greater one taste, here the presentation is of the inseparability of appearances and mind that is relevant in this context. At this point, śamatha is that when appearances arise, you rest right with them, freely without any grasping or any judgments. Vipaśyanā is your recognition or certainty that cuts through misinterpretations you might have about the inseparability of appearances and emptiness. Appearances have the nature of emptiness, and emptiness has the manifestation of appearances. The experience of their indivisibility is the unification of śamatha and vipaśyanā. On the basis of such experiences and realizations, the followers of the Dakpo Kagyu present and use the expressions "whatever appears is dharmakāya" and "all possible appearances are the dharmakāya" as dharma to be realized.

This is taught in the sūtras, tantras, and esoteric instructions. The *Heart Sūtra* proclaims:

> Forms are empty. Emptiness is forms. Forms are not other than emptiness. Emptiness is not other than forms.[986]

It is said in the Prajñāpāramitā texts:

> There is no thusness of forms apart from forms. That being so, forms and the thusness of forms are not dual and cannot be made dual. They are not individual and are not separate.[987]

The *King of Samādhi, Which Elaborates on the Equality That Is the Nature of Phenomena*, states:

> Forms demonstrate awakening.[988]

It continues:

> Forms and awakening are the same:
> you will not find them to be different things.[989]

And:

> All phenomena naturally
> are the same as nirvāṇa.[990]

In his commentary on that text, Mañjuśrīkīrti points out:

> The dharmatā of forms is awakening. Awakening is forms.[991] [328]

He continues:

> Sounds and nirvāṇa are not dual and are not separate.[992]

The *King of Samādhi* says:

> [Bodhisattvas] do not see [the tathāgatas] as other than form or as other than the nature of forms. They do not see the nature of forms and the tathāgatas as other than each other.[993]

The *Two-Part [Hevajra Tantra]* teaches:

> Meditate with certainty that every thing, inanimate and animate—
> grasses, twigs, vines and all—
> [have no other] nature than your own:
> genuine suchness.
>
> Their genuine [nature] is nothing else.
> Reflexive awareness is great bliss.[994]

The *Vajra Pañjarā* observes:

> All that appears individually—forms and so forth—
> are only appearances of this mind.[995]

The *Sampuṭa* says:

Looking at forms,
listening to sounds,
speaking or laughing,
experiencing different tastes,
or engaging in any kind of activity
never happen outside of the mind.

Yogins and yoginīs who know that
will always experience yoga.
This is the sublime bodhicitta,
glorious, vajra Vajrasattva,
the awakening of perfect buddhas.[996] [329]

The *Tantra of the Inconceivable Connateness* says:

The connateness of mind-itself is the dharmakāya.
The connateness of appearances is the radiance of the dharmakāya.
Therefore, the inseparability of appearances and mind is connate.[997]

The Great Brahman [Saraha] states:

Earth, water, fire, wind, and space
do not exist apart from the one taste of the connate.
Existence and nirvāṇa are not thought of as dual.
That's said to be the abiding state of the dharmadhātu.[998]

The Śavara [Saraha] expounds:

All appearances and sounds are like illusions,
mirages, and reflections: they have no real characteristics.
The perceiver of illusions is mind-itself, space,
without end or middle: no one can know this.[999]

Virūpa observes:

All dualistic appearances and characteristics—happiness, sadness, and the rest—
are the display of intrinsic mahāmudrā, dharmatā.[1000]

Tilopa exclaims:

> Skandhas, dhātus, and āyatanas [330]
> spring from and dissolve into
> the nature of mahāmudrā.[1001]

Nāropa states:

> These phenomena that appear and are possible
> are nothing apart from the reflexively aware mind.[1002]

The *Summary Verses* of Nāropa and Maitrīpa explain:

> Appearances, free in themselves, are the dharmakāya.[1003]

And:

> Once this is seen and realized,
> all that can possibly appear is mahāmudrā.[1004]

Maitrīpa proclaims:

> The various appearances and this essence of mind
> don't exist even at the moment they meet: this is mahāmudrā.[1005]

The exalted Marpa declares:

> These illusory contrivances of external appearances
> are realized to be unborn mahāmudrā.[1006]

The Exalted One [Milarepa] sings:

> When external appearances, however they appear,
> are not realized, they are delusory appearances.
> Clinging to them as external objects causes bondage. [331]
> With realization, everything appears as an illusion—
> appearing objects arise as aids for the mind.[1007]

The exalted Gampopa sings:

> These appearances and sounds, imputed latent tendencies:
> know for sure they are the ultimate.[1008]

There are many such vajra sayings of the precious Kagyu, but I will not elaborate more for fear of being excessive.

C) Eliminating Flaws and Identifying the Point of the Meditation

This has three parts:

1) The Explanation of Mistakes in Meditation
2) The Explanation of the Problems of Partial Meditation
3) The Identification of Flawless Meditation

1) The Explanation of Mistakes in Meditation

As explained in earlier sections on śamatha, we should sustain a one-pointed mind with its experiences of bliss, clarity, and nonconceptuality, free from the faults of dullness and agitation. Even though that may be a special type of samādhi that produces supercognitive abilities, miraculous powers, and the like, if that samādhi is not embraced by bodhicitta, it is difficult for it to become a cause for complete awakening. Even when it is so embraced, that samādhi will not develop along the distinguished path to awakening because, since our mind is not directed towards emptiness, that samādhi does not become a direct cause for liberation. Nāgārjuna explains:

> Those who don't know emptiness
> are not receptive vehicles for liberation.
> Those confused beings will circle
> in the prison of existence as one of six kinds of beings.[1009] [332]

The vipaśyanā of severing a root or basis of mind, or the vipaśyanā that [sees] the absence of the two types of self-entity, is essential to understanding emptiness. Śamatha by itself, without any connection to vipaśyanā, does not become meditation on emptiness and mahāmudrā. As cited before, the *King of Samādhi* states:

> Even though the worldly cultivate samādhi,
> they do not destroy the notion of a self.*[1010]

Those who have heard [the dharma] just a little and studied with a guru for only a short period of time can develop an approximation of meditation, but the natural, automatic consequence of not knowing how to sustain that is that they will lose certainty in vipaśyanā, and their mindfulness and alertness in samādhi will become slack. They will presume that various kinds of experience that are not meditation are meditation. There are many such mistakes. Therefore, I will discuss them now.

For some of us, sustaining meditation increases our dullness and sluggishness. At first, large and small forms, which are visual objects, may be unclear and seem rather vague. Then they become increasingly unclear and, in the end, appearing forms cease because our visual consciousness dissolves. Similarly, other kinds [of objects], such as auditory forms, can become unclear and in the end disappear. Finally, once the six consciousnesses, which engage their six types of objects, cease, we end up with no appearances and no mindfulness—it's as if we have fainted. This is like when a lake freezes, the sparkling, brilliant quality of the water and the distinctions of the things under the water become blurred.

Alternatively, we may have slightly more lucidity and flashes of mindfulness. [333] The appearances of forms, sounds, and so forth do not cease but they become indistinct and vague. Without vivid alertness, we become confused, or dazed, or idle. All those qualities are said to belong to the category of the mental affliction of bewilderment and to be part of its related secondary mental afflictions.

Another possibility is that we have no sense of awareness or perception of anything, such as whether what is appearing to the six modes of consciousness is clear or unclear. We may rest with no mindfulness, no active application to anything. That resting, which is similar to those previously described, is a kind of stagnation and, therefore, is not suitable as meditation. Since it seems to be predominantly a state of confusion, it is said to be part of the causes for being [reborn as] an animal.[1011] The *Precious Garland* informs us:

> Confusion mainly results in becoming an animal.[1012]

*See p. 216.

On the other hand, we may have somewhat different [experiences]. We may have a lucid quality of mind or various kinds of vivid appearances but not the mindfulness we need or the sharp clarity of alertness. Since that will not become a virtuous one-pointed mind and here is also not something unvirtuous, it is included within the unspecified [or neutral] mental states. Similarly, when our mindfulness and alertness are not clear and we simply rest with appearances, neither blocking them nor encouraging them, that too must be included within the mental formation of equanimity [or indifference]. Therefore it too is an unspecified [or neutral] mental state.

It is explained that subsequent conditions can change unspecified karma into another kind of karma [that is, positive or negative] but it will not become one definite type of result. Some explain that [unspecified karma] and stable karma are the same, however that is not quite right because there is a big difference between those two. [334] In the best-case scenario, it's possible that those two mental states will gravitate towards being causes for afflicted meditative absorption that is without cognitive discriminations. In spite of that, here they are never suitable as the meditation to be practiced since they will not become even the flawless samādhis of the four meditative concentrations and the formless realm. The *Entrance to the Bodhisattva's Way of Life* explains:

> The mind lacking [the realization of] emptiness
> may cease but it will arise again,
> just as [we do from] absorption without discriminations.[1013]

That is said to be the reason why gods who have interrupted their operative consciousnesses along with the associated factors are called "those without cognitive discriminations."

Another possibility is that the mind that is between an earlier thought having ceased and a subsequent one not having arisen may remain just blank. Although many mistake that for meditation, they are wrong. Since that state lacks the certainty of vipaśyanā, it is like deep sleep, fainting, or being drunk. Or it is simply nonconceptual in a way that is similar to the mind that is suddenly shocked. Even though some sharp mental lucidity may arise within that state, it is really just clever stillness and not meditation in which the mind is directed towards emptiness.

If we only have vipaśyanā certainty, without having had śamatha experiences of thoughts self-pacifying, we may be forcefully blocking thoughts, and even subtle manifestations of thoughts and appearances will seem to be interruptions and arising as enemies. It will be very difficult to prolong the continuity of such samādhi. [335] While that may be considered suitable as meditation for some beginners, it is not said to be meditation in which the abiding state is determined, not at all. The exalted Gampopa teaches:

> During stillness, nonconceptuality is prolonged. If you prolong nonconceptuality as the essence [of mind], you do not understand the key point of the dharma.[1014]

He also says:

> Some regard blocking every thought as it arises and resting with the mind wrapped up in nonconceptuality as a positive thing. That cannot serve as the path. It will cripple wisdom.[1015]

Alternatively, we may simply rest in the stillness of the mind suffused with bliss. We may just rest in pure emptiness without attending to any thoughts of the three times. Or we may rest our mind in the vivid appearances that give us the idea that we can see all external and internal things. Such [experiences] may occur individually or all together. In brief, no matter how excellent our samādhi of bliss, clarity, or emptiness may be, when it lacks vipaśyanā certainty it is not the meditation to be practiced here. The exalted Gampopa states:

> What is called "[a mind to which experiences or objects] appear yet are not ascertained" becomes a cause for nonanalytical cessation. It is uncertain where we will be born as a result.[1016]

This will also be explained again.*

Another possibility is that with whatever appears to the mind, with everything that arises, and even when there are no manifestations, we make sure we are never separated from the perception of emptiness and the total lack of reality. Here, that is not the meditation to be practiced. That is simply a reliance on continuous mindfulness that presumes the mind to be empty—it is not vipaśyanā certainty. Even if there is certainty, since that

*See "The Way Those [Experiences] Become Strayings," pp. 366–73.

involves repetitively generating a belief in emptiness and the lack of reality, it leads to a massive nihilistic view. It is refuted by statements from Nāgārjuna: [336]

> Those for whom emptiness is a view
> are said to be unable to accomplish anything.[1017]

He also says:

> If emptiness is seen incorrectly,
> those of little intelligence are ruined.[1018]

And:

> Those who assert nonexistence proceed to negative states.[1019]

In this context, without having carefully analyzed these issues, a certain person [Sakya Paṇḍita], on the basis of having heard some kind of explanation, states:

> The fool's meditation on mahāmudrā
> usually is a cause for being [born as] an animal.
> If not that, they may be born in the formless realm
> or else they may descend into the cessations of śrāvakas.[1020]

Those remarks contain very flawed statements and simply reflect his desire to say something [critical].

We may ask, Why is that? It is because, were it the case that meditating on mahāmudrā brought about birth as an animal, mahāmudrā would be the cause of becoming an animal. Then, it would mean that it is improper for fools to meditate on mahāmudrā and, if that is so, it also means that it is improper for fools to undertake listening, reflection, and meditation. Finally, it would also mean that there is a common locus that is the cause for being born as animals, being born in the formless realm, and achieving the cessation of śrāvakas and, that being so, they are all of equal status.

He also claims:

> Our mahāmudrā
> is the wisdom arisen from abhiṣeka.[1021] [337]

Furthermore, it would also be improper for fools to meditate on the wisdom arisen from abhiṣeka and fools would not be suitable recipients of abhiṣeka.[1022] If they are not suitable recipients, then statements such as the following are incorrect. The *Two-Part [Hevajra Tantra]* teaches:

> The deluded, those who engage in reprehensible acts
> [... one day will certainly become accomplished].[1023]

And fools who do meditate on the wisdom arising from abhiṣeka would be creating the causes for [being born] as animals and so forth because [Sakya Paṇḍita] claims that a fool's meditation on mahāmudrā is a cause for [being born] as animals and so forth, and he asserts that the wisdom arising from abhiṣeka is mahāmudrā.

Even though [Sakya Paṇḍita] likes to say that if someone does not know how to meditate on mahāmudrā that is what will happen, his statement is still flawed. For example, if someone does not understand how to meditate on the Mahāyāna path, it is possible that they are creating causes for the Hīnayāna. However, that does not justify saying that meditating on the Mahāyāna path is a cause for the Hīnayāna. Also if someone does not understand how to practice the genuine dharma, it is possible that they will be born in the negative states, but that does not justify saying that practicing the genuine dharma is the cause of the negative states.

Furthermore, the causes for being born in the formless realm must be mundane vipaśyanā with both calm and coarse aspects and the absorptions in which the clear appearances of the actual meditative concentrations of each of the four spheres has been attained. Since those are said to be absorptions of meditative concentration that are difficult for even śrāvaka arhats to achieve, it is most unreasonable to put them in the same class with the causes for [being reborn as] an animal.

Moreover, if the cessations referred to in the line "they may descend into the cessations of śrāvakas" are the cessations of śrāvaka nonreturners and arhats, those require the vipaśyanā that has the element of [knowing] the lack of a self of persons. [338] Therefore, it cannot be that [those cessations] are in the same class as the causes for [being reborn as] an animal. It would be difficult for a fool to practice meditation that is the cause for such cessations. Such ideas are in direct contradiction with what is said in the final *Stages of Meditation*:

> It is impossible for the mind of an ordinary being who has

> not attained the fourth meditative concentration to reach cessation.[1024]

Therefore [those statements by Sakya Paṇḍita] are just baseless talk.

To look at this again: if the śrāvaka cessations he speaks about are the śrāvaka cessations that feature in some common stories, those are simply ordinary tales and, in fact, are not about śrāvakas. Those cessations are not the śrāvaka cessations. For such reasons, again we all should leave our mind in its natural state and speak properly.

This certain person [Sakya Paṇḍita] also says:

> These days, some take the pointing out of mahāmudrā
> to be the brief stopping of thoughts
> that occurs when their mind has been transformed
> through their devotion to their guru.
>
> It is possible that such things are [the blessings] of māras
> or that they come with the gathering of certain dhātus.[1025]

Those are ill-considered remarks because they mean accepting that there is a common locus for the guru's blessings and the blessings of māras, because being consumed by such doubts is most unfortunate, and because (as explained above) nonconceptuality that is not recognized by vipaśyanā is not asserted to be mahāmudrā. It is also absurd to put forth that everything that comes with the gathering of the dhātus is inauthentic because that would invalidate all the methods for arousing wisdom through wind-mind abiding and dissolving in the avadhūti, and because it means that he is refuting the very mahāmudrā that he asserts. [339]

2) The Explanation of the Problems of Partial Meditation

There are some who consider simply resting quietly with the mind's quality of vibrant, sharp clarity and not thinking about anything to be mahāmudrā meditation. That is a śamatha samādhi free from the faults of dullness and agitation. It is not really mahāmudrā meditation since it lacks the vipaśyanā certainty and is just an experience of the mind's empty clarity.

If, within a state where thoughts are pacified on the spot, you have the experience of, and certainty in, the essence of mind or awareness being clear yet free from identification, that can be considered a beginner's meditation. However, it is not exactly meditating on the uncontrived essence of the abiding-state awareness since it implies that, no matter what, there must be nonconceptuality in which thoughts and appearances seem to be blocked. With that approach, it will be difficult to give rise to meditation during postmeditative attainment.

There are some who find it is necessary to stop or draw in the manifestations of thoughts or appearances when they occur in order to rest in clarity without conceptuality. Others assert that to rest in sharp clarity-emptiness they must hold mindful awareness continuously. If undistracted mindful awareness arises right with the essence of mind—with the impact of a rock crushing bones—that will serve as a beginner's meditation. [340] However, it is highly likely that thoughts and appearances will arise as enemies because misinterpretations about the essence of thoughts and appearances have not been severed. Therefore, [that beginner's meditation] is a limited experience in which there is excessive tightening without having discovered the key point of relaxing into the mind's basic nature.

Nevertheless, if you are skilled in nurturing such spiritual practice, with familiarization that meditative equipoise will progress. Gradually, the manifestations of thoughts and appearances will vanish as self-pacified. Finally, you will come to the point when your misinterpretations about thoughts and appearances will be severed. Yet for some, your mind's manifestations are vivid and plentiful from the start. [If] you are not grounded in the experience of the abiding state of those and are uncomfortable sustaining meditation, there is the danger that you will reach a point of exhaustion with your meditation. Therefore, you must recognize the connateness of the manifestations of nonconceptual mind, thoughts, and appearing objects, and sever your misinterpretations about them. Particularly, if only nonconceptuality is pointed out during the pointing-out instructions, most will understand that to be the ideal all the time. Since that may make them feel very constrained, it is not really recommended. It is important to emphasize the recognition of the manifestations of thoughts and appearances.

3) The Identification of Flawless Meditation

This has three parts:

a) The Way the Abiding State of Mind Is Taught to Be Ordinary Mind
b) Identifying the Features of That Ordinary Mind

c) The Presentation That Not Wavering from That [Ordinary Mind] Is Mahāmudrā Meditation

a) The Way the Abiding State of Mind Is Taught to Be Ordinary Mind

Although the uneducated generally assume that what is called "ordinary mind" is the regular, normal, confused mind, it is not that at all. [341] The term "ordinary" (*tha mal*) is *prākṛta* [in Sanskrit], which is used for both "nature" (*rang bzhin*) and "ordinary" (*tha mal*). Therefore, it means the "natural mind." And that means it is naturally luminous. It is the mind that is neither contrived nor adulterated by anything. It is settled in its natural state and rests in its own basic nature, its own state.

The use of the expression "ordinary mind" for that mind is not confined to the followers of the Dakpo Kagyu. It is used by others, as seen in many citations including the following. The *Tantra of Nonabiding Suchness* says:

> The nature of ordinary mind is the most sublime of fruitions.
> If left uncontrived, it achieves the result of the three kāyas.
> If let loose and free, it is the consummate wisdom.
> It is uncontrived mind-itself, the state of all vajras.
> The import of remaining in naturalness is inexpressible.
> This is the mother of all buddhas of the three times.[1026]

The glorious Śavara [Saraha] says:

> Ordinary mind in its own intrinsic state
> is not spoiled by contrived focuses.
> The naturally pure mind needs no contrivance.
> Don't grasp at it, don't release it: leave it as it is.[1027]

The mahāsiddha Kuddāla teaches:

> Ordinary mind awakens in the middle of the heart. [342]
> When the six consciousnesses are pure, bliss is continuous.
> Conceptuality is pointless and the cause of suffering.
> Remain in the intrinsic state without meditating.[1028]

The Great Exalted One [Milarepa] sings:

> By sustaining ordinary mind again and again,
> confused ignorance is forgotten and vanishes.[1029]

The exalted Gampopa declares:

> This practice where ordinary mind is all that's needed
> is discovered through the kindness of the Buddha in human form.[1030]

b) Identifying the Features of That Ordinary Mind

Although there are many references to ordinary mind, there are few who clearly identify it and, therefore, I will discuss it here. The exalted Gampopa explains in his *Grand Dharma Lectures*:

> Nowadays, if we wish for liberation from saṃsāra, we must recognize ordinary mind since it is the root of all phenomena. What is called "ordinary mind" is our own mind unadulterated by any phenomenon and unsullied by any worldly consciousness. Not covered up by dullness, sluggishness, or thoughts, it remains in its own spot. If we recognize it, it is reflexively aware wisdom. [343] If we don't realize it, it is connate ignorance. When we realize it, it is called awareness, the essence, connate wisdom, ordinary mind, the intrinsic state, freedom from elaborations, and luminosity.[1031]

He continues with an identification of the essence of ordinary mind, its synonyms, and a lengthy discussion about how, when that is recognized, it is superior to most virtues.[1032]

"Unadulterated by any phenomenon" means mind is not corrupted by intellectualization related to the analyses of philosophical tenets or by the experiences of bliss, clarity, nonconceptuality, and so forth. "Unsullied by any worldly consciousness" means mind is not adulterated by the dregs of mental afflictions (such as attachment and aversion) or the intellect with such momentary thoughts as, "I will do this," "I am doing that."

"Not covered up by dullness, sluggishness, or thoughts" means that mind's abiding mode, or way of being, is not obscured by the confusion created by dullness or sluggishness, or by being distracted with the usual thoughts involving discursiveness or agitation. "Remains in its own spot" means that the essence, the basic nature, or way of being of mind—just what it is—stays right within its own way of being without being spoiled by additional efforts to encourage one thing or prevent something else.

In this context, the exalted Yang Gönpa teaches:

> "Nonconceptual wisdom" is a dharma term. "Naked ordinary mind" is the foolish talk of kusālis. In fact they are the same.[1033]

On the other hand, on the basis of just a few instances of some random remarks by previous masters of the practice lineage, these days some think that "ordinary mind" is only nonconceptual and that is how they explain it. They seemed to have missed seeing the meaning of ordinary mind taught by the exalted Dakpo uncle and nephews. [344] While the exalted Dakpos do teach that the mind's way of being is not obscured by the usual thoughts of percepts and perceivers, in a general sense blocking conceptuality and creating nonconceptuality is not the meaning of ordinary mind and noncontrivance. The exalted Gampopa says in his instructions to Ācārya Gomchung:

> In brief, do not block or encourage anything [in relation to ordinary mind], be it existence or nonexistence, being empty or not empty, thoughts or nonconceptuality, something good or bad, something positive or negative. Do not make any alterations of any kind. Ordinary mind, left to be just as it comes, is itself uncontrived.[1034]

The exalted Gampopa also teaches:

> Among the three, ordinary mind, noncontrivance, and the intrinsic state, ordinary mind is the original mind not influenced by philosophical tenets. Noncontrivance means to let [mind] be just as it is without making any alterations.[1035]

We may, however, wonder, What is the meaning of the exalted Yang Gönpa's statement? In the expression "naked ordinary mind," "naked" signifies the essence or nature. Since that [mind] is free from thoughts involving terms and referents, and it is not mistaken, it is the same as nonconceptual wisdom. The dharmatā of [all things] in general is called "nonconceptual wisdom." If we recognize that, since it abides within each and every phenomenal entity, we will then recognize that whatever manifestations of thoughts and appearances happen to arise that they are of that [dharmatā] nature, which is nothing other than wisdom itself. This is the thought of Yang Gönpa since he also says:

> In brief, ordinary mind—"being just as you are," which no one can fabricate—recognizes itself all by itself. That is what is called the arising of mahāmudrā meditation.[1036]

First, no matter what, we must fully recognize the abiding state of mind-itself, thoughts, and appearances (as discussed previously). [345] Without that we are like a blind person with wide-open eyes trying to examine the features of a form. Right now we may not have developed assurance and confidence in the nature of ordinary mind and uncontrived mind. If, however, we have such recognitions, we will develop deep certainty that the way of being, or abiding mode, of the mind—not adulterated or altered by the intellect involved in blocking or encouraging—is itself the mode of being of ordinary mind, and that is the way of being of the dharmakāya. By practicing properly with that [certainty, full recognition of ordinary mind] will manifest.

It is taught that approaching this in any other way makes it difficult to precisely realize the way of being of ordinary mind, as the exalted Yang Gönpa explains:

> There are many gurus who can arouse special experiences and samādhis and point them out to be the meditation. But gurus who know how to point out ordinary mind as the meditation are as rare as daytime stars.[1037]

When ordinary mind is recognized, various expressions are used such as "seeing the essence of mind." Once we have mastered familiarizing ourselves with that mode of seeing, finally it won't matter whether a nonconceptual state arises or not: even the mind involved with conceptuality—such as the mind of a regular person without any dharma—will be recognized and free, without any compartmentalization or corruption, as the exalted Gampopa states:

> The perceiving mind functioning powerfully
> without any compartmentalization or corruption
> is the actual vividness of the buddhas' faces and arms.[1038]

The exalted Gomchung declares: [346]

> One, original mind,
> two, ordinary mind,
> and, three, mind as the perceiving subject:
> when we recognize those three,
> it is our own mind directly identifying itself.
> That seeing is wisdom.
>
> Mind-itself is seen to be the natural essence
> of the uncontrived intrinsic state.
> Just this with conceptuality
> is seen to be its vivid brilliance.
> In brief, the mind of one without any dharma at all
> is exactly this.[1039]

The exalted Tsangpa Gyare says:

> The mind of just any old person
> is the dharmakāya.
> The guru can reveal it but even that's not necessary.
> You can verify it yourself.[1040]

Although there are many similar statements in the practice lineage, I will not elaborate now since they can be understood from the explanations that will follow.

c) The Presentation That Not Wavering from That [Ordinary Mind] Is Mahāmudrā Meditation

Thus, what we call "meditation" means that, within a state where ordinary mind is recognized and reflexively aware mindfulness does not waver from that nature, we sustain that naturally settled mind without contrivance, no matter what happens or comes up suddenly. As Gampopa says:

> Know right now that meditation
> is this undistracted ordinary mind.[1041] [347]

Therefore, if you have drifted from sustaining the naturally settled mind with the mindfulness of recognizing it just as it is, and you then try to fabricate that or patch it back together and meditate, that is not in keeping with the meaning of uncontrived mind. It will not become meditation on the abiding state. Nevertheless, you should not allow yourself to be distracted, even for an instant, with your routine, confused mind, which involves clinging. The *King of the Tantras of Secret Amṛta* states:

> Natural, empty luminosity
> is not found through meditation
> and is not found through not meditating.
>
> Meditation is discernment.
> Not meditating is discernment.
> There's not even a particle's worth of something to meditate upon,
> not even a moment's worth of distraction.[1042]

The Śavara [Saraha] teaches:

> Don't regard anything as a flaw.
> Practice nothing whatsoever.
> Don't seek signs.
> Although you are taught nonmeditation,
> don't let yourself become lazy or indifferent.
> Meditate continuously with mindfulness.[1043]

The *Accomplishment of the Purpose of Meditation* explains:

> When meditating, don't meditate on anything.
> Calling that "meditation" is simply as a conventional expression.[1044]

That being so, no matter what your state of mind is as you experience unsettling circumstances—be it a mental state of pure emptiness, sparkling bliss, swirling thoughts, or brilliant appearances—none of it creates any uncertainty about the natural expression of the abiding state. By recognizing [ordinary mind] itself, and with reflexively aware mindfulness not wandering from that, everything is sustained without fabrication and in a relaxed way. [348] [Those who think it] necessary to rest in nonconceptuality by drawing in discursive thoughts or blocking appearances are referred to by the exalted Tsangpa Gyare as [practitioners of] "iron-hook meditation." They have trained in meditation but are somewhat limited. The essence of mind and the manifestations of thoughts and appearances are most certainly not discrete things that stand on their own. As shown by the analogies of light radiating from the sun or waves rising up on the ocean, thoughts and appearances are the various natural expressions of mind's awareness. Thus, whatever arises or appears in the naturally settled mind is in fact neither good nor bad.

When there is stillness, recognize just that right within the stillness and sustain it with reflexively aware mindfulness. When there is movement, do the same right within the movement. When there are appearances, do the same right with appearances. There is no need to change anything or fabricate something, as explained by the exalted Gampopa:

> Don't put any effort into preventing something or creating anything. If there is nonconceptuality, that's fine. If there are all kinds of thoughts, that's fine. Remaining without contrivance is itself free from dualistic perception. When you have the understanding that thinks, "Isn't this nondual wisdom itself?" that's the recognition of the very essence of mind, its basic nature, its way of being.
>
> If you understand that, there's no need for an object of meditation. Not cast away, not made to remain, meditation occurs automatically. Because the various thoughts arise unhindered, nondual wisdom arises unhindered.[1045]

The exalted Gomchung also states:

> The essence of lucid awareness
> has nothing to be removed, no wandering, no interruption.
> Within it, memories and thoughts—
> however they occur—
> are all of its essence.
> If ordinary mind is not distracted,

> all memories and thoughts are awareness.
> There's no need to see them as problems.[1046] [349]

Nevertheless, we may wonder, Is it enough to be mindful of whatever arises in the mind right from the beginning without being guided according to the stages of instruction? That may be sufficient for those of the instantaneous type since doing just that [serves as] the pointing out. However, most who are not guided according to the stages of instruction do not sever their misinterpretations about the abiding modes of mind-itself, thoughts, and appearances. Also, the experiences and certainty of seeing the essence of those will not arise. Therefore, although they may have some generalized mindfulness, nothing will develop because they don't have recognition and reflexively aware mindfulness. This point is stated decisively by the exalted Gampopa:

> Is there a difference between the regular thoughts that worldly people have and the regular ordinary mind that yogins and yoginīs have? If there isn't, you may wonder why worldly people are not self-liberated. Worldly people do not have the instructions that yogins and yoginīs have and, therefore, they do not recognize nonduality. They only have the dualistic perception that blocks or creates. Even if they receive instructions, since they have no confidence that nondual wisdom arises as various, unpredictable [appearances or thoughts], no state of liberation will arise from the thoughts involving dualistic perception. Dharma practitioners train themselves through the sufferings of dualistic perceptions involved in listening, reflecting, and meditating.
>
> Yogins and yoginīs disconnect from things to be blocked or encouraged, and thus nondual wisdom arises as the varieties of unpredictable thoughts, as great bliss. The difference between those two groups comes from this key point.[1047]

That completes the explanation of the process of pointing out. [350/351]

11

Sustaining Mahāmudrā

iii. The Way to Sustain the Practice of Meditation

This has four parts:

A) The Necessity of Sustaining [Meditation] Once Recognition [Develops] in Spiritual Practice
B) Specifically, the Methods for Sustaining Meditation During Equipoise and Postmeditative Attainment
C) Eliminating Deviations and Strayings in Meditation
D) Enhancement: Concluding That [Mind] Is Unborn

A) The Necessity of Sustaining [Meditation] Once Recognition [Develops] in Spiritual Practice

This has three sections:

1) The Reasons That Sustaining Meditation Is Necessary Once It Has Developed
2) A General Discussion of How to Sustain [Meditation] with Mindfulness, Alertness, and Conscientiousness
3) Specifically, the Presentation That Mindfulness Is Crucial

1) The Reasons That Sustaining Meditation Is Necessary Once It Has Developed

It is explained that once we develop meditation, if we carry on in an ordinary way or engage in inferior actions, we will come to be like the most degenerate people. Our virtues will decline, and we will again be bound to saṃsāra, as the Great Brahman [Saraha] observes:

> KYE MA. Once you've realized the abiding state, if you take up what is unworthy,
> you're like royalty descending from your throne to sweep up the dirt.
> Discarding inexhaustible great bliss,
> you're bound by your contact with saṃsāra's pleasures.[1048]

The exalted Tsangpa Gyare concurs:

> Meditation that is left ownerless once it has developed
> is like wealth swept away by wind,
> a lion gone off with the dogs,
> a precious jewel submerged in mud.[1049]

Not only that, it is taught that when we have discovered the view of nonelaboration and yet continue to make efforts that are primarily directed towards reference points—physical or verbal spiritual practices and the like—we are missing the point, like someone who pursues trinkets when they have already found jewels. [352] The Great Brahman [Saraha] declares:

> KYE MA. Having seen their own mind free from elaborations,
> yogins and yoginīs who persist in pursuing elaborations
> are like those who seek trinkets despite having found a precious gem.
> Though they apply themselves, they never [reach] the core spot.[1050]

Tilopa teaches:

> The state beyond the intellect isn't seen by means of intellectual phenomena.
> The state of nonaction isn't realized through the phenomena of activities.[1051]

The Exalted Lord [Atīśa] says:

> When your mind is stabilized in meditative equipoise as one,
> do not emphasize physical and verbal virtues.[1052]

The Exalted One [Milarepa] sings:

> When freedom from elaborations dawns in your mind,
> don't chase conventional terms and expressions—
> there's the danger you'll get stuck in the shackles of the eight worldly values.[1053]

He continues:

> When meditating upon mahāmudrā,
> don't exert yourself in spiritual practices involving your body or speech—
> there's the danger nonconceptual wisdom will disappear.
> Remain in the uncontrived intrinsic state.[1054]

Furthermore, in the same way that we must continue to rub sticks together until fire appears, [we must continue to meditate] as long as we have not perfected the liberating qualities of mind. An abundance of characteristics is not exactly conducive since that won't enhance the absence of characteristics. [353] Ācārya Śūra says:

> If you repeatedly slack off,
> fire will not appear from friction.
> The process of yoga is the same:
> do not stop until you reach what is exceptional.[1055]

Repeatedly contemplating and cultivating the object of meditation over a period of time is praised. The *Ornament of Clear Realization* teaches:

> The path of meditation is one of repeated
> reflection, deliberation, and validation
> during the branches of ascertainment
> and the paths of seeing and meditation.[1056]

2) A General Discussion of How to Sustain [Meditation] with Mindfulness, Alertness, and Conscientiousness

All occasions of meditation should involve resting with mindfulness, alertness, and conscientiousness, as is said in the sūtras:

> If you always turn to mindfulness and alertness,
> you will not be affected by mistaken notions.[1057]

The *Entrance to the Bodhisattva's Way of Life* advises:

> To those who wish to protect their mind
> I say: guard your mindfulness and alertness
> even if it comes down to your life.
> Vow to do that.[1058] [354]

Mindfulness. This is the mental state of not forgetting the object for practice. Here it is [specifically] the mental formation that guards against unvirtue and engages in virtue, as the *Sūtra of the Questions of Ratnacūḍa* teaches:

> Mindfulness does not allow any mental afflictions to arise. Mindfulness does not give the work of māras any chances. Mindfulness does not go down bad paths or misleading paths. Mindfulness does not act like a door opening the possibilities for unvirtuous minds or mental events. That is true mindfulness.[1059]

Mindfulness has many divisions. The *Compendium of Dharma Sūtra* describes the mindfulness that is part of the path to awakening and its enumerations:

> What is true mindfulness on the path to awakening? It is the mindfulness that realizes phenomena. It is what discerns phenomena. It is that which analyzes phenomena. It accompanies phenomena. It reflects upon phenomena. It considers phenomena. That mindfulness realizes the characteristics belonging to each and every phenomenon.[1060]

The *Sūtra of the Questions of Akṣayamati* discusses the distinctions of the true mindfulness on the path of noble ones:

> What is true mindfulness? It is the mindfulness that rests closely with something. It is unshakeable, straightforward, and does not vacillate. It sees the shortcomings that flaw saṃsāra. It leads to

> the path that connects with nirvāṇa. What is mindful, sound, and does not forget the noble path is called "true mindfulness."[1061] [355]

Furthermore, the *Compendium of Dharma Sūtra* presents the bodhisattvas' foundation of mindfulness:

> Child of good family, what is the bodhisattvas' foundation of mindfulness? What is mindfulness? What is the abode of mindfulness? I will answer those questions. Child of good family, mindfulness is the bodhisattvas' recognition that phenomena are unborn. Bodhisattvas have the aspiration to know the unborn. Their mindfulness is fully trained through their recognition of the unborn. Always imperturbable, their mindfulness is unwavering. Its depth and limits are unfathomable. It is hard for the worldly, śrāvakas, and pratyekabuddhas to comprehend.[1062]

Although there are many such enumerations, what is relevant now [is to mention] the following [three types of mindfulness]. There is the mindfulness [or recollection] that looks to the past, as presented in the *Four Hundred Verses*:

> Things seen do not reappear
> and [their perceiving] mind does not arise again.
> Thus what is called mindfulness [or recollection]
> is simply being deceived about a deceptive object.[1063]

Dharmakīrti refers to the mindfulness that apprehends by linking previous and latter [moments]:

> That which is other than the deluded sense [consciousnesses]
> and, linking entities together,
> doesn't identify them as separate is deluded:
> that is mindfulness, which is conceptual.[1064]

The higher abhidharma [that is, the *Compendium of Abhidharma*] explains the particular mindfulness that ascertains objects:

> What is mindfulness? It is not forgetting a familiar object. Its function is to be undistracted.[1065]

Among those three, the first two are conceptual mindfulness and, therefore, are necessary during investigation and analysis. They are, however, to be abandoned during meditative equipoise. The latter is described as the mindfulness that is practiced during śamatha and, thus, is the mindfulness that is definitely necessary during meditative equipoise. [356]

[Alertness]. On the basis of that [mindfulness], we examine the conduct of our three doors and give rise to the alertness that differentiates the bases to be adopted or rejected. The *Entrance to the Bodhisattva's Way of Life* teaches:

> When mindfulness sits at the mind's door
> for the sake of guarding it,
> alertness will come.[1066]

It also provides a definition of alertness:

> Repeatedly examine
> the condition of your body and mind.
> That alone sums up the definition
> of what it means to protect alertness.[1067]

Here it is important to cultivate primarily the mindfulness and alertness that sustain the abiding state of mind and that properly undertake abandoning and adopting during enhancing conduct. Lacking such mindfulness and alertness is problematic, as the *Entrance to the Bodhisattva's Way of Life* explains:

> Those whose minds are devoid of alertness
> may listen, reflect, and meditate,
> and yet, like water leaking out from a cracked vase,
> none of it remains in their memory.
>
> Those who have studied, who have faith,
> and much perseverance,

but who are flawed by a lack of alertness,
will be stained by downfalls.

The thief "no alertness"
shadows diminished mindfulness.
Like a thief stealing any merit we have amassed,
it sends us to the negative states.[1068]

[Conscientiousness]. Those with that type of mindfulness and alertness develop conscientiousness. [357] The essence of conscientiousness is that it protects our mind from afflictive phenomena and enables us to fully practice worldly and transcendent virtues. The *Sūtra on the Inconceivable Secret Teachings of the Tathāgatas* says:

> Conscientiousness disciplines our mind, protects others' minds, dispels our predilection for the mental afflictions, and arouses our delight in the dharma.[1069]

It continues:

> To be conscientious is to be without improper thoughts and without thoughts involving unvirtuous and evil qualities.[1070]

The *Moon Lamp Sūtra* teaches:

The root of all the qualities said to be virtuous—
ethical discipline, listening, giving, and patience—
is conscientiousness.
The Sugata called it "the bestower of treasure."[1071]

The *Letter to a Friend* says:

Miserliness, deceitfulness, idleness,
overt pride, desire, aggression,
and being inflated about your family, looks, learning, youth,
or power should be seen as your enemies.

The Muni declared conscientiousness to be the source of amṛta
and its lack, the abode of death.

Therefore, be conscientious continuously and with respect
so that your virtuous qualities may increase.[1072] [358]

On the basis of those approaches there are the following sayings in the teachings of the practice lineage that we should know:

- Revulsion is the foot or owner of meditation.
- Devotion is the head or enhancement of meditation.
- Mindfulness is the lookout or main practice of meditation.
- Kindness, compassion, and bodhicitta are the activity of meditation.
- Consideration and integrity are the armor of meditation.

It is critical that we apply ourselves to abandoning distractions and to practicing the meditation of letting our mind settle into its natural state.

3) Specifically, the Presentation That Mindfulness Is Crucial

Generally speaking, mindfulness is important for listening, reflecting, and meditating. It is also important specifically for nurturing meditation. We must tighten our mind one-pointedly and be mindful because, when we lose our mindfulness, the object for practice also slips away. The *Letter to a Friend* teaches:

Lord, the Sugata taught that mindfulness scrutinizing the body
is the single path to follow.
Adhere to that and protect it well.
All dharma is destroyed by the loss of mindfulness.[1073]

The exalted Gampopa says:

The king of mindfulness meditates on the view without distraction.
Apply yourself to that without being diverted by various circumstances.
Seek nothing apart from the stream of unwavering mindfulness.[1074]

The exalted Pakmo Drupa states: [359]

If you are not mindful in this lifetime,
the four māra-thieves will encircle you,
and you risk losing the gem of wisdom.[1075]

The exalted Drikungpa [Jikten Sumgön] teaches:

> The main path of the buddhas of the three times
> is uninterrupted mindfulness.
> If you don't know undistracted mindfulness,
> nothing will come of what you do physically or verbally.[1076]

Mindfulness is explained as twofold: the mindfulness that leads to mindfulness and the mindfulness that focuses on mindfulness. The first is simply to initiate the intention of being mindful of the object of mindfulness. The latter is the actual mindfulness that brings the object of mindfulness to mind and is then not distracted from it. As a beginner, we may have a slight sense of the former coming before the latter but, once we are familiar with them, they arise together.

The practice lineage refers to those types of mindfulness as mindfulness involving effort and effortless mindfulness. The first is said to be the mindfulness that solidifies, or enforced mindfulness, and the mindfulness applied to emptiness, or the mindfulness recognizing [emptiness]. The latter is true mindfulness, or the mindfulness of unification, and the mindfulness that is free from or transcends the intellect.[1077] Thus there are four, which are described as follows:

- The first [mindfulness that solidifies or enforced mindfulness] is when, by enforcing mindfulness, the mind rests within experience along with certainty.
- The second [mindfulness applied to, or recognizing, emptiness] is when whatever arises and whatever appears is recognized to be empty and the continuity of conclusive certainty is maintained.
- The third [true mindfulness or mindfulness of unification] is when, once even the subtle maintenance of effort and certainty is liberated as wisdom, the realization of unification arises naturally without relying on being mindful. [360]
- The fourth [mindfulness that is free from or transcends the intellect] is when all states of mind—those involving an object of meditation and a meditator, and so on—are purified in the nature of the great intrinsic state, equality, and continuous mindfulness becomes the wheel of wisdom.

The scholar-siddha Orgyenpa correlates those four types of mindfulness with the four yogas of meditation and presents the divisions into twelve yogas as a description of how the four types of mindfulness improve. He states that meditation is profound when the latter types of mindfulness develop as a natural outcome of the earlier types.

Among those types of mindfulness, in this context for beginners, the emphasis is on enforced mindfulness. Later, once we are certain that everything that arises is unborn, mindfulness applied [to emptiness] is enough. Both have a phase when they must be generated through great effort and a phase when mindfulness arises naturally on its own. The exalted Götsangpa considers the first type to be a continually maintained mindfulness, which is like a cormorant catching fish. He calls it stacking mindfulness up on top of mindfulness because, in addition to the force of the previous [moment of] mindfulness, mindfulness must be generated again.

We may now wonder, Here it is said that mindfulness is important. What is the meaning of the many statements in the scriptures, including *Unraveling the Intent*, about nonmindfulness and nonattention? Those are relevant for meditative equipoise and, therefore, the meaning of "nonmindfulness" [should be understood] in that context. The *Sūtra of the Questions of Sāgaramati* says:

> The foundation of mindfulness is taught
> to be nonmindfulness and nonattention.[1078]

It is said in the *Sūtra on the Buddha's Deliberations*:

> Mañjuśrī was asked: "What is it like to abide in the foundation of mindfulness?" [361]
>
> He replied: "There is no mindfulness of phenomena. There is no attention."[1079]

It continues:

> Cultivate the recollection of the buddhas that is without mindfulness and without attention.[1080]

There are many such ways that nonmindfulness and nonattention are taught to be recollection and the foundation of mindfulness. As discussed above, the distinctions of true mindfulness are that it is the foundation of mindfulness, unshakeable, straightforward, not vacillating, mindful, sound, and does not forget the path. In that context, the pacification of the distractions of vacillating recollections and thoughts is referred to with the term "nonmindfulness," but that is not a nonmindfulness that is a type of confusion that forgets or loses its object, or what occurs when we faint or sleep.

The meaning of nonattention [or not engaging the mind] is described in the following. The *Dhāraṇī: Access to the Nonconceptual* teaches:

> Child of good family, why is the expanse of nonconceptuality called nonattention? When the characteristics of conceptuality are truly transcended, that is what arises. Since that demonstrates the true transcendence of conceptuality, it is referred to by the term "nonattention."[1081]

The [first] *Stages of Meditation* comments:

> When the *Dhāraṇī: Access to the Nonconceptual* says, "By not engaging the mind, the characteristics of forms and so forth are abandoned," the nonengaging of mind that is intended is the nonobservation that occurs when investigating with prajñā. It is not a mere absence of attention.[1082]

Accordingly, the abandonment of the movements of mind and the separation from all conceptuality is referred to with the term "nonattention," but that does not mean there is a complete absence of mental functions, as the Great Brahman [Saraha] states:

> Yogins and yoginīs: rest as one with the intrinsic mind.[1083]

The Śavara [Saraha] declares:

> Whenever the intrinsic mind is purified, . . .[1084] [362]

Furthermore, the *Śrāvakabhūmi* explains the meaning of nonmindfulness and nonattention as being without characteristics and as nonconceptuality:

> In order to turn from characteristics and be without distractions, from the beginning focus and be nonmindful and nonattentive.[1085]

The final *Stages of Meditation* teaches:

> If nonmindfulness and nonattention are considered to be mere absences of mindfulness and attention, we must analyze how those absences occur. Absence [or nonexistence] cannot serve as a cause. Does nonconceptuality come about from the absence of characteristics and the absence of attention? If just such [mere absence] is considered nonconceptuality, then someone who has fainted would enter nonconceptuality since mindfulness and attention are absent.[1086]

To summarize those numerous explanations, it is said that nonmindfulness and nonattention refer to sustaining the stream of nonconceptual wisdom that is discovered by first analyzing with prajñā. The final *Stages of Meditation* says:

> Therefore, the nonmindfulness and nonattention found within the genuine dharma are seen to be preceded by discernment of what is true. Consequently, only discernment of what is true is able to bring about nonmindfulness and nonattention, nothing else. Thus, when yogins and yoginīs examine with true prajñā, they do not see that ultimately any phenomenon arises during the three times. At which point they enter nonmindfulness and nonattention. Entering those, they realize emptiness. Realizing that, they abandon the webs of wrong views.[1087]

We must understand how to abandon the recollections, thoughts, and attention that involve percepts and perceivers and how to cultivate the continuity of nonconceptual mindfulness and attention. [363] To consider all mindfulness and attention to be what are to be stopped is absurd and unacceptable.

B) Specifically, the Methods for Sustaining Meditation During Equipoise and Postmeditative Attainment

This has five parts:

1) Identifying Equipoise and Postmeditative Attainment
2) Delineating the General Ways to Sustain [Meditation]
3) The Methods for Sustaining Meditative Equipoise

4) The Methods for Sustaining Postmeditative Attainment
5) Delineating the Way to Mix Equipoise and Postmeditative Attainment

1) Identifying Equipoise and Postmeditative Attainment

Equipoise and postmeditative attainment are only properly differentiated starting with freedom from elaborations meditation. Since the phase of one-pointedness is primarily one of meditative experiences, it does not have true equipoise and postmeditative attainment. Nevertheless, it is said to be possible to differentiate the equipoise and postmeditative attainment of this level. Meditative equipoise is when, free from the faults of dullness and agitation, we rest in the essence of the connateness of mind-itself, which was previously pointed out. Then, without any contrary recollections, thoughts, or attention, the mind remains in its natural state as long as the distractions of characterizing or conceptualizing do not arise. The Lord [Atīśa] states in his *Instructions on Madhyamaka*:

> Everything that could be a flaw (such as dullness or agitation) has been cleared away. At this point, mind does not think about anything, it does not grasp at anything. Mindfulness and attentiveness are cast aside. As long as the enemy, or thief, of characterizing or conceptualizing does not arise, rest mind that way.[1088]

The way to cast aside mindfulness and attention is as follows. As explained above, it is not that we should completely eliminate the mindfulness and attention that do not waver from the object but rather that anything else—the recollections, thoughts, and mental activities that show up suddenly—should be eliminated.

As long as our mindfulness does not wander, thoughts do not appear but, if we are even slightly distracted, thoughts pop up immediately. [364] When we are very distracted, all kinds of thoughts and appearances involved with the characterizing process occur. Those are simply the deluded mental states referred to as the normal postmeditative mind and appearances. When we again arouse our earlier mindfulness and hold those unobstructed thoughts and appearances with the light touch of mindfulness, thoughts and appearances are unified emptiness and appearances, unceasing, without any identified essence. Since that is achieved again after it has lapsed, it is called postmeditative attainment. It is commonly said that meditative equipoise is like space and postmeditative attainment is like an illusion.

When we are one-pointedly undistracted right within the essence [of mind] that is meditative equipoise even if it occurs between meditation sessions. When, during the actual meditation session, we hold [the essence of mind] with the light touch of mindfulness after having been slightly distracted, that is considered postmeditative attainment. The exalted Zhang proclaims:

> Resting in unceasing empty clarity,
> vibrant and crisp without center or edge,
> like the middle of clear open space,
> is the meditative equipoise of the first yoga.
>
> When a thought appears within that,
> even if you are meditating on your cushion, that is postmeditative attainment.
> If you remain in vibrant, crisp clarity-emptiness
> while talking, moving, or sitting around,
> you remain in a state of meditative equipoise.[1089]

At this point, on the basis of being habituated to the stream of mindfulness of this level, something like the mixing of equipoise and postmeditative attainment will occur. While this is not true equipoise and postmeditative attainment, it is called the "constant flow of experience."

Here, the point of mahāmudrā is that we don't tamper with our recognition of the abiding state of whatever arises (regardless of whether it is conceptual or nonconceptual)—alterations and abandoning or adopting are never appropriate. [365] Nevertheless, these days when we are practicing as beginners, until we have mixed the equipoise and postmeditative attainment of realization, the primary focus during our actual meditation sessions should be meditative equipoise, that is, one-pointedly sustaining the essence [of mind]. During other periods, such as between meditation sessions, postmeditative attainment should be our primary focus, that is, cultivating the integration of thoughts and appearances with the path. We should understand this to be the intention of the practice lineage. Most of us will find that practicing this way will provide a firm footing for meditative equipoise and make postmeditative attainment decisive. Since each of those enhances the other, this is a very effective way to develop meditation. Therefore, here I will continue to give explanations in keeping with this approach.

2) Delineating the General Ways to Sustain [Meditation]

The way to sustain meditation in a general sense is described by the exalted Gampopa using the term "the three skills." The first is to be skilled in initiating meditation.[1090] Sit properly in the physical posture. In accordance with what was taught previously in the context of śamatha, arouse strong faith and intention through seeing the virtues of samādhi. Dispel the pains of any other mental states, and rest.

In the middle, be skilled in tending experience. Nakedly maintain the essence of mind, adjusting for mental dullness or agitation. Be free from the dankness of stagnate experiences. [366]

In the end, be skilled in suspending meditation. Repeatedly sustain [meditation] with clarity for short periods of time. Part from your meditation when it is going well. Don't allow yourself to grow to dislike it. Those comments are made for beginners.

The exalted Gampopa teaches:

> First, relax your mind and body deeply, not making any effort or trying to practice anything.[1091]

Rest naturally settled without being excessively tight with your physical posture. With your mind, be free from ambition and any effort related to an object of meditation. Let your mind relax in its own basic state with spaciousness and vibrancy.

He continues:

> In the middle, remain in a natural state of freshness with no hesitations.[1092]

Put aside any doubts about what [mind] may or may not be. Do not alter the primordial abiding state of mind, its fresh nature, just as it is.

And he concludes:

> In the end, recognize all impressions and sensations to be unborn.[1093]

With the mindfulness that recognizes all impressions and sensations occurring with the experiences of unsettling circumstances, [know] that as soon as they manifest, they do not exist with any essence that arises, abides, or ceases: they are free in the intrinsic state.

The exalted Gampopa also says:

> Be as wide-open as the sky.[1094]

Let your sense of appearances [and your perspective] be spacious and vibrant. He continues:

> Be as vast as the earth.

Make the scope of your mindfulness and alertness vast. And:

> Be firm like a mountain.

Leave your mind immobile. And:

> Be luminous like a candle flame.

Arouse sharp clarity, the essence of awareness. Finally:

> Be free from stains like a crystal.

Let your mind rest in its vivid brilliance free from the obscurations of experiences.

Those ways of practicing are, for the most part, suitable for any type of equipoise or postmeditative attainment and, therefore, they are taught as the general way to sustain [meditation]. [367]

3) The Methods for Sustaining Meditative Equipoise

This has two parts:

a) The Presentation of Various Methods for Sustaining the Essence [of Mind]

b) The Explanations Summarizing the Vital Points of Those [Methods for Sustaining Meditative Equipoise]

a) The Presentation of Various Methods for Sustaining the Essence [of Mind]

This has three sections:

i) The Explanation of the Six Methods for Sustaining the Essence [of Mind]

ii) The Explanation of Famous Methods for Resting

iii) The Explanation of Other Ways to Sustain [the Essence of Mind]

i) The Explanation of the Six Methods for Sustaining the Essence [of Mind]

Tilopa's famous instructions on the six ways to rest say:

> Don't reflect, don't think, don't speculate.
> Don't meditate, don't analyze—rest naturally.[1095]

"Don't reflect" means don't pursue thoughts about things that are gone: doing so only distracts your mind. "Don't think" means don't fabricate or make judgments about present mental appearances: that will cause your mind—which is what should remain in equipoise—to come under the sway of [discursive] conditions. "Don't speculate" means don't anticipate thoughts of what you will do in the future: if you speculate, your mind will go to those objects and become unstable. These three points are very well known. The Great Brahman [Saraha] states:

> Cast away thoughts and their objects,
> and you'll rest like a small child.[1096]

He also says:

> This mind that cannot be seen to be external or internal
> cannot be thought about by anything or thought to be anything.
> I sing this song of the vajra pinnacle about resting naturally.[1097]

And:

> Being free from meditative concentration, what could be contemplated?[1098]

The Śavara [Saraha] expounds: [368]

> Thus it is that throughout the three times
> sustaining the intrinsic state free from extremes, without mental activity,
> is labeled with the term "meditation."[1099]

"Don't meditate" means don't meditate on anything that is an object of the intellect, such as something with characteristics or something without characteristics. Such meditation causes attention [or mental activity] involving percepts and perceivers. The Great Brahman [Saraha] says:

> KYE MA. Don't say suchness free from any nature exists in meditation.
> If you conceive of an object of meditation and a meditator as a duality,
> the mind grasping dualism rejects its bodhicitta.
> People who do that defile themselves.[1100]

And:

> The mind without meditation and object of meditation is free from any nature.
> Being the consummate, with no hopes or fears, it is vajra mind.[1101]

The Śavara [Saraha] states:

> Unrealized minds have nothing to meditate upon.
> Realized ones have neither an object of meditation nor a meditator,
> just as space cannot observe space.[1102]

Virūpa announces:

> In the expanse of mind's dharmatā there's nothing that's "this";
> therefore, there's no object of meditation, no meditator.[1103] [369]

"Don't analyze" means that [while resting] in that state where elaborations have been pacified, don't again examine or analyze. If you do, your intellectualizations will create dualistic appearances and the characterization process. The Great Brahman [Saraha] explains:

> The unstained essence, untainted by extremes,
> is not an object of analysis: its nature is primordially pure.
> Analyze and a poisonous snake bites, that's all.[1104]

He also says:

> Analyzing mind in terms of being one or many
> eliminates lucidity and perpetuates existence.
> Those who knowingly enter that pit
> deserve our compassion.[1105]

And:

> The mind not analyzing abides like space.
> Space has no abode: it is beyond labels.
> There's no need to examine or analyze the free mind.[1106]

The Śavara [Saraha] observes:

> The analyzing mind binds mind-itself.[1107]

Virūpa says:

> The nature is inexpressible, the essence is beyond all dependent
> phenomena:
> they can't be examined or analyzed—no examples can show them.[1108]

"Rest naturally" means to remain without contrivance right within mind's nature, or way of being, however that is. Not doing that corrupts the abiding state with intellectual constructs. [370] The Great Brahman [Saraha] explains:

> Rest naturally: be just as you are.
> The result is unobstructed, present from the start within yourself.[1109]

He also states:

> Don't adulterate the naturally pure mind with meditative concentrations.
> You reside in bliss—don't torment yourself.[1110]

The Śavara [Saraha] declares:

> The naturally pure mind needs no alteration.
> Don't grasp at it, don't release it: leave it as it is.[1111]

Virūpa teaches:

> Ultimate naturalness, free from attachment, is the state to cultivate.
> Do not abandon, practice, fixate, train, or block.
> Cultivate your own nature comfortably—it is the genuine sublime state.[1112]

Maitrīpa says:

> Remain in the uncontrived nature, the natural state.[1113]

Those methods for resting the mind include most of the key points for sustaining the essence of mind one-pointedly, and they are magnificent methods for determining dharmatā. Tilopa states:

> Don't think, don't reflect, don't analyze. [371]
> Don't meditate, don't engage, don't hope or fear.
> The mental fabrications grasping those liberate in their own spot.
> They settle right within original dharmatā.[1114]

ii) The Explanation of Famous Methods for Resting

Gampopa's *Dharma Lecture: [Abundant Virtue]* presents four methods:

> When looking at your mind, the essence: Let your mind remain relaxed. Rest in freshness. Rest freely. Rest loosely.[1115]

Remain relaxed. Knowing how to relax your mind is a very profound method for cutting through misinterpretations about the mind's way of being and its uncontrived essence. Gampopa says:

> The best relaxation is the best meditation. Intermediate relaxation is intermediate meditation. Inferior relaxation is inferior meditation.[1116]

We may ask, Why is that? If we can let go and relax in a natural way right within whatever arises or occurs in the mind, without creating any expectations, all operative [sense] consciousnesses will cease and we will settle nonconceptually into spaciousness tranquility. At that time, if the sharpness of unborn awareness does not lapse, that is the nature of the inseparability of śamatha and vipaśyanā and the connateness of mind-itself. The mahāsiddha Zhang teaches:

> When your mind lets go and relaxes,
> an experience of clarity free of conceptuality
> dawns like the center of clear open space.
> That's the dharmakāya, luminosity.[1117] [372]

The Great Brahman [Saraha] states:

> If the mind twisted into knots
> is relaxed, it's free—there is no doubt.[1118]

He also says:

> When mind is fettered you are bound.
> It can be liberated—have no doubts.
> What binds fools
> sets the wise free.[1119]

Tilopa teaches:

> Be relaxed in the uncontrived intrinsic state.
> Relax your bonds and there's no doubt: you will be liberated.[1120]

He continues:

> Mind, like the center of space, transcends being an object of reflection.
> Remain relaxed in that state, not discarding or keeping anything.
> When mind is without reference point, that is mahāmudrā.
> When you are accustomed to and familiar with this, you achieve unsurpassable awakening.[1121]

Rest in freshness. This means to rest evenly in the primordial abiding mode. Let the essence, or nature, of the connateness of mind-itself—which was pointed out by the guru and is originally free from elaborations and unidentifiable—be just as it is. This is analogous to how pure gold, whose original condition, whatever that is, cannot be altered subsequently by melting, cutting, and so forth. [373] In some cases this [resting in freshness] is described as being without hesitation, like a pigeon entering her nest. Others say it means to rest without contrivance. The Great Brahman [Saraha] says:

> For those who contemplate suchness free from a root
> receiving the guru's instructions is sufficient.[1122]

He also teaches:

> Meditate on wisdom, self-arisen and inconceivable,
> and you meditate on all the results.[1123]

The Śavara [Saraha] declares:

> Whenever the intrinsic mind is purified,
> you have entered the realization of me, the śavara.[1124]

Virūpa states:

> Being connate from the outset, there's nothing to seek elsewhere:
> mind-itself is empty of names, free from elaborations, mahāmudrā.[1125]

Rest freely. Let the abiding state of mind—its way of being, however that is—remain in a natural way, as it is comfortable. If it is bound by reference points or expectations, it becomes intractable. This is analogous to when someone is put in prison, their only wish is to escape but, if they are set free, they will remain comfortably in a natural way. The Great Brahman [Saraha] says:

> What is bound wants to run in the ten directions.
> When let go, it stays still and motionless.
> I understand these camel-like perversities.[1126]

This is similar to the earlier point to rest naturally.* [374]

Rest loosely. Let the mind go without any fixation or clinging, without the bonds of blocking or encouraging anything, not taking mind to be or not be something, not taking it to be positive or problematic. Like loosening the rope that binds hay, let mind settle loosely into its natural condition whatever that is. In this regard, the Great Brahman [Saraha] instructs:

> If you have an attachment, let it go.[1127]

He also says:

> Entities and nonentities are bonds for sugatas.
> Not separating existence and equality,
> yogins and yoginīs, rest as one with the intrinsic mind.[1128]

Additionally, the exalted Gampopa teaches:

> From time to time, rest in freshness, without contrivance, loosely.[1129]

Although resting without contrivance is similar to resting freely, it [specifically] means that when an unsettling circumstance or appearance comes

*See pp. 323–24.

up, by sustaining just that without any contrivance, it will free itself within the spontaneously existent intrinsic state. Resting without contrivance is [to remain in] clarity without grasping, like the mind of a small child. Accordingly, the Śavara [Saraha] says:

> Ordinary mind in its own intrinsic state
> is not spoiled by contrived focuses.
> The naturally pure mind needs no contrivance.[1130]

He also states:

> Don't hold your breath, don't bind your mind.
> Let your uncontrived mind be like that of a small child.[1131]

Maitrīpa proclaims:

> The uncontrived, intrinsic mind is the dharmakāya. [375]
> The contrived mind will not achieve natural union [yoga].
> Thus leave it be in a blissful space.[1132]

Maitrīpa says:

> Other than settling within without distraction,
> there are no physical or verbal contrivances and no meditation.
> [Despite] saying, "I'm resting evenly," or, "I'm not resting,"
> there's nothing to fix with a remedy and no meditation.[1133]

iii) The Explanation of Other Ways to Sustain [the Essence of Mind]

Nāgārjuna presents four [ways to sustain the essence of mind]: being without conceptuality, without meditating, without contrivance, and loose:

> Don't think at all, don't speculate about anything.
> Don't contrive—remain naturally loose.
> Noncontrivance is the natural, unborn treasure,
> the nondual path of prajñāpāramitā.[1134]

Finding Ease in Mind-Itself lists three ways: being without distraction, without contrivance, and free:

> Listen child, about your thoughts:
> since here they neither bind nor liberate a self,
> be undistracted, without contrivance, and free.
> KYE HO. Your weariness will be eased.[1135]

The exalted Gampopa presents a threefold approach of resting without conceptuality, motionless, and in lucid awareness:

> Remain like a cloudless sky. [376]
> Remain like an ocean without waves.
> Remain like a candle flame in still air.[1136]

The *Instructions on the Four Syllables of Mahāmudrā* presents six modes [of resting]:

> Rest effortlessly in the uncontrived intrinsic state, like a garuḍa soaring through space. Rest motionless, like an ocean without waves. Rest with sparkling clarity, like the sun free from clouds. Rest with the recognition that all impressions and sensations are mind, like waves on water. Rest in unimpeded clarity with no clinging, like a small child looking at a shrine hall. Rest in awareness that leaves no trace, like a bird gliding through the sky.[1137]

The scholar-siddha Chegompa explains many points about the methods for resting, including the following:

- the four: rest with sparkling clarity, without thoughts, uncontaminated, and without support;
- the three: rest uncontrived, unadulterated, and in the intrinsic state;
- the three: rest fresh, loose, and in natural brilliance;
- the two: rest in nonmeditation and nondistraction.[1138]

However, since it seems that those can be understood from what was taught and what will be presented, I will not elaborate on them individually.

The teachings of the earlier masters of the practice lineage contain various methods for sustaining [the essence of mind]. Some emphasize the quality of stillness, described as buoyant, expansive, quiet, radiant, and loose. Others emphasize intense clarity, described as vivid, vibrant, radiant, crisp, naked, and sharp. Here, [the focus is on how] beginners one-pointedly sustain the essence [of mind] during meditative equipoise so we should be guided by the following instructions. The exalted Gampopa says:

> When training, first cultivate vibrant mental clarity. Next train in nondistraction. Then train in never being distracted from the essence of awareness. When you have become accustomed to that, confidence will arise within.[1139] [377]

He also teaches:

> Vibrant clarity is an experience. Not being distracted from that is stillness. Realization is when prajñā sees that no essence exists.[1140]

In brief, bliss, clarity, and nonconceptuality that don't connect directly with the very essence of mind, like a rock pulverizing bones—no matter how good they are—are appearances without ascertainment. Even [if they do connect] right with the essence [of mind], if we are not resting one-pointedly, they are said to be just conceptual understandings. The sayings of the Exalted One [Milarepa] include:

> Whatever that is, it's not it.
> It's the trunk, not the fruit.
> It's a good quality but it's not nonconceptual.[1141]

It is taught that no matter how long we are able to sustain meditative equipoise, the point is that we need to bring out clarity-awareness right within the essence of mind and have the quality of stillness that is not distracted from that. Succinctly put, for beginners this is the one-pointed mind in which śamatha and vipaśyanā are inseparable.

b) The Explanations Summarizing the Vital Points of Those [Methods for Sustaining Meditative Equipoise]

This has three parts:

- i) The Approach of Not Meditating with Mental Formulations
- ii) Why Being Undistracted Right within the Nature Is Necessary
- iii) The Way Those Two [Approaches] Summarize the Vital Points of Meditation

i) The Approach of Not Meditating with Mental Formulations

To sustain meditation on mahāmudrā our mind must simply not stray from its way of being, its natural condition, however that may be. The various reasons why the actual abiding state is not something that can be newly fabricated through intellectual elaborations and then meditated upon have already been presented. [378] However, I will discuss this a little bit again.

- Since the abiding state of mind has no bias, do not meditate with prejudice or partiality towards its manifestations, be they appearances, emptiness, awareness, or the like.
- Since the nature of mind has nothing to be identified, do not meditate with any identification of something being so, not being so, needing to be adopted, or needing to be discarded.
- Since the nature of mind has nothing to be ascertained, do not meditate with any ascertainment or reference points, such as letting some things go and retaining others.
- Since the nature of mind has absolutely nothing to transform, do not meditate with uncertainties and judgments, such as those involving hopes or fears.
- Since the nature of mind has nothing positive or negative, do not meditate with the fabrications of blocking or producing things.
- Since the nature of mind has nothing to be focused upon, do not meditate with anything produced by a focus or effort.

To summarize, since the abiding state of mind has nothing upon which to meditate, do not meditate on anything. If you meditate, no matter what type of meditation you do, it will simply create mental formations, objects of meditation, characteristics, clinging, and fixation. And those are wholly unsuitable in the view and meditation of the abiding state. The sūtras state:

> To meditate on prajñāpāramitā means not meditating on any phenomenon.[1142]

The *Guhyasamāja* observes:

> Since there are no entities, there is no meditation.
> Meditating is not meditation.

> Since entities are devoid of entityness,
> meditation is unobservable.[1143]

The *Vajra Pañjarā* instructs:

> Do not meditate on emptiness.
> Do not meditate on nonemptiness.[1144]

The Great Brahman [Saraha] says:

> If you have an attachment, let it go.[1145] [379]

He also observes:

> Whatever you focus on will itself obscure liberation.[1146]

And:

> If the mind that thinks, "This is attractive,"
> takes that to heart and cherishes it,
> even pain the size of a sesame seed husk
> will cause constant affliction.[1147]

The Śavara [Saraha] says:

> With mahāmudrā, where mind doesn't do anything,
> there's not even an atom's worth of something to meditate on, so don't meditate.[1148]

Virūpa teaches:

> If we bring the abiding state to mind, fixate on experiences,
> or focus and meditate on suchness, we deviate.[1149]

Tilopa advises:

> Don't think: behold the phenomenon of the breakthrough.[1150]

Maitrīpa says:

> Other than settling within without distraction,
> there are no physical or verbal contrivances and no meditation.
> [Despite] saying, "I'm resting evenly," or, "I'm not resting,"
> there's nothing to fix with a remedy and no meditation.[1151] [380]

ii) Why Being Undistracted Right within the Nature Is Necessary

Even though there is nothing to meditate upon that can be contrived by the mind, we still need undistracted mindfulness that keeps us from slipping into a typical, ordinary state. As long as we have not mastered familiarization with mindfulness, an undistracted mind on its own won't be able to distinguish [between slipping into an ordinary state and not doing so]. Therefore, we must have the mindfulness that is not distracted from the point of meditation for each particular level of the four yogas of meditation. At this juncture, we need to be undistracted from the connateness of mind-itself, which was pointed out previously. However, as beginners who have not cut through our misinterpretations about just how things are, we should be undistracted right within the experiences we have on our particular level, such as those of the one-pointed mind. The Great Brahman [Saraha] proclaims:

> KYE MA. Look: [mind] itself reveals suchness to itself.
> If your undistracted mind's looking slips away,
> your distracted mind won't realize suchness.
> You will lose the jewel of suchness in the thicket of objects.[1152]

The Śavara [Saraha] says:

> KYE MA. The undistracted mind looks at itself.[1153]

Virūpa teaches:

> Remain undistracted in a state not thinking of anything, existent or nonexistent.[1154]

Tilopa states:

> To be undistracted is the king of meditation.[1155]

Maitrīpa says:

> Other than settling within without distraction, . . .[1156] [381]

There may be some of inferior intelligence who have experiences of nondistraction and yet do not recognize that they are distracted from the nature [of mind]. We may wonder, What are those [experiences] like?

- Since the abiding state of mind transcends being an object of conceptual understanding, when your intellect and thoughts consider and pay attention to objects of conceptual understanding, you are slightly distracted from the nature [of mind].
- Since the nature of mind is beyond being consciousness, when your intellect and thoughts engage with objects that are cognized by the consciousness, you are slightly distracted from the nature [of mind].
- Since the nature of mind is not an object of reflection or investigation, when your intellect and thoughts pay attention to emptiness, the unborn, and so forth that are the objects of investigation and analysis, you are slightly distracted from the nature [of mind].
- Since the nature of mind is not a reference point, when your intellect and thoughts concentrate on experiences such as bliss, clarity, and nonconceptuality that are specifically used as reference points, you are slightly distracted from the nature [of mind].

In brief, since the abiding state of mind is beyond all forms of attention [or mental activity], anything you take to mind that is contrived or produced by your intellect and thoughts—whether it is something with or without characteristics—is a form of attention [or mental activity].* Even resting with the idea, "I will not do anything with my mind," creates mental activity and distracts you slightly from the nature [of mind]. The Great Brahman [Saraha] explains:

> When the stains of mentation are purified, there is the connate state.
> At that time you don't encounter anything discordant.[1157]

*In this section, "attention," "mental activity," "do (something) with mind," "engage with mentation," "take (something) to mind" are all used to translate *yid la byed pa*; and "mentation" translates *yid*.

He also says:

> When mentation is no longer mentation,
> unsurpassable awakening is attained.[1158]

Virūpa declares:

> If you engage suchness with mentation and fall into the two extremes, [382]
> you will circle in saṃsāra—those are the roots of existence.
> Look at the essence of mentation, the basis and root of all.
> Not seeing anything by looking and free from mental activity, you are certainly liberated.[1159]

He also states:

> If you take something to mind—emptiness, the unborn,
> transcendence of the intellect, being beyond extremes—
> you will not dwell in the abiding state but be rather far from it.[1160]

Śavara advises:

> Look! Look! Do not look at anything.
> Meditate! Meditate! Do not meditate on anything.[1161]

We may now wonder, What is a beginner, within whose mindstream such transcendence of the intellect has not arisen, to do? Although the fundamental state is as just described, those of us who have not developed [realization of that] should, for the time being, nurture our experiences of, and certainty in, the connateness of mind-itself, which was previously pointed out. We should dispel the hindrances of strayings and deviations. At some point, through the process of the four yogas, the unmistaken abiding state, free from the intellect, will manifest. We can know this from the analogies of the moon on the first lunar day, a lion's cub, and a small child. And we will know this from the explanations to come. [383]

iii) The Way Those Two [Approaches] Summarize the Vital Points of Meditation

Nonmeditation and nondistraction contain all the previously described methods for resting. Not meditating on anything contains not reflecting, not thinking, not speculating, not contriving, not adulterating, not analyzing, and so forth. Being undistracted from the nature [of mind] includes freshness, looseness, one's own nature, the abiding mode, the fundamental state, and so forth.

Leaving the mind in its natural condition without meditating is śamatha. Not being distracted from the nature [of mind] is vipaśyanā. Nonmeditation and nondistraction becoming of equal taste contains all the points related to unifying śamatha and vipaśyanā. In the Sūtra context, this [state in which nonmeditation and nondistraction are unified] is referred to as nonconceptual wisdom, nonconceptual and unmistaken awareness, and emptiness of inherent nature. In the Mantra context, it is referred to as connate wisdom, natural luminosity, and total emptiness. In this context, it is referred to as the connateness of mind-itself, essence of mind, abiding state of mind, and the like. These [that is, nonmeditation and nondistraction] are a wondrous approach to meditative equipoise. The *Verses That Summarize the Prajñāpāramitā Sūtras* states:

> Sentient beings say, "I see space."
> Yet how is space seen? Examine this matter.
> The Tathāgata taught that that is how to see phenomena.
>
> No other analogy can express such seeing.
> Those who see that way see all phenomena.[1162] [384]

The *Samputa* teaches:

> If you rest in nonconceptual samādhi,
> you rest without stains like space.[1163]

The *Commentary on Bodhicitta* explains:

> The mind free from reference point
> rests with the characteristics of space.

> Meditating on space
> is described as meditating on emptiness.[1164]

The *Praises of the Dharmadhātu* says:

> Once we abandon conceptions and what is conceptualized
> in the mind, the principal phenomenon,
> we should meditate on phenomena's lack of nature
> as the dharmadhātu.[1165]

The *Entrance to the Bodhisattva's Way of Life* teaches:

> Once neither entities nor nonentities
> remain before the mind,
> since there is no other form,
> there is peace, free from reference point.[1166]

The Exalted Lord [Atīśa] advises:

> In the dharmadhātu, free from elaborations,
> rest your mind free from elaborations.[1167]

We can also refer to previous citations from texts by the mahāsiddhas. I will not elaborate more.

What we should understand now as beginners is that since not meditating is associated with śamatha and relaxing, in excess it can cause dullness. And since being undistracted is associated with vipaśyanā and tightening, in excess it can produce agitation. [385] We must know the ways to dispel dullness and agitation, the ways to sustain śamatha and vipaśyanā equally, and so on, according to what has already been explained in the context of the general explanation of śamatha and vipaśyanā.* Now it is said we must sustain meditative equipoise in which tightness and looseness are balanced, as illustrated by the example of a brahman spinning threads. There are many related sayings, including this one from the exalted Gampopa:

*See "The Ways to Prevent Dullness and Agitation," pp. 28–29, and "The Way To Unify Śamatha and Vipaśyanā," pp. 40–42.

Don't create contrivances: rest loosely.
Don't be on the lookout: rest freely.
Don't do anything with your mind: rest without reference point.[1168]

The exalted Pakmo Drupa teaches:

Meditating on the intrinsic dharmakāya
is like a brahman spinning threads:
rest loosely in uncontrived freshness.

If any sullying faults occur—
becoming stagnant where you rest or wandering off to what's to be let go—
cultivate unification with the connate state.[1169]

Regarding this, a certain person [Sakya Paṇḍita] says:

Resting loosely in uncontrived freshness,
like a brahman spinning threads,
is for them called mahāmudrā.

When I examine the meaning, I see
resting in freshness as being the wool.
Making that into threads is a contrivance.
Therefore the analogy is flawed.[1170] [386]

And yet it seems that he is the one who is mistaken: he doesn't recognize that spinning threads is an analogy for balancing tightness and looseness, doesn't understand the sense of freshness, and doesn't comprehend that just a bit of such resting is not considered mahāmudrā.

Furthermore, the way to sustain meditative equipoise is as the exalted Götsangpa teaches:

Look nakedly at your mind.
Through looking, nothing is seen—there is no thing.
Rest loosely in a state of nonexistence.
Rest without clinging in sheer openness.[1171]

When mind looks nakedly at mind, no nature of mind is seen at all and there is no thing. Within that experience, leave awareness loosely in its natural condition. Not letting that become a neutral state, rest with sheer mindfulness and awareness. Without any reference point for this meditation, [mind] is open. Rest with no fixation or clinging to something to be blocked or something to be produced. That is a concise summary of the key points and is very well regarded.

4) The Methods for Sustaining Postmeditative Attainment

This has four parts:

a) Identifying the Mindfulness of Postmeditative Attainment
b) How That [Mindfulness] Sustains Meditation
c) The Process of Taking Thoughts as the Path
d) The Way Postmeditative Attainment Manifests as Illusionlike

a) Identifying the Mindfulness of Postmeditative Attainment

We may wonder, After resting in one-pointed equipoise within the essence of the connateness of mind-itself as our main practice during meditation sessions, what should we do during the subsequent periods between sessions? Here, at first we should arouse our exertion and train in continuous mindfulness and alertness, as the exalted Drikungpa [Jikten Sumgön] advises:

> If you are skilled in mindfulness, you are skilled in meditation.
> My children, value your mindfulness.[1172] [387]

Moreover, in this context, being mindful of the object of mindfulness is primarily the experience of, and certainty in, the connateness of mind-itself, which was previously pointed out. Nevertheless, there is a slight difference now. Within a moment of mindfulness that preserves the energy or light touch of being mindful of that spiritual practice, do not entertain any reification—don't block or encourage anything—with the thoughts that may suddenly arise with unsettling situations or with the vivid appearances of forms, sounds, and so on. This is like, for example, the mind of a small child looking at a shrine room. With spacious, vibrant mindfulness that is lucid yet without clinging, expand your mental scope and hold that. In brief, sustain the spiritual practices of [being mindful of] the connateness of thoughts and the connateness of appearances, which were previously pointed out.

This is explained in the *Entrance to the Bodhisattva's Way of Life*:

> What is seen, heard, and cognized
> is not what is negated here.
> Here what is negated is the idea of reality,
> the cause of suffering.[1173]

b) How That [Mindfulness] Sustains Meditation

We may wonder, How should that mindfulness sustain spiritual practice? The analogy is the way skilled shepherds care for their animals. Although the animals move around easily as they graze and they may even wander, the shepherds do not need to do anything arduous, such as herding them or chasing them.[1174] Simply not losing sight of them is enough to protect them. Similarly, here it's not that the manifestations of thoughts or appearances are rounded up and then stopped or made to vanish as if we are narrowing in on the essence [of mind]. [388] Nor is it that thoughts and appearances are to be solidified in their normal mode by following them, getting distracted, losing the light touch of mindfulness, or attempting to prevent or promote them. You should have certainty: as each and every object of the six modes of consciousness arises, its manifestation is clear and at the same time its nature cannot be identified. Be mindful [aware], without grasping, that all thoughts are empty movements and all appearances are empty appearances. That certainty and mindfulness sustain [thoughts and appearances] just as they are, without alterations. The exalted Götsangpa presents this in an easily understood way that captures the meaning:

> Whenever yet another thought arises,
> recognize its essence immediately
> and relax right into that.
> There's no doubt: it's free on the spot.
>
> Look nakedly at external objects.
> They are your mind and like illusions.
> Rest without clinging right with whatever appears.
>
> Liberate awareness that's between [those two].
> [Thought-]movements are like breezes, not [solid] things.

Not clung to, movements are fine.
That's called thoughts arising as meditation.

Recognize their essence and you're free from blocking and
producing.
There is nothing to meditate on: just do not wander.
Be undistracted within a state of nonmeditation.[1175]

Practice simply embracing the four types of activities and anything else you do with the light touch of mindfulness. At first, as beginners, distraction will predominate. However, the force of arousing strong mindfulness of the essence [of mind] during meditative equipoise and relying on continuous mindfulness involving effort here in the context of postmeditative attainment will generate naturally occurring mindfulness. In the end, clarity-emptiness and appearance-emptiness will arise vividly, without any distractions, right with most thoughts and appearances themselves. [389]

If that seems to be hard to develop no matter what, it may be that despite your claims to have cut through misinterpretations about the connateness of thoughts and the connateness of appearances, you have not done so at all. Therefore, within the meditative equipoise of [recognizing] the essence [of mind], again cause any kind of thought or appearance to manifest and do what is needed: investigate the origin, abiding, and departure of those manifesting [thoughts or appearances] and look at their essence. Practice as before by determining [the nature of] thoughts and appearances. This point is explained by the Great Brahman [Saraha]:

All phenomena designated by the intellect are empty in and of
themselves.
Devoid of conditions, imputations do not exist.
When you know thusness, liberation in the natural state,
nothing's seen or heard—there's no such nature.[1176]

He also says:

Know the single thusness of what appears as self and other.
Embrace that suchness without distraction.
Since even that torments the mind, let it go.
Without any fixation, you can take up bliss.[1177]

The Śavara [Saraha] observes:

> In the same way all rivers, the Ganges and others,
> become of one taste in the salt ocean,
> know that all analyzing minds and mental events
> are of one taste in the dharmadhātu.[1178]

Virūpa teaches: [390]

> Thus, all conventional phenomena, all possible appearances,
> have no essence: they're merely names, symbols, and imputations.[1179]

c) The Process of Taking Thoughts as the Path

The exalted Gampopa teaches that there are three ways thoughts are incorporated into the path: as the impact of meeting, as the aftereffect, and as nonexistent fantasies.[1180]

As the impact of meeting. This is presented from the perspective of those who are slightly familiar with postmeditative attainment. The analogy is the recognition that occurs when two longtime friends or relatives meet directly on the road: it happens immediately, they don't need to examine [each other to decide] whether it is that person or not. Similarly, the very moment a thought or appearance arises it is liberated within the unborn mind—there's no need to examine it. The Great Brahman [Saraha] says:

> In front, behind, and in all ten directions,
> whatever you see is suchness.[1181]

And:

> What radiates from mind
> is of the nature of the protector.
> Are water and waves different?[1182]

Maitrīpa states:

The various appearances and this essence of mind
don't exist even at the moment they meet: this is
mahāmudrā.[1183]

As the aftereffect. This is presented from the perspective of those who are not very familiar with [postmeditative attainment]. The analogy is that of snow melting and becoming water when it falls on a hot stone or a lake. In the same way, even though [when a thought arises] at first your mindfulness decreases and you are slightly distracted, if you then look at whatever thought or appearance arose, it will immediately be of one taste with the unborn mind. The Great Brahman [Saraha] says: [391]

Just like a crow flying from a ship
circles and circles, and lands there again . . .[1184]

The Śavara [Saraha] teaches:

Just like a crow flying from a ship
circles in many directions yet returns,
though the mind of desire pursues thoughts
it returns to the intrinsic, original mind.[1185]

As nonexistent fantasies. This is presented from the perspective of those who are very familiar [with postmeditative attainment]. The analogy is that of fire in a forest: while a small fire is threatened by wet wood, fierce winds, and the like, when a strong fire races through a forest, it is aided by the trees, grasses, and fierce winds. Correspondingly, even when most of our thoughts and appearances manifest as unborn, again we should conjure up or arouse thoughts and appearances that weigh heavily on our mind or are very unpleasant. They too will manifest as the play of the unborn mind. The Great Brahman [Saraha] states:

Like flames spreading through a forest,
know that all that appears before you
is connate with emptiness, the root of mind.[1186]

Maitrīpa teaches:

> Mental afflictions are great wisdom:
> like a forest for a fire, they aid yogins and yoginīs.[1187]

He continues:

> Appearances, free in themselves, are the dharmadhātu.
> Thoughts, free in themselves, are great wisdom.
> Nondual sameness is the dharmakāya.[1188] [392]

This point is explained in detail by the exalted Pakmo Drupa:

> If you integrate thoughts into the path
> and meditate during four sessions,
> it is taught that your experience will be one of four:
> the meeting of old friends, snow on hot rocks,
> fire consuming a forest, or bliss, clarity, and emptiness.
>
> First, "the meeting of old friends" refers to
> when two close friends
> bump into each other on the road:
> they recognize each other immediately.
>
> Similarly, yogins and yoginīs
> determine that the very moment a thought arises
> it is their own mind, emptiness.
> That is called "the impact of meeting."
>
> Second, "snow on hot rocks" refers to
> that snow falls from clouds
> and yet as soon as it hits hot rocks
> immediately it becomes water.
>
> Likewise, when a thought arises from a distraction,
> just after it occurs, it is known to be mind.
> Without any effort, it is realized
> to be mind-itself, dharmakāya free from elaborations.
> That is called "the aftereffect."

Third, "fire consuming a forest" refers to
when fire rages through a forest,
trees, grasses, sentient beings,
clean ground, unclean ground,
all are consumed without any thought.
No matter what happens—winds or hail—
the fire doesn't die out, it is aided by all that.

In the same way, when the firestorm of realization blazes,
all thoughts, good and bad,
percepts and perceivers, the afflictions of desire and aggression, [393]
are consumed in the unborn state,
without any adopting or rejecting, blocking or producing.
The more thoughts, the more assistance
you have for realization to arise.[1189]
That is called "nonexistent fantasies."

When realization is firm,
[mind] is clear yet unimpeded, free from extremes.
It is blissful, clear, and nonconceptual without fixation.
Even being pricked by a needle arouses bliss.

When there's no change no matter what you do
during the day or night, between sessions, walking, or sitting,
that is the fourth experience: "bliss and clarity."

Those are the ways experiences occur.[1190]

d) The Way Postmeditative Attainment Manifests as Illusionlike

This has two parts:
- i) The Explanation of the Meaning of Illusionlike
- ii) The Way Postmeditative Attainment Manifests as Illusionlike

i) The Explanation of the Meaning of Illusionlike

Some assert that being like an illusion means that while something does not exist in fact, it is ascertained as a mere appearance for the deluded mind.

Others assert that illusionlike means that when we are steeped in experiences of stillness or experiences of emptiness and a thought or appearance arises, it seems amorphous and hazy. Still others maintain that it means to sustain the recollection of, and belief in, the thought that whatever occurs or appears in the mind is illusionlike.

The first are incorrect. They lean towards nihilism because, other than simply not blocking immediate appearances, they take even what is merely dependently originated to be in fact nonexistent. The second are wrong because, not having determined the nature of appearances, they just have experiences [of things seeming to be illusionlike]. The third are also not right because they simply presume that appearances are illusionlike. [394]

We may ask, How is it then? Generally speaking, the phrase "illusionlike" is used when dharmatā and omniscience are described as illusionlike and when entities (such as forms) are taught to be illusionlike. In the first instance it means that, although they are affirmed as being merely existent, conventionally they do not appear. In the latter case, it means that they do not exist in terms of their own nature and yet they appear conventionally. In this context, it is the latter sense that is being used. The *Verses That Summarize the Prajñāpāramitā Sūtras* say:

> Know the five skandhas to be like illusions.
> Don't take illusions to be one thing and skandhas to be
> another.[1191]

The *King of Samādhi* teaches:

> Like mirages and cities of gandharvas,
> illusions and dreams,
> all characteristics you entertain are empty of any essence.
> Know all phenomena are this way.[1192]

Although many examples of illusions are taught, here I will use one that it is easy to understand. The horses and elephants conjured up by illusionists have never had the nature, or essence, of horses and elephants. In terms of [the perception of] the way they appear, there is no difference between the audience (whose vision has been distorted by the power of substances and mantras) and illusionists: the horses and elephants appear undeniably to both of them. On the other hand, in terms of [understanding] the way they actually are, there is a difference: one group believes in and takes those horses and elephants to have [real] characteristics [that is, to be real] and the other does not. Here, just like an illusionist's [experience of] those visual appearances, [our perception of] the way things appear—the appearing objects (such as forms and sounds) and the thoughts occurring in our mind as we experience unsettling circumstances—is similar to that of an ordinary person. [395] However, in terms of [understanding] the way things are, since we have severed our misunderstandings and [know] that those [thoughts and objects] have never existed with their own nature or essence, we experience them as appearing yet being without any nature—as being like illusions. The *King of Samādhi* states:

> Illusionists conjure up forms,
> creating various horses, elephants, and chariots.
> Those appear despite not existing at all.
> Know all phenomena are this way.[1193]

ii) The Way Postmeditative Attainment Manifests as Illusionlike

Generally speaking, [the experience of things being] illusionlike must arise based on the sense consciousnesses perceiving appearances and the mind ascertaining emptiness. Keeping with the same analogy: illusionists perceive the appearances of conjured-up horses and elephants with their visual consciousness, and they ascertain the nonexistence of those seeming horses and elephants with their mental consciousness. On the basis of those two, they are certain that what appear as horses and elephants are simply false appearances.

Similarly, now during the postmeditative attainment of yogins and yoginīs, all thoughts (related to unsettling circumstances) and appearances (forms, sounds, and so on) manifest undeniably to the visual and other sense consciousnesses based on the interdependence of causes and conditions. Holding them with the light touch of mindfulness of our previous experiences (and certainty) in which we determined the connateness of thoughts and of appearances, those thoughts and appearances are recognized to be emptiness: they are empty of any essence or nature of their own. The convergence of those two allows postmeditative attainment to arise as illusionlike. The Śavara [Saraha] explains: [396]

> When you examine objects, since they are devoid of the three reference points,
> like dreams and illusions, [you see] they are not real.
> When you're free from attachments, [they bring] joy, not sadness,
> just like the illusory objects created by a magician.[1194]

He also says:

> All appearances and sounds are like illusions,
> mirages, and reflections: they have no real characteristics.
> The perceiver of illusions is mind-itself, space.[1195]

To cultivate the emptiness component that gives rise to that [postmeditative attainment experience of things being illusionlike], primarily we need certainty in our ascertainment of the unborn essence of the connateness of mind-itself. Therefore, it is important to apply ourselves to [recognizing] that essence [of mind] during meditative equipoise. It is also important to apply ourselves to [recognizing] the essence of the connateness of thoughts and of appearances during postmeditative attainment. To cultivate the appearance component, there's nothing that needs to be specifically done since the arising and perception of our usual thoughts and appearances happens naturally, in keeping with the interdependence of causes and conditions and through the force of habituation. Nevertheless, some, due to their excessive fixation on emptiness, take even the dependent origination of actions and their results to be nonexistent. They are great nihilists, which is always unsuitable. They must develop the ascertainment of clear appearances with even the most subtle dependent origination of actions and results.

In brief, it is essential that we instill within ourself an understanding that actions and their results are infallible, and that we combine this with a conviction about emptiness, that all phenomena lack a nature. This is described as a source of wonderment, as the *Commentary on Bodhicitta* states:

> Those who understand this emptiness of phenomena
> and also attend to actions and their results
> are more amazing than amazing,
> more wondrous than wondrous.[1196] [397]

That being the case, earlier scholars explain the exclusion of a nature, or essence, of phenomena to be freedom from elaborations, which they refer to as spacelike emptiness. They also explain that while [phenomena] are empty of a nature or essence, manifestations of forms and so forth appear, which they refer to as illusionlike emptiness. Based on that, it is common for many present-day practitioners of the definitive meaning to refer to "spacelike meditative equipoise" and "illusionlike postmeditative attainment." Also, in some instances, that nonconceptual meditative equipoise is described using the term "transcendent wisdom" and illusionlike postmeditative attainment by the term "mundane wisdom."

Based on the sayings in the practice lineage, "sustain the mind naturally settled without contrivance" and "sustain the mind experiencing unsettling circumstances without altering it," some mistakenly sustain, in an oblivious way, their regular mind when it is agitated by unsettling circumstances and objects. Other mistakenly sustain the deluded mind, which is ignorant of the mind's abiding state, without any alteration, however it happens to manifest. Since neither distinguish between phases [of the path] and what is to be adopted and what is to be rejected, their approaches are quite absurd.

During the phase when we have correctly realized the abiding modes of the mind's essence, nature, and characteristic and, having really stabilized those, we are able to take all circumstances as the path, there are occasions when it is appropriate to take literally the instructions to sustain whatever arises in the mind without contrivance or tampering, without adopting or discarding, and to sustain the mind experiencing unsettling circumstances without altering it.

On the other hand, it is explained that if we can't connect directly with sharp clarity right within the essence of mind, like a rock pulverizing bones, we should dispel any stagnate experiences of bliss and clarity that may arise occasionally, and sustain [our practice] having dispersed the dankness of experiences. This is because if we sustain our usual deluded mind without alteration in an oblivious way, we will not transcend the causes of saṃsāra. [398] With this point in mind, the exalted Drikungpa [Jikten Sumgön] teaches about the different types of noncontrivance [or nonmodification]:

> Not modifying mental afflictions and thoughts
> is the way of being in the three realms of saṃsāra.
> Not modifying excellent experiences
> is a cause for birth in the higher states of the gods.

> Not modifying the abiding state of mind
> is to rest in the ground of nirvāṇa.
> Not modifying nondual saṃsāra and nirvāṇa
> is the unification of training in the Mahāyāna.
>
> Finally, not modifying transcendence of the intellect
> is the final fruition of beyond training,
> the source of effortless benefit for others
> in self-arising spontaneous existence.[1197]

We may ask now, What then is the meaning of the previous statements? The expression "sustain the mind naturally settled without contrivance" means when you are aware of the abiding state of mind, sustain that in a natural way without subjecting it to any extraneous contrivance or tampering. The expression "not altering the mind experiencing unsettling circumstances" means you continue to be aware of the abiding state of the mind experiencing objects, no matter what occurs, and then do not adulterate that by grasping, which would involve blocking one thing or encouraging another.

Similarly, the saying "blend right with the experience of unsettling circumstances" means you should hold the light touch of mindfulness of the essence right with those very [circumstances]. "Relax right with the arising of unsettling circumstances" means, by relaxing any clinging involving preventing or promoting those [circumstances], you settle right within the nature.

In brief, if you continuously apply mindfulness of the essence to the postmeditative mind and postmeditative appearances, all thoughts and appearances involving undistracted mindfulness will be postmeditative attainment. When you have continuous awareness of the abiding state, you can sustain whatever arises during postmeditative attainment in a natural way, and you will have certainty right with the experience of unsettling circumstances—without doing anything, such as altering them. [399] That is why having mindfulness that is not distracted from the nature is critical at all times, and why mindfulness is the main practice of meditation. The exalted Gampopa explains:

> The king of mindfulness meditates on the view without distraction.
> Apply yourself to that without being diverted by various
> circumstances.

> Seek nothing apart from the stream of unwavering mindfulness.[1198]

He also comments:

> As long as the stake of clinging is not extracted,
> thoughts will gather karma.
> Posting the lookout of undistracted mindfulness is something good.[1199]

5) Delineating the Way to Mix Equipoise and Postmeditative Attainment

Since there are many ways experiences arise in the minds of individuals, it is difficult to describe precisely how equipoise and postmeditative attainment are mixed. I also have not seen many other explanations. Nevertheless, in some of the questions and answers with exalted Gampopa we find:

> [Yogin Chöyung] asked: "What does it mean to mix the meditative equipoise of the essence with postmeditative attainment?"
>
> [Gampopa] replied: "If, no matter which of the four daily activities you are doing, you are not separated from luminosity and the essence is always present, they have mixed."
>
> [Yogin Chöyung] asked: "Sometimes when mindfulness fades we start thinking. Once we regain mindfulness, the essence is present. Is that not mixing?"
>
> [Gampopa] replied: "That is not mixing."[1200]

The exalted Drikungpa [Jikten Sumgön] teaches: [400]

> Those who have equipoise and postmeditative attainment
> are called bodhisattvas.
> Those who do not have equipoise and postmeditative attainment
> are called siddhas and buddhas.[1201]

It is clear that the true, authentic mixing of meditative equipoise and postmeditative attainment does not occur until the phases of greater one-taste meditation and nonmeditation because it is taught that, even during greater freedom from elaborations, the postmeditative mind is not solely a state of luminosity in which conceptuality is pure and because, during intermediate one taste, the postmeditative mind sometimes experiences appearances with the solidification of dualistic perception.

The exalted Gomtsul asked the exalted Gampopa:

> [Gomtsul] asked: "How do we assess the mixing of meditative equipoise and postmeditative attainment? Is it being able to perform our daily activities without being separated from one-pointed meditative equipoise? Or is it that postmeditative attainment is aided by thoughts? Is it that postmeditative attainment is like dreams and illusions? Or is it that during postmeditative attainment what appear as thoughts are recovered as that [meditative equipoise]?"
>
> [Gampopa] replied: "If it arises the first way that is excellent, and that may just be possible. The middle ones qualify. In the last case, if thoughts become ordinary and then [awareness of their abiding state] is not recovered, meditative equipoise and postmeditative attainment have not mixed."[1202]

If we consider the sayings of the previous masters of the practice lineage, it is clear that it is not wrong to use the expression "mixing meditative equipoise and postmeditative attainment" for what occurs during the phase of greater freedom from elaborations. The mixing of meditative equipoise and postmeditative attainment does not require that all of postmeditative attainment be only luminosity. Being aided by illusionlike thoughts qualifies. Also, even if our postmeditative mind is momentarily distracted, when then it is aware of its abiding state and recovers, that qualifies. It is taught that all that happens at the level of greater freedom from elaborations and above. [401]

Furthermore, greater freedom from elaborations is a time when meditative equipoise and postmeditative attainment mix due to the fact that recognizing the nature of phenomena is said to be the mixing of meditative equipoise and postmeditative attainment, as the *Verses That Summarize the Prajñāpāramitā Sūtras* says:

> This does not have the presumption of what is called "meditative equipoise" or "rising [from that]." Why? Because the nature of phenomena is recognized.[1203]

Greater freedom from elaborations can also be considered to be a time when meditative equipoise and postmeditative attainment mix because it is taught that when dharmatā is realized, meditation occurs without mindfulness or distraction, as the Śavara [Saraha] says:

> When you realize your own suchness,
> even the distracted mind is mahāmudrā.[1204]

Here, however, I will describe the mixing of meditative equipoise and postmeditative attainment for each level [of the four yogas] in relation to the way experiences develop.

During one-pointed meditation, since fixating on experiences has not been purified, there is no authentic meditative equipoise and postmeditative attainment but there is the meditative equipoise and postmeditative attainment specific for its levels. During intermediate one-pointedness, [the experience of] the postmeditative mind is that previous coarse thoughts and appearances have vanished and, consequently, there is little arising of solidification. Most thoughts and appearances self-liberate in their natural brilliance. That is asserted to be the slight mixing of meditative equipoise and postmeditative attainment of this level. Greater one-pointedness is said to be when there is a constant flow of experience. Therefore, the meditative equipoise and postmeditative attainment of these levels must be mixed.

Freedom from elaborations meditation is explained to be when authentic meditative equipoise and postmeditative attainment occur. During intermediate freedom from elaborations, although the postmeditative mind does not always experience the essence of purified thoughts, for the most part it maintains applied mindfulness. At that time, it is easy and comfortable to cultivate spiritual practice with excellent experiences of awareness-emptiness and appearance-emptiness. That is asserted to be a slight mixing of meditative equipoise and postmeditative attainment. During greater freedom from elaborations, which is the purification of experience, the constant flow day and night must be posited as the mixing of meditative equipoise and postmeditative attainment. [402]

During intermediate one taste, the postmeditative mind has few delusions and experiences most appearances as meditation. That is asserted to be a slight mixing of meditative equipoise and postmeditative attainment. During greater one taste, the postmeditative mind experiences all appearances as empty clarity, without clinging and like illusions. That is posited as the mixing of meditative equipoise and postmeditative attainment. For those reasons, the exalted Gampopa, his two nephews [Gomtsul and Gomchung], the exalted Pakmo Drupa, the exalted Tsangpa Gyare, and their students teach that meditative equipoise and postmeditative attainment are mixed during the phase of one taste.

There are many other distinctions between the spiritual practices of freedom from elaborations and one taste, and what is elevated during their respective meditative equipoises and postmeditative attainments. These can be understood from the explanations that will come later.*

That completes the explanation of the way to sustain spiritual practice.

*See "How the Realizations of the Four Yogas Develop," pp. 425–76.

12

Eliminating Deviations and Strayings

C) Eliminating Deviations and Strayings in Meditation

This has two parts:

1) Eliminating Deviations and Strayings in Samādhi
2) Clearing Away Obstructing Hindrances

1) Eliminating Deviations and Strayings in Samādhi

This has two sections:

a) Eliminating the Four Deviations
b) Eliminating the Three Strayings

a) Eliminating the Four Deviations

This has two divisions:

i) Identifying the Four Deviations
ii) The Presentation of the Methods for Not Deviating in Those Ways

i) Identifying the Four Deviations

Generally speaking, the explanations of each of the four deviations in relation to emptiness use the terms "fundamental deviations" for the deviations of [leaving emptiness as] a theoretical understanding, an abstract idea, and "temporary deviations" for the mistaken ways of cultivating experiences [of emptiness].

The two types of deviations from emptiness as the basic nature of knowable objects are as follows. [Since emptiness is the basic nature of knowable objects] we meditate on the inseparability of appearances and emptiness. When we are ignorant of the way that emptiness and dependent origination are nondual—which is called "emptiness endowed with the most sublime of manifestations"—we may conclude that emptiness is only something primordially nonexistent: a total absence, never covered by faults or positive qualities. And, therefore, we dismiss [the validity of] the causes and results of virtue and evil. [403] Or we may deviate from the basic nature, which is that phenomena are primordially pure, primordially liberated, and so forth, and, carried away by our assessment of such [one-dimensional] emptiness, not develop proficiency with dependent origination on the conventional level. Those are the fundamental deviations.

On the basis of study and reflection, we may correctly understand emptiness (the object of meditation) as an abstract idea, as an intellectual object for ourselves. We may also know how to explain that approach to others. But that [basic nature of emptiness] has become like something that exists somewhere else. We don't recognize that abiding nature right within our own awareness and aren't confident about it right within our own experience. That is the temporary deviation.

Deviating from emptiness as the path is twofold as follows. [Since emptiness is the path] we meditate on the inseparability of the path and fruition. Since ground, path, and fruition are inseparable and complete as one nature in the abiding state of our mind, the resultant dharmakāya exists spontaneously as an innate quality of mind's nature. Not realizing that, we believe that by taking emptiness as the path and meditating upon it now, we will attain something else as the result: buddhahood with its three kāyas and five wisdoms. That is the fundamental deviation.

Although the practice of meditation on the abiding state, just as it is, is what we are to sustain, not being confident in that, we hope for something else or something superior to that and go looking elsewhere. Or we manufacture something "superior" in the abiding state of the mind's nature—such as bliss, clarity, or nonconceptuality—and meditate on that instead. Those are the temporary deviations.

Deviating from emptiness as the remedy is twofold as follows. [Since emptiness is the remedy] we meditate on the inseparability of the factors to be abandoned and their remedy. The basic nature of the mental afflictions, what are to be abandoned, is itself the remedy: emptiness. Not understanding that when we are aware of that very nature [emptiness], mental afflictions (what are to be abandoned) arise as wisdom (the remedy), we take mental afflictions and emptiness to be different things.

We reject mental afflictions and, as their remedy, we meditate on emptiness, something separate. [404] Or we work out that those mental afflictions do not inherently exist and rest in that. Those are the fundamental deviations.

When thoughts related to unsettling circumstances arise, we do not sustain the mindfulness that recognizes their nature. Instead, we either destroy the thought itself or we draw it in and place it within our meditation. Those are the temporary deviations.

Deviating from emptiness as the seal is twofold as follows. [Since emptiness is the seal] we meditate on the inseparability of method and wisdom. Being unaware that [emptiness] is the very essence of phenomena (those involving reference points and those that do not), first we take a virtuous quality (such as generosity) to involve reference points and the characterization process. Then we dissect it using reasoning. Or we intellectually fabricate its lack of inherent existence by reciting the *svabhāva* mantra or the like. Those are the fundamental deviations.

While sustaining meditation, we may not keep to the proper sequence and not take [whatever arises] as the path. Instead we recreate some past [experience of emptiness] and bring that to mind thinking, "This is meditation." Or, not taking postmeditative mental states as the path, first we are distracted and don't notice, then we interrupt the discursiveness of thoughts with meditation, thinking that is meditation.[1205] Those are the temporary deviations.

These illustrate the ways beings deviate in meditation.

ii) The Presentation of the Methods for Not Deviating in Those Ways

Among those ways of deviating, the fundamental deviation from emptiness as the basic nature of knowable objects is a very flawed wrong view. The Great Brahman [Saraha] declares:

> Those who grasp at what doesn't exist are even more foolish.[1206]

Nāgārjuna teaches that to be a major nihilistic view:

> If emptiness is seen incorrectly,
> those of little intelligence are ruined.[1207] [405]

He also states that its result is to be born in the negative states:

> Those who assert nonexistence proceed to negative states.[1208]

The exalted Gampopa teaches:

> Even though you may not fixate on emptiness, the basic nature of knowable objects,
> you may not have realized reality.[1209]

The other ways of deviating do not bring about that type of wrong view but, since they do not lead to meditation that is conclusive about the abiding state, we should avoid them.

Not Deviating from Emptiness as the Basic Nature of Knowable Objects

[We avoid this deviation by understanding the meaning of] "mahāmudrā." Our basic nature is unborn: it does not exist as anything at all since it is empty of any phenomenon involving existence, nonexistence, permanence, annihilation, truth, or falsity. And yet its unimpeded radiance manifests as a variety of dependent arisings on the conventional level. By understanding that emptiness is the core of dependent origination and dependent origination is of the nature of emptiness, we do not deviate from emptiness as the basic nature of knowable objects. The *Fundamental Treatise on the Middle* sums this up:

> There is no existent phenomenon
> that is not dependently originated.
> Therefore, there is no existent phenomenon
> that is not empty.[1210]

The *Commentary on Bodhicitta* adds:

> The conventional is taught to be emptiness,
> and emptiness itself is the conventional.[1211]

Not Deviating from Emptiness as the Path

By knowing that mahāmudrā, the nature of ordinary mind, is the governing principle of all phenomena related to ground, path, fruition, and so forth, or that it is the very essence, we do not deviate from emptiness as the path. The Great Brahman [Saraha] declares:

> With mind, enquire into mind for this intrinsic wisdom,
> the one taste of the bhūmis, paths, and buddhahood.[1212] [406]

He continues:

> Meditate on wisdom, self-arisen and inconceivable,
> and you meditate on all the results.[1213]

He concludes:

> The result is unobstructed, present from the start within yourself.
> There's no need to be caught up in remedies with hopes and fears.[1214]

Āryadeva explains:

> One entity has the essence of all entities.
> All entities have the essence of one entity.[1215]

The exalted Gampopa says:

> Know right now that this clarity-emptiness—
> the essence of reflexive awareness—is the dharmakāya.
> Know right now that your mind—
> pure and beginningless—is the result.
>
> E MA. The expanse of the precious mind:
> at the time of being the cause, it is the actual result.[1216]

Not Deviating from Emptiness as the Remedy

When we recognize that all phenomena are of one nature in the natural expression of intrinsic mahāmudrā, we understand the nature of connateness—the equal taste of mental afflictions (what are to be abandoned) and wisdom (the remedy)—and thus do not deviate from emptiness as the remedy. The *Two-Part [Hevajra Tantra]* teaches:

> There is not the slightest difference
> between the nature of pure wisdom
> and the thoughts of saṃsāra.[1217] [407]

It also says:

> Saṃsāra is anger and the rest.
> The dharma[tā] of those is nirvāṇa.[1218]

Nāgārjuna states:

> Saṃsāra is not even slightly
> different from nirvāṇa.[1219]

Maitrīpa observes:

> Mental afflictions are great wisdom.[1220]

Not Deviating from Emptiness as the Seal

When, through understanding that intrinsic mahāmudrā is the governing principle of all phenomena, we know the reason that the basic nature of all the roots of virtue (those that involve characteristics and so on) is never anything other than emptiness, which is naturally pure, all phenomena are sealed. Subsequently, we will not deviate into sealing with an emptiness that is conceptually contrived by an individual person. Virūpa says:

> All dualistic appearances and characteristics—happiness, sadness, and the rest—
> are the display of intrinsic mahāmudrā, dharmatā.
> Since that display is neither real nor permanent,
> it never goes beyond the seal of emptiness, the abiding state.[1221]

The Śavara [Saraha] states:

> All karmic formations are primordially the dharmadhātu.[1222]

Maitrīpa explains:

> Once this is realized,
> all that can possibly appear is mahāmudrā:
> the great pervasive infinite dharmakāya.[1223] [408]

Furthermore, the exalted Gampopa teaches:

> Experience can deviate [from] realization, and realization can deviate into experience.[1224]

The first occurs when, using specialized techniques such as those of breath control, we meditate on the essence of mind-itself and the positive experiences of bliss, clarity, and nonconceptuality arise. We have confidence in those and take them to be sublime. Thinking there can be nothing higher, we continue to practice while fixating on those experiences.

The latter occurs when, on the basis of our guru's blessings, we realize that the essence of mind does not exist as anything and cannot be identified. Within such [realization] experiences of bliss, clarity, and so forth can naturally arise. If they do and we are pleased, or if they don't and we are unhappy, we may direct our efforts towards them and rest our mind there instead. The exalted Drikungpa [Jikten Sumgön] says:

> In samādhi, bliss and clarity
> are sometimes present, sometimes not.
> If we meditate with the hope they will come,
> we're like children gazing at a rainbow,
> which grows fainter and fainter until it finally disappears.[1225]

In this context, a certain person [Sakya Paṇḍita] says:

> The thought, "I will abandon the four deviations,"
> is not mahāmudrā.
> [But] if we don't have that thought, we can't abandon them.
> If we could give them up without that thought,

why wouldn't mahāmudrā
arise effortlessly in all sentient beings?
Therefore, whatever is mahāmudrā
has no deviations and strayings.
If it does, it's not mahāmudrā.[1226]

That statement reflects nothing more than his desire to say something [critical]. We may ask, Why [is he wrong]? The previously cited quotation from Maitrīpa and his statement, "Thoughts, free in themselves, are great wisdom,"[1227] explain the context in which thoughts are mahāmudrā: when the suchness of thoughts is recognized. [409] Here, as a general matter, it is not asserted that the usual sense of the thought, "I will avoid the deviations," is itself mahāmudrā. [Sakya Paṇḍita's] statements are just what he insists upon saying. If the absence of thoughts [nonconceptuality] is unable to relinquish what is to be abandoned, the following citations would be incorrect, such as the *Ornament for the Mahāyāna Sūtras*:

The power of the nonconceptual wisdom of the wise
continuously extends to all equally,
eliminating the tangled mass of their flaws,
just as a strong antidote [neutralizes] poison.[1228]

The *Entrance to the Bodhisattva's Way of Life* observes:

Emptiness is the remedy for the darkness
of the afflictive and cognitive obscurations.
Those who wish to attain omniscience quickly
should meditate on emptiness.[1229]

And if the absence of thoughts [nonconceptuality] is unable to relinquish what is to be abandoned, it means that all meditation on nonconceptual wisdom would be pointless since it could not relinquish the objects to be abandoned. It is also laughable to suggest that sentient beings don't have thoughts. And by saying whatever is mahāmudrā doesn't have deviations and strayings, he refutes his own statement:

The fool's meditation on mahāmudrā
usually is a cause for being [born as] an animal.[1230]

Furthermore, if no deviations and strayings can occur in mahāmudrā, applying the reasoning of equivalency means that it would impossible to deviate from, or err in relation to, the bhūmis and paths. In that case, many more contradictions with the scriptures and reasonings would follow. [410]

b) Eliminating the Three Strayings

This has three parts:

i) The Explanation of Specific Instances of Experiences That Are Strayings
ii) The Way Those [Experiences] Become Strayings
iii) The Presentation of the Methods for Not Straying in Those Ways

i) The Explanation of Specific Instances of Experiences That Are Strayings

Broadly speaking, when we cultivate meditation without letting it become routine and distinguish between brilliant states of mind and sullied ones, all kinds of experiences can arise in our mind. In particular, it is explained that many wonderful types of experiences can occur for practitioners with an excellent orientation in terms of their channels, winds, and so forth, for those who rely on specialized techniques (such as breath control), and for the few whose great diligence in meditation is not interrupted by distraction and laziness. When various latent tendencies of karma and mental afflictions are activated, objects [normally appearing for] the six modes of consciousness appear as mental objects. There may appear many different kinds of objects for the five physical sense faculties, such as visual experiences of forms, auditory experiences of sounds, olfactory experiences of smells, and the like. And there is an endless variety of thoughts that can arise, like waves on water. But those who vacillate between meditating and being seduced by appearances will only have a tiny bit of experiences. Since it is clear that not all people are the same, the specific experiences they have won't be the same. Nevertheless, now I will draw from teachings that summarize experiences into three types.

Blissful [or pleasurable] experiences. Your body may be pervaded by bliss [or pleasure]. Objects you touch may arouse bliss. You may feel so blissful you can't tell whether you have a body or not. Your mental joy may cause you to laugh. You might be at ease mentally and all appearances might seem delightful. The bliss [or pleasure] of simply not knowing whether it is day or night may fill your body and mindstream.

Experiences of clarity. Your mind may sparkle, like a crystal, and you may have many different clear visions. You may have the sense that you can see objects both near and far even at night. You may experience visual appearances [in meditation] with characteristics you can [actually] touch and see.[1231] You can have experiences of illumination similar to that of radiant light. [411] You might also think you have the supercognitive ability of knowing other people's minds.

Although some explain empty forms that are latent tendencies to be part of the experiences of emptiness, it seems better to consider those to be experiences of clarity.

Experiences of nonconceptuality. You may have the perception that all animate and inanimate things are empty. Appearing objects—forms, sounds, and so forth—can seem amorphous and vague. You might have the sense that you don't exist, that you and all appearances are expressions of emptiness. Experiences of such utter emptiness that even the subtlest thoughts have dissolved may occur—like a clear open sky.

Some assert that once we have received the blessing of the three vajras, experiences and signs arise in our three doors [body, speech, and mind] as harbingers of realizing the abiding state. It is said:

> Once the intrinsic abiding state manifests just a bit,
> concordant experiences arise in dreams
> because the profound abiding state, the nature of the four vajras,
> is the nature of all manifestations.
>
> When vajra body has blessed your body,
> many different physical manifestations will occur naturally,
> such as trembling, shaking, floating, moving, jumping, and running.
>
> When vajra speech has blessed your speech,
> many different verbal expressions will occur naturally,
> such as discoursing, laughing, crying, wailing, and shouting. [412]

> When vajra mind has blessed your mind,
> supreme samādhi and supercognitions develop.[1232]

Although there are many such explanations, and even though it is possible that [such experiences] will occur for a few due to their practice of breath control and the interdependence of their channels and winds, they will not happen for everyone.

In this practice tradition, those experiences are explained by categorizing them as being either experiences of just śamatha, experiences connected to śamatha and vipaśyanā, or experiences intrinsic to realizations. The exalted Gampopa teaches:

> The experiences of stillness are as follows. Using [the techniques of] the path of method, winds enter the avadhūti, the force of which generates bliss, clarity, and nonconceptuality. Bliss is a defiled bliss that spreads throughout your body and mind. Clarity is your experience of that. Nonconceptuality is the expanding of nonconceptual samādhi without mindfulness.[1233]

He also says:

> The force of the winds entering the avadhūti [result in] signs, such as the eight benefits or the five signs. They arise through cultivating the unification of śamatha and vipaśyanā but not during the intermittent stillness that focuses on a subtle object.[1234]

He concludes:

> When realization occurs it's impossible for experiences not to do so as well. Realization is that when you see clearly the essence of mind-awareness, you will think that you should have recognized what was taught to be "it" from the first. Then your experiences of bliss are of undefiled, natural great bliss. Clarity is that sense that it's just vividly right there, something you feel you could grasp in your hand. Nonconceptuality is untainted by even the smallest thoughts. That is the arising of the nonduality of experience and realization.[1235] [413]

ii) The Way Those [Experiences] Become Strayings

When any of those experiences of bliss, clarity, or nonconceptuality develop (either altogether or separately), if we take them to be sublime and intentionally cultivate them with attachment and fixation—feeling pleased when they develop and unhappy when they don't—they will cause us to stray from the abiding state. The reason is that, generally, all reference points block the attainment of liberation and, specifically, conceptualizing good karma (like bliss, clarity, and nonconceptuality) will be a cause for the happy states and conceptualizing bad karma (such as the mental afflictions) will be a cause for the negative states. In brief, all attachments and reference points are said to be ways we go astray on the path. The Great Brahman [Saraha] teaches:

> Whatever you focus on will itself obscure liberation.
> What's labeled "good" is a sickness dragging you into saṃsāra.
> Labeling an inferior action does not stop its maturation.[1236]

He continues:

> KYE MA. Do not attach yourself to the things you desire.
> That's an illness afflicting the sublime mind of great bliss.
> When your mind is impassioned about an object it desires,
> the stainless mind is struck by the weapon of desire.[1237]

He also says:

> If the mind that thinks, "This is attractive,"
> takes that to heart and cherishes it,
> even pain the size of a sesame seed husk
> will cause constant affliction.[1238] [414]

Virūpa explains:

> If we bring the abiding state to mind, fixate on experiences,
> or focus and meditate on suchness, we deviate.[1239]

Specifically, I will now discuss which experiences causes us to stray into particular situations. Since bliss creates the causes for being born in the desire realm, clarity the causes for the form realm, and nonconceptuality the causes for the formless realm, they are not causes for perfect buddhahood. It is explained that once we've had a break from the sufferings of the lower states for a time and have experienced the happiness of the three realms, we will return to cycling endlessly in the three lower states. The exalted Gampopa teaches:

> The three strayings of experience are as follows. When we have experiences of physical bliss, mental bliss, and bliss pervading our body, being attached to those, overly fixating upon them, and taking them to be supreme are the substantial causes for [being reborn in] the desire realm. If we die in such circumstances we will stray into the desire realm. Once we have enjoyed the pleasures of the desire realm, it won't be hard for us to wander endlessly in the three lower states.
>
> When we have experiences of clarity free from dullness and sluggishness, being attached to those and taking them to be sublime lead us to stray into the form realm. Once we have experienced its pleasures and enjoyments, we will easily fall to lower states.
>
> When we have experiences of not being disturbed by the winds of thoughts, fixating on those and taking them to be superior are the substantial causes for [being reborn in] the formless realm. If we die in those circumstances we will stray into the formless realm. Once we have experienced the pleasures and enjoyments there, we will wander endlessly in the three lower states.[1240]

The exalted Pakmo Drupa states:

> Having sought the company of genuine gurus
> and practiced their instructions, [415]
> bliss may fill your body and mind.
> Fixating on that and cultivating it,
> you will stray into the places of the desire realm.
>
> Brilliant clarity, like the sky, arises.
> Like the moon rising internally and externally,
> there may be no difference between opening and closing your eyes.

If, being attached to and fixated upon that,
you practitioners sustain it,
you will stray into the form realm.

You may look externally and internally,
yet there won't be the slightest thought:
you see the dharmakāya, free from particles.
If you consider what you enjoy and don't enjoy
and specifically sustain that experience,
you will stray into the formless realm.[1241]

In keeping with the practice tradition, the exalted Ling Repa says:

Some great meditators, like simple-minded children,
latch onto the vivid appearances of their rainbowlike
experiences,
not recognizing them to be seductive points where they go
astray.[1242] [416]

The exalted Barawa explains in detail:

As for the strayings from mahāmudrā:
Resting evenly with the thought,
"All phenomena are infinite like space,"
we stray into Limitless Space.

Thinking, "Consciousness is limitless,"
we stray into Limitless Consciousness.
Meditating with the thought, "Phenomena are nothing,"
we stray into Nothingness.

Resting evenly with the thought,
"Phenomena are neither existent nor nonexistent,"
we stray into the sphere of Neither Existent nor Nonexistent.

Meditating in samādhi
with discernment, analysis involving fixations,
joy, ease, and a one-pointed mind,
we stray into the first meditative concentration.

> Meditating in samādhi
> with tranquility, joy, ease, and a one-pointed mind,
> we stray into the second meditative concentration.
>
> Meditating in samādhi
> free from discernment and analysis,
> with equanimity, mindfulness, alertness,
> ease, and a one-pointed mind,
> we stray into the third meditative concentration.
>
> Purified equanimity, purified mindfulness,
> the sensation of there being neither pleasure nor pain,
> and a one-pointed mind
> are the fourth meditative concentration.
>
> Resting the mind on just the nonconceptuality
> that comes from blocking the objects appearing for the six consciousnesses [417]
> is the absence of true mindfulness
> and is straying into the cessation without cognitive discriminations.
>
> A blank, open mind
> that is completely neutral
> causes us to stray into an unmindful, neutral state.
>
> A glazed, sluggish, uncertain state—
> one merely without thoughts and with no clarity—
> causes us to stray into becoming animals.[1243]

Furthermore, the exalted Pakmo Drupa says:

> Even though we meditate without fixating
> on bliss, clarity, or nonconceptuality,
> it's still possible that we'll become śrāvakas or pratyekabuddhas.[1244]

The exalted Yang Gönpa explains:

> We may cling to bliss, grasp at clarity, or fabricate nonconceptuality. If we fixate on those three, we will stray into the three

> realms. Even without such fixations, if we do not see our own face—[our mind's] abiding state—we will stray into the results of śrāvakas and pratyekabuddhas.[1245]

Although we do find in the exalted Gampopa's lectures that he said that analytical emptiness and a lack of love and compassion can cause us to stray into the Hīnayāna, it is explained that to attain the results of śrāvakas and pratyekabuddhas we need both śamatha and the vipaśyanā that focuses on the nonexistence of a self. And we must relinquish our mental afflictions. Sustaining, with no fixation, the bliss, clarity, and nonconceptuality that are devoid of vipaśyanā is an ordinary mundane meditative concentration. Therefore, we can conclude that it isn't feasible that such [meditative concentration] will bring the attainment of the level of a śrāvaka or pratyekabuddha arhat.

We may then wonder, What does the exalted Gampopa mean when he says there is the danger that "[a mind to which experiences or objects] appear yet are not ascertained" can become a cause for cessation? His *Abundant Auspiciousness: A Collection of Dharma Lectures* explains that the cessation he refers to is a nonanalytical cessation: [418]

> A guru with the eye of dharma who has directly perceived mind-itself to be emptiness ascertains bliss, clarity, and nonconceptuality as being unborn. If [those experiences] are not ascertained as unborn, they are what are called "[experiences or objects that] appear yet not ascertained." They lead to a nonanalytical cessation and, since that is a common path, it is uncertain where we will be born as a result.[1246]

Nonanalytical cessations are described in the *Treasury of Abhidharma* as follows:

> The complete prevention of arising
> is a different cessation: it is nonanalytical.[1247]

The *Explanation of the "Treasury of Abhidharma"* says:

> What completely prevents the arising of future phenomena is a cessation that is different from separation: it is nonanalytical and it is a cessation. It is not attained through analysis.[1248]

When the conditions are not complete, the arising of a future phenomenon, be it defiled or undefiled, is blocked. That is a cessation that is of a different substance from an analytical cessation.

The reasons that it is uncertain where we will be born as a result of such [a nonanalytical cessation] are explained in the *Entrance to the Bodhisattva's Way of Life*:

> The mind lacking [the realization of] emptiness
> may cease but it will arise again,
> just as [we do from] absorption without discriminations.[1249]

The *[King of Samādhi] Sūtra* teaches:

> Even though the worldly cultivate samādhi,
> they do not destroy the notion of a self.
> Mental afflictions return to disturb them,
> as they did for Udraka, who meditated in samādhi.[1250] [419]

Those without cognitive discrimination. Those who are born as a god without cognitive discriminations, those in states in which mental factors are blocked, and those in the meditative absorption that is without cognitive discriminations are in meditative absorptions in which mind and mental factors cease because, relying on the fourth meditative concentration, they perceive the absence of cognitive discriminations to be liberation.

The meditative absorption of cessation. This is a state without cognitive discrimination in which beings rely on the sphere of Neither Discrimination nor Nondiscrimination and, feeling weary of discriminations and feelings, and perceiving their state as the actualization of peace, they are absorbed in the meditative absorption in which mind and mental factors are pacified.

Although those are meditative absorptions, in this context they are considered to be strayings. Since they do not have [the understanding] of the absence of self, they are unable to pacify their belief in a self, the root of saṃsāra. Because they are unable to do that, their karma and mental afflictions reoccur and they continue to circle in saṃsāra, as Dharmakīrti says:

If there is self, other is cognized.
From the pair of self and other come clinging and anger.
The connections with these two
produce all faults.[1251]

The point here is that saṃsāra is not transcended even by those whose minds attain the Pinnacle Existence, like the example of the samādhi practiced by Udraka.

Analytical cessation. This is described as a cessation attained through analysis of the four truths with the prajñā of the uninterrupted paths, a cessation that is free from defiled phenomena.

All that being the case, those who do not understand the distinctions of the different types of cessations are confused by the statement that there is the danger that "[a mind to which experiences or objects] appear yet are not ascertained" can become a cause for cessation. Most of the numerous discussions by unlearned people about that referring to the cessations of śrāvakas and pratyekabuddhas is just the chatter of fools. And yet there is one well-known scholar [Sakya Paṇḍita] who says:

[The fool's meditation on mahāmudrā
usually is a cause for being [born as] an animal.
If not that, they may be born in the formless realm]
or else they may descend into the cessations of śrāvakas.[1252] [420]

And then there are those who repeat such nonsense. Nevertheless, all that seems to be the talk of people who do not understand that only śrāvaka nonreturners and arhats have the ability to enter the śrāvaka meditative absorption of cessation and that that meditative absorption of cessation requires the vipaśyanā that realizes the absence of a self of persons. If such people understood that they would regret drawing comparisons between [the cessations of śrāvakas and pratyekabuddhas] and the causes for being born as an animal.

Also Dorje Sherab, [propounder] of the Single Intent, teaches:

[Even] without attachment to experiences of bliss we can achieve
the desire realm. [Even] without clinging to clarity we can achieve

> the form realm, and [even] without fabricating nonconceptuality
> we can achieve the formless realm.[1253]

Implicit in that statement is that being attached to the experiences of bliss, grasping at the experiences of clarity, and fabricating nonconceptuality lead to major problems.

Therefore, nonconceptuality in which the unborn [nature] is not ascertained can be the catalyst for clinging to emptiness and a strong nihilistic view. Its result will be to descend into the lower states. Although it may be free from attachment and fixation, it is a mental state of equanimity [or indifference] included within bliss, clarity, and nonconceptuality, and it is an unspecified [neutral] mental state. The reasons that those are strayings have been discussed already in the section on eliminating flaws in meditation.*

Finally, the exalted Gampopa states:

> Even though you may be free from fixating on the emptiness
> of percepts and perceivers, knowable objects, you may not see the
> true point.
> Even though you may experience meditation free from duality,
> you may not see the true point.
>
> Although the view free from conceptualization
> is called "beyond extremes," that's mentally fabricated.
> Great meditators who haven't cut their bonds
> may have excellent samādhi but it's a cause of their saṃsāra. [421]
>
> Dharma practitioners without compassion
> may be very diligent but they are on the śrāvakas' path.[1254]

iii) The Presentation of the Methods for Not Straying in Those Ways

Most experiences, which are part of bliss, clarity, and nonconceptuality, become strayings due to the following circumstances. When we aren't certain that all those experiences are free from an essence that arises or ceases, that they have no nature that can be identified, and that they are unborn empti-

*See "The Explanation of Mistakes in Meditation," pp. 288–94.

ness, we go astray by reifying, or taking to be real, those meditative experiences that, born of latent tendencies, arise as mere conventionalities through the interdependence of the channels, winds, and bindus in the body. Therefore, we should sustain [our meditation] with the continuous mindfulness that ascertains everything to be unborn, without the clinging that reifies. By doing so we will keep from straying. As cited above, Gampopa teaches:

> Ascertain bliss, clarity, and nonconceptuality to be unborn. If [those experiences] are not ascertained as unborn they are what are called "[experiences or objects that] appear yet not ascertained."[1255]

He also says:

> Generally speaking, it is explained that any straying into the three realms, the four meditative concentrations, and the four spheres occurs based on just a bit of clinging to those states. Straying into being a śrāvaka is the straying of analytical emptiness. Abiding without clinging to an essence has no straying.[1256]

And:

> Generally, since strayings involve fixation or grasping, you should rid yourself of fixations and grasping. Remain utterly without fixation, without any clinging. Remain utterly without anything to adopt or reject. Resting uncontrived in that way is referred to with the term "meditation." As the *Lamp [for the True View]* says: [422]
>
> > Resting without contrivance in equanimity
> > is called "meditation" just as a convention.[1257]

Now we might think, Isn't it sufficient to only ascertain the unborn [nature]? It can't really be necessary to have the experiences of bliss, clarity, and nonconceptuality. That's not quite right. The following citations demonstrate that both realizations and experiences are necessary. The exalted Gampopa explains:

> Without bliss, clarity, and nonconceptuality, even if we ascertain the essence of the unborn, it is as my guru Milarepa says:

> Whatever that is, it's not it.
> It's the trunk, not the fruit.
> It's a good quality but it's not nonconceptual.[1258]

The Great Lord [Atīśa] sings:

> Without the latent tendencies of definite training, yogins and yoginīs see nothing.
> They are like bees drinking from sky flowers.[1259]

In that case, we may ask, How should it be? As [Gampopa] says:

> The view connects to realization.[1260]

Do not leave the abiding state of mind, its essence and nature, as being a freedom from extremes or a freedom from elaborations that is just mentally fabricated or intellectually derived. Look with prajñā and directly realize that mind has no essence at all. It is beyond being an object that can be expressed verbally or conceptually. As for [the cultivation of] the view, [Gampopa] continues:

> Meditation connects to experiences.[1261]

It is taught that what is realized is not to be left far away as just a theoretical understanding: it must be experienced vibrantly, clearly, right within awareness. [423] Again, the exalted Gampopa says:

> When training, first cultivate vibrant mental clarity. Next train in nondistraction. Then, train in never being distracted from the essence of awareness. When you have become accustomed to that, confidence will arise within.[1262]

And:

> Vibrant clarity is an experience. Not being distracted from that is stillness. Realization is when prajñā sees that no essence exists.[1263]

Those types of experiences are called "experiences intrinsic to realization" or the "experiences intrinsic to the essence." They are explained as being meditation in which experiences and realizations are inseparable, free from strayings and errors. They are discussed by the exalted Gampopa:

> Now you may ask, What are the experiences connected to meditation? They are called "experiences intrinsic to the essence," "experiences intrinsic to the connate state," "experiences intrinsic to the natural state," "experiences intrinsic to mahāmudrā." What do they refer to? They refer to the essence of your own mind. What is that? It is not something existent: it does not have even one-hundredth of a hair tip's worth of something to be identified. It is not nonexistent: it is something that is experienced and is realized. The essence of mind is clarity-emptiness, unidentifiable. It must arise uninterruptedly as empty clarity. When it does, meditation is connected to experiences. When it is said that experiences and realizations are simultaneous, that's what is meant.[1264]

That being so, some say:

> Bliss, clarity, and nonconceptuality
> are three places to go astray in meditation.
> Bliss, clarity, and nonconceptuality
> are three pinnacles in meditation.[1265] [424]

The first sentence refers to experiences that involve fixation and clinging, and the latter one to experiences intrinsic to realization.

In this context, a certain person [Sakya Paṇḍita] says:

> If merely cutting off the three strayings
> brought mahāmudrā,
> the cessation of śrāvakas would be that.[1266]

That statement reflects nothing more than his desire to say something [critical]. His statement is a false statement because, although we assert that the three strayings must be cut off in mahāmudrā meditation, we do not accept that merely severing the three strayings results in mahāmudrā. The three places to go astray are the three realms, and there are others [besides those following the Mahāmudrā path] who do not stray there [such as śrāvakas] and yet it is not an occasion to make a special mention of the śrāvakas' cessation. [However, since he has,] those who are able to enter the śrāvakas' absorption of cessation are the nonreturners who physically actualize [nirvāṇa] and the arhats with twofold liberation. Since they have the remainder of a body of the desire realm or the form realm, they have not relinquished the three places to go astray.

This certain person [Sakya Paṇḍita] also says:

> The prajñāpāramitā [sūtras] teach,
> "you should become familiar with emptiness
> but do not actualize emptiness."
>
> If you meditate on just emptiness
> you will not realize emptiness itself.
> Even if you realize emptiness
> you will fall into the cessation of śrāvakas.[1267] [425]

That is not correct. We cannot become familiar with emptiness without actualizing emptiness. Therefore, that is a falsification of the teachings in the prajñāpāramitā [sūtras]. Here [our mahāmudrā] meditation on emptiness endowed with the most sublime of manifestations does not involve the flaws of meditation on just emptiness. The last two flaws [that is, meditating on just emptiness not leading to the realization of emptiness and, even if it does, then leading to the cessation of śrāvakas] come back to him with his view that asserts [the ultimate] to be an analytical emptiness, a nonaffirming negation. The "Unchanging Primordial Wisdom" chapter of the *Kālacakra Tantra* explains that analytical emptiness is the emptiness of a nihilistic view and, therefore, it is to be abandoned.[1268]

2) Clearing Away Obstructing Hindrances

This has two parts:

a) Clearing Away the General Hindrances to Samādhi
b) Clearing Away Other Inner and Outer Hindrances

a) Clearing Away the General Hindrances to Samādhi

Broadly speaking, regardless of the particular samādhi we are sustaining, we must combine both arousing clarity with the focus (the object of cultivation), without that being obscured, and stabilizing that clarity, without being swayed by distractions. The hindrances for the first are created by all types of dullness, and the hindrances for the latter by all forms of agitation. Thus, dullness and agitation are the root hindrances for sustaining samādhi. To look at their internal divisions: the category of dullness includes dullness itself, sluggishness, feeling dazed, drowsiness, and idleness. The category of agitation includes agitation itself, remorse, doubt, pleasure-seeking, and malice. For beginners they are hindering problems and must be dispelled. The ways to identify those and remedy them have been explained already in the section of the general explanation of śamatha and vipaśyanā.*

For those who have become realized through recognizing the nature of phenomena such [faults] arise as meditation because they are aware of the nature of dullness, agitation, and so forth. [426] The Great Exalted One [Milarepa] sings:

> Physician-Teacher, do not dispel dullness and agitation: they are the meditation.
> Dispelling the flaws of scattering, sluggishness, dullness, or agitation
> is like lighting a candle during the day.[1269]

The exalted Gampopa states:

> When dullness or agitation arise, look at that itself.[1270]

b) Clearing Away Other Inner and Outer Hindrances

The *Vairocanābhisambodhi* says:

> There are two types of hindrances:
> those of the external sphere and those of the internal.[1271]

*See pp. 19–29.

It continues:

> You should know that
> the internal ones are diseases—
> pulmonary congestion, choking, vomiting,
> dropsy illnesses, loss of appetite, and the like—
> that have unbearable qualities,
> such as those of cold or hot winds.
>
> The great external hindrances
> are humans and nonhumans.
> Those thorns to wisdom
> appear in order to destroy the world
> with their various kinds of behavior.
> They create confusion for any who undertake austerity.[1272]

As is said, there are two categories of hindrances: the external ones of humans and nonhumans, and the internal ones of illnesses and thoughts.

In the first category, humans are [specifically] our relatives, companions, and others who deceive us, who draw our mind into the seductiveness of worldly appearances. It can also refer to our enemies and thieves who, by harming us, cause us to give up on our spiritual practices. Nonhumans include māras with imperceptible [forms]—such as those who create the magical displays of bhūtas and hungry ghosts—and māras with perceptible [forms]—such as yetis and predatory animals—all of whom cause us to be overpowered by obstacles. [427]

In the second category, the hindrance of illness occurs when the four elements in our body are disturbed or become unbalanced. The various illnesses that arise from wind, bile, phlegm, and their combinations create obstacles for us. The hindrance of thoughts is the random arising of thoughts involving the five mental afflictions that cannot be checked by remedies or incorporated into the path through the view or meditation. They bring us under the sway of the eight worldly values. We should recognize that all of these are obstacles and dispel their specific faults.

The scholar-siddha Chegompa's saying "the māra of torpor has gotten into your head" refers to when our experiences in our spiritual practices are unclear. "The māra of speech has entered your tongue" means we enjoy talking and, specifically, are unable to keep our experiences secret. "The māra of discursiveness has entered your heart" means our mind pursues objects and cannot settle in naturalness. "The māra of traveling has entered your feet" means we cannot stand to stay in isolation and long to travel. When those arise, we should meditate on our guru at our head, throat, heart, and head, respectively, and supplicate strongly that the specific hindrance be pacified. It is taught that they will be pacified.

In brief, if something harms the progress of our excellent qualities of the view or meditation, it is said to be a hindrance that obstructs the supreme siddhi even though it may be the development of merit or the development of a common siddhi. Therefore, we should dispel such faults using the appropriate remedy or by integrating them into the path.

That completes the explanation of eliminating deviations and strayings in meditation.

13
Enhancement

D) Enhancement: Concluding That [Mind] Is Unborn

This has two parts:

1) Breaking Through to the Unborn Transparency [of Mind]
2) Refinement through the Conducts That Integrate [All Experiences] into the Path

1) Breaking Through to the Unborn Transparency [of Mind]

This has five sections: [428]

a) The Meaning of the Term "Breakthrough" and Its Timing
b) The Place for the Breakthrough: The Abiding State of the Basic Nature
c) What Constitutes the Breakthrough: Looking at the Essence of Mind
d) The Actual Breakthrough to the Unborn Transparency [of Mind]
e) Blending [Equipoise and Postmeditative Attainment] into a Constant Flow Day and Night by Means of That [Breakthrough]

a) The Meaning of the Term "Breakthrough" and Its Timing

The term "breakthrough" means to have reached a conclusion without any lingering doubts. In this context, it means to have cut through conceptual elaborations about your own mind (such as that it arises, abides, or ceases, or that it has three periods of time) and to have reached the conclusion that it is a great unborn transparency,[1273] as Tilopa says:

> Don't think: behold the phenomenon of the breakthrough.[1274]

The meaning of this is taught in the following citations. The Great Brahman [Saraha] observes:

> For those who contemplate suchness free from a root
> receiving the guru's instructions is sufficient.[1275]

He also says:

> Today, through the glorious guru's teachings,
> I realize the primordial, unborn nature.[1276]

And the Śavara [Saraha] teaches:

> Thus it is that throughout the three times
> [there is just] the intrinsic state free from extremes, without mental activity.[1277]

Tilopa says:

> When mind is without reference point, that is mahāmudrā.[1278]

Maitrīpa states:

> Phenomena are uniform, like space.
> That is called "mahāmudrā."[1279] [429]

In this practice tradition, [breakthroughs] are the thought of the instructions in *Revealing the Hidden Characteristics of Mind* and other works by the unequaled Dakpo [Gampopa].[1280] Later, numerous variations of the meditation techniques for breakthroughs were formulated by those of the practice tradition.

The timing of breakthroughs. [Breakthroughs are] when, as practitioners, we have purified stagnate experiences of bliss, clarity, or nonconceptuality, and we arouse brilliant clarity in our awareness. Then, meditation on spacelike clarity-emptiness is an unbroken flow. Or, that experience [of spacelike clarity-emptiness] is an unbroken flow even with the allure of daytime appearances. Whenever we are mindful right within the movements of thoughts, movements are empty clarity, empty movements.

Whenever we are mindful right with the appearances of the objects for the six modes of consciousness, appearances are vivid empty appearances. In brief, when all thoughts are empty clarity and appearances are empty appearances, and we experience all as illusionlike with decisive certainty, that is a breakthrough.

Breakthroughs may [be attempted] prematurely. If we lack the firm footing of experience and certainty right within awareness and simply rely on a theoretical understanding, we will turn into someone whose high view is just words, whose talk of emptiness is that of someone complacent about the dharma. This will muddle our mind and we will come under the sway of our own conceited delusions. Even though others may see us as someone with realization, it is said that we have become a jaded "dharma expert," someone with an inflated external presence who is empty on the inside, like a vacant house with padlocked doors. We haven't achieved anything lasting in relation to our aim. We just deceive ourselves.

Breakthroughs may not occur even after a long time. Worthy ones with the karmic continuity [of spiritual practice] experience their mind and appearances as the ācārya. Once their fixations on and clinging to experiences are self-purified, they attain liberation. However, most [meditators] develop strong clinging to their certainty about their experiences, thinking that they are excellent. They fall into the straying called "great meditators getting stuck in the sweetness of experience." As the exalted Tsangpa Gyare says:

> Many understand meditation, few understand letting go.[1281] [430]

When these instructions on breakthroughs are heard in this context, they are methods of instantaneous liberation for those with the karmic continuity [of spiritual practice]. For everyone else, they will enhance their progression through the four yogas. These are special instructions for advancing our spiritual practice. With them, it is said that we can achieve our aim in just a few days, which otherwise might take years of meditation for those of us with a distorted vision of the intrinsic state.

b) The Place for the Breakthrough: The Abiding State of the Basic Nature

Breakthroughs [are directed at] the unborn abiding state, the ground of all phenomena. That has already been discussed in the earlier sections on determining the essence, or nature, of mind.* Here, I will discuss this again briefly. All phenomena comprising existence and peace are only appearances of your mind. The essence, nature, or basic state of your mind is that it does not come into being as something inherently real: not as an entity, a nonentity, an appearance, emptiness, existent, nonexistent, and so on. It is free from all characteristics, such as being something perceived or a perceiver. It is devoid of movement—it doesn't transfer, change, depart, or arrive. Since it doesn't change in the three times, it is uninterrupted. Like space, it is not tainted or altered by anything. The Great Brahman [Saraha] states:

> [I] Saraha constantly shout,
> "The connate nature
> is neither an entity nor a nonentity."[1282]

The Śavara [Saraha] explains: [431]

> Without exception, everything—
> what moves and doesn't move, what wavers and does not,
> entities, nonentities, appearances, and emptiness—
> never, at any moment or time, moves beyond being of the nature of space.
>
> Though we say, "space, space,"
> the essence of space doesn't exist in any way.
> It transcends being an object that can be shown
> to exist, not exist, to be not existent and not nonexistent, or anything other than those.
>
> Thus, there isn't the slightest distinction between
> space, mind, and dharmatā.
> The different words are simply temporary labels:
> unreal, nothing more than false terms.[1283]

Virūpa expounds:

> Mind-itself is empty of names, free from elaborations: mahāmudrā.

*See "Determining the Essence of Mind, the Root," pp. 224–37.

It's similar to the nature of space in being primordially empty of names.
Inherently unborn, beyond entities with characteristics,
it's like space, pervading all without movement or change.
At all times it's empty and, from the outset, devoid of self.[1284]

It is not that [mind] suddenly changes to being that way. The basic state of mind, from the beginning, remains that way, as it is, without changing. [432] An analogy is space: no matter what terms we use for space—such as being empty or not empty—there is no one who can say, "The nature of space is exactly this." Thus Tilopa teaches:

For example, we use the term "empty" to refer to space,
but space cannot be described as being "like this."
Similarly, your mind is said to be luminous,
yet there is no basis to which the expression "it exists like this" applies.
In that way, the nature of mind is primordially like space.[1285]

From the start, mind and all phenomena, which arise from mind, are devoid of any nature and, therefore, are without arising, ceasing, or abiding. [Mind] is the great unborn transparency, which cannot be attained or lost, moved or transformed—by anything, be it mindfulness, distraction, or something else. As the Śavara [Saraha] explains:

If mind exists, it follows that phenomena exist.
In the absence of mind, who realizes dharma?

When we search for mind and what appear as phenomena,
nothing is found—there isn't even a searcher.
What is nonexistent neither arises nor ceases in the three times.
It doesn't become something else.
It's the abiding state of natural great bliss.[1286]

He also says:

The nature of space, primordially pure,
has nothing to be abandoned or attained.[1287] [433]

c) What Constitutes the Breakthrough: Looking at the Essence of Mind

This has two parts:

i) Looking at the Essence of Thoughts and Appearances
ii) Looking at the Essence of the Object of Meditation and the Meditator

i) Looking at the Essence of Thoughts and Appearances

Generally speaking, since this path is a path of blessings, we must arouse strong devotion to our gurus. Specifically, since the enhancement of our meditation depends on our devotion, devotion is the one common tradition throughout all the practice lineages. The exalted Drikungpa [Jikten Sumgön] teaches:

> What enhances mahāmudrā
> is devotion to genuine gurus.[1288]

He continues:

> If the sun of devotion doesn't shine
> on the snowy mountain of the gurus' four kāyas,
> streams of blessings will not flow.
> Dedicate yourself to devotion.[1289]

The Great Brahman [Saraha] in his *Dohā for the Queen* sings:

> The realization that all varieties of phenomena are of one taste in emptiness
> is aroused by the genuine gurus themselves.
> With a devoted mind, place on the Brahman spot on your head
> these sublime exalted ones, who are like the bills of swans [in extracting the essence].[1290]

There are many such statements.

At this point, during whatever spiritual practices you do and particularly during guru yoga, begin by arousing the devotion in which you see your gurus as the dharmakāya. Make fervent supplications to realize all possible appearances are the dharmakāya. [434] Next, as described before, cultivate one-pointed equipoise, which is the means for resting in the essence, and differentiate between brilliant states of mind and sullied ones. Then, in a spacious and vibrant state of mind—when your awareness is undistracted and your meditation is without reference point—there may arise a subtle thought that doesn't create great mental pleasure or pain, or you should cause one to arise. Without clinging or wandering, look fixedly at its essence while its manifestation is vivid. Similarly, there may arise a clearly evident coarse thought, the kind that creates the miseries associated with mental joys and sorrows, or you should cause one to arise. Look again and again to see if there is any difference between the essence of a subtle thought and that of a coarse thought. When you sever misinterpretations regarding that, look to see if there is any difference between the essence of those [thoughts] and the essence of the still mind.

Similarly, look at the many different kinds of thoughts involved with the mental afflictions (desire and so forth) and those related to the eight worldly qualities of pleasure and pain. Sometimes block thoughts. Sometimes increase them. Sometimes pursue just one stream of thought. Do various things, and look at the essence of each to eliminate your misinterpretations.

Similarly, examine the external objects that appear. Through a variety of physical postures and your eyes being open or closed, gazing right or left, and so forth, there are many types of appearances that can arise: forms of various sizes, colors, shapes, and qualities, sounds of various strengths, qualities, and melodies, and so on. Look to see if there is a difference between their essence and the essence of mind. Explore each of those techniques, and in a few days you will sever your misinterpretations.

The aim to be attained by doing that. No matter what manifestations of thoughts or appearances occur, without feeling the need to block them or terminate them, you must be absolutely certain that while being vivid manifestations, their essence is unidentifiable: they are just empty clarity, empty appearances, reflexive awareness. [435] This point has already been explained in the sections pointing out the connateness of thoughts and appearances.* It is also explained by the following. The Great Brahman [Saraha] says:

*See pp. 277–88.

Know that all that appears before you
is connate with emptiness, the root of mind.[1291]

The Śavara [Saraha] advises:

In the same way all rivers, the Ganges and others,
become of one taste in the salt ocean,
know that all analyzing minds and mental events
are of one taste in the dharmadhātu.[1292]

Virūpa teaches:

[Mind-itself] is devoid of memories, thoughts, or characteristics,
which are like the water of a mirage.
Neither bound nor liberated, it does not move from its intrinsic
state.[1293]

Tilopa states:

For example, mist and clouds vanish into space.
They go nowhere and reside nowhere.
Similarly, when the masses of thoughts rising up in the mind
are seen to be the mind itself, the waves of thoughts vanish.[1294]

Maitrīpa observes:

From the unborn, a thought suddenly appears. [436]
That very thought is the essence of the expanse.[1295]

Maitrīpa also explains:

The various appearances and this essence of mind
don't exist even at the moment they meet: this is mahāmudrā.[1296]

ii) Looking at the Essence of the Object of Meditation and the Meditator

Here the object of meditation is actually your own mind. It's not enough to simply to engage your mind with the thought, "[mind] is without arising, ceasing, or abiding; it is something that transcends the intellect, which cannot be identified," and have certainty about your understanding. You must immediately cut through misinterpretations right within your experience using direct yogic perception. As before, in a state of undistracted awareness, spacious and vibrant, repeatedly look to see just how the essence of that object of meditation is when you are looking fixedly and nakedly, without wandering or clinging. And look directly at the essence of the mind doing the action of meditation. If those two seem to be dualistic appearances—such that they are in a reciprocal relationship or one is external, the other internal—you have not severed your misinterpretations. Look again. Simply put, you must conclude that mindfulness-awareness—in which the object of meditation and the one becoming familiar [the meditator] are undifferentiated and inseparable—appears just like an illusion. Mindfulness-awareness is simply designated with such terms but, actually, it is primordial, open emptiness in which there is nothing to be identified and not even a hair tip's worth of instantiation.

Once you sever your misinterpretations in that way, look to see if there is a difference in your mind during any of the three times. When you examine where your past mind has gone, from where your future mind will arise, and how your present mind abides, if you see what seems to be the arising, ceasing, or abiding of a mind in the three times, you should reexamine that well. You have not gained assurance about this point. [437] Since there has never been any interruption in the unidentifiable nature [of mind], it is inseparable during the three time periods. You must conclude that [mind] is a single transparent state throughout the three times, like space.

In the same fashion, examine the mind that is the perceiving subject with the thought, "I, me," and the mind that is the perceiving subject with the thought, "other, them." If those manifest as dualistic appearances—such that one seems to be external and the other internal or they are in a reciprocal relationship—you have not severed your misinterpretations. Look again. Conclude that everything is mind-itself, which, from the start, is groundless and rootless: it is an unrivaled single state, self-arising and self-liberating, a nonexistent openness.

Thus, you conclude that the object of meditation and the meditator, the mind during the three times, and the mind [perceiving] dualistic appearances of self and other are only separate as words. Any separateness is just ascribed by the intellect. They are an undifferentiated continuum. Mind-itself—whose essence does not exist as anything and yet can arise as anything due to conditions—is illusionlike. Its essence is neither confused nor liberated. It is not tainted by flaws or virtues. It cannot be attained or lost, met with or departed from. Intentionally focus for a few days and, without blocking or encouraging anything, sustain whatever arises in a loose, naturally settled state free from fabrication or contrivance. You will develop certainty about your conclusions. The Great Brahman [Saraha] exclaims:

> KYE MA. Don't say the suchness free from any nature exists in meditation.
> If you conceive of an object of meditation and a meditator as a duality,
> the mind grasping dualism rejects its bodhicitta.
> People who do that defile themselves.[1297]

And:

> The mind without meditation and object of meditation is free from any nature.
> Being the consummate, with no hopes or fears, it is vajra mind.[1298] [438]

And:

> Sublime great bliss
> has neither self nor other.
> In front, behind, and in all ten directions,
> whatever you see is suchness.[1299]

The Śavara [Saraha] says:

> Realized ones have neither an object of meditation nor a meditator.
> Just as space cannot observe space,
> emptiness does not meditate on emptiness.
> The nondual mind is like water [mixed] with milk:
> continuous great bliss in which diversities are of one taste.[1300]

Virūpa comments:

> In the expanse of mind's dharmatā there's nothing that's "this";
> therefore, there's no object of meditation, no meditator.[1301]

He continues:

> When there's nothing seen and no seer, differences are free on the spot.
> When someone practicing has vanished, effort and striving are gone.
> When a result to be attained has vanished, you're freed from all hopes and fears.
> When "I" and "me" have been eradicated, you're victorious in the battles with māras.
> When reifications have subsided in their own place, you're freed from saṃsāra and nirvāṇa.[1302] [439]

d) The Actual Breakthrough to the Unborn Transparency [of Mind]

Once you have conclusive certainty in what was explained above, destroy any clinging you may have to certainty about the object of meditation. Relax your mindfulness, which is doing the action of meditating. Similarly, give up any expectations about the object of your practice and put aside your strivings as a practitioner. Let go of the object of realization, and pacify the mind that is doing the realizing.[1303]

In brief, dispense with notions of, "This is it," and mental formations that think, "It's like this." Cast off your ambitions and any wishes you may harbor about meditation, mindfulness, experiences, or awareness. Do not even have the intention, "I won't do anything with my mind." Remain comfortably with your ordinary, normal mind unfabricated, uncontrived, just left to be as it is with no fuss. Whatever normal thoughts and appearances arise, simply let them be as they come—don't try to manipulate them, change them, or establish them with a mind intent on preventing or promoting something.

Don't pursue mental activities. When your mind is distracted, don't worry about that, don't regard it as a problem, don't even examine it.[1304] When you are mindful, let that be uncontrived ordinariness that isn't anything: not an object of meditation, not an object of experience, not an object of action. Eat, move about, and sleep in a state free from conceptualizing as much as you can—don't entertain ideas like, "I will do this, I am doing that" or any coarse mental formulations.[1305]

Don't do any other physical activities or work. Except for maybe offering tormas and supplications a little bit, put aside all your other daily recitations and spiritual practices. Observe silence. Sleep in a free, uncontrived ordinariness devoid of any ambition.

Letting go of all mental activities, remain just as you are for a few days. Your attachments to good experiences or grasping at joyful sensations will unravel. [440] Your clinging to negative, confused thoughts as problems and your annoyance with them will subside. Whatever ordinary state of mind you have, or arises, or manifests, it is of the nature of meditation, an expression of emptiness. Actually, there is no arising or cessation, nothing to be separated from or to attain, nothing to abandon or adopt. There is no distracted mind or undistracted mind, no being mindful or not being mindful, no experience or lack of experience, no realization of the point or lack of realization. Therefore, when all the appearances of the world arise as objects for the mind, they are self-arising, self-occurring. When they subside, they are self-pacifying, self-liberating. This is the unrivaled, single transparent state. Everything is of the nature of meditation. Meditation is a constant flow; meditation never goes away. That is the conclusive certainty you must develop.

In this context, some block mental activities too forcefully and, consequently, remain in a stagnant śamatha. Others restrict their winds and mind internally, causing themselves to suffer uncomfortable meditative experiences and mental stress. They should lighten their moods in whatever ways they need, be gentle with what comes up in their minds for a time, and refresh themselves.

If a flawless experience occurs, you can allow it to continue for a few days. From time to time, look to see if there are occasions when your mind is not meditating. If you recognize that there are times that are not meditation, such as when you are distracted or sleeping, again examine the essence and nature of those periods of not meditating. Recognize their abiding state.

These points are described frequently by the Great Brahman [Saraha], who says:

> Meditate on wisdom, self-arisen and inconceivable,
> and you meditate on all the results.[1306]

He continues:

> When the mind without activities seeks nothing,
> there's no need to seek virtues: it's free from discordant elements. [441]

Suchness isn't found through the tantras or śāstras.
The mind without ambitions is free from the stains of causes.[1307]

And:

Mind in its essence is free from faults and virtues.
That state needs no actions at all.
The mind that's let go of actions is sublime great bliss.[1308]

And:

When mentation is no longer mentation,
unsurpassable awakening is attained.[1309]

And:

When your mind is unmoving, stable in its own place,
it's self-liberated from the things of saṃsāra.[1310]

He concludes:

If you know that seeing, hearing, touching, recollecting,
eating, smelling, wandering, going, staying,
talking idly, and speaking in reply are mind,
the expressions of the one [mind] won't disturb you.[1311]

The Śavara [Saraha] observes:

Seeing the suchness of the phenomena of saṃsāra and nirvāṇa,
thoughts with hopes or fears collapse—
they're devoid of nature.
What's the use of striving to adopt or reject?[1312] [442]

He also says:

KYE HO. For yogins and yoginīs of the nondual intrinsic state
what things could there be to adopt or reject?
I don't hold onto phenomena or reject them.
I don't say, "Child, you must do this."[1313]

Virūpa teaches:

> With no object of realization and no realizer, you're separated from bias and extremes.
> With no separation or nonseparation, there is the intrinsic state of equality.
> Once you definitely realize that, no stains linger.
> Since variations are clearly the dharmakāya, the idea to reject or accept doesn't occur.
>
> With no meditation and no nonmeditation, nothing is tainted by characteristics.
> Don't ever rely on appearing or nonappearing objects.
> Having no notions of an actor and actions is freedom from reference points.
> The absence of a mind with hope and fear reverses all attachments.[1314]

He continues:

> Once there are no mental activities, there are no stains and no doubts.
> With the purification of the knower and knowable objects, dharmatā directly manifests.[1315]

He also states:

> Ultimate naturalness, free from attachment, is the state to cultivate.
> Don't abandon, practice, fixate, train, or block.
> Cultivate your own nature comfortably—it is the genuine sublime state.[1316]

Tilopa declares: [443]

> Mind is not to be contrived or uncontrived.
> Know that the intrinsic state is the absence of mental objects.[1317]

He continues:

Don't think, don't reflect, don't analyze.
Don't meditate, don't engage, don't hope or fear.
The mental fabrications grasping those liberate in their own spot.
They settle right within original dharmatā.[1318]

He concludes:

Ambitions obscure: you won't see luminosity.
Vows kept conceptually impair the true samaya.
Don't do anything with your mind and you'll be free from ambition,
self-arising and self-pacifying, like waves on water.

If you don't transgress the state of not resting and not focusing,
you won't transgress samaya—you'll be a lamp in darkness.
When you're free from ambition and don't dwell in extremes,
you behold all dharma contained in the piṭakas.[1319]

There are many such statements by the mahāsiddhas.

The exalted Gampopa teaches:

Don't adopt or reject anything, don't seek a path.
When no result is seen, hopes and fears subside.
Recognize misinterpretations, and deceptions about what is false
scatter.[1320] [444]

He continues:

First, since mind-itself does not exist,
who recognizes the wisdom of stillness and movement?
Thus, all that has been done and is being done
is merely the difficult task of farming in space.[1321]

And:

Being without reference points is to let go into openness.
Being without perceived objects is to discard the mindful perceiver.
Being in nonmeditation is to remain ordinary.

Since there is no owner, nothing can be right or wrong.[1322]

And:

Since there is no cultivation of an ocean of mindfulness, there is no fear of distraction.
Since there is no alternating between equipoise and postmeditative attainment, there are no sessions and breaks.
Whatever occurs is neither adopted nor rejected in dharmadhātu.
Know the false structures, the misinterpretations of all.[1323]

Finally he states:

When you realize there is no mind, appearances are set free.
When you don't evaluate, thoughts arise and release.
When you don't have ambitions, everything is equal.
When you realize that, your meditation is continuous.[1324]

There are many such statements. Those who wish for more should look at *Revealing the Hidden Characteristics of Mind*.[1325] [445]

e) Blending [Equipoise and Postmeditative Attainment] into a Constant Flow Day and Night by Means of That [Breakthrough]

The constant flow of meditation that was explained above blends meditative equipoise and postmeditative attainment during the day, and it will also blend them during the night. The ways to sustain meditative equipoise and postmeditative attainment are, for the most part, as were presented earlier.* Nevertheless, here in the context of a breakthrough, there is some concern that if your applied mindfulness is very rigid, it will arouse experiences and you will then fixate on those experiences. Therefore, when you are mindful, let go of any expectations—don't even set up the intention to let go. With no fuss or fabrication, and in keeping with the approach that the best relaxation means the best meditation, cultivate not separating meditative equipoise and postmeditative attainment. As the exalted Zhang states:

*See "The Methods for Sustaining Meditative Equipoise" and "The Methods for Sustaining Postmeditative Attainment," pp. 321–51.

Mahāmudrā meditation
does not contain dictates, "do it this way."
It has no beginning, middle, or end.
Whenever you are mindful, rest relaxed.[1326]

We may wonder, If we do that, will we stray into a blank lack of mindfulness and not be meditating? You will not have that problem. Generally speaking, the relaxation that occurs when you are mindful is mindfulness that disrupts fixations. Since remaining in a state free from mental activities is the true mindfulness of the abiding state just as it is, [this mindfulness with relaxation] is very different from enforced mindfulness or applied mindfulness, as the Śavara [Saraha] explains:

With mahāmudrā, where mind doesn't do anything,
there's not even an atom's worth of something to meditate on, so
don't meditate.
This is the supreme meditation, never apart from the actual
nonmeditation.[1327]

On the other hand, if your postmeditative mind sometimes lapses into distractions, once you apply the mindfulness of postmeditative attainment, you will be aware of the abiding state of all those [distractions], and that is sufficient. And if you recover [mindfulness], that state is included within the mixing of meditative equipoise and postmeditative attainment. This is referred to with the term "the constant flow of meditation." [446]

Similarly, a constant flow [of meditation] during the day can be blended with [practice] at night. When you start to fall asleep, first you will need to apply some effort to fall asleep while doing your daytime spiritual practice of [remaining] without any mental activities. If sleep and dreams then arise as the path, that is sufficient. However, while it's possible that will occur, in this context it won't happen for most people. Therefore, even though your sleep lacks mindfulness and your dreams are deluded, if you recognize their abiding state as soon as you wake up that is sufficient. This is referred to with the term "a constant flow day and night." The questions and answers with the exalted Gampopa contains the following exchange:

[Yogin Chöyung] asked: "When we are not mindful, the essence is not apparent. [When] we are mindful of our regular thoughts

> are all our previous thoughts purified or not? Is relentless mindfulness necessary or not?"
>
> [Gampopa] replied: "As soon as you are mindful of your normal thoughts that were not embraced with mindfulness, they are purified. It isn't necessary for you to be relentlessly mindful. Nevertheless, if mindfulness creates nondistraction, it is helpful as a condition for the mixing of meditative equipoise and post-meditative attainment. Even when you aren't being mindful, thoughts never harm, obscure, or interrupt."[1328]

He also says:

> Since luminosity is an innate quality during sleep and dreams, that is sufficient. After you wake up, look at whatever was not embraced by mindfulness. By being confident that it is nothing other than luminosity, there is a flowing river [of practice].[1329]

Many of the questions and answers [with Gampopa] relate to eliminating doubts about these situations.

If you are greatly concerned about whether you have achieved mindfulness or are lost in distraction, your [attempt at] a breakthrough may be somewhat premature since [that shows] you have not realized the uninterrupted mode of the mind's nature or abiding state. The exalted Gampopa explains:

> When you are distracted, that's delusion in its usual sense. [447]
> When you are mindful, the essence is something obtained elsewhere.
> Those kinds of things are ignorance involving dualistic phenomena.
> I don't understand such attaining or straying in meditation.
>
> If dualistic phenomena existed, [it would make sense] to know what to adopt and abandon,
> and eliminating them would be a mistake on our part.[1330]

He also says:

> What is attained through mindfulness and the delusion created by distraction

> are simply perceived by the intellect: actually, there's nothing to be
> attained or lost.[1331]

When you have developed certainty in the breakthrough, continue in that breakthrough state for five days, without doing anything that involves conceptual characteristics or any other kinds of mental activities. Then take a comfortable break for a day or so. Next, alternate between [intensifying] the breakthrough and taking a break, first for seven days each, and then for ten days each. [Cultivate] the breakthrough with your recognition of the abiding state until it continues as a constant flow during the day. Once that happens, it will gradually occur at night due to your habituation to it. Once you are very habituated to this, it is said that you will be able to thoroughly mix [your practice] with both the day and night.

The purpose of breakthroughs. Having eliminated all dualistic perception—such as there being an object of meditation and a meditator, an object of experience and an experiencer, an object of realization and a realizer—and all fixations and clinging (such as grasping at emptiness), your aim is to completely let go into the abiding state of the ground. For individuals of the highest or intermediate calibers, realization of the abiding state, free from dualistic apprehension, will arise in a matter of days. Since that depends on the degree of your training, it does not occur in one set way. [448]

Some are unable to give rise to such realizations no matter what. It is explained that they should practice for some time following what was explained previously about cultivating spiritual practices during meditative equipoise and postmeditative attainment. Later on, by meditating in a way that repeatedly dissociates from any clinging—such as grasping at appearances or at emptiness—realization will gradually dawn.

When we have a genuine realization of the abiding state, that is the ultimate essence of the Buddha's teachings found in the sūtras, tantras, and esoteric instructions. Thus, [the approach of this practice tradition] is more profound than that of other paths or other lineages.

2) Refinement through the Conducts That Integrate [All Experiences] into the Path

This has three parts:

a) The Explanation of the Timing and Conducts for Integrating [All Experiences] into the Path
b) The Explanation of the Universal Vital Points for Integrating [All Experiences] into the Path
c) The Explanation of the Six Types of Path Integration

a) The Explanation of the Timing and Conducts for Integrating [All Experiences] into the Path

The timing of path integration. Generally, once we see the essence of the connateness of mind-itself and, specifically, once we fully see the essence of the connateness of thoughts and appearances, most postmeditative mental states and appearances will arise as postmeditative attainment as long as we are mindful of [or recollect] our spiritual practices. This is the point at which we should undertake to integrate [all that we experience] into the path because, until we have recognized the three modes of connateness, we will be unable to integrate the mind experiencing unsettling circumstances into the path.

The timing of when it is necessary [to practice] path integration. Although we may have the realization of seeing the essence [of mind during] meditation, we may also remain completely ordinary, having succumbed to the lure of the appearances of this life and having rigid fixations to our attachments and aversions. When our mind is disturbed by intense situations and plagued by concerns, it can be difficult to incorporate those into the path just as they are. When we are comfortable and at ease, we may slip into not noticing our latent thoughts. In brief, we should undertake path integration when it is difficult to incorporate those [states of mind] into the path spontaneously by being mindful of [or recollecting] our spiritual practice and when our usual thoughts involved with anxieties—our hopes or fears—cause our mindstream to be unworkable. [449]

When we are staying in seclusion and meditation arises as a constant flow, we should engage in conduct that integrates [difficulties] right with that situation in order to stabilize and enhance our practice. At that time, whenever concerns arise in our mind, they are to be integrated with the path. Otherwise, if we are mindful without distractions during meditative equipoise and postmeditative attainment, we might discard sustaining the natural expressions of the abiding state, and we could end up in one of the deviations described above by applying path integration involving remedies, subversive meditations, and the like.

The timing for engaging in conduct. It is taught that conduct is to be undertaken once we have achieved heat and signs, as is stated in the *Two-Part [Hevajra Tantra]*:

> Once you have attained some heat,
> if you want to engage in conduct
> and wish to become accomplished,
> undertake the conduct in this way.[1332]

This practice tradition also says that conduct must be linked with timing. Some who have not recognized the essence of their mind [undertake conduct] when they have had just some kind of śamatha experience. Others, without even that, wander in charnel grounds and at crossroads for the sake of fame, recognition, and gains. They may start out with tenacity but will later become complacent. None of them will enhance their spiritual practices authentically because they neither recognize the essence of their thoughts, which are what are to be integrated into the path, nor recognize the abiding state of their mind, the place where integration occurs.

The purpose of conduct. Conduct is not undertaken simply for the sake of taking sense pleasures as the path. It is done to equalize the taste of mental stability and wavering as the essence of dharmatā, as the *Two-Part [Hevajra Tantra]* explains: [450]

> The explanation of conduct
> that employs an intimidating form
> was not given so that you could indulge.
> [Its purpose is] to see if your mind
> is one that wavers or is stable.[1333]

The actual conducts. In the Vajrayāna, the father tantras present three types of conduct: elaborate conduct, unelaborate conduct, and very unelaborate conduct. The mother tantras also present three types: secret conduct, conduct of discipline, and conduct that is victorious in all directions. In the [Seven] Siddhi [Texts] and the [Sixfold] Essence Cycle, four types of conduct are mentioned: excellent conduct, secret, or hidden, conduct, conduct of discipline with awareness, and conduct that is victorious in all directions. Furthermore, other enumerations are taught, such as the four types of conduct: the conduct for beginners, conduct of mastering wisdom, conduct of greatly mastering wisdom, and conduct of liberation. If practitioners are also Secret Mantra practitioners with a connection to the profound instructions of the generation and perfection processes, it is clear that those conducts may also be suitable as conducts for them as mahāmudrā practitioners because the [Seven] Siddhi [Texts, the Sixfold] Essence [Cycle], the dohās of the Great Brahman [Saraha], and the mahāmudrā texts of the lord Śavaripa, Virūpa, and Tilopa teach those types of conduct.

However, that is interpreted in this practice tradition as follows. In keeping with the Kālacakra [system's] almost virtual prohibition of conduct involving desire for those observing [monastic] vows, practitioners observing [monastic] vows must not transgress their training [when undertaking] conduct to enhance their meditation. It is explained that this [prohibition] applies to just the secret conduct since the excellent conduct, the unelaborate and very unelaborate conducts, and the conduct that is victorious in all directions are harmonious with the intent [and vows of monastics]. [451]

The locations. When conduct is undertaken in pleasing and comfortable places, such as monasteries or villages, the external and internal interdependent connections are not complete. Powerful thoughts and mental afflictions don't come up in our mind in such places and, without those, we don't have anything challenging to integrate into the path of Mahāmudrā. For the most part, our mind will just remain at ease in a state of laziness and idleness. Even though we meditate for many years or throughout our lifetime, [our meditation] won't be effective right on the spot. When we are happy and at leisure, our cultivation of spiritual practice is something we do on the side. But if a situation involving mental afflictions arises, we find that we are pulled into an ordinary state. Therefore, it is said that spending just one month practicing secret conduct mixing that with the situations we encounter in dangerous places with difficult terrain is more effective for enhancing meditation than meditating for three years in villages or monasteries.

Consequently, we should go to terrifying and forbidding mountain peaks or mountain hermitages, dangerous places where the magical displays of nonhumans appear, scary and frightening charnel grounds with corpses and skeletons, the base of a solitary tree that is controlled by nāgas, evil spirits, and the like, abandoned towns and crossroads where hungry ghosts and demons gather, and other such places.[1334] We should begin with the practice of the offerings and generosity of a kusāli, then give up ordinary conversation and undertake [the practice of conduct].

The confidence [needed] to undertake conduct. The early Kadampa masters teach that we need five qualities while wandering in mountain hermitages:

1. a lack of hypocrisy in our ethical behavior
2. the ability to withstand adverse circumstances through applying remedies
3. proficiency with the oral instructions
4. the ability to restore our health through our faith
5. the ability to dispel subtle harms through our own abilities[1335]

The exalted Gampopa explains:

> You need these four: confidence in the oral instructions, confidence in your own abilities, confidence in your experiences, and confidence in the view.[1336] [452]

The mahāsiddha Zhang teaches:

> When, on your own, you are proficient with the oral instructions,
> are unaffected by the hordes of external and internal māras,
> and can maintain pure ethical conduct without hypocrisy,
> then wander alone in mountain retreats.[1337]

The actual conduct has five modes:

1. *Conduct like that of a wounded deer.* Wounded deer don't associate with others in their herd and withdraw their minds, remaining apart. Similarly, you should act alone, having given up close companions and withdrawing your mind from the concerns of this life—such as subjugating your enemies, caring for your friends, and

keeping up good relations with your patrons.

2. *Lionlike conduct.* Lions are untroubled by other groups of animals, be they wild herbivores or carnivores. Similarly, do not be afraid of the obstacles presented by any situation, whether they be external ones created by humans or nonhumans, or internal ones, such as the movements of thoughts.
3. *Conduct like the wind blowing through open space.* Just as the wind blows through open space fluidly, transparently, and without being obstructed by objects, let your mind be transparent and open without any attachment or clinging to your body, possessions, pleasures, gain, or fame.
4. *Spacelike conduct.* Just as space is without support, you should not hold onto any reference point (such as thinking, "I will do this," or "I am doing that") and should not have any object of meditation, such as those with characteristics or those without characteristics. [453]
5. *Conduct like that of a crazy person.* In the same way that someone insane has no fixed reference points, you should have no fixations—no affirming or adopting something positive and no negating or rejecting what is unwholesome.

It is taught that those five modes of conduct are the means by which we can take whatever situations and appearances occur as the path and enhance our practice of the abiding state.

b) The Explanation of the Universal Vital Points for Integrating [All Experiences] into the Path

In this context, what we integrate into the path are our normal thoughts of something perceived and a perceiver, which are obscured by ignorance, because they are what drag us down in saṃsāra, as the *Vairocanābhisambodhi* states:

> Thoughts, great ignorance,
> are what plunge us into the ocean of saṃsāra.[1338]

When we do not lapse into regular thinking and we integrate our thoughts into the path using the key instructions, they arise as the essence of wisdom and purify saṃsāra. As the *Two-Part [Hevajra Tantra]* says:

> Concepts purify concepts,
> and existence purifies itself.[1339]

The Great Brahman [Saraha] declares:

> The great wisdom of thoughts
> dries up the ocean of saṃsāra.[1340]

Nāropa and Maitrīpa proclaim:

> Thoughts, free in themselves, are great wisdom.[1341] [454]

We may think, It was said previously that pointing out thoughts to be the dharmakāya is sufficient. If that's the case, why is it necessary to again integrate them into the path? It is possible that some instantaneous-type practitioners are always liberated by just that [pointing-out instruction]. However, most practitioners will need to penetrate the vital point by again integrating thoughts into the path. When you are cultivating mindfulness of your spiritual practice, it may be that most subtle thoughts are purified as wisdom. However, some coarse thoughts during that [meditation] and most of the thoughts of your postmeditative mind will not be purified in your practice. Moreover, in the midst of unrestrained thoughts, you will be able to do little more than bring [those thoughts] into meditation for a few short, fleeting moments. And, having lapsed into regular thinking, you then may stray further by sealing [those thoughts] with a theoretical understanding, thinking, "This is the dharmakāya," "This is wisdom."

It is explained that during the phase of freedom from elaborations meditation, although subtle thoughts arise as the dharmakāya through undistracted mindfulness itself, powerful thoughts of desire or aggression may not arise fully as the dharmakāya. Even during one taste, thoughts that are stirred up by intense situations may not become part of your spiritual practices. Since that can happen even for those who have reached elevated states of meditation, it is important to integrate thoughts into the path. Nowadays, some see something of the essence of meditation early on and then meditate for many years but, being unable to progress, they become discouraged. That happens because they did not grasp the vital point of path integration. For those reasons, new meditators and great meditators alike must be skilled in the vital point of path integration and greatly value it.

Its vital point depends on being skillful in cultivating the stream of mindfulness within a specific context, as the exalted Drikungpa [Jikten Sumgön] points out:

> My children, if I summarize everything, it will be nothing other than this. What is it? If you are skilled in being mindful, you are skilled in meditation.[1342]

He continues:

> In yoga's flowing river
> undistracted mindfulness is crucial.[1343]

Since all forms of path integration are variations of integrating thoughts into the path, the root of all path integration is integrating thoughts with the path. [455] In the same way that if we know that one reed is hollow, we know that all reeds are hollow, we should know that all specific instances of thought are the same.

With this point in mind, the exalted Gampopa primarily taught integrating thoughts into the path as the dharmakāya and considered that to include all other instances of path integration. It is not that Gampopa did not teach the six types of path integration that are found in the practice tradition these days. Gampopa's teachings called *Esoteric Instructions on the Five Nails*,[1344] which were written down as notes by his disciples, contain instructions on integrating obstacles into the path, illness into the path, death into the path, mental afflictions into the path, thoughts into the path, and severing the four demons, which is integrating god-demons into the path. Furthermore, he discussed these in various places throughout his precious Collected Works. Later, certain of the exalted Rechungpa's esoteric instructions were extracted as a treasure [that is, were discovered as hidden teachings] by the exalted Tsangpa Gyare and became greatly renowned in the glorious Drukpa system under the name "Equal Taste."

There are three vital points essential to all path integrations.

1. First, identify thoughts. No matter what good or bad situations occur, or how they appear, start with recognizing thoughts and not just letting things be as they are.
2. In the middle, let go of any sense of self. Whatever arises, do not distort it by having attachment or aversion towards it or by trying

to block or establish it. Give up the entanglements of a belief in a self. Without seeing or holding anything as problematic or meritorious, rest right with that [thought] without being affected by the intellect. [456]

3. In the end, avoid the difficult passages of hope and fear. Do not entertain hopes or fears, such as hoping that by practicing in that way something will happen or fearing that nothing will, or hoping that things will manifest as the path or fearing that they won't. Even if subtle thoughts involving hopes or fears come up, let go without fabrication or contrivance right within whatever occurs and be set free without clinging.

We should be aware of these three modes in all instances of path integration.

c) The Explanation of the Six Types of Path Integration

This has six parts:

i) Integrating Thoughts into the Path: The Instructions for Turning Bad Omens into Auspicious Ones
ii) Integrating Mental Afflictions into the Path: The Instructions for Transforming Poison into Amṛta
iii) Integrating God-Demons into the Path: The Instructions for Converting Obstacles into Siddhis
iv) Integrating Suffering into the Path: The Instructions on Bodhicitta
v) Integrating Illness into the Path: The Instructions for Equalizing the Elements
vi) Integrating Death into the Path: The Instructions That Point Out the Mother and Child Dharmatās

i) Integrating Thoughts into the Path: The Instructions for Turning Bad Omens into Auspicious Ones

Thoughts purify thoughts, as the *Two-Part [Hevajra Tantra]* says:

> Just as water that has entered the ear
> will be extracted by more water,
> likewise, thoughts of entities
> will be purified by ascertainment.[1345]

The method of purification. Do not regard thoughts as things to be given up—take them as the path by integrating thoughts into thoughts that [reflect] their own inherent nature. The exalted Gampopa states:

> Do not reject the internal mind's thoughts. Regard thoughts as useful. Regard thoughts as indispensible. See them as necessary. See them as something dear to your heart. If you do that, thoughts will be thoughts that [reflect] their own inherent nature. Thoughts will be your friends. Thoughts will be your path. Thoughts will be fuel for your prajñā.[1346]

Although the exalted Gampopa taught numerous ways to integrate thoughts into the path, in this context his procedure is as follows. [457]

First identify thoughts. When a subtle or coarse thought of any kind, virtuous or unvirtuous, arises in your mind, it may cause uneasiness and your mind to clearly experience pleasure or discomfort. If that happens, don't just let that thought be as it is: recognize it directly with mindfulness.

In the middle, let go of any sense of self. Disengaging from that thought, drawing your mind in, and meditating on remedial nonconceptual wisdom is not it. Analyzing a thought in terms of its origin, abiding, departure, and so forth, and determining it to be without any essence is not it. First letting a thought go, then pursuing it and sustaining it with mindfulness is not it. The true spiritual practice is to simply recognize a thought and let that thought be, however it is, without any compartmentalization or corruption. Do not regard it as a problem or a virtue. Even if it stops, don't stop. Don't follow it. Don't tamper with it in any way. Without any clinging, sustain vividness, crispness—loosely, spaciously, with vibrancy.

By doing that, no matter what thought arises, you do not need to abandon it or adopt it, block it or encourage it, alter it or manipulate it, change it or establish it. That thought itself clearly arises as meditation. This is what is meant by incorporating thoughts into the path. Maitrīpa explains:

> From the unborn, a thought suddenly appears.
> That very thought is the essence of the expanse.
> From the beginning those two are not separate.
> Those two are of equal taste, I teach.[1347] [458]

The exalted Gampopa proclaims:

> Undistorted thoughts are naturally dharmatā.
> Know that uncontrived, they are free in their own place.[1348]

The exalted Götsangpa teaches:

> Whenever another thought arises,
> recognize its essence immediately
> and relax right into that.
> There's no doubt: it's free on the spot.[1349]

He also says:

> [Thought-]movements are like breezes, not [solid] things.
> Not clung to, movements are fine.
> That is called thoughts arising as meditation.
> Recognize their essence and you're free from blocking and producing.[1350]

Those who are unable to do that may find, at first, that turbulent thoughts disturb their mind and unsettle their spiritual practice. Since thoughts and karmic winds operate together, those are just experiences of disturbed karmic winds. Actually, there is nothing that is not included within spiritual practice. The natural, automatic [result] of this process is that [thoughts] will be incorporated into the path comfortably as part of your spiritual practice. When you have become habituated to that, by just recognizing a thought, it will be part of your spiritual practice.

In the end, avoid the difficult passages of hope and fear. When integrating thoughts into the path in that manner, do not be anxious, hoping that they will arise as the path or fearing they will not. Do not try to dissect or connect anything at all. Without judgments or clinging, let things go without a trace.

We should be aware of these modes [of instruction] when training in any of the other forms of path integration. [459]

ii) Integrating Mental Afflictions into the Path: The Instructions for Transforming Poison into Amṛta

The *Two-Part [Hevajra Tantra]* says:

> Just as those burned by a cooking [fire]
> should endure fire again,
> those who burn with the fires of passion
> should endure passion's fires.[1351]

The *Sampuṭa* states:

> Desire purifies desire,
> aggression cleanses aggression,
> bewilderment purifies bewilderment,
> pride purifies pride,
> jealousy cleanses jealousy.
> The Vajra Holder and the others purify everything.[1352]

Once mental afflictions are integrated into the path, since they are of equal taste with dharmatā, their manifestations as mental afflictions are experienced as their essences: the five wisdoms. Having purified desire into the discriminating wisdom, aggression into the dharmadhātu wisdom, bewilderment into mirrorlike wisdom, pride into the wisdom of equality, and jealousy into the wisdom that accomplishes all activities, the states of the five victorious ones are evident. The *Sampuṭa* continues:

> The wisdoms and afflictions become the same.
> They are five families:
> five wisdoms and five buddhas.[1353] [460]

Therefore, if you apply the instructions for path integration, even when you avail yourself of the six types of objects as sense pleasures, you won't be tainted by the deficiencies of those objects. Instead they will be like poison transformed into amṛta. The *Two-Part [Hevajra Tantra]* teaches:

> The incorrigible actions of people,
> whatever they are, will cause bondage.

[But] with methods, those very [actions]
will free beings from their bondage in saṃsāra.[1354]

The Great Brahman [Saraha] observes:

Availing ourselves of objects, we are not sullied by objects,
like utpālas are untouched by muddy water.
Yogins and yoginīs take refuge in what is the root.
How can poison harm the one with the mantra for poison?[1355]

He also says:

Just as water from the salty oceans
becomes sweet after it is taken up by the clouds,
a stable mind that benefits others
turns the poison of objects into amṛta.[1356]

The actual path integration. Desire: identify when your mind is passionately in the throes of desire, when you are attached to, and fixated upon, an attractive external object or sentient being and wish to possess that object or person. Aggression: identify when your mind bears deep-seated dislike of and animosity towards an object or situation, such as an enemy or hindrance. Bewilderment: identify when your mind is unclear (as when feeling befuddled or idle) or is in a temporary state of torpor, such as when feeling sleepy, dull, or sluggish. Pride: identify the mindset when you feel impressed with yourself and superior to others, such as when you think, "Me!" on the basis of attachment to yourself and you feel proud that you are better than others. [461] Jealousy: identify the abrasive state of mind that keenly feels loss and unhappiness in relation to others' prosperity and wealth.

Once you have identified those, apply the previous instructions about letting go of a sense of self, avoiding the difficult passages of hope and fear, and so forth.

Sometimes you should use the method of arousing stronger than usual attachment or aggression towards an object of desire or aversion (the reference points for your mental afflictions), thereby creating powerful mental afflictions. Allow intense attachment or aggression to build up, or intentionally generate it, such that your breathing becomes uncomfortable, your facial expression changes, and your body trembles and shakes. Then identify that thought and so forth.

It is taught that the stronger the mental afflictions, the more effective the path integration will be and the greater the purification of the usual [seemingly] existent mental afflictions, as Maitrīpa says:

> Mental afflictions are great wisdom:
> like a forest feeds a fire, they aid yogins and yoginīs.[1357]

The way [to know if you have] successfully incorporated [mental afflictions into the path] or not is as described above.

iii) Integrating God-Demons into the Path: The Instructions for Converting Obstacles into Siddhis

It is said:

> Thoughts are hindering spirits.
> All hindering spirits come from thoughts.[1358]

Nāropa teaches:

> What the obstacles of illness and spirits
> come down to are thoughts. [462]
>
> When you are sick, sickness lies in the thought.
> When you feel harmed, the harm is found in the thought.
> When you die, death is in the thought.
> When you are born, birth is in the thought.
>
> Pleasure and pain and all the rest,
> everything is thought.
> Mind does not exist as anything.
> If you cut through the ground and root of thoughts,
> illnesses and spirits won't occur.[1359]

The Great Exalted One [Milarepa] teaches:

The appearances of demons, the perception of demons, and the
thought of demons:
They appear, yet they appear from the yogin himself.
They dissolve, yet they dissolve into the yogin himself.

Again all hindering spirits are the magical display of mind:
if they are not realized to be empty self-appearances
and are taken to be autonomous demons, the yogin is deluded.[1360]

Rock Rākṣasī observes:

If the propensities of your own confused mind
didn't cause your thoughts to manifest as enemies,
how could I, Rock Rākṣasī, appear as your enemy?

Again these māras of latent tendencies will arise from your mind.
If you don't know the suchness of mind,
I won't go just because you tell me to.[1361] [463]

As said, all perceptions of demons are the magical display of your own thoughts. What seem to be forms of gods or demons are the visions of a mind solidifying its thoughts. An analogy is when you take a rope to be a snake, that rope appears to you as a snake.

The causes and conditions for that [are a combination of mental and physical]. It is said that when winds enter the channel locations related to the three poisonous mental afflictions in your physical body (which is the result of fully matured karma), you experience delusive appearances and conceptual perceptions that correspond to those [mental afflictions]. Bewilderment causes you to perceive and experience appearances of nāgas and earth-lord types, aggression causes the evil spirits and male spirit types, and desire causes the female spirit types, such as rākṣasīs.[1362] Later, when those are incorporated into the path, they will be experienced as part of your spiritual practice. Your fearful thoughts will vanish, the atmosphere will be warm, your gloom will disappear. Once the harm they cause is pacified, they come under your power. All that happens like the rising and falling of the balance arm of a scale.

The way to integrate demons into the path. Although in *Annihilating* *the Four Demons*[1363] Gampopa explains the approach of determining that demons lack any nature, which is not exactly in keeping with this context of equalizing taste. However, his presentation of the way to penetrate the vital point in relation to demons that says, "rest uncontrived in a state in which a thought appearing as a demon and your own mind are not a duality"[1364] and the section on taking god-demons as the path seem to be exactly the point in this context.

The actual path integration. When the magical displays of god-demons actually appear, or your mind is clearly depressed with the worry that that they will (even though nothing is happening), or your fears are overwhelming you and you're starting to panic, immediately recognize that mind. That very mind can be relied upon as your true spiritual practice. Cultivate that and so on, following the previous instructions. [464]

Downplay the magical displays regardless of their size. Imagine even more frightening magical displays, almost inconceivable ones: that heaven and earth collide, that you are being beaten and slaughtered by armies of demons with their weapons, burned by fires, dragged through water, and so forth. Magnify those terrifying appearances and bring them into your practice as instructed above.

iv) Integrating Suffering into the Path: The Instructions on Bodhicitta

In *The [Grand Collection of] Dharma Lectures*, the exalted Gampopa teaches integrating suffering into the path by seeing the suffering of saṃsāra as kind, integrating the nature of suffering into the unborn state, and cultivating love, compassion, and bodhicitta on the basis of suffering.[1365] Although overall that is consistent with this point, here I will present the instructions in keeping with the general approach to path integration.

Broadly speaking, all beings—yourself and others—are plagued by the three types of suffering. Specifically, you can see directly with your own senses that beings create suffering for each other by killing, slaughtering, and exploiting each other. Even when they are not tormenting each other in those ways, you can see that beings suffer gripped by various kinds of unbearable misery related to their own karma. When you hear about such things, without having any feelings of affection for those beings, you become afraid that will happen to you due to your own karma and mental afflictions. You become terribly distressed. In order to pacify your karma and mental afflictions and attain liberation, you feel inspired to practice the path. That is the mindset of the Hīnayāna. Recognizing that all those suffering beings are your kind parents, you feel great affection for them, and then extend that love and compassion to all beings. [465] That is the attitude of the Mahāyāna.

Regardless of which attitude you have, when you experience vivid pain in your mind, identify it and integrate it into the path using the approach described already. In the end, while in a state that maintains the experiences of your spiritual practice, arouse bodhicitta motivated by your love and compassion for all sentient beings, and make excellent aspiration prayers for the welfare of others.

This is very laudable as Nāgārjuna teaches:

> If you and others in this world
> wish to attain unsurpassable awakening,
> you need bodhicitta, its root,
> firm as the mighty king of mountains,
> compassion stretching throughout all directions,
> and wisdom not based on duality.[1366]

Furthermore, in this context, while the radiance of your affection that cannot bear the suffering of sentient beings is unceasing, you are aware that its essence, or nature, is emptiness—it does not exist as anything at all. That is said to be the unification of emptiness and compassion, or bodhicitta that is emptiness imbued with the heart of compassion. The *Two-Part [Hevajra Tantra]* says:

> Indivisible emptiness and compassion
> is called bodhicitta.[1367]

The *Vajra Pañjarā* states:

> Whenever the mind meditates
> on the inseparability of emptiness and compassion,
> that is the teachings of the buddha,
> dharma, and saṅgha.[1368]

The *Sampuṭa* declares: [466]

The nature without elaborations
is renowned as "prajñā."
Compassion is what benefits sentient beings,
like a wish-fulfilling gem.[1369]

The Great Brahman [Saraha] observes:

Those who remain in emptiness without any compassion
do not discover the sublime path.
Yet those who only meditate on compassion
never attain liberation from this saṃsāra.

Whoever can unite the two
abides in neither saṃsāra nor nirvāṇa.[1370]

The Śavara [Saraha] states:

In the nonjudgmental sphere of realization
tears flow naturally from overwhelming compassion
when the misery of ignorant beings is so clear.
Switch places with others and do what is useful.[1371]

v) Integrating Illness into the Path: The Instructions for Equalizing the Elements

Overall, the causes of disease are produced by karma and mental afflictions that are brought on by ignorance. The conditions at the start of any illness are the displaced movements of the karmic winds. Those disturb the four elements and create an imbalance in the [body's] constitution. [467] The results are pain, the sensations of mental or physical illnesses, and the like. Illnesses are categorized as those that develop from wind, those that come from bile, those that come from phlegm, and those that are compounds. Altogether, there are four hundred and four types of diseases.

Although many methods for treating illnesses are explained in the medical systems, in this context the approach is as follows:

- Treat the cause of illness. Since ignorance is the cause, the profound way to treat that is to cultivate awareness-wisdom.

- Dispel its conditions. Since the disturbances of the karmic winds are the conditions, the profound way to purify those right where they are is to sustain the uncontrived, intrinsic state of mind using the technique of bringing together the winds and mind.
- Destroy its results. Since the sensations of suffering are the results, the profound way to cast them off with no remainder, with nothing left, is to meditate on emptiness, the abiding state.

For those reasons, regardless of the type of illness and whether it is new or chronic, the profound way to heal an illness is to integrate it into the path.

Integrating illness into the path. The exalted Gampopa teaches [the following three points]:

- First, downplay the illness. Imagine something even greater and more unbearable than your [present] painful illness.
- In the middle, undermine the illness. Examine its origin, abode, departure, color, and shape.
- In the end, integrate the illness into the path. Recognize that the one who is sick is the mind, that the one perceiving the illness is the mind, and that mind is unborn, like space.[1372]

Overall, that is consistent with this point except that here the causes and conditions of illness, the modes of illness, and so forth are not examined and analyzed in terms of their origin, abode, departure, and so on. Not slipping into feeling attachment or aversion for an illness, or blocking or encouraging one, identify the clear painful physical or mental sensations of illness. Those can be relied upon as the true meditation. Sustain that as vibrant clarity without altering or manipulating it with a mind bent on preventing or promoting something. [468] At times, undermine all sense of self, be it a sense of the one who is sick, the one who feels pain, or the experiencer. Remain without contrivance in a state in which no essence is identified. To downplay the illness, do as was described above. Finally, do not entertain hopes or fears, such as hoping that you will be cured of your illness or fearing that you will not be. Be certain about the great equality [of all things].

These days, as a means for becoming grounded in the experience of integrating illness into the path, it is taught that we should train by integrating into the path the pain of sitting for a long time in the vajra position or any other physical discomfort that we may intentionally create for ourself. It is also taught that by sustaining practice for a long time directly with an illness without losing the vital point, eventually we won't need to regard pain and belief in a self as enemies or things to be rejected.[1373] They will arise as meditation. When the hot and cold elements are equalized, serious illness and the enhancement of our spiritual practice occur simultaneously.

Here it is explained that equalizing [the elements enables] us to dispense with medical treatments for illness. In the end, this is in keeping with the point of equalizing the taste in which hopes and fears are rejected. It is the practice of the mahāsiddhas. There are numerous stories of many masters, such as the exalted Drikungpa and the exalted Götsangpa, who were very ill and were cured only through [their ability] to equalize [the elements].

Nevertheless, these days integrating illness into the path is a special quality of yogins and yoginīs, and it is wrong to adopt the dharma of fools who say the support for awakening [that is, our body] is without [or beyond] death or no-death. Therefore, on the conventional level, we should rely on the methods for treating diseases and establishing the right interdependent connections, and practice rejecting hopes and fears right within awareness of the ultimate. That accords with the point and is reasonable.[1374] [469]

vi) Integrating Death into the Path: The Instructions That Point Out the Mother and Child Dharmatās

By being accustomed to integrating all the appearances and thoughts that occur during the circumstances of your life with your spiritual practice and, particularly, by being familiar with integrating into the path the dissolution process that happens as you fall asleep and [the ensuing] luminosity, you will be well prepared to experience integrating death into the path without abandoning it, just as children know how to crawl into their mothers' laps. Therefore, right now apply yourself to taking all varieties of thoughts and appearances—be they congenial or not, be they clear or not—as your path.

As you approach the time when death will be the focus of your path, you should let go of any attachments you might have, such as to your homeland or possessions. If you are wealthy, make offerings to please your gurus and present tormas to satisfy the yidams, ḍākinīs, and dharma protectors. To your vajra brothers and sisters, offer enjoyable gaṇacakras and give them everything you own. Cast far away any negative objects or situations and properly arrange positive interdependent connections. When death approaches, prepare to integrate it into the path by taking up the vital points of the body, [that is, adopting] the sleeping position of a lion or sitting upright. Arouse great devotion towards your guru visualized on top of your head.

What is to be integrated into the path. Integrate the awareness that you are separating from this life to which you have clung. Integrate your anxious thoughts about dying, which cause your heart to chill. And integrate the sequence of visions of the dissolution process related to the four elements, then illumination, radiance, and so on.

The way to integrate death into the path. [470] If your anxieties make you feel averse to this upsetting prospect, if your mind is set on clinging to a sense of self, thinking, "There is this and that," or if you are [wrapped up] in the hopes and fears of hoping you will recognize luminosity and fearing that you won't, those will hinder your ability to integrate death into the path. First, simply identify those thoughts and experiences. Then, relying on whatever arises as your true spiritual practice, follow the process explained above, beginning with sustaining that without clinging or manipulating anything with a mind bent on preventing or promoting something.

It is taught that while this topic is discussed in many of the Mahāyāna esoteric instructions for mind training and there are numerous esoteric instructions for transferring at the time of death, none of those are more profound than sustaining whatever arises without clinging.

After the completion of the dissolution process, natural luminosity will dawn spontaneously and automatically, mixing with the luminosity that you have practiced on the path as mother and child, like water poured into water, or space merging with space. That is said to be awakening as the dharmakāya, the meaning of which is expressed in the following citations. The [*Laghusaṃvara*] *Tantra* says:

> "Death" is a thought.
> It leads us to the celestial abodes.[1375]

It is also said:

> A single moment makes the difference:
> instantly, complete buddhahood [is attained].[1376]

The exalted Gampopa declares:

> With one thought following on another
> how can there be death?
> In the pure dharmakāya,
> how can there be death?
>
> In the disappearance of a rainbow painting,
> how can there be death?
> In the mind without birth or death,
> how can there be death?[1377] [471]

Even if your habituation to integrating death into the path is minimal and you're unable to awaken in the state of inseparable space-awareness, it is taught that whatever path integration you have practiced previously will enable you to have control over the bardos and connecting with your next rebirth. At the very least, you will be someone with karmic continuity in your next life due to the power of interdependence.

That completes the explanation of enhancement by breaking through to the unborn and by path integration. [472/473]

14

Realization and the Four Yogas

iv. The Way Realization Develops through Sustaining Meditation

This has three parts:

A) The Divisions of the Development of Realization
B) How the Realizations of the Four Yogas Develop
C) How the Bhūmis and Paths Are Traversed through Those [Four Yogas]

A) The Divisions of the Development of Realization

If we cultivate well those meditations on mahāmudrā that were explained, without deviating or going astray, it is said that the realization of the four yogas will develop sequentially in keeping with the three ways realization arises, which correspond to the type of practitioner we are. Since, as practitioners, we are divided into those whose previous training has been superior, moderate, or lesser, we are classified as instantaneous, bypassing, or gradual types.

The instantaneous way of development. First, during śamatha, or while being guided in vipaśyanā, or when the pointing-out [instructions are given], understandings, experiences, and realizations occur simultaneously. What arises instantaneously may be just one-pointedness, or it may be up to freedom from elaborations, up to one taste, or even up to nonmeditation. It is explained that what develops is stable. It occurs in the same way that when sunlight reaches a canyon, the fog there dissipates and the soil and rocks become warm all at the same time.

The bypassing way of development. Understandings, experiences, realizations, and the four yogas arise suddenly without the later phases necessarily being based on the earlier ones. It is said that this development is not stable, that there is considerable fluctuation. It is like, for example, the sun appearing and disappearing between clouds. [474] Nevertheless, it is taught that if these practitioners meditate with determination, practice in solitude for a long time, stay in retreat, arouse devotion towards their gurus, and supplicate ardently, they will achieve stable realization. It is also explained that if they are unable to meditate for a long time and do not stabilize realization in this lifetime, genuine realization will occur in the bardo.

The gradual way of development. Understandings, experiences, realizations, and the four yogas arise sequentially. Once the earlier ones are stabilized, the latter ones develop. It is said that progress is slow. Although the essence [of mind] is seen slightly, the objects of abandonment are not given up right away and the remedies are not mastered. The analogy is the sun rising over the horizon: as soon as it appears, it does not heat the entire earth or melt all that is frozen.

It is said that if both the latter two types arouse devotion and determination, the vital point of blessings will cause them to become like the instantaneous type without any difficulties. It is also said that realizations can occur in a variety of ways, such as realization happening at unpredictable times to be followed by conclusiveness, or realization occurring but there being no certainty or assessment of it because it is not recognized. Therefore, it is important to consult with gurus and experienced fellow practitioners.

The differences between understanding, experience, and realization. Regardless of the phase of our spiritual practices, high or low, understanding is when an abstract idea of the object of that practice arises correctly as a mental object and we have inferential understanding. Experience is when something similar to the actual [object of practice] is properly grounded in experience and experienced right within awareness. Realization is when, without being mistaken about the actual [object of practice], there is direct realization of, and conclusiveness about, the fundamental state. As the exalted Tsangpa Gyare states:

> Understanding involves examination and analysis.
> Experience is of the highs and lows of bliss and clarity.
> Realization is the recognition of the abiding state.[1378] [475]

Their differences are comparable to the following analogy. Through hearing stories about a place, like Bodh Gaya in India, an abstract image of it arises. Once we actually go there, we see its overall layout.[1379] When we have detailed certainty about the way things are there, we have full comprehension.

It is also taught that regardless of the phase of our spiritual practice, when it arises clearly right within awareness, that is experience. When we rest one-pointedly in that very state, without being distracted, that is meditative equipoise. When, through looking with discerning prajñā, we are convinced that nothing—be it the object seen or the seer—exists with any essence, that is realization. The exalted Gampopa explains the differences between experience and realization:

> Vibrant clarity is an experience. Not being distracted from that is stillness. Realization is when prajñā sees that no essence exists.[1380]

And:

> [Pakmo Drupa] asked: "What is the difference between experience and realization?"
>
> [Gampopa] replied: "Experience does not transcend being a mental object. Like the sun in the midst of clouds, bliss, clarity, and nonconceptuality are sometimes heightened, sometimes reduced, sometimes still. By sustaining those without fixation, the stains of the mind are purified and realization starts to dawn. Realization is when the nonduality of appearances and mind [are realized] right within the mind. That continues in a state of luminosity. When there is no object of meditation and no meditator, that is said to be the simultaneity of realization and attainment."[1381]

Concerning this, a certain person [Sakya Paṇḍita] says:

> Some say, "There are three:
> experience, understanding, and realization.
> Experience is inferior, understanding is middling,
> and realization is best."
>
> This requires some examination.
> If "experience" is used to mean having experiences, [476]

then all who have minds
have experiences.

If it is used to mean what is experienced in meditation,
then it is present from the lesser path of accumulation
through the path of perfection.

However, if it is the wisdom
of intuitive reflexive awareness,
that experience is only found in noble beings.

Understanding and realization
are synonymous terms that are of one essence [that is, are identical].
They are simply variant translations
of one Sanskrit term by the lotsāwas.[1382]

That is illogical for the following reasons. Not having seen those three [experience, understanding, and realization] referred to as terms [denoting] what is inferior, middling, or superior, it seems to be a dubious statement, one involving misinterpretations. Since it has not been determined that experience is necessarily inferior, it is not necessary to mention the experiences of noble beings and others. However, having mentioned them, it would be appropriate to distinguish the differences between their experiences and realizations. This practice tradition asserts that there are experiences intrinsic to realization and there is a phase when experiences and realizations are inseparable. If understanding and realization are the same in all instances, many absurd consequences follow: the divisions [of the dharma] into that of scripture and realization must be referred to as the divisions [of the dharma] into that of scripture and understanding, the realizations on the bhūmis and paths must be referred to as the understandings of those [levels], and so on. Since there are reasons for translating [a term] according to its meaning in a specific context, the lotsāwas and paṇḍitas translated [one Sanskrit term] differently.

[Sakya Paṇḍita] also says:

If clear and unclear thoughts
are being referred to as understanding and realization, then say
that.[1383]

That statement is also illogical for the following reasons. According to him, the difference between clear and unclear thoughts must be the difference between understanding and realization, and yet that contradicts what he said above [about them being synonyms]. It is very absurd to refer to unclear thoughts as realization, which is what [must be concluded] according to the order [of the terms] in his composition. His statement also means that all realizations of nonconceptual wisdom must be asserted to be conceptual. [477]

B) How the Realizations of the Four Yogas Develop

This has three parts:

1) The Way the Subject of the Four Yogas Is Presented in the Sūtras and Tantras
2) The Common Presentation of the Rationale for the Four Yogas
3) The Explanation of the Divisions of the Four Yogas

1) The Way the Subject of the Four Yogas Is Presented in the Sūtras and Tantras

The *Descent into Laṅkā* gives a presentation of four yogas:

> The Bhagavān said: "Mahāmati, bodhisattva mahāsattvas endowed with four qualities are yogins and yoginīs of the great yoga. What are the four? To meditate upon appearances as one's own mind. To abandon the view [that phenomena] arise, abide, and perish. To realize that external entities are nonentities [that is, do not exist]. To hold the intention to internalize the wisdom of the noble ones. Mahāmati, bodhisattva mahāsattvas endowed with those four qualities are yogins and yoginīs of the great yoga."[1384]

I will explain those one by one. Meditating on appearances as mind describes the yoga of one-pointedness because that is in keeping with the qualities of the yoga of one-pointedness. The same text continues:

> Mahāmati, that being so, how do bodhisattva mahāsattvas become skilled in meditating upon appearances as being their own mind? They do so by considering as follows. These three

> realms are simply one's own mind. [Mind] is devoid of a self and "mine," it is without movement, and is free from anything to be adopted or rejected. It is tainted by overly fixating on the latent tendencies of negative propensities, which are conceptual elaborations [held] throughout beginningless time. It is linked with enjoying the various forms of the three realms. [Mind] appears in keeping with the conceptualizations of the body, possessions, abodes, and beings.[1385] [478]

Abandoning the view [that phenomena] arise, abide, and perish describes the yoga of freedom from elaborations because that is in keeping with the qualities of the yoga of freedom from elaborations. The same text continues:

> Mahāmati, how do bodhisattva mahāsattvas abandon the view [that phenomena] arise, abide, and perish? They do so by considering as follows. Just like the arising of illusions or forms in a dream, all entities do not [truly] come into being because there is no self, no other, and not even both [self and other from which they arise]. Bodhisattvas follow [or understand] that [entities] are simply appearances of their own mind and see that external entities do not exist. Having seen that entities do not exist, they see that the consciousnesses have nothing to engage and that conditions are neither a mass nor do they amass. They see that the three realms arise from the conditions of thoughts. Because they do not observe any external or internal phenomena and they see the absence of any nature, they turn away from the view [that phenomena] arise. Realizing the nature of phenomena to be an illusion and so forth, they achieve patience in relation to unborn phenomena.[1386]

Realizing that external entities are nonentities [that is, do not exist] describes the yoga of one taste because that is in keeping with the qualities of the yoga of one taste. The same text states:

> Mahāmati, how do bodhisattva mahāsattvas become skilled in realizing that external entities are nonentities [that is, do not exist]? They do so by considering as follows. All entities are like mirages, dreams, and floaters. All entities are caused by overly

> fixating on the various latent tendencies of thoughts related to negative propensities, which are conceptual elaborations [held] throughout beginningless time. Thus they become bodhisattvas who truly see "the absence of nature."[1387] [479]

Holding the intention to internalize the wisdom of the noble ones describes the yoga of nonmeditation because that is in keeping with the qualities of the yoga of nonmeditation. The same text says:

> Mahāmati, how do bodhisattva mahāsattvas hold the intention to internalize the wisdom of the noble ones? They do so as follows. Having achieved patience in relation to unborn phenomena, they abide on the eighth bhūmi. Because they have internalized the fulfillment of the realization of mind, mentation, the mental consciousness, the five topics, the nature, and the twofold absence of self, they have also attained a mental body.[1388]

Similarly, the *Descent into Laṅkā* says:

> By relying on mind alone,
> you do not conceive of outer referents.
> Resting with thusness as your object,
> you transcend mind alone as well.
>
> Once you transcend mind alone,
> you go beyond the absence of appearances.
> Yogins and yoginīs who abide in the absence of appearances
> see the Mahāyāna.[1389]

Explanations of those verses found in the *Stages of Meditation* and *Instructions on Prajñāpāramitā* are in keeping with the meaning of the four yogas.[1390]

The *Tantra of the Great River of the Inconceivable Secrets of Ālikāli* correlates the four samādhis, the four levels of the path of preparation, and the four yogas:

> Through the samādhi of a majestic lion,
> clear cognition—one-pointed, unmoving, and lucid—

awakens from within as reflexively aware wisdom.
Once heat is attained, there is mastery over birth.

Second, with the illusionlike samādhi
and through the great equipoise free from elaborations,
the inconceivable samādhi arises as the expressive power.
Having attained peak, progress is uninterrupted.

Third, through the heroic-stride samādhi,
the realization of the tenth bhūmi arises: the one taste of the many.
The children of the victors of the three times benefit others.
By stabilizing patience, the suffering of the three realms is dispelled.

Fourth, with the vajralike samādhi [480]
and through exertion in the practice of nonmeditation,
immeasurable pure lands of omniscient buddhas are achieved.
That is the unsought, spontaneously existent great [level of] supreme qualities.[1391]

The *Two-Part [Hevajra Tantra]* refers to one-pointedness when it says:

Like the way a river's current flows
or a candle's flame is bound,
yogins and yoginīs remain continually
in the yoga of suchness, day and night.[1392]

It describes freedom from elaborations:

In essence, there are neither forms nor those who see them.
There are no sounds and no hearers.[1393]

And:

This has no beginning, middle, or end.
It is without existence and without nirvāṇa.[1394]

About one taste, it says:

Meditation is one taste, equality.[1395]

It refers to nonmeditation when it says:

> There is no meditator and no meditation.[1396]

The Great Brahman [Saraha] teaches one-pointedness:

> Cast away thoughts and their objects,
> and you'll rest like a small child.[1397]

He refers to freedom from elaborations:

> For those who contemplate suchness free from a root . . .[1398]

To one taste:

> Since everything is of equal taste,
> there is nothing higher than inconceivable wisdom.[1399]

And to nonmeditation:

> Being free from meditative concentration, what could be contemplated?[1400]

We should know, as those references demonstrate, that all teachings in the sūtras, tantras, and esoteric instructions on resting evenly in the one-pointed mind are teachings on one-pointedness, all teachings on the absence of arising and freedom from extremes are about freedom from elaborations, all descriptions of equality and the lack of reality are about one taste, and all instructions on being without adopting or rejecting, dispelling or establishing, are instructions on nonmeditation.

The exalted Yang Gönpa and others state that the four yoga process is a dharma of realization of the exalted Dakpo Rinpoche [Gampopa], that the terminology is used explicitly in the tantras, and that the features [of the four yogas] are found [in the tantras] exactly in that way.[1401] [481] Most are familiar with that much. However, [we should acknowledge] the great kindness of the exalted Gampopa for categorizing precisely the experiences and realizations of each of the four yogas and their gradations, and for laying these out in a way that is easy to understand even for practitioners these days. The names and general characterizations of the features of the four yogas are seen from early on since they appear in the previously cited passage from the *Tantra of the Great River of the Inconceivable Secrets of Ālikāli*. Also, the Great Lord [Atīśa] explains the four yogas in the instructions he gave on connate union to Gönpawa, and the stages of four yogas appear in the songs of the Great Exalted One [Milarepa].

Although we find many approaches to meditation involving various types of śamatha and vipaśyanā practices both in earlier times and now, I have never seen in another lineage what is found in this tradition in terms of assessing experiences and realizations once they have arisen in meditation, methods for enhancement, and ways of delineating the gradations of realization. This is clearly an unexcelled special feature of the Dakpo Kagyu.

2) The Common Presentation of the Rationale for the Four Yogas

This has two parts:

a) Identifying the Essence of Each of the Four Yogas
b) Explaining the Distinctive Features of Each [of the Four Yogas]

a) Identifying the Essence of Each of the Four Yogas

Generally speaking, the topic of the four yogas appears in many esoteric instructions, such as those that the exalted Gampopa gave to the exalted Gomtsul, the exalted Gomchung, and the exalted Pakmo Drupa; the instructions of the exalted Zhang (a student of the exalted Gomtsul); and those of the exalted Tsangpa Gyare (a student of the mahāsiddha Ling Repa) and his students. I will explain the four yogas referring to the thought of those instructions while primarily relying on the instructions of the exalted Gompas, elder and younger [Gomtsul and Gomchung]. [482]

First, the identification of the essence [of each of the four yogas]. Overviews are given by the exalted Gomchung:

> Vivid stillness is one-pointedness.
> Severing misinterpretations is freedom from elaborations.
> The absence of something to be abandoned or adopted is one taste.
> The purification of experience is nonmeditation.[1402]

And by the exalted Gampopa:

> The instantaneous lucid, unimpeded mind is the yoga of one-pointedness. The realization that the essence of awareness is unborn and beyond existence or nonexistence is the yoga of freedom from elaborations. The realization that, although there are various appearances, they are of the same nature is the yoga of the one taste of the many. The realization that the inseparability of appearances and emptiness is unceasing is the great meditative equipoise.[1403]

Next are summaries of the descriptions given in the many presentations.

One-pointedness. It is the vivid, vibrant, crisp resting in a state of empty clarity with the awareness that the mind's stillness and movements are commingled. It is like space in being without middle or edge. The exalted Pakmo Drupa teaches:

> First, when one-pointedness arises in your mindstream,
> there is a vibrancy and crispness beyond words.
> Like open spaces, it is clear without any materiality.[1404]

The exalted Zhang says:

> When the yoga of one-pointedness arises,
> you realize the nature of your own mind.
>
> Resting in unceasing empty clarity,
> vibrant and crisp, without center or edge,
> like the middle of clear open space,
> is the meditative equipoise of the first yoga.[1405]

Freedom from elaborations. Once we are liberated from the conceptual elaborations of the characterization process and taking percepts and perceivers, or external and internal phenomena, to arise, abide, and cease, we cut through our misinterpretations about the unborn emptiness of everything. The exalted Pakmo Drupa comments:

> Next, freedom from elaborations arises.
> The holy ones call it "seeing the essence."

Although it is explained that when the essence free from elaborations, the expanse of saṃsāra and nirvāṇa, [483]
is realized, one is a buddha and when not realized, one is a sentient being,
there is nothing other than a single essence free from elaborations.

Free from the extremes of permanence or annihilation and the elaborations of birth and cessation,
there is no duality of things to be adopted and things to be rejected.
Everything external and internal are devoid of the extremes of elaborations and are the middle path.[1406]

The exalted Zhang explains:

When the yoga of freedom from elaborations arises,
you realize the essence of your own mind.
It is uninterrupted awareness, free from elaborations.
Your mind—which is without arising or cessation, with nothing to adopt or reject—
abides as the dharmakāya.
That is the meditative equipoise of the second yoga.[1407]

One taste. This is when the phenomena of saṃsāra and nirvāṇa—all appearances and possibilities—are equal in the intrinsic state. There is no negating or confirming, abandoning or adopting, related to [phenomena] being empty or not empty, being free or not free from the elaborations of arising or cessation. The exalted Pakmo Drupa explains:

Meditating in that way, the one taste of the many will arise.
The various appearances and nonappearances, mind and emptiness,
being empty and not empty are of one taste: indivisible emptiness.

Realization or no realization are of one taste—there's no equipoise and postmeditative attainment.
Meditation and no meditation are of one taste: a sphere of purity.
Elaborations and freedom from elaborations are of one taste: the dharmadhātu.[1408]

The exalted Zhang says:

When the yoga of one taste arises,
you realize the characteristic of your own mind.
You realize that from your own mind—the dharmakāya, free from elaborations—
the profusion of saṃsāra and nirvāṇa appears.

This is because the whole array of thought and no thought,
appearances and no appearances, resting and no resting,
empty and not empty,
clarity and no clarity
is of one taste in the dharmakāya, luminosity.[1409]

Nonmeditation. Once the stains of all our previous meditative experiences are purified, path realizations mix with the natural abiding state, and there is neither meditative equipoise and postmeditative attainment nor mindfulness and distraction. [484] The exalted Pakmo Drupa teaches:

Having become familiar with that, the ultimate manifests.
Awareness is stripped to its singularity with no support.
This awareness free from elaborations is meditation.
Since there's no object of meditation or meditator observed externally or internally,
the mind that is the object of meditation dissolves into luminosity.
That is the incomparable essential nature transcending the intellect.[1410]

The exalted Zhang elaborates:

When the yoga of nonmeditation arises,
the essence of awareness is devoid of support.
Yogins and yoginīs have nothing to meditate upon.
There is no meditator either—all is openness.

You will know that the saying,
"buddhahood with its three kāyas and five wisdoms
is complete within yourself,"
from now on applies to you.[1411]

Since it seems that the many descriptions found in the practice lineage identifying the four yogas are mostly in agreement, I will not elaborate more.

b) Explaining the Distinctive Features of Each [of the Four Yogas]

This has eight parts:

i) The Distinctive Features of Their Realizations
ii) The Range of Experiences
iii) The Way the Postmeditative Mental States Manifest
iv) The Stains to Be Purified
v) The Way Postmeditative Attainment Is Purified
vi) The Distinctive Features of Their Meditative Equipoises and Postmeditative Attainments
vii) Their Distinctions in Terms of Time
viii) Other Explanations of Their Distinctive Features

i) The Distinctive Features of Their Realizations

The exalted Gomchung states:

> During one-pointedness the essence is realized.
> During freedom from elaborations the nature is realized.
> During one taste the characteristic is realized.
> The realization of nonmeditation is a constant flow.[1412]

Generally speaking, at this point we should understand the presentation of the essence, nature, and characteristic of mind according to what has already been explained.* Here they are [realized] as follows:

- During one-pointedness, realizing the essence of mind means developing confidence and certainty in your experience of mind being nonconceptually clear and unidentifiable.
- During freedom from elaborations, realizing the nature of mind means being aware that mind is unconditioned—free from arising, abiding, and ceasing—and that it lacks any nature.
- During one taste, realizing the characteristic of mind means being aware that all the myriad representations of mind's latent tendencies that appear are of equal taste within the unborn state. And it means being aware that the unceasing expressive power of emptiness is the interdependent display of myriad appearances. [485]

*See "Determining the Abiding State of Mind," pp. 259–67.

- During nonmeditation, there is the continuous realization of the great intrinsic state, the equality of everything, without distinguishing between an object of experience and an experiencer, an object of realization and a realizer.

This is as the exalted Gampopa teaches:

> Among the essence, nature, and characteristic of mind, its essence is that it is clear yet nonconceptual. Its nature is that it is free from arising, abiding, and ceasing. Its characteristic is that it appears as both saṃsāra and nirvāṇa. During one-pointedness, the essence is realized. During freedom from elaborations, the nature is realized. During one taste, the characteristic is realized.[1413]

Alternatively, the exalted Pakmo Drupa, the exalted Zhang, and others explain that the nature is realized during one-pointedness and the essence is realized during freedom from elaborations. However, since the essence and nature of mind are identical in essence but are discrete isolates, there is no difference [between the statement by Gampopa and those by Pakmo Drupa and others].

We might now wonder, Are the realizations of one-pointedness and freedom from elaborations the same? They are not. Although right within the essence of awareness itself they are similar, there are significant differences between them, such as whether fixations and clinging to experiences have been purified or not, and whether external and internal phenomena have been realized to be unborn or not, as we will learn from the presentations to come.

ii) The Range of Experiences

The exalted Gomchung says:

> One-pointedness may be enveloped in darkness. [486]
> Freedom from elaborations might get caught up in adhering to an
> emptiness that is nonexistence.
> One taste can be knocked off course by the waves of mixing.
> Nonmeditation's sun may be obscured by clouds.[1414]

The meaning of that verse. As long as we have not seen the essence, one-pointedness may simply arise as resting vividly and vibrantly in the mind's empty clarity. However, that kind of experience can obscure and prevent the development of conviction and certainty in that mind, which is the essence of awareness, clear and unimpeded. Like being enveloped in darkness, we do not see what is to be seen.

In some cases of freedom from elaborations, we fixate on external and internal phenomena as empty. Being under the sway of experiences in which we are certain about that, we can become unskillfully neglectful or scornful of the side of appearances and the interdependent connections between actions and their results. We get caught up in adhering to an emptiness that is nonexistence, a nihilistic view.

During one taste, some of us lose the objects that are our references for devotion and compassion when we experience and realize appearances and mind to be the same. Being ignorant of the method aspect—pure perception, compassion, and so on—it is said that we fall to the Hīnayāna. This is a dangerous situation, like being knocked off course by waves.

In some types of nonmeditation, realization without an object of meditation or a meditator may have arisen and yet, if illusionlike dualistic appearances are still present, like clouds blocking the sun, what obscures realization has not vanished.

iii) The Way the Postmeditative Mental States Manifest

The exalted Gomchung says:

> The postmeditative mental state during one-pointedness is solid.
> The postmeditative mental state during freedom from elaborations is illusory.
> The postmeditative mental state during one taste is empty.
> The postmeditative mental state during nonmeditation is compassion.[1415]

During one-pointedness, since fixations on inner experiences have not been purified, the postmeditative mental state will not have destroyed taking the things that are perceived and perceivers to be real. There will be reification and the appearances of solidity. [487]

During freedom from elaborations, since phenomena are realized to be unborn emptiness, the postmeditative mental state will be of the appearances of mere objects and perceiving subjects, but those will arise as illusionlike and not be taken to be real.

During one taste, the postmeditative mental state for some may not be one of recognizing appearances as the nondual unification of appearances and emptiness. The force of not having purified clinging to emptiness previously means that there will be a one-dimensional emptiness, and the postmeditative mental state will manifest as emptiness.

During nonmeditation, since meditative equipoise and postmeditative attainment mix, there will not be a postmeditative mental state in the usual sense but there will be manifestations of nonreferential compassion as a mere postmeditative attainment. Therefore, this postmeditative mental state is referred to with the term "arising as compassion." The *Verses That Summarize the Prajñāpāramitā Sūtras* states:

> Know these skandhas to be empty and unborn from the beginning.
> When not in equipoise, engage compassionately in the realm of
> sentient beings.
> In that interval, do not transgress the Buddha's dharma.[1416]

The Great Brahman [Saraha] sings:

> The sacred tree of nondual mind
> spreads throughout the three realms;
> its flowers of compassion yield the fruit of benefit for others.
> Its name is "sublime altruism."[1417]

The exalted Tsangpa Gyare states:

> From freedom from elaborations through intermediate
> nonmeditation,
> any remaining reifications arise as illusions.
> At the highest nonmeditation, there is no movement of
> appearances.[1418]

Since it is asserted that even during nonmeditation postmeditative appearances manifest as illusionlike, the mental state during such postmeditative attainment must manifest as illusionlike compassion.

iv) The Stains to Be Purified

The exalted Gomchung states:

> One-pointedness has the stain of reification.
> Freedom from elaborations has the stain of not recognizing.
> One taste has the stain of experiences.
> Nonmeditation has the stain of objects of knowledge.[1419]

It is taught that one-pointedness has the stain of reification because fixating on experiences and certainty have not been purified. [488] Some types of freedom from elaborations have the stain of not recognizing unification because our certainty in grasping emptiness causes us to feel comfortable with the emptiness component during our spiritual practice but uncomfortable with the appearance component.

One taste has the stain of experiences appearing as illusionlike during its subtle apprehension of emptiness that is not unified [with appearances] and even when there is such unification.

Some types of nonmeditation involve what is called "not recognizing nonconceptuality with postmeditative appearances," which is explained as remaining in the nonconceptual, neutral ālaya consciousness. Since that is the aspect of dharmatā not arising as reflexive clarity, it is said to be the stain of objects of knowledge.

v) The Way Postmeditative Attainment Is Purified

The exalted Gomchung teaches:

> One-pointedness has separation and no achievement.
> Freedom from elaborations has both separation and achievement.
> One taste has no separation but does have achievement.
> Nonmeditation has neither separation nor achievement.[1420]

During one-pointedness, when enforced mindfulness is distracted, meditation is lost; therefore, there can be separation [from meditation]. Even when we are mindful, we only recover the continuum of spiritual practice of this level and do not achieve true meditation.

During freedom from elaborations, when applied mindfulness strays, meditation is lost; therefore, there can be separation [from meditation].

When we are mindful we achieve true meditation, which sees the unborn essence; thus there is achievement.

During one taste, even if we are not mindful right with postmeditative appearances, our stream of realization is unbroken; therefore, there is no separation [from meditation]. As soon as we apply true mindfulness, appearances arise as emptiness; thus there is achievement.

During nonmeditation, since mindfulness arises as the wheel of wisdom, there is no separation from meditation. Since whatever appearances arise are themselves sufficient, there is no newly achieved meditation. [489]

vi) The Distinctive Features of Their Meditative Equipoises and Postmeditative Attainments

The exalted Gomchung says:

> One-pointedness has the meditative equipoise and postmeditative attainment of its own level.
> During freedom from elaborations, meditative equipoise and postmeditative attainment are distinct.
> During one taste, meditative equipoise and postmeditative attainment mix.
> Nonmeditation is only meditative equipoise.[1421]

Since nonconceptual wisdom, properly speaking, does not develop during one-pointedness, there is no true meditative equipoise at this level. Since appearances are not realized to be unborn and, therefore, postmeditative appearances do not manifest as illusionlike, there is no true postmeditative attainment either. Nevertheless, the spiritual practice of one-pointedness according to its own level has a meditative equipoise and a postmeditative attainment, which is the mindfulness that occurs after being distracted.

Freedom from elaborations is being free from perceiving phenomena dualistically as objects and perceiving subjects, and it is when nondual wisdom arises transparently. Since that is nonconceptual wisdom, freedom from elaborations has true meditative equipoise. Although dualistic appearances of objects and perceiving subjects do arise for the postmeditative mind, they do so as unreal and illusionlike. That is true postmeditative attainment. Thus its meditative equipoise and postmeditative attainment are distinct.

With one taste, during meditative equipoise all dualistic phenomena—such as appearances and emptiness—remain nondual. When the postmeditative mind applies the mindfulness of unification, nondual appearance-emptiness arises, like an illusion. That is referred to with the expression "the mixing of meditative equipoise and postmeditative attainment."

During nonmeditation, although there are manifestations of appearances, since they arise from within meditative equipoise, they do not occur anywhere but within meditative equipoise. There is only meditative equipoise.

In this context, we should be aware that the exalted Zhang teaches:

> When you remain within the intrinsic mind, [490]
> you can jump, run, and even talk
> and remain in a state of meditative equipoise.
> If you disconnect from the intrinsic mind,
> even if you are meditating on your cushion, that is postmeditative attainment.[1422]

He also says:

> No matter how high your realization,
> as long as you are still familiarizing yourself,
> there will be meditative equipoise and postmeditative attainment,
> there will be mindfulness and its absence,
> there will be distraction and its absence.
>
> When there's no more familiarization to be done,
> that's called nonmeditation.[1423]

During the first three yogas, when we remain within the actual [experience or realization] of one of those levels, even if we jump, run about, or talk, that is meditative equipoise. If we lose the actual [experience or realization], even though we may be meditating on our cushions, that is said to be postmeditative attainment. As long as we have the need to familiarize ourselves with something, there will be meditative equipoise and postmeditative attainment, mindfulness and no mindfulness, distraction and no distraction. Actual nonmeditation is explained to be unification beyond training.

vii) Their Distinctions in Terms of Time

The exalted Gomchung states:

> One-pointedness is the time of meditating with solidification.
> Freedom from elaborations is the time of meditating in equipoise
> and postmeditative attainment.
> One taste is the time of meditating on unification.
> Nonmeditation is the time of actualization.[1424]

During one-pointedness, experiences accompanied by conviction are cultivated through continuous mindfulness while remaining in meditative equipoise. The postmeditative mind primarily employs "summoning meditation" using enforced mindfulness. Therefore, one-pointedness is said to be meditation with solidification.

During freedom from elaborations, applied mindfulness is strengthened. Meditative equipoise is sustained as spacelike and postmeditative attainment as illusionlike. Meditative equipoise and postmeditative attainment are cultivated as two separate things.

During one taste, all states of meditative equipoise and postmeditative attainment are cultivated as unified by the true mindfulness that recognizes the nonduality of appearances and emptiness. [491]

During nonmeditation, that realization is brought to completion, and unification manifests. The exalted Gampopa explains:

> One-pointedness is the time of spontaneous existence.
> Freedom from elaborations is the time of nonduality.
> One taste is the time of inconceivability.
> Nonmeditation is the time of purity.[1425]

viii) Other Explanations of Their Distinctive Features

The exalted Tsangpa Gyare teaches:

> One-pointedness has the highs and lows of experiences.
> It is a mundane path when karma is amassed.
>
> Freedom from elaborations is when you see your homeland.
> For most, meditation is engaged with alternately.

During one taste, appearances arise as meditation.
It is when [meditation] becomes a constant flow.

Nonmeditation is the seat of the dharmakāya.
For most, nonmeditation is something nominal.[1426]

Thus Tsangpa Gyare asserts that one-pointedness is a mundane path, freedom from elaborations is when the ground abiding state is seen, one taste is when appearances arise as meditation, nonmeditation is the actual dharmakāya, and the nonmeditation of most [practitioners] these days is something nominal. He also describes how the signs and excellent qualities arise during the cultivation of the four yogas:

If you sustain one-pointedness for a long time,
you can't help but reverse your fixation to sense pleasures,
and you will have some of the excellent qualities of the ṛṣis,
such as supercognitive abilities and miraculous powers.

If you sustain the realizations of freedom from elaborations,
[you will see] the great spectacle of indeterminate false appearances.
Depending on the strength of your training and acuity of your
faculties,
you will develop some of the excellent qualities of the bodhisattvas.
That is the field for the arising of compassion free from attachments.

If you sustain one taste for a long time,
[you will see] the great spectacle of the buddhas' pure lands.
Whether you roll about, stand on your head, or wander around,
you never leave the victors' seat.
The whole array of interdependent causes and conditions
is laid out, [like] brocade in the midday sun.
You will have some of the buddhas' excellent qualities.
Immeasurable benefit for others will occur. [492]

If you proceed to the highest nonmeditation,
you will perfect your actions and excellent qualities will manifest.[1427]

The exalted Yang Gönpa explains how the four yogas purify the eight modes of consciousness:

> During one-pointedness, you will separate from the skandha of forms and will purify the five sense consciousnesses. During freedom from elaborations, you will separate from the skandhas of feelings and discriminations, and will purify the mental consciousness. During one taste, you will separate from the skandha of formative forces and will purify the afflictive mentation. During nonmeditation, you will separate from the skandha of the consciousnesses and will purify the ālaya consciousness.[1428]

He delineates the differences between the experiences and realizations of the four yogas:

> The experiences and realizations of one-pointedness are stained.
> Freedom from elaborations differentiates between experiences and realizations.
> One taste unifies experiences and realizations.
> Nonmeditation is a constant flow of realization.[1429]

He describes the way the causes and results manifest for the four yogas:

> During one-pointedness, there are solidified causes and results. During freedom from elaborations, there are illusionlike causes and results. During one taste, there are spacelike causes and results. During nonmeditation, they are known to be groundless dependent arisings.[1430]

Regarding this point, some say:

> Once the essence of mind is seen, karmic causes and results do not occur, just as seeds cannot be planted in space.[1431]

They are quite wrong for the following reasons. Although the expression "recognizing the essence of mind" is used during one-pointedness meditation, since fixations have not yet been purified, practitioners on that level accumulate the karma of solidification. Even though it is explained that seeing the essence of the mind, just as it is, is the realization of freedom from elaborations, practitioners on that level have separations, achievements, and alternations, so there are still occasions when they accumulate the usual [seemingly] existent karma. [493] It is also taught that even the attainment of the realization of one taste may have fleeting moments of solidified appearances and, therefore, practitioners on that level have moments when they amass karma.

Consequently, as long as our mind has any grasping, we accumulate karma, as the *Precious Garland* states:

> As long as you cling to the skandhas,
> you will take them to be an "I."
> If you believe in an "I," you create karma.
> From karma, there will be birth.[1432]

The exalted Gampopa states:

> As long as the stake of clinging is not extracted,
> thoughts will gather karma.
> Posting the lookout of undistracted mindfulness is something good.[1433]

That being so, we amass karma in keeping with the degree and mode of clinging that we have in our mind. Until we realize that appearances are illusions, we experience the causes and results of fixations or the causes and results of solidification. Once we have such realization, until we perfect it, we have causes and results that are mere appearances or we have illusionlike causes and results. As the exalted Gampopa teaches:

> The dividing line between the presence or absence of causes and results is as follows. As long as you haven't realized dharmatā and that appearances are illusionlike, you will have the causes and results of fixations. Even when you realize the truth of dharmatā and that appearances are illusionlike, as long as you haven't perfected your familiarization [with these realizations], you will have causes and results that are mere appearances. To sum this all up, until you realize the dharmakāya, you will have causes and results. Once you realize the dharmakāya, there will not even be the words "causes and results."[1434]

Some may think about this and say, Once emptiness is realized, one is a noble being and it isn't logical that noble beings can newly amass karma since it is said:

> Noble ones abandon the sufferings
> of sickness, aging, and death.[1435]

They are confused about the distinctions between abandoning suffering and having abandoned it. [494] When we have become accustomed to emptiness, our coarse reification is destroyed and we do not accumulate the karma of solidification. However, as long as we have not cleared away our latent tendencies, we will amass subtle karma that is illusionlike. The *Entrance to the Bodhisattva's Way of Life* states:

> By familiarizing yourself with the latent tendencies of emptiness,
> you will abandon the latent tendencies for existence.
> By familiarizing yourself with "nothing exists at all,"
> that too will eventually be abandoned.[1436]

It also says:

> Those who conjure up an illusory woman
> may experience desire for her.
>
> Those conjurers have not abandoned
> their latent tendencies of mental afflictions towards knowable objects.
> Thus, when they see that [illusory woman],
> their latent tendencies for emptiness are weak.[1437]

That completes the explanation of the way realization develops through those [four yogas] and the common exposition of the four yogas.

15

The Four Yogas in Detail

3) The Explanation of the Divisions of the Four Yogas

This has two parts:

a) How the Four Yogas Are Divided

b) The Explanation of Their Divisions

a) How the Four Yogas Are Divided

The presentation of the four yogas as twelve levels by dividing each [yoga into three] does not appear in the present-day Collected Works of the exalted Dakpo [Gampopa], however, it is clear in the records of his instructions. His oral instructions to the exalted Gomchung divides each of the four yogas into highest, intermediate, and lowest, and the exalted Pakmo Drupa divided each of the yogas into lesser, intermediate, and greater.

This presentation continued and figures prominently in the teachings of the exalted Tsangpa Gyare and his lineage of disciples. The exalted Rangjung Dorje's lineage disciples and particularly the exalted Khachö Wangpo present the twelve yogas and also divide them into twenty-four by distinguishing between experiences and realizations. Thus, nowadays these explanations are well known in this precious practice lineage. It is wonderful how applicable they are to the gradations and classifications of experiences and realizations that occur during our spiritual practice. [495]

Since the exalted Pakmo Drupa's way of classifying the twelve yogas is the most famous, I will present that approach.

- During lesser one-pointedness, we see the essence of the mind's bliss and clarity. During the intermediate level, we attain mastery of that samādhi. During the greater level, those experiences become a continuous flow.

- During lesser freedom from elaborations, we realize our mind is unborn. During the intermediate level, we realize that it is free from a root. During the greater level, we cut through all misinterpretations about everything internal and external.
- During lesser one taste, saṃsāra and nirvāṇa blend as one. During the intermediate level, the root of percepts and perceivers is severed. During the greater level, all phenomena are pacified in the state of equality.
- During lesser nonmeditation, we are separated from an object of meditation and a meditator. During the intermediate level, we reach the level of spontaneous existence. During the greater level, the two types of luminosity mix.

We will understand the meaning of those points from the explanations to come.

The sequence of twelve yogas is not something definite like the rungs of a ladder. For example, even when we have not perfected the experiences and realizations of greater one-pointedness, either lesser or intermediate freedom from elaborations may develop. While not having perfected the experiences and realizations of greater freedom from elaborations, lesser or intermediate one taste may arise. Not having perfected the experiences and realizations of greater one taste, lesser or intermediate nonmeditation may develop. Thus it is not clear that what develops will always follow the sequences described in the commentaries.

Most descriptions of the way experiences and realizations develop are provided by the earlier masters of the practice tradition who adhered to solitude and roused the experience of planting the victory banner of practice. Teachings given from the perspective of the gradual type of individuals are not necessarily relevant for those who are the instantaneous or bypassing types. In particular, since it seems that the majority of practitioners these days have succumbed to laziness and distraction, it's not certain that they will experience the development [of the four yogas] just described. [496]

Nevertheless, even today those with great natural intelligence, who have received the blessing of their gurus, can give rise to the essence of true realization. Since it is important for us to be able to assess the level of our spiritual practice, I will provide explanations based on the teachings of the earlier masters of the practice tradition.

b) The Explanation of Their Divisions

This has five parts:

i) The Yoga of One-Pointedness
ii) The Yoga of Freedom from Elaborations
iii) The Yoga of One Taste
iv) The Yoga of Nonmeditation
v) The Summary of Common Key Points

i) The Yoga of One-Pointedness

This has three sections:

(A) The Divisions of One-Pointedness
(B) The Way Experiences Arise
(C) The Methods for Sustaining Those

(A) The Divisions of One-Pointedness

The meaning of "one-pointedness." [This yoga] is called "one-pointedness" because it is when undistracted mindfulness of the abiding state of mind is one-pointed, or because it is when there is the one-pointed awareness in which stillness and movements are mixed.

If we wonder, Doesn't that contradict the explanation that the abiding state is realized during freedom from elaborations? There is no such problem because there are many significant differences between [the yoga of one-pointedness and the yoga of freedom from elaborations], such as the difference between the object of meditation being simply our own mind and it being all external and internal phenomena, and between clinging to objects of experience and certainty, and being free from that.

Some confuse the explanation that śamatha is the one-pointed mind—in which context the mind rests one-pointedly in a nonconceptual state and has the sharp, vivid clarity of alertness—with the one-pointedness of this context. Others mistake [this one-pointedness] for the certainty that arises with an understanding of emptiness within that śamatha. [497] The first are incorrect because, although that [one-pointed mind] is the mere arising of flawless śamatha, it is completely devoid of the certainty of vipaśyanā. The latter are also wrong because [their certainty] is nothing but a simple understanding in which the mind is directed towards emptiness—they too lack the vipaśyanā certainty in which the essence of mind-itself is seen.[1438]

Therefore, this [yoga of one-pointedness] must be awareness resting one-pointedly on what is seen when the essence of mind is seen, and it must have the mindfulness-awareness that recognizes and mixes stillness and movements as being of equal taste, because, as [the exalted Gomchung] says:

> During one-pointedness, the essence is realized.[1439]

The exalted Yang Gönpa explains the way to cultivate one-pointedness:

> The mind's movements as thoughts are the door to its abiding state. Recognition of [mind] itself is the key point of practice. Encountering [mind's] own face, [mind] mixes with itself. Look to see whether there are any recollections or thoughts that are not [mind] itself. There will come a time when meditation blends the distinction between stillness and movements.[1440]

This yoga of one-pointedness has three levels:

1. Lesser one-pointedness starts when samādhi [focusing on] the essence of mind—clarity and emptiness, and accompanied by experiences of bliss—arises and yet is difficult to sustain. It includes the phase when meditation occurs as long as you meditate.
2. Intermediate one-pointedness is when samādhi occurs sometimes even though you are not meditating, and when meditation makes it stable. Thus you attain mastery [of one-pointedness].
3. Greater one-pointedness is when the experiences of that samādhi manifest continuously. Meditative equipoise and postmeditative attainment, your four daily activities, and the cycle of day and night pass completely in that state of clear, empty awareness.[1441]

The exalted Tsangpa Gyare determines whether the realizations of each of the four yogas have been perfected or not by considering six pairs of criteria, twelve specific points:

1. Whether the essence has been seen or not
2. Whether mastery has been achieved or not

3. Whether thoughts arise as meditation or not
4. Whether excellent qualities have developed or not
5. Whether there is proficiency with the conventional or not
6. Whether the seeds for the rūpakāyas have been planted or not [498]

Since those are excellent criteria and very applicable, I will use them here. In this context they are as follows:

1. The essence of mind is emptiness since it does not exist as anything at all. Its manifestations are clarity because they are unimpeded.[1442] When that very mind—which is the inseparability of clarity and emptiness, like the center of space—is itself aware of itself and the certainty confident about that arises, you have seen the essence of one-pointedness. If you rest vividly and vibrantly in the experiences of bliss, clarity, and nonconceptuality but do not have the assurance that is certain about reflexive awareness, your experiences, which appear yet are not ascertained, are like that of children seeing the moon reflected in water. You have not seen the essence of one-pointedness.
2. When samādhi of bliss, clarity, or nonconceptuality, with reflexive awareness and certainty, continues throughout the day and night, you have achieved mastery of one-pointedness. If that only happens sporadically, you have not achieved mastery of one-pointedness.
3. When the arising of thoughts and the appearances of objects become meditation simply by being mindful without the need to reject them and you can enter into the luminosity experienced during sleep, thoughts have arisen as meditation. If the manifestations of thoughts and appearances are drawn in by mindfulness and then must be forced into meditation, thoughts have not arisen as meditation.
4. When your mind has turned away from the eight worldly values, insects and microorganisms no longer inhabit [your body] externally or internally, and you are able to demonstrate various kinds of miraculous powers (such as supercognitive abilities, totalities, and overpowerings), you have developed the excellent qualities of one-pointedness. If your mind is unworkable, you haven't achieved mental tranquility, and you aren't able to demonstrate the common

signs, you have not developed these excellent qualities.

5. When, in your postmeditative mind, you feel certain about the interdependent connections between all external and internal causes and their results (both large and small)—which unerringly arise, being manifestations of the lucidity of samādhi—and you are able to correctly engage with adopting and rejecting them, you have proficiency with the conventional. If you do not have certainty about such interdependence and are careless about adopting or rejecting causes and results, you do not have this proficiency.
6. When your postmeditative mind is one of compassion that references sentient beings and you make vast aspiration prayers to be of benefit to others, you have planted the seeds of the rūpakāyas. [499] If, being obscured by certain types of experiences in samādhi, it is difficult to arouse compassion and you seek peace and happiness for yourself alone, you have not planted the seeds of the rūpakāyas.

(B) The Way Experiences Arise

During lesser one-pointedness, the meditative equipoise of mind's clarity and emptiness with experiences of bliss involves ascertainment and fixations. That is what is sustained. When thoughts and appearances arise within those experiences, for the most part, they do not become established and are free in being self-dissolving and self-liberating. You have the certainty that thinks, "This is meditation." Sometimes thoughts are not liberated. Most postmeditative appearances include experiences of joy and delight and manifest as solid. When your postmeditative mental states are embraced by mindfulness and include experiences of clarity and emptiness, you label them, thinking, "These are empty. These are appearances of mind." Your dreams may be somewhat more clear and lucid, but otherwise they are not very different from your previous dreams. Some have many different kinds of dreams and less identification of them. Sometimes it is difficult to rest evenly, and you might think, "I just can't meditate." Other times you think, "My meditation is excellent." Thus your spiritual practice can fluctuate greatly. You should arouse devotion for your gurus, pure perception towards your fellow practitioners, and compassion for sentient beings.

During intermediate one-pointedness, when you cultivate a samādhi of clarity and emptiness with experiences of bliss, it is a stable meditation. Sometimes even without meditating samādhi comes easily. Within this experience, thoughts and appearances occur less than before, and whatever arises is self-liberating. [500] Postmeditative appearances are vibrant, spacious appearances combined with experiences of empty clarity. Sometimes they manifest as solid. When your postmeditative mind is mindful, meditation comes easily. [Meditative] experiences may or may not arise in your dreams. Some may have fewer dreams. You feel enthusiastic about meditating.

During greater one-pointedness, a samādhi of clarity and emptiness with experiences of bliss is uninterrupted. All thoughts dissolve into that state. All postmeditative appearances occur in that state. Most dreams take place in that state. You have certainty that fixates on what you perceive to be good, and you have many experiences of emptiness, such as mind being bliss-emptiness and awareness-emptiness, thoughts being clarity-emptiness, and appearances being appearance-emptiness. You also may have many experiences in which you think, "All phenomena are like dreams and illusions." You can develop some defiled excellent qualities, such as a little bit of supercognitive abilities. You may think, "There is no meditation better than this." You give rise to devotion, pure perception, and so forth.

(C) The Methods for Sustaining Those

During the three levels of one-pointedness, you should be diligent about staying in retreat in the mountains, sealing yourself into retreat, and observing silence. If you are affected by serious "contaminations" [or negative influences], your mind will be unworkable and your prajñā obscured. Since even minor "contaminations" can make your samādhi unclear and create many hindrances and problems, you should be very careful to avoid contaminations. If you are affected by contaminations you must dispel them. With most instances of dullness and agitation you can apply the methods for the removing the particular problem and should repeatedly look at its essence. If you feel a great deal of sluggishness, since that [indicates] a larger problem, you should do the following to clear it up: make appropriate confessions of negative actions, receive abhiṣekas from your gurus, and take the samādhi abhiṣeka many times. [501] Offer gaṇacakras, make offerings, and engage in acts of generosity. You should discuss this with your gurus and experienced fellow practitioners.

If you have significant troubles, don't want to discuss them with your gurus and experienced practitioners, and develop wrong views, those are obstacles of māras. You must make a special effort in taking refuge. Revitalize your disenchantment [with saṃsāra], your [determination for] definite release [from saṃsāra], your devotion, pure perception, and compassion. Then meditate. You should also rest for a few days to recover from any fatigue you may be experiencing and do some type of physical exercise.

Following that, like a cormorant [focused on] catching fish, one-pointedly cultivate some kind of enforced mindfulness or applied mindfulness, as was explained earlier for samādhi.* Do not pursue an analytical understanding, nonconceptual stillness, anything you have experienced, or the allure of what appears to the postmeditative mind. Do not be attached to good experiences, and don't regard bad ones as problems. No matter what arises in your mind, sustain it without any clinging, which involves trying to block or encourage something. Since stagnate experiences will obscure the essence [of your mind], disperse the dankness of experiences again and again. Arouse sharp awareness and sustain a fresh mind unaffected by contrivances. From time to time, read the vajra songs and biographies of the previous masters of the practice tradition to see how they underwent hardships with fortitude and established their practice. Be determined to practice as they did.

It is taught that those who practice the yoga of one-pointedness for many years but do not progress to freedom from elaborations should give up the three attachments.

Give up attachment to your sense of self. Cut your ties to anything you are attached to in this life. Withdraw from human company. Dispense with your attachments to friends and your aversion for enemies. Let go of any worldly entanglements. Offer your body to your gurus. Stop cherishing your skandhas, and practice the offerings and generosity of a kusāli.

Give up attachment to your possessions. [502] With whatever wealth and possessions you have, make pleasing offerings to your gurus, present satisfying offering tormas and gaṇacakras to the yidams and others, and give everything you own to please your vajra brothers and sisters. Give up all the pleasure you desire, the food you crave, the wealth for which you long.[1443] Care nothing for food, clothing, or conversation. Undertake conduct like

*See pp. 313–14.

that of a [wounded] deer, as explained above.* Leave behind places of distraction and where you experience attachment and aversion, such as your homeland. If you are unable to stand to give up anything, observe silence for a few years.

Give up attachment to samādhi. Destroy all good experiences that you believe to be joyful and delightful. Conclude that, in terms of the abiding state, whatever arises is neither good nor bad. Do not be distracted from and do not meditate upon the natural state of naked mind-itself, which is free from experiences.

The exalted Gampopa teaches:

> When training, first cultivate vibrant mental clarity. Next train in nondistraction. Then train in never being distracted from the essence of awareness. When you have become accustomed to that, confidence will arise within.[1444]

The exalted Tsangpa Gyare explains:

> Once you get to one-pointedness,
> dismantle your experiences and meditate without meditating.[1445]

During one-pointedness, experiences can be points of going astray when they are mistaken for realization. Practitioners of inferior intelligence and those who have spent only a short amount of time with their gurus may get stuck in the sweetness of experience. They spend their lives practicing superficially and don't recognize the essence of mind or, if they do at first, they lose it. The exalted Gampopa states:

> Although the view free from conceptualization
> is called "beyond extremes," that's mentally fabricated.
> Great meditators who haven't cut their bonds
> may have excellent samādhi but it's a cause of their saṃsāra.[1446]

The exalted Drikungpa [Jikten Sumgön] declares:

*See p. 403.

> Not modifying excellent experiences
> is a cause for birth in the higher states of the gods.[1447] [503]

It is also critical not to cling or be attached to the naked abiding state of mind. The Great Brahman [Saraha] advises:

> If you have an attachment, let it go.[1448]

The exalted Gampopa says:

> Great meditators who cling to dualities
> have experiences but miss the point.[1449]

Practicing that way will gradually enhance your spiritual practice. At some point, the experiences of one-pointedness along with any fixations will be purified, and you will be liberated from the dualistic perception of regarding emptiness as the object and your mind as the perceiving subject. Then the realizations of freedom from elaborations meditation will arise.

ii) The Yoga of Freedom from Elaborations

This has three sections:
- (A) The Divisions of Freedom from Elaborations
- (B) The Way Experiences Arise
- (C) The Methods for Sustaining Those

(A) The Divisions of Freedom from Elaborations

The meaning of "freedom from elaborations." [This yoga] is called "freedom from elaborations" because the abiding state of mind is, like space, free from the elaborations of arising, abiding, and ceasing, permanence and annihilation, going and coming, and so on, as is stated in the *Fundamental Treatise on the Middle Way*:

> There is no cessation or origination,
> no annihilation or permanence,
> no coming or going,
> no discreteness or sameness:
> elaborations are pacified and there is peace.[1450]

Some assert that the absence of the conceptual elaborations of percepts and perceivers is the meaning of freedom from elaborations. Others state that certainty in the recognition that all phenomena are empty is the meaning of freedom from elaborations. Both are wrong. If the former were the case, mere nonconceptual śamatha would be freedom from elaborations. If the latter were correct, even fixations involving certainty about emptiness and the lack of reality would be freedom from elaborations. [504]

It is, therefore, taught that during freedom from elaborations the nature of mind is realized. And it is explained that the nature of mind is an unconditioned phenomena, which, like space, does not move or change. It is said in the sūtras:

> Profound, peaceful, free from elaborations, luminous, and unconditioned . . .[1451]

The *Highest Continuum* remarks:

> The luminous nature of mind
> is unchanging like space.[1452]

This yoga of freedom from elaborations has three levels:

1. Lesser freedom from elaborations is when you have realized that the essence of mind is free from the elaborations of arising and ceasing, but you are not yet free from experiences in which you have the certainty that grasps that [freedom from elaborations] as emptiness. You also have hope and fears: the fear that you will wander in saṃsāra and the hope that you will attain nirvāṇa.
2. Intermediate freedom from elaborations is when your experiences of grasping mind as appearances or as emptiness have been purified, and you realize that mind-itself has no ground, that it is free from a root. Nevertheless, you still cling to your hopes and fears in relation to the appearances of external objects.
3. Greater freedom from elaborations is when, having been liberated from holding onto the certainty that grasps the external and internal phenomena of saṃsāra and nirvāṇa as empty, you are free from hopes and fears and have severed all misinterpretations.

Determining whether freedom from elaborations has been perfected or not:

1. Seeing the essence of mind to be free from elaborations is to be liberated from holding onto certainty. When, having severed the root of someone experiencing freedom from elaborations, a state in which all elaborations have been purified continues smoothly, you have seen the essence of freedom from elaborations. Since grasping at emptiness or having certainty are experiences of freedom from elaborations, if you have any trace of those, you have not seen its essence.
2. When you have no hopes or fears and not even a bit of grasping at emptiness, and you have eliminated all misinterpretations about everything being free from elaborations, you have achieved mastery of freedom from elaborations. If you recognize the nature of thoughts as unborn but still have hopes and fears in relation to appearing objects and have not purified the experiences of grasping emptiness, you have not achieved mastery of freedom from elaborations. [505]
3. When, having recognized all thoughts to be empty movements and all appearances to be empty appearances, your postmeditative mental state and appearances manifest like your realizations during meditative equipoise, thoughts have arisen as meditation. If you are unable to incorporate your realizations during meditative equipoise into the path right with your postmeditative mind and appearances, thoughts have not arisen as meditation.
4. When, through encountering the path conditions for awakening excellent qualities (such as those associated with the path of methods), you connect the signs of accomplishment with realization, you have developed the excellent qualities of freedom from elaborations. Despite having realized the nature of dharmatā, if, due to not encountering the path conditions, you lack the appearing quality of the signs of accomplishment, you have not developed these excellent qualities.
5. When, since emptiness arises as causes and results and the essence of mind does not exist as anything, you feel confident with interdependent connections that conditions can transform into anything, you have proficiency with the conventional. If, being obscured by the ignorance that is confused about causes and their results, you

do not understand the interdependent connections between causes and results, you do not have this proficiency with the conventional.

6. When, with the unceasing expressive power of emptiness arising as nonreferential compassion, in your postmeditative mind you know how to establish the illusionlike interdependent connections of arousing bodhicitta, aspiration prayers, and so on, you have planted the seeds of the rūpakāyas. If you have realized emptiness but find it difficult to arouse compassion and do not establish the interdependent connections for benefiting others, you have not planted the seeds of the rūpakāyas.

(B) The Way Experiences Arise

During lesser freedom from elaborations, even though the essence of each and every phenomenon is free from the elaborations of arising, abiding, and ceasing, you hold onto the notion that everything is empty. In your postmeditative mental state, your perceptions of friends and enemies, attachments and aversions, seem solid. Your sleep and dreams are mostly confused, and you have many highs and lows in your spiritual practice. Sometimes you feel faith and confidence in your gurus, fellow practitioners, and your own spiritual practice, and at other times it's possible that doubts arise. [506]

During intermediate freedom from elaborations, those experiences of grasping at emptiness are purified and your fixations are minimal. Having severed the root of thoughts, you have eliminated your misinterpretations in relation to movements, but you still have some solidified hopes and fears with appearances. Your postmeditative mental states and dreams are varied, both deluded and undeluded. You continue to have some highs and lows, such as having faith or doubts in your gurus, fellow practitioners, and your spiritual practice. Sometimes you may even think, "There is no buddhahood to be attained, no hells in which to be born."

During greater freedom from elaborations, having cut through the root of all phenomena of saṃsāra and nirvāṇa, you eliminate misinterpretations about everything external and internal, and are without hopes and fears. Feeling no pleasure or pain about such things as whether all phenomena are empty or not empty, you evenly maintain a spacious mind. Appearances manifest as empty, without any self-entity. Your postmeditative mind is not necessarily only a vibrant, lucid mind in which all thoughts have been purified, yet you have continuous meditation throughout the entire day with excellent experiences of awareness-emptiness, appearance-emptiness. Nevertheless, since your mindfulness is not necessarily unbroken, you still need to rely on some degree of applied mindfulness. You may have some delusion and grasping during your dreams. Sometimes you may think, "There is no buddhahood to be attained, no hells in which to be born. I have realized the abiding state." You understand even deeply profound dharma. Mind-itself arises as your guru. Appearances become aids for your spiritual practice. You have few fixations on anything, and your mind turns away from the eight worldly values. However, it is taught that at this point there is the danger of thinking you do not need a guru, becoming proud and arrogant, having distain for others, and the like. [507]

(C) The Methods for Sustaining Those

During the three levels of freedom from elaborations, cast off the three attachments and apply yourself to practicing in isolation, observing silence, and sealing yourself into retreat. It is explained that other than offering a few tormas and supplications to your gurus, you will not enjoy many different kinds of spiritual practices involving characteristics. It is important to put those aside for a time, hold the light touch of applied mindfulness, and sustain the essence of freedom from elaborations without distraction or clinging.

From time to time, you should create conditioned virtue, such as that which comes from making offerings or being generous. Cultivate devotion, pure perception, and compassion, and contemplate the interdependent connections between causes and their results. Discuss the profound [dharma] with your gurus and fellow practitioners with realization. Read and sing the vajra songs of the lineage of siddhas. If you start to feel somewhat unhappy, that you want to travel or eat [something special], or begin to despair, you should do some form of the blazing and dripping meditations of the path of method, practice the supreme caṇḍālī, or do some physical exercises.

Once the realization of greater freedom from elaborations has developed, if you do not make further progress despite cultivating that for years, again you must give up the three attachments, receive abhiṣekas, confess any impaired or broken [vows], and so forth. Supplicate [your guru] that your realization advances. Meditate upon yourself as the yidam and contemplate the sufferings of the hells. Determine those to be mind and rest evenly in freedom from elaborations. Similarly, contemplate the pleasures of the gods and rest in freedom from elaborations. Reflect upon the way things are in saṃsāra and rest in freedom from elaborations. Consider the state of affairs of nirvāṇa and rest in freedom from elaborations. Sometimes go to the top of a mountain and relax in freedom from elaborations. Other times go somewhere with many people and let go within freedom from elaborations. Retain cycles of breath, gaze vacantly, and relax in freedom from elaborations. Those are all explained as ways to enhance [realization]. [508]

Furthermore, it is said that you should intensify your awareness, mix that with various appearances, and meditate on freedom from elaborations, as the exalted Gampopa explains:

> During the yoga of freedom from elaborations, it is important not to remain indifferent: intensify your awareness.[1453]

The exalted Tsangpa Gyare also teaches this:

> Once you reach the time of freedom from elaborations,
> mix with dualistic phenomena and meditate.[1454]

Additionally, the exalted Yang Gönpa instructs:

> Do not lose fresh, undistracted mindfulness. Don't meditate and don't fabricate the abiding state. Do not make statements about inconceivable awareness. Not distorting [awareness] with analysis, give it free rein. There will come a time when the mother and child of meditation free from elaborations will meet.[1455]

Those instructions mean that you should intensify applied mindfulness and neither lose nor be distracted from the essence of freedom from elaborations. Since its abiding state can't be fabricated, don't newly meditate on anything else. Without analyzing awareness, which is indescribable, inconceivable, and inexpressible, sustain it as free-flowing.

By practicing in that way, at some point, without preventing or promoting the phenomena of saṃsāra and nirvāṇa in any way—as elaborations or freedom from elaborations, as empty or not empty, as something to abandon or to adopt—whatever appears will, without compartmentalization or corruption, manifest as the yoga of one taste, the essence of mahāmudrā.

iii) The Yoga of One Taste

This has three sections:

(A) The Divisions of One Taste
(B) The Way Experiences Arise
(C) The Methods for Sustaining Those

(A) The Divisions of One Taste

The meaning of "one taste." In the general presentations, one taste is explained as being that all phenomena (which include saṃsāra and nirvāṇa, all appearances and possibilities) are of one taste: emptiness, dharmatā. The Great Brahman [Saraha] teaches:

> The realization that all varieties of phenomena are of one taste in emptiness
> is aroused by the genuine gurus themselves.[1456] [509]

The Śavara [Saraha] says:

> In the same way all rivers, the Ganges and others,
> become of one taste in the salt ocean,
> know that all analyzing minds and mental events
> are of one taste in the dharmadhātu.[1457]

However, in this context the meaning of one taste is as follows. [This yoga] is called "one taste" because the many dualistic phenomena, in all their various permutations (such as appearances and nonappearances), are one taste: the essence of unification. As the exalted Pakmo Drupa says:

> The various appearances and nonappearances, mind and emptiness,
> being empty and not empty are of one taste: indivisible emptiness.
>
> Realization and no realization are of one taste: there's no meditative equipoise and postmeditative attainment.
> Meditation and no meditation are of one taste: a sphere of purity.
> Elaborations and freedom from elaborations are of one taste: the dharmadhātu.[1458]

The exalted Zhang teaches in a similar way.*

Some say that, like the one taste of the general presentations, one taste in this context means that the essence of all phenomena is of one taste: emptiness. That is wrong. If that were the case, that type of yoga would be the yoga of one taste. However, if that is said, intermediate freedom from elaborations would also have to be said to be the yoga of one taste because the same criteria applies to both.

Furthermore, although during freedom from elaborations all phenomena are realized to be empty, there is no realization of unification since it is explained that we are comfortable with the empty component and slightly uncomfortable with the appearance component. It is taught that once true one taste is realized, appearances are not compartmentalized or corrupted—the unification of appearances and emptiness arises. Therefore, the correct meaning of one taste in this context is that the many dualistic phenomena are of one taste: unification.

This yoga of one taste has three levels: [510]

1. Lesser one taste is when, despite having realized that all dualistic phenomena (such as saṃsāra and nirvāṇa) are of one taste in being of the essence of mahāmudrā, unification, you have an experience of that and the entanglements of the certainty grasping that.[1459]
2. Intermediate one taste is when holding onto certainty about the experience of the many as being of one taste is purified. Appearances of perceived objects are not put aside as something external, and the mind perceiving those is not set apart as internal. The inseparability of appearances and mind is clearly evident.
3. Greater one taste is when, through realizing the many to be of one taste and that realization of one taste arising as the appearances of many, all possible appearances are pacified in the intrinsic state of equality.

Determining whether one taste has been perfected or not:

1. When, without blocking or encouraging anything, rejecting or adopting, you recognize that whatever appears is the intrinsic state of equality—reflexive clarity without an object—you have seen the

*See p. 433.

essence of one taste. If you have any sense of something to be mixed with equality and an experience of mixing, and any holding onto certainty, you have not seen the essence of one taste.

2. When all appearances manifest as the natural expression of that intrinsic state of equality, you have achieved mastery of one taste. If, because you're not free from being entangled with remedies that prevent or promote, one taste does not arise as the many, you have not achieved mastery of one taste.
3. When, having purified your perception of objects and perceiving subjects (such as appearances and mind) as being dualistic appearances, you are fine with whatever arises—with no fears about being bound by what manifests to the six modes of consciousness or hopes for liberating those—thoughts have arisen as meditation. If what manifests to the six modes of consciousness requires the mindfulness of recognition for attainment or liberation, thoughts have not arisen as meditation.
4. When, through truly mixing your body, appearances, and mind, you achieve miraculous powers, such as emanating and transforming, you have developed the excellent qualities of one taste. If, even though you have developed the realization of one taste, the signs of accomplishment fail to emerge because the path conditions for awakening excellent qualities are weak, you have not developed these excellent qualities. [511]
5. Emptiness arises as causes and results. When, through realizing clearly the interdependent connections between causes and their results, you recognize the manifestations of instantaneous awareness to be the dividing line between saṃsāra and nirvāṇa, you have proficiency with the conventional. If, because you have not cleared away the ignorance that is confused about causes and their results, emptiness does not arise as the causes and results of multiplicity, you do not have this proficiency with the conventional.
6. When, because emptiness arises as compassion, all-pervasive compassion arises effortlessly and you have opened the treasure chest of benefiting others, you have planted the seeds of the rūpakāyas. If, because the expressive power of your realization fails to manifest as compassion, the method aspect (such as compassion) is weak and you cannot benefit others, you have not planted the seeds of the rūpakāyas.

(B) The Way Experiences Arise

During lesser one taste, although you have realized everything to be of the essence of the intrinsic state, you have experiences of that and hold onto your certainty. In the context of your postmeditative mental state, spiritual practice may not always be easy when what appear to the six modes of consciousnesses are agitated by intense objects or situations. Although free, percepts and perceivers may manifest to some degree as solidified appearances, and their latent tendencies may cause some delusion and grasping in dreams. Sometimes you experience your body, appearances, and mind as inseparable. It is also said that it is possible that your attention to causes and their effects and your devotion and compassion decline.

During intermediate one taste, you are liberated from the dualistic perception of an object of realization and a realizer, an object of experience and an experiencer. You cut through the root of taking appearances and mind to be dual. Your postmeditative mind and dreams are less deluded than before, and perceptions of solidity do not arise very much. It is said that you may have the ability to benefit or harm external beings to be trained. [512]

During greater one taste, throughout the day and night, there is the realization that the myriad appearances of the unimpeded expressive power of intrinsic equality are nondual, free from reification. Since meditative equipoise and postmeditative attainment have fully mixed, there is a continuously flowing yoga. Manifestations of nonconceptuality arise as brief experiences of just clarity, appearances without ascertainment. For the postmeditative mind, appearances that do not involve grasping are illusionlike clarity-emptiness. Sometimes there are subtle dualistic appearances that involve alertness of that [clarity-emptiness]. Your dreams may arise freely but indistinctly, and at other times you don't have any dreams. At this point subtle supercognitive abilities develop. It is taught that you may receive prophesies from yidam deities and ḍākinīs, and that your jealousy has been eradicated.

(C) The Methods for Sustaining Those

During the three levels of one taste, you should mostly practice in isolation though sometimes also be in the company of others. The way to enhance [your realization] is, for the most part, the same as it was during greater freedom from elaborations. Although it may seem that there is no difference between meditating and not meditating, being mindful or not, it is crucial that you remain in isolation and, with true mindfulness, sustain the essence of realization without distraction. During lesser and intermediate one taste, it is possible that you may look down upon the aspects of method—adopting or rejecting causes and results, devotion, pure perception, compassion, and so forth—therefore you should cultivate those energetically. It is important to set up excellent interdependent connections, avoid everything morally wrong, and correctly engage in adopting what is virtuous and rejecting negative actions, as the exalted Gomtsul instructs:

> Although you have realized the state of nonduality,
> please do not neglect virtuous things.
> Even though you have realized the state of nonmeditation, [513]
> please do not forsake service [to your guru] as method.
>
> Although your conduct is not to adopt or reject,
> please do not create evil situations for others.
> Even though the result is without hopes or fears,
> please do not let your mental afflictions run free.[1460]

If you realize greater one taste but are unable to bring about benefit or harm and the signs (such as supercognitive abilities or the prophecies of ḍākinīs) do not arise, you have either impaired your samaya or you have been affected by the "contaminations" of others. You must make strong confessions and intensify your [commitment to] refrain [from further impairments]. Make a thousand tsa-tsa or more, and offer a flower to each along with the supplication, "May my contaminations be pacified." You should also do other types of virtue and dhāraṇī rituals that dispel contaminations.

Once the marks and signs develop, if you become smug or feel pleased or displeased, you have been infected by māras. Reflect that everything—be it creating benefit, inflicting harm, or māras—is your own mind and that, like space, mind has no center or edge. Again, when one taste arises, you won't fear thoughts or take pleasure in good qualities, and problems will be unable to bring you down you.[1461] Later, if you have strong jealousy, many mental afflictions, coarse thoughts, sharp pains, pleasure and displeasure, since your mind has been infected by māras, recognize that and concentrate on your spiritual practice. Recognize that everything that does not accord with meditation is a māra. Thus it is said.[1462]

The exalted Gampopa teaches that the realization of one taste is to be intensified:

> During the yoga of the one taste of the many, it is imperative that you do not mix [that] with an object of understanding or abstract image, that you experience it internally.[1463]

The exalted Tsangpa Gyare explains that we should make vast aspiration prayers for the benefit of others and set up excellent interdependent connections:

> When you get to the yoga of one taste,
> sow the seeds of the welfare of beings.
> Even though you have no considerations for yourself, [514]
> set up interdependent connections despite their unreality.[1464]

The exalted Yang Gönpa teaches that we must let go of any grasping no matter what arises or appears:

> The five senses arising with their objects are unimpeded radiance.
> What is born from not grasping at objects is the unborn basic state.
> Attachment to appearances may be unceasing but reverse it:
> meditate naturally settled.
> Empty appearances arising free from the intellect is the path of
> natural expressions.
> Do not see appearances as problems, let go of clinging.
> There will come a time when you will arrive in the valley of one taste
> meditation.[1465]

We should be aware of all those instructions.

By practicing in that way, the stains of experience will be purified, path realizations and the natural abiding state will mix, and the realization of nonmeditation—without meditative equipoise and postmeditative attainment, mindfulness or distraction—will dawn.

iv) The Yoga of Nonmeditation

This has three sections:

(A) The Divisions of Nonmeditation
(B) The Way Experiences Arise
(C) The Methods for Sustaining Those

(A) The Divisions of Nonmeditation

The meaning of "nonmeditation." In the general presentations, nonmeditation is so designated because it means there are no entities that are objects of meditation upon which to focus, or because it means that objects of meditation have no nature. The *Kālacakra* [commentaries] and *Guhyasamāja Tantra* say:

> Since there are no entities, there is no meditation.
> Meditating is not meditation.
> Since entities are devoid of entityness,
> meditation is unobservable.[1466]

Nonmeditation also means the absence of the duality of an object of meditation and a meditator, as the Great Brahman [Saraha] states:

> KYE MA. Don't say suchness free from any nature exists in meditation.
> If you conceive of an object of meditation and a meditator as a duality,
> the mind grasping dualism rejects its bodhicitta.[1467] [515]

For those reasons some assert those two modes to be the meaning of the yoga of nonmeditation. They are wrong. If the former were the case, the yoga of freedom from elaborations onwards would be the yoga of nonmeditation. If the latter were the case, the phase of one taste would also be the yoga of nonmeditation.

We may then ask, What is it? During one taste there is a subtle mental state with an object of meditation and a meditator. When that is purified and there is only realization without meditative equipoise and postmeditative attainment, without mindfulness or nonmindfulness, since you are free from any effort in meditation, that is called "nonmeditation." The Śavara [Saraha] explains:

> Realized ones have neither an object of meditation nor a meditator.
> Just as space cannot observe space,
> emptiness does not meditate on emptiness.
> The nondual mind is like water [mixed] with milk:
> continuous great bliss in which diversities are of one taste.[1468]

The exalted Zhang observes:

> When the yoga of nonmeditation arises,
> the essence of awareness is devoid of support.
> Yogins and yoginīs have nothing to meditate upon.
> There is no meditator either—all is openness.[1469]

This nonmeditation has three levels:

1. Lesser nonmeditation is when, without needing to be mindful or intentionally rest in equipoise, there is no distinction between objects of meditation and a meditator since appearances arise as meditation. This phase continues as long as you have the slight sense of grasping at the experiences of [all things being] illusionlike.
2. Intermediate nonmeditation is when, free from such grasping, your realization of nonmeditation continues throughout the day and night, and you reach the very state of spontaneous existence. Post-meditative appearances are subtle aspects of the consciousnesses manifesting as reflexive clarity.
3. Greater nonmeditation is when those subtle aspects of the consciousnesses become wisdom, the two luminosities mix, and there is only that infinite expanse [of luminosity]. [516]

Determining whether this nonmeditation has been perfected or not:[1470]

1. When the realization of nonmeditation has nothing about which to be mindful, nothing to become familiar with, and experiences are purified, you have seen the essence of nonmeditation. The continued presence of even a little bit of something with which to become familiar or something to become clarity means that you have not seen the essence of nonmeditation.
2. When that realization has been purified of even the subtlest of dualistic appearances and is never without recognition of the mind, it is always indivisible from wisdom. You have achieved mastery of nonmeditation. Not being free from subtle dualistic appearances and having even a trace of not recognizing nonconceptuality means you have not achieved mastery of nonmeditation.
3. When, without abandoning everything, the ālaya consciousness is purified as the wisdom of the dharmadhātu, thoughts have arisen as meditation. If you have any subtle dormant tendencies for con-

ceptually grasping at a body, appearances, and mind and even a small amount of the stains of experiences, thoughts have not arisen as meditation.

4. When, through your body becoming a rūpakāya of wisdom (a rainbow body) and your mind becoming the dharmakāya (luminosity), pure lands appear as a vast display, you have developed the excellent qualities of nonmeditation. There being any vestiges of your body and mind, or the environment and its inhabitants, as impure appearances and having any trace of grasping means that you have not developed these excellent qualities.
5. When you have perfected the qualities of a buddha (such as the strengths and fearlessnesses), you have proficiency with the conventional. If the three seals—maturation sealing the body, latent tendencies sealing appearances, consciousnesses sealing the mind—obscure the excellent qualities of buddhahood, you have not purified the conventional and do not have this proficiency.
6. When, having awakened as the dharmakāya (the inseparability of the dhātu and wisdom), your inexhaustible ornamented wheels of [awakened] body, speech, and mind bring uninterrupted benefit to sentient beings, you have brought the potential of the seeds of the rūpakāyas to fruition. If that has not occurred and you still rely on the pure lands, you have not ripened the potential of the seeds of the rūpakāyas.

Consequently, it is explained that because the perfection of the realization of nonmeditation and the attainment of complete buddhahood occur simultaneously, the full attainment of nonmeditation does not occur in this lifetime. [517] The nonmeditation that occurs in this lifetime is simply a nominal nonmeditation, as the exalted Tsangpa Gyare says:

> Nonmeditation is the seat of the dharmakāya.
> For most, nonmeditation is something nominal.[1471]

Furthermore, when the exalted Gomtsul was asked by Len-gom about the differences between the four yogas, he said:

> One-pointedness is the recognition of the nature of mind.
> Freedom from elaborations is the recognition of the nature of
> emptiness.

> One taste is the recognition of the nature of appearances.
> As for nonmeditation, I have no idea.[1472]

Thus he made no comments about nonmeditation. Among the students of the exalted Pakmo Drupa, it is said that three and a half had the realization of one taste.[1473] Even the exalted Götsangpa, the mahāsiddha Orgyenpa, and others would only comment up to one taste, nothing more. These days, claims to have realized one taste and nonmeditation seem to be just the foolish talk and arrogance of those who have not understood the presentations of the four yogas precisely. They are not to be trusted.

(B) The Way Experiences Arise

During lesser nonmeditation, most dualistic appearances have been purified and there is no need to intentionally meditate or be mindful: everything arises as meditation. For the most part there is no wavering from meditation. In the context of postmeditative appearances, it is explained that what is called "not recognizing nonconceptuality" is an aspect of the ālaya consciousness, a residual ignorance or unawareness. It is a nonconceptual, neutral mind. That is said to be the stains of negative propensities. It is also explained that the postmeditative mind is unable to amass karma but it does give rise to fleeting moments of illusionlike perceiving thoughts, which have not been purified as wisdom. During dreams there may be some slight bit of reification, which is a lack of recognition. [518]

During intermediate nonmeditation, those subtle illusionlike dualistic appearances are purified and the realization of nonmeditation flows throughout the day and night. With postmeditative appearances, there is the most subtle lack of recognition of nonconceptuality, which is referred to as "that [subtle nonconceptuality] arising as reflexive clarity." It is also called "perfection that accords with the basic state." It is explained that it is the most subtle stain of negative propensities and that it is present at night as well.

During greater nonmeditation, that most subtle lack of recognition of nonconceptuality is purified as wisdom. Natural luminosity and the luminosity of realization mix, becoming an infinite expanse of wisdom. It is explained that, as benefit for yourself, you [attain] the dharmakāya, which is termed "awakening." By perfecting its display without any limitation and gathering the interdependent connections of pure appearances for those to be trained, the reflected appearances of the rūpakāyas manifest for the benefit of others. Benefit for beings arises spontaneously for as long as saṃsāra exists.

(C) The Methods for Sustaining Those

Although the three modes of nonmeditation are as was just presented, it is explained that the final nonmeditation that arises in this lifetime is the nonmeditation that is simply vivid certainty in the absence of meditative equipoise and postmeditative attainment. Through the clear understanding that your own mind is a buddha, you gain the deep conviction that there is no object of abandonment to reject, no remedy to apply, no object to purify, no mind doing the purification, no dying, and no not dying. Other than that [no higher level of nonmeditation] arises.

As for the way to cultivate those experiences, the exalted Gampopa says: [519]

> During the yoga of nonmeditation it is important not to get stuck in the sweetness of experience. Don't fixate on experiences.[1474]

Since Gampopa teaches that even in this phase we must beware of fixating on experiences, it is vital not to block or promote, or fixate in any way on, experiences, be they good or bad. Even dormant aspects of not recognizing mind must be purified so that they are never apart from recognition. True mindfulness, or undistracted mindfulness transcending the intellect, is the root of meditation. Consequently, it is said that, no matter what happens in life, you should plant the victory banner of meditation practice and take through to perfection the ordinary mind of undistracted nonmeditation.

The exalted Tsangpa Gyare explains that the way to cultivate spiritual practice on the levels of lesser and intermediate nonmeditation is the same as during one taste:

> The lower nonmeditations are similar to one taste.
> Their spiritual practices are the same.
> The highest nonmeditation is buddhahood.
> It is free from all striving.[1475]

The exalted Yang Gönpa says:

> Look: are the objects to be meditated upon and the mind meditating dual right within awareness? Separate nondual awareness from a support. Evenly sustain mind without mindfulness. There will come a time when meditation will flow day and night.[1476]

He teaches that awareness in which the objects of meditation and the meditator are inseparable has no support and is without reference point. Evenly sustain the mind that is without mindfulness and without attentiveness: without grasping, let it be free-flowing. The meanings of nonmindfulness and nonattention were already explained.*

In a general sense, something similar to nonmeditation's continuous flow of meditative experience occurs during one-pointedness. Nonmeditation's inseparability of the object of meditation and a meditator occurs during freedom from elaborations. Nonmeditation's absence of meditative equipoise and postmeditative attainment, when whatever appears manifests as meditation, occurs during one taste. [520] We should understand that those are types of meditative experience and why they are not the nonmeditation of realization.

Broadly speaking, the divisions of the four yogas must be explained through experience.[1477] They are much more difficult [to present] than other scriptural expositions. In particular, it is very difficult to explain the latter yogas when they have not arisen as mental objects. However, for these presentations I have taken the instructions of the exalted Gompas, elder and younger [Gomtsul and Gomchung], as the basis and, relying on the teachings of earlier undisputed siddhas, I have discussed them in detail.

v) The Summary of Common Key Points

As previously cited, the *Precious Garland* says:

> As long as you cling to the skandhas . . .
> [you will take them to be an "I."
> If you believe in an "I," you create karma.
> From karma there will be birth.][1478]

*See pp. 313–16.

And the *Commentary on Valid Cognition* states:

> If there is self, other is cognized.
> [From the pair of self and other come clinging and anger.
> The connections with these two
> produce all faults].[1479]

The *Entrance to the Bodhisattva's Way of Life* observes:

> Whatever harm there is in the world
> and however much fear and suffering there is
> all comes from the belief in a self.
> What am I to do with this great demon?[1480]

As stated, holding onto the belief in a self and other is the root of saṃsāra. As long as we have not pacified our belief in a self, we repeatedly recreate it and circle like a [water] wheel, never becoming free from saṃsāra.

Some who desire liberation don't recognize that their belief in a self is the root of their karma and mental afflictions and don't understand those are what are to be eliminated. Desiring to eliminate suffering—which is the result of karma and mental afflictions—they abandon unvirtuous actions and cultivate conditioned virtue, such as listening to and reflecting upon [the dharma]. However, if their attitude and behavior are flawed, it is uncertain what will result. [521] Even if their attitude and behavior are excellent, that [approach] will not actually be able to pacify their belief in a self, though it may become indirect causes that are methods for pacifying a belief in a self.

There are a few practitioners of meditation who state that the actual method for pacifying the belief in a self is to meditate on the lack of self. However, by intensely generating certainty that holds onto nonexistence—which negates clinging to existence—they increase their clinging and descend into a grand nihilistic view.

There are also some who desire good meditation practice and gain experiences in meditation but, because they then fixate on those, they do not keep straight to the main path and instead wander off into the four deviations and three strayings. Clinging in meditative equipoise is the root of the deviations and strayings. Clinging during the postmeditative mental states amasses karma and then becomes the cause for saṃsāra.

Therefore, since all faults and flaws are the result of entertaining mental fixations, it is crucial that we not fixate, as the Great Brahman [Saraha] says:

> If the mind that thinks, "This is attractive,"
> takes that to heart and cherishes it,
> even pain the size of a sesame seed husk
> will cause constant affliction.[1481]

And:

> Those who grasp at existence are like cattle.
> Those who grasp at what doesn't exist are even more foolish.[1482]

He concludes:

> If you have an attachment, let it go.[1483]

For those reasons it is taught that the sublime path for yogins and yoginīs is to remain without any clinging no matter what appears or what arises, be it visions in meditation (those involving characteristics or without characteristics) or just normal appearances based on ordinary latent tendencies. The exalted Gampopa states:

> Whatever arises, do not cling at all.
> There is no higher place of offering than this supreme path.[1484] [522]

It is taught that if we become accustomed to sustaining a state free from clinging, many excellent qualities will develop: the karmic appearances of our latent tendencies will be purified, thoughts will simultaneously arise and be liberated, at that time the stains of conceptual elaborations will not taint our mindstream, whatever appears will be the play of the dharmakāya, and so forth. The exalted Gampopa teaches:

> Whatever can and does appear as the solidification of latent tendencies
> is pure in its own spot, without being abandoned, when you are accustomed to not clinging.
> Whatever your mind holds onto is a seed for characteristics.
> When you don't grasp at anything, arising and liberating are simultaneous.[1485]

And:

When your mind doesn't hold onto anything, no matter what appears,
the stains of elaborations don't taint your mindstream.[1486]

And:

Not defiled for an instant by the stains of dualistic perception,
whatever there is, is itself the power of the dharmakāya.[1487]

He also says:

When you don't evaluate, thoughts arise and release.
When you don't have ambitions, everything is equal.
When you realize that, your meditation is continuous.
Since you have neither birth nor death, you are the king of transitions.
Since you don't cling to characteristics, luminosity is continuous.[1488]

The way liberation is attained when clinging subsides. When clinging to a self internally and clinging to "mine" externally are extinguished, that stops the appropriated skandhas, which are the link with the next birth. When the skandhas that link with the next birth are extinguished, birth is extinguished. That being extinguished, karma and mental afflictions are extinguished and liberation is attained, as the *Fundamental Treatise on the Middle Way* says:

When notions of "I" and "mine" are extinguished
in relation to inner and outer,
the appropriated [skandhas] cease.
Since those are extinguished, birth is extinguished.
Since karma and afflictions are extinguished, there is liberation.[1489]

Thus, [the instructions that say] no clinging, no fixation, no focus, no characteristics, no reference point, no blocking or encouraging, no abandoning or adopting, no hopes or fears, and no aims all make the same critical point. We should be certain exactly how they are to be applied. [523] We must know that during each phase of the four yogas it is key that, while we are not distracted from our specific spiritual practices, we do not entertain any clinging.

C) How the Bhūmis and Paths Are Traversed through Those [Four Yogas]

The exalted Gampopa, the uncle, and his nephews did not explicitly teach the correspondences between the four yogas of meditation and the bhūmis and paths that are discussed within the philosophical yānas. The exalted Gomtsul's student, the mahāsiddha Zhang, however, says:

> Mahāmudrā is itself [attained in] a single stride.
> The confused make the mistake of delineating it
> in terms of the bhūmis and paths.
> But to indulge the confused
> I will delineate substitutes for
> the bhūmis and paths of the philosophical vehicles even here.[1490]

Mahāmudrā, the essence of dharmatā, is a path of a single stride. Since dharmatā cannot be divided in terms of its essence, it is said that, on the level of the definitive meaning, it is not possible to delineate the stages of bhūmis and paths. The *Commentary on the "Entrance to the Middle Way"* observes:

> Being of the nature of cognition, those [bodhisattva bhūmis] cannot be divided by means of their own essences. As is said [in the *Sūtra on the Ten Bhūmis*]:
>
>> Just as the wise cannot see or describe
>> a track left by birds in the sky,
>> the bhūmis of bodhisattvas cannot be described—
>> thus how could they be heard of?[1491]

The *Commentary on the "Ornament for Clear Realization"* states:

> Because something different from what has been actualized on the path of seeing is not observed, [the paths of] seeing and meditation are not different. Thus a true path of meditation is not presented.[1492]

Those statements accord with the explanation that there are no divisions in terms of the essence. Nevertheless, for those with confused minds who think, "How are the bhūmis and paths crossed through the practice of meditation?" [Zhang Rinpoche] says, "I will delineate" the equivalents of bhūmis and paths in the four yogas [using] the bhūmis and paths of the philosophical yānas. [524]

How they are delineated. The same person [Zhang Rinpoche] continues:

> The full development of realization
> is the path of seeing, the bhūmi of Very Joyful.
> Familiarization with the realization of equal taste
> is the path of meditation.
> Once there is no meditation, that is the path of perfection.[1493]

His explicit presentation is that the arising of the realization of nonduality, or unification, is the path of seeing and the first bhūmi. Being accustomed to that is the path of meditation and the second bhūmi through the tenth. Nonmeditation is the path of perfection and the bhūmi of buddhahood. He does not provide an explicit correlation for freedom from elaborations. We may think, Is freedom from elaborations considered the path of seeing and the first bhūmi? If that is the case, then by implication one-pointedness is the path of preparation.

The exalted Tsangpa Gyare teaches:

> Even though the path does not require bhūmis and the like,
> if they are to be presented, they should be asserted as follows.
> The offering of maṇḍalas is the path of accumulation.
> The development of experiences is the path of preparation.
> Freedom from elaborations is the path of seeing.
> The dawning of realization is the path of meditation.
> One taste is the eighth bhūmi.
> Nonmeditation is the eleventh, the path of perfection.[1494]

Thus he considers that, starting with the preliminary practices, gathering the accumulations and purifying negative actions are the path of accumulation. One-pointedness is the path of preparation. Freedom from elaborations is the path of seeing. Beginning with the dawning of the realization of unification, all of one taste is the path of meditation. Lesser and intermediate nonmeditation are the ninth and tenth bhūmis. Greater nonmeditation corresponds to the eleventh bhūmi, the path of perfection.

The exalted Götsangpa states:

> Gathering the accumulations and the like is the path of accumulation and the bhūmi of beginners. One-pointedness is the path of preparation and the bhūmi of engagement through belief. Freedom from elaborations is the path of seeing and the first bhūmi. One taste is the second bhūmi through the seventh, and lesser and intermediate nonmeditation are the three remaining ones, all of which are the path of meditation. Greater nonmeditation is the path of perfection, the bhūmi of buddhahood.[1495] [525]

Some divide the twelve levels of the four yogas into those of experience and those of realization, making twenty-four divisions. The twelve yogas of experience correspond to the four levels of the path of preparation. Of the twelve yogas of realization, the three levels of one-pointedness correspond to the first three bhūmis; the three levels of freedom from elaborations correspond to the fourth, fifth, and sixth bhūmis; the three levels of one taste correspond to the seventh, eighth, and ninth bhūmis; and the three levels of nonmeditation correspond to the tenth bhūmi through the twelfth.

My thoughts about this are as follows. The paths presented in the philosophical yānas, which are traversed in stages, are designated in terms of excellent qualities, a mode of appearance. Here, the meditative path of intrinsic equality, which is traversed in a single stride, is designated in terms of the natural essence. Ultimately they are the same even though on a temporal level they manifest in dissimilar ways. They differ in that the philosophical yānas are presented from the perspective of awakening after three incalculable aeons and here, once the interdependent connections have been gathered, awakening occurs without many rebirths intervening. An analogy can be found in ordinary roads with the differences between main highways and shortcuts.

Nevertheless, a rough correlation can be made in terms of the equivalents of bhūmis and paths as follows:

- The period from entering the path through the three levels of one-pointedness is the path of accumulation and the bhūmi of beginners.
- The three levels of freedom from elaborations are the path of preparation and the bhūmi of engagement through belief.
- The three levels of one taste and lesser and intermediate nonmed-

itation are the paths of seeing and meditation and the first bhūmi through the tenth.

- Greater nonmeditation is the path of perfection and the bhūmi of buddhahood.

Those designations are clearly excellent. It is difficult to delineate a dividing line between greater freedom from elaborations and lesser one taste, and between greater one taste and lesser nonmeditation. Yet, if we look at the present-day explanations in light of the stages of the twelve yogas, during greater freedom from elaborations there is not the slightest bit of the true realization of unification, equal taste. [526] Without that, it is somewhat uncomfortable to designate freedom from elaborations as the path of seeing and the first bhūmi, since dharmatā has not been properly realized. Learned ones, please examine this matter again.[1496]

However, we may now wonder, Is that in keeping with the teachings of the exalted Tsangpa Gyare and Götsangpa? [When they correlate freedom from elaborations to the first bhūmi] they have in mind the completion of freedom from elaborations. At that point, since all fixations on experiences (such as grasping at emptiness) have been purified and the realization of equal taste, unification, has arisen, it must be considered one taste. When present-day explanations designate lesser and intermediate freedom from elaborations as the path of seeing, I think it is difficult to consider the experiences of those [two levels] as equivalents of the [first] bhūmi.

Now a certain person [Sakya Paṇḍita] states:

> Some say, "There are four: one-pointedness,
> freedom from elaborations, one taste, and nonmeditation.
> One-pointedness is the path of seeing.
> Freedom from elaborations continues through the seventh bhūmi.
> One taste is the three pure bhūmis.
> Nonmeditation is the bhūmi of buddhahood."[1497]

And concludes:

> [This correlation] contradicts all the sūtras and tantras.[1498]

Although he makes this refutation, I have not seen that the renowned previous masters of the practice tradition teach that way. Even if there is [such a teaching], since there are many forms of the four yogas, correlating the four yogas of the realization of emptiness [to the bhūmis and paths] in terms of their congruent qualities does not have the flaw of contradicting the sūtras and tantras because the sūtras and tantras do not say that such correlations are impermissible. His depiction does not complement the conventional designations of the present day because it is not found in the sūtras and tantras.

Also this certain person [Sakya Paṇḍita] says:

> [To assert that] the path of seeing arises in this life
> but its excellent qualities manifest after death
> is the fiction of fools.[1499]

To say that the explanation that those who attain the path of seeing do not attain the twelve sets of one hundred excellent qualities of the first bhūmi in this life but do attain them in the next "is the fiction of fools" simply reflects his desire to say something [critical] while at the same time not being certain.[1500] [527] The reasons are as follows. There is no teaching that those who attain the path of seeing immediately attain its excellent qualities when they have not departed from this life. The teaching that a special feature of that birth [that is, the one after attaining the path of seeing] being that it is most likely to be as a cakravartin king is in reference to attainments in future lives, not what is attained in this life. For example, someone who attains the path of seeing in a female form does not change her physical body into that of a cakravartin king when she has not departed from this life. If those who attain the path of seeing must be able to actually display the whole extent of the excellent qualities described for the first bhūmi, it would be necessary to say—without even considering Indian and Tibetan paṇḍitas and siddhas—that none of the bodhisattvas in the Teacher's retinue attained the bhūmis (such as the path of seeing). And yet that is not what happened.[1501] The *Sūtra on the Ten Bhūmis* teaches that it is most likely that those who attain the first bhūmi will be born in their next life as a cakravartin king. At that time, having renounced their home and become monastics, they dwell in forests and attain the twelve sets of one hundred excellent qualities, such as one hundred samādhis.[1502] Since the text says, "it is most likely," it is not certain that that will be the case for everyone. [Those who think otherwise] seem not to have applied their intelligence to this and related teachings. It would be a grave mistake to imply that the *Sūtra on the Ten Bhūmis* is the fiction of fools.[1503]

Furthermore, we find in some places the example of a garuḍa chick not being freed from its eggshell [used to illustrate] that, even though we have fully realized our mind to be the dharmakāya, the excellent qualities of buddhahood do not appear in this lifetime.[1504] That example demonstrates the key point of not being free from the three seals (such as the seal of the body), that when luminosity becomes manifest at the time of death we arise in the illusory form of the saṃbhogakāya, and so forth. A certain person [Sakya Paṇḍita] regards those explanations as unreasonable, saying:

> It is amazing that the light rays of the sun today
> shine forth tomorrow instead.[1505]

His objection is completely unacceptable because it dismisses the teachings that, through the Mantra path, death becomes the dharmakāya and the bardo the saṃbhogakāya. [528] And because it renders illogical statements such as the Guhyasamāja [Cycle's] *Questions of the Four Goddesses*:

> When your karmic body has disintegrated,
> at that point, through your own power,
> a similar body will manifest
> and, pervading the animate and inanimate,
> it will be equal to space.
> Know that to be so.[1506]

And the statement in the *Sampuṭa*:

> When the karmic body is destroyed,
> it becomes the deity.[1507]

With this point in mind, the exalted Zhang says:

> The moment you realize nonduality,
> suffering does not vanish
> and the powers of your excellent qualities do not appear.
> And yet who can deny that saying, "It is not the path of seeing"?
>
> The moment the sun rises,
> it is unable to melt ice
> and the earth and stones don't become warm.
> But who can deny it saying, "There is no sun"?[1508]

That statement is consistent with the facts. Other analogies include the moon on the first lunar day, which is not complete in all aspects but is still the moon. Small babies do not have all the skills of adults but they are humans. Lion cubs have not mastered all their powers but they are lions.

In regard to this the exalted Tsangpa Gyare states:

> Śrāvakas are of two types: ornamented and unornamented.
> Bodhisattvas are renowned and unrenowned.
> In the Mantra [path] there is secret conduct and conduct in a crowd.
> Excellent qualities are of two kinds: those that are described and
> those that can be shown.
>
> The excellent qualities of the bhūmis and paths are intentionally
> ambiguous.
> The degrees of great meditators' purification and strengths
> result in the mixture of the presence or absence of miraculous powers
> and the accomplishment of benefit for beings or lack thereof.[1509]

There are many such teachings, the meaning of which can be summarized as follows. The excellent qualities of the bhūmis and paths taught in the philosophical yānas are intentionally ambiguous. Since those [excellent qualities] and the paths are not identical, the signs of the path are not identical. [529] In the same way that śrāvakas are ornamented and unornamented, and bodhisattvas are renowned and unrenowned, great meditators, due to the different degrees of their previous purification and strengths, appear variously: some develop miraculous powers in this life and some do not. The achievement of excellent qualities, such as miraculous powers, requires exertion in the mundane paths and the Mantra path.

That completes the explanation of the divisions of the four yogas and how the bhūmis and paths are traversed through those [four yogas]. This concludes the explanation of the way to cultivate mahāmudrā, the definitive meaning.

Colophon

Now I will say:

For fortunate ones desiring liberation, the door to the teachings well
known to scholars
is proper comportment, listening, reflection, and meditation.
However, the most highly praised method for eradicating cyclic
existence
is meditation on the ultimate definitive meaning.

Meditating on emptiness as an analytical emptiness, a nonaffirming
negation,
something that seals, an inanimate emptiness, and the like
is, for the most part, negated in the glorious *Kālacakra*.
And there are some who oppose [what is taught in the Seven] Siddhi
[Texts] and [Sixfold] Essence [Cycle].

Meditating on emptiness endowed with the most sublime of
manifestations
is lauded and praised by the followers of the Great Brahman of the
Noble Land,
the Dakpo Kagyu of this Snowy Land,
and all unbiased scholars and siddhas.

The definitive meaning of that is called mahāmudrā.
The term and its meaning are well known
in many sūtras, tantras, Indian texts, and this practice tradition.
Numerous extensive and abbreviated texts on its stages of meditation
have spread far and wide.

And yet seeing the rarity of commentaries
that are definitive about this term and its meaning,

[I resolved to compose this text, out of] the highest faith in this kind of thorough exposition
and to eliminate the uncertainties of the few who have wrong views or doubts.

Nowadays, in these times,
most scholars are ignorant of the key points of experience.
Some realized ones have not studied any sūtras or tantras.
Even among those who combine both, it is rare to find someone with an altruistic attitude.

Although I lack a great deal of training in the scriptural tradition [530]
and lack the excellent experiences and realizations [that come from] meditating for a long time,
I am familiar with the teachings of the precious Kagyu
and have acted [that is, undertaken this composition] only with the highest intentions.

If in this I have committed faults due to misunderstandings,
wrong ideas, or doubts, may the holy ones be patient.
May the flawless citations and the reasonings [established through] the power of [their relationship to real] things
refute faulty explanations and allow the teachings to shine.

Those who are addled by the demons of partiality,
who in thought and deed find fault with what is right,
who say that what is, is not, and turn truth into a lie
should feel ashamed in front of those with unbiased intelligence.

If there is an amassment of excellence here,
it is worthy of the praise of learned and accomplished beings
and particularly those of the Dakpo lineage.
May the wise study and reflect upon it.

May the virtue of actively contemplating and engaging in this approach
blaze increasingly like the sun,

dispelling the darkness of ignorance in all beings
and increasing the light of their reflexively aware wisdom.

May I, in all my successive lives, attain without hindrance
the excellent fortune to practice this sublime path.
May I realize the dharmakāya without too much delay
and be of benefit to infinite beings.

Considering the scarcity of commentaries elucidating the ways to cultivate mahāmudrā, the definitive meaning, and motivated by an altruistic intention to dispel the mistaken understandings of those harboring wrong understandings and arouse certainty in those with confidence in this practice tradition, I, the one called "Gampopa Mang-gala," began the composition of this text at a virtuous time. It was completed on an excellent day during the waxing phase of the third month of the Ox Year* in the isolated spiritual hermitage called Nāgakoṭa, which is below the glorious Daklha Gampo, the great residence prophesied by the Victor. The secretary for the composition was the one known as Loppön Tubten Palbar, who has devotion to this path and is a holder of the Secret Mantra piṭakas. May this bring excellence and virtue to each and every being.

*1565 or 1577.

Mahāmudrā: Dispelling the Darkness of Ignorance

Wangchuk Dorje, the Ninth Karmapa

Introduction

Although you attained full awakening innumerable ages ago,
you emanate the kāyas necessary to train disciples.
Merely hearing your names dispels the fears of saṃsāra:
I bow with all my heart to the precious Kagyu.

With prostrations to gurus and the lineage,
and in response to the urging of a student longing for liberation,
I will say a little something about the single path trod by all buddhas,
the innermost heart of the Vajrayāna: mahāmudrā.

The elixir of the mind of all buddhas of the three times is contained within the instructions transmitted from the Buddha down to my root guru orally, from "one ear to another." The warmth of their blessings has not vanished. These methods enabling us to attain the uncommon level of unification, Vajradhara, in one lifetime are the practices of mahāmudrā found intact in the precious Kagyu tradition. To expand on these, there are three parts:

I. Preliminaries
II. Main Practices
III. Conclusion

1

Preliminaries

One: Taking Refuge and Arousing Bodhicitta

In the sky in front, visualize a wish-fulfilling tree with one trunk and five spreading branches. On the central branch are the gurus; to the front are the yidams; to the right, the buddhas; to the rear, the dharma; and to the left, the saṅgha. Each are surrounded by many of their own kind.

Imagine that you are standing in front as the leader with all your mother sentient beings gathered around and joining you in taking refuge. [304] Recite a suitable refuge liturgy. With the awareness that all sentient beings have been your parents, take refuge and arouse bodhicitta, wishing that all beings have happiness, are free from suffering, and will achieve unsurpassable awakening. In that state of mind, recite:

> In the Buddha, dharma, and supreme assembly,
> [I take refuge until awakening.
> Through the merit of generosity and the rest,
> may I attain buddhahood for the sake of beings.]

Meditating on the four immeasurables, chant:

> May all sentient beings have happiness and the causes of happiness.
> [May they be free from suffering and the causes of suffering.
> May they never be parted from the genuine happiness that is free from suffering.
> May they abide in great equanimity, free from prejudice, attachment, and aggression.]

In the end, meditate that the objects of refuge melt into light and dissolve into you.

That was the first session: taking refuge and arousing bodhicitta, which purify your mindstream.

Two: Vajrasattva Meditation

Meditate that guru Vajrasattva is on your head. He is white, holding a vajra at his heart with his right hand, resting a bell on his hip with his left, and adorned with the major and minor marks. Supplicate him:

> Guru Vajrasattva, please purify my negative actions and obscurations.

Also perform an appropriate confession. Meditate that white amṛta flows from the big toe of Vajrasattva into your head and fills your body. All your negative actions and obscurations depart, and the space left behind is filled with amṛta. Pleased, the guru melts into light. The body, speech, and mind of Vajrasattva and your body, speech, and mind mix inseparably.

That was the second session: the meditation and recitation of Vajrasattva, which purify negative actions and obscurations.

Three: Maṇḍala Offering

For the maṇḍala [offering, first set up] the practice maṇḍala by arranging five offering piles on it. Meditate that the gurus are in the center, the yidams are to the front, the buddhas to the right, the dharma to the rear, and the saṅgha to the left. On another maṇḍala, arrange offering piles while reciting: [305]

> The earth is perfumed with scented water [and strewn with flowers,
> adorned with Mount Meru, the four continents, the sun and the moon.
> Imagining this as the buddha realm, I offer it
> so that all beings may enjoy that pure realm].

Using that and other suitable maṇḍala rituals, make offerings, actual and imagined. Supplicate:

> Grant your blessings that, through the power of such offerings,
> I may fulfill the two accumulations and perfect experiences and realizations.

Imagine that the deities of the practice maṇḍala melt into light and dissolve into you.

That was the third session: applying yourself to the instructions for maṇḍala [offerings], which enable you to fulfill the two accumulations.

Four: Guru Yoga

Meditate that your root guru is on your head, either in their normal form or in the form of a yidam, whichever you prefer. Above your guru's head are all the gurus up to Vajradhara, either arranged one above the other or gathered around in a group. Supplicate with unbounded devotion and extraordinary longing, forcefully and for a long period, to ensure that your outlook is transformed.

Meditate that the lineage gurus, buddhas, bodhisattvas, and assemblies of vīras, ḍākinīs, dharma protectors, and guardians dissolve into your root guru, who becomes the embodiment of them all. Present outer, inner, and secret offerings and the sevenfold service. Take refuge, arouse bodhicitta, and supplicate fervently, reciting:

> My mother sentient beings, who equal the extent of space, supplicate the guru, the precious buddha.
> [My mother sentient beings, who equal the extent of space,] supplicate the guru, the all-pervasive dharmakāya.
> [My mother sentient beings, who equal the extent of space,] supplicate the guru, the saṃbhogakāya of great bliss.
> [My mother sentient beings, who equal the extent of space,] supplicate the guru, the compassionate nirmāṇakāya.

Think that the guru dissolves into you, and that the guru's body, speech, and mind and your body, speech, and mind blend without distinction. Rest within a state free from conceptual elaborations. Since [guru yoga] is the means for realizing mahāmudrā, apply yourself to it.

That was the fourth session: guru yoga, which brings blessings. [306]

Five: Contemplation of Death and Impermanence

If you do not contemplate impermanence, your mind will not turn away from this life. If you do not turn away from that, you will not be liberated from saṃsāra. [Reflect on Nāgārjuna's] observation:

> Many things endanger this life,
> more impermanent than water bubbles blown by wind.
> That you inhale again after you exhale
> and wake up from sleep, are marvelous things.[1510]

Generally speaking, all conditioned phenomena are impermanent and, in particular, since the life-force of beings is as ephemeral as water bubbles, you never know when yours will be destroyed. It is not even certain that you will not die right now. When you die, nothing other than the dharma will be of any help. If you engage in futile worldliness and activities for just this life, you will not transcend the causes of suffering. Now, promise yourself that the moment your mind wanders to concerns about food, clothing, or similar things of this present life, you will remember death. From time to time, count how many of your relatives and close friends have already died. Think about how they died and that once they were taken to cemeteries nothing remained of their physical body. You are not beyond this natural situation. When [by contemplating that] you tremble with fear, like someone caught by their executioner, your mind will not be distracted, and you will give up concerns for this life. Meditate intently on this.

That was the fifth session: the meditation on death and impermanence.

Six: Contemplation of Karma

Next, it is imperative that you are not confused about what is to be taken up and what is to be rejected in terms of the karmic process of causes and results. Beings experience the results of the actions they have done—their actions ripen for them alone. Those who engage in the ten unvirtuous activities are reborn in the negative states. [Depending on which of] the three poisons [is involved], the frequency [of their actions], the gravity of the object, and the scale [of their actions], beings are born as hell beings, hungry ghosts, or animals. Once born in those states, they experience the sufferings specific [to the state], which are difficult to imagine. Those who engage in major, intermediate, or minor virtuous actions are reborn in the desire realm as gods or humans, in the form realm, or the formless.

You should at all times examine your three doors. Take delight in whatever virtuous actions you have done, and put an end to unvirtuous actions or [karmically] unspecified [or neutral] ones. Without mixing up what is to be abandoned with what is to be adopted, what is to be undertaken with what is to be shunned, sever the stream of unvirtue and set in motion a continuous flow of virtue with your three doors. That is the point of the Buddha's teachings and what enables us to accomplish the aim of our practice. Therefore, train yourself with a subtle awareness of what is to be adopted or rejected in the context of the karmic process of causes and results.

That was the sixth session: the discussion of the karmic process of causes and their results.

Seven: Contemplation of the Deficiencies of Saṃsāra

Following that, if you do not contemplate the deficiencies of saṃsāra, you will not develop revulsion for it and the determination to be released from it. Without those catalysts, [meditation] experiences and realizations will not arise in your mindstream, and you will lack the circumstances for them to arise. To prevent that, you must contemplate the sufferings of saṃsāra.

Sentient beings born in the hells suffer in eight hot hells, eight cold hells, the occasional and neighboring hells, and elsewhere. Hungry ghosts are thirsty and famished. Animals are slaughtered. Humans are born, age, get sick, and die. The gods must leave [their elevated state] and descend. Demigods suffer due to wars and fights. The six classes of beings are tormented unceasingly by the sufferings related to sufferings (which are the many manifest sufferings they experience), by the sufferings related to changes ([which occur with] what appears to be happiness), and by the sufferings related to conditioned existence ([which occur with] whatever has an indifferent feeling).

Thus, even if you were to attain the heights of a cakravartin king, Brahmā, Indra, or the like here in saṃsāra, you would not escape suffering. Think, "Now I will do whatever it takes to permanently separate myself from this state." Certain that saṃsāra is like a prison cell or a pit of fire, apply yourself to the methods for liberation. [308]

However, even if you attain the awakening of the Hīnayāna, which is superior to [saṃsāra], you have not reached the level of final happiness. Now, you must, no matter what, attain the unsurpassable awakening. To do so, resolve, "Since all beings, each and every one, have been my kind parents [in one lifetime or another] throughout beginningless time, I will establish them in unsurpassable, true, perfect awakening, which is definite and lasting happiness." Arouse bodhicitta without any artifice, and apply yourself to that.

That was the seventh session.

Eight: Contemplation of the Opportunities of Human Life

This precious human existence, which is the support for being able to practice [the dharma] in that way, is extremely difficult to acquire. Therefore, not succumbing to the lure of idleness and laziness, you should concentrate intently on [dharma] practice. What will you do if the leisures and opportunities [of your human life] are lost to the demon of death and impermanence, and you are left empty-handed? Since this human existence is so hard to obtain and so easily destroyed, exert yourself at all times and in every situation to make your attainment of its leisures and opportunities meaningful.

That was the eighth session.

Nine: The Causal Condition

Among the four conditions [necessary] for dharma practice, the causal condition is to strenuously cultivate weariness with and revulsion for saṃsāra and take up [the life of] a renunciate. This is based on having tamed your mindstream through [recognizing] impermanence and seeing the general and specific characteristics of the phenomena of saṃsāra.

That was the ninth session.

Ten: The Dominant Condition

Study with a genuine spiritual mentor—a guru who is an individual in a lineage, a guru [in the form of] the words of the Sugata, a guru who is the ultimate dharmatā, or a guru who [manifests as] symbolic appearances—and practice their instructions correctly. Since to be guided by a genuine spiritual mentor is the dominant condition, train in that way.

That was the tenth session.

Eleven: The Object Condition

Here, we must eliminate any biases towards what is established through conventions or conceptual imputations. What does not contradict anything and yet is superior to everything is the primordial abiding state, which is called "the natural state of dharmatā." [309] Develop conviction in that. Since the object condition is that unmistaken object of meditation, develop certainty in it.

That was the eleventh session.

Twelve: The Immediate Condition

Within a state free from any fixation to meditation, arouse your perseverance and fortitude, but do not harbor the signs of hopes or fears, such as thinking, "I am meditating," "I will meditate," "I was meditating," "It would be good if something happened," or "If nothing happens that is bad." Being free from hopes and fears is the immediate condition. Therefore, practice within an uncontrived state.

That was the twelfth session and completes the preliminaries.

2

Main Practices

This has two parts:

A. Śamatha

B. Vipaśyanā

A. Śamatha

One: Essential Points for Body and Mind

In general, although there are many methods for developing samādhi, if you know one [set of] essential points, hindrances and obstacles will not arise, your śamatha and vipaśyanā will be flawless, and experiences and realization of innate wisdom will arise without exertion. Since the dharma can be taught by means of Vairocana's kāya, the method for effortlessly giving rise to the samādhis of the generation and perfection processes and to experiences of bliss, clarity, and nonconceptuality is, for beginners, to rely upon the essential points of the physical posture.

- To control the downward-expelling winds, place your legs either in the vajra posture or the bodhisattva posture.
- To cause the earth winds to abide in the madhyamā, straighten your spine like [a stack of] coins.
- To bring the water winds into the madhyamā, hold your hands in the mudrā of meditative equipoise below your navel and raise both your shoulders.
- To draw the fire winds into the madhyamā, draw up your neck so that it resembles an iron hook.
- To bring the wind winds into the madhyamā, gaze out at the level of the tip of your nose with your eyes neither wide open nor shut, and let your tongue and lips rest naturally, or press your tongue against your palate.

By holding those essential points for the body, the movements of thoughts are self-purified and many excellent qualities, such as nonconceptuality, arise. Maintaining just those essential points for the body brings physical and mental tranquility. [310] Do not be too tightly focused or too taut.

Begin by exhaling a small amount of stale breath. Then rest without putting any effort into exhaling or inhaling. Recall the preliminaries in a generalized way. Don't bring past activities to mind. Don't speculate about the future, thinking, "I will do this" or "I should do that." Relax in the ordinary mind of the present: unfabricated freshness. Leave it just as it is without adopting or rejecting anything. Your mind will become workable and samādhi will arise.

Since those essential points for the body and mind are the foundation stone for meditation, apply yourself to them.

That was the first session.

Two: Resting with a Visual Support

If your mind is unable to rest on that, direct your gaze to any appropriate external object of meditation, such as a twig, pebble, statue of the Buddha, candle flame, or the sky. Do not consider the color, shape, and so forth of the focal support. Avoid getting too tight or drifting about. Simply use the focal support to remain without distraction. Cut off the movements of any extraneous thoughts.

Alternatively, either draw or visualize in front a white OṂ, red ĀḤ, and blue HŪṂ or white, red, and blue bindus (whichever set you prefer) as the essences of the body, speech, and mind of all buddhas.

In brief, settle your mind by focusing one-pointedly on any suitable form that your mind finds congenial for concentration. The way to settle is as follows: the basic nature is nothing at all and there is nothing to be grasped by the intellect. If your mind rests, leave it be. If it moves, let it go. Without acting as a "minder," let it be free.

Cut off all conceptualizations, such as thinking, "I am meditating," "I am not meditating," or hoping that your mind will rest, or feeling anxious that it won't rest. Without any object of meditation whatsoever and without letting yourself be distracted for even an instant, maintain the light touch of mindfulness and meditate.

Leave [your meditation] when it is going well. Do short sessions frequently. It is important to train yourself by repeatedly resting in equipoise with vibrant clarity infused with enthusiasm, and then suspending [your meditation] before you become exasperated with it. [311]

If you are comfortable concentrating on one of those focal supports, do that. If you prefer to concentrate using all of them sequentially, that's also fine. Concentrating with one may be sufficient—it is not required that you use each and every one of them [as if you are going through] an alphabetic list. In brief: concentrate on a form, any one of them.

That was the second session.

Three: Resting with Other Focal Supports

Concentrate on those [visual objects] and also on sounds (auditory objects), smells (olfactory objects), tastes (gustatory objects), and tangible objects (objects for the body), one after another. When focusing on sounds, smells, and so forth, direct your mind to just the clear sound, a distinct scent, and so on. Hold your mind with the iron hook of undistracted mindfulness and just leave it naturally settled—do not study the object's qualities, size, or other attributes. Settle your mind on whatever object seems appropriate. Stop while your mind's clarity is still heightened and take a break. Don't let your mind become fuzzy.

Between sessions maintain the continuity of mindfulness, and let your gaze rest towards the tip of your nose. Physically, when you are moving about or sitting around, and verbally, when you are talking, don't do too much or do anything too intensely. Mentally, cut off any deliberations involved with conceptualizing. Gradually you will become accustomed to meditative equipoise.

That was the third session.

Four: Counteracting Dullness and Agitation

The faults of dullness and agitation are removed [by the following methods]. Meditate that there is a round, glistening, glowing white bindu, the size of pea, at the point between your eyebrows, and focus your mind there. From time to time, direct your mind to a round, shiny black bindu, the size of a pea, under your mat. When you are experiencing dullness, direct your awareness to the white bindu, and gaze into space. Sit in a breezy spot and sprinkle water on yourself. Wear light clothing and eat smaller amounts of nutritious food. Do not sit near a fire or in the sun. When your mind is agitated and very scattered, direct your gaze and focus to the black bindu. Keep yourself warm during your activities, get massages, and eat larger amounts of nutritious food. When you have neither dullness nor agitation, direct your attention and your eyes to a small blue bindu, or substance, at the edge of some shade directly [in front]. [312]

In all those cases, first simply set your intention, thinking "I will meditate in this way," whether it be on a bindu or something else. Next, if it is clear, that is the best. If it is not, bring the object to mind, thinking, "It is present." After that, without doing any investigating, let [your mind] settle into itself right with that [object], undistracted and in a natural way. When your clarity is heightened, break off the session. Then meditate again. Do short, frequent sessions. Concentrate your mind.

That was the fourth session.

Five: Resting Without Support

To focus without a support, look vacantly into the space in front. Do not use any reference point, and do not mentally contemplate anything. Simply be undistracted. Do not dwell on existence or nonexistence, the past or the future. With great perseverance, place the lookout of undistracted mindfulness, and remain at ease in buoyant, uncontrived freshness. Rest without being diverted for an instant, as if you were threading a needle. Do not waver: be like an ocean without waves. Do not make any effort: be like a garuḍa soaring in space. Leave aside your hopes and fears.

When you aren't distracted, thoughts won't arise. But if you are distracted, a thought will appear suddenly. As soon as that happens, recognize it, look nakedly at it, and settle your mind as before. No matter what thought arises, recognize it. And, without doing anything to it—trying to stop it or encourage it, enjoy it or not enjoy it—rest right within it. Look at it with your eye of prajñā. Use the thought itself as the support for concentrating your mind, and rest. Sustain [this meditation] without slipping into being too tight or too loose.

That was the fifth session.

Six: Breath As a Support

[Another] method for concentrating your mind is based on the breath. Retain the vase breath and rest without distraction. If you are unable to do that, concentrate on counting and so forth. Count your breath moving in, moving out, and resting internally. Start with twenty-one [cycles], and then gradually increase to one hundred and more. Focus on your nostrils, and count your breath without letting your attention wander anywhere else. [313] When concentrating on filling [with breath] and releasing it, [begin by] expelling your breath three times. Then, inhale and retain what you can, pressing it down below your navel. When you can no longer hold it, release it fully. Do that repeatedly without distraction.

If dullness or agitation arises, apply the [appropriate] method for dispelling them. If you are not able to initiate resting using the techniques [given above], you should use other objects suitable for meditation.

Individuals are not necessarily all [the same] type. Some immediately "get" the instructions and develop [śamatha]. Others meditate a lot but have difficulty making any progress. For those who persevere without getting discouraged, it's impossible not to progress. Experienced gurus must be able to [give instructions about how to] dispel hindrances and enhance the development [of meditation] according to their students' abilities.

Through sustaining [meditation] in that way, [three levels of resting will develop]. On the first level of resting, you will have many coarse thoughts, which are like water falling from a mountain cliff. During the second level, your coarse thoughts will subside. At times, a thought may pop up suddenly, but you will notice it and immediately it will be self-pacified. Like a large river, meditation just continues flowing. Finally, both subtle and coarse thoughts subside, and there is a steady nonconceptual state. Within a state of bliss, clarity, and nonconceptuality, there will arise stillness that is quiet, serene, vivid, vibrant, crisp. Until such stillness develops, you must arouse exertion. Once it has developed, keep practicing without interruption.

That was the sixth session.

Seven: Tightening, Loosening, and Subverting

If the three levels of resting do not develop, increase your exertion and practice by tightening, loosening, and using subversive meditation.

Tightening means to intensify your physical posture, gaze, and awareness. Tighten with [self-]control: do not let yourself be distracted for a second. Focus as if you were crossing a river on a bridge made of a single plank. Without any object of meditation, arouse a strong flow [of meditation] with just the right amount of tension. Not allowing yourself to be distracted for even an instant, do frequent, short sessions. [314]

Loosening uses trulkhor and gazes [but] has no reference point for meditation at all. Regardless of what occurs, leave your mind at ease in its own state, without contrivance, with no sense of ownership or fuss. Be buoyant and relaxed, naturally settled, comfortable, effortless. Rest at ease, like a small child with a full stomach or a sheaf of hay when its rope has been cut. Within that state, arouse flashes of mindfulness simply free from wandering. Don't do any meditation other than that. Leave [your mind] in its own state. Make your short sessions a bit longer. [While] you are resting quietly, interrupt that and take a break. Between sessions, simply maintain the light touch of mindfulness.

You may also [need] to use subversive meditation. When you aren't distracted, thoughts don't arise. As soon as you are distracted or a situation suddenly presents itself, many thoughts appear. When that happens, you may wonder, "Should I get rid of them?" Don't reject them—see them as useful. Allow them to come, saying, "Come, come, as many as you can." Notice them as they arise, one after another. Even if you were to reject them, they wouldn't go away. They cannot be chased down. Be free from hopes and fears, such as taking delight in stillness, being upset with movements, fearing that your meditation will not progress, or hoping that it will go well. Take the thought itself to be a support for concentration. Blocking thoughts in order to create nonconceptuality does not work. You must take the thought itself as your object and rest right there. Once thoughts vanish, being self-pacified, nonconceptuality will arise as a matter of course. Practice in that way.

That was the seventh session.

Eight: Authentic Śamatha

Next, the way śamatha develops and is pointed out is as follows. Authentic śamatha is the mental state in which all distractions involving thoughts and the conceptualizing of characteristics have been pacified. Free from dullness, agitation, and sluggishness, that mind rests one-pointedly in its nonconceptual essence. Previously, śamatha involved effort. Now, without relying on any effort, it comes easily, is comfortable and spacious, and continues with ease.

Even when you get up from your meditation, your mind doesn't change in any way: you continue to abide in that same state [of śamatha]. [315] While walking, sitting, and so forth, your mind is slow yet resplendent, loose, unconstrained, and serene. Appearances seem to float by, vague and amorphous. If you do not intentionally pay attention to objects, you won't notice their details. Your mind does not wander.

The experiences of bliss, clarity, and nonconceptuality may be present in equal proportions or one may predominate. Many different visual experiences, auditory experiences, supercognitive abilities, and even miraculous powers may develop. Any of the ten signs and the like may occur.[1511] Thus, the arising of flawless śamatha in your mindstream is the foundation for the development of all excellent qualities, including vipaśyanā.

At this time, no matter what good or bad experiences you have—be they physical illness, mental suffering, positive or negative dreams, supercognitive abilities, miraculous powers, bliss, clarity, or nonconceptuality—do not cling to them. Be certain that they have no essence. Do not entertain happy thoughts or sad ones. If you fixate on experiences, you create the root for circling in one of the three saṃsāric realms, and you will not be liberated from cyclic existence. The outsiders [non-Buddhists] have this much [that is, these experiences] but they are not benefited by them. In brief, if you fixate on any of your experiences or realizations, you will destroy yourself.

Within a state free from any attachment to those [experiences] and devoid of entangling fixations, prolong [your meditation]. Propel it with the oar of exertion. If you can meditate while you have difficulties, your excellent qualities will exceed your imagination. Therefore, train yourself accordingly. Both the master and the student must be unmistaken about the actual way to give rise to experiences, understanding, and realization, thus ensuring recognition.

Mainly, the following are most important: Do not be attached to sense pleasures for the sake of this lifetime. Have uncontrived devotion for your guru. Perfect your bodhicitta with the six kinds of beings. Free from distraction, maintain the light touch of mindfulness. Feeling you can't delay, shorten your perspective and maintain your convictions. Don't be swayed by the [usual] human concerns or the eight worldly qualities.

If you practice that way, free from errors, experiences and realizations will arise effortlessly. Apply yourself accordingly.

That was the eighth session. [316]

B. Vipaśyanā

One: Looking with Stillness

Hold the essential points for the body as before. Your gaze is very important in this context. Without blinking, letting your eyes wander or flutter, look vacantly with bulging eyes into the center of the empty space directly in front. Remain quietly within flawless stillness, with your mind naturally settled in its own state, without contrivance, with no sense of ownership or fuss. Intensifying that slightly, arouse a flash of undistracted mindfulness, brilliant and sharp.

When your śamatha is going well, look closely at the nature of your mind. Does it have a color, form, or shape? Does it arise, cease, or abide? Is it existent? Nonexistent? Does it reside externally or internally? Or is it something to be known apart from just that stillness? It may be an emptiness that cannot be identified as anything, a nothingness.[1512] Alternatively, it may be that, within stillness, the mental state that cannot be identified is vivid, crisp, stark, something you do not know how to describe. The nature of stillness may be a stupefied dark mental state. Or it may be clear, sharp, and naked.

This [approach] contains all the critical and key points related to the abiding state. And yet those with just a theoretical understanding, who have only heard [the instructions], and who use lofty dharma jargon have a mindstream bound by the eight worldly qualities that they [try to pass off] as fabulous experiences and realizations. Pretending something has arisen in their mindstream when it has not, they pull the wool over their own eyes and deceive themselves. If they are monastics, they have impaired their vows by lying about their attainments.

Therefore, [be rigorous] in your practice, [like] pulverizing bones with a rock. It is not something "out there" to be patched together by conceptuality. It must be genuine experiences and realizations arising within you, "right here," through the force of meditation. Tighten up your awareness and look. Then take a break. Again, look. Look at the nature of the still mind. In this context, the approach to settling [your mind] is to remain clear, lucid, and radiant, like the sun free from clouds. At times, energize your awareness, and strive to look at its nature. [317]

Since this is the first way to give the pointing-out instructions, gurus should closely check and question the students according to their abilities. Some have trained but they can be deceptive and should be repeatedly questioned. Understandings, [meditation] experiences, realizations, and experiences should be pointed out, without being mixed with dharma terminology. Students should make efforts accordingly.

To look at the nature of mind is the first session.

[Two: Looking with Movement]

To cut through a root or basis [of mind], pointing-out instructions should be given in relation to movements directly or once the movements of thoughts have been investigated. The essential points for the body, the gaze, and conduct are the same as before. Within a blissful, clear, and nonconceptual state, vivid and relaxed, a fleeting thought may suddenly appear, or you should arouse a thought about something suitable. Look at the nature of that active mind. Look at when it is active. Look at where it is active. What is its color and shape? What are its origin, resting place, and destination like? Does it reside externally? Or is it internal, within the body? If it is internal, is it in the center of the heart? Or somewhere else?

Examine this by asking yourself: Wherever it is, outside or inside the body, how does mind rest and how is it active? Is mind an entity? Is it a nonentity? Does it arise? Cease? Have a color or shape? If so, what are those like? Is it "something" about which you think, "It does not have [such attributes]"? Or, even though there is nothing thought of as, "This is it," is there still something known that does not arise, cease, and so on?

When you look at thoughts, is it that all thoughts are empty, free from conceptual elaborations, without arising or ceasing? Or is it that having looked at a thought, it vanishes without a trace? Or is that all thoughts arise without being identified? If they arise without being identified, is there the thought, "There is nothing to identify," at that time or not?

Once a thought appears or you have caused one to appear, look at its nature without blocking it or grasping at it. When you have happy ones or sad ones, look at their nature. Create many thoughts, and look. When strong ones, such as those involving the five poisonous mental afflictions, arise or you create them, also look. [318] Is there a difference between the thought itself, the object of the thought, and the immediately preceding thought or mind? Look to be certain that you cut your misinterpretations from within.

If you see the nature of thoughts as naked clarity-awareness, look: is there a difference between the naked clarity-awareness that you saw before while resting and the naked clarity-awareness that you see now with thoughts? If you are not certain, look carefully. Drawing a thought in and placing it in clarity-awareness is not [the way] to look. To see that a suddenly arising thought is of the same nature as the original, ordinary mind—which is not adulterated in any way—is it.

In brief, in keeping with the way [the student's experiences] develop, both the master and student must differentiate [between correct and mistaken development. In that way,] you will gain certainty and cut through a basis and root. Apply yourself to those pointing-out instructions for looking and to those ways of looking.

That was the second session.

Three: Looking with Appearances and the Body

In order that the inseparability of appearances and mind may be pointed out, you should look [at your mind] right with appearances. The essential points for the body and the gaze are as before. Direct your focus and eyes one-pointedly to a specific object, be it a column, vase, sacred image, Mount Meru, or some other suitable form in the space in front. Look directly at it. Then rest awhile with relaxed attention. Again, look.

Similarly, look at the nature of sounds, which are objects for your ears. Look at pleasing sounds, displeasing sounds, loud ones, soft ones, various ones, existent ones, nonexistent ones, those uttered by yourself and by others, and so on. Also, look at the fragrant and foul odors that appear as objects for your nose, the delicious and unsavory tastes experienced by your tongue, and the sensations of pleasure and discomfort, hot and cold, sickness and pain that are tangible objects experienced by your body. Whatever occurs, look at that.

When you do so, do those appearances stop? Or do you and the appearances appear to be separate? Do appearances come to the mind? Or does mind reach out to appearances, thinking, "This appears"? Or do you say that since appearances and mind are inseparable, there is just vivid appearance-emptiness, no objects?

Alternate between looking at the thought that is looking and looking at any one of the five objects. Can you see any difference between those two? Look: what is the difference between the appearing object and the perceiving thought? [319] When you look at an object, if it is clearly out there, is there "something" that you think is that way? Or, without there being any such thought, is it that there seems to be no difference between the unceasing and transparent object and the looking mind, which is free, without grasping, and of no particular significance?[1513] In that case, is there not even the thought, "There is no distinction"? If there is "something" about which you think, "That object is clearly out there," look: what exactly is that "something" you think is that way like?

Also look at your body and mind. Are they the same or different? If they are the same, is it that the body, something born and perishable, and the mind, something not born, not perishable, and permanent, are the same? If they are different, the body and mind must be identifiable as separate from each other. How is it that the mind, while not having a specific location, pervades the whole body and experiences sensations? If the body is the support and mind is the supported, and the body is external and mind is internal, then they are like a person and their clothing. When sensations are experienced, if you think that it is only the body that experiences sensations, then a corpse would also experience sensations. On the other hand, you may think that the mind experiences sensations. If [mind and body] are different, [how is it that] the mind, which cannot be killed or cut, can experience the body being pricked with a thorn? Would that not be like saying that when someone's clothing (the support) is burned, the person (the supported) is also burned?

You must look well and reach a conclusion. At this point, you should recognize that all thoughts and feelings are mind, like waves on water, and rest in that. In order to become certain about the abiding state, while resting in that [recognition] look as has been described.

That was the third session.

Four: Looking with Stillness and Movement

When your mind rests vividly in clarity-emptiness, look at its nature. Then cause a thought to stir, and look at its nature. Look: is the nature of stillness and the nature of movement the same or different? Having looked in that way, if you see them as different, how are they different? Is it that stillness and movements arise in alternation with their strengths being equally matched, like strings stretched out on a flat surface? [320] Or is stillness like the ground and movement what grows from it, like a tree? Or are they both like a snake or rope, which can be coiled [or not], so that when one is present, the other is not? Is it that when there is stillness, there is no movement? And when there is movement, there is no stillness?

Movement is the busyness of all kinds of rambling thoughts, and stillness is to rest without movement. Therefore, they are very different from each other. If you think that their natures are different, look: Do they have distinctive colors, shapes, and so forth? Do they differ in terms of their arising, abiding, or ceasing? Do they differ in being past, future, or present? Or do they differ in being permanent or impermanent?

Alternatively, if you know thoughts to be meditation, [you see] stillness and movements to be nothing other than of the same nature. Their way of arising is to appear in alternation. When there is stillness, there is no movement, and when there is movement, there is no stillness. Like water and waves, they are only the modes, or actions, of a single mind. That is all there is. If you realize that both stillness and movements are never anything other than naked empty clarity, you have slight realization.

Nevertheless, [you must check:] Is there empty clarity because you have drawn in a thought and placed it in meditation? Or does empty clarity follow the disappearance of a thought? Or is it that a sudden thought is empty clarity? If you think that it is like either of the first two, you should continue to energetically supplicate your guru, and again exert yourself in looking. By doing so, it is certain that you will see [the nature of thoughts] at some point.

By practicing those ways of looking at the nature, [experiences and realizations will arise differently for the three types of individuals]. The bypassing type [might experience] vipaśyanā first, then śamatha, sometimes neither, sometimes both. The instantaneous type, through the force of their previous training, develop śamatha and vipaśyanā simultaneously through merely being presented with symbols. The gradual type progress in stages. Here the presentation is from the perspective of the latter. [Gurus] should instruct [their students] having assessed the way [their experiences and realizations] develop.

Looking involves having clarity but being without grasping, like a small child gazing at a shrine hall. Within that state, be very diligent about looking. [321] Cast aside laziness. Have revulsion, no needs, determination to be released, devotion, and faith. Stabilize undistracted mindfulness. Within an uncontrived state, do not be bound by any hopes or fears. Do not just have a vague sense about what is to be practiced. Only pursue what will benefit you in your future lives. If you exert yourself in these ways of looking at your mind, the wisdom of vipaśyanā will definitely develop quickly—there is no way that it will not.

That is how to determine [the natures of] both stillness and movement.

This is the fourth session.

Five: Pointing-Out Instructions in Relation to Stillness

Those who have looked at the nature [of stillness, movement, and so forth] and practiced those key instructions for mind probably will not need pointing-out instructions. [Recognition of the mind's nature] will emerge spontaneously from within. Some, however, may have [that recognition] but not know it. Others—who have an intellectual understanding, a dry sense based on what they have heard, and the desire for excellent experiences and realizations to quickly develop—may express themselves flawlessly using dharma terminology despite not having had any [experiences]. Since there are such dangers, gurus must differentiate between these [kinds of practitioners]. Students also must engage the practice by penetrating its essential points.

The first way to give the pointing-out instructions relates to the first [approach of] looking at the nature. Use the ways of looking at the nature of the resting mind and so forth, as described above. The nature of stillness is a brilliant, sharp, and naked state—not mere emptiness. Within that state of stillness, the unidentified mind is vivid, open, stark, crisp, and relaxed. It is not something that can be said to have this color or that shape, nor can it be described verbally, by saying, "It is like this." Nevertheless, while not being identifiable, the clear, unobstructed mind is vibrant, crisp, naked, stark, and sharp.

What is seen that cannot be seen, what is experienced that cannot be experienced, and what is known that cannot be known is nothing about which you can think, "It is exactly like this." And yet there is something that arises within you, even though it is not something you can talk about by saying, "It is this way." It may be that with deep conviction [you experience] lucid, quiet stillness: clear yet empty, without being identified.

If that is merely an understanding, nothing will come of it, because it won't inspire confidence. If it arises from within, that is it: vipaśyanā has dawned within stillness. Therefore, the only thing to do is to see the nature directly, [like] pulverizing bones with a rock. [322] If you [receive] pointing-out instructions too soon, they will remain as objects of a theoretical understanding and you will become jaded. That will undermine any guidance someone else may give later. Without receiving the pointing-out instructions and cutting through the stream of thoughts, you will not see the nature. Without seeing the nature, the pointing out cannot happen. If you do not recognize [what is pointed out], your meditation will not become your path.

When you have good experiences, look. When you have bad ones, repeatedly clarify [or recall the instructions]. Training in the ways to sustain practice is called "being guided." Once meditation is understood, that is called "completing the guidance." By maintaining nondistraction in such a state [of meditation], you will develop experiences and realizations without difficulties. Thus, seeing the nature produces certainty and eliminates doubts.

In order to bring that about, now what is to be pointed out is as follows. Generally speaking, meditation consists of śamatha (*zhi gnas*) and vipaśyanā. When your mind remains relaxed in its natural condition, all thoughts are pacified (*zhi*) in their own place, and mind rests (*gnas*) clearly and quietly in its natural state. Your mind does not engage in the distractions of this worldly life. It is comfortable and buoyant. Your mental afflictions are completely pacified (*zhi*). To the degree that you remain one-pointedly in the nature of what is virtuous, you have mastery. You may have no sense of the coming and going of breath. That is exceptional śamatha. It is primarily an experience and, while it does not function as realization, it is essential.

By sustaining [śamatha] without fixation and not letting it slip into dullness, agitation, or a neutral state of indifference, [you see that] the nature of mind is free from being something that can be thought about or described as having a color or shape, such that you could say, "It is this way." Like the pleasure experienced by a young person, what you know and experience isn't something that you can describe as an intellectual object, saying, "It is like this." It is unified clarity and emptiness, without identification or the extremes of conceptual elaborations. It cannot be altered by any dharmic concepts or be sullied by worldly ideas. A mental state that is not affected by stagnant nonconceptuality and śamatha is naturally settled and free in its own place. It is the root of all excellent qualities. That is called ordinary mind or [just] mind. [323] Not recognizing it is to be ignorant and in saṃsāra. Recognition is called awareness-wisdom or nirvāṇa, connate wisdom, the intrinsic state, luminosity, or vipaśyanā. Now, [those] are the primary indications of the distinction between saṃsāra and nirvāṇa.

Having received the pointing-out instructions from the guru, the disciple's recognition is like that of reuniting with an old friend. That recognition is called recognizing the mind. It doesn't occur because the disciple has great prajñā or because the guru is skilled in giving instructions. [It occurs because] this is how [the mind] has always been. Previously, that wasn't recognized because it was obscured by mental afflictions and thoughts. Now, since thoughts are interrupted and [the nature of mind] has been pointed out, there is recognition.

This unidentified vibrant clarity of mind is its nature. While not existing, it vividly appears—that is mind's characteristic. The essence of emptiness, clarity, and awareness is sparkling, vivid, continuous.[1514] That is [mind's] essence. If you maintain a naked recognition of that at all times without wavering, one of the unimaginable benefits is that vipaśyanā will dawn within stillness. Since that is the recognition [of what is pointed out: the nature of mind during stillness], it is the first set of the actual pointing-out instructions. It is important to penetrate the vital points, bring them into experience, and maintain [recognition] constantly. Therefore, recognize and sustain that.

That was the fifth session.

Six: Pointing-Out Instructions in Relation to Nonconceptuality and Conceptuality

The second way of looking cuts through a basis and root. This set of pointing-out instructions is given in relation to nonconceptuality and in relation to movement or thoughts (that is, once a thought arises or you have caused a thought to arise). Among these two, the first is as follows.

First: Nonconceptuality

Looking at mind in a nonconceptual state—quiet, vibrantly clear stillness, free from dullness or agitation—there is not even the thought, "This is what is thought of as being without color or shape, what has no arising or ceasing." When there is something known without any arising or ceasing, vipaśyanā has dawned within nonconceptuality. [324]

Second: Conceptuality

Those who say that all movements of thoughts are empty, free from arising or cessation, may just be using the jargon of emptiness. If [thoughts] vanish without any trace—without their arising, abiding, or ceasing, shape, or color being identified—a little [experience of vipaśyanā in relation to thoughts] has developed. If the arising [of a thought] and its freeing are simultaneous, without being identified as such—without even the thought, "There is nothing to be identified"—with no sense of that being significant, and with no clinging, that is recognition [of what is being pointed out].

Furthermore, thoughts and the objects of thoughts, the mind at rest and in motion, a previous state of mind or previous thoughts are neither good nor bad, they are not different in even the slightest way: they are realized to be naked clarity-awareness. It is not that thoughts become empty clarity after they are drawn in or after they disappear. The very thought that suddenly appears is realized to be, or manifests as, empty clarity. That is recognition [of what is being pointed out].

Now, all three—the movements of thoughts, stillness, and the nature of thoughts themselves—are stripped down to empty clarity. There are no differences at all beyond [those created by] the mind misinterpreting, and grasping at, its own lack of recognition of the nature of thoughts and nonconceptuality. Previously, since you did not recognize the nature of thoughts, they were not meditation. They were ignorance. Now, when you do recognize that, thoughts themselves are meditation and are awareness-wisdom. Now make thoughts the basis of your meditation.

Earlier, thoughts obscured themselves and you did not see [their nature]. What is superior to meditating upon nonconceptuality is now knowing how to meditate on concepts. Recognize [the nature of] whatever thoughts arise. If thoughts don't arise, remain within their not arising. You need not provoke them. If they arise, rest right within their arising. You need not dissolve them. Don't create hopes and fears. Make thoughts the essence of your meditation. Thoughts are not beyond the mind. Mind self-liberates. Its essence is naked clarity-emptiness, the dharmakāya, with nothing to be liberated or means of liberation. Realizing that is the dawning of vipaśyanā within thoughts. It is the recognition of the unification of clarity and emptiness as the dharmakāya. [325]

In brief, recognize the nature of whatever arises. Rest right within that, sustaining it without contrivance, without wandering. That is the second set of the actual pointing-out instructions. Recognition is not enough: you must sustain it.

That was the sixth session.

Seven: Pointing-Out Instructions in Relation to Appearances and Body

The third set of pointing-out instructions introduces the inseparability of appearances and mind in relation to appearances. Looking at any of the five types of external objects, you see that objects are unceasing and transparent without the thought, "That object is out there." The mind that looks at them is free without any grasping. Those two are neither the same nor different. There is not even the thought that they are neither [the same nor different].

Not being the same or different, body and mind are inseparable. They are unified clarity-emptiness, appearance-emptiness, like the moon reflected in water. Sensations (such as of hot and cold) are also appearances. It is simply that, not knowing them to be appearance-emptiness, the mind endlessly labels them and grasps at them. Realize that in actuality there is no basis of designation for the sensations [experienced] by the body or mind.

Direct your gaze and attention to whatever appears. Then relax somewhat and rest. At first, the details of those objects will be clear. Next, since you may not really want to keep looking, you might feel nauseous or find that your vision has gone "numb," and so [objects] vanish on their own. Then, when you look [again] for a while, appearances become vivid with no clinging: they vanish into their own state. At that point, if you and appearances are inseparable—vivid appearance-emptiness without being objects—[you are experiencing] the reflexive-appearances of the abiding state, the characteristics of mind. External appearances and the internal mind are not different. The self-radiance of mind manifests freely.

When appearances are grasped as objects, the perceiving mind is deluded. At that time, it is not that [appearances] have become something separate: they appear [as external objects] because the mind has deluded itself. [Appearances] are simply mental appearances—appearances, or objects, do not have even the slightest bit of existence as some object that is other [than mind]. [326] Previously, being obscured by ignorance or the mind's grasping, you did not see [the nature of appearances]. Now, having severed the continuum of fixated conceptuality, you recognize the nature without an object. Not fixating on appearances, they appear utterly empty and vividly without being objects. This is referred to as "the connateness of appearances is the radiance of the dharmakāya."

Now sustain this without fabrication. Let your six modes of consciousness be free. Sustain your practice right with appearances. In that state, rest your mind without contrivance in its fundamental state, buoyant and at ease. Don't try to deliberately make that into something ecstatic, dazzling, void, or fantastic. Don't dream about the past. Don't speculate about the future. Don't ponder the present. Don't meditate on intellectual constructs.[1515] Don't engage in analysis about what is or is not.

When mind is naturally settled, loose and fresh, with no effort or caretaking, it rests in its own nature. Remain in the state of the inseparability of appearances and emptiness, the inseparability of sound and emptiness, the inseparability of bliss and emptiness, the inseparability of awareness and emptiness, and the inseparability of clarity and emptiness.

The direct realization of the inseparability of appearances and emptiness—with no blocking of, or grasping onto, appearances—is the dawning of vipaśyanā within appearances. It is the recognition of the unification of appearances and emptiness as the dharmakāya. On the basis of continuously sustaining that, special experiences and realizations will develop.

Those are the pointing-out instructions given in relation to appearances, the third set of pointing-out instructions. Cultivate them in your practice.

That was the seventh session.

Eight: Pointing-Out Instructions in Relation to Stillness and Movement

Having looked at stillness and movements in terms of whether they are the same or different, the [corresponding] pointing-out instructions are as follows. When you investigate the sameness or difference of stillness and movement, once you understand that thoughts are meditation, stillness and movements are nothing but the same. They manifest in alternation: when there is stillness, there is no movement; when there is movement, there is no stillness. As for their agent: they are created by one mind. The nature of both is nothing other than naked empty clarity. [327]

It is not that you draw in your thoughts and then see them as naked empty clarity. Nor is it that after thoughts or recollections disappear they become empty clarity. When you realize, or it is, that a suddenly arising thought is itself naked empty clarity, you know the abiding state of mind. That is called the collapse of the distinction between stillness and movement. Therefore, whether your mind rests quietly in a nonconceptual and clear state, moves with thoughts, or is [seen to be] the essence of the thoughts themselves, it is nothing other than naked empty clarity.

- Now, you realize that, in fact, all objects and appearances have no existence other than as the magical displays of mind, like [the relationship between] waves and water. You have recognized [the pointing out] that appearances are mind.
- Through examining the nature of that mind in terms of going, abiding, and arising, you realize that it does not exist anywhere. Like horses and elephants in dreams, it does not actually exist. You have recognized [the pointing out] that mind is empty.
- When you realize that the myriad [appearances] manifest unceasingly and are spontaneously existent within the empty and lucidly clear state, like the moon reflected in water, you have recognized [the pointing out] that emptiness has spontaneous existence.
- Through being merely spontaneously existent in that way, spontaneously existent clarity-awareness-emptiness does not move from unchanging great bliss, free from elaborations. When you are certain that arising and liberating are simultaneous, like a snake uncoiling, you have recognized [the pointing out] that what is spontaneously existent is self-liberating.

The mind that is pointed out is the ordinary mind, which thinks all sorts of things, is keenly aware, and vividly clear. That very mind is unified clarity and emptiness, great bliss, what is called "emptiness endowed with the most sublime of manifestations" or "mahāmudrā." Recognizing that is referred to as "realizing mahāmudrā." Without any object of meditation whatsoever and without being distracted for even an instant, leave sharp awareness in its own place. Do not create any hopes or fears, neither hoping for the best nor fearing the worst. Be totally relaxed and sustain the very nature of ordinary mind. In that instant you will see mahāmudrā, unified bliss-emptiness, like the center of a clear, cloudless sky. [328]

Now śamatha and vipaśyanā are united, and your experiences and realizations are perfected. Since you have entered the path to liberation, you have accomplished your goal.

Emptiness is the nature of mind, clarity is its characteristic, and [their] unification is its essence. It is free from all extremes of elaborations, such as good and bad; arising, ceasing, and abiding; existence and nonexistence; and permanence and impermanence. It transcends speech or thought and is beyond identification. And yet there is something to be experienced: it is sharp, naked clarity, which is of the nature of bliss, clarity, and nonconceptuality. It is the embodiment of great wisdom, the dharmatā of the great self-arising [of all phenomena], the basic abiding state of all knowables, correct cognition, thusness, equality, great bliss, tathāgatagarbha, prajñāpāramitā, omniscience, the ultimate, and emptiness endowed with the most sublime of manifestations. Since all phenomena are realized to be mind, it is Cittamātra. Since it is free from any extreme or center, it is Great Madhyamaka. Since it is difficult for everyone to realize, it is Secret Mantra. Since it destroys all confusion, it is the Vajrayāna. Because it beholds the heart of the buddhas [buddha nature], it is called the dharmakāya.

In brief, now you have recognized [the pointing out of] mahāmudrā: great bliss, equality free from elaborations, nondual wisdom, what is free from the elaborations of dualistic perception. This hovers above those whose devotion has struck the vital point. It circles those who are insatiable in their supplications. It descends into those who have truly received blessings. Not hidden and not beyond direct perception, it is your innate quality, naked and unobscured. Now that you have recognized this [pointing out], you have arrived at ground mahāmudrā, seen the essence of path mahāmudrā, and determined resultant mahāmudrā. Sustain this with joy. You have now made your attainment of a human body meaningful. You have entered the path to liberation and brought saṃsāra to an end. This is excellent. It is important to rejoice and to cultivate this over a long period. [329]

Those are the pointing-out instructions based on looking at stillness and movement, which point out that appearances are mind, mind is empty, emptiness has spontaneous existence, and that what is spontaneously existent is self-liberating [as found in the texts on] mahāmudrā and *Pointing Out the Dharmakāya*.[1516] Maintain your practice of them continuously. You must take them to the end, making sure that they become part of your mindstream and are not just a patch of theoretical understanding.

That was the eighth session.

Those are the pointing-out instructions for the main practices of śamatha and vipaśyanā. First, there are the techniques for looking. Then, the pointing-out instructions are given collectively, one after the other, in accordance with the overall development [of experiences]. Alternatively, the pointing-out instructions can be given one by one in accordance with each [experience] that develops. Here, without utilizing many words, the ways to look are grouped together. The pointing-out instructions are also arranged altogether in a progressive manner that corresponds to the resolution of doubts and the signs [in meditation], like an alphabetized list or checklist. I wrote this in keeping with the timing and way [experiences and realizations typically] develop.

If the pointing-out instructions are given at the beginning, people can become complacent about them and turn into jaded dharma "experts." Since I fear that such persons will never develop anything in their mindstream, the pointing-out instructions should be given as they are laid out here to eliminate that [possibility].

That concludes the main practices.

3

Conclusion

One: Enhancement

During meditative equipoise, if your mindfulness becomes unfocused in not wandering, leave it for a bit. During postmeditative attainment, when you are distracted, you should alternate between meditative equipoise and sustaining nondistraction.

During your contemplations on death and impermanence, the mind thinking, "At death, body, speech, and mind die," should identify the nature of death and the mind at the time of death. [Seeing that death is] merely designated by the mind, you are freed from any notions of permanence or impermanence. By contemplating the deficiencies of saṃsāra in a similar way, you will know that saṃsāra and nirvāṇa are like nearby mountains and faraway mountains in a dream. [330]

When cultivating heartfelt love and compassion with the understanding that all sentient beings have been your parents and when cultivating bodhicitta—from aspiring and engaging up through [realizing its ultimate fruition]—recognize their natures and rest without contrivance. By remaining in the recognition that the essence of brilliant bodhicitta (the manifestation) is free from elaborations—with nothing to do—emptiness and compassion are inseparable.

During the generation process (which is the path of the vase abhiṣeka, one of the four abhiṣekas), visualize yourself as the yidam using any one of the four rituals for generation. When meditating that the environment and beings are deities and sounds are mantras, look at their clarity and their nature. Those being free from thought is the practice of unifying the generation and perfection processes. Meditate joining the generation process with mahāmudrā and luminosity. At all times—when you are walking, moving around, lying down, sitting, or talking—recognize the very nature [of whatever occurs] and mix it with mahāmudrā.

The one-pointed practice of the inseparable generation and perfection processes, or inseparable śamatha and vipaśyanā, is the excellent conduct. When that has been stabilized, to practice with awareness in dangerous isolated areas, keeping your view, meditation, and conduct concealed, is secret conduct. When you have stabilized that to the point where you are undistracted [in those circumstances], mix your practice with distractions by going where many people gather. Integrating that as your path is group conduct, which has three levels (greater, intermediate, and lesser), distinguished by degrees of stability or the lack of stability. The greater level does not have definite signs but, once the greater degree of the path of preparation has been achieved, if you practice with elaborations, adopt the attire of a heruka. Do not think that some things are to be eaten and others not, about cleanliness or filth, faults or virtues. Mix with intense situations and practice. Gradually, you will progress from the path of preparation to the attainment of the path of seeing. From your own perspective, since you are victorious over māras, mental afflictions, and the Hīnayāna, you are victorious in all directions. From the perspective of others, through your greater degree of group conduct, you are of immense benefit to sentient beings. Thus, conduct is developed by mahāmudrā itself. [The practice of] individuals of the highest abilities has no need of enhancement because it is free from an object of meditation and a meditator. For those not like that, there are many means of enhancement to be learned from the guru's oral instructions. [331]

Those are the ways to enhance [your experiences and realizations] by joining [mahāmudrā practice] with alternating between meditative equipoise and postmeditative attainment, with the paths of the common yānas, the Mantra system, and the four types of conduct. Practicing those with perseverance will bring enhancement.

That was the first session.

Two: Five Mistaken Ideas, Three Skills, and Three Kāyas

Eliminating Five Mistaken Ideas

To clear away hindrances, do as follows:

- Be free from any fixation to objects, be they virtuous objects, unvirtuous, and so forth.

- [Know that] the three times do not exist. Also give up the thought, "I will attain awakening at such and such a time." Be certain that awakening occurs in an instant.
- Do not regard your mind as something ordinary. Know that from the beginning its essence is that of the five wisdoms.
- Do not regard your skandhas, dhātus, and āyatanas as unclean. Have the certainty that from the outset they are gods and goddesses, male and female tathāgatas.
- Give up the desire to be liberated through just study and reflection. Resolve to be liberated through meditation and the gurus' blessings.

Those are the five mistaken ideas about objects, time, essence, nature, and prajñā to be eliminated.

Developing Three Skills

Sit properly in the physical posture. When [your mind] is still, look at its nature within that stillness and rest in equipoise. When it is active, look at its nature within that activeness and rest in equipoise. At the beginning, that is how to be skilled in initiating meditation.

Do not adhere to one type of samādhi or physical posture: they should be changed. Do not let yourself become exhausted. In the middle, be skilled in suspending [your meditation].

No matter what kind of good experiences arise, do not fixate on them. In the end, be skilled in sustaining experiences.

Recognizing the Three Kāyas

The myriad appearances of mind are the nirmāṇakāya. Its awareness is the saṃbhogakāya. Its emptiness is the svabhāvakāya. The inseparability [of those three aspects] is the dharmakāya. Be certain that all of saṃsāra and nirvāṇa, all apparent existence, is of the nature of those [four kāyas]. Determine that all phenomena have no arising, ceasing, or abiding, that they are free from the extremes of conceptual elaborations. Rest evenly without any hopes or fears, without rejecting or adopting anything.

That was the second session. [332]

Three: Three Strayings and Four Deviations

The Three Strayings

If you fixate on bliss, clarity, or nonconceptuality, you will stray into the three realms. Therefore, regardless of whether good or bad experiences arise, do not take [any of them] to be supreme.

The Four Deviations in Relation to Emptiness

You may think and meditate that the nature of all phenomena becomes emptiness through your ascertainment [of emptiness] based on the reasoning that they are neither one nor many. Or, having analyzed [phenomena], you may think about and meditate on nonexistence that is simply the negation of existence, saying, "This is the emptiness of everything." That is deviating from emptiness as the basic nature. Since it will cause you to have a crude [understanding] of actions and their results, give up that grasping at nonexistence and meditating on an intellectually constructed emptiness. Look at the nature of grasping at nonexistence, and do not fabricate.

Not realizing that objects to be abandoned and their remedies are both empty, when the many mental afflictions and negative thoughts arise in your mindstream, you may think, "These are stealing the life-force of liberation," and take them to be your enemies. Thinking, "They must be destroyed by emptiness," you take the two [mental afflictions and emptiness] to be objects to be abandoned and the remedy, and then meditate on emptiness. Meditating on emptiness in that way is to deviate from emptiness as the remedy.[1517] Recognize the very [nature of] those mental afflictions or the very [nature of] the thought that takes the objects to be abandoned and their remedies as separate, and rest without blocking or encouraging anything.

Not realizing that the ground, path, and result are all empty, you might think, "The best path for the attainment of buddhahood is emptiness. If I realize this, it is the supreme path. All other paths are inferior." In that way you ignore the aspect of method. That is deviating from emptiness as the path. Recognize the nature of the thought that fixates on emptiness, that takes [emptiness] to be sublime among paths. Looking in that way, you will see that everything is empty. Recognize emptiness, without [discriminating between] objects to be abandoned and remedies, or [something being] superior or inferior.

You might seal phenomena with an intellectually created emptiness or with a mantra whose [import] you have not experienced, and simply think, "Everything is empty." Or you may think, "Since everything is empty, nothing exists. What could conditioned virtuous actions possibly do?" With that, you deny karmic causes and results. That is deviating from emptiness as the seal. Look directly at the thought, "This is emptiness," and, recognizing it, remain in its own essence, which is nonconceptual. [333]

It is not that these intellectually created emptinesses are always inappropriate. If, as a beginner, you do not engage in intellectually created meditations, you will not be able to realize emptiness despite having been taught about it from the beginning. Once you become familiar with it, eventually the realization of emptiness will arise automatically. Therefore, it is fine to meditate on intellectually created emptiness [in the beginning]. However, in the end, it is a deviation from mahāmudrā and must be abandoned.

Those are the hindrances of the four deviations. Do not confuse what is to be abandoned with what is to be adopted. Without making assumptions, rest without contrivance right within whatever arises. Not wavering from that fresh state, do not adopt a rigid physical posture or retain your breath. Be relaxed. Do not prevent or promote, reject or adopt any thoughts, be they virtuous, nonvirtuous, or unspecified [neutral]. Let whatever arises unfold naturally without any grasping. Remain free.

That was the third session.

Four and Five: Five Difficult Passages and Three Hindrances[1518]

The Five Difficult Passages Where Enemies Manifest

Once thoughts and mental afflictions arise properly as meditation, there may be times when your thoughts are rough and numerous. If they become wild and your meditation cannot tame them, thoughts have arisen as enemies. You should recognize the essence of thoughts and the thoughts themselves. Rather than regarding them as problems, consider them to be useful. Make them your real meditation and their nature will manifest as the dharmakāya, free from elaborations. Practice that way.

Previously any mental afflictions that arose were purified by emptiness. There may come a time when mental afflictions, such as desire, arise uncontrollably. Mental afflictions have arisen as enemies. Recognize the essence of whatever mental affliction appears. By remaining in that without stopping or producing anything, [mental afflictions] will be purified on the spot without being abandoned. Their vivid manifestation will be self-purified right within bliss, clarity, nonconceptuality, or emptiness, as explained in the context of integrating thoughts into the path. Practice like that.

When you examine, analyze, and search for mind, nothing is found. [334] Seeing that all phenomena do not exist, you may dismiss [the relative validity of] what is to be abandoned, remedies, virtue, and evil, and emphasize experiences of emptiness. Everything—yourself and others—becomes empty and, not knowing what to do, you grasp at emptiness. That is emptiness arising as an enemy or glibness. If you recognize that grasping at emptiness and remain without blocking or encouraging anything, it will dissipate. Rest in that way.

While you know that appearances are dependently originated, you still might reify emptiness and feel constricted. Or you might fixate on and be fearful of whatever appearances you see, becoming deeply uneasy with [appearances]. Appearances have arisen as enemies. If you recognize appearances, your reification of them, and the essence of those, and also rest without blocking or establishing anything, this will clear up.

Through your meditation, you may develop faith, compassion, and so forth to a greater degree than other people. When those [qualities] are not purified as mahāmudrā, they can lapse into being very ordinary. You may feel compassion for others who do not have such virtues and think that now there is greater benefit in working for the welfare of others than there is in your [own practice of mahāmudrā]. Although you are not accomplished, you cast aside [the cultivation of] your own virtues and set about trying to benefit others. Compassion has arisen as an enemy. Recognize the mind that has such heartfelt compassion and rest without suppressing or promoting anything. In a state where that vivid compassion is clear in being of the nature of mahāmudrā, make vast aspiration prayers. That will banish this enemy and create the auspicious connections for benefiting others.

When you have not determined the view, you may decide, "I must train in the minor subjects, such as grammar and valid cognition, and then I will realize the primordial view," and put aside your meditation. Cause and result have arisen as an enemy. Apply yourself to both the view and meditation. By cultivating those without hope or fear, you will vanquish [this enemy]. Practice accordingly.

The Three Hindrances

There are also the hindrances of illnesses, demons, and to samādhi, and [the flaws of] dullness, agitation, or sluggishness. No matter what arises, examine its nature, color, shape, origin, abiding, and departure—without affirming or negating anything. [335] Be certain that nothing has inherent existence. Alternatively, you can practice taking and sending [to dispel illnesses or demons]. Or, without any hopes or fears whatsoever—such as being afraid that you will get sick or hoping for relief—take illnesses and demons to be the four kāyas and practice.

For dullness, agitation, and the like, [adjust] your focus or activities. If you are [experiencing] dullness, employ methods that agitate. If you are agitated, use methods that bring dullness. Or dispel them by looking at the essence of dullness or agitation and resting in that.

Although there are many ways to dispel hindrances, I have not written about them here for fear of being wordy. You should learn them from your guru's oral instructions.

Summary

Those of the highest abilities have no hindrances to remove because they realize everything to be the intrinsic state, free from elaborations. It is taught that all these difficult passages arise during the phase of one taste. They are also said to be signs that mahāmudrā practitioners have purified into emptiness the flare-ups of their latent tendencies of mental afflictions and thoughts, which had been "solidified" in their mindstreams. The Path and Result and other [traditions] teach that, generally speaking, during the perfection process with characteristics, [hindrances and difficult passages] arise due to the interdependence of the channels, winds, bindus, and mind gathering through the force of [practices corresponding to] the respective class of a particular mental affliction or thought.

There are many deviations, difficult passages, and hindrances of illnesses, demons, and to samādhi but probably most are included in just these. You should know the ways to dispel problems as explained.

Those are the processes for dispelling the three strayings, four deviations, five difficult passages, and three hindrances. You should recognize your problems and virtues, and exert yourself as needed. Do not mix up the objects to be adopted with those to be rejected.

That was the fifth session.

Six: Development of Virtues and Progression on the Path

Development of Virtues

The virtues of the preliminaries are that they enable you to achieve their specific benefits and that they support the development of subsequent [phases of] the path. Furthermore, meditating on the difficulty of acquiring the leisures and opportunities [of a precious human rebirth] and meditating on death and impermanence turn your mind away from this lifetime. By contemplating karma and its results, you gain confidence in its process and would risk your life to avoid [creating negative actions]. Through reflecting on the deficiencies of saṃsāra, you become weary with its three realms. Once you are determined to be released [from saṃsāra], your sole desire is to attain awakening. [336] By cultivating love, compassion, and bodhicitta, you develop the intention to only benefit sentient beings, with no desire for your own happiness.

When you exert yourself in the yoga of the one hundred syllables, signs that you have purified your negative actions appear in actuality and in your dreams, and experiences and realizations arise. Through [the practice of offering] maṇḍalas, you achieve physical wellbeing, mental lucidity, decreased desires, and limitless merit. By meditating on guru yoga, your devotion blazes from within, samādhi and blessings come, and experiences and realizations arise effortlessly. Whether the main practices develop or not depends on this [guru yoga].

In the main practices, the virtues of śamatha are as follows. When flawless experiences of bliss, clarity, and nonconceptuality develop, you have little craving for food and clothing, [your body] glows, your mind is supple, you achieve the five eyes, supercognitive abilities, and so forth, and your mental afflictions and thoughts are suppressed.

As for the virtues of vipaśyanā: Those of the highest abilities progress through the bhūmis and paths all at once. For those of intermediate abilities, they develop in a nonlinear way: sometimes all at once, sometimes sequentially. Those of the lowest abilities develop gradually, proceeding sequentially from the bhūmi of beginners to the tenth bhūmi.

Progression on the Path

Progression [on the paths and bhūmis] occurs in accordance with the way the twelve levels of the four yogas manifest.

During lesser one-pointedness, you may be able to rest as long [as you wish] in bliss, clarity, or nonconceptuality. Or, when resting in meditation, sometimes nothing happens even though you are meditating. At other times, even though you are not meditating, [meditation experiences] occur. You have not yet fully mastered samādhi. During intermediate one-pointedness, distractions do not disturb you and you rest solidly. When you meditate, [meditation experiences] occur. You have mastered samādhi.

During greater one-pointedness, [samādhi] is continuous and even intense situations do not distract you. All thoughts are pacified in that state. Sleep is also mixed with that state [of samādhi], and your conduct is not separate from it either. Since the flow of experiences is unbroken, you may have a realization that causes you to think, "Now this is greater nonmeditation." However, that is only an experiential realization, not actual realization. This is the period of [the paths of] accumulation and preparation. [337] Since you don't really recognize the nature of mind, śamatha experiences in which emptiness is grasped predominate.

Sustaining those experiences without fixation purifies them. All aspects of resting with bliss, clarity, or nonconceptuality are completely destroyed, and you see the truth of dharmatā. Once threefold emptiness—that of bliss, clarity, and nonconceptuality—is pacified in not being an object, the nature of awareness appears vividly, like something removed from its covering or a treasure discovered. This is the attainment of the path of seeing belonging to the Mahāyāna. It is called "freedom from elaborations."

At this point, you are not completely free from the entanglements of the grasping that fixates on emptiness. As soon as you see the nature of mind even slightly, that is lesser freedom from elaborations. When that [grasping at emptiness] is purified completely and you have correct realization, ordinary mind manifests clearly without being an object. That is intermediate freedom from elaborations. Once that [realization] becomes stable and your discomfort with appearances and comfort with thoughts are purified, you realize that everything is empty: there is not a single phenomenon that is not empty. You sever all misinterpretations about external and internal phenomena right within emptiness. This is greater freedom from elaborations.

During the postmeditative attainment of those [three levels], appearances manifest as illusions. You realize the nature of bodhicitta and relinquish the eighty-two objects to be abandoned on [the path of] seeing. You will not take birth in, or return to, saṃsāra (cyclic existence) except through the power of your aspiration prayers. This is the attainment of the first bhūmi, Joyful, and the path of seeing.

By sustaining that over time, you will rise up to one taste. At this point, your comfort with phenomena's lack of inherent existence, or nonexistence, and your slight discomfort with the unimpaired freshness of arising thoughts are both purified. The freshness of whatever arises—regardless of whether it is empty or not, free from elaborations or not—is sufficient. The essence of realizations about phenomena is one taste. To realize that all the qualities of the path, in their entirety, are complete in either appearances or emptiness is lesser one taste. Now, what was experienced on that [previous level] is blended with the quality of certainty, and both are purified. Matter is not put aside as something external, and awareness is not set apart as internal. [338] Everything—including appearances and mind, consciousnesses and wisdoms—blends as one in the purity of dharmatā. In brief, existence and peace are equal. Saṃsāra and nirvāṇa are fused inseparably. This is intermediate one taste. The many arise as one taste. From that, dependently originated appearances, the skillful means, radiate, and the one taste arises as many. This is greater one taste and is the attainment of patience in relation to unborn phenomena. It is the period from the second bhūmi to the seventh. Some explain that it includes the eighth.

At this point, although meditative equipoise and postmeditative attainment have blended, there is still the stain of grasping at emptiness during postmeditative attainment. Once that has been purified, there is not even the slightest difference between what is to be attained and the means of attainment, meditative equipoise and postmeditative attainment, distraction and nondistraction: all are pure within the dharmadhātu. The absence of all characteristics of an object of meditation and a meditator is lesser nonmeditation and the eighth bhūmi. At this point it is possible that during sleep there are occasionally slight stains related to grasping. When those are purified, there is the single state of wisdom's great equipoise. This is intermediate nonmeditation and the ninth and tenth bhūmis.

Next, the sword of prajñā-wisdom slashes the cognitive obscurations along with their dormant tendencies. Mother luminosity (the utterly pure dharmadhātu) and child luminosity (mirrorlike wisdom) blend. You manifest the awakening of a buddha, unification beyond training. This is greater nonmeditation, the bhūmi of a buddha. You have traversed the eighth, ninth, tenth, and eleventh bhūmis. You manifest the natural purity of the intrinsic, connate state: the dharmakāya. You actualize the natural purity of thoughts, the minds of sentient beings: the saṃbhogakāya. You demonstrate the natural purity of seeming appearances, objects influenced by conditions: the nirmāṇakāya. Through your three kāyas, or limitless kāyas, your inconceivable altruistic activity will effortlessly and nonconceptually spread throughout the reaches of space, bringing benefit to others for as long as saṃsāra is not emptied. That is the ultimate virtue. [339]

Therefore, if you exert yourself in the methods that generate the virtues of the preliminary practices up through nonmeditation, one after another, furthering those that have arisen so they do not lapse, all those virtues will arise. Accordingly, generate diligence and practice.

That was the sixth session.

Seven: Final Remarks

Ground, Path, and Resultant Mahāmudrā

In actuality, mind-itself is innately thusness or mahāmudrā—the only [distinction] is whether the twofold purity, primordially present, is realized or not. This innate quality is mahāmudrā at the time of the ground. Mind-itself, from when you start to cultivate the path up through the tenth bhūmi, is mahāmudrā at the time of the path. When you awaken from the sleep of ignorance and actualize the true nature, that is mahāmudrā at the time of the result.

View, Meditation, Conduct, and Result

To be free from percepts and perceivers and see the true abiding state is the view. To meditate on that nature without distraction is the meditation. To be free of doing things and things to do and to sustain that during any one of the four types of conduct is the conduct. To have no hopes or fears—no fears of falling to the lower states of saṃsāra or wishes to attain the elevated state of a buddha—and no sense of an object of meditation and a meditator is the result. Understand the meaning of the view, meditation, conduct, and result in that way, and arouse your diligence.

Advice

Have the devotion of total trust in your guru and the revulsion that is free from any attachment to saṃsāra and this life. Rely on undistracted mindfulness at all times. Be without needs and shorten your perspective. If the eight worldly values, thoughts of this life, or pretenses arise in your mind, crush them. Decisively cut your ties to this life. Until you have no sense of ownership about [or investment in] the development of your meditation, apply yourself to sustaining it continuously.

Experiences and Realizations

Although there are many differences between experiences and realizations, [simply put, their differences are as follows]. If there is a meditator, your mind, and meditation—bliss, clarity, nonconceptuality, or emptiness as objects of meditation or objects of experience—that is experience. If the meditator and the meditation not being two [separate things] is directly realized—and is not simply an assumption—that is realization. [340] Experiences and realizations must be distinguished. It is important to nurture [experiences or realizations] with constant effort within a state that neither fixates nor regards them as sublime.

Four Mudrās

Karmamudrā is a path for those of dull faculties and the means for achieving the siddhis of the desire realm. Samayamudrā and dharmamudrā are paths for those of intermediate faculties and methods for achieving the siddhis of the ultimate Akaniṣṭha.

Mahāmudrā is a path for those of sharp faculties and the method for achieving the supreme siddhi. It is the inseparability of appearances and emptiness, bliss and emptiness, awareness and emptiness, and clarity and emptiness—free from all conceptual elaborations. It cannot be shown by a guru, cannot be understood by a disciple, and cannot be communicated by words. It is beyond being something [about which we could say,] "It is this, not that." Being great bliss—which cannot be identified and yet is something experienced—it pervades all the phenomena of saṃsāra and nirvāṇa, all that can appear. This is the great transcendence of the intellect. Although mind, thoughts, and the dharmakāya abide together primordially, we did not realize that. Now the guru's instructions show us that they are inseparable, unified, blended as one. Those [instructions on] mahāmudrā are called "connate union."

The Lineage

These [mahāmudrā teachings] were transmitted from Vajradhara to Tilopa, Nāropa, Marpa, Milarepa, and Gampopa. What was transmitted from Gampopa to Gomtsul and others became the Zhang Kagyu Mahāmudrā and Barom Mahāmudrā. What was transmitted from Pakmo Drupa became the Drikung Kagyu Mahāmudrā, Taklung Kagyu Mahāmudrā, Chen-nga Kagyu,[1519] Mar[tsang and] Ye[lpa] Kagyu, Shukseb Kagyu, Tropu Kagyu, and Yabzang Kagyu. What was transmitted from Ling Repa, Tsangpa Gyare, and others became the Drukpa Kagyu. In particular, what was transmitted from Gampopa to Dusum Khyenpa and has continued uninterruptedly to my guru the omniscient Könchok Yenlak is the Karma Kamtsang Mahāmudrā, distinguished instructions from which the heat of blessings has not faded and the moisture of the ḍākinīs' breath has not evaporated. [341] Since these [instructions] combine the special transmissions of the many mahāmudrā [teachings] that have spread, they are called mahāmudrā, connate union. They are endowed with lineage, are the source of numerous virtues, and famous throughout Jambudvīpa, like the sun and moon. You can be assured that if you practice these [rigorously, like] pulverizing bones with a rock, experiences and realizations will arise spontaneously. Practice accordingly.

That was the seventh session.

Samdey Lama Rabjam Mrawa Samten Kunga persistently requested me, saying, "Please teach [mahāmudrā] by emphasizing the pointing-out instructions that pinpoint the practice, without using scriptural quotations and so forth." In response, although I have no experiences myself, [I] Mipam Chöwang, also [known as] Vajreśvara [Wangchuk Dorje], dutifully wrote this during my meditation sessions at Zhokha Or House in accordance with the teachings of the previous gurus.

Here, the sessions can be condensed to twenty, twenty-two, or twenty-five.

By this merit, may I and all sentient beings, who have been my mothers, wholeheartedly turn away from our attachments to pleasurable objects and see the nature of our mind.

ŚUBHAM ASTU SARVA-JAGATĀM[1520]

Abbreviations

BDRC	Buddhist Digital Resource Center. Formerly known as Tibetan Buddhist Resource Center. www.tbrc.org
Biography DK Delhi	Shākya Gelong Zangpo, *An Abbreviated Biography of Dakpo Tashi Namgyal*. In Phyag rgya chen po'i sgom rim gsal bar byed pa legs bshad zla ba'i 'od zer (Delhi: Drikung Kagyu Publications, 2004), iii–xxxiv. BDRC W29341.
Biography DK Lhasa	Shākya Gelong Zangpo, *An Abbreviated Biography of Dakpo Tashi Namgyal*. In the Drikung Kagyu Great Treasury of Dharma (Lhasa: n.a, 2004), vol. 76, 341–585. BDRC W00JW501203.
Biography DLG	Shākya Gelong Zangpo, *An Abbreviated Biography of Dakpo Tashi Namgyal*. A probable Daklha Gampo edition (date and publication information unknown). BDRC W00EGS1016800.
DDI	Wangchuk Dorje, Ninth Karmapa, *Dispelling the Darkness of Ignorance* (*Ma rig mun sel).*
DDI PP	Wangchuk Dorje, Ninth Karmapa, *Dispelling the Darkness of Ignorance*. Collection of Commentaries from Newly Printed Old Text at Palpung (dPal spungs dpe rnying gsar bskrun las khrid yig phyogs bsgrigs) (Upper Bhattu, India: dPal spungs gsung rab nyams gso khang, 2006), vol. 3, 375–420. BDRC W1KG4336.
DDI RD	Wangchuk Dorje, Ninth Karmapa, *Dispelling the Darkness of Ignorance.* Rigpe Dorje Practice Series. (Kalimpong: Rigpe Dorje Publications, 2010), vol. 10, 303–40.
D/Dg.T.	Derge Tengyur (sDe dge bstan 'gyur).
Dg.K.	Derge Kangyur (sDe dge bka' 'gyur).
DNZ	Jamgön Kongtrul Lodrö Taye, Treasury of Instructions (gDams ngag rin po che'i mdzod). 18 vols. Shechen printing. (Delhi: Shechen Publications, 1999).
GTCD	*Great Tibetan-Chinese Dictionary* (*Bod rgya tshig mdzod chen* mo). Edited by Zhang Yisun et al. 3 vols. (Beijing: Mi rigs dpe skrun khang, 1985).
H.K.	Lhasa Kangyur (Lha sa bka' 'gyur). Lha sa: Zhol bka' 'gyur par khang, 194–.
JIABS	*Journal of the International Association of Buddhist Studies.*
JIATS	*Journal of the International Association of Tibetan Studies.*

JIP	*Journal of Indian Philosophy.*
Great Treatise	Tsongkhapa, *Great Treatise on the Stages of the Path to Awakening* (*Lam rim chen mo / Byang chub lam rim che ba / sKyes bu gsum gyi nyams su blang ba'i rim pa thams cad tshang bar ston pa'i byang chub lam gyi rim pa*). (Delhi: Tibetan Cultural and Religious Publication Centre, 2004).
MB	Dakpo Tashi Namgyal, *Moonbeams of Mahāmudrā* (*Phyag chen zla ba'i 'od zer*).
MB DK	Dakpo Tashi Namgyal, *Moonbeams of Mahāmudrā.* (Delhi: Drikung Kagyu Publications, 2004). BDRC W29341.
MB DLG	Dakpo Tashi Namgyal, *Moonbeams of Mahāmudrā.* Reproduced Dvags lha sgam po blocks, from the library of rTogs ldan Rin po che of sGang sngon Monastery, Ladakh. (Bir, India: D. Tsondu Senghe, The Bir Tibetan Society, 1978). BDRC W4CZ15298.
MB PP	Dakpo Tashi Namgyal, *Moonbeams of Mahāmudrā.* (mDo khams sde dge: dPal spungs dgon pa, n.d.). BDRC W3CN631.
MB RD	Dakpo Tashi Namgyal, *Moonbeams of Mahāmudrā.* Rigpe Dorje Practice Series. (Kalimpong, India: Rigpe Dorje Publications, 2010), vol. 13.
MB TsRP	Dakpo Tashi Namgyal, *Moonbeams of Mahāmudrā.* rTsibs ri'i par ma (dKar rnying gi skyes chen du ma'i phyag rdzogs kyi gdams ngag gnad bsdus nyer mkho rin po che'i gter mdzod) (Darjeeling: Kargyu Sungrab Nyamso Khang, 1978–1985), vol. 3. BDRC W20749.
MB VVI	Dakpo Tashi Namgyal, *Moonbeams of Mahāmudrā.* (Varanasi: Vajra Vidya Institute Library, 2005).
NG RD	Wangchuk Dorje, *Ocean of Definitive Meaning.* Rigpe Dorje Practice Series. (Kalimpong: Rigpe Dorje Publications, 2010), vol. 2.
N.K.	Narthang Kangyur (sNar thang bka' 'gyur).
P.K.	Peking Kangyur (Pe cin bka' 'gyur).
Toh.	*A Complete Catalogue of the Tibetan Buddhist Canons.* Edited by Hakuju Ui et al. (Sendai, Japan: Tohoku University, 1934).
TOK	Jamgön Kongtrul Lodrö Taye, Treasury of Knowledge (*Shes bya mdzod / Shes bya mtha' yas pa'i rgya mtsho*). 3 vols. (Beijing: Mi rigs dpe skrun khang, 1982).
T. PD.	Tengyur Pedurma (bsTan 'gyur dpe bsdur ma).
TsRP	rTsib ri'i Par ma (dKar rnying gi skyes chen du ma'i phyag rdzogs kyi gdams ngag gnad bsdus nyer mkho rin po che'i gter mdzod rtsibs ri'i par ma). Edited by La dwags Khri dpon Padma chos rgyal. 30 volumes. (Darjeeling: Kargyu Sungrab Nyamso Khang, 1978–1985). BDRC W20749.

Notes

Many passages from canonical works cited in *Moonbeams* differ semantically from the recensions found in the Kangyur and Tengyur. Unless otherwise stated, the *Moonbeams* citation is used for the translation.

1. *Phyag chen zla ba'i 'od zer.* The full title is *Moonbeams of Eloquence: Clarifying the Way to Cultivate Mahāmudrā, the Definitive Meaning* (*Nges don phyag rgya chen po'i sgom rim gsal bar byed pa'i legs bshad zla ba'i 'od zer*).
2. *Ma rig mun sel.* The full title is *Mahāmudrā: Dispelling the Darkness of Ignorance* (Phyag *rgya chen po ma rig mun sel*).
3. Traleg Kyabgon, *Moonbeams of Mahamudra*, xv.
4. For an overview of Marpa Kagyu mahāmudrā, see Kongtrul, *Treasury of Knowledge: Esoteric Instructions*, 208–31. On Shangpa Kagyu mahāmudrā, see Harding, *Niguma: Lady of Illusion*, 143–52; and Kongtrul, *Treasury of Knowledge: Esoteric Instructions*, 245–46. On the Geluk mahāmudrā tradition, see R. Jackson, *dGe ldan-bKa' brgyud Tradition*; and Dalai Lama and Berzin, *The Gelug/Kagyü Tradition.* Other excellent overviews of mahāmudrā are found in R. Jackson, "Mahāmudrā in India and Tibet" and "Brief History of Mahāmudrā Studies."

   It should be noted that in the Tibetan translation of mahāmudrā, *phyag rgya chen po* (pronounced "chak-gya chenpo"), *phyag rgya* translates "mudrā" (seal) and *chen po* means "great," "mahā." As was often the case in their translations, the Tibetan translators added an extra word *phyag*, the honorific for "hand," to their translation of mudrā. Although Tibetan commentators sometimes explain "*phyag*" and "*rgya*" as conveying distinct meanings, a Sanskrit source corroborating this has yet to be found.

   This is a topic discussed by some Tibetan scholars. For example, in *Replies to the Questions of Tok-den Gyalpo* (*rTogs ldan rgyal po'i dris lan*), 407–8, Sakya Paṇḍita states that the famous quote attributed to the *Mahāmudrā-tilaka,* "'Mudrā' (*phyag*) is the wisdom of emptiness. 'Mudrā' (*rgya*) is free from the phenomena of saṃsāra" (*phyag ni stong pa'i ye shes yin/ rgya ni 'khor ba'i chos las grol*), is not found in the *Mahāmudrā-tilaka* and is something falsified by Tibetans. See this citation in *Moonbeams*, p. 115.
5. For translations of some of these songs, see Saraha's *Dohā for the King* (Thrangu, *A Song for the King*), *Dohā for the Queen* (R. Jackson, "Saraha's *Queen Dohās*"), *Dohā for the People* (R. Jackson, *Tantric Treasures*; and Schaeffer, *Dreaming the*

Great Brahmin), *Body Treasury*, *Speech Treasury*, and *Mind Treasury* (Braitstein, *Adamantine Songs*); Tilopa's *Ganges Mahāmudrā* (Brunnhölzl, *Straight from the Heart*; and Nyenpa, *Tilopa's Mahamudra Upadesha*); Nāropa's *Summary of the View* and *Summary Verses on Mahāmudrā* (Thrangu, *Songs of Nāropa*); and Maitrīpa's *Golden Garland of Mahāmudrā* (Mathes, *Fine Blend*). For translations of Maitrīpa's texts, see Mathes, *Fine Blend*; and for a translation of the life stories of the mahāsiddhas, see Dowman, *Masters of Mahāmudrā*.

6. See Glossary of Enumerations for lists of the texts included in each collection.
7. Phyag chen rgya gzhung. See Mathes "The Collection of 'Indian Mahāmudrā Works.'"
8. For a discussion of the life of Saraha, see Braitstein, *Adamantine Songs*; and Schaeffer, *Dreaming the Great Brahmin*.
9. For biographies of Maitrīpa, see Mathes, *Fine Blend*; Passavanti, "Life of Maitrīpā/Maitreyanātha"; and Tatz, "Life of the Siddha-Philosopher Maitrīgupta."
10. On the life of Tilopa, see Brunnhölzl, *Straight from the Heart*; and Torricelli, *Life of the Mahāsiddha Tilopa*.
11. For the life of Nāropa, see Guenther, *Life and Teaching of Nāropa*.
12. Marpa most likely was born circa 1011 and died in the 1090s. For Marpa's biography, see Nālandā Translation Committee, *Life of Marpa*. For the ten variant dates for Marpa's life found in Kagyu histories, see Roberts, *Mahāmudrā and Related Instructions*, 629n33.
13. See Roerich, *Blue Annals*, 843–44 and 855–61; and Roberts, *Mahāmudrā and Related Instructions*, 11–13.
14. On the life of Milarepa, see Quintman, *Life of Milarepa* and *Yogin and the Madman*; and Lhalungpa, *Life of Milarepa*.
15. On the life of Gampopa, see Kragh, *Tibetan Yoga and Mysticism*; and Sherpa, "Gampopa, the Monk and the Yogi."
16. See Roerich, *Blue Annals*, 460.
17. *Bodhipathapradīpa*, *Byang chub lam sgron*.
18. See Sørensen and Dolma, *Rare Texts from Tibet*, 46–50.
19. *Deb ther sngon po*, 547. See also Roerich, *Blue Annals*, 459–60.
20. *pha rol tu phyin pa'i lugs*. *Deb ther sngon po*, 846. See also Roerich, *Blue Annals*, 724.
21. *Replies to Dusum Khyenpa's Questions* (*Du gsum mkhyen pa'i zhus len*). Collected Works of Gampopa, text 10/tha, 23b–24a.
22. Sherpa, "Gampopa, the Monk and the Yogi," 132–33.
23. *Analysis of the Three Vows* (*sDom pa gsum gyi rab tu dbye ba'i bstan bcos*). See *Moonbeams*, pp. 141 and 128–30. For the full accounts of Sakya Paṇḍita's criticism of Kagyu mahāmudrā, see D. Jackson, *Enlightenment by a Single Means*, 162; and Rhoton, *Clear Differentiation*, 118–19. For a biography of Sakya Paṇḍita, see Stearns, *Luminous Lives*.
24. Many other Kagyu masters replied to Sakya Paṇḍita's criticisms, including Mikyö Dorje and Pema Karpo. See Higgins and Draszczyk, *Mahāmudrā and the Mid-*

dle Way, 327–31 and 364–65; and Draszczyk, "Some Dwags po Mahāmudrā Responses to Sa skya Paṇḍita."

25. For discussion of this famous debate, see Bretfeld, "The 'Great Debate' of bSam-yas"; D. Jackson, "Sa-skya Paṇḍita the 'Polemicist'"; Meinert, "Legend of *Cig car ba* Criticism"; Wangdu, Pasang, and Diemberger, *dBa' bzhed*; Ruegg, "Historiography and Doxography"; and van Schaik, "Great Perfection and the Chinese Monk."
26. *dBa'/sBa bzhed.* See Wangdu, Pasang, and Diemberger, *dBa' bzhed.*
27. In *Lamp for the Eyes of Meditative Concentration* (*bSam gtan mig sgron*), Nubchen Sangye Yeshe divides the Buddhist path into four stages: gradual (the Indian Buddhist path as laid out by Śāntarakṣita, Kamalaśīla, and others), instantaneous (Ch'an Buddhism), mahāyoga, and atiyoga. See Dalton and van Schaik, *Lighting the Lamp*; and Meinert, "Structural Analysis of the bSam gtan mig sgron."
28. See van Schaik, *Tibetan Zen*, 12–17.
29. *Analysis of the Three Vows* (*sDom pa gsum gyi rab tu dbye ba'i bstan bcos*). Sakya Collected Teachings, vol. 12a, 60.21–61.2. See *Moonbeams*, p. 130.
30. See *Moonbeams*, pp. 128–33.
31. *Replies to the Exalted Pakmo Drupa's Questions* (*rJe phag mo gru pa'i zhus len*). Collected Works of Gampopa, text 11/da, 11a.
32. See Roerich, *Blue Annals*, 724–25. Maitrīpa is said to have rediscovered the *Highest Continuum* (*Mahāyānottaratantraśāstra*, *Theg pa chen po rgyud bla ma'i bstan bcos*) and the *Differentiation of Phenomena and Their Nature* (*Dharmadharmatāvibhāga*, *Chos dang chos nyid rnam 'byed*) inside an old stūpa and to have received instructions on them from their author Maitreya. See also Brunnhölzl, *When the Clouds Part*, 82–84.
33. See Mathes, "Blending Sūtras with Tantras," 224–25. See also Mathes, "Can Sūtra Mahāmudrā be Justified" and *Fine Blend.*
34. *Analysis of the Three Vows*, 60.21–61.2. See *Moonbeams*, p. 130.
35. See Shakabpa, *Tibet*, 73–91; and van Schaik, *Tibet*, 112–24. It is said that Daklha Gampo was destroyed in 1718 during the Dzungar Mongol invasion of that period.
36. See Kragh, "Significant Leap"; and Schaeffer, *Culture of the Book.*
37. For details of Dakpo Tashi Namgyal's life and training, see the translation of *An Abbreviated Biography of Dakpo Tashi Namgyal*, pp. lxv–lxxviii.
38. See *An Abbreviated Biography of Dakpo Tashi Namgyal*, pp. lxix and lxx.
39. *Sunrays of Eloquence: An Explanation of the King of Tantras, The Glorious Hevajra* (*dPal kye'i rdo rje zhes bya ba'i rgyud kyi rgyal po'i 'grel pa legs bshad nyi ma'i 'od zer*).
40. *Jewel-Light Rays of Eloquence: A Summation of the General Points of Secret Mantra, Vajrayāna* (*gSang sngags rdo rje theg pa'i spyi don mdor bsdus pa legs bshad nor bu'i 'od zer*). For an English translation, see Roberts, *Mahāmudrā and Related Instructions*; and, for a French translation, see Charrier, *Lumière de diamant.*
41. *Clarifying the Suchness of the Innate State: A Major Instruction Manual on the*

Definitive Meaning, Mahāmudrā (*gNyug ma'i de nyid gsal ba / Nges don phyag rgya chen po'i khrid yig chen mo gnyug ma'i de nyid gsal ba*). For an English translation, see Schmidt, *Clarifying the Natural State.*

42. *Clarifying the Suchness of the Great Secret: A Major Instruction Manual on the Profound Path of the Six Dharmas* (*Zab lam chos drug gi khrid yig chen mo gsang chen gyi de nyid gsal ba*). For an English translation, see Chang, *Teachings of Tibetan Yoga.*
43. On the origins of this and its fallacy, see D. Jackson, "Which bKra shis rnam rgyal." For continuing evidence of this conflation, see the entry for Dwags po Bkra shis rnam rgyal in Buswell and Lopez, *Princeton Dictionary of Buddhism*, 277–78: "In his early years he studied with Sa skya teachers and was abbot of Na lan dra monastery."

    Also see the inside flap of the Vajra Vidya 2005 and Lhasa 2009 editions of *Moonbeams*, which misidentify the author of *Moonbeams* as being born in 1398, studying with twenty-five gurus, including Rongtön Sheja Kunrik, and dying in 1458—mistaking the *Moonbeams*' author for the Sakya Dakpo Paṇchen Tashi Namgyal, second abbot of Nālendra monastery. *Dvags po paṇ chen bkra shis rnam rgyal ni/ bod rang byung bdun pa'i sa stag ste spyi lo 1398 lor yab ston pa rab gsal dang/ yum gza' a mtsho gnyis kyi sras su sku 'khrung/ rong stong shes bya kun gzigs* [presumably should be *rong ston shes bya kun rig*] *sogs mkhas grub kyi bla ma nyer lnga bsten/. . . mthar rab byung brgyad pa'i sa stag ste spyi lo 1458 lor sku gshegs so.*
44. For a French translation of Tashi Namgyal's biography, see Charrier, *Lumière de diamant*, 309–26.
45. Dvags po bka' 'bum. Most of the works included in this collection are not authored by Gampopa but are records of his teachings written by his students. See Kragh, "Significant Leap" and *Tibetan Yoga and Mysticism*; and Sherpa, "Gampopa, the Monk and the Yogi."
46. *The Flag of Renown*: *The Biography of Gampopa* (*Chos kyi rje dpal ldan sgam po pa chen po'i rnam par thar pa yid bzhin gyi nor bu rin po che kun khyab snyan pa'i ba dan thar pa rin po che'i rgyan gyi mchog*). Collected Works of Gampopa, text 3/ga.
47. Phyag chen rgya gzhung.
48. 'Bri gung bka' brgyud chos mdzod chen mo. This collection was later expanded and it now contains four volumes of the Collected Works of Dakpo Tashi Namgyal.
49. *rGyud bla ma'i 'grel bshad de kho na nyid rab tu gsal ba'i me long.*
50. *Lam rim chen mo.* Hereafter abbreviated as *Great Treatise.*
51. For a discussion of stages of the path and stages of the doctrine texts, see D. Jackson, "*bsTan rim* ('Stages of the Doctrine')" and *Stages of the Buddha's Teachings*, 1–16.
52. These sections are called parts 1 and 2 in this translation and are then divided into chapters; neither type of division is found in the Tibetan original but are introduced into the English translation for ease of navigation. They follow, for the most part, similar divisions made in Lhalungpa, *Mahāmudrā*, and Traleg Kyabgon, *Moonbeams of Mahāmudrā.*

53. *bsTan bcos lung gi nyi 'od.* Collected Works of Gampopa, text 37/ji.
54. *Thar pa rin po che'i rgyan.* Collected Works of Gampopa, text 38/nyi.
55. The canonical citations that do not appear in either Gampopa's Collected Works or the *Great Treatise* are from over thirty different texts and, given the spelling variants and misattributions, it may be that they are from a single yet-unidentified source or from multiple sources that Dakpo Tashi Namgyal used as his "source" material for part 1.

    One small point that may help the future identification of a source is that there are five citations attributed to the first *Stages of Meditation* that are not found in that text but which are found in the middle *Stages of Meditation.* None of those citations are found in either Gampopa's Collected Works or the *Great Treatise,* whereas almost all the accurate attributions of citations to the first *Stages of Meditation* in *Moonbeams* are also found in the *Great Treatise.*
56. *Abhidharmasamuccaya, Chos mngon pa kun las btus pa.* Toh. 4049. D 4049: vol. 134, 48b.3. *Moonbeams,* pp. 25 and 309. For discussions of the definitions of the term and its uses in early Buddhism, see Anālayo, "Mindfulness in Early Buddhism"; Bodhi, "What Does Mindfulness Really Mean?"; R. Gethin, "On Some Definitions of Mindfulness"; and Harvey, "Mindfulness in Theravāda."
57. Dakpo Tashi Namgyal cites three sources for these nine states: *Ornament for the Mahāyāna Sūtras, Compendium of Abhidharma,* and *Śrāvakabhūmi.*
58. *Moonbeams,* p. 103.
59. gSang spyod kyi skor. Unidentified collection of instructions or texts associated with Maitrīpa's student Vajrapāṇi.
60. *Moonbeams,* p. 152.
61. *Moonbeams,* p. 177.
62. *Moonbeams* has two names for this section: "Objects of Meditation Without Characteristics" is used when the topic is first listed, and "Śamatha Without Characteristics" is used when the explanation is given. The translation has followed the latter in both instances. See n. 702.
63. *Moonbeams,* p. 244.
64. *Moonbeams,* p. 251.
65. *Moonbeams,* p. 253.
66. *Moonbeams,* p. 257.
67. *Uncommon Amṛta of Speech* (*Zhal gyi bdud rtsi thun mong ma yin pa*). Collected Works of Gampopa, text 19/dza, 18b. *Moonbeams,* p. 260.
68. *Moonbeams,* p. 269.
69. The term is not attested to in Sanskrit texts. See Kragh, *Tibetan Yoga and Mysticism,* 100, 288, 326–27, 333, 366–97, and 533–36; and Roberts, *Mahāmudrā and Related Instructions,* 153–168. The term could also be translated as "uniting with the connate."
70. *Moonbeams,* p. 282.
71. *Core of Mahāmudrā: The Instructions on the Ultimate Essence* (*mDo sngags kyi sgom don bsdus pa*). Collected Works of Gampopa, text 23/'a, 8a. *Moonbeams,* p. 291.

72. *Uncommon Amṛta of Speech.* Collected Works of Gampopa, text 19/dza, 7b. *Moonbeams*, p. 291.
73. Although *Moonbeams* cites this as being from the *Compendium of Dharma Sūtra*, it is not found there. It is found in the *Sūtra of the Teaching of Akṣayamati* (*Akṣayamatinirdeśasūtra, bLo gros mi zad pas bstan pa'i mdo*). Toh. 175, H.K. 176. See H.K. 176: vol. 60, 254a.2–4. *Moonbeams*, p. 308.
74. *Dharmasaṃgītisūtra, Chos yang dag par sdud pa'i mdo*. Toh. 238, H.K. 239. H 239: vol. 65, 70a.5–70b.2. The H.K. recension reads . . . *mi bskyod pa drang pa . . . gting dang 'gram mi rtogs pa* . . . ; the *Moonbeams* citation (MB VVI 355.6) reads . . . *mi bskyod pa dran pa . . . gting dang mtha' mi rtogs pa . . . Moonbeams*, p. 309.
75. *Moonbeams*, p. 316. For more discussion of nonattention, or lack of mental engagement, (*amanasikāra, yid la mi byed pa*), see Mathes, *Fine Blend* and "Maitrīpa's Amanasikārādhāra"; and Brunnhölzl, *When the Clouds Part*, 171.
76. *Consummate Sublime Path of Mahāmudrā Composed by the Unborn Zhang Rinpoche* (*sKye med zhang rin po ches mdzad pa'i phyag rgya chen po'i lam mchog mthar thug*). DNZ, vol. 8, 450.3–4, and TsRP, vol. 4, 89.4–90.1. The DNZ recension reads . . . *gsal stong ma 'gags sal le ba/ sing nge ye re 'dug pa de* . . . ; the *Moonbeams* citation (MB VVI 364.11–12) reads . . . *gsal stong ma 'gags mtha' dbus med/ sing nge ye re gnas pa de* . . . Note that the *Moonbeams* citation reads as does the TsRP. *Moonbeams*, p. 318.
77. *Moonbeams*, p. 330.
78. *Moonbeams*, p. 336.
79. *Moonbeams*, p. 373.
80. *Moonbeams*, p. 381.
81. *Moonbeams*, pp. 382–83.
82. *Moonbeams*, p. 392.
83. *Dohā for the Queen.* D 2264: vol. 52, 33b.1. *Moonbeams*, p. 393.
84. *Revealing the Hidden Characteristics of Mind* (*Sems kyi mtshan nyid gab pa mngon du phyung ba*). Collected Works of Gampopa, text 14/pha, 3b. *Moonbeams*, p. 395.
85. *Revealing the Hidden Characteristics of Mind*, 5b. *Moonbeams*, p. 396.
86. *Moonbeams*, p. 429.
87. See, for example, Pakmo Drupa's *Long Four Yogas* (*rNal 'byor bzhi chen mo*); Jikten Sumgön's *Longer Instructions on the Four Yogas* (*rNal 'byor bzhi'i zhal gdams chen mo*); Tsangpa Gyare's *Instructions on the Four Yogas Bestowed on Tuk-kyi Dorje* (*rNal 'byor bzhi'i zhal gdams thugs kyi rdo rje la gnang ba*); and Yang Gönpa's *Treasury of the Ultimate Essence: The Stages of the Four Yogas of Mahāmudrā* (*Phyag rgya chen po rnal 'byor bzhi'i rim pa snying po don gyi gter mdzod*).
88. *Moonbeams*, p. 483.
89. The full title is the *Unsurpassable Complete Path: Commentary on the Main Practice of Connate Mahāmudrā* (*Phyag rgya chen po lhan cig skyes sbyor gyi dngos gzhi'i khrid yig zab don rgya mtsho'i lam tshang bla na med pa*). English translation by Gerardo Abboud, titled *The Royal Seal of Mahamudra Volume One: A Guidebook for the Realization of Coemergence.*

90. *Earrings of the Accomplishments [of] the Practice Lineage: A Summary Catalog and Index [Showing] How the Three Volumes of Indian Mahāmudrā Texts on the Abiding State Were Arranged as a Literary Source* (*gNas lugs phyag rgya chen po'i rgya gzhung glegs bam gsum yi ge'i 'byung gnas su ji ltar bkod pa'i dkar chag bzhugs byang mdor bsdus pa sgrub brgyud grub pa'i rna rgyan*). See Mathes, "Collection of 'Indian Mahāmudrā Works,'" 97–106.
91. See Kongtrul, *Treasury of Knowledge: Foundations of Study and Practice*, 221–57.
92. *Lion's Roar That Destroys the Deviations of Renunciants Meditating on the Seminal Heart* (*sNying tig sgom pa'i bya bral gyi go shor tshar gcod seng ge'i ngar ro*); and *rGyab brten padma dkar po*. See van Schaik, *Approaching the Great Perfection*, 86, 88, and 105–107.
93. See Thrangu Rinpoche, *Essentials of Mahamudra, Moonbeams of Mahamudra, Moonlight of Mahamudra: Volume III,* and *Moonlight of Mahamudra: Volume IV*; and Traleg Kyabgon, *Moonbeams of Mahamudra.*
94. See R. Jackson, "The Indian Mahāmudrā 'Canon(s)'"; and D. Jackson, *Enlightenment by a Single Means.*
95. *Nges don rgya mtsho / Lhan cig skyes sbyor gyi zab khrid nges don rgya mtsho'i snying po phrin las 'od 'phro.*
96. *Chos sku mdzub tshugs / Phyag rgya chen po lhan cig skyes sbyor gyi khrid zin bris snying po gsal ba'i sgron me bdud rtsi'i nying khu chos sku mdzub tshugs su ngo sprod pa.*
97. *Feast for the Fortunate: An Easy Way into the "Chariot of the Dakpo Siddhas," A Commentary on the "Entrance [to the Middle Way]"* (*'Jug ṭikā dvags brgyud grub pa'i shing rta bde bar 'dren byed skal bzang dga' ston*). For an English translation, see Dewar, *Karmapa's Middle Way.*
98. *Youthful Play: An Explanation of the "Treasury of Abhidharma"* (*mNgon par mdzod kyi rnam bshad gzhon nu rnam rol / Chos mngon pa mdzod kyi rnam par bshad pa chos mngon rgya mtsho'i snying po mkhyen rtse'i zhal lung gzhon nu rnam rol legs bshad chos mig rnam 'byed grub bde'i shing rta zhes bya ba bzhugs so*). For an English translation, see Choephel, *Jewels from the Treasury.*
99. See Callahan, *Ocean of the Definitive Meaning*, 85; and Thrangu Rinpoche, *Essentials of Mahamudra*, 26.
100. Available from http://dharmacloud.tsadra.org.
101. Available from http://dharmacloud.tsadra.org.
102. http://dharmadownload.net/pages/english/Texts/texts_0127.htm.
103. http://dharmadownload.net/karmapa/09_Karmapa/9th%20Karmapa%20pages/06_9th_karmapa_text_MarigMunsel.htm.
104. *Gangs can 'dir ston pa'i rgyal tshab dpal sgam po pa'i khri gdung dzin pa'i dam pa rnams kyi gtam Bai durya'i phreng ba.* There are two editions of this text found on BDRC: a probable Daklha Gampo edition (date and publication information unknown) (BDRC W00EGS1016800); and an edition in the Drikung Kagyu Great Treasury of Dharma, vol. 76: 341–585 (Lhasa 2004) (BDRC W00JW501203). The former is hereafter referred to as "Biography DLG." The

latter is also reprinted in Sørensen and Dolma, *Rare Texts from Tibet*, 191–247, and hereafter cited as "Biography DK Lhasa."

Dakpo Tashi Namgyal's biography, extracted from the *Garland of Vaiḍūrya*, is also printed with *Phyag rgya chen po'i sgom rim gsal bar byed pa legs bshad zla ba'i 'od zer*, iii–xxxiv (Delhi: Drikung Kagyu Publications, 2004) (BDRC W29341); and with *dPal kye rdo rje zhes bya ba'i rgyud kyi rgyal po'i 'grel pa legs bshad nyi ma'i 'od zer*, iii–xxxiv (Delhi: Drikung Kagyu Publications, 2004) (BDRC W29342). These editions are based on the probable Daklha Gampo edition and are hereafter cited as "Biography DK Delhi." These two editions are the only ones containing the title *mNyam med sgam po pa chen po'i rnam rol khams gsum chos kyi rgyal po dvags po bkra shis rnam par rgyal ba'i rnam thar mdor bsdus*, and they include the introduction of Western dates, which are found in the translation in parentheses.

105. Two page numbers occurring together divided by a slash (e.g., 36/37) means that one of the pages in the Tibetan text is blank.
106. http://dharmadownload.net/pages/english/Sungbum/002_Dhakpo%20Kabum/Dhakpo%20Kabum.htm.
107. See Kragh, *Tibetan Yoga and Mysticism*, 195.
108. 1562–1593. See Gyamtso, *Hundred Tertöns*, 169–72.
109. *Dam tshig gi bka' rgya*. Text not found.
110. For biographical information on Rigdzin Gödem (1337–1409), see Dudjom, *Nyingma School of Tibetan Buddhism*, 780–83; and on Sangye Lingpa (1340–1396) and Zhigpo Lingpa (1524–1583), see Gyamtso, *Hundred Tertöns*, 153–58 and 167–69.
111. Sho mo yar shog gi mgur. This song appears in the *Ocean of Kagyu Songs / Rain of Wisdom* (*bKa' brgyud mgur mtsho*), in the chapter, "The Three Men of Kham," although this prophecy is not contained in that account. See Nalanda Translation Committee, *Rain of Wisdom*, 277–80.

    The three men of Kham (*khams pa mi gsum*) are Dusum Khyenpa, the first Karmapa, also known as U-se; Pakmo Drupa, also known as Khampa Dor-gyal; and Sal-tong Shogom, "the guru who originated the Traleg Khyapgön tülku line" (Nalanda Translation Committee, *Rain of Wisdom*, 333).
112. Biography DK Delhi (2a.3): *mnga' bdag* should be *sde bdag*. See Biography DLG (29a.5) and Biography DK Lhasa (74a.6).
113. *sTag seng kha sprod kyi gdams pa*.
114. *gCod yul stan thog gcig*.
115. In this context, lay precepts or *poṣadha* (*gso sbyong*, "purification-renewal") refers to eight vows, which include celibacy, taken for one day. See Kongtrul, *Treasury of Knowledge: Buddhist Ethics*, 100–1. In other contexts, *poṣadha* is the monastic confession ceremony. See Kongtrul, *Treasury of Knowledge: Buddhist Ethics*, 131–33.
116. dPal sdong. dPal sdong seems to be an alternate spelling for dPal gdong. Śrīmukha is the name for the seventh year (Water Bird) in the sixty-year cycle.
117. The *Garland of Vaiḍūrya* states in the biography of the sixteenth throne-holder,

Gampo Chöje Sönam Lhundrup (1488–1552), that his older brother was Dedak Chenmo Chögyal Wangpo. See Biography DLG (45b.7); and Sørensen and Dolma, *Rare Texts from Tibet*, 223 and 225.

118. *Mañjuśrī-nāmasaṁgīti*, *'Jam dpal mtshan brjod.*
119. *dad pa'i sa*, *śraddha bhūmi.*
120. *smyung bar gnas pa.* A two-day fasting ritual of the Eleven-Faced Avalokiteśvara.
121. *rgyu mtshan rtsis.* The reference is unclear.
122. *Thar pa rin po che'i rgyan.*
123. *Bodhicaryāvatāra*, *Byang chub sems dpa'i spyod pa la 'jug pa.*
124. *Zab mo nang don.*
125. sNyug la legs bshad gling. The monastery founded by Karma Tinle (1456–1539). Alternative names are Nyukla Lekshe Ling (sMyug la legs bshad gling) and Rinchen Riwo Lek-she Ling (Rin chen ri bo legs bshad gling).
126. *bsdus pa brtsis pa.* This is a tentative translation.
127. *Phar phyin lung chen don mthun.* This is Smṛtijñānakīrti's *Teaching on the Eight Clear Realizations as the Concordant Topics of the [Prajñāpāramitā Sūtras in] 100,000, 25,000, and 18,000 [Lines]* (*Prajñāpāramitāmātṛkā-śatasāhasrikābṛhacchāsanapañcaviṃśatisāhasrikāmadhyaśāsanāṣṭādaśasāhasrikālaghuśāsanāṣṭasamānārthaśāsana*, *'Bum dang nyi khri lnga stong pa dang khri brgyad stong pa gsum don mthun par mngon rtogs brgyad du bstan pa*).
128. *mNgon pa mdzod kyi gzhung ṭīkā dang bcas.*
129. *gSum brgya pa* by Vinītadeva; *Kā ri kā lnga bcu'i gzhung dang 'bru ṭīkā* by Kamalaśīla.
130. *gsan yig.*
131. Tana (rTa rna) monastery, founded in 1068 by Yelpa Yeshe Tsekpa, belongs to the Yelpa Kagyu.
132. *kāvya*, *snyan ngag.*
133. gSang sngags rgyud 'bum.
134. *Phyag chen lhan cig skyes sbyor* by Rangjung Dorje. For an English translation, see Roberts, *Mahāmudrā and Related Instructions*, 153–73.
135. *Chos drug gser zhun ma* by Rangjung Dorje.
136. *rLung sems gnyis med kyi khrid.* The root text, *Nondual Wind-Mind* (*rLung sems gnyis med*), is by the Third Karmapa, Rangjung Dorje.
137. *rDo rje phreng ba.*
138. *Mi tra brgya rtsa.* A compilation of one hundred Secret Mantra texts by Mitrayogin. See Roerich, *Blue Annals*, 1030–39; and Willis, *Enlightened Beings*, 211n419.
139. Chos bzhi rtsa 'grel.
140. bKa' gdams glegs bam.
141. *Gab pa mngon phyung / Sems kyi mtshan nyid gab pa mngon du phyung ba.* Collected Works of Gampopa, text 14/pha. Tashi Namgyal cites this text as one of the sources for instructions on breakthroughs in *Moonbeams*. See chapter 13, p. 382.
142. Sa ga zla ba. The name of the fourth lunar month of the Tibetan calendar, an espe-

cially holy month because it is said that the Buddha was born, attained awakening, and passed away (parinirvāṇa) on its fifteenth day (the full moon).

143. *bsnyen rdzogs.*
144. *yantra, 'phrul 'khor.* Yogic exercises, in this case the ones associated with caṇḍālī yoga (*gtum mo'i rnal 'byor*).
145. *sku 'bum.* Also referred to as *gdung 'bum.* See *Great Treasure for the Faithful: Description of the Wonders of Daklha Gampo* (*Dvags lha sgam po'i ngo mtshar gyi bkod pa dad pa'i gter chen*). Drikung Kagyu Great Treasury of Dharma, vol. 75: 440.4.
146. Biography DK Delhi (8b.4): *de rnams kyi* should be *de rnams kyis.* See Biography DLG (52a.6).
147. Gomde Nang is the Barom Kagyu monastery of Potrang Nangso Chenmo (Pho brang nang so chen mo). Its two branches (*ya gnyis*) are Nangchen Tsang (Nang chen tsang) and Tsang-sar Tsang (Tsang sar tsang). Oral communication from Lama Tashi Topgyal, a Barom Kagyu lama.
148. Las stod. Biography DK Delhi (9b.3): *la stod* should be *las stod.* See Biography DLG (52b.5); and Biography Lhasa (79b.1).
149. Sönam Gyatso (1475–1511) was the fifteenth throne-holder and Sönam Lhundrup's older brother.
150. 'Dzam gling dpal 'bar.
151. Biography DK Delhi (11a.2): *ri zhol skya ser* should be *ri zhol gyi skya ser.* See Biography DLG (53b.7); and Biography DK Lhasa (80a.6).
152. Biography DK Delhi (11a.3): *sgrig srol gyi* should be *sgrig srol gyis.* See Biography DLG (53b.7); and Biography DK Lhasa (80b.1).
153. gSang sngags pho brang.
154. gTso 'khor gsum pa.
155. *tshe dbang brgya rtsa.*
156. The two Drikung Khang-tok (Khang thog) are Tel (Thel) and Yangri (Yang ri). Oral communication from Khenchen Nyima Gyaltsen. Tel is an alternative spelling for Til (mThil), one of the main Drikung monasteries and founded by Jikten Sumgön. The Yangri hermitage was expanded into a monastery by Rinchen Puntsok (1509–1576), the seventeenth Drikung throne-holder. See Gruber, *From the Heart of Tibet*, 190–91.
157. Tsewa (rTse ba) is probably Drikung Tse, established as a monastery by Rinchen Puntsok.
158. Tup-wang Tenzin had commissioned a statue of Gomtsul in honor of their uncle Sönam Lhundrup's passing in 1552. See the *Garland of Vaiḍūrya*, Drikung Kagyu Great Treasury of Dharma, vol. 76, 73b4–5 and 86a4.
159. bLa ma lha khang.
160. rJe nyid kyi 'dra sku phyag nas ma. This is probably the statue that Dakpo Tashi Namgyal had made of his own likeness and the one referred to in the *Great Treasure for the Faithful.* See Drikung Kagyu Great Treasury of Dharma, vol. 75: 449.4: *rje bkra shis rnam rgyal gyi 'dra sku phyag nas ma.* Its name also indicates

that it was blessed by Dakpo Tashi Namgyal (oral communication from Ringu Tulku).

161. *thub pa gnas bcu.* The *GTCD* says *thub pa gnas bcus bskor/ dgra bcom pa bcu drug gis skor ba'i sangs rgyas shākya thub pa'i sku brnyan.*

162. *gdan rabs.*

163. *gdung 'bum.*

164. mThong ba don ldan.

165. These are probably *Clarifying the Suchness of the Innate State: A Major Instruction Manual on the Definitive Meaning, Mahāmudrā* (*Nges don phyag rgya chen po'i khrid yig chen mo gnyug ma'i de nyid gsal ba*) and *Clarifying the Suchness of the Great Secret: A Major Instruction Manual on the Profound Path of the Six Dharmas* (*Zab lam chos drug gi khrid yig chen mo gsang chen gyi de nyid gsal ba*). See Schmidt, *Clarifying the Natural State*, and Chang, *Teachings of Tibetan Yoga*, respectively.

166. There are four volumes of the Collected Works of Dakpo Tashi Namgyal in the Drikung Kagyu Great Treasury of Dharma, vols. 71–75 (du, nu, pu, phu, bu), printed in Lhasa, 2004 (BDRC W00JW501203); and a three-volume Collected Works of Dakpo Tashi Namgyal printed at Palpung (BDRC W3CN631).

167. Thigs khang chen mo.

168. ltung bshags.

169. *rgyal.* Puṣya is the name of one of the lunar mansions.

170. Khri rin po che bKra shis kun grags (1571/72–1599), Dakpo Tashi Namgyal's nephew and his successor as throne-holder.

171. *Mos gus kyi dpal ster*; text not identified. This is the end of Dakpo Tashi Namgyal's Biography in the *Garland of Vaiḍūrya.* What follows is only found in Biography DK Delhi.

172. *MB* VVI (21.10): *snyams* should be *snyoms.* See *MB* DLG (2.5) and *MB* TsRP (3.3).

173. Bracketed text from the table of contents in *MB* VVI (1.2).

174. *Daśabhūmikasūtra, Sa bcu pa'i mdo.* Toh. 44, H.K. 9. (Chapter 31 of the *Avataṃsaka Sūtra.*) H.K. 94: vol. 43/03, 145b.4. The H.K. recension reads . . . *'di ltar khams gsum pa 'di ni sems tsam ste*; the *Moonbeams* citation (*MB* VVI 24.11–12) reads *kye rgyal ba'i sras dag/ khams gsum po 'di dag ni sems tsam mo.* The *Moonbeams* citation is identical to one found in Gampopa's *Sunrays of Scriptural Citations* (*bsTan bcos lung gi nyi 'od*). Collected Works of Gampopa, text 37/ji, 9b.

175. *Vajrapañjarā / Ārya-ḍākinī-vajrapañjarā-mahātantrarāja-kalpa-nāma, rDo rje gur / 'Phags pa mkha' 'gro ma rdo rje gur zhes bya ba'i rgyud kyi rgyal po chen po'i brtag pa.* Toh. 419, H.K. 379. H.K. 379: vol. 79, 400a.5. The H.K. recension reads . . . *sangs rgyas med cing gang zag med*; the *Moonbeams* citation (*MB* VVI 24.14–15) reads . . . *sems can med cing sangs rgyas med.* The *Moonbeams* citation is identical to one found in Gampopa's *Sunrays of Scriptural Citations*, 9b.

176. *Sampuṭa-nāma-mahātantra, Yang dag par sbyor ba zhes bya ba'i rgyud.* Toh. 381, H.K. 396. H.K. 396: vol. 81, 390a.2. Also cited in Collected Works of Gampopa.

177. *Treasury of Dohā: Instructions on Mahāmudrā* (*Dohakoṣa-nāma-mahāmudro-padeśa, Do ha mdzod ces bya ba phyag rgya chen po'i man ngag*). Toh. 2273. D 2273: vol. 52, 122a.6–7. Note that the author is cited here as Ri khrod dbang phyug (Lord of Hermits), and later always as Sha wa ra, ("The Śavara [Saraha]"). Although there is some uncertainty as to whether this text was authored by Saraha or Śavaripa, the Dg.T. colophon says it was spoken by the Great Hermit (Ri khrod pa chen po), Saraha.

178. *Laṅkāvatārasūtra, Lang kar gshegs pa'i mdo*. Toh. 107, H.K. 110. The first two lines are H.K. 110: vol. 51, 264b.3. The third and fourth lines are probably H.K. 110: vol. 51, 264b.1–2, where the H.K. recension reads *phyi rol don mthong log pa ste/ don med sems ni 'ba' zhig go*. The *Moonbeams* citation (*MB* VVI 25.14–15) reverses these two lines and reads *don yod ma yin sems nyid de/ phyi rol don mthong log pa yin*. The *Moonbeams* citation is identical to the one found in Gampopa's *Sunrays of Scriptural Citations*, 9a.

179. Citation not located in this text or the Kangyur. The verse is found in Bhavapa's *Ritual for the Great Uniting with the Great Chief of Yakṣas, Blue-Clad Vajrapāṇi* (*Mahāyakṣasenāpatinīlāmbāradharavajrapāṇimahāgaṇavidhi, gNod sbyin gyi sde dpon chen po lag na rdo rje gos sngon po can gyi sbyor ka chen po'i cho ga*) (Toh. 2174; D 2174: vol. 50, 26b.1–2); and Śrīghoṣa's *Lamp Eliminating the Darkness of Extremes* (*mTha'i mun sel sgron pa*) (Toh. 4448; D 4448: vol. 212, 384b.1). The first two lines are found in Gampopa's *A Major Collection of Dharma Lectures* (*Tshogs chos chen po*). Collected Works of Gampopa, text 8/nya, 41a.

180. *Dohā for the King* (*rGyal po do ha*). Also known as *Treasury of Dohā: Songs on Conduct* (*Dohakoṣa-nāma-caryāgīti, Do ha mdzod ces bya ba spyod pa'i glu*). Toh. 2263. D 2263: vol. 52, 27b.4.

181. *Hevajra-tantra-rāja-nāma, dPal brtag pa gnyis pa / Kye'i rdo rje zhes bya ba rgyud kyi rgyal po* (Part I) and *Kye'i rdo rje mkha' 'gro ma dra ba'i sdom pa'i rgyud kyi rgyal po* (Part II). Toh. 417 and 418, H.K. 378a and 378b. H.K. 378b: vol. 79, 364b.2–3. Also cited in Collected Works of Gampopa.

182. H.K. 396: vol. 81, 374b.7–375a.2.

183. *Praises of the Dharmadhātu*. (*Dharmadhātustava, Chos dbyings bstod pa*). Toh. 1118. D 1118: vol. 1, 63b.6.

184. H.K. 110: vol. 51, 207a.5 and 185b.3–185b.4. The H.K. recension reads *me long la ni ji ltar gzugs/ snang yang yod pa ma yin ltar/ bag chags dag gis me long la/ byis pas sems ni rnam gnyis mthong/ sems kyi snang ba mi shes pas/ rnam par rtog pa rnam gnyis skye/* and *rnam par rtog pa'i bag chags 'brel/ sems las byung ba sna tshogs pa/ mi la phyi rol snang ba ni/ 'jig rten pa yi sems tsam mo/ phyi rol gyi ni snang ba med/ lus dang longs spyod gnas lta bu/ sems ni sna tshogs par snang ba/ sems tsam du ni ngas bshad do*.

The *Moonbeams* citation (*MB* VVI 27.10–15) reads *me long la ni gzugs snang yang/ yod pa min par snang ba ltar/ sems kyi snang bar ma shes par/ rnam par rtog pa gnyis su skye/ rnam rtog bag chags 'brel ba yis/ sna tshogs sems las byung ba yi/ mi rnams la ni phyi rol snang/ 'jig rten pa yi sems tsam mo/ phyi rol snang ba yongs *med de/ sems ni sna tshogs rnams su shar/ lus la longs spyod gnas 'dra ba/ sems tsam du ni ngas bshad do.*

The *Moonbeams* citation is identical to one found in Gampopa's *Sunrays of Scriptural Citations*, 9a.

185. *Avataṃsakasūtra, Phal po che / Phal po che'i mdo / Sangs rgyas phal chen / Sangs rgyas phal po che zhes bya ba shin tu rgyas pa chen po'i mdo.* Toh. 44, H.K. 94. H.K. 94: vol. 42, 69b.2–3. The H.K. recension reads . . . *sems ni phung po byed pa ste/ . . . ji snyed pa'i/ 'jig rten 'di dag sems kyis bris*; the *Moonbeams* citation (*MB* VVI 27.17–18) reads . . . *sems kyi phung pos byas pa ste/ . . . ji snyed pa/ de snyed thams cad sems kyis bris.* The *Moonbeams* citation is almost identical to one found in Gampopa's *Sunrays of Scriptural Citations*, 9a–b, which reads . . . *sems kyis phung po byas pa ste/ . . .* The translation follows the H.K. recension and Gampopa's citation.

186. *Ratnameghasūtra, dKon mchog sprin gyi mdo.* Toh. 231, H.K. 232. H.K. 232: vol. 64, 129b.5–6. The H.K. recension reads *'jig rten sems kyis bris pa ste/ sems ni sems kyis mi mthong ngo/ dge ba'am yang ni mi dge ba'i/ las ni sems kyis bsags pa'o/ sems ni 'gal me lta bur 'khor/ sems ni rta ltar 'khyams pa yin/ sems ni nags kyi me ltar tshig . . .*; the *Moonbeams* citation (*MB* VVI 28.2–5) reads *'jig rten sems kyis khris pa ste/ sems kyis sems ni mi mthong ngo/ dge ba'am ni mi dge ba'i/ las ni sems kyis bsags pa yin/ sems ni 'gal me bzhin du 'khor/ sems ni rlabs dang 'dra bar g.yo / sems ni nags kyi me bzhin bsreg . . .* The *Moonbeams* citation is identical to one found in Gampopa's *Sunrays of Scriptural Citations*, 2b.

187. H.K. 379: vol. 79, 418a.5–6. The H.K. recension reads *thog med srid pa'i bag chags kyis/ phyi rol don ni rnam par brtags/ sems kyis thams cad rnam par brtags/ sems ni kun tu 'gro bar brjod*; the *Moonbeams* citation (*MB* VVI 28.7–8) reads *thog ma med pa'i srid gyur nas/ phyi rol don du brtags pa ste/ thams cad sems kyi rnam 'phrul zhing/ sems nyi kun tu song ba'o.* The *Moonbeams* citation is identical to one found in Gampopa's *Sunrays of Scriptural Citations*, 3b.

188. H.K. 379: vol. 79, 418a.3. The H.K. recension reads . . . *gzugs sogs so sor 'dod pa yi/ sems nyid du ni 'dod par bya*; the *Moonbeams* citation (*MB* VVI 28.9–10) reads . . . *gzugs sogs so sor snang ba rnams/ sems 'di kho na snang ba yin.* The *Moonbeams* citation is identical to one found in Gampopa's *Sunrays of Scriptural Citations*, 9b.

189. *sDong po bkod pa.* Toh. 44, H.K. 94. Although *Moonbeams*, probably following Gampopa's *Sunrays of Scriptural Citations* (5a), states that this citation is from the *Gaṇḍavyūha*, which is chapter 45 of the *Avataṃsaka Sūtra*, it is not found there, but it is found in chapter 15 of the *Avataṃsaka Sūtra*. H.K. 94: vol. 41, 303b.5–304a.6.

190. *MB* VVI (29.17): *yongs* should be *yengs*. See *MB* DLG (8.4) and *MB* TsRP (14.3).

191. *Mañjuśrīvikrīḍitasūtra, 'Jam dpal rnam par rol pa'i mdo.* Toh. 96, H.K. 97. Citation not found in this text. It is found (attributed to the *Play [of Mañjuśrī] Sūtra*) in Gampopa's *Sunrays of Scriptural Citations*, 5b–6a.

192. *Bodhicaryāvatāra, byang chub sems dpa'i spyod pa la 'jug pa.* Toh. 3871. D 3871: vol. 105, 23a.7. Also cited in Collected Works of Gampopa.

193. D 3871: vol. 105, 10b.7. The Dg.T. recension reads . . . *gang gis chos . . .* ; the

Moonbeams citation (30.6) reads . . . *gang gi* . . . Also cited in Collected Works of Gampopa.

194. *Suhṛllekha, bShes pa'i spring yig.* Toh. 4496. D 4182: vol. 173, 45b.4. Also cited in Collected Works of Gampopa.

195. *Abhidharmakośakārikā, Chos mngon pa'i mdzod kyi tshig le'ur byas pa.* Toh. 4089. D 4089: vol. 140, 18b.7.

196. *De kho na nyid bstan pa'i mdo.* Citation and text are not found in the Kangyur. The citation is found (attributed to the *Sūtra Revealing Suchness*) in Gampopa's *Sunrays of Scriptural Citations*, 7a.

197. *Mahoṣṇīṣa, gTsug tor chen po'i mdo.* Presumably this is Toh. 236, H.K. 237. Citation not found in this text. It is found (attributed to the *Sūtra of the Great Uṣṇīṣa*) in Gampopa's *Sunrays of Scriptural Citations*, 7a.

198. *rTogs pa rgyas pa'i mdo* (no Sanskrit title; translated from Chinese). Toh. 265, H.K. 267. H.K. 267: vol. 67, 543b.7–544a.1. The H.K. recension reads *thang gcig sangs rgyas thun zhugs na/ khams gsum gnas pa'i sems can rnams/* . . . ; the *Moonbeams* citation (*MB* VVI 31.6–8) reads *thangs gcig bsam gtan thun zhugs na/ khams gsum gang ba'i mi rnams la/* . . . The *Moonbeams* citation is identical to one found in Gampopa's *Sunrays of Scriptural Citations*, 7a.

199. *MB* VVI (31.10): *'chang* should be *'char.* See *MB* DLG (9.4).

200. *Prajñāpāramitā-saṃcayagāthā, 'Phags pa mdo sdud pa / Shes rab kyi pha rol tu phyin pa sdud pa tshigs su bcad pa.* Toh. 13, H.K. 17. H.K. 17: vol. 34, 214b.5–6. *MB* VVI (31.13): *'dog* should be *'dor* and *rigs* should be *rig.* See *MB* DLG (9.5), *MB* VVI (211.10), and H.K. (214b.5). Also cited in Collected Works of Gampopa.

201. *Daśacakrakṣitigarbha, Sa'i snying po'i 'khor lo bcu pa.* Toh. 239, H.K. 240. H.K. 240: vol. 65, 213b.5–6. Also cited in Collected Works of Gampopa.

202. *Dharmasaṃgītisūtra, Chos yang dag par sdud pa'i mdo.* Toh. 238, H.K. 239. H.K. 239: vol. 65, 80a.7. Also cited in Collected Works of Gampopa.

203. *Mahāyānasūtrālaṃkāra, Theg pa chen po mdo sde'i rgyan.* Toh. 4020. D 4020: vol. 123, 23a.4.

204. *Saṃdhinirmocanasūtra, dGongs pa nges 'grel.* Toh. 106, H.K. 109.

205. *Byams pa'i chos sde.* See entry in Glossary of Enumerations under 5.

206. *Sa sde lnga.* See entry in Glossary of Enumerations.

207. *Abhidharmasamuccaya, Chos mngon pa kun las btus pa.* Toh. 4049.

208. *Prajñāpāramitopadeśa, Sher phyin gyi man ngag.* Toh. 4079.

209. Three texts each called the *Stages of Meditation* and referred to as the first, second, and third *Stages of Meditation* (*Bhāvanākrama, dBu ma'i sgom pa'i rim pa/ sGom pa'i rim pa*). Toh. 3915–17.

210. H.K. 109: vol. 51, 53b.7. H.K. 109: vol. 51, 53b.7–54a.1. The H.K. recension reads . . . *de dag thams cad bsdus par rig par bya'o/ bcom ldan 'das/ zhi gnas dang/ lhag mthong rgyu gang las byung pa lags*; the *Moonbeams* citation (*MB* VVI 16–17) reads . . . *de dag thams cad zhi gnas dang lhag mthong gis bsdus par rig par bya'o.* The *Moonbeams* citation is identical to the one found in Kamalaśīla's middle *Stages of Meditation* (*sGom rim bar pa*). Toh. 3916. D 3916: vol. 110, 44b.1. Also cited in the *Great Treatise.*

211. *sGom rim bar pa.* D 3916: vol. 110, 44a.7. Also cited in the *Great Treatise.*

212. *Mahāyānaprasādaprabhāvanasūtra, Theg chen la dad pa'i mdo.* Toh. 144, H.K. 146. H.K. 146: vol. 57, 36a.6–7. The H.K. recension reads *rigs kyi bu/ byang chub sems dpa' gang la la theg pa chen po'i phyir theg pa chen po la dad pa skye ba de thams cad ni/ mi g.yengs pa'i sems kyis chos kyi don la rtog pa las skye bar rnam grangs 'dis de ltar rig par bya'o.* The *Moonbeams* citation (*MB* VVI 34.16–19) reads *rigs kyi bu rnam grangs 'dis kyang 'di ltar byang chub sems dpa' rnams kyi theg pa chen po la dad pa theg pa chen po las 'byung ba gang ci yang rung ba de thams cad ni/ rnam par ma g.yengs pa'i sems kyi chos kyi don dang/ chos yang dag par bsams pa las byung bar rig par bya'o.* The *Moonbeams* citation is identical to the one found in Kamalaśīla's middle *Stages of Meditation.* D 3916: vol. 110, 45a.3. *MB* VVI (34.18): *sems kyi don* probably should be *sems kyis don.* See D 3916: vol. 110, 45a.3. Also cited in the *Great Treatise.*

213. *sGom rim tha ma.* Toh. 3917. D 3917: vol. 110, 55b.6–56a.1. Also cited in the *Great Treatise.*

214. H.K. 109: vol. 51, 54a.1–2. Also cited in the *Great Treatise.*

215. There are five mentions of these four causes of śamatha in the Collected Works of Gampopa: *Abundant Auspiciousness: A Collection of Dharma Lectures* (*Tshogs chos bkra shis phun tshogs*) (text 4/nga, 4a); *Replies to Dusum Khyenpa's Questions* (*Du gsum mkhyen pa'i zhus len*) (text 10/tha, 30a); *Replies to the Exalted Pakmo Drupa's Questions* (*rJe phag mo gru pa'i zhus len*) (text 11/da, 9b); *Core of Mahāmudrā: The Instructions on the Ultimate Essence* (*sNying po don gyi gdams pa phyag rgya chen po'i 'bum tig*) (text 23/'a, 5b); and *Esoteric Instructions on the Twofold Abiding State and Esoteric Instructions on Twofold Armor* (*gNas lugs gnyis kyi man ngag dang go cha gnyis kyi man ngag*) (text 31/ki, 20b).

216. D 3916: vol. 110, 45b.2 and 46a.4. Bracketed words from the middle *Stages of Meditation* (D 3916: 45b.2). Also cited in the *Great Treatise.*

217. D 4020: vol. 123, 17b.7–18a. The Dg.T. recension reads . . . *bde ba'i yon tan ldan*; the *Moonbeams* citation (*MB* VVI 38.7) reads . . . *bde ba'i yo byad ldan.* The *Moonbeams* citation is identical to the one in the *Great Treatise*, 484.

218. H.K. 109: vol. 51, 54b.2–54b.6. Also cited in the *Great Treatise.*

219. D 4049: vol. 134, 51a.5–6. Also cited in the *Great Treatise.*

220. D 4049: vol. 134, 52a.1–2. The Dg.T. recension reads . . . *yid la gcags pa* . . . ; the *Moonbeams* citation (*MB* VVI 40.4) reads . . . *yid la bcags pa* . . .

221. D 4049: vol. 134, 51a.5. Also cited in the *Great Treatise.*

222. *Abhidharmakośa-bhāṣya, Chos mngon pa'i mdzod kyi bshad pa.* Toh. 4090. D 4090: vol. 140, 65b.7. Also cited in the *Great Treatise.*

223. D 3916: vol. 110, 47b.7–48a.1. Also cited in the *Great Treatise.*

224. D 4049: vol. 134, 51b.7–52a.1.

225. D 4049: vol. 134, 49b.1–2.

226. H.K. 109: vol. 51, 54b.7–55a.2.

227. H.K. 109: vol. 51, 55a.2–55b.1. The H.K. recension reads . . . *rnam par rtog pa dang/ nyong mongs pa dang nyer ba'i nyon mongs pa* . . . *gnas ngan len gyi lus* . . . ; the *Moonbeams* citation (*MB* VVI 42.5) reads . . . *rnam par rtog pa dang/ nyer ba'i*

nyon mongs pa . . . gnas ngan len gyi tshogs . . . The translation includes the words found in the H.K. recension (which are missing from the *Moonbeams* citation) in brackets.

228. *Madhyāntavibhāga, dBus mtha' rnam 'byed* by Maitreya. Toh. 4021. D 4021: vol. 123, 43a.4. Also cited in the *Great Treatise.*
229. D 4021: vol. 123, 43a.3.
230. D 4049: vol. 134, 49a.2. Also cited in the *Great Treatise.*
231. *A Detailed Commentary on "The Explanation of the Five Skandhas."* (*Pañcaskandha-prakaraṇavaibhāṣyā, Phung po lnga'i rab tu byed pa bye brag tu bshad pa*). Toh. 4066. D 4066: vol. 136, 215a.2–3. Also cited in the *Great Treatise.*
232. *Nyan thos kyi sa* by Asaṅga. Toh. 4036. See D 4036: vol. 128, 163a.2–6.
233. D 4049: vol. 134, 48b.3. Also cited in the *Great Treatise.*
234. *Madhyāntavibhāga-ṭīkā, dBus dang mtha' rnam par 'byed pa'i 'grel bshad* by Sthiramati. Toh. 4032. D 4032: vol. 124, 274b.1–2. Also cited in the *Great Treatise.*
235. D 3871: vol. 105, 11b.2. Also cited in the *Great Treatise.*
236. D 3871: vol. 105, 14b.1. Also cited in the *Great Treatise.*
237. D 4049: vol. 134, 48a.7. Also cited in the *Great Treatise.*
238. D 4036: vol. 128, 144b.1–2. Also cited in the *Great Treatise.*
239. D 4036: vol. 128, 144b.2–3. Also cited in the *Great Treatise.*
240. D 4036: vol. 128, 144b.3. The Dg.T. recension reads . . . *sems bying ba . . .* ; the *Moonbeams* citation (*MB* VVI 46.11) reads . . . *sogs bying ba . . .* The translation follows the Dg.T. recension. Also cited in the *Great Treatise.*
241. *Sa'i dngos gzhi / rNal 'byor spyod pa'i sa las dngos gzhi'i sa mang po* by Asaṅga. Toh. 4035. D 4035: vol. 127, 134a.2–5. The Dg.T. recension reads . . . *zhi gnas la ma goms pa. . .* ; the *Moonbeams* citation (*MB* VVI 47.1) reads . . . *zhi gnas la goms pa . . .* The *Moonbeams* citation is identical to the one in the *Great Treatise*, 523–24.
242. D 4035: vol. 127, 134a.5–7. The Dg.T. recension reads . . . *rab tu 'dzin pa la yongs su byang bar ma byas pa de'i phyogs . . .* ; the *Moonbeams* citation (*MB* VVI 47.8) reads . . . *rab tu 'dzin pa la byang bar ma byas pa'i de'i phyogs . . .* The *Moonbeams* citation is identical to the one in the *Great Treatise*, 524.
243. *sGom rim dang po.* Toh. 3915. D 3915: vol. 110, 31b.2–3. Also cited in the *Great Treatise.*
244. *Pāramitāsamāsa, Phar phyin bsdus pa / Pha rol tu phyin pa bsdus pa* by Āryaśūra. Toh. 3944. D 3944: vol. 111, 229a.5. Also cited in the *Great Treatise.*
245. *Madhyamakahṛdayakārikā, dBu ma'i snying po'i tshig le'ur byas pa* by Bhāvaviveka. Toh. 3855. D 3855: vol. 98, 4a.7. The Dg.T. recension reads . . . *spang pa nyid du bya*; the *Moonbeams* citation (*MB* VVI 48.6) reads . . . *yangs pa nyid du bya.* The citation in the *Great Treatise* (520) reads . . . *yengs pa nyid du bya.*
246. D 4036: vol. 128, 153b.2. Also cited in the *Great Treatise.*
247. See D 4036: vol. 128, 39a.7–39b.7.
248. D 3915: vol. 110, 31b.3–4. Also cited in the *Great Treatise.*
249. D 3855: vol. 98, 4a.7. The Dg.T. recension reads *g.yengs pas g.yeng . . .* ; the *Moonbeams* citation (*MB* VVI 49.2) *g.yengs pa g.yengs . . .* The translation follows the

Dg.T. recension. See also Bhāvaviveka's *Blaze of Reasoning: Commentary on the "Heart of the Middle Way"* (*Madhyamakahṛdayavṛttitarkajvālā, dBu ma'i snying po'i 'grel pa rtog ge 'bar ba*). Toh. 3856. D 3856: vol. 98, 57b.7. The bracketed words in the translation are drawn from the *Blaze of Reasoning*. The *Moonbeams* citation is identical to the one in the *Great Treatise*, 52.

250. D 3944: vol. 111, 229a.5. Also cited in the *Great Treatise*.

251. H.K. 109: vol. 51, 41a.1–3. The H.K. recension reads . . . *sems gang gis yid la byed pa'i sems* . . . ; the *Moonbeams* citation (*MB* VVI 49. 14) reads . . . *sems can gang gis yid la byed pa'i sems* . . . The translation follows the H.K. recension. Also cited in the *Great Treatise*.

252. H.K. 109: vol. 51, 41a.3–7. Also cited in the *Great Treatise*.

253. H.K. 232: vol. 64, 146a.7. The H.K. recension reads . . . *yang dag pa ji lta ba bzhin du chos la so sor rtog pa'o*; the *Moonbeams* citation (*MB* VVI 50.6) reads . . . *yang dag par so sor rtog pa'o*. The *Moonbeams* citation is identical to the one in the *Great Treatise*, 472.

254. D 4020: vol. 123, 19a.3–4. Also cited in the *Great Treatise*.

255. D 4020: vol. 123, 31a.2–3. Also cited in the *Great Treatise*.

256. *Explanation of the "Ornament for the Mahāyāna Sūtras"* (*Sūtrālaṃkārabhāṣya, mDo sde'i rgyan gyi bshad pa*). Toh. 4026. D 4026: vol. 123, 229a.3–4.

257. *MB* VVI (50.19): *'byed cing 'byed pa'i sems* should be *'byed cing dpyod pa'i sems*. See *MB* DLG (23.3) and *MB* TsRP (43.5).

258. *Byang chub sems dpa'i sa* by Asaṅga. Toh. 4037. D 4037: vol. 129, 59a.5–59b.1. The Dg.T. recension reads . . . *sems nges par btags na* . . . *mos pas na* . . . *sems 'jog par byed pa dang/ yang dag par 'jog par byed pa na* . . . *ting nge 'dzin du byed rtse gcig tu byed cing mnyam par 'jog pa 'di ni* . . . ; the *Moonbeams* citation (*MB* VVI 51.5–9) reads . . . *sems nges par btad na* . . . *mos pa na* . . . *sems 'jog par byed pa dang bsdus te 'jog pa nas* . . . *ting nge 'dzin du byed pa'i bar 'di ni* . . . The *Moonbeams* citation is identical to the one in the *Great Treatise*, 473.

259. H.K. 109: vol. 51, 40b.1–3. Also cited in the *Great Treatise*.

260. D 4079: vol. 138, 154b.4–5. Also cited in the *Great Treatise*.

261. D 3916: vol. 110, 46b.7–47a.2. Also cited in the *Great Treatise*.

262. H.K. 109: vol. 51, 41a.7–41b.2. Also cited in the *Great Treatise*.

263. H.K. 109: vol. 51, 41b.2–4. Also cited in the *Great Treatise*.

264. D 4079: vol. 138, 154b.5–6. The Dg.T. recension reads . . . *dben par gnas la* . . . *yid kyis brjod pa* . . . ; the *Moonbeams* citation (*MB* VVI 53.5–6) reads . . . *dben par gnas bcas la* . . . *yid kyi brjod pa* . . . The *Moonbeams* citation is identical to the one in the *Great Treatise*, 538.

265. D 4079: vol. 138, 154b.6–7. The Dg.T. recension reads . . . *shin tu byangs pas nyer bar thob pa* . . . ; the *Moonbeams* citation (*MB* VVI 53.9) reads . . . *shin tu byangs pa thob pa* . . . The *Moonbeams* citation is identical to the one in the *Great Treatise*, 798.

266. H.K. 109: vol. 51, 54b.5–6.

267. D 4020: vol. 123, 19a.5. Also cited in the *Great Treatise*.

268. D 4026: vol. 123, 191a.6–191b.1.
269. D 4049: vol. 134, 99a.4.
270. H.K. 109: vol. 51, 43a.1–2. Also cited in the *Great Treatise.*
271. H.K. 109: vol. 51, 43a.2–5. Also cited in the *Great Treatise.*
272. D 4049: vol. 134, 99a.5–6.
273. D 4036: vol. 128, 134a.1–4. The Dg.T. recension reads . . . *chos rnam par 'byed par byed pa dang . . . spyad pa rnam par sbyong ba'i dmigs pa . . .* ; the *Moonbeams* citation (55.19–56.1) reads . . . *chos rnam par 'byed pa dang . . . spyad pa rnam par sbyong ba'i dmigs pa . . .* The *Moonbeams* citation is identical to the one in the *Great Treatise,* 770. The translation, however, follows the Dg.T. recension in reading *spyad pa rnam par sbyong ba'i dmigs pa.*
274. D 4036: vol. 128, 135a.3–4. Also cited in the *Great Treatise.*
275. D 4020: vol. 123, 21b.7. Also cited in both Collected Works of Gampopa and *Great Treatise.*
276. D 4182: vol. 173, 45b.4. Also cited in Collected Works of Gampopa.
277. D 3871: vol. 105, 23b.1–23b.2. Also cited in both Collected Works of Gampopa and *Great Treatise.*
278. This may be a reference to statements by Tsongkhapa in his *Great Treatise.* See Lamrim Chenmo Translation Committee, *Great Treatise,* vol. 3, 78.
279. *MB* VVI (57.17): *yin* should be *yan.* See *MB* DLG (29.2) and *MB* TsRP (55.3).
280. D 4049: vol. 134, 99a.7. Also cited in the *Great Treatise.*
281. D 4035: vol. 127, 156a.7–156b.1. Also cited in the *Great Treatise.*
282. D 3915: vol. 110, 30b.6–7. Also cited in the *Great Treatise.*
283. D 3916: vol. 110, 45a.4–5. Also cited in the *Great Treatise.*
284. *MB* VVI (59.19): *ni* should be *mi.* See *MB* DLG (31.1).
285. D 3916: vol. 110, 44b.1–3. The Dg.T. recension reads . . . *shes rab kyi snang ba byung ba med par 'bag la nyal legs par choms mi srid pa'i phyir bag nyal legs par choms par mi 'gyur ro . . .* ; the *Moonbeams* citation (*MB* VVI 60.3–4) reads . . . *shes rab kyi snang ba byung ba med par bag nyal legs par choms par mi 'gyur ro . . .* The *Moonbeams* citation is identical to the one in the *Great Treatise,* 479. The *Unraveling the Intent* citation is found in H.K. 109: vol. 51, 67a.5.
286. D 3916: vol. 110, 44b.5–7. The Dg.T. recension's citation reads . . . *ting nge 'dzin tsam gyis chog par 'dzin pa ni . . . gzhan la rjes su mthun pa thos pa ni . . .* ; the *Moonbeams* citation (*MB* VVI 60.9–14) reads *ting nge 'dzin tsam gyis chog par 'dzin pa thob pa ni . . . gzhan las rjes su mthun pa thob pa ni . . .* The translation follows the Dg.T. recension's citation in reading *rjes su mthun pa thos pa ni* (which is in keeping with the H.K. recension). This citation is found in H.K. 56: vol. 37, 310b.5–311a.2. Also cited in the *Great Treatise* with some differences.
287. *Zla ba sgron me'i mdo.* Also known as the *King of Samādhi Sūtra* (*Samādhirāja-sūtra, Ting nge 'dzin gyi rgyal po'i mdo*). Toh. 127, H.K. 129. H.K. 129: vol. 55, 33b.6. The Dg.T. recension reads *zhi gnas stobs kyis bskyod pa med gyur cing/ lhag mthong gis ni ri bo lta bur gyur;* the *Moonbeams* citation (*MB* VVI 60.19–20) reads *zhi gnas stobs kyis g.yo ba med par 'gyur / lhag mthong gis ni ri dang 'dra bar gyur.* The

Moonbeams citation is identical to the one in the middle *Stages of Meditation.* D 3916: vol. 110, 45a.7–45b.1. Also cited in the *Great Treatise.*

288. *MB* VVI (61.4): *re* should be *de.* See *MB* DLG (32.1).
289. D 4036: vol. 128, 148b.4–7. The Dg.T. recension reads . . . *mnyam par bzhag pa'i rnam pa dgu po . . .* ; the *Moonbeams* citation (*MB* VVI 61.12) reads . . . *mnyam par bzhag pa'i rnam pa dgu pa . . .* The translation follows the Dg.T. recension. Also cited in the *Great Treatise.*
290. D 3917: vol. 110, 59b.1–2. Also cited in the *Great Treatise.*
291. D 4079: vol. 138, 154b.7–155a.2. The Dg.T. recension reads . . . *zung du 'jug pa'i lam . . .* ; the *Moonbeams* citation (*MB* VVI 62.8) reads . . . *zung du 'brel ba'i lam . . .* The Moonbeams citation is identical to the one in the *Great Treatise*, 803.
292. *MB* VVI (63.6): *brtag ma yin par bshad* should be *brtags yin par bshad.* See *MB* DLG (33.7–34.1), and *MB* TsRP (64.6).
293. H.K. 109: vol. 51, 54a.3–4.
294. H.K. 109: vol. 51, 54a.5–6. The H.K. recension reads . . . *byams pa/ 'ching ba rnam pa gnyis po mtshan ma'i 'ching ba dang/ gnas ngan len gyi 'ching ba las rnam par thar par byed pa yin no*; the *Moonbeams* citation (*MB* VVI 64.16–17) reads . . . *byams pa/ mtshan ma'i 'ching ba dang/ gnas ngan len gyi 'ching ba ste 'ching ba rnam pa gnyis las rnam par grol ba'o.*
295. H.K. 17: vol. 34, 214b.5–6. *MB* VVI (65.3): *rigs* should be *rig.* See *MB* VVI (211.10) and H.K. (214b.5). Also cited in Collected Works of Gampopa.
296. D 4182: vol. 173, 42b.4. Also cited in Collected Works of Gampopa.
297. D 3947: vol. 111, 240a.1–2.
298. H.K. 17: vol. 34, 210a.3–4. Also cited in Collected Works of Gampopa.
299. H.K. 17: vol. 34, 214b.6. Also cited in Collected Works of Gampopa.
300. D 4037: vol. 129, 113a.4–5. Also cited in Collected Works of Gampopa.
301. H.K. 15: vol. 34, 154a.4–5. Also cited in Collected Works of Gampopa.
302. *Replies to Dusum Khyenpa's Questions*, 24a. *MB* VVI (66.14): *gtan* should be *gtam.* See *MB* DLG (36.4) and *Replies to Dusum Khyenpa's Questions* (text 10/tha, 24a).
303. D 3947: vol. 111, 239b.7–240a.1. Also cited in the *Great Treatise.*
304. D 3915: vol. 110, 30b.7–31a.1. Also cited in the *Great Treatise.*
305. This may refer to the explanation in the *Great Treatise*, 491.
306. *MB* VVI (68.16): *spyad spyod* should be *spyad sbyong.* See *MB* DLG (38.2).
307. Although most editions of *Moonbeams* read *mi dge ba rnams las rnam smin yid du mi 'ong ba 'byung ba gnas ma yin pa*, the translation follows *MB* RD (68.15) and the *Great Treatise* (493.6) (from which this section appears to be drawn), which read *mi dge ba rnams las rnam smin yid du 'ong ba 'byung ba gnas ma yin pa.*
308. *Nam grus zhus pa'i mdo.* Text not found in the Kangyur.
309. D 4036: vol. 128, 77a.5–6. The Dg.T. recension reads . . . *khams rab tu dbye ba . . .* ; the *Moonbeams* citation (71.2) reads . . . *khams kyi rab tu dbye ba . . .* The *Moonbeams* citation is identical to the one in the *Great Treatise*, 496.
310. D 4036: vol. 128, 77a.7. *MB* VVI (71.3): *spang* should be *spyad.* See *MB* DLG (39.7). Also cited in the *Great Treatise.*

311. D 4036: vol. 128, 77a.7–77b.3. Also cited in the *Great Treatise.*

312. D 4036: vol. 128, 77b.3–5. The Dg.T. recension reads . . . *skyob par 'dod pa* . . . ; the *Moonbeams* citation (72.1) reads . . . *skyo bar 'dod pa* . . . The *Moonbeams* citation is identical to the one in the *Great Treatise*, 498. *MB* VVI (71.17): *rigs pa* should be *rags pa*. See *MB* DLG (40.4).

313. D 4036: vol. 128, 122a.4. Also cited in the *Great Treatise.*

314. D 3947: vol. 111, 240a.1. Also cited in the *Great Treatise.*

315. *Synopsis of the Pāramitās* (*Pāramitāsamāsa, Phar phyin bsdus pa / Pha rol tu phyin pa bsdus pa*). Toh. 3944. D 3944: vol. 111, 229a.4–5. Also cited in the *Great Treatise.*

316. *A Work on the Requisites for Samādhi* (*Samādhisambhāraparivarta, Ting nge 'dzin gyi tshogs kyi le'u*). Toh. 3924. D 3924: vol. 110, 90a.4–6. Also cited in the *Great Treatise.*

317. H.K. 129: vol. 55, 22b.1–2. The H.K. recension reads *sku lus dag ni gser gyi mdog 'dra bas/ 'jig rten mgon po kun nas rab tu mdzes/ dmigs pa de la gang gi sems 'jug pa/ byang chub sems dpa' de ni mnyam bzhag yin*; the *Moonbeams* citation reads *gser gyi kha dog lta bu'i sku lus kyis/ 'jig rten mgon po kun tu mdzes pa ste/ dmigs pa de la gang gis sems 'jug pa/ byang chub sems dpa' de mnyam bzhag ces bya*. The *Moonbeams* citation is identical to the one in the middle *Stages of Meditation* (D 3916: vol. 110, 47b.4–5) and the *Great Treatise*, 501.

318. D 3917: vol. 110, 57a.3–4. The Dg.T. recension reads . . . *sems gtad te bzhag* . . . ; the *Moonbeams* citation (*MB* VVI 74.2) reads . . . *sems bzhag* . . . The *Moonbeams* citation is identical to the one in the *Great Treatise*, 500.

319. D 3915: vol. 110, 31a.5. Also cited in the *Great Treatise.*

320. Although *Moonbeams* refers to this source text as *mDo sde rgyan gyi 'grel pa*, it is Vasubandhu's *Explanation of the "Ornament for the Mahāyāna Sūtras"* (*Sūtrālaṃkārabhāṣya, mDo sde'i rgyan gyi bshad pa*). Toh. 4026. D 4026: vol. 123, 227a.2. The Dg.T. reads . . . *gnyis pas 'phro ba* . . . ; the *Moonbeams* citation (*MB* VVI 13–14) reads . . . *gnyis pas sems 'phro ba* . . . The *Moonbeams* citation and title reference is identical to the one in the *Great Treatise*, 505.

321. D 3855: vol. 98, 4a.6. Also cited in the *Great Treatise.*

322. *Praise of Confession* (*Deśanāstava, bShags pa'i bstod pa*). Toh. 1159. D 1159: vol. 1, 205b.5. The Dg.T. recension reads . . . *dkrugs pa ni ji ltar bgyi*; the *Moonbeams* citation (*MB* VVI 75.9) reads . . . *dkrugs pas ni ci zhig bgyi.* The *Moonbeams* citation is identical to the one in the *Great Treatise*, 509.

323. D 1159: vol. 1, 205b.6–7. The Dg.T. recension reads . . . *dkrugs pa ni ji ltar bgyi*; the *Moonbeams* citation (*MB* VVI 75.14) reads . . . *dkrugs pas ni ci zhig bgyi.* The *Moonbeams* citation is identical to the one in the *Great Treatise*, 509.

324. I am reading *de dag pa yid byed bzhi yod tshul* following *MB* DLG (43.4), *MB* DK (124.3), and the *Great Treatise* (529 and 535), from which this section seems to be drawn. *MB* VVI (75.17) and *MB* TsRP (84.1) read *de dag pa yid byed bzhi yong tshul.*

325. D 4021: vol. 123, 43a.3–5. Also cited in the *Great Treatise.*

326. D 4020: vol. 123, 19a.5. Also cited in both Collected Works of Gampopa and *Great Treatise.*

327. *MB* VVI (77.10): *'phro zhing yongs* should be *'phro zhing yengs.* See *MB* DLG (44.5).

328. D 4020: vol. 123, 19a.5. Also cited in both Collected Works of Gampopa and *Great Treatise.*

329. *MB* VVI (77.14): *yengs ni gtong* should be *yengs mi gtong.* See *MB* DLG (44.6).

330. D 4020: vol. 123, 19a.5. Also cited in both Collected Works of Gampopa and *Great Treatise.*

331. D 4020: vol. 123, 19a.5. Also cited in both Collected Works of Gampopa and *Great Treatise.*

332. *MB* VVI (78.3): *mang yang bsdus* should be *yang yang bsdus.* See DLG (44.7).

333. D 4020: vol. 123, 19a.5. Also cited in both Collected Works of Gampopa and *Great Treatise.*

334. D 4020: vol. 123, 19a.5–6. Also cited in the *Great Treatise* and partially in Collected Works of Gampopa.

335. D 4020: vol. 123, 19a.6. Also cited in the *Great Treatise* and partially in Collected Works of Gampopa.

336. D 4020: vol. 123, 19a.6. The Dg.T. recension reads *brnab sems yid mi bde la sogs . . .* ; the *Moonbeams* citation (78.18) reads *chags sems yid mi bde la sogs . . .* The *Moonbeams* citation (79.18) is identical to the citations found in the *Instructions on Prajñāpāramitā* (D 4079: vol. 138, 155b.1–2) and the *Great Treatise,* 531. The citation found in Collected Works of Gampopa (*Sunrays of Scriptural Citations,* 17b) reads *brnab sems yid mi bde la sogs . . .*

337. D 4020: vol. 123, 19a.6–7. Also cited in both Collected Works of Gampopa and *Great Treatise.*

338. D 4020: vol. 123, 19a.7. Also cited in the *Great Treatise.*

339. See D 4036: vol. 128, 133b.1–5.

340. D 4036: vol. 128, 133b.5–7. The Dg.T. recension reads . . . *bsgrims te 'jug pa dang/ skabs su 'chad cing 'jug pa dang . . . rtsol ba med par 'jug pa'o/ . . .* ; the *Moonbeams* citation (81.5–6) reads . . . *bsgrims te 'jug pa dang/ bar du 'chad cing 'jug pa dang . . . lhun gyis grub par 'jug pa'o/ . . .* The *Moonbeams* citation is identical to the one in the *Great Treatise,* 535. Also cited in the *Great Treatise.*

341. D 3947: vol. 111, 239b.7–240a.1. Also cited in the *Great Treatise.*

342. D 3944: vol. 111, 229a.3–4. The Dg.T. recension reads . . . *zhing ngal bso na/ gtsubs pas me phyin me 'gyur te . . .* ; the *Moonbeams* citation (82.8) reads . . . *zhing ngal so na/ gtsubs pas me phyin me 'gyur te . . . MB* VVI (82.8): *mi phyin* should be *me phyin.* See *MB* DLG (47.7) and Dg.T. recension. Also cited in the *Great Treatise.*

343. D 4020: vol. 123, 19a.3. Note that the Dg.T. recension reads *yid kyi brjod pas . . . brjod med par*; the *Moonbeams* citation (*MB* VVI 84.9–10) reads *yid kyi brjod pa . . . brjod med pa.* The translation follows the Dg.T. recension.

344. D 4026: vol. 123, 191a.2–4.

345. *Madhyamakopadeśa, dbU ma'i man ngag*. Toh. 3929. See D 3929: vol. 110, 95b.7–96a.2.
346. *Bodhisattvayogacarācatuḥśatakaṭīkā, bZhi brgya pa'i rgya cher 'grel pa / Byang chub sems dpa'i rnal 'byor spyod pa bzhi brgya pa'i rgya cher 'grel pa*. Toh. 3865. D 3865: vol. 103, 190b.2–3. Also cited in the *Great Treatise*.
347. *mDo sil bu*. Citation and text not found in the Kangyur. The citation is found (attributed to the *Sūtra of Fragments*) in Gampopa's *Ornament of Precious Liberation* (*Thar pa rin po che'i rgyan*). Collected Works of Gampopa, text 38/nyi, 98a.
348. Citation and text not found in the Kangyur. The citation is found (attributed to the *Sūtra of Fragments*) in Gampopa's *Ornament of Precious Liberation*, 98a.
349. *Commentary on Valid Cognition* (*Pramāṇavārttikakārikā, rNam 'grel / Tshad ma rnam 'grel gyi tshig le'ur byas pa*). Toh. 4210. D 4210: vol. 174, 116a.1–2. Also cited in both Collected Works of Gampopa and *Great Treatise*.
350. *Ratnāvalī, Rin chen 'phreng ba* by Nāgārjuna. Toh. 4158. D 4158: vol. 172, 108a.5–6. Also cited in Collected Works of Gampopa with differences; first two lines cited in the *Great Treatise*.
351. *Commentary on Valid Cognition*. D 4210: vol. 174, 116a.3. Also cited in the *Great Treatise*.
352. *Catuḥśatakaśāstra, bZhi brgya pa / bsTan bcos bzhi brgya pa* by Āryadeva. Toh. 3846. D 3846: vol. 97, 16a.5. Also cited in the *Great Treatise*.
353. D 3861: vol. 102, 210a.4. Also cited in the *Great Treatise*.
354. *Prajñā-nāma-mūlamadhyamakakārikā, rTsa sher / dBu ma rtsa ba'i tshig le'ur byas pa shes rab ces bya ba* by Nāgārjuna. Toh. 3824. D 3824: vol. 96, 10b.6–7. Also cited in the *Great Treatise*.
355. D 3824: vol. 96, 10b.7–11a.1. Also cited in the *Great Treatise*.
356. D 4158: vol. 172, 108a.2. Also cited in Collected Works of Gampopa.
357. D 4158: vol. 172, 108a.6–7. Also cited in Collected Works of Gampopa.
358. D 3824: vol. 96, 18a.1. Also cited in the *Great Treatise*.
359. D 3824: vol. 96, 10b.6. Also cited in the *Great Treatise*.
360. D 3824: vol. 96, 10b.6. Also cited in the *Great Treatise*.
361. D 3824: vol. 96, 18a.2. Also cited in the *Great Treatise*.
362. D 3861: vol. 102, 210a.6–7. Also cited in the *Great Treatise*.
363. D 3824: vol. 96, 10b.6. Also cited in the *Great Treatise*.
364. D 3861: vol. 102, 212a.7. Also cited in the *Great Treatise*.
365. Citation not found in the first *Stages of Meditation*. It is found in the middle *Stages of Meditation*. D 3916: vol. 110, 48b.2–4. Note *MB* VVI (90.18): *bdag ni phung po* should be *gang zag ni phung po*. See Dg.T. recension (48b.3) and *MB* DLG (53.4).
366. D 3824: vol. 96, 1b.3. Also cited in the *Great Treatise*.
367. D 3824: vol. 96, 12a.4. Also cited in the *Great Treatise*.
368. D 3824: vol. 96, 12a.4–5. Also cited in the *Great Treatise*.
369. D 3861: vol. 102, 209a.6. Also cited in the *Great Treatise*.
370. D 3824: vol. 96, 8b.5. Also cited in the *Great Treatise*.
371. *Commentary on Valid Cognition*. D 4210: vol. 174, 132a.4.
372. *Bodhicittavivaraṇa, Byang chub sems 'grel* by Nāgārjuna. Toh. 1800. D 1800:

vol. 35, 39a.3–4. Bracketed words are from Smṛtijñānakīrti's *Explanation of the "Commentary on Bodhicitta"* (*Bodhicittavivaraṇaṭīkā, Byang chub sems kyi 'grel pa'i rnam par bshad pa*). Toh. 1829. D 1829: vol. 36, 126a.7–126b.5.

373. D 1800: vol. 35, 39a.4–5. *MB* VVI (92.17): *gzhan ma gzhan du* should be *gzhan la gzhan du.* See Dg.T. recension (39a.4).

374. The first two lines are H.K. 110: vol. 51, 264b.3. The third and fourth lines are probably H.K. 110: vol. 51, 264b.1–2. For textual differences see note 178. Also cited in Collected Works of Gampopa.

375. H.K. 129: vol. 55, 43a.2–3. The H.K. recension reads *rta dang glang po'i shing rta*; the *Moonbeams* citation (*MB* VVI 93.9) reads *rta dang glang po shing rta.*

376. Citation not found in the first *Stages of Meditation*. It is found in the middle *Stages of Meditation.* D 3916: vol. 110, 48b.4–7. *Moonbeams* (*MB* VVI 93.13 and 93.17): *phung po dang* should be *phung po lnga dang*; and *ngo bo nyid med par bzung* should be *ngo bo nyid nges par bzung.* See Dg.T. 3916 (48b.4 and .6).

377. D 3824: vol. 96, 8a.6–7. Also cited in the *Great Treatise.*

378. Ratnakūṭa, dKon mchog brtsegs pa. (The Heap of Jewels is a section of the Kangyur, which includes Toh. 45–93.) This citation is in the *Discourse for Kāśyapa* (*Kāśyapa-parivarta-sūtra, 'Od srung gi le'u zhes bya ba'i mdo*). Toh. 87, H.K. 87. H.K. 87: vol. 40, 231a.4–6. The translation follows the H.K. recension in reading *bla'i*, not *sla'i* as found in the *Moonbeams* citation (*MB* VVI 94.10). See H.K. recension (231a.5). The *Moonbeams* citation is identical the one in Gampopa's *Ornament of Precious Liberation*, 102a.

379. D 1800: vol. 35, 40a.5–6. The translation is based Chödrak Yeshe's *Elucidating the Word-Meaning: An Explanation of the "Commentary on Bodhicitta"* (*Byang chub sems 'grel gyi rnam par bshad pa tshig don gsal ba*). Collected Works of Chödrak Yeshe, vol. 2, 670. Other explanations would warrant different translations.

380. D 3947: vol. 111, 240a.4–5. The Dg.T. recension reads *thabs bsgoms dbang gis bdag nyid kyis/ gang gis shes rab rnam bsgoms pa/ de ni byang chub myur thob kyi . . .* ; the *Moonbeams* citation (*MB* VVI 94.17–95.2) reads *thabs goms dbang gi bdag nyid kyi/ gang gis shes rab rnam bsgoms na/ des ni byang chub myur thob kyi . . .* The translation follows the Dg.T. recension. The citation in Gampopa's *Esoteric Instructions on the Twofold Abiding State and Esoteric Instructions on Twofold Armor* (*gNas lugs gnyis kyi man ngag dang go cha gnyis kyi man ngag*) (Collected Works of Gampopa, text 31/ki, 102a) reads *thabs goms dbang gis bdag nyid kyi/ gang gis shes pa rnam sgoms na/ des ni bde ba myur thob kyi . . .*

381. D 3824: vol. 96, 15a.6–7. Also cited in the *Great Treatise.*

382. D 3824: vol. 96, 13b.1–2.

383. D 3824: vol. 96, 9a.2–3. Also cited in the *Great Treatise.*

384. *Commentary on the "Differentiation of the Two Truths"* (**Satyadvaya-vibhaṅga-vṛtti, bDen gnyis rnam par 'byed pa'i 'grel pa*) by Jñānagarbha. Toh. 3882. D 3882: vol. 107, 6a.6.

385. D 4158: vol. 172, 109b.5. The Dg.T. recension reads *gnas med chos 'dis skrag pa yis/. . . yod dang med las ma 'das pa . . .* ; the *Moonbeams* citation (*MB* VVI 96.3–4) reads *gnas med chos 'dis skrag gyur pa'i/. . . yod dang med par 'dzin pas na . . .*

386. H.K. 110: vol. 51, 217b.7–218a.1 and H.K. 110: vol. 51, 289b.6–290a.1. In both instances the H.K. recension reads *phyi rol dngos po dngos med min* . . . ; the *Moonbeams* citation (*MB* VVI 96.9) reads *phyi rol dngos po yod med min* . . . . The *Moonbeams* citation is identical to one found in *Sunrays of Scriptural Citations*, 13b.

387. D 3871: vol. 105, 31b.4–5. The Dg.T. recension (31b.5) reads . . . *mo gsham bu mo'i* . . . ; the *Moonbeams* citation (*MB* VVI 96.13) reads . . . *mo sham bu yi*. . . The bracketed word in the first line is from Khenpo Shenga's *Annotations on the "Entrance to the Bodhisattva's Way of Life"* (*Byang chub sems dpa'i spyod pa la 'jug pa'i mchan 'grel*), 192. Also cited in Collected Works of Gampopa.

388. D 3871: vol. 105, 32a.4. Also cited in Collected Works of Gampopa.

389. Citation not found in the first *Stages of Meditation*. It is found in the middle *Stages of Meditation* (and is attributed to that text on p. 251). D 3916: vol. 110, 48b.7–49a.6. The Dg.T. recension reads . . . *chos brtags pa mtha' dag ni/* . . . *bzung du med pa/ brtan du med pa/* . . . *brtan du med pa* . . . *gzugs can ma yin pa gang yin pa de'i ngo bo nyid* . . . ; the *Moonbeams* citation (*MB* VVI 96.17–97.16) reads . . . *chos gdags pa mtha' dag ni/* . . . *bzung du med pa/ bstan du med pa/* . . . *bstan du med pa* . . . *gzugs can ma yin pa de'i ngo bo nyid* . . . The translation follows the Dg.T. recension in its reading of *brtags pa*. The *Discourse for Kāśyapa* citation: H.K. 87: vol. 40, 242a.2–4.

390. D 4020: vol. 123, 6b.5–6.

391. D 4026: vol. 123, 146b.2–3.

392. *Dharmatā-svabhāva-śūnyatācala-pratisarvāloka-sūtra*, *Chos nyid mi g.yo ba'i mdo / Chos nyid rang gi ngo bo stong pa nyid las mi g.yo bar tha dad par thams cad la snang ba'i mdo*. Toh. 128, H.K. 130. H.K. 130: vol. 55, 270b.1–2 and 272a.5–6. Also cited in Collected Works of Gampopa.

393. H.K. 17: vol. 34, 191b.2–3. Also cited in both Collected Works of Gampopa and *Great Treatise*.

394. H.K. 17: vol. 34, 191a.7. Also cited in Collected Works of Gampopa.

395. *Dharmadhātu-prakṛti-asaṃbheda-nirdeśa*, *Chos kyi dbyings kyi rang bzhin dbyer med pa bstan pa'i mdo*. Toh 52, H.K. 52. H.K. 52: vol. 36, 234a.4–5, 234a.6, and 234a.7–234b.1. The H.K recension reads *sems de gzugs can ma yin/ bstan du med pa/ snang ba med/ thogs pa med/ gnas med/ rnam par rig byed ma yin/ nang na yang med/ phyi rol na med/ gnyis ga med par yang dmigs su med* . . . *gang yang dag pa ma yin zhing yongs su grub pa ma yin pa de la ci rnams par grol ba yod snyams 'am*. . . *chos kyi dbyings kyi rang bzhin la ni kun nas nyong mongs par 'gyur pa yang med la rnam par byang bar 'gyur ba yang med do*. The *Moonbeams* citation (*MB* VVI 99.17–100.1) reads *sems ni gzugs can ma yin bstan du med pa snang ba med thogs pa med rnam par rig byed ma yin/ nang na mi gnas phyi rol na mi gnas gnyis ka'i bar na mi gnas pa'i phyir/ yongs su dag pa ma yongs su ma grub pa yin shing/ de la rnam par grol ba med de chos kyi dbyings kyi rang bzhin no*. The *Moonbeams* citation is identical to the one in Gampopa's *Ornament of Precious Liberation*, 101b.

396. *Yum la bstod pa*. Although *Praises to the Mother* may be referring to *Praises of Prajñāpāramitā* (*Prajñāpāramitāstotra*, *Shes rab kyi pha rol tu phyin ma'i bstod*

pa) by Nāgārjuna (or Rāhulabhadra) (Toh. 1127), this famous line is not found in that text. It is found in Ānandagarbha's *Ritual for the Maṇḍala of Prajñāpāramitā* (*Prajñāpāramitāmaṇḍalopāyikā, Shes rab kyi pha rol tu phyin pa'i dkyil 'khor gyi cho ga*) (Toh. 2644; D 2644: vol. 68 254b.40–254b.5); and Ratnakīrti's *Praises to the Deities of the Four Yogas* (*Yogacaturdevastotra, sByor ba bzhi'i lha la bstod pa*) (Toh. 1170; D 1170: vol. 1, 247b.5). The attribution of this citation to *Praises to the Mother* is found in Gampopa's *Ornament of Precious Liberation*, Collected Works of Gampopa 101b.

397. D 3824: vol. 96, 16a.6–7. The Dg.T. recension reads *de ni mya ngan 'das par brjod*; the *Moonbeams* citation (*MB* VVI 100.5) reads *de ni mya ngan 'das pa'o*. The *Moonbeams* citation is identical to the one in Gampopa's *Ornament of Precious Liberation*, 105a.

398. *Song of the View of Dharmadhātu* (*Dharmadhātudarśanagīti, Chos kyi dbyings lta ba'i glu*). Toh. 2314. D 2314: vol. 52, 255a.1–2. The Dg.T. recension reads *zab zhing spros bral de bzhin nyid/ . . . ma skyes ma 'gags gzod nas dag/ rang bzhin mya ngag 'das pa yis/ . . . blo mig zhib mo rtog bral ba*; the *Moonbeams* citation (*MB* VVI 100.7-9) reads *zab cing spros bral de nyid do/ . . . ma skyes ma 'gags gdod nas dag/ rang bzhin mya ngag 'das pa yi/ . . . blo mig zhib mos rtog bral bas*. The *Moonbeams* citation is identical to the one in Gampopa's *Ornament of Precious Liberation*, 105a–b. *MB* VVI (100.9): *rtag bral bas* should be *rtog bral bas*. See *MB* DLG (60.1).

399. *Lamp for the Path of Awakening*. D 3947: vol. 111, 240a.5. Also cited in Collected Works of Gampopa.

400. *Nam mkha lta bu'i ting nge 'dzin gyi mdo*. Citation and text not found in the Kangyur. The citation is found (attributed to the *Spacelike Samādhi Sūtra*) in Gampopa's *Sunrays of Scriptural Citations*, 18b.

401. *Ting 'dzin dam pa'i mdo*. This may be the *Sūtra of the Supreme, Genuine Samadhi* (*Samādhi-agrottama, Ting nge 'dzin mchog dam pa*). Toh. 137, H.K. 139. However, the citation is not found in that text or the Kangyur. The citation is found (attributed to the *Sūtra of Genuine Samādhi*) in Gampopa's *Sunrays of Scriptural Citations*, 18b.

402. H.K. 15: vol. 34, 128a.3 and 129b.1. The H.K. recension (129b.1) reads . . . *gang la yang mi sems la rnam par mi rig pa* . . . ; the *Moonbeams* citation (*MB* VVI 101.10) reads . . . *gang la yang mi sems rnam par mi dmigs pa* . . . The Moonbeams citation is identical to the one in Gampopa's *Ornament of Precious Liberation*, 105b.

403. *Aṣṭasāhasrikāprajñāpāramitā, brGyad stong pa / Shes rab kyi pha rol tu phyin pa brgyad stong pa*. Toh. 12, H.K. 11. H.K. 11: vol. 29, 266a.2. The H.K. recension reads . . . *chos thams cad mi sgom pa lags so*; the *Moonbeams* citation (*MB* VVI 101.11–12) reads . . . *chos gang yang mi sgom pa lags so*. The Moonbeams citation is identical to the one in Gampopa's *Ornament of Precious Liberation*, 105b.

404. H.K. 11: vol. 29, 266a.1–2. Also cited in Collected Works of Gampopa.

405. H.K. 11: vol. 29, 446a.1. Also cited in Collected Works of Gampopa.

406. *Nam mkha' rin po che'i mdo*. Citation and text not found in the Kangyur. The

citation is found (attributed to the *Sūtra of Precious Space*) is found in Gampopa's *Ornament of Precious Liberation* (104a). Citation is also in Maitreya's *Ornament of Clear Realization* (D 3786: vol. 80, 10a.3–4) and his *Highest Continuum* (D 4024: vol. 123, 61b.5–6).

407. H.K. 94: vol. 44, 121b.3–4. The H.K. recension reads *rgyal ba'i spyod yul 'di la 'jug par gyis su 'dod pa/ des ni nam mkha' 'dra bar bsam pa yongs su sbyongs* . . . ; the *Moonbeams* citation (*MB* VVI 101.19–102.1) reads *rgyal ba'i spyod yul 'di la gang zhig 'jug 'dod pas/ de ni bsam pa nam mkha' lta bu rnam par sbyongs* . . . The *Moonbeams* citation is identical to the one in Gampopa's *Sunrays of Scriptural Citations,* 19a.

408. D 4020: vol. 123, 6b.7. The Dg.T. recension reads *rtsa ba chos kyi dbyings la blo gros bzhag* . . . ; the *Moonbeams* citation (*MB* VVI 102.5) reads *rtsa ba chos kyi dbyings la blo bzhag nas* . . . The translation follows the Dg.T. recension. The bracketed line is the first line of this verse.

409. D 1800: vol. 35, 40a.6–7. The Dg.T. recension reads *sems la dmigs pa med pa yi/ gnas pa nam mkha'i mtshan nyid yin/ de dag stong nyid bsgom pa ni/ nam mkha' bsgom par bzhed pa yin*; the *Moonbeams* citation (*MB* VVI 102.9–10) reads *dmigs pa dang ni bral ba'i sems/ nam mkha'i mtshan nyid la gnas te/ nam mkha' sgom par byed pa ni/ stong pa nyid ni sgom par bzhed.* The *Moonbeams* citation is identical to the one in Gampopa's *Sunrays of Scriptural Citations,* 20a.

410. *Lamp That Summarizes Conduct* (*Caryāsaṃgrahapradīpa, sPyod pa bsdus pa'i sgron ma*). Toh. 3960. D 3960: vol. 111, 313a.5. The Dg.T. recension reads *chos nyid spros pa dang bral ba* . . . ; the *Moonbeams* citation (*MB* VVI 102.12) reads *chos dbyings spros dang bral ba la* . . . The *Moonbeams* citation is identical to the one in Gampopa's *Sunrays of Scriptural Citations,* 18b.

411. H.K. 17: vol. 34, 190a.6–7. Also cited in Collected Works of Gampopa.

412. H.K. 129: vol. 55, 42b.4–5.

413. H.K. 129: vol. 55, 43a.2–3. The H.K. recension reads . . . *rta dang glang po'i shing rta* . . . ; the *Moonbeams* citation (*MB* VVI 104.11) reads . . . *rta dang glang po shing rta* . . . The Moonbeams citation is identical to the one in Gampopa's *Ornament of Precious Liberation,* 106a; and the *Great Treatise,* 749.

414. H.K. 17: vol. 34, 190a.3–4. Also cited in Collected Works of Gampopa.

415. See D 4036: vol. 128, 133b.5 (which is cited on pp. 60–61) and 134a.1. *MB* VVI (105.5): *bzhi sa* should be *bzhis.* See *MB* DLG (63.2).

416. Citation not found in the Collected Works of Götsangpa. It is found (attributed to Götsangpa) in Gö Lotsāwa's *Mirror Illuminating Suchness: A Commentary on the "Highest Continuum"* (*rGyud bla ma'i 'grel bshad de kho na nyid rab tu gsal ba'i me long*). Stuttgart: Franz Steiner Verlag, 59.23–24. *MB* VVI (108.7): *'jog don* should be *'jog sgom.* See *MB* DLG (64.3).

417. See D 3915: vol. 110, 34b.4 and .6.

418. See D 4026: vol. 123, 191a.3.

419. *MB* VVI (110.4) reads *dpyad pa rnam sbyongs* (as do all extant editions). Nevertheless, since *dpyad pa rnam sbyongs* ("purifying analysis") is not one of the four

objects of meditation—even though the *Moonbeams* citation on p. 36 of the *Śrāvakabhūmi*'s presentation of these four incorrectly lists *dpyad pa rnam*—this may be a scribal error for *spyad pa rnam sbyongs* ("purifying behavior"). The mistake here is probably a carryover from the misquote. The translation assumes that it should be *spyad pa rnam sbyongs*.

420. D 3915: vol. 110, 31a.5.

421. *MB* VVI (111.11): *zhi gnas* should be *zhi nas*. See *MB* DLG (66.7).

422. *'Od srungs kyis zhus pa*. This is the *Discourse for Kāśyapa*. (*Kāśyapa-parivarta-sūtra, 'Od srung gi le'u zhes bya ba'i mdo*). Toh. 87, H.K. 87. H.K. 87: vol. 40, 232b.4–5. The H.K. recension reads *dper na shing gnyis rlung gis drud pa las/ me byung bas ni de nyid sreg par byed/ de bzhin shes rab dbang po skyes nas kyang/ so sor rtog pa de nyid sreg par byed*. The *Moonbeams* citation (*MB* VVI 111.14–17) reads *shing gnyis drud pa las ni me 'byung ste/ byung ba de yis de gnyis sreg pa ltar/ de bzhin shes rab dbang po skyes nas kyang/ skyes pa de yis de gnyis bsreg par byed*. The bracketed words drawn from Sthiramati's *Extensive Explanation on the "Discourse for Kāśyapa."* See D 4009: vol. 116, 229b.5–6.

423. D 3861: vol. 102, 210a.1–2.

424. Citation not found in the first *Stages of Meditation*. It is found in the middle *Stages of Meditation*. D 3916: vol. 110, 50b.4-6. The Dg.T. recension reads *gal te sems bying par gyur pa brtsal bar ... bying bar gyur na rtsal bar bya'o/ mnyam par gyur na brtsal bar mi bya'o/ ... de'i tshe zhi gnas chung bas mar me ...* The *Moonbeams* citation (*MB* VVI 112.9-13) reads *gal te sems bying par gyur pa bsal bar ... bying bar gyur na bsal bar bya'o/ ... de'i tshe/ de'i phyir de kho na shin tu mar me ...* The bracketed words are from the Dg.T. recension.

425. D 3916: vol. 110, 50b.6–7.

426. H.K. 109: vol. 51, 42b.4–5.

427. H.K. 109: vol. 51, 42b.7–43a.1. The H.K. recension reads ... *de bzhin nyid du ...*; the *Moonbeams* citation (*MB* VVI 113.6) reads ... *de bzhin du ...* The translation follows the H.K. recension.

428. *Explanation of Just the Maitreya Chapter from "Unraveling the Intent"* (**Saṃdhinirmocanasūtre-āryamaitreyakevalaparivartabhāṣya, dGongs pa nges par grel pa'i mdo las / 'Phags pa byams pa'i le'u nyi tshe bshad pa*). Toh. 4033. D 4033: vol. 124, 321a.6–7. The Dg.T. recension reads ... *lhag mthong gis dmigs pa'i sems la dmigs pa'i phyir ... lhag mthong gis dmigs pa'i sems kho na la dmigs pas*; the *Moonbeams* citation (*MB* VVI 113.8–9) reads ... *lhag mthong gi dmigs pa'i sems la dmigs pa'i phyir ... lhag mthong gi dmigs pa'i sems kho na la dmigs pas*. The corresponding section in *Unraveling the Intent* (H.K. 109: vol. 51, 41b.6) reads *lhag mthong gi dmigs pa'i sems la dmigs pa'i phyir ro*, as does Wonch'uk's *Extensive Commentary on "Unraveling the Intent"* (*Gambhīrasaṃdhinirmocanasūtraṭīkā, dGongs pa zab mo nges par 'grel pa'i mdo rgya cher 'grel pa*). Toh. 4016. D 4016: vol. 119, 102b.2.

429. D 3915: vol. 110, 34b.4–7. The Dg.T. recension reads ... *zhi gnas kyis dmigs pa ... mun pa bsal ba bzhin du sgrib pa 'byung ngo ... ci zhe na ... rnal 'byor pa rnams kyi zhi gnas skabs ...*; the *Moonbeams* citation (*MB* VVI 115.15–116.5) reads ...

zhi gnas kyi dmigs pa . . . mun pa bsal ba bzhin du 'byung ngo . . . ces zhe na . . . rnal 'byor pa rnams kyi gnas skabs . . . The translation follows the Dg.T. recension in reading . . . *rnal 'byor pa rnams kyi zhi gnas skabs . . .*

The quoted statement, "When you rest evenly in that, you know what is true just as it is" (*de ni mnyam par bzhag na yang dag pa ji lta ba bzhin rab tu shes so*), is found in numerous Tengyur treatises, including Asaṅga's *Yogāchāryābhūmi* (D 4039: vol. 131, 237a.1): *sems mnyam par bzhag na yang dag pa ji lta ba bzhin du mthong bar 'gyur ro*; Vasubandhu's *Explanation of the "Ornament for the Mahāyāna Sūtras"* (D 4026: vol. 123, 198a.23): *sems mnyam par bzhag na yang dag pa ji lta ba bzhin du rab tu shes so*; and Vasubandhu's *Explanation of the "Treasury of Abhidharma"* (D 4090: vol. 141, 66a.2-3): *sems mnyam par bzhag na yang dag pa ji lta ba bzhin du rab tu shes.*

430. D 3915: vol. 110, 33b.6–7. Sūtra citation not found in the Kangyur. It is found in Jñānakīrti's *Entrance to Suchness* (*Tattvāvatārākhyasakalasugatavacastātparyavyākhyāprakaraṇa, De kho na nyid la 'jug pa zhes bya ba bde bar gshegs pa'i bka' ma lus pa mdor bsdus te bshad pa'i rab tu byed pa*). Toh. 3709. See D 3709: vol. 78, 65a.1, where the author states that this is from the *Mother of the Bhagavān* (*bCom ldan 'das yum*).
431. D 3915: vol. 110, 34b.6–7.
432. This seems to be a reference to a statement by Tsongkhapa in the *Great Treatise*, 704–5. See Lamrim Chenmo Translation Committee, *Great Treatise*, vol. 3, 260.
433. In his *Abundant Virtue: A Collection of Dharma Lectures* (*Tshogs chos yon tan phun tshogs*) (Collected Works, text 6/cha, 16b), Gampopa says that there are two types of nonarisings: negated nonarisings (*bkag pa skye med*) and natural nonarisings (*rang bzhin skye med*). The first are emptiness arrived at through determining the "established conclusion" regarding the self-entities of persons and phenomena. Those do not include natural nonarisings. The second is the self-liberating within emptiness through meditating on the path of method (such as caṇḍālī). The manifestation of oneself as a buddha is a natural nonarising. That includes negated nonarisings.
434. *Pramāṇasamuccaya, Tshad ma kun las btus pa zhes bya ba'i rab tu byed pa*, by Dignāga. Toh 4203. D 4203: vol. 174, 13a.3. The Dg.T. recension reads . . . *thub pa'i bstan las cher bsrings nyams par byas ma yin*; the *Moonbeams* citation (*MB* VVI 117.11) reads . . . *de ni thub pa'i bstan la chos srid nyams pa'ang yin.*
435. *Entrance to the Two Truths.* D 3902: vol. 109, 72b.1–2. The Dg.T. recension reads *mngon sum dang ni rjes su dpag/ sangs rgyas pa yis de gnyis gzung/ gnyis pos stong nyid rtogs so shes/ tshu rol mthong ba'i rmongs pa smra*; the *Moonbeams* citation (117.13–14) reads *mngon sum dang ni rjes su dpag/ shes pa gnyis kyi sgo nas ni/ stong nyid mthong bar 'gyur ro shes/ tshu rol mthong ba'i rmongs pa smra.*
436. *Kālacakra Tantra / Glorious Kālacakra, King of Tantras: Issued from the Supreme, Original Buddha* (by Mañjuśrī Yaśas) (*Laghutantra / Laghukālacakra / Paramādibuddhoddhṛta-śrīkālacakra-nāma-tantrarāja, bsDus pa'i rgyud / Dus 'khor nyung ngu / mChog gi dang po'i sangs rgyas las phyung ba rgyud kyi rgyal po dpal dus kyi 'khor lo*). Toh. 362 and 1346.

437. This seems to be drawn from the *Great Treatise,* 773. See Lamrim Chenmo Translation Committee, *Great Treatise,* vol. 3, 331.

438. This "someone else" seems to be Tsongkhapa. See his first refutation in *Great Treatise,* 773–81 and Lamrim Chenmo Translation Committee, *Great Treatise,* vol. 3, 331–37.

439. *MB* VVI (119.3): I am reading *rtsom 'jog* as *tsom 'jog,* which is used by Tsongkhapa in his rebuttal of this position. See the *Great Treatise* (773–74).

440. This seems to be drawn from the *Great Treatise,* 781. See Lamrim Chenmo Translation Committee, *Great Treatise,* vol. 3, 337.

441. This is probably Tsongkhapa. See his second refutation in *Great Treatise,* 781, and Lamrim Chenmo Translation Committee, *Great Treatise,* vol. 3, 337–38.

442. This seems to be drawn from the *Great Treatise,* 781–82. See Lamrim Chenmo Translation Committee, *Great Treatise,* vol. 3, 338.

443. This is probably Tsongkhapa. See his third refutation in *Great Treatise,* 782, and Lamrim Chenmo Translation Committee, *Great Treatise,* vol. 3, 338.

444. This seems to be drawn from the *Great Treatise,* 782. See Lamrim Chenmo Translation Committee, *Great Treatise,* vol. 3, 338–39.

445. This is probably Tsongkhapa. See his fourth refutation in *Great Treatise,* 782–83, and Lamrim Chenmo Translation Committee, *Great Treatise,* vol. 3, 339.

446. Citation not found in the *Stages of Meditation.* It is found in Kamalaśīla's *Entering Yoga Meditation* (*Yogabhāvanāvatāra, rNal 'byor bsgom pa la 'jug pa*). Toh. 3918. D 3918: vol. 110, 70a.1. The Dg.T. recension reads *chos thams cad don dam par rang bzhin med par bsam mo . . .* ; the *Moonbeams* citation (*MB* VVI 121.19) reads *chos thams cad rang bzhin med par bsam mo . . .*

447. D 3824: vol. 96, 8a.6–7. Also cited in the *Great Treatise.*

448. D 3824: vol. 96, 13b.1–2.

449. D 3824: vol. 96, 8b.7–9a.1.

450. D 3824: vol. 96, 9a.2. *MB* VVI (122.9): *rtag par lta* should be *rtag par 'dzin.* See *MB* VVI (95.12) and the Dg.T. recension. Also cited in both Collected Works of Gampopa and *Great Treatise.*

451. D 1800: vol. 35, 40a.5–6. The translation is based on Chödrak Yeshe's *Elucidating the Word-Meaning: An Explanation of the "Commentary on Bodhicitta"* (670). Other explanations would warrant different translations.

452. D 3824: vol. 96, 15a.2. Also cited in both Collected Works of Gampopa and *Great Treatise.*

453. *Mūlamadhyamakavṛttiprasannapadā, dBu ma'i rtsa ba'i 'grel pa tshig gsal ba* by Candrakīrti. Toh. 3860. D 3860: vol. 102, 164b.4.

454. Citation not found in the *Fundamental Treatise on the Middle Way.* It is found in Nāgārjuna's *Precious Garland* (D 4158: vol. 172, 109a.2–3). The Dg.T. recension reads *med pa pa ni ngan 'gror 'gro/ yod pa pa ni bde 'gror 'gro*; the *Moonbeams* citation (*MB* VVI 123.1) reads *yod pa po ni bde 'gror 'gro/ med pa po ni ngan 'gror 'gro.* Found in Gampopa's *Ornament of Precious Liberation* (102b) attributed to the *Precious Garland.*

455. D 4033: vol. 124, 321a.6–7. See note 428 for textual differences.

456. D 1118: vol. 1, 65a.6. The Dg.T. recension reads . . . *rang bzhin med pa nyid* . . . ; the *Moonbeams* citation (*MB* VVI 123.16) reads . . . *rang bzhin med nyid las* . . .

457. *Dohā for the Queen* (*bTsun mo Do ha*). Also known as *Dohākoṣopadeśagīti* (*Mi zad pa'i gter mdzod man ngag gi glu*). Toh. 2264. D 2264: vol. 52, 29a.3. The Dg.T. recension reads . . . *rang bzhin gdod nas rnam pa kun gyi dpyad bya min* . . . ; the *Moonbeams* citation (*MB* VVI 123.19) . . . *rang bzhin gdod nas dag pas kun gyis dpyad bya min* . . .

 The translation follows the Dg.T. recension in reading *kun gyi*, which is also found in Karma Tinle's *Mirror That Reveals the Liberation of Mind: The Middle-Length Commentary on the Queen's Dohā* (*bTsun mo do ha'i t'i ka 'bring po sems kyi rnam thar ston pa'i me long*). Sarnath: Vajra Vidya Institute Library, 124.

 MB VVI (123.20): *btses pa* should *gtse pa*. See *MB* VVI (369.6) and the Dg.T. recension.

458. Citation not found in works by Nāgārjuna. It is found in Śāntideva's *Entrance to the Bodhisattva's Way of Life*. D 3871: vol. 105, 31a.1.

459. H.K. 17: vol. 34, 189b.7–190a.1.

460. *Dohā for the People* (*dMangs do ha*). Also known as *Songs in a Treasury of Dohās* (*Dohakoṣagīti, Do ha mdzod kyi glu*). Toh. 2224. D 2224: vol. 51, 75a.2–3. Also cited in Collected Works of Gampopa.

461. *Dohā for the People*. D 2224: vol. 51, 71b.2. The Dg.T. recension reads . . . *yod pa de yang* . . . ; the *Moonbeams* citation (*MB* VVI 124.16) reads . . . *yod na de yang* . . . The Moonbeams citation is identical to one found in Gampopa's *Sunrays of Scriptural Citations* (18a), and Gampopa's *Ornament of Precious Liberation* (105a).

462. D 1800: vol. 35, 40a.3.

463. D 3861: vol. 102, 210a.2.

464. D 3929: vol. 110, 96a.2.

465. D 1800: vol. 35, 41a.3. The Dg.T. recension reads . . . *de dag thar pa'i rten ma yin* . . . ; the *Moonbeams* citation (*MB* VVI 126.10) reads . . . *de dag thar pa bsten ma yin* . . . The translation follows the Dg.T. recension.

466. *Dṛṣtisaṃkṣipta, lTa ba mdor bsdus pa*. Toh 2304. D 2304: vol. 52, 245b.1. The Dg.T. recension reads *de ltar lta ba ma nor na* . . . *dkyus bstan pa yi rta bzhin no* . . . *lta ba dngos dang ma mthun na* . . . *dmus long dmigs bu med pa bzhin*; the *Moonbeams* citation (*MB* VVI 126.15–17) reads *de ltar lta ba ma nor bas* . . . *dkyu sa bstan pa rta bzhin no* . . . *lta ba dngos su ma mthun na* . . . *dmus long mig bu med pa bzhin*.

467. *Guhyasamāja Tantra* (*Sarvatathāgatakāyavākcittarahasyaguhyasamājanāmamahākalparāja, gSang 'dus / De bzhin gshegs pa thams cad kyi sku gsung thugs kyi gsang chen gsang ba 'dus pa zhes bya ba brtag pa'i rgyal po chen po*). Toh. 442, H.K. 416a. The cited verse is probably H.K. 416a: vol. 82, 494a.5–6: *rang sems rnams ni dmigs pa la/ chos rnams thams cad rab tu gnas/ nam mkha' rdo rje'i gnas sems 'di/ chos med chos nyid med pa'o.*

 The *Moonbeams* citation resembles Ratnākaraśānti's citation in his *Instructions on Prajñāpāramitā* (D 4079: vol. 138, 161a.7–161b.1): *rang gi sems ni brtags pas na/ chos kun sems la rab tu gnas/ chos 'di nam mkha'i rdo rjer gnas/ chos dang chos nyid med pa'o*, and may be drawn from there. The *Moonbeams* citation (*MB* VVI 127.5–6) reads *rang gi sems ni brtag pa na/ chos kun rang gi sems la gnas/ chos 'di nam mkha'i rdo rjer gnas/ chos dang chos nyid med pa'o.*

468. *Vajra Pañjarā* (*Vajrapañjarā* / *Ḍākinī–vajrapañjarā-mahātantrarāja-kalpa-nāma*, *rDo rje gur* / *mKha' 'gro ma rdo rje gur zhes bya ba'i rgyud kyi rgyal po chen po'i brtags pa*). Toh. 419, H.K. 379. H.K. 379: vol. 79, 400a.4. The H.K. recension reads *sems kyi rin chen bskul . . .* ; the *Moonbeams* citation (*MB* VVI 127.8) reads *rin chen sems kyis bskul . . .*

469. H.K. 110: vol. 51, 270a.1–3. The H.K. recension reads *sems tsam la ni gnas nas ni/ phyi rol don la mi brtag go/ yang dag dmigs la gnas nas ni/ sems tsam las ni 'da' bar bya/ sems tsam las ni 'das na ni/ snang ba med las 'da' bar bya/ rnal 'byor snang ba med gnas na/ theg pa chen po mi mthong ngo.* The *Moonbeams* citation (*MB* VVI 127.11–14) reads *sems tsam la ni brten nas ni/ phyi rol don la mi brtag go/ de bzhin nyid kyi dmigs gnas nas/ sems tsam las kyang 'da' bar bya/ sems tsam las ni 'das nas su/ snang ba med la 'da' bar bya/snang med gnas pa'i rnal 'byor pa/ de yis theg pa chen po mthong.*

Note that the *Moonbeams* citation is almost identical to the citation attributed to this text in Bhāvaviveka's *Precious Lamp of Madhyamaka* (*Madhyamakaratnapradīpa, dbU ma rin po che'i sgron ma*) (Toh. 3854; D 3854: vol. 97, 280a.4); Nāgārjuna's *Stages of Meditation* (*Bhāvanākrama, bsGom pa'i rim pa*) (Toh. 3908; D 3908: vol. 110, 4a.1–2); and Kamalaśīla's first *Stages of Meditation* (D 3915: vol. 110, 33a.3–4). The Dg.T. 3854 recension of the citation reads . . . *de bzhin nyid la brten nas ni/ . . . sems tsam las ni 'das gyur na/ snang ba med la gnas par 'gyur . . .* The Dg.T. 3908 recension of the citation reads . . . *de bzhin nyid dmigs nas ni/ sems tsam las ni 'da' bar bya/ . . . snang ba med las 'da' bar bya . . .* The Dg.T. 3915 recension of the citation reads *sems tsam la ni rab brten nas/ . . . sems tsam las kyang bzla bar bya/ sems tsam las ni bzlas nas su/ snang ba med las bzla bar bya . . .*

Regarding the last line having a negative or not: Suzuki, *Laṅkāvatāra Sūtra*, 247n2, says that one Sanskrit manuscript replaces "not" (*na*) with "he" (*sa*). On the other hand, fifteen texts in the Tengyur cite this quotation (with or without attribution) without the negative (each citation is slightly different, often resembling the *Moonbeams* citation more than the H.K. recension). These include, in addition to the aforementioned texts, Jñānakīrti's *Entrance to Suchness* (*Tattvāvatārākhyasakalasugatavacastātparyavyākhyāprakaraṇa, De kho na nyid la 'jug pa zhes bya ba bde bar gshegs pa'i bka' ma lus pa mdor bsdus te bshad pa'i rab tu byed pa*) (Toh. 3709; D 3709: vol. 78, 64b.5); and Ratnākaraśānti's *Instructions on Prajñāpāramitā* (D 4079: vol. 138, 161a.5–6).

For a translation of Kamalaśīla's commentary on these lines in his first *Stages of Meditation*, see Brunnhölzl, *Center of the Sunlit Sky*, 300–2.

470. D 4020: vol. 123, 6b.5.

471. *Dohā for the People.* D 2224: vol. 51, 72b.5.

472. D 3917: vol. 110, 62a.7.

473. H.K. 87: vol. 40, 232b.3–4. Also cited in the *Great Treatise.*

474. D 3916: vol. 110, 49b.5–6. Also cited in the *Great Treatise.*
475. Citation not found in the Kangyur. It is found in numerous Tengyur treatises, where it is sometimes attributed to the Buddha. See the first *Stages of Meditation* (D 3915: vol. 110, 34b.6). Also see note 429 for more information.
476. D 3915: vol. 110, 34b.4.
477. *Compendium of Dharma Sūtra.* H.K. 239: vol. 65, 106a.4–5.
478. D 3915: vol. 110, 33b.6–7. Sūtra citation not found in the Kangyur. It is found in Jñānakīrti's *Entrance to Suchness.* See D 3709: vol. 78, 65a.1, where it is attributed to the *Mother of the Bhagavān* (*bCom ldan 'das yum*).
479. This verse is also found on p. 81 where it is attributed to the *Sūtra of Genuine Samādhi.*
480. *Lamp That Summarizes Conduct.* D 3960: vol. 111, 313a.5. The Dg.T. recension reads *chos nyid spros pa dang bral ba* . . . ; the *Moonbeams* citation (*MB* VVI 129.17) reads *chos dbyings spros dang bral ba la* . . .
481. *Song of the View of Dharmadhātu.* D 2314: vol. 52, 255a.2. The Dg.T. recension reads *blo mig zhib mo rtog bral ba* . . . ; the *Moonbeams* citation (*MB* VVI 130.1) reads *blo mig zhib mos rtog bral bar* . . .
482. D 3929: vol. 110, 95b.5–96b.2. The Dg.T. recension reads . . . *shes rab nyid snang ba med pa cing 'od gsal ba* . . . ; the *Moonbeams* citation (*MB* VVI 130.13) reads . . . *shes rab de nyid kyang snang ba med pa 'od gsal ba* . . . The translation follows the Dg.T. recension.
483. Citation not found in the *Stages of Meditation.* It is found in Kamalaśīla's *Entering Yoga Meditation.* D 3918: vol. 110, 70a.1–2. See note 446 for textual differences.
484. H.K. 129: vol. 55, 22b.2–3.
485. D 3916: vol. 110, 50a.1 and D 3917: vol. 110, 58b.5. The passage from the *Jewel Cloud Sūtra* is probably H.K. 232: vol. 64, 146a.2–3. The H.K. recension reads [*sems*] *de dang de dag la ngo bo nyid yongs su btsal na stong par rtogs so/* . . . *de de ltar rtog pas mtshan ma med pa la rnal 'byor du byed do*; the middle and final *Stages of Meditation* and the *Moonbeams* citation (*MB* VVI 132.1–3) read *sems gang gis rtog pa de yang ngo bo nyid kun tu btsal na stong par rtogs te/ de ltar rtogs pas mtshan ma med pa'i rnal 'byor la 'jug go.* Also cited in the *Great Treatise.*
486. D 3917: vol. 110, 63a.7. Also cited in the *Great Treatise.*
487. D 3916: vol. 110, 49b.4. The Dg.T. recension reads *rnam par dpyad de dngos po gang* . . . *don dam par nges par mi 'dzin pa*; the *Moonbeams* citation (*MB* VVI 132.5–6) reads *rnam par dpyad de gang* . . . *don dam par mi 'dzin pa.*
488. *Avikalpapraveśadhāraṇīṭīkā, rNam par mi rtog par 'jug pa'i gzungs kyi rgya cher 'grel pa.* Toh. 4000.
489. D 3947: vol. 111, 240b.4. The Dg.T. recension reads *chos rnams thams cad skye med pa'i* . . . ; the *Moonbeams* citation (*MB* VVI 132.11) reads *chos rnams thams cad rkyen med pa'i* . . . The translation follows the Dg.T. recension.
490. This is stated by Buddhaguhya in his *Entrance to the Meaning of the Tantras* (*Tantrārthāvatāra, rGyud kyi don la 'jug pa*). Toh. 2501. See D 2501: vol. 54, 4b.5.

491. *Gaganagañjaparipṛcchāsūtra, Nam mkha' mdzod kyis zhus pa.* Toh. 148, H.K. 149. H.K. 149: vol. 57, 363b.4–364a.1. The H.K. recension reads *shin tu 'dod chags . . . shin tu de bzhin nyid . . . shin tu yang dag pa'i mtha'i . . . shin tu nam mkha'i*; the *Moonbeams* citation (*MB* VVI 134.9–10) reads *'dod chags . . . de bzhin nyid . . . yang dag pa'i mtha'i . . . nam mkha'i. MB* VVI (134.4): *bskyon pa* should be *bskyod pa.* See *MB* DLG (83.7) and H.K. (363.4).

492. *Śrīguhyasiddhi / Sakalatantrasambhavasaṃcodanī-śrīguhyasiddhi, gSang ba grub pa / rGyud ma lus pa'i don nges par skul bar byed pa dpal gsang ba grub pa* by Padmavajra. Toh. 2217. D 2217: vol. 51, 14b.1. The Dg.T. recension reads *bzhi pa gong na med pa'i rgyu . . .*; the *Moonbeams* citation (*MB* VVI 134.12) reads *bzhi pa gong na med pa'i rgyud . . .* The translation follows the Dg.T. recension.

493. *Mahāmudrā-tilakaṃ, Phyag rgya chen po'i thig le.* Toh. 420, H.K. 380. Citation not found in the Kangyur. The first line is found in *Tantra Prophesying the Intent* (*Sandhivyākaraṇa-tantra, dGongs pa lung bsten pa'i rgyud*). Toh. 444, H.K. 418. H.K. 418: vol. 83, 160b.2. The last three lines (with one difference) are found in Tilopa's *Teachings of the Formless Vajra Ḍākinīs* (*Vajraḍākiniṣkāyadharma, rDo rje mkha' 'gro lus med pa'i chos*). Toh. 1527. D 1527: vol. 23, 85a.6, and it reads . . . *rgya ni 'khor ba'i rgya dang bral . . .* ; the *Moonbeams* citation (*MB* VVI 134.18) reads . . . *rgya ni 'khor ba'i chos las 'grol . . .*

494. *Pañcakrama, Rim pa lnga pa* by Nāgārjuna. Toh. 1802. D 1802: vol. 35, 48a.4–5. The Dg.T. recension reads *rang gis rang gi ye shes ni . . .* ; the *Moonbeams* citation (*MB* VVI 135.1) reads *rang gis rang rig ye shes ni . . .*

495. H.K. 416a: vol. 82, 439a.1–2.

496. *Tattvadaśaka, De kho na nyid bcu pa.* Toh. 2236. (Note this is attributed to Advayavajra, a later name for Maitrīpa.) Citation not found in this text. It is found (unattributed) in Jñānakīrti's *Entrance to Suchness.* D 3709: vol. 78, 43a.7–43b.1. The Dg.T. recension reads . . . *mnyam sbyor ba'i/ bsgom pa nyid rnal 'byor mchog gi ni/ phyag rgya chen po'i mnyam sbyor ba*; the *Moonbeams* citation (*MB* VVI 135.12–13) reads . . . *mnyam sbyor ba/ sgom pa mchog gi rnal 'byor pa/ phyag rgya chen po mnyam sbyor ba.*

497. *Padmani-nāma-pañjikā, Padma can zhes bya ba'i dka' 'grel* by Kālacakramahāpāda. Toh. 1350. D 1350: vol. 13, 83a.6–7.

498. *Pointing Out the Essence: An Ultimate Treasury* (*sNying po'i ngo sprod don dam gter mdzod*). Collected Works of Gampopa, text 25/ra, 1b. *MB* VVI (136.3): *chos nyid rab grol* should be *chos nyid rang grol.* See *MB* DLG (85.2) and Collected Works of Gampopa edition.

499. *Theg sgron.* Text not found.

500. *Jñānasiddhi-nāma-sādhanopāyikā, Ye shes grub pa zhes bya ba'i sgrub pa'i thabs.* Toh 2219. D 2219: vol. 51, 38b.5-6.

501. *Yogasaptanāmacaturabhiṣekhaprakaraṇa, sByor ba bdun pa zhes bya ba dbang bzhi'i rab to byed pa* by Vitapāda. Toh 1875. D 1875: vol. 44, 72b.3–4.

502. *Sādhana for the Siddhi of Wisdom.* D 2219: vol. 51, 38b.5.

503. Citation not found in a text attributed to Maitrīpa. It is found (with some textual

differences) in Saraha's *Dohā Song on View, Meditation, Conduct, and Fruition* (*Bhāvanādṛṣṭicaryāphaladohagītikā, lTa bsgom spyod pa 'bras bu'i do ha'i glu*). Toh. 2345. D 2345: vol. 53, 3a.7–3b.1.

The Dg.T. recension reads *zung 'jug phyag rgya blo 'das chen po ni/ bde gsal mi rtog nam mkha' lta bu ste/ khyab cing rgya chen snying rje chen po'i ngo/ snang yang rang bzhin med pa chu zla bzhin/ gsal yang tha snyad mtha' dbus kun dang bral/ gang gis ma gos dri med re dogs bral/ lkugs pa'i rmi lam bzhin du smra mi shes.*

The *Moonbeams* citation (*MB* VVI 137.7–13) reads *zung 'jug blo 'das phyag rgya chen po ni/ gsal la mi rtog nam mkha' lta bu yis/ khyab cing rgya che snying rje chen po ni/ snang la rang bzhin med pa chu zla bzhin/ gsal la tha snyad mtha' dbus kun bral/ gang gis ma gos dri med re dogs bral/ lkugs pa'i rmi lam bzhin du smra mi shes.*

504. *Mahāyānottaratantraśāstra, rGyud bla ma / Theg pa chen po rgyud bla ma'i bstan bcos.* Toh. 4024. D 4024: vol. 123, 56b.6–7.

505. *bDe mchog 'byung ba.* Toh. 373, H.K. 389. H.K. 389: vol. 81, 6b.3.

506. *Jñānagarbha, Ye shes snying po.* Toh. 421, H.K. 381. H.K. 381: vol. 79, 475b.2–3.

507. D 2219: vol. 51, 38b.5. The Dg.T. recension reads ... *snang bas me long shes bya'o*; the *Moonbeams* citation (*MB* VVI 139.1) reads ... *snang ba me long shes bya'o.* The translation follows the Dg.T. recension.

508. H.K. 380: vol. 79, 471b.6–472a.1. The H.K. recension reads ... *gang zhig dri med shes pa min* ... ; the *Moonbeams* citation (*MB* VVI 139.10) reads ... *gang zhig dag pa ma shes pa* ...

509. D 1800: vol. 35, 41a.3. For textual differences, see note 465.

510. *Summary Verses on Mahāmudrā* (*Mahāmudrāsañcamitha* [sic], *Phyag rgya chen po'i tshig bsdus pa*). Not included in the Tengyur. In the Eight Dohā Treasures (*Do ha mdzod brgyad / Do ha mdzod brgyad ces bya ba phyag rgya chen po'i man ngag gsar bar ston pa'i gzhung*). TsRP, vol. 4, 45.5–6. The TsRP recension reads *gang gis* ... ; the *Moonbeams* citation (*MB* VVI 140.4) reads *gang gi* ...

Dakpo Tashi Namgyal refers to two texts of this name (see e.g., p. 280), one by Maitrīpa, the other by Nāropa. Of the four consulted editions of texts with that name, two are attributed to Nāropa, one to Maitrīpa, and one is unattributed. The four texts are almost identical although the differences are notable. See the Bibliography under Nāropa for three of the four consulted editions, and Maitrīpa for the fourth.

Since it is not clear what Dakpo Tashi Namgyal's source was for this and other citations from the *Summary Verses on Mahāmudrā* attributed to Maitrīpa, unless otherwise noted, I use the *Summary Verses on Mahāmudrā* in the Eight Dohā Treasures (TsRP) when the reference is to Maitrīpa's *Summary Verses on Mahāmudrā* since that is the only edition whose colophon credits Maitrīpa with authorship.

511. *Summary Verses on Mahāmudrā*, 46.4. *MB* VVI (140.7): *mi rtogs* should be *ma rtogs*. See *MB* DLG (87.6) and TsRP edition.

512. *Sāgaramati-paripṛcchā-nāma-mahāyāna-sūtra, bLo gros rgya mtshos zhus pa zhes bya ba theg pa chen po'i mdo.* Toh. 152, H.K. 153. H.K. 153: vol. 58, 118b.5.

513. H.K. 153: vol. 58, 120a.7–120b.1. The H.K. recension reads ... *nam mkha'i dkyil*

dang bye brag med . . . ; the *Moonbeams* citation (*MB* VVI 140.14) reads . . . *nam mkha'i dkyil ltar bye brag med* . . .

514. H.K. 153: vol. 58, 39b.1–2. The H.K. recension reads *ngar 'dzin pa yongs su dag pas nang yongs su dag pa dri ma med pa'i phyag rgya dang*; the *Moonbeams* citation (*MB* VVI 140.16) reads *ngar 'dzin pa yongs su dag pas dri ma med pa'i phyag rgya dang*. The translation follows the H.K. recension because the second of the twenty mudrās is the mudrā that is stainless and externally pure by virtue of having purified belief in a self (*ngar 'dzin pa yongs su dag pas phyi yongs su dag pa dri ma med pa'i phyag rgya*).

515. H.K. 153: vol. 58, 41a.7–41b.1. The H.K. recension reads . . . *gdod nas byung ba med* . . . ; the *Moonbeams* citation (*MB* VVI 141.1) reads . . . *gdod nas skye ba med* . . . The translation follows the H.K. recension.

516. *Maitreyaprasthānasūtra, Byams pa 'jug pa'i mdo*. Toh. 198, H.K. 199. H.K. 199: vol. 61, 443b.4.

517. See H.K. 149: vol. 57, 363b.6–364a.1.

518. *Bu mo rin chen gyis zhus pa / Theg pa chen po'i man ngag bu mo rin chen gyis zhus pa* is an alternative title for the *Instructions on the Mahāyāna* (*Mahāyānopadeśasūtra, Theg pa chen po'i man ngag gi mdo*). Toh. 169, H.K. 170. H.K. 170: vol. 59, 481b.7–482a.1.

519. *Bhadrakalpikasūtra, bsKal bzang / bsKal pa bzang po pa*. Toh. 94, H.K. 95. H.K. 95: vol. 47, 22b.5–6 and 24b.4.

520. *Varmavyūhanirdeśasūtra, Go cha'i bkod pa bstan pa*. Toh. 51, H.K. 51. See H.K. 51: vol. 36, 216a.7, 220b.5–6, and 221b.2–3.

521. *Mañjuśrīmūlatantra, 'Jam dpal gyi rtsa ba'i rgyud*. Toh. 543, H.K. 501. H.K. 501: vol. 88, 318b.3, 324b.1, 325a.4, 334a.4, and *passim*.

522. *Mahāvairocanābhisambodhi-vikurvatī-adhiṣṭhāna-vaipulya-sūtra-indrarājā, rNam snang mngon byang / rNam par snang mdzad chen po mngon par rdzogs par byang chub pa rnam par sprul pa byin gyis rlob pa shin tu rgyas pa mdo sde'i dbang po'i rgyal po*. Toh. 494, H.K. 462. H.K. 462: vol. 86, 243a.5 and 333a.2.

523. *Dus 'khor rtsa rgyud*. The root *Kālacakra Tantra* (*Ādibuddhatantra, Dang po'i sang rgyas*) is said to have contained 12,000 verses and, while not existing as a separate text now, many verses from it are found in Puṇḍarīka's *Stainless Light* (*Vimalaprabhā, Dri ma med pa'i 'od*) (Toh. 845 and Toh. 1347) and other works related to the Kālacakra system. This verse is cited in the *Stainless Light*. D 1347: vol. 12, 242b.1–2.

524. The first two lines are found in *Stainless Light*. D 1347: vol. 12, 159b.2. The second two are found in *Summary of the [Kālacakra] Initiation* (*Sekoddeśa, dBang mdor bstan pa*). Toh. 361, H.K. 370. H.K. 370: vol. 79, 24a.3–4 as part of the following verse: *las kyi phyag rgya'i snyoms 'jug dang/ ye shes phyag rgya'i dmigs pa dang/ phyag rgya chen po gcig sbyor bas/ mi 'gyur ba de 'phel bar 'gyur*. The *Moonbeams* citation (*MB* VVI 142.12–13) reads *las kyi phyag rgya'i rab sbyor dang/ ye shes phyag rgya'i rjes chags dang/ phyag rgya chen mos gcig sbyor ba/ mi 'gyur ba de 'phel bar 'gyur*.

525. D 2217: vol. 51, 10a.6–7.

526. *Pradarshanānumatoddeshaparīkṣā* / *Āryamañjuśrīpradarshana, Rang gi lta ba'i 'dod pa mdor bstan pa yongs su brtag pa* / *'Phags pa 'jam dpal gyi rang gi lta ba* by Narendrakīrti. P.K. 4610, N.K. 3400. N.K. 36a.6–7. The N.K. recension reads *las kyi phyag rgya g.yon can gdug/ ye shes phyag rgya de bzhin te/ rnam par rtog ma dor byas nas/ phyag rgya chen po brten par byos.* The *Moonbeams* citation (142.18–19) reads *las kyi phyag rgya g.yon can gdug/ ye shes phyag rgya de bzhin du/ rnam rtog mang ba dor byas nas/ phyag rgya chen po bsten par byos.*

These lines are cited (attributed to the *Synopsis of Our View Asserted by Mañjuśrī*) in *Illuminating the Unmoving Heart: A Commentary for Entering the Glorious Tantra of "Stainless Light"* (*Śrīmadvimalaprabhātantrāvatāraṇīvāda-hṛdayāloka, dPal ldan dri ma dang bral ba'i 'od kyi rgyud la 'jug pa'i bshad sbyar mi g.yo ba'i snying po snang ba*). Author unknown. Toh. 1349. Dg.T. 1349: vol. 13, 33b.7–34a.1. The Dg.T. 1349 recension reads *las kyi phyag rgya g.yo can gdug/ ye shes phyag rgya de bzhin te/ rnam par rtog mang dor byas nas/ phyag rgya chen po brten par byos.*

527. *Illuminating Lamp* (*Pradīpoddyotana-nāma-ṭīkā, sGron gsal* / *sGron ma gsal bar byed pa zhes bya ba'i rgya cher bshad pa*) by Candrakīrti. Toh. 1785. D 1785: vol. 30, 32a.5.

528. *rDo rje phreng ba*. Toh. 445, H.K. 417. H.K. 417: vol. 83, 62b.5. The H.K. recension reads . . . *phyag rgya chen po mngon par brjod* . . . ; the *Moonbeams* citation (*MB* VVI 143.6) reads . . . *phyag rgya chen po ma nor brjod* . . .

529. *Candraguhyatilaka, Zla gsang thig le.* Toh. 477, H.K. 446. H.K. 446: vol. 84, 87b.1–2.

530. *Sarvabuddhasamayogaḍākinīmāyāśambaravṛttisamayogālaṃkāra, Sangs rgyas mnyam sbyor gyi 'grel pa* / *Sangs rgyas thams cad dang mnyam par sbyor ba mkha' 'gro ma sgyu ma bde mchog gi 'grel pa mnyam sbyor gyi rgyan* by *Pramuditāvajra. Toh. 1660. *Moonbeams* (*MB* VVI 143.12) refers to the author in Tibetan as Garab Dorje (dGa' rab rdo rje), and the Dg.T. lists the author as Rabtu Ga-way Dorje (Rab tu dga' ba'i rdo rje). For instances of four mudrās in this text, see D 1660: vol. 26, 390b.2, 391a.7, and 391b.1.

531. Abhayākaragupta's commentary is *Abhayākara's Source Commentary: A Detailed Explanation of the "Buddha-kapāla, King of Tantras"* (*Buddhakapālamahātantrarājaṭīkā-abhayapāddhati, Sangs rgyas thod pa'i rgyud kyi rgyal po chen po'i rgya cher 'grel pa 'jigs pa med pa'i gzhung 'grel*). Toh. 1654.

532. Nāropa's commentary is the *Commentary on the Difficult Points: Summarizing the Essence of the Vajra Words* (*Vajrapādasāra-saṃgraha-pañjikā, rDo rje'i tshig gi snying po bsdus pa'i dka' 'grel*). Toh. 1186. See D 1186: vol. 4, 62a.5–6.

533. *Caturmudrāniścaya, Phyag rgya bzhi gtan la dbab pa.* Toh. 2225. The Tengyur recension's colophon identifies the author as Nāgārjunagarbha, not Maitrīpa. See D 2225: vol. 51, 77a.6. However, Mathes, "Collection of 'Indian Mahāmudrā Works,'" 94n19, says: "The attribution of the *Caturmudrāniścaya* to Nāgārjuna was already controversial in the 11th century. Thus we find this text included in the collection of Maitrīpa's works, the *Advayavajrasaṃgraha.*"

534. *Analysis of the Three Vows* (*sDom pa gsum gyi rab tu dbye ba'i bstan bcos*). Sakya Collected Teachings, vol. 12a, 61.2–5.

535. *Ganges Mahāmudrā* (*Phyag chen gang ga' ma*). Also known as the *Esoteric Instructions on Mahāmudrā* (*Mahāmudropadeśa, Phyag rgya chen po'i man ngag*). Toh. 2303.

536. *Mahāmudrapādametha* [sic] / *Mahāmudrāsañcamitha* [sic], *Phyag rgya chen po'i tshig bsdus pa*. DNZ, vol. 7, 47–48. See also note 510.

537. *Ye shes gsal byed.* Text not found.

538. D 1347: vol. 11, 108a.4.

539. H.K. 417: vol. 83, 64b.6–65a.1. The H.K. recension reads . . . *go 'phang bsten* . . . ; the *Moonbeams* citation (*MB* VVI 146.8) reads . . . *go 'phang ste* . . . The translation follows the H.K. recension.

540. H.K. 417: vol. 83, 65a.1–3.

541. H.K. 417: vol. 83, 65a.3–4. The H.K. recension reads . . . *ye shes chen po rab gsol ba* . . . ; the *Moonbeams* citation (*MB* VVI 146.18) reads . . . *ye shes chen po rab rtsol ba* . . . .

542. *Commentary on the Profound Meaning: Detailed Explanation of the "Glorious Vajramālā," a Mahāyoga Tantra* (*Śrīvajramālāmahāyogatantraṭīkāgaṃbhīrārthadīpikā, rNal 'byor chen po'i rgyud dpal rdo rje phreng ba'i rgya cher 'grel pa zab mo'i don gyi 'grel pa*). Toh. 1795.

543. H.K. 380: vol. 79, 471a.4–5. The H.K. recension reads . . . *mi shes mun pa 'jig byed pa/ gsang ba kun ni gsung pa la* . . . ; the *Moonbeams* citation (*MB* VVI 147.4–5) reads . . . *mi shes mun pa med byed pa/ gsang ba kun gyis gsung pa la* . . .

544. H.K. 380: vol. 79, 471a.5–471b.1. The H.K. recension reads . . . *rtag tu shar ba char yang mchog* . . . ; the *Moonbeams* citation (*MB* VVI 147.14) reads . . . *rtag tu shar ba rgyar yang mchog* . . . The translation follows the H.K. recension.

545. See H.K. 380: vol. 79, 471b.1–472a.1.

546. *Great, Wondrous Clarification of the Glorious Profound Principles* (*Śrīguhyārthaprakāśamahādbhūta, dPal zab mo'i don gsal ba rmad du byung ba chen po*). Toh. 1200. See Dg.T. 1200: vol. 8, 153a.4–154a.1.

547. *Jñānatilaka-yoginī-tantrarājā-paramamahādbhutaṃ, Ye shes thig le rnal 'byor ma'i rgyud kyi rgyal po chen po mchog tu rmad du byung ba*. Toh. 422, H.K. 382. H.K. H.K. 382: vol. 80, 53a.1–2.

548. *Jñānatilakapañjikāguhyatattva, Ye shes thig le'i dka' 'grel gsang ba'i de kho na nyid* by Jñānaparama. Toh. 1203. D 1203: vol. 8, 261b.5–6.

549. D 1203: vol. 8, 262a.1–2.

550. *Buddhakapālatantrasya pañjikājñānavatī, Sangs rgyas thod pa'i rgyud kyi dka' 'grel ye shes ldan pa*. Toh. 1652. D 1652: vol. 26, 146b.5. The Dg.T. recension reads *phyag rgya chen po blo chen ma* . . . ; the *Moonbeams* citation (*MB* VVI 148.12) reads *phyag rgya chen po'i blo chen ma* . . . The translation follows the Dg.T. recension because that accords with the *Buddha-kapāla* (H.K. 400: vol. 82, 41b.5).

551. D 1350: vol. 13, 83a.6.

552. *Sekanirdeśapañjikā, dBang bskur ba nges par bstan pa'i dka' 'grel.* Toh. 2253. D 2253:

vol. 51, 154a.2–4. The Dg.T. recension reads . . . *dpyad pas 'ongs pa* . . . and . . . *goms par byas bas* . . . ; the *Moonbeams* citation (*MB* VVI 148.19–20) reads . . . *dpyad pas ma 'ongs pa* . . . and . . . *goms par byas ba* . . .

553. *Sarvabuddha-samāyogaḍākinī-jālasaṁvara-nāma-uttaratantra*, *Sangs rgyas mnyam sbyor / Sangs rgyas thams cad dang mnyam par sbyor ba mkha' 'gro ma sgyu ma bde ba'i mchog ces bya ba'i rgyud bla ma.* Toh. 366, H.K. 376.

554. Sakya Paṇḍita's *Letter to the Buddhas and Bodhisattvas of the Ten Directions* (*Phyogs bcu'i sangs rgyas dang byang chub sems pa thams cad la phul ba'i yi ge*). Sakya Collected Works (Sa skya'i bka' 'bum), vol. 12, 7a.5.

555. *Analysis of the Three Vows*, 60.4–5.

556. *mDo sde brgyad bcu khungs.* Tibetans, such as Butön and Sakya Paṇḍita, consider Heshang Moheyan to be the author of this text. See Sakya Paṇḍita's *Letter to the Holy Beings* (*sKyes bu dam pa rnams la spring ba'i yi ge*) (Sakya Collected Works, vol. 12: 155.1); and *Butön's History of Buddhism in India and Its Spread to Tibet* (trans. Stein and Zangpo, *Butön's History of Buddhism*, 286). However, a Dunhuang manuscript cites the author as Puk Yeshe Yang (sPug ye shes dbyangs). See Tauscher, "Manuscript of the 'Gondhla Kanjur,'" 2007, 82–84; and Dalton and van Schaik, *Tibetan Tantric Manuscripts*, 299–300. *MB* VVI (150.4): *cu* should be *bcu.* See *MB* DLG (94.6).

557. *Analysis of the Three Vows*, 60.8.

558. Source unidentified.

559. *Analysis of the Three Vows*, 60.21–61.2.

560. *MB* VVI (151.3): *ma thungs* should be *ma tshud.* See *MB* DLG (95.4), *MB* TsRP (188.3), and *MB* DK (243.5).

561. Source unidentified.

562. D 3917: vol. 110, 61b.1–4. The Dg.T. recension reads . . . *sbyin pa la sogs pa spyod pa ni skye bo blun po'i* . . . and . . . *theg pa chen po thams cad kyi rtsa ba ni* . . . ; the *Moonbeams* citation (*MB* VVI 151.18 and 20) reads . . . *sbyin pa la sogs pa spyad pa ni blun po'i* . . . and . . . *theg pa thams cad kyi rtsa ba ni* . . . The *Moonbeams* citation is identical to the one in the *Great Treatise* (775) except that the *Great Treatise* reads . . . *skye bo blun po'i* . . .

563. *MB* VVI (152.8): *dang nyid* should be *rang nyid.* See *MB* DLG (96.5) and *MB* TsRP (190.5).

564. Presumably this is a reference to Sakya Paṇḍita's account in his *Clarifying the Sage's Intent* (*Thub dgongs / Thub pa'i' dgongs pa rab tu gsal ba*). Sarnath, Varanasi: Sakya Students' Union, 94–98. See also D. Jackson, *Clarifying the Sage's Intent*, 489–92, and *Enlightenment by a Single Means*, 177–80.

565. *Analysis of the Three Vows*, 59.21–60.1.

566. *Sādhana for the Siddhi of Wisdom.* D 2219: vol. 51, 45b.5–6. The Dg.T. recension reads . . . *gang phyir 'di de thams cad du* . . . *ngo bo nyid mkhyen pa'o* . . . ; the *Moonbeams* citation (*MB* VVI 155.1–2) reads . . . *gang phyir bde de thams cad du* . . . *ngo bo nyid mkhyen pa'i* . . . The translation follows the Dg.T. recension in reading *mkhyen pa'o.*

567. *MB* DLG (98.7) reads . . . *'jig bde'i tshor ba yin*, whereas *MB* TsRP (195.3) and *MB* VVI (155.7) read . . . *'dzag bde'i tshor ba yin.*
568. Citation found in *Illumination of the Unmoving Heart: A Commentary for Entering the Tantra of the "Stainless Light."* D 1349: vol. 13, 20b.6–7.
569. The "Achievement of Unchanging Wisdom" is the third section of chapter 5 in Puṇḍarīka's *Stainless Light*. D 1347: vol. 12, 223a.6–7.
570. See *Clarifying the Sage's Intent*, 102 and 116, and D. Jackson, *Stages of the Buddha's Teachings*, 496 and 511.
571. Phyag chen brda brgyud kyi skor. Unidentified.
572. gSang spyod kyi skor. Unidentified collection of instructions or texts associated with Maitrīpa's student Vajrapāṇi.
573. *Dohā for the Queen*. D 2264: vol. 52, 32b.6–7.
574. *Dohā for the Queen*. D 2264: vol. 52, 30b.4–5.
575. *Dohā for the People*. D 2224: vol. 51, 71b.6–7.
576. *Dohā for the People*. D 2224: vol. 51, 71a.7. The Dg.T. recension reads . . . *gsang sngags bsten pa ci dgos*; the *Moonbeams* citation (*MB* VVI 157.19) reads . . . *gsang sngags bsten pas ci.* The translation follows the Dg.T. recension.
577. See D 2264: vol. 52, 31.531b.6.
578. *Replies to Dusum Khyenpa's Questions*, 23b–24a. The Collected Works edition reads . . . *yang gsum ste dbang po brtul po dad pa can tshogs kyi lam* . . . ; the *Moonbeams* citation (*MB* VVI 158.19) reads . . . *yang lam gsum ste dbang po brtul po tshogs kyi lam* . . . The translation includes both.
579. See *The Flag of Renown: The Biography of Gampopa* (*Chos kyi rje dpal ldan sgam po pa chen po'i rnam par thar pa yid bzhin gyi nor bu rin po che kun khyab snyan pa'i ba dan thar pa rin po che'i rgyan gyi mchog*) by Sönam Lhundrup (Collected Works of Gampopa, text 3/ga, 119); and *A Grand Collection of Dharma Lectures* (*Tshogs chos legs mdzes ma*) (Collected Works of Gampopa, text 5/ca, 2a and 2b). Note that since the latter work was collected and written down by Lek-dze ("Grand One" or "Handsome One"), it could also be called *Lek-dze's Collection of Dharma Lectures.*
580. Source unidentified.
581. D 3916: vol. 110, 48a.5.
582. *Entrance to the Two Truths*. D 3902: vol. 109, 72b.5.
583. D 1802: vol. 35, 50b.6–7. The Dg.T. recension reads *sna tshogs mdo dang rgyud las ni/* . . . *thams cad stong gnas 'di nyi la* . . . ; the *Moonbeams* citation (*MB* VVI 160.8–10) reads *sna tshogs mdo dang rgyud rnams su/* . . . *thams cad stong pa 'di nyi la* . . .
584. *sGrib pa rnam sel gyis bcom ldan 'das la bstod pa.* Citation and text not found in the Kangyur or Tengyur.
585. *rDo rje ting nge 'dzin gyi mdo.* Citation and text not found in the Kangyur. The citation is found (attributed to the *Vajra Samādhi Sūtra*) in Gampopa's *Sunrays of Scriptural Citations* (21b), and Gampopa's *Ornament of Precious Liberation* (108a).

The citation is also found in Vimalamitra's *Import of Instantaneous, Nonconceptual Meditation* (**Sakṛtprāveśikanirvikalpabhāvanārtha, Cig car 'jug pa rnam par* *mi rtog pa'i bsgom don*). Toh. 3910. D 3910: vol. 110, 12b.6. The recension found in the *Import of Instantaneous, Nonconceptual Meditation* reads *sems stong pa nyid du mi g.yon pha rol . . .* ; the *Moonbeams* citation (*MB* VVI 160.19) reads *stong pa nyid du mi g.yos na/ pha rol . . .*

586. *Brahmaviśeṣacintiparipṛcchā, Khyad par sems kyis zhus pa'i mdo / Tshangs pa khyad par sems kyis zhus pa'i mdo*. Toh. 160, H.K. 161. Exact citation not found in this text. The closest is H.K. 161: vol. 59, 141a.1–3: *chos thams cad gtong ba med pa'i sbyin pa la mos so/ chos thams cad bsrung ba med pa'i tshul khrims la mos so/ chos thams cad rlom sems med pa'i bzod pa la mos so/ chos thams cad rtsom pa med pa'i brtson 'grus la mos so/ chos thams cad mnyam pa nyid kyi ting nge 'dzin la mos so/ chos thams cad rnam par mi rtog pa'o zhes shes rab la mos so.*

The *Moonbeams* citation is identical to one found in Gampopa's *Sunrays of Scriptural Citations* (21b) and Gampopa's *Ornament of Precious Liberation* (108a).

A nearly identical citation (also attributed to the *Sūtra of the Questions of Brahmaviśeṣacintin*) is found in Vimalamitra's *Import of Instantaneous, Nonconceptual Meditation*. D 3910: vol. 110, 12b.6–7. The recension there reads . . . *sbyin pa/ mi gnas pa ni tshul khrims/ ci yang bye brag mi phyed pa ni bzod pa/ . . . ma chags pa ni ting nge 'dzin/ mi gnyis pa ni shes rab*; the *Moonbeams* citation (*MB* VVI 161.1–3) reads . . . *sbyin pa'o/ tha dad ma yin ni tshul khrims/ bye brag mi byed pa ni bzod pa'o/ . . . ma chags pa ni bsam gtan/ mi rtog pa ni shes rab.*

587. *Dohā for the People*. D 2224: vol. 51, 71b.2. The Dg.T. recension reads . . . *bstan bcos snying la 'chad pa'ang de yin no*; the *Moonbeams* citation (161.6) reads. . . *bstan bcos snying la 'chang pa'ang de yin no.* The consulted commentaries by Tibetan authors follow the Dg.T. recension.

There are two commentaries in the Tengyur that contain this line: Avadhūtipa's *Explanation of the "Song That Is the Ultimate Essence of the Treasury of Dohās"* (*Dohakoṣahṛdayārthagītāṭīkā, Do ha mdzod kyi snying po don gyi glu'i 'grel pa*) (Toh. 2268; D 2268: vol. 52, 70a.6); and Advayavajra's *Explanation on Difficult Points in the "Dohā Treasury."* (*Dohakoṣapañjikā, Do ha mdzod kyi dka' 'grel*) (Toh. 2256; D 2256: vol. 51, 186a.7). The first reads. . . *bstan bcos snying las 'chang pa'ang de yin no*; the latter reads . . . *bstan bcos rnying la 'chad pa'ang de yin no.*

Looking at R. Jackson, *Tantric Treasures*, 62, we see that the Apabhraṃśa word *purāṇeṃ* is used, which should be rendered into Tibetan as *rnying* ("old"), not *snying* ("heart"). The Tibetan *rnying pa* was used to translate "purāṇa" (a class of works in Sanskrit verse, comprising mainly Hindu myths, legends, history, and ritual). The translation follows the Dg.T. recension in reading *'chad pa* and the Apabhraṃśa for purāṇa. A translation of the line as it appears in *Moonbeams* would be "Holding the śāstras in your heart is it as well."

588. *Rab tu mi gnas pa'i rgyud*. Citation and text not found in the Kangyur. The citation is found (attributed to the *Tantra of Nonabiding*) in Gampopa's *Ornament of Precious Liberation*, 109a.

589. *rDo rje mkha' 'gro*. Toh. 370, H.K. 386. H.K. 386: vol. 80, 518a.1–3. The H.K. recension reads . . . *bzlas pa bya/ rnal ma'i sbyor ba rtogs gyur na/ bcos ma'i sbyor*

ba phyi rol nas . . . ; the *Moonbeams* citation (*MB* VVI 161.16) reads . . . *bzlas pa bya/ bcos ma'i sbyor phyi rol ba . . .*

590. *rDo rje snying 'grel.* Also known as the *Commentary That Summarizes the "Hevajra Tantra"* (*Hevajrapiṇḍārthaṭīkā, Kye'i rdo rje bsdus pa'i don gyi rgya cher 'grel pa*). Toh. 1180. D 1180: vol. 2, 58a.4.

591. H.K. 378a: vol. 79, 341b.6–7.

592. H.K. 378a: vol. 79, 352b.4–5.

593. *Amṛta-guhyatantrarāja, gSang ba bdud rtsi rgyal po'i rgyud / gSang ba bdud rtsi'i rgyud kyi rgyal po.* Toh. 401. Dg.K. 401: vol. 79, 234a.4. The Dg.K. recension reads . . . *sems kyi de nyid shes gyur na . . .* ; the *Moonbeams* citation (*MB* VVI 162.16) reads . . . *sems kyi de nyid rnyed gyur pas . . .* The *Moonbeams* citation is identical to one found in Gampopa's *Ornament of Precious Liberation,* 109a.

594. *Dohā for the People.* D 2224: vol. 51, 71a.4–7. The Dg.T. recension reads *dge tshul dge slong gnas brten zhes bya bas/ . . . byed ching 'jug/ . . . kha cig theg chen de la rgyug byed cing/ de ni gzhung lugs tshad ma'i bstan bcos yin/ . . . la la nam mkha'i khams la rtog par snang/ gzhan yang stong nyid ldan par byed pa de.* The *Moonbeams* citation (*MB* VVI 163.1–11) reads *dge slong dge tshul gnas brten zhes bya ba'i/ . . . byed ching 'dug/ . . . gzhan dag theg chen de la rgyu byed de/ de ni gzhung lugs mtshan ma'i bstan bcos te/ . . . la la nam mkha'i khams la rtog par byed/ gzhan dag stong nyid lta bar byed pa ste.*

595. *Ganges Mahāmudrā.* D 2303: vol. 52, 243b.7. The Dg.T. recension reads *'dul ba'i sde gnod la sogs chos rnams dang*; the *Moonbeams* citation (*MB* VVI 163.19) reads *'dul ba mdo sde sde gnod sna tshogs kyi.*

596. *Abhidhāna-uttaratantra, mNgon par brjod pa'i rgyud bla ma.* Toh. 369, H.K. 385. H.K. 385: vol. 80, 140a.3–4. The H.K. reads *phyag rgya che dang nges par rol/ sgom pa mngon du gyur pa yis/ . . . skye ba 'di la dngos grub 'gyur*; the *Moonbeams* citation (*MB* VVI 164.5–6) reads *phyag rgya che la nges par rol/ sgom pa mngon du gyur pa yin/ . . . skye ba 'di la mngon du 'gyur.* The *Moonbeams* citation is almost identical to one found in Gampopa's *Sunrays of Scriptural Citations,* 24b.

597. *Kālacakropadeśa-sūryacandrasādhana, Dus kyi 'khor lo'i gdams ngag nyi ma zla ba bsgrub pa* by Bhekuni. Toh. 1369. D 1369: vol. 14, 219b.5–6.

598. *Anāvila-tantrarājā, rNyog pa med pa / rGyud kyi rgyal po rnyog pa med pa.* Toh. 414, H.K. 399.

599. U rgyan. Generally identified as the Swat Valley in Pakistan.

600. Be ta'i grong khyer. Vedalī is located in present-day Andhra Pradesh, an area generally associated with Nāgārjuna. On the question of whether this is Vidarbha (in present-day Maharashtra), see Mabbett, *Problem of the Historical Nāgārjuna.*

601. dPal gyi ri. A mountain in Andhra Pradesh, associated with Nāgārjuna and Saraha, and where Śavaripa lived. According to Dowman, *Masters of Mahāmudrā,* 122 and 393, Śrī Parvata was, along with Kāñňī, "the most important tantric power place on the sub-continent to both Buddhists and *śaiva-śāktas.*"

602. *MB* VVI (166.20): *bsan* should be *gsan.* See *MB* DLG (106.6).

603. The Root Symbols (*brDa rtsa*) and Secret Conduct (*gSang spyod*) instructions, or collection of texts, coming from Vajrapāṇi have not been identified.
604. *MB* VVI (167.7): *ma las 'das* should be *mi las 'das*. See *MB* DLG (107.1).
605. Tilopa's *Esoteric Instructions on the Six Dharmas* (*Ṣaḍdharmopadeśa, Chos drug gi man ngag*) (Toh. 2330) state that the four sets of instructions, or transmissions (*bka' babs bzhi*), are Nāgārjuna's instructions on illusory body and luminosity, Kṛṣṇācārya's instructions on caṇḍālī, the mahāsiddha Kambala's instructions on dreams, and the instructions from the ḍākinī Subhaginī (also known as Sukhasiddhi) on bardos and transference. There are other accounts, see Torricelli, "Chos drug and bKa'-babs bzhi Material," 68–70.
606. Luyipa transmitted the Cakrasaṃvara abhiṣeka, explanation of the tantra, and its practice instructions (*sgrub yig*) to the king Dārikapa and his minster Ṭeṅgipa, and they were transmitted to Vajraghaṇṭā (rDo rje dril bu pa), Kurmapāda (Ru sbal zhabs), Jayandhara, Kṛṣṇācārya (Nag po spyod pa), Vijayapāda (rNam rgyal zhabs), and then to Tilopa. See Roerich, *Blue Annals,* 380. There was also a transmission of the Cakrasaṃvara abhiṣeka that Tilopa received that came through Luyipa to Ṭeṅgipa, Kambala (Lawapa), Indrabhūti, Kacapa, Vajraghaṇṭā, Jālandhara, Kṛṣṇācārya, Kuśalana to Tilopa. This did not pass down to Marpa Lotsāwa but did to Butön, who was the holder of seven lineages of the Cakrasaṃvara abhiṣeka. See Roerich, *Blue Annals*, 385.
607. Za hor. Sahor, the Persian word for "city," is identified as Sābhār/Savar/Śabhar, a subdistrict northwest of present-day Dhakar, Bangladesh. See Roerich, *Blue Annals*, 241. It has also been identified with the Kangra district of present-day Himachal Pradesh.
608. For this story, see Torricelli and Naga, *Life of the Mahāsiddha Tilopa*, 46–56.
609. According to Nāropa's biography, the seven like himself are Maitrīpa, Śāntibhadra, Ḍombīpa, Śāntipa, Chiterwa (sPyi ther ba) from Nepal, Prajñāsinha, and Ākarasiddhi from Kashmir. See Guenther, *Life and Teaching of Nāropa*, 99.
610. May Tsönpo (Mes tshon po), Ngok Chödor (rNgog chos rdo), and Tshur-tön Wang-nge (Tshur ston dbang nge) were, along with Milarepa, the four pillar-like disciples of Marpa. May, Ngok, and Tshur received and continued Marpa's exegetical transmission (*bshad pa'i bka'*), whereas Milarepa received and continued Marpa's practice transmission (*sgrub pa'i bka'*). Ram is presumably Ram Tsanchen (Ram tsan can), who along with Ngok, was a major transmitter of Marpa's *Hevajra Tantra* teachings. Go-lek (mGo legs) was a relative and known as Marpa Go-lek. See Nalanda Translation Committee, *Life of Marpa*, and Roerich, *Blue Annals*, 403–16.
611. See H.K. 129: vol. 55, 20a.1–5 and 82b.2–83b.6.
612. Although *Moonbeams* references *mDo snying rje pad dkar*, which might be construed to mean the *White Lotus of Compassion* (*Karuṇāpuṇḍarīka, sNying rje padma dkar po*; Toh. 112), this prophesy is found in *White Lotus of Great Compassion* (*Mahākaruṇāpuṇḍarīka, sNying rje chen po'i padma dkar po*). Toh. 111, H.K. 114. See H.K. 114: vol. 52, 133a.6–133b.6 and 134a.6–134b.1. I am grateful to Peter Alan Roberts for alerting me to this.

613. The Lohit river is in Assam and Arunachal Pradesh. It begins in eastern Tibet and is a major right bank tributary of the Brahmaputra river.

614. Jīvaka (*'Tsho byed*, "Healer"). Prior to becoming a monk, Gampopa was a physician and is often referred to as Dakpo Lhaje (Dvags po lha rje, "Physician from Dakpo"). Lhaje (*Lha rje*, "Lord of Gods") is an honorific title bestowed on physicians by King Trisong De-tsen.

615. *MB* VVI (173.12): *snang shes* should be *snang shas*. See *MB* DLG (111.7) and TsRP (221.6).

616. Citation not found in a work by Nāgārjuna. It is found (unattributed) in Bodhibhadra's *A Work on the Requisites for Samādhi*. D 3924: vol. 110, 81b.4.

617. D 4089: vol. 140, 18b.7.

618. D 3915: vol. 110, 28a.3–5. The Dg.T. recension reads ... *de nas des bye brag* ... *de la ma yin du zin na* ... *the tshom yang ma btsal bas* ... *mu stegs can rnams kyis sgom pa dang 'dra'o*; the *Moonbeams* citation (*MB* VVI 174.12–15) reads ... *de nas bye brag* ... *de la ma yin du zin* ... *the tshom yang ma bsal bas* ... *mu stegs can rnams kyi sgom pa dang 'dra'o.*

619. *Caryāmelāpakapradīpa*, *sPyod pa bsdus pa'i sgron ma* by Āryadeva. Toh. 1803. D 1803: vol. 35, 60b.5.

620. H.K. 378b: vol. 79, 374b.5–7. The H.K. recension reads ... *de rjes kye yi rdo rje brtsal* ... ; the *Moonbeams* citation (*MB* VVI 175.8) reads ... *de rjes kye yi rdo rje bstan* ...

621. *Ka* [or *bKa'*] *dpe snga ma* (Toh. 2331) and *Pravacanottaropamā*, *Ka* [or *bKa'*] *dpe phyi ma* (Toh. 2332). The former—also known as *Truly Valid Words: The Esoteric Instructions of the Ḍākinīs* (*Ājñāsaṁyakpramāṇa-nāma-ḍākinyupadesha* / *Ābhapramāṇasaṁyag-nāma-ḍākinyupadesha*, *bKa' yang dag pa'i tshad ma zhes bya ba mkha' 'gro'i man ngag*)—has no authorship colophon in its Tengyur recension but the colophon of the edition found in the DNZ (DNZ, vol. 7, 89.5) states that the author is Tilopa. The latter is by Nāropa. This citation is found only in the former. D 2331: vol. 52, 271a. 3–5.

622. Gampopa's Collected Works contains four texts of his dialogues with students: *Replies to Dusum Khyenpa's Questions*; *Replies to the Exalted Gomtsul's Questions* (*rJe sgom tshul gyi zhus len*) (Collected Works of Gampopa, text 9/ta); *Replies to the Exalted Pakmo Drupa's Questions*; and *Replies to Yogin Chöyung's Questions* (*rNal 'byor chos g.yung gi zhus lan*) (Collected Works of Gampopa, text 12/na).

623. The Fivefold Mahāmudrā is primarily practiced in the Drikung Kagyu based on the teachings of Pakmo Drupa and Jikten Sumgön. *MB* VVI (177.2): *sgo bstan* should be *sgo bstun*. See *MB* DLG (114.1).

624. H.K. 380: vol. 79, 434b.4.

625. *Buddha-kapāla*, *Sangs rgyas thod pa*. Toh. 424, H.K. 400. H.K. 400: vol. 82, 16b.2–3.

626. *MB* VVI (178.20): *kha mnon* should be *kha ma non*. See *MB* DLG (115.4).

627. *Ganges Mahāmudrā*. D 2303: vol. 52, 243a.1–2. The Dg.T. recension reads *kye ho 'jig rten chos la legs ltos dang/* ... *chags sdang nye 'brel kun spongs la*; the *Moonbeams*

citation (*MB* VVI 179.4) reads *kye ho 'jig rten chos la legs rtogs dang/ . . . chags sdang 'brel ba kun chod la.*

628. This often-quoted passage is found in numerous sūtras, including the *Basis of the Minor Vinaya* (*Vinaya-kṣudraka-vastu, 'Dul ba phran tshegs kyi gzhi*). Toh. 6, H.K. 6. H.K. 6: vol. 11, 76b.6–77a.2. It is also in Dharmatrāta's *Collection of Meaningful Expressions* (*Udānavarga, Ched du brjod pa'i tshoms*) (Toh. 326, H.K. 330; H.K. 330: vol. 72, 361a.2); Vasubandhu's *Explanation of the "Treasury of Abhidharma"* (D 4090: vol. 140, 184b.4–5); and Atīśa's *Teaching on Refuge* (*Śaraṇagama-nadeśanā, sKyabs su 'gro ba bstan pa*) (Toh. 3953; D 3953: vol. 111, 298b.6–299a.1).
629. D 3944: vol. 111, 218b.6.
630. *Precious Garland.* D 4158: vol. 172, 113b.1.
631. H.K. 94: vol. 46, 265a.4–5.
632. D 4158: vol. 172, 117b.3–5. The Dg.T. recension reads *rje'u chos sum . . . dus sum byin ba bas . . .*; the *Moonbeams* citation (*MB* VVI 181.12) reads *rje'u tshong sum . . . dus sum sbyin pas kyang . . .*

    MB VVI (181.13) *thabs* should be *thangs.* See *MB* DLG (117.3) and *MB* TsRP (232.6).
633. *sPyan ras gzigs kyi rtogs brjod.* In the *Compendium of Dharma Sūtra.* H.K. 239: vol. 65, 130a.7–130b.1. The H.K. recension reads *byang chub sems dpas chos gcig rab ru gzung zhing rab tu rtogs par bgyis na/ bcom ldan 'das/ sangs rgyas kyi chos thams cad de'i lag mthil du mchis pa lags so/ chos gcig po'i gang she na/ 'di lta ste/ snying rje chen po'o.* The *Moonbeams* citation (*MB* VVI 182.1–3) reads *chos gcig yod na sangs rgyas kyi chos thams cad lag mthil tu bzhag pa lta bur 'gyur te/ gcig gang zhe na/ 'di lta ste/ snying rje chen po'o.* The *Moonbeams* citation is identical to one found in Gampopa's *Ornament of Precious Liberation*, 41b.
634. *Entrance to the Middle Way.* D 3861: vol. 102, 201b.2–3.
635. *Vīradattaparipṛcchāsutra, dPas byin gyis zhus pa'i mdo.* Toh. 72, H.K. 72. H.K. 72: vol. 39, 352b.2–3. The H.K. recension reads . . . *de ni de bas lhag par 'gyur*; the *Moonbeams* citation (*MB* VVI 182.11) reads . . . *de ni de bas khyad par 'phags. MB* VVI (18.9): *dpa' sbyin* should be *dpas byin.*
636. H.K. 72: vol. 39, 352b.3–5. The H.K. recension reads . . . *rin chen dag gis rab bkang ste/ 'jig rten mgon la phul ba bas . . .* ; the *Moonbeams* citation (*MB* VVI 182.14) reads . . . *rin chen dag gis yongs bkang ste/ bde gshegs rnams la phul ba bas . . .* The *Moonbeams* citation is identical to one found in Gampopa's *Ornament of Precious Liberation*, 62b. *MB* VVI (182.13): *mi gang gi* should be *mi gang gis.* See the H.K. recension and the *Ornament of Precious Liberation.*
637. A similar verse is found in the *Account of the Noble Deeds of Puṇyabala* (*Puṇyabala-avadāna, bSod nams kyi stobs kyi rtogs pa brjod pa*). Toh. 347, H.K. 355. H.K. 355: vol. 76, 8a.4, 9b.4, and 30a.4: *bsod nams bsags na bde bar 'gyur/ de phyir mis ni bsod nams bya/ de yang yang dang yang du bya/ de nyid la ni 'dun pa bya.* The *Moonbeams* citation (*MB* VVI 183.15–16) reads *bsod nams bsags pas bde ba thob/ de phyir mi yis bsod nams bsag/ de yang yang dang yang du bsag/ de ring nyid la bstun te bsag.*
638. H.K. 17: vol. 34, 204a.1. The H.K. recension reads *de dag dge ba'i rtsa ba ji srid ma rdzogs pa/ de srid stong nyid dam pa de ni thob mi byed*; the *Moonbeams* citation

(*MB* VVI 183.18–184.1) reads *ji srid dge ba'i rtsa ba ma rdzogs par/ de srid stong nyid dam pa 'thob mi 'gyur.*

639. *Tathāgatācintyaguhyanirdeśa, De bzhin gshegs pa gsang ba'i mdo.* Toh. 47, H.K. 47. Only the second sentence of the *Moonbeams* citation is found in H.K. 47: vol. 35, 154b.2–3. The *Moonbeams* citation is identical to one found in Kamalaśīla's final *Stages of Meditation*, which is attributed to the *Sūtra on the Inconceivable Secret Teachings of the Tathāgatas* (*Tathāgatācintyaguhyanirdeśa, De bzhin gshegs pa gsang ba'i mdo / De bzhin gshegs pa'i gsang ba bsam gyis mi khyab pa bstan pa'i mdo*). Toh. 3917. D 3917: vol. 110, 61a.2–3.

640. D 4158: vol. 172, 115a.1. The Dg.T. recension reads *sangs rgyas rnams kyi gzugs sku ni/ bsod nams tshogs las byung ba ste*; the *Moonbeams* citation (*MB* VVI 184.8) reads *gzugs kyi sku ni mdor bsdu na/ rgyal po bsod nams tshogs las 'khrungs.*

641. H.K. 330: vol. 72, 363a.3.

642. H.K. 330: vol. 72, 334b.2–3. The H.K. recension reads . . . *sdig pa'i las de'i rnam smin dag* . . . ; the *Moonbeams* citation (*MB* VVI 185.16) reads . . . *sdig las de yi rnam smin dag* . . .

643. *Caturdharmanirdeśa, Chos bzhi bstan pa'i mdo.* Toh. 249, H.K. 250. H.K. 250: vol. 66, 90a.7–90b.2. The H.K. recension reads . . . *kun tu spyod pa dang/ sor chud par byed pa'i stobs dang/ rten gyi stobs so*; the *Moonbeams* citation (*MB* VVI 186.3) reads . . . *kun tu spyod pa dang/ nyes pa la zlog pa dang/ rten gyi stobs so.* The *Moonbeams* citation is identical to one found in Gampopa's *Ornament of Precious Liberation*, 53b.

644. *Subāhu-paripṛcchā-nāma-tantra, dPung bzang gis zhus pa zhes bya ba'i rgyud.* Toh. 805, H.K. 761. H.K. 761: vol. 96, 173a.5–7. The H.K. recension reads . . . *mar me phyung ba yis* . . . *stong na gnas* . . . ; the *Moonbeams* citation (*MB* VVI 187.1–3) reads . . . *mar me chung ba yis* . . . *stong nas bsags* . . .

645. A similar statement is found in the *Collection of Meaningful Expressions* (H.K. 330: vol. 72, 344a.2): *sdig pa chung byas bdag nyid kyi/ phyi bzhin mi 'ong ma sems shig/ chu yi thigs pa lung ba yis/ bum chen gang ba ji bzhin du.* However a more similar one is found in the *Mahāparinirvāṇa Sūtra* (*Mahāparinirvāṇa-mahāsūtra, Yongs su mya ngan las 'das pa chen po'i mdo*). Toh. 119, H.K. 368. H.K. 368: vol. 78, 187b.6–7: *sdig pa phra mo chung ngu la/ mi gnod snyam du brnyes mi bya/ chu yi thigs pa zags pa yang/ snod chen khad kyis gang bar 'gyur.* The *Moonbeams* citation (*MB* VVI 187.8–9) reads *sdig pa shin tu chung ngu la'ang/ mi gnod snyam du brnyes mi bya/ chu yi thigs pa bsags pas kyang / snod chen khad kyis 'gang bar 'gyur.*

646. *Susiddhikara-mahātantra-sādhanopāyika-paṭala, Legs grub / Legs par grub par byed pa'i rgyud chen po las sgrub pa'i thabs rim par phye ba.* Toh. 807, H.K. 764. H.K. 764: vol. 96, 236b.4–5.

647. *Sarvaguhyavidhigarbhālaṃkāra-nāma, sNying po rgyan / gSang ba thams cad kyi spyi'i cho ga'i snying po rgyan* by Mañjuśrīkīrti. Toh. 2490. D 2490: vol. 53, 238a.6–7. The Derge recension reads *pad dkar zla ba'i dbus gnas shing/ rdo dril bu rgyan spras pa'i/* . . . *'bum phrag tu ni* . . . ; the *Moonbeams* citation (*MB* VVI 187.14–18) *pad dkar zla ba'i gdan steng du/* . . . *'bum phrag gcig tu* . . .

648. *Mañjuśrī-nāmasaṁgīti / Mañjuśrījñānasattvasya-paramārtha-nāmasaṃgīti,*

mTshan brjod / *'Jam dpal mtshan brjod* / *'Jam dpal ye shes sems dpa'i don dam pa'i mtshan yang dag par brjod pa*. Toh. 360, H.K. 369. H.K. 369: vol. 79, 11a.3–4. The H.K. recension reads . . . *bla ma'i mchog* . . . ; the *Moonbeams* citation (*MB* VVI 188.11–12) reads. . . *bla ma'i rab*. . . *MB* VVI (188.11) should read *rim gro,* not *ri mor.* See the Dg.T. recension.

649. This well-known verse is found in *Maṇḍala* (**Maṇḍala-nāma, Maṇḍala bzhugs*) by Saṃvarabhadra. Toh. 2121. D 2121: vol. 49, 161a.6–7.

650. Bhavideva (Bha vi lha) is another name for Aśvaghoṣa. This citation is found in Aśvaghoṣa's *Compendium of Root Downfalls in the Vajrayāna* (*Vajrayānamūlāpattisaṃgraha, rDo rje theg pa rtsa ba'i ltung ba bsdus pa*). Toh. 2478. D 2478: vol. 53, 179a.7.

651. *Fifty Verses for the Guru* (*Gurupañcāśikā, bLa ma lnga bcu pa*). Toh. 3721. D 3721: vol. 79, 10a.1–2.

652. *Vajrahṛdaya-alaṃkāra-tantra, rDo rje snying po rgyan gyi rgyud.* Toh. 451, H.K. 788. H.K. 788: vol. 96, 449a.2.

653. H.K. 379: vol. 79, 432b.6–7. The H.K. recension reads *rdo rje sems dpa' ji lta bar/ de ltar slob dpon gzugs 'dzin te/ sems can rjes su bzung dmigs nas/ phal pa'i gzugs su gnas so*; the *Moonbeams* citation (*MB* VVI 189.9–10) reads *gang nyid rdo rje sems dpa' zhes/ de nyid slob dpon gzugs su 'dzin/ sems can phan gdags dmigs nas ni/ tham mal pa yi gzugs su gnas.*

654. Citation not found in a text by Bhavideva (or Aśvaghoṣa). It is found in Atīśa's *Detailed Explanation of the Root Downfalls* (*Mūlāpattiṭīkā, rTsa ba'i ltung ba'i rgya cher 'grel pa*). Toh. 2487. D 2487: vol. 53, 192b.7–193a.1.

655. H.K. 386: vol. 80, 430b.1–3.

656. For an almost identical passage, see the *Caturpīṭha* (*Caturpīṭha-mahāyoginītantrarāja, rNal 'byor ma'i rgyud kyi rgyal po chen po dpal gdan bzhi pa*). Toh. 428, H.K. 404. H.K. 404: vol. 82, 118b.4–6. Commentaries on these lines are found in Bhavabhadra's *Reasons for Recollection: Commentary on the "Caturpīṭha"* (*Catuḥpīṭhatantrarājasya ṭīkāsmṛtinibandha, rGyud kyi rgyal po dpal gdan bzhi pa'i 'grel pa dran pa'i rgyu mtshan*) (Toh. 1607; D 1607: vol. 24, 243b.2–6); and Kalyāṇavarman's *Explanation of the "Caturpīṭha"* (*Catuḥpīṭhaṭīkā, gDan bzhi pa'i rnam par bshad pa*) (Toh. 1608; D 1608: vol. 25, 43b.5–7).

657. See Ratnākaraśānti's *Handful of Flowers: Explanation of the "Guhyasamāja"* (*Kusumāñjaliguhyasamājanibandha, gSang ba 'dus pa'i bshad sbyar snyim pa'i me tog*). Toh. 1851. D 1851: vol. 41, 76a.4–5.

658. D 1802: vol. 35, 53b.4. *MB* VVI (190.7): *yang dag brtsi* should be *yang dag brtsam.* See *MB* DLG (122.7).

659. The exact citation not found in the Kangyur or Tengyur. A similar statement is found in the *Guhyasamāja Tantra,* H.K. 416a: vol. 82, 513b.3: *sangs rgyas bcom ldan 'das de rnams kyi sku dang/ gsung dang/ thugs rdo rje las byung ba'i bsod nams kyi phung po ji snyed pa de bas kyang slob dpon gyi ba spu'i bu ga gcig gi bsod nams khyad par du 'phags so.*

660. H.K. 396: vol. 81, 372b.3. The H.K. recension reads . . . *de dang de nyid dbul bar bya*; the *Moonbeams* citation (*MB* VVI 190.14) reads . . . *de dang de ni bla mar dbul.*

661. H.K. 788: vol. 96, 449b.4. The H.K. recension reads *de bas thabs ni thams cad kyis/ rdo rje 'dzin pa bla ma mchog*; the *Moonbeams* citation (*MB* VVI 190.15) reads *de bas 'bad pa thams cad kyis/ bla ma rdo rje 'dzin pa mchod.*

662. *Fifty Verses for the Guru.* D 3721: vol. 79, 10b.6–7.

663. *Daśadharmakasūtra, Chos bcu pa'i mdo.* Toh. 53, H.K. 53. H.K. 53: vol. 36, 270b.7.

664. *Ratnolkādhāraṇīsūtra, dKon mchog ta la la'i gzungs.* Toh. 145/847, H.K. 100. H.K. 100: vol. 48, 492b.5–7. The H.K. recension reads *dad pa sngon 'dren ma ltar . . .* ; the *Moonbeams* citation (*MB* VVI 191.11) reads *dad pa sngon 'gro ma ltar . . .*

665. H.K. 94: vol. 45, 251a.6–251b.6. The H.K. recension reads *byang chub sems dpa'i dbang po brtan pa'i myu gu skyed par byed pa'o/ dge ba'i bshes gnyen rnams ni bdag ngan song gi g.yang sa thams cad nas skyob pa'o/ dge ba'i bshes gnyen rnams ni bdag chos mnyam pa nyid kyi tshul khong du chud par bya ba la gzhog pa'o/ dge ba'i bshes gnyen rnams ni bdag la lam bde ba dang/ mi bde ba ston pa'o/ dge ba'i bshes gnyen rnams ni bdag la theg pa chen po yongs su ston pa'o/ dge ba'i bshes gnyen rnams ni bdag la byang chub sems dpa' kun tu bzang po'i spyod pa'i gdams ngag gis 'doms pa'o/ dge ba'i bshes gnyen rnams ni bdag la thams cad mkhyen pa nyid kyi grong khyer gyi lam ston pa'o/ dge ba'i bshes gnyen rnams ni bdag thams cad mkhyen pa'i gnas su phyin par skyel ba'o/ dge ba'i bshes gnyen rnams ni bdag chos kyi dbyings kyi tshul rgya mtsho la 'jug par byed pa'o/ dge ba'i bshes gnyen rnams ni bdag la dus gsum gyi shes bya rgya mtsho'i tshul rab tu ston pa'o/ dge ba'i bshes gnyen rnams ni bdag la 'phags pa'i tshogs kyi dkyil 'khor thams cad rab tu ston pa'o/ dge ba'i bshes gnyen rnams ni bdag gi dkar po'i chos thams cad rnam par 'phel bar byed pa'o zhes de de ltar ngu zhing smre sngags 'don pa'i tshe.*

The *Moonbeams* citation (*MB* VVI 192.2–9) reads *gzhon nu nor bzang/ dge ba'i bshes gnyen rnams ni bdag ngan song gi thams cad las skyob pa'o/ chos mnyam pa nyid rtogs par byed pa'o/ lam bde ba dang mi bde ba ston pa'o/ kun tu bzang po'i spyod pas 'doms pa'o/ thams cad mkhyen pa'i grong khyer gyi lam ston pa'o/ thams cad mkhyen pa'i gnas su skyel ba'o/ chos kyi dbyings kyi rgya mtshor 'jug pa'o/ dus gsum gyi shes bya'i rgya mtsho ston pa'o/'phags pa'i tshogs kyi dkyil 'khor ston pa'o/ dge ba'i bshes gnyen ni bdag gi dkar po'i chos thams cad 'phel bar byed pa'o/ zhes rjes su dran zhing ngu bar byed.*

666. H.K. 378a: vol. 79, 347b.4–5.

667. *Five Stages.* D 1802: vol. 35, 48a.3. The Dg.T. recension reads *ri dbang rtse nas dga' zhig lhung gyur na/ . . . bla ma'i drin gyis phan pa'i lung thob na . . .* ; the *Moonbeams* citation (*MB* VVI 192.16–18) reads *ri dbang rtse nas thur du lhung gyur na/ . . . bla ma'i drin gyis phan pa'i lam rnyed na . . .*

668. *A String of Pearls: A Collection of Dharma Instructions* (*Khrid chos mu tig tsar la brgyus pa*). Collected Works of Gampopa, text 13/pa, 1b.

669. *Treatise Containing a Garland of Amṛta-Advice and [the Means for] Annihilating the Four Demons* (*bsTan bcos gros 'debs bdud rtsi'i phreng ba dang 'dre bzhi rtsad gcod*). Collected Works of Gampopa, text 33/gi, 8b–9a.

670. *A String of Pearls: A Collection of Dharma Instructions*, 3b.

671. Citation not found in this text. Rangjung Dorje cites the *Presentation of Ati* (*A ti*

bkod pa'i rgyud) as the source for the same passage in his *Pointing Out the Three Kāyas* (*sKu gsum ngo sprod*). Collected Works of Rangjung Dorje, vol. 11/A, 2b.1–2.

672. Source not found.
673. See D 4049: vol. 134, 92b.2–4.
674. D 3871: vol. 105, 10b.3–4.
675. D 4182: vol. 173, 41a.2–3.
676. *Śīlasaṃyuktasūtra*, *Tshul khrims dang ldan pa'i mdo* / *Tshul khrims yang dag par ldan pa'i mdo*. Toh. 303, H.K. 306. H.K. 306: vol. 72, 196b.5–6. The H.K. recension reads . . . *gzugs mthong mi rung ltar* . . . ; the *Moonbeams* citation (*MB* VVI 196.7) reads . . . *gzugs mthong mi 'gyur ba* . . . The *Moonbeams* citation is identical to one found in Gampopa's *Ornament of Precious Liberation*, 76a.
677. The *Sūtra on the Inconceivable Secret Teachings of the Tathāgatas* (H.K. 47: vol. 35, 272a.3); *Sūtra of the Questions of Subāhu* (*Subāhu-paripṛcchā-nāma-mahāyāna-sūtra*, *Lag bzangs kyis zhus pa zhes bya ba theg pa chen po'i mdo*) (Toh 70, H.K. 70; H.K. 70: vol. 39, 299a.4–5); and the *Sūtra Teaching Great Compassion* (*Tathāgat-amahākaruṇānirdeśasūtra*, *sNying rje chen po bstan pa'i mdo*) (Toh. 147, H.K. 148; H.K. 148: vol. 57, 201b.6–7) contain the following: *mig gis gzugs rnams mthong nas* [or *na*] *mtshan mar mi 'dzin cing mngon rtags su mi 'dzin pa yin*. The *Moonbeams* citation (*MB* VVI 196.14) reads *mig gis gzugs rnams mthong ste mtshan mar mi 'dzin mngon rtags su mi 'dzin*.
678. D 3871: vol. 105, 14b.1–2.
679. H.K. 17: vol. 34, 201b.1.
680. Almost identical passages are found in the *Prajñāpāramitā in Eight Thousand Lines* (H.K. 12: vol. 30, 236b.3); and *Prajñāpāramitā in Ten Thousand Lines* (*Daśasāhasrikā-prajñāpāramitā*, *Shes rab kyi pha rol tu phyin pa khri pa*) (Toh. 11, H.K. 13; H.K. 13: vol. 32, 437b.5–6).
681. Source not found.
682. D 4182: vol. 173, 42b.2. The Dg.T. recension reads . . . *'tshag phyir ma lags* . . . ; the *Moonbeams* citations read variously as . . . *mtshag phyir ma lags* . . . and . . . *mchog phyir ma lags* . . . The translation follows the Dg.T. recension. *MB* VVI (197.14): *rig pa yis* should be *rigs pa yis*. See *MB* DLG (127.7) and the Dg.T. recension.
683. See the *Śrāvakabhūmi*. D 4036: vol. 128, 29b.5–38b.1.
684. H.K. 17: vol. 34, 214b.4–5.
685. D 4182: vol. 173, 42b.2–3.
686. *MB* VVI (198.20): *mi brjod pa* should be *mi brjed pa*. See *MB* DLG (128.7).
687. *MB* VVI (200.2): *mchod na* should be *ma chod na*. See *MB* DLG (129.5).
688. *MB* VVI (204.5): *sbyor* should be *spyod*. See *MB* DLG (132.1).
689. This citation is found only in the first text, the *Earlier Authoritative Text*. D 2331: vol. 52, 271a.4. See note 621.
690. *Lamp for the Path of Awakening*. D 3947: vol. 111, 239b.7–240a.1.
691. *Vajra Song Summarizing the Six Dharmas: Instructions by the Great Scholar-siddha Nāropa for the Lord of Yogins Marpa Lotsāwa* (*mKhas grub chen po nA ro*

tA pas rnal 'byor gyi dbang phyug mar pa lo tsA la gdams pa'i chos drug dril ba rdo rje'i mgur). DNZ, vol. 7, 108.2.

692. In his *Ocean of Definitive Meaning* (*Nges don rgya mtsho*, 142), Wangchuk Dorje, the ninth Karmapa, attributes this to Dusum Khyenpa, the First Karmapa.

693. This may refer to a statement in the *Great Treatise* (486): "Leave your lips and teeth just as they are, in their ordinary way" (*so dang mchu ni rang lugs su tha mal bar bzhag go*).

694. See the middle *Stages of Meditation* (D 3916: vol. 110, 46b.6–7) and the final *Stages of Meditation* (D 3917: vol. 110, 57a.2–3).

695. H.K. 417: vol. 83, 17b.1–2.

696. *Illuminating the Suchness of Connate Cakrasaṃvara* (*Cakrasaṃvarasahaja-tattvāloka, dPal 'khor lo sdom pa'i lhan cig skyes pa'i de kho na nyid snang ba*). Toh. 1504. D 1504: vol. 22, 271a.7.

697. *Authoritative Text in Verse on the Six Dharmas: Instructions of the Mahāsiddha Nāropa* (*Grub chen na ro pa'i gdams ngag chos drug skor gyi bka' dpe tshigs su bcad pa*). DNZ, vol. 7, 97.1–2. The DNZ recension reads . . . *li ri bzhin du . . . re'u mig*. . . ; the *Moonbeams* citation (*MB* VVI 209.15–17) reads . . . *li gri bzhin du* . . . *re mig* . . . The translation follows the DNZ recension.

698. See D 4036: vol. 128, 131b.1–3.

699. Citation not found in the Kangyur. A very similar verse is found in the *Garland of Light* (*Ālokamālaprakaraṇa, sNang ba'i phreng ba*) by Kambala. Toh. 3895. D 3895: vol. 108, 59a.1–2: *chos 'di yongs su ma bsgoms pas/ chos nyid thob par mi 'gyur te/ ma 'thung skom pa ji ltar bzlog*. The *Moonbeams* citation (*MB* VVI .6–7) reads *chos 'di bsgoms par ma gyur na/ chos nyid mthong bar mi 'gyur te/ ma 'thung skom pa ji ltar sel*.

700. H.K. 17: vol. 34, 214b.5–6.

701. D 4021: vol. 123, 43a.4.

702. The translation uses the outline heading as it appears on p. 195: "Śamatha Without Characteristics" (*mtshan med kyi zhi gnas*), not as it appears here: "Objects of Meditation Without Characteristics" (*mtshan med kyi dmigs pa*), because the heading "Śamatha Without Characteristics" seems to fit the contents of the section better than "Objects of Meditation Without Characteristics."

703. *Ganges Mahāmudrā*. D 2303: vol. 52, 243a.5.

704. See, for example, the *Great Treatise*, 494, and Lamrim Chenmo Translation Committee, *Great Treatise*, vol. 3, 38.

705. D 3924: vol. 110, 90a.3–4.

706. D 3924: vol. 110, 90a.6.

707. D 3924: vol. 110, 90a.5–6.

708. See the first *Stages of Meditation*. D 3915: vol. 110, 31b.6.

709. *Bhadrapālaparipṛcchāsūtra, bZang skyong gis zhus pa'i mdo*. Also known as the *Sūtra on the Samādhi in Which the Buddhas of the Present All Stand Before One* (*Pratyutpannabuddhasaṃmukhāvasthitasamādhisūtra, Da ltar gyi sangs rgyas mngon sum du bzhugs pa'i ting nge 'dzin gyi mdo*. Toh 133, H.K. 135, H.K. 135:

vol. 56, 36b.1–4. The H.K. recension reads . . . *de bzhin du bzang skyong/ . . . de bzhin gshegs pa dgra bcom pa yang dag par rdzogs pa'i sangs rgyas de dag sangs rgyas kyi gdan la bzhugs shing chos ston par yang yid la bya'o/ des rnam pa thams cad kyi mchog dang ldan pa/ . . . sku yongs su grub pa dang ldan par de bzhin gshegs pa rnams . . . de bzhin gshegs pa dgra bcom pa yang dag par rdzogs pa'i sangs rgyas kyi skyes bu chen po'i mtshan re re'ang bsod nams rgyas bskyed par blta'o.*

The *Moonbeams* citation (*MB* VVI 215.1–6) reads . . . *de bzhin du/ . . . de bzhin gshegs pa de dag yid la bya ste/ sangs rgyas gdan la bzhugs shing chos 'chad pa/ rnam pa'i mchog thams cad dang ldan pa/ . . . sku phun sum tshogs pa dang ldan pa'i de bzhin gshegs pa rnams . . . de bzhin gshegs pa'i mtshan rnams re re yang bsod nams rgyas bskyed pa bsgom par bya'o.*

710. See endnote 317.

711. See D 3917: vol. 110, 57a.3–4 and 61a.5.

712. See the first *Stages of Meditation.* D 3915: vol. 110, 31b.6.

713. *Ganges Mahāmudrā.* D 2303: vol. 52, 243b.3. The Dg.T. recension reads *lus kyi bya ba yo thong . . . brag ca . . .* ; the *Moonbeams* citation (*MB* VVI 216.4–5) reads *lus kyi bya ba yongs thong . . . brag cha . . .*

714. *Entrance to Yoga* (*Yogāvatāra, rNal 'byor la 'jug pa*). Toh. 4074. D 4074: vol. 138, 127a.2. The Dg.T. recension reads . . . *gnyi ga gnyis min . . .* ; the *Moonbeams* citation (*MB* VVI 216.8) reads . . . *gnyis dang gnyis min . . .*

715. *Ganges Mahāmudrā.* D 2303: vol. 52, 243a.4–5. The Dg.T. recension reads *blo dman skye bo don la . . .* ; the *Moonbeams* citation (*MB* VVI 217.17) reads *blo dman skye bo ngang la . . .*

716. D 4090: vol. 141, 11b.1. This is the summary verse for the commentary on *Treasury of Abhidharma*, chapter 6, verse 12d. The bracketed words in the first line of the translation are from verse 12a.

717. H.K. 240: vol. 65, 190b.7–191a.1.

718. H.K. 240: vol. 65, 192a.4–5.

719. H.K. 389: vol. 81, 12a.6–12b.1. The H.K. recension reads *rnal 'byor ma ni mnyam gzhag pas/ . . . sgrub po sgra . . .* ; the *Moonbeams* citation (*MB* VVI 219.4–6) reads *rnal 'byor pa ni mnyam gzhag las/ . . . sgrub pos sgra . . .*

720. H.K. 386: vol. 80, 413b.7–414a.1. The H.K. recension reads *dgang ba yis ni lus bkang na/ dug dang rims kyis . . . bum pa can gyis sgo bcings na/ sgo yi sbu gu dag par 'gyur*; the *Moonbeams* citation (*MB* VVI 220.4–5) reads *dgang ba yis ni lus dag nas/ dug dang rims kyi . . . bum pa can gyi rlung bcings na/ sgo yi bu ga 'gag par 'gyur.* The translation follows the H.K. recension and relies on the explanations given on that recension in Bhavabhadra's *Commentary on "The King of Tantras, the Glorious Vajra Ḍāka"* (*Vajraḍāka-nāma-mahātantrarājasyavṛtti, rGyud kyi rgyal po chen po dpal rdo rje mkha' 'gro zhes bya ba'i rnam par bshad pa*). Toh. 1415. D 1415: vol. 19, 133a.7–133b.3. *MB* VVI (220.4): *rigs* should be *rims.* See *MB* DLG (142.6) and *MB* TsRP (286.1).

A translation based on the *Moonbeams* citation would be:

> When filling purifies your body,
> poisons and the fevers of flu are vanquished.
> When the breath of the vase is bound,
> the openings of your [sense] doors are blocked.

721. H.K. 389: vol. 81, 12b.1–2. The H.K. recension reads *yang na bum pa'i rnal 'byor gyis/ rtag tu 'chi bdag las rgyal bya/ bdag nyid rig pas rkang mthil bar/ kun tu rlung gi dgang bya ste/ bum pa can la brtan byas nas*; the *Moonbeams* citation (*MB* VVI 220.7–9) reads *yang na bum pa can sbyor bas/ thams cad du ni 'chi las rgyal/ bdag nyid rigs pas rkang mthil bar/ thams cad rlung gis kun bkang ste/ bum pa can la brtan bcas nas. MB* DLG (142.6) reads . . . *bdag nyid rig* . . .
722. H.K. 389: vol. 81, 13a.1–2. The H.K. recension reads *steng dang 'og du rgyu ba'i rlung/ kha sbyor du ni yid kyis byas/ de yi sbyor bas goms byed na* . . . ; the *Moonbeams* citation (*MB* VVI 220.12–13) reads *steng dang 'og du 'gro ba'i rlung/ yid kyis kha sbyor du bya ste/ de yi rnal sbyor goms pa yis* . . .
723. D 1346: vol. 11, 76b.1–2. The Dg.T. recension reads *kha yang bkab ste sna yi bug pa gnyis* . . . *shugs kyis bkug ste* . . . *mtshungs pa* . . . *dus kyis* . . . *ro ni mnyam par 'gyur/* . . . *sogs pa dang ni bkres dang skom pa 'phrog ste* . . . ; the *Moonbeams* citation (*MB* VVI 220.15–221.1) reads *kha yang btsum ste sna yi bu ga gnyis* . . . *shugs kyis dkrugs te* . . . *mtshungs pa'i* . . . *dus kyi* . . . *ro mnyam 'gyur/* . . . *sogs pa bkres pa dang ni dang skom pa 'phrog ste* . . . The translation follows the Dg.T. recension in reading *bkug*, not *dkrugs*, and *dus kyis*, not *dus kyi*.
724. *Authoritative Text in Verse on the Six Dharmas: Instructions of the Mahāsiddha Nāropa*, 97.3.
725. *MB* VVI (222.2): *byid* should be *bying*. See *MB* DLG (144.1).
726. *MB* VVI (222.8): *ni rigs* should be *ci rigs*. See *MB* DLG (144.3).
727. Citation not found in this text. It is found in Tāranātha's *Hundreds of Light Rays: An Addendum to Tongwa Dönden's "Vajrayoginī Commentary"* (*rDo rje'i rnal 'byor gyi 'khrid yig mthong ba don ldan gyi lhan thabs 'od brgya 'bar ba*) (Collected Works of Tāranātha, vol. 7, 326) attributed to Carpati (Tsarpaṭi), one of the eighty-four mahāsiddhas. Tāranātha comments:

    > Make your previous conceptual mind a nonconceptual mind. Then do nothing at all: without signs, without seeing, do not do anything. (*sems sngar rtog bcas de sems min pa rtog med du byed cing/ de'i tshe ci med cang med/ rtags med mthong med du mi bya/*)

728. D 2224: vol. 51, 74a.2–3. The Dg.T. recension reads . . . *tshul du gnas par bya*; the *Moonbeams* citation (*MB* VVI 223.4) reads . . . *tshul du bzhag par bya*.
729. D 2224: vol. 51, 72b.6–7.
730. Citation not found in this text. It is found in the following four texts belonging to the *Kālacakra Tantra* cycle: Yaśobhadra's *Difficult Points That Condense the Essence of the Vajra Lines* (*Vajrapadasārasaṃgrahapañjikā, rDo rje'i tshig gi snying po bsdus pa'i dka' 'grel*) (Toh. 1186; D 1186: vol. 4, 121a.5–6); Avadhūtipa's *Explanation of the Difficult Points of the Tantra of the Six-Branch Yoga, the Kālacakra*

Esoteric Instructions (*Kālacakropadeśayogaṣaḍaṅgatantrapañjikā, Dus kyi 'khor lo'i man ngag sbyor ba yan lag drug gi rgyud kyi dka' 'grel*) (Toh. 1373; D 1373: vol. 14, 240b.2); Anupamarakṣita's *Six-Branch Yoga* (*Ṣaḍaṅgayoga, sByor ba yan lag drug pa*) (Toh. 1387; D 1387: vol. 14, 297b.3–4); and Vajrapāṇi's *Commentary That Summarizes the Meaning of the "Laghutantra"* (*Lakṣābhidhānāduddhṛta-laghutantrapiṇḍārthavivaraṇa, mNgon par brjod pa 'bum pa las phyung ba nyung ngu'i rgyud kyi bsdus pa'i don rnam par bshad pa*) (Toh. 1402; D 1402: vol. 16, 131a.6–7).

731. D 2224: vol. 51, 74a.4.
732. *MB* VVI (224.5): *rnyed bde* should be *rnyed pa de*. See *MB* DLG (154.4).
733. *MB* VVI (225.17): *'di* should be *'dir*. See *MB* DLG (146.6).
734. *MB* VVI (226.6): *zhong* should be *shor*. See *MB* DLG (147.1).
735. *MB* DLG (147.2), *MB* TsRP (295.2), and *MB* DK (363.5) read *bying ba phra mo ma chod pa'i bying zhad yin la*; *MB* RD (201.14) reads *bying ba phra mo ma chod pa'i bying zhad mi rtog*; and *MB* PP (85b.5–6) reads *bying ba phra mo mchod pa'i bying zhad yin la*. *MB* VVI (226.7) reads *bying ba phra mo mchod pa'i bying zhad mi rtag* (*mchod* should be *ma chod*). The translation follows *MB* DLG.
736. D 3944: vol. 111, 229a.5.
737. D 3855: vol. 98, 4a.7. The Dg.T. recension reads ... *spang pa nyid du bya*; the *Moonbeams* citation (*MB* VVI 226.16) reads ... *yangs pa nyid du bya*. The citation in the *Great Treatise* (520) reads ... *yengs pa nyid du bya*.
738. *MB* VVI (226.17): *song yang phra ba ma ma sel na* should be *sol yang phra ba ma sol na*. See *MB* DLG (147.5) and *MB* TsRP (296.1).
739. D 4021: vol. 123, 43a.4–5.
740. D 3916: vol. 110, 50b.1 and D 3917: vol. 110, 59a.5.
741. D 3916: vol. 110, 50b.2 and D 3917: vol. 110, 59a.7.
742. D 4020: vol. 123, 19a.6. For textual variations see note 336.
743. D 3855: vol. 98, 4a.7. The Dg.T. recension reads *g.yengs pas g.yeng* ... ; the *Moonbeams* citation (*MB* VVI 228.6) reads *g.yengs pa g.yengs* ... The translation follows the Dg.T. recension. See also Bhāvaviveka's *Blaze of Reasoning*. D 3856: vol. 98, 57b.7. The bracketed words in the translation are drawn from the *Blaze of Reasoning*.
744. D 3944: vol. 111, 229a.5.
745. *MB* VVI (228.16–17): *sa le brgya* should be *sa le ba rgya*. See *MB* DLG (148.7).
746. *MB* VVI (228.18): *'chang* should be *'char*. See *MB* DLG (149.1).
747. *MB* VVI (229.7): *cig tu ... gtun* should be *zhig tu ... gcun*. See *MB* DLG (149.3).
748. *MB* VVI (229.12): *snga rabs* should be *sngar bas*. See *MB* DLG (149.5).
749. *Dohā for the People*. D 2224: vol. 51, 73a.4.
750. *Dohā for the People*. D 2224: vol. 51, 73a.5. The Dg.T. recension reads *thong bar gyur ... go bzlog*; the *Moonbeams* citation (229.18) reads *thongs bar gyur ... go log*.
751. Citation not found in a text attributed to Maitrīpa. It is found in Saraha's *Dohā Song on View, Meditation, Conduct, and Fruition*. D 2345: vol. 53, 3b.4. The Dg.T. recension reads ... *ras bal 'dab ma bzhin du glod la zhog*; the *Moonbeams* citation (*MB* VVI 229.22) reads *ras bal bzhin du ma bcos glod la zhog*.

752. This may refer to one of the statements in *Great Treatise* (508). See Lamrim Chenmo Translation Committee, *Great Treatise*, vol. 3, 51.

753. *Ganges Mahāmudrā*. D 2303: vol. 52, 243b.2.

754. *Dohā for the People*. D 2224: vol. 51, 71b.2. The Dg.T. recension reads . . . *yod pa de yang* . . . ; the *Moonbeams* citation (*MB* VVI 230.8) reads . . . *yod na de yang* . . .

755. *Consummate Sublime Path of Mahāmudrā Composed by the Unborn Zhang Rinpoche* (*sKye med zhang rin po ches mdzad pa'i phyag rgya chen po'i lam mchog mthar thug*). (Hereafter cited as *Consummate Sublime Path of Mahāmudrā*.) DNZ, vol. 8, 441.2–3, and TsRP, vol. 4, 71.6–72.1. The DNZ and TsRP recensions read *shes pa lhod kyis glod tsam na* . . . *dkyil ltar gnas* . . . ; the *Moonbeams* citation (*MB* VVI 230.11–12) reads *shes pa lhod kyis glod pa'i dus* . . . *dkyil ltar 'char* . . .

756. *MB* VVI (231.6): *skrag med du* ("fearlessly") may possibly be an error and should be *bkrag med* ("amorphous"). Although all consulted editions of *Moonbeams* read *skrag med du*, the parallel section of Dakpo Tashi Namgyal's *Clarifying the Suchness of the Innate State* (*gNyug ma'i de nyid gsal ba*) (Rigpe Dorje Practice Series, vol. 11, 36.4–5) has *bun ne ba* ("hazy"), which is similar to *bkrag med*, and therefore the translation assumes *bkrag med* is correct.

757. *Moonbeams* cites the text as *Dus bzhi mnyam sbyor*, however, no text of that name is found, and this quotation is found in Nāgārjuna's *Delineating the Four Empowerments* (*Sekacatuḥprakaraṇa*, *dBang bzhi pa'i rab tu byed pa*). Toh. 1799. D 1799: vol. 35, 36b.7. *MB* VVI (232.8): *'thong* should be *'thor*. See *MB* DLG (151.5).

758. *MB* VVI (232.16): *dran shes bya* should be *dran shes phye*. See *MB* DLG (151.7).

759. D 3871: vol. 105, 11b.2.

760. D 4032: vol. 124, 274b.2.

761. D 3916: vol. 110, 47b.5–6.

762. D 4036: vol. 128, 132a.3–4.

763. D 4036: vol. 128, 132a.4–5.

764. D 4021: vol. 123, 43a.4–5.

765. D 3916: vol. 110, 50b.4; and D 3917: vol. 110, 60a.2–3.

766. D 3916: vol. 110, 48a.3. The Dg.T. recension reads . . . *rnal du 'jug pa* . . . ; the *Moonbeams* citation (*MB* VVI 238.4) reads . . . *rnal du 'dug pa* . . . The *Moonbeams* citation is identical to the one in the *Great Treatise*, 526.

767. *Ganges Mahāmudrā*. D 2303: vol. 52, 243b.6–7. The Dg.T. recension reads . . . *gcong rong chu dang 'dra/* . . . *dal bus 'bab/ tha ma chu bran ma bu* . . . ; the *Moonbeams* citation (*MB* VVI 239.3–5) reads . . . *gcong rong 'bab chu 'dra/* . . . *dal zhing g.yo/ tha ma chu rnams ma bu* . . .

768. *MB* VVI (239.8): *las can* should be *lang can*. See *MB* DLG (156.7) and *MB* TsRP (313.6).

769. D 4020: vol. 123, 19a.5.

770. *MB* VVI (242.7): *rgyun gyur* should be read *rgyur gyur*. See *MB* DLG (159.3) and *MB* TsRP (318.6).

771. See D 4036: vol. 128, 163a.2–6.

772. See D 4036: vol. 128, 163.4a–167.2.

773. D 3915: vol. 110, 32b.3–7.

774. D 3871: vol. 105, 23b.1–23b.2.
775. Source unidentified.
776. Source unidentified.
777. *MB* VVI (244.9): *las* should be *lam. See MB* DLG (161.1).
778. D 3915: vol. 110, 32b.1–3. the Dg.T. recension reads . . . *khyad par thob pas* . . ; the *Moonbeams* citation (245.10) reads . . . *khyad par thob pa'i* . . . The translation follows the Dg.T. recension.
779. D 3915: vol. 110, 30b.6–7.
780. D 3916: vol. 110, 45a.4.
781. *Varṇārhavarṇe* (*Varṇārhavarṇe bhagavato buddhasya stotre śakyastava, Sangs rgyas bcom ldan 'das la bstod pa bsngags par 'os pa bsngags pa las bstod par mi nus par bstod pa*). Toh. 1138. D 1138: vol. 1, 96a.3–4. *MB* VVI (246.14): *gang 'byung* should be . . . *yang 'byung*. See *MB* DLG (162.7).
782. D 3916: vol. 110, 44b.1–3. The Dg.T. recension reads . . . *shes rab kyi snang ba byung ba med par 'bag la nyal legs par choms mi srid pa'i phyir bag nyal legs par choms par mi 'gyur ro* . . . ; the *Moonbeams* citation (*MB* VVI 247.12–13) reads . . . *shes rab kyi snang ba byung ba med par bag nyal legs par choms par mi 'gyur ro* . . . The *Moonbeams* citation is identical to the one in the *Great Treatise,* 479. The *Unraveling the Intent* citation: H.K. 109: vol. 51, 67a.5.
783. D 3916: vol. 110, 44b.7–45a.1.
784. H.K. 129: vol. 55, 44a.7–44b.2. The H.K. recension reads . . . *de ni nyon mongs phyir yang rab tu ldang/ lhag spyod kyis ni* . . . *gal te bdag med chos la rab rtog cing/ de dag brtags nas gal te sgom byed na/ 'bras bu mya ngan 'das thob rgyu de yin/ rgyu gzhan de dag zhi bar 'gyur mi srid*. The *Moonbeams* citation (*MB* VVI 248.2–8) reads . . . *de ni nyon mongs phyir zhing rab 'khrug ste/ lhag spyod kyi ni* . . . *gal te chos la bdag med so sor rtog/ so sor de brtags gal te sgom pa na/ de ni mya ngan 'das thob 'bras bu'i rgyu/ rgyu gzhan gang yin des ni zhir mi 'gyur*. Note that the *Moonbeams* citation is identical to the one found in the *Great Treatise*, 564–65.
785. This may refer to the explanation in the *Great Treatise*, 565. See Lamrim Chenmo Translation Committee, *Great Treatise*, vol. 3, 108.
786. See H.K. 109: vol. 51, 54a.1–2.
787. See D 3916: vol. 110, 46a.3–4.
788. *Akṣayamatinirdeśasūtra, bLo gros mi zad pas bstan pa'i mdo.* Toh. 175, H.K. 176. H.K. 176: vol. 60, 231a.6, 231a.7–231b.1, and 231b.5–6. The H.K. recension reads . . . *mdo sde gang dag zab mo mthong bar dka' ba khong du chud par dka' ba bstan*; the *Moonbeams* citation (*MB* VVI 249.18) reads . . . *mdo sde gang dag zab mo blta dka' ba rtogs par dka' ba bstan.* The *Moonbeams* citation is identical to the *Great Treatise* (568–69), and Kamalaśīla's *Illumination of Madhyamaka* (*Madhyamakāloka, dbU ma snang ba*) (Toh. 3887; D 3887: vol. 107, 149a.7–149b.1).
789. H.K. 176: vol. 60, 231b.6–232a.4 with numerous small differences. The *Moonbeams* citation is identical to the *Great Treatise* (569), and both are almost identical to Kamalaśīla's *Illumination of Madhyamaka* (D 3887: vol. 107, 149b.1–3).
790. H.K. 129: vol. 55, 33b.1–2.

791. H.K. 378a: vol. 79, 347b.4–5.
792. H.K. 378a: vol. 79, 348b.2–3.
793. H.K. 239: vol. 65, 97a.7–97b.2. The H.K. recension does not contain *byang chub sems dpa' rnam par gnon pa'i blo gros kyis gsol ba/ bcom ldan 'das/* and reads *gang chos zhes bya ba'i chos 'di ni yul na mi gnas . . . rag las pa ni med pa ma yin no/ . . . bzung ba dang/ shin tu mthar gtugs pa dang/ shin tu thul ba dang/ shin tu mnyam par brtsam pa . . .* The *Moonbeams* citation (*MB* VVI 253.8–12) reads *byang chub sems dpa' rnam par gnon pa'i blo gros kyis gsol ba/ bcom ldan 'das/ chos chos zhes bgyi ba'i chos gang lags de ni yul na mi gnas . . . rag las pa ni ma gtogs so/ . . . bzung ba dang/ mthar gtugs pa dang/ shin tu 'dul ba dang/ shin tu mnyam par bzhag pa . . .* The translation follows the H.K. recension in reading *rag las pa ni med pa ma yin no.* The *Moonbeams* citation is identical to one found in Gampopa's *Sunrays of Scriptural Citations*, 1b.

Almost identical citations (attributed to this sūtra) are found in Śāntideva's *Compendium of Training* (*Śikṣāsamuccaya, bsLab pa kun las btus pa*) (Toh. 3940; D 3940: vol. 111, 70a.1–70a.2–3); and Prajñākaramati's *Explanation of the Difficult Points of the "Entrance to the Bodhisattva's Way of Life"* (*Bodhicaryāvatārapañjikā, byang chub kyi spyod pa la 'jug pa'i dka' 'grel*) (Toh. 3872; D 3872: vol. 105, 91b.3–4).
794. H.K. 232: vol. 64, 129b.4. The H.K. recension reads *chos thams cad kyi thog mar sems 'gro ste/ sems yongs su shes na . . .* ; the *Moonbeams* citation (*MB* VVI 253.15–16) reads *sems ni chos thams cad kyi sngon du gro ste/ sems yongs su shes na . . .*
795. *Ātyayajñāna, 'Da' ka ye shes*. Toh. 122, H.K. 124. H.K. 124: vol. 54, 226a.7.
796. *Dohā for the People.* D 2224: vol. 51, 72b.5.
797. *Dohā for the People.* D 2224: vol. 51, 76a.6–7.
798. *Ganges Mahāmudrā.* D 2303: vol. 52, 243a.3–243a.4.
799. D 3871: vol. 105, 10b.7.
800. D 3871: vol. 105, 10b.7–11a.1.
801. H.K. 110: vol. 51, 269a.1–2. The H.K. recension reads *rnyog pa spangs . . . sang rgyas zhes nga 'chad*; the *Moonbeams* citation (255.11–12) reads *rtog pa spangs . . . sang rgyas zhes pa 'chad.*
802. Citation not found in the Kangyur or Tengyur. It is found (attributed to the *Kālacakra Root Tantra*) in Gampopa's *Sunrays of Scriptural Citations*, 11a.
803. Chapter 5, verse 65. D 1346: vol. 11, 87a.3–87a.4.
804. *Vajraḍāka-guhyatantrarāja, rDo rje mkha' 'gro gsang ba'i rgyud kyi rgyal po*. Toh. 399. Dg.K.: vol. 79, 231.3.
805. H.K. 378b: vol. 79, 367a.1–2.
806. *'Jam dpal zhal lung*, by Buddhaśrījñāna. Also known as *Oral Teachings: Meditation on the Suchness of the Two Stages* (*Dvikramatattvabhāvanā-nāma-mukhāgama, Rim pa gnyis pa'i de kho na nyid bsgom pa zhes bya ba zhal gyi lung*). Toh. 1853. D 1853: vol. 42, 3a.7–3b.1.
807. *Rāṣṭrapālaparipṛcchāsūtra, Yul 'khor skyong gis zhus pa'i mdo*. Toh. 62. Citation not found in this text. It is found in the *Bodhisattva's Piṭaka*. H.K. 56: vol. 37,

34a.4. The H.K. recension reads *gang la gnas te sems sgom pa* . . . ; the *Moonbeams* citation (*MB* VVI 256.13) reads *gang la brten te sems sgom du* . . . The citation is found twice in Gampopa's *Sunrays of Scriptural Citations*, 11a and 19b. The first citation is attributed to the *Sūtra of the Questions of Rāṣṭrapāla* and the second to the *Bodhisattva's Piṭaka*. Both citations read *gang la brten nas sems bsgom pa* . . .

808. H.K. 379: vol. 79, 400a.4–5. The H.K. recension reads *sems kyi rin chen bskul* . . . *skye bar sangs rgyas dam pa nyid*; the *Moonbeams* citation (*MB* VVI 256.18–257.1) reads *rin chen sems kyis bskul* . . . *skye ba dam par sangs rgyas nyid.*

809. H.K. 379: vol. 79, 416a.6. The H.K. recension reads *stong pa snying rje tha dad med/ gang du sems ni rab bsgom pa/* . . . ; the *Moonbeams* citation (*MB* VVI 257.2) reads *stong nyid snying rje dbyer med par/ gang du sems ni rnam sgom pa/* . . .

810. D 4020: vol. 123, 6b.5–6.

811. D 1800: vol. 35, 39a.7–39b.3.

812. Citation not found in the first *Stages of Meditation*. It is found in the middle *Stages of Meditation*. D 3916: vol. 110, 48b.7–49a.3.

813. See, for example, the final *Stages of Meditation*, 58a.5–58b.3.

814. *Dohā for the Queen*. D 2264: vol. 52, 30b.3.

815. Source not found.

816. Source not found.

817. *Dohā for the Queen*. D 2264: vol. 52, 29b.1–2. The Dg.T. recension reads . . . *sems kyis de nyid rtogs par mi 'gyur te*; the *Moonbeams* citation (*MB* VVI 261.19) reads . . . *sems kyis de nyid mthong ba med.* The translation follows the Dg.T. recension, which is also found later in *MB* (see *MB* VVI 380.12). *MB* VVI (261.18): *kyi* should be *kyis*. See *MB* DLG (173.5).

818. D 3915: vol. 110, 34b.4.

819. H.K. 87: vol. 40, 240b.4.

820. *Ratnacūḍaparipṛcchāsūtra, gTsug na rin po ches zhus pa'i mdo*. Toh. 91, H.K. 91. H.K. 91: vol. 40, 375b.2.

821. *Trayastriṃśatparivartasūtra, Sum cu rtsa gsum pa'i le'u*. Toh. 223, H.K. 224. H.K. 224: vol. 63, 215a.7–215b.1. The H.K. recension reads . . . *chos nyid mthong ba med* . . . ; the *Moonbeams* citation (*MB* VVI 262.10) reads . . . *chos nyid mthong ba na* . . . The *Moonbeams* citation is identical to the citation in Gampopa's *Sunrays of Scriptural Citations*, 16a.

822. D 3916: vol. 110, 49b.7–50a.1 and D 3917: vol. 110, 58b.3–5. See H.K. 232: vol. 64, 146a.1–3. The H.K. recension reads . . . *gnas gang dang gang la sems 'jug cing sems mngon par dad pa'i gnas* . . . *sems de gang yin pa de'ang yongs su brtags na stong pa'o/ gang gis brtags pa de yang stong par rtogs so/ de de ltar rtog pas mtshan ma med pa la rnal 'byor du byed do.* The middle and final *Stages of Meditation* and the *Moonbeams* citation (*MB* VVI 132.1–3) read . . . *gnas gang dang gang du sems 'phros shing sems mngon par dga' pa'i gnas* . . . *sems gang yin pa de yang brtags na stong par rtogs so/ sems gang gis rtog pa de yang ngo bo nyid kun tu btsal na stong par rtogs te/ de ltar rtogs pas mtshan ma med pa'i rnal 'byor la 'jug go.*

823. *Dharmadhātu-prakṛti-asaṃbheda-nirdeśa-nāma-mahāyāna-sūtra, Chos kyi dbyings kyi rang bzhin dbyer med pa bstan pa*. Toh. 52, H.K. 52. H.K. 52: vol. 36, 233b.4–

234a.5. The H.K. recension reads . . . *yang dag par yongs su grub pa yod snyam mam/* . . . ; the *Moonbeams* citation (*MB* VVI 263.16) reads . . . *yang dag par yongs su grub pa med snyam mam/* . . . The translation follows the H.K. recension.

824. H.K. 87: vol. 40, 240b.4–241a.1. The H.K. recension reads . . . *sems ni dpyad du med* . . . ; the *Moonbeams* citation (*MB* VVI 264.2) reads . . . *sems ni bcad du med* . . . The translation follows the H.K. reading.

825. H.K. 87: vol. 40, 240a.3–5.

826. *Ratnacūḍaparipṛcchāsūtra, gTsug na rin po ches zhus pa'i mdo.* Toh. 91. H.K. 91: vol. 40, 375b.2–7. The H.K. recension reads *de sems kun du tshol ba na sems nang na yang yang dag par rjes su mi mthong/ sems phyi rol na yang yang dag par rjes su mi mthong/ sems phyi dang nang na yang yang dag par rjes su mi mthong/ phung po rnams la yang sems yang dag par rjes su mi mthong/ khams rnams la yang sems yang dag par rjes su mi mthong/ skye mched rnams la yang sems yang dag par rjes su mi mthong* . . . The *Moonbeams* citation (*MB* VVI 264.9–12) reads *de sems kun du 'tshol ba ni sems de nang na yang dag par rjes su mi mthong/ de bzhin du sbyar te/ sems de phyi rol na/sems de phyi nang na/phung po rnams las/ khams rnams las/ skye mched rnams las yang dag par rjes su mi mthong* . . . The *Moonbeams* citation is identical to the citation in Gampopa's *Sunrays of Scriptural Citations,* 15b–16a.

827. *Mahāvairocanābhisambodhi, rNam snang mngon byang / rNam par snang mdzad chen po mngon par rdzogs par byang chub pa.* Toh. 494, H.K. 462. H.K. 462: vol. 86, 180b.4–7.

828. Gods (*lha*), nāgas (*klu*), yakṣas (*gnod sbyin*, "harmful spirits"), gandharvas (*dri za*, "divine musicians"), asuras (*lha ma yin*, "demigods"), garuḍas (*nam mkha' lding*), kiṃnaras (*mi'am ci*, "half-horse, half-human"), and mahoragas (*lto 'phye chen po*, "great snakes") are the eight classes of gods and demons (*lha srin sde brgyad*).

829. H.K. 462: vol. 86, 179b.5–180a.7. The H.K. recension reads . . . *sangs rgyas rnams kyis ma gzigs/ mi gzigs/ gzigs par mi 'gyur te/* . . . *mig la mi gnas/ rna ba la mi gnas/ sna la mi gnas/ lce la mi gnas/ lus la mi gnas* . . . ; the *Moonbeams* citation (*MB* VVI 265.10 and 18) reads . . . *sangs rgyas rnams kyis ma gzigs gzigs par mi 'gyur te/* . . . *mig la mi gnas lus la mi gnas* . . .

830. D 1800: vol. 35, 40a.1–3.

831. D 1803: vol. 35, 75a.2–3. The Derge recension reads . . . *kha phyir bstas pa rnams kyi spyod yul ma yin pa/ shin tu zab pa/ mchog tu bzung ba dka' ba/* . . . *sems gang yin pa de'i ngo bo nyid ni rtsa ba med pa* . . . ; the *Moonbeams* citation (*MB* VVI 266.17–18) reads . . . *kha phyir bstas pa rnams kyi spyod yul ma yin pa/ mchog tu bzung ba dka' ba/* . . . *sems gang yin pa de ni/ rtsa ba med pa* . . .

832. D 1803: vol. 35, 85a.1.

833. *Tathāgatamahākaruṇānirdeśasūtra, sNying rje chen po bstan pa'i mdo.* Toh. 147; H. 148. H.K. 148: vol. 57, 210a.7. The H.K. recension does not have *sems ni*, which is found in the *Moonbeams* citation (*MB* VVI 267.9).

834. *Maitreya-paripṛcchā, Byams zhus kyi mdo.* Toh. 85, H.K. 85. Citation not found in the Kangyur. It is found (attributed to the *Sūtra of the Questions of Maitreya*) in Gampopa's *Sunrays of Scriptural Citations,* 16a.

835. H.K. 462: vol. 86, 180a.6–7.

836. *Dohā for the People.* D 2224: vol. 51, 72b.6.
837. *Treasury of Dohā: Instructions on Mahāmudrā.* D 2273: vol. 52, 123a.7.
838. *MB* VVI (268.2): *rtogs pa* should be *rtog pa. See MB* DLG (178.7).
839. *Ganges Mahāmudrā.* D 2303: vol. 52, 243a.5–7. The Dg.T. recension reads *dper na nam mkha'i dkyil ni brtag byas na/ mtha' dang dbus su 'dzin pa 'gag par 'gyur/ de bzhin sems kyis sems la brtag byas na/ rnam rtog tshor 'gag rtog med gnas gyur na/ bla med byang chub sems kyi rang bzhin mthong/ dper na sa rlung sprin ni nam mkhar dengs/ gar yang song med gar yang gnas pa med/ . . .* The *Moonbeams* citation (*MB* VVI 268.4–10) reads *dper na nam mkha'i dkyil bltas mthong ba 'gag par 'gyur/ de bzhin sems kyis sems la bltas byas na/ rnam rtog tshogs 'gag rtog bla med byang chub thob/ dper na khug sna sprin rnams nam mkha'i khams su dengs/ gar yang song ba med cing gang du'ang gnas pa med/ . . .*
840. *Ganges Mahāmudrā.* D 2303: vol. 52, 243b.1–3. The Dg.T. recension reads *dper na nam mkha' stong par rab rtags kyang/ . . . brjod par 'di 'dra grub ces brtags gzhi med . . .* ; the *Moonbeams* citation (*MB* VVI 268.11–14) reads *dper na nam mkha' stong par tha snyad rab rtags kyang/ . . .'di 'drar grub ces tha snyad gdags gzhi med . . .*
841. *Treasury of Dohā: Instructions on Mahāmudrā.* D 2273: vol. 52, 123a.5–6.
842. H.K. 87: vol. 40, 232.4–5. See note 422 for textual differences. The bracketed words are drawn from Sthiramati's *Extensive Explanation on the "Discourse for Kāśyapa."* See D 4009: vol. 116, 229b.5-6.
843. H.K. 109: vol. 51, 10a.1–2. The H.K. recension reads *so so rang rig mtshan nyid spyod yul te/ brjod du med cing tha snyad yongs chad pa/ . . .* ; the *Moonbeams* citation (*MB* VVI 269.14–15) reads *so so rang rig mtshan med spyod yul te/ brjod du med cing tha snyad spong chad pa/ . . .*
844. *Sandhivyākaraṇa-tantra, dGongs pa lung bsten pa'i rgyud.* Toh. 444, H.K. 418. H.K. 418: vol. 83, 123b.5–6. The H.K. recension reads . . . *slar yang de nyid la gsungs pa/ . . . gnyis ga ming du'ang 'gyur ma yin . . .* ; the *Moonbeams* citation (*MB* VVI 269.19–20) . . . *slar yang de nyid legs byas pa/ . . . gnyis ka min du 'gyur ba min . . .* The *Moonbeams* citation is identical to the citation in Gampopa's *Sunrays of Scriptural Citations,* 12a. Note that *Moonbeams* (*MB* VVI 269.18) refers to this text as *dGongs pa lung bsten pa'i mdo* as does Gampopa's *Sunrays of Scriptural Citations.*
845. H.K. 378a: vol. 79, 348b.2.
846. H.K. 378a: vol. 79, 348a.5–6.
847. Citation not found in the Tengyur. It is found (attributed to Tilopa) in Gampopa's *Esoteric Instructions on the Twofold Abiding State and Esoteric Instructions on Twofold Armor* (2a); *Pointing Out the Root of Mahāmudrā* (*Phyag rgya chen po'i rtsa ba la ngo sprad pa*) (Collected Works of Gampopa, text 24/ya, 7a); and Wangchuk Gyaltsen's *Great Bliss of Stainless Eloquence: A Biography of Nāropa* (*NA ro pa'i rnam thar dri med legs bshad bde chen*) (58a.1–2).
848. H.K. 17: vol. 34, 199a.1–2.
849. *Dohā for the People.* D 2224: vol. 51, 72a.7.
850. *Treasury of Dohā: Instructions on Mahāmudrā.* D 2273: vol. 52, 122b.1–2.
851. D 2273: vol. 52, 122b.6–7.

852. *Summary of the View.* D 2304: vol. 52, 244b.5 and 1.
853. Citation and text not found in the Kangyur. It is found (attributed to the *Sūtra of Genuine Samādhi*) in Gampopa's *Sunrays of Scriptural Citations*, 18b.
854. Source not found.
855. *Summary Verses on Mahāmudrā*, 45.3–4. Also cited in Gampopa's *Sunrays of Scriptural Citations*, 14a.
856. H.K. 110: vol. 51, 185b.3–185b.4. See note 184 for textual differences.
857. H.K. 379: vol. 79, 400a.6–400b.1. The H.K. recension reads . . . *reg bya'i rang bzhin te/ chos kyi dbyings ni mchog tu zhi/ 'di ni rin chen mchog tu brjod/ . . . 'di dag thams cad sems las skyes/ thub pa 'di ni gzhan mi 'gyur*; the *Moonbeams* citation (*MB* VVI 273.13–16) reads . . . *reg bya skyes pa'i dngos/ rin chen sems 'dir brjod nyid de/ chos dbyings mchog tu zhi nyid do/ . . . thams cad sems 'di'i dngos po las/ thub pas gzhan du ma gsungs so.*
858. The first two lines are H.K. 110: vol. 51, 264b.3. The third and fourth lines are probably H.K. 110: vol. 51, 264b.1–2. For textual differences see note 178.
859. H.K. 379: vol. 79, 418a.5–6. See note 187 for textual differences.
860. *Dohā for the King.* D 2263: vol. 52, 27b.4–5.
861. *Treasury of Dohā* (*Dohakoṣa, Do ha mdzod*). Toh. 2280. D 2280: vol. 52, 135a.5–6. *MB* VVI (275.6): *mig gi nang* should be *mig gi nad.* See *MB* DLG (183.4).
862. H.K. 379: vol. 79, 418a.3. See note 188 for textual differences.
863. D 1800: vol. 35, 39b.2.
864. *Dohā for the People.* D 2224: vol. 51, 72b.5. *MB* VVI (276.4): *gang las* should be *gang la.* See Dg.T. and *MB* DLG (183.6).
865. *Dohā for the People.* D 2224: vol. 51, 74b.7. The Dg.T. recension reads . . . *srid dang mnyam zhing* . . . ; the *Moonbeams* citation (*MB* VVI 276.9) reads . . . *srid dang mnyam nyid* . . .
866. See the *Prajñāpāramitā in One Hundred Thousand Lines* (*Śatasāhasrikā-prajñāpāramitā, Shes rab kyi pha rol tu phyin pa stong phrag brgya pa*) (Toh. 8, H.K. 9; H.K. 9: vol. 14, 451a.3); *Prajñāpāramitā in Twenty-Five Thousand Lines* (*Pañcaviṃśatisāhasrikā-prajñāpāramitā, Shes rab kyi pha rol tu phyin pa stong phrag nyi shu lnga pa*) (Toh. 9, H.K. 10; H.K. 10: vol. 26, 169a.2); *Prajñāpāramitā in Eighteen Thousand Lines* (*Aṣṭādaśasāhasrikā-prajñāpāramitā, Shes rab kyi pha rol tu phyin pa khri brgyad stong pa*) (Toh. 10, H.K. 12; H.K. 12: vol. 30, 108b.3); and *Prajñāpāramitā in Eight Thousand Lines* (*Aṣṭasāhasrikāprajñāpāramitā, brGyad stong pa / Shes rab kyi pha rol tu phyin pa brgyad stong pa*) (Toh. 12, H.K. 11; H.K. 11: vol. 29, 4b.5). In the first three texts, the H.K. recension reads *sems de sems ma yin te/ sems kyi rang bzhin 'od gal ba'i phyir ro*; the *Moonbeams* citation (*MB* VVI 276.12) reads *sems ni sems ma mchis te/ sems kyi rang bzhin 'od gal ba lags so.* The *Moonbeams* citation is almost identical to one found in Gampopa's *Sunrays of Scriptural Citations*, 10a.
867. Source unidentified.
868. Citation not found in a text by Āryadeva. It is found (unattributed) in Bodhibhadra's *Commentary on the "Compendium on the Heart of Wisdom"* (*Jñānasārasamuccaya-*

nāma-nibandhana, Ye shes snying po kun las btus pa zhes bya ba'i bshad sbyar) (Toh. 3852; D 3852: vol. 97, 33b.3–4); Haribhadra's *Illumination of the "Ornament for Clear Realization"* (*Āṣṭasāhasrikāprajñāpāramitāvyākhyānābhisamayālaṃkārāloka, Shes rab kyi pha rol tu phyin pa brgyad stong pa'i bshad pa mngon par rtogs pa'i rgyan gyi snang ba*) (Toh. 3791; D 3791: vol. 85, 314b.1–314b.2); and his *Commentary on the "Ornament for Clear Realization"* (*Abhisamayālaṃkāra-nāma-prajñāpāramitopadeśaśāstravṛtti, Shes rab kyi pha rol tu phyin pa'i man ngag gi bstan bcos mngon par rtogs pa'i rgyan zhes bya ba'i 'grel pa*) (Toh. 3793; D 3793: vol. 86, 130a.6–7). On p. 284 the same citation is attributed to Nāgārjuna.

869. D 3846: vol. 97, 9b.6.
870. *Satyadvayāvatāra, bDen pa gnyis la 'jug pa.* Toh. 3902. D 3902: vol. 109, 72a.6. The Dg.T. recension reads . . . *cung zad yod pa ma yin te*; the *Moonbeams* citation (*MB* VVI 277.9) reads . . . *gcig kyang yod pa ma yin no.*
871. H.K. 129: vol. 55, 71a.6 and 66a.7. The H.K. recension (71a.6) reads *ji ltar bdag gi 'du shes rig/ de bzhin kun tu blo yang gtong/ chos kun de yi rang bzhin te/ rnam par dag pa nam mkha' bzhin* and (66a.7) *gcig gyis kyang ni thams cad shes/ gcig gis kyang ni thams cad mthong*; the *Moonbeams* citation (*MB* VVI 277.13–16) reads *ji ltar khyod kyis bdag gi 'du shes ni/ shes pa de bzhin kun la blos sbyar bya/ chos rnams thams dad de yi ngo bo nyid/ yongs su dag pa nam mkha' lta bu yin/ gcig gyis kyang ni thams cad shes/ gcig gis kyang ni thams cad mthong.* The *Moonbeams* citation is found verbatim in Candrakīrti's *Lucid Words.* See D 3860: vol. 102, 43b.1–2.
872. D 1800: vol. 35, 40b.2–3.
873. D 1800: vol. 35, 41a.1.
874. *MB* VVI (279.17): *rang kham* should be *rang kha ma.* See *MB* DLG (186.2) and *MB* DK (452.2).
875. *MB* VVI (283.17): *sems nyid de yang sgom 'gags pas* should be *sems nyid de yang sgo ma 'gags pas.* See *MB* DLG (189.5) and *MB* TsRP (380.2).
876. *Dohā for the People.* D 2224: vol. 51, 73a.7. The Dg.T. recension reads . . . *g.yo zhing 'phyar la* . . . ; the *Moonbeams* citation (*MB* VVI 286.18) reads . . . *g.yo zhing 'char la* . . .
877. *Summary Verses on Mahāmudrā,* 45.3–4. Also cited in Gampopa's *Sunrays of Scriptural Citations,* 14a.
878. D 1800: vol. 35, 39b.5–6.
879. *Dohā for the King.* D 2263: vol. 52, 26b.7–27a.1. The Dg.T. recension reads . . . *rlung gis brgyab* . . . *de ltar rgyal pos* . . . ; the *Moonbeams* citation (*MB* VVI 288.2–4) reads . . . *rlung gis rgyab* . . . *de bzhin rgyal po* . . .
880. *Dohā for the People.* D 2224: vol. 51, 72a.7.
881. *Dohā for the People.* D 2224: vol. 51, 75a.6–7.
882. 3916: vol. 110, 49a.3–5.
883. The middle *Stages of Meditation* only cites the first three sentences of the passage. See D 3916: vol. 110, 49a.6. The entire passage is found verbatim in Candrakīrti's *Lucid Words.* See D 3860: vol. 102, 14a.7–14b.2. See also H.K. 87: vol. 40, 242a.2–6 which varies from the *Moonbeams* citation and the *Lucid Words* recension.

884. *Saddharmarājasūtra, Chos kyi rgyal po'i mdo / Dam pa'i chos kyi rgyal po'i mdo.* Toh. 243, H.K. 244. H.K. 244: vol. 66, 3b.6–4a.7. The H.K. recension reads *sangs rgyas zhal na rigs kyi bu pho rnams grol thar par 'dod na/ 'dod pa'i yan lag bcad la sems gnyis su mi bsam par gcig tu bsam ste yod pa bsam pa'i sems btang ngo/ sems kyi ngo bo nyi kyi tshul ni/ stong pa ste/ sems kyi ngo bo nyid kyi nang na 'gro ba'ang med do/ gtong ba yang med na ci'ang thob pa med do/ de'i ming ni/ byang chub bo/... byang chub sems dpa' nam mkha' mdzod kyis sangs rgyas la gsol pa/ bcom ldan 'das/ sems can kyi 'du mched dang/ shes rab kyi legs nyes skye nus shing/ lan bon ldang ba'i gnas lags te/ phyi nang mu gnyis kyi chos so cog gcig gi nang du gcig zhugs nas ci'i slad nas de'i nang na blang ba dang btang ba ma mchis zhes bgyir rung/ sangs rgyas kyis byang chub sems dpa' nam mkha' mdzod la bka' stsal pa/ rigs kyi bu pho/ bsam gtan gcig tu 'dus pa'i nang du zhugs la kun gyis phyi nang du brtags na tha mar yong med do/ de'i ci'i phyir zhe na/ nang du bltas/ nang du brtags na yang dag pa'i ngo bo nyid la skye ba med.*

The *Moonbeams* citation (*MB* VVI 290.19–291.6) reads *rigs kyi bu grol ba dang thar pa 'dod na 'dod pa'i yan lag bcad la sems gnyis su mi bsam par gcig tu bsam ste/ yod bsam pa'i sems skyang stong ngo/ sems kyi ngo bo nyid ni stong pa ste/ 'gro ba yang med/ btang ba yang med/ thos pa yang med de/ de'i ming ni byang chub bo/ gsol pa/ sems kyi 'du shes bsam gyis mi khyab pa mchis na/ de la 'gro ba dang btang ba dang thob pa med ces bgyi ba ji ltar lags/ bka' stsal pa/ bsam gtan gcig tu 'dus pa'i nang du zhugs la nang du blta zhing nang du brtags na/ yang dag pa'i ngo bo nyid la skye ba med. MB* VVI (290.20): *bcang* should be *bcad.* See *MB* DLG (193.2).

885. *Dam pa'i chos yongs su 'dzin pa'i mdo.* No text of that exact name is found in the Kangyur. This citation is found in the *Sūtra on Obtaining the Roots of Virtue* (*Kuśalamūlasaṃparigraha, dGe ba'i rtsa ba yongs su 'dzin pa'i mdo*). Toh. 101, H.K. 104. H.K. 104: vol. 50, 83a.4–83b.5. The H.K. recension reads ... *mkhas rnams dbu mas spyod par byed* ... ; the *Moonbeams* citation (*MB* VVI 291.13) reads ... *mkhas rnams dbu mar dpyod par byed* ... The *Moonbeams* citation is identical to one attributed to the *Sūtra on Holding the Genuine Dharma* found in Gampopa's *Sunrays of Scriptural Citations*, 12b–13a.

886. See D 4036: vol. 128, 134a.1. *MB* VVI (294.5): *zhig* should be *bzhi.* See *MB* DLG (197.6).

887. See H.K. 109: vol. 51, 41a.5–6 and p. 30.

888. D 4036: vol. 128, 134a.2–4. The Dg.T. recension reads ... *chos rnam par 'byed par byed pa dang* ... *spyad pa rnam par sbyong ba'i dmigs pa* ... ; the *Moonbeams* citation (295.6) reads ... *chos rnam par 'byed pa dang* ... *spyad pa rnam par sbyong ba'i dmigs pa* ... The *Moonbeams* citation is identical to the one in the *Great Treatise*, 770. The translation follows the Dg.T. recension in reading *spyad pa rnam par sbyong ba'i dmigs pa.*

889. H.K. 109: vol. 51, 43a.2–5.

890. *Commentary on Valid Cognition.* D 4210: vol. 174, 116a.3.

891. *Four Hundred Verses.* D 3846: vol. 97, 16a.5.

892. *Upadeśa-mañjari, Man snye / Man ngag snye ma* by Abhayākaragupta. Toh. 1198.

D 1198: vol. 7, 7b.3. *MB* VVI (299.8): *rnams kyis stong pa nyid* should be *rnams kyi stong pa nyid*. See *MB* DLG (201.3) and the Dg.T. recension.

893. *Uncommon Amṛta of Speech* (*Zhal gyi bdud rtsi thun mong ma yin pa*). Collected Works of Gampopa, text 19/dza, 18b.

894. *Esoteric Instructions: Illuminating Mahāmudrā* (*Phyag rgya chen po gsal byed kyi man ngag*). Collected Works of Gampopa, text 21/zha, folio 5b.

895. *Verses on the Four Yogas Requested by Geshe Nyang Gom* (*rNal 'byor bzhi'i tshigs bcad ma dge bshes nyang sgom gyis zhus pa*). Collected Works of Pakmo Drupa, vol. 4/nga, text 10.9.

896. *The Profound Inner Principles* (*Zab mo nang gi don*). Collected Works of Rangjung Dorje, vol. 7/ja, 311.1.

897. H.K. 416a: vol. 82, 439a.1–3.

898. D 1800: vol. 35, 38b.3. The Dg.T. recension reads . . . *bdag dang phung sogs rnam rig gi* . . . ; the *Moonbeams* citation (*MB* VVI 300.17) reads . . . *bdag dang phung po rnam rig gi* . . .

899. D 3902: vol. 109, 73a.2. *MB* VVI (301.4): *rig pas btags na* should be *rigs pas brtags na*. See *MB* DLG (202.4) and the Dg.T. recension.

900. Citation not found in a text by Āryadeva. It is found (unattributed) in Bodhibhadra's *Commentary on the "Compendium on the Heart of Wisdom"* (D 3852: vol. 97, 33b.3); Haribhadra's *Commentary on the "Ornament for Clear Realization"* (D 3793: vol. 86, 130a.6); and two other texts in the Tengyur.

901. D 3846: vol. 97, 9b.6.

902. D 3902: vol. 109, 72a.6.

903. H.K. 11: vol. 29, 4b.5.

904. H.K. 110: vol. 51, 299a.1–2.

905. *Upāli-paripṛcchā-sūtra, Nye bar 'khor gyis zhus pa'i mdo*. Toh. 68, H.K. 68. H.K. 68: vol. 39, 243b.7–244a.1.

906. D 4024: vol. 123, 57b.1.

907. *Jñānālokālaṃkāra, Ye shes snang ba rgyan*. Toh. 100, H.K. 103. H.K. 103: vol. 49, 513a.2–4. The H.K. recension reads . . . *byang chub ni/ sems kyi rang bzhin 'od gsal ba nyid kyis rang 'od gsal ba yin te/ ci'i phyir 'od gsal ba zhes bya zhe na/* . . . ; the *Moonbeams* citation (*MB* VVI 302.11–13) reads . . . *byang chub ni sems rang bzhin gyis 'od gsal ba nyid kyis rang gyis 'od gsal ba yin te/ ci'i phyir rang bzhin gyis 'od gsal ba zhes bya zhe na/* . . . The *Moonbeams* citation is almost identical to one found in Gampopa's *Sunrays of Scriptural Citations*, 10a. The only difference is that the *Moonbeams* citation (*MB* VVI 302.12) reads . . . *'od gsal ba nyid kyis rang bzhin* . . . whereas the citation in *Sunrays of Scriptural Citations* reads . . . *'od gsal ba nyid kyi rang bzhin* . . . The translation follows the latter.

908. H.K. 462: vol. 86, 179b.6–7. The H.K. recension (and *Moonbeams* p. 231) read . . . *yongs su dag pa yin te/ de ni/ nang na yang med/ phyi rol na yang med/ gnyis ga'i bar na yang mi dmigs so*; the *Moonbeams* citation (*MB* VVI 302.16–17) reads . . . *yongs su dag pa yin ste/ de ni nang dang phyi dang gnyis ka'i bar na'ang mi dmigs so*.

909. H.K. 462: vol. 86, 180a.7–180b.1. The H.K. recension reads . . . *sems kyi rang bzhin gang yin pa de ni byang chub kyi rang bzhin te/ gsang ba pa'i bdag po/ de ltar na/ sems dang . . . byang chub 'di ni . . .* ; the *Moonbeams* citation (*MB* VVI 302.19–20) reads . . . *sems kyi rang bzhin gang yin pa de ni byang chub kyi sems so/ de bas na sems dang . . . byang chub kyi sems ni . . .*

910. H.K. 416a: vol. 82, 439b.5.

911. D 2304: vol. 52, 244a.6–7.

912. D 2304: vol. 52, 244b.3.

913. *Dus 'khor 'grel chen.* This is Puṇḍarīka's *Stainless Light* (*Vimalaprabhā / Vimalaprabhā-nāma-mūlatantrānu-sāriṇī-dvādashasāhasrikā-laghu-kālacakra-tantrarāja-tīkā, Dri ma med pa'i 'od / bsDus pa'i rgyud kyi rgyal po dus kyi 'khor lo'i 'grel bshad rtsa ba'i rgyud kyi rjes su 'jug pa stong phrag bcu gnyis pa dri ma med pa'i 'od ces bya ba*). Toh. 845 and Toh. 1347. D 1347: vol. 11, 272a.7–272b.2.

914. H.K. 369: vol. 79, 8a.4. The H.K. recension reads *thams cad ye shes kung rig mchog/ rnam par shes pa'i chos nyid 'das*; the *Moonbeams* citation (*MB* VVI 304.11–12) reads *kun shes kun rig dam pa'o/ rnam par shes pa'i chos nyid 'das*. The exact form of the *Moonbeams* citation is found in six commentaries on this text contained in the Tengyur.

915. H.K. 369: vol. 79, 11a.6.

916. *Background Teachings on the Ten Instructions That Resemble a Mighty King* (*dBang gi rgyal po lta bu'i gdams pa bcu chos kyi rgyab chos*). Collected Works of Jikten Sumgön, vol. 8, 363.2–3. Jikten Sumgön attributes these lines to the *Garland of Amṛta* (*bDud rtsi 'phreng ba*), a text not found in the Kangyur or Tengyur.

917. H.K. 109: vol. 51, 10a.1–2. The H.K. recension reads *so so rang rig mtshan nyid spyod yul te*; the *Moonbeams* citation (*MB* VVI 304.19) reads *so so rang rig mtshan med spyod yul te*.

918. *Cakrasaṃvara-guhyācinta, gSang ba bsam gyis mi khyab pa'i rgyud / dPal 'khor lo sdom pa'i gsang ba bsam gyis mi khyab pa'i rgyud*. Toh. 385. Dg.K. 196a.6.

919. D 2304: vol. 52, 245a.3.

920. D 2304: vol. 52, 245a.6. The Dg.T. recension reads . . . *zhing khams rnam par dag pa dang/ dkyil 'khor rnam 'phrul la sogs pa/ ngo mtshar dngos gzhi de nyid de/ . . .* ; the *Moonbeams* citation (*MB* VVI 306.4–6) reads . . . *zhing khams dag par snang ba dang/ dkyil 'khor rnam 'phrul sna tshogs pa/ ngo mtshar che ba'i rnam 'phrul dag/ . . .*

921. *Dohā for the People*. D 2224: vol. 51, 72b.5. *MB* VVI (306.10): *gang las* should be *gang la*. See Dg.T. and *MB* DLG (206.1).

922. H.K. 396: vol. 81, 374b.7–375a.2.

923. *MB* VVI (307.2): *blo brdeg* should be *glo brdeg*. See *MB* DLG (206.3).

924. D 4024: vol. 123, 58b.7–59a.1. The Dg.T. recension reads . . . *sa nang rin chen gzugs . . .* ; the *Moonbeams* citation (*MB* VVI 307.10) reads . . . *sa la ser gyi gzugs . . .*

925. H.K. 378b: vol. 79, 366b.4.

926. *Praises of the Dharmadhātu*. D 1118: vol. 1, 64a.3–4.

927. Citation not found in the Kangyur. It is found (attributed to the *Descent into*

Laṅkā) in Lho Layakpa Jangchub Ngödrup's *Ornament That Clarifies the Heart: A Commentary on the "Text Known as the Four Dharmas of Dakpo"* (*Dvags po'i chos bzhir grags pa'i gzhung gi 'grel pa snying po gsal ba'i rgyan*), Rigpe Dorje Institute Series, bLo gros mtha' yas pa'i mdzod, vol. 3, 235.

928. H.K. 378b: vol. 79, 359b.2–3.

929. *Yum la bstod pa.* Although *Praises to the Mother* may be referring to *Praises of Prajñāpāramitā* (*Prajñāpāramitāstotra, Shes rab kyi pha rol tu phyin ma'i bstod pa*) by Nāgārjuna (or Rāhulabhadra) (Toh. 1127), this famous line is not, however, found in that text. It is found in Ānandagarbha's *Ritual for the Maṇḍala of Prajñāpāramitā* (D 2644: vol. 68 254b.4–254b.5), where it ends with "I take refuge in" rather than "I pay homage to"; and Ratnakīrti's *Praises to the Deities of the Four Yogas* (*Yogacaturdevastotra, sByor ba bzhi'i lha la bstod pa*). Toh. 1170. D 1170: vol. 1, 247b.5.

930. Citation not found in the Tengyur. It is found (attributed to Tilopa) in Gampopa's *Esoteric Instructions on the Twofold Abiding State and Esoteric Instructions on Twofold Armor* (2a); *Pointing Out the Root of Mahāmudrā* (7a); and Wangchuk Gyaltsen's *Great Bliss of Stainless Eloquence: A Biography of Nāropa* (58a.1–2).

931. H.K. 378a: vol. 79, 347b.4.

932. H.K. 378a: vol. 79, 352b.2

933. *Sahajasiddhi, Lhan cig skyes pa grub pa.* Toh. 2223. D 2223: vol. 51, 68b.6.

934. *Sahajasiddhipaddhati, Lhan cig skyes grub kyi gzhung 'grel* by Lakṣmī. Toh. 2261. D 2261: vol. 52, 15a.7–15b.1. *Moonbeam*'s title reference includes the name of the root text's author: *Indra bodhi'i lhan cig skyes grub kyi gzhung 'grel.*

935. *Commentary on Bodhicitta.* D 1800: vol. 35, 40b.2–3.

936. *Commentary on Bodhicitta.* D 1800: vol. 35, 41a.1.

937. *Abundant Virtue: A Collection of Dharma Lectures*, 12a–12b.

938. Texts by Gomchung not found. This statement is found in Gampopa's *Core of Mahāmudrā: The Instructions on the Ultimate Essence*, 2b. The Collected Works text reads *rang sems lhan cig skyes pa* . . . ; the *Moonbeams* citation (*MB* VVI 312.13) reads *sems nyid lhan cig skyes pa* . . .

939. *Dohā for the King.* D 2263: vol. 52, 27a.2.

940. *Treasury of Dohā: Instructions on Mahāmudrā.* D 2273: vol. 52, 122b.3–4.

941. *Treasury of Dohā.* D 2280: vol. 52, 134a.5–6.

942. *Connate Union* (*Lhan cig skyes sbyor*). Collected Works of Pakmo Drupa, vol. 4/ nga, text 10.1.

943. *MB* VVI (315.2): *bslang* should be *bslad.* See *MB* DLG (211.5).

944. D 4020: vol. 123, 31a.2–3.

945. H.K. 109: vol. 51, 42b.4–5.

946. *Tathāgatajñānamudrāsamādhisūtra, Ye shes phyag rgya'i mdo.* Toh. 131, H.K. 133. Citation not found in the Kangyur. It is found (attributed to the *Sūtra on the Wisdom Mudrā*) in Gampopa's *Sunrays of Scriptural Citations*, 18b.

947. H.K. 109: vol. 51, 42b.3–4. The H.K. recension reads . . . *ji tsam gyis na/ gcig tu lhag mthong sgom pa lags/ gang gi tshe rgyun chags su yid la byed pas sems kyi mtshan*

nyid la byed pa'o; the *Moonbeams* citation (*MB* VVI 316.17–18) reads . . . *ji tsam gyis na sgom pa lags/ gang gis rgyun chags su yid la byed pas sems kyi mtshan nyid la yid byed pa'o.*

948. H.K. 129: vol. 55, 20b.5. The H.K. recension reads . . . *gzhon nu/ ting nge 'dzin/ ting nge 'dzin ces bya ba ni 'di ste/ sems nges par rtogs pa dang/ skye ba med pa dang/* . . . ; the *Moonbeams* citation (*MB* VVI 31.19–20) reads . . . *gzhon nu ting nge 'dzin zhes bya ba ni 'di ste/ sems nges par rtogs pa skye ba med pa pa'o* . . . This is identical to the citation in Gampopa's *Sunrays of Scriptural Citations*, 18b.
949. H.K. 129: vol. 55, 73a.1–2. The H.K. recension reads . . . *bzung du med cing bstan du med* . . . ; the *Moonbeams* citation (*MB* VVI 317.1) reads . . . *bzung du med cing brjod du med* . . . This is identical to the citation in Gampopa's *Sunrays of Scriptural Citations*, 18b.
950. Text and citation not found in the Kangyur or Tengyur. The citation is found (attributed to the *Spacelike Samādhi Sūtra*) in Gampopa's *Sunrays of Scriptural Citations*, 18b.
951. H.K. 94: vol. 44, 121b.3–4. The H.K. recension reads *rgyal ba'i spyod yul 'di la 'jug par gyis su 'dod pa/ des ni nam mkha' 'dra bar bsam pa yongs su sbyongs* . . . ; the *Moonbeams* citation (*MB* VVI 317.8–9) reads *rgyal ba'i spyod yul 'di la gang zhig 'jug 'dod pas/ de ni bsam pa nam mkha' lta bu rnam par sbyongs* . . . The *Moonbeams* citation is identical to the citation in Gampopa's *Sunrays of Scriptural Citations*, 19a.
952. *Lalitavistara, rGya cher rol pa.* Toh. 95; H.K 96. H.K. 96: vol. 48, 305b.7–306a.1. The H.K. recension reads . . . *zab zhi rdul bral* . . . *bdud rtsi'i chos ni bdag gis thos par gyur*; the *Moonbeams* citation (*MB* VVI 317.14) reads . . . *zab zhi spros bral* . . . *bdud rtsi lta bu'i chos shig kho bos rnyed.* The *Moonbeams* citation is identical to citations simply attributed to "the sūtras" in Gampopa's *The Grand Collection of Dharma Lectures*, 29b and 34a.
953. H.K. 396: vol. 81, 481a.3–4. The H.K. recension reads . . . *lam rig rnam par rtog mi bya/ rnam rtog gti mug* . . . ; the *Moonbeams* citation (*MB* VVI 317.17) reads . . . *rnam rig rnam par rtog mi bya/ rnam rtog ma rig* . . . The *Moonbeams* citation is identical to the citation in Gampopa's *Sunrays of Scriptural Citations*, 8b.
954. H.K. 389: vol. 81, 69b.1–3. The H.K. recension reads . . . *mkha' mtshungs nam mkha'* . . . ; the *Moonbeams* citation (*MB* VVI 318.8) reads . . . *mkha' gzugs nam mkha'* . . .
955. D 2304: vol. 52, 245a.3–5.
956. D 2304: vol. 52, 244b.5–7.
957. D 2304: vol. 52, 245a.1 and 244b.3–4. The Dg.T. recension reads . . . *rang rig min phyir* . . . ; the *Moonbeams* citation (*MB* VVI 319.5) . . . *rang rig yin phyir* . . .
958. D 2304: vol. 52, 244b.3 and 245a.1–2.
959. *Phyag rgya chen po rab tu mi gnas pa'i rgyud.* Citation and text not found in the Kangyur. The citation (attributed to the *Tantra of Nonabiding Suchness, Rab tu mi gnas pa de kho na nyid kyi rgyud*) is found in Jikten Sumgön's *Ornament for the Illumination of Wisdom That Dispels the Darkness of Ignorance: Pointing Out*

Connate Union (*Phyag rgya chen po lhan gcig skyes sbyor gyi ngo sprod ma rig mun sel ye shes snang ba'i rgyan*). Collected Works of Jikten Sumgön, vol. 9, 481.3–5.

960. *MB* VVI (320.6): *rang kham* should be *rang kha ma. See MB* DLG (214.7–215.1).
961. H.K. 176: vol. 60, 247a.6.
962. H.K. 153: vol. 58, 45a.2–3.
963. H.K. 153: vol. 58, 137a.3–4. The H.K. recension reads . . . *rtogs pa ni/ byang chub bo/ bcom ldan 'das/ de lta bas na/ byang chub sems dpas byang chub la ring ba'i 'du shes mi bgyi'o*; the *Moonbeams* citation (*MB* VVI 321.9–10) reads . . . *rtogs pas byang chub ste/ de bas na byang chub sems dpa' byang chub la ring ba'i 'du shes mi bya'o.*
964. *Sarvadharmāpravṛttinirdeśa*, *Chos thams cad 'byung ba med par bstan pa.* Toh. 180, H.K. 181. H.K. 181: vol. 60, 463a.4–5.
965. H.K. 181: vol. 60, 463a.6. The H.K. recension reads . . . *'dod chags gnyis ni gnyis su med*; the *Moonbeams* citation (*MB* VVI 321.14) reads . . . *'dod chags gnyis su med.*
966. Citation not found in the Heap of Jewels. It is found in the *Sūtra That Gathers All Intentions* (*Sarvatathāgata-citta-jñāna-guhyārtha-garbha-vyūha-vajra-tantra-siddhi-yogāgama-samāja-sarvavidyāsūtra-mahāyānābhisamaya-dharmaparyāya-vivyūha, mDo dgongs pa 'dus pa / De bzhin gshegs pa thams cad kyi thugs gsang ba'i ye shes don gyi snying po rdo rje bkod pa'i rgyud rnal 'byor grub pa'i lung kun 'dus rig pa'i mdo theg pa chen po mngon par rtogs pa chos kyi rnam grangs rnam par bkod pa zhes bya ba'i mdo*). Toh. 829, H.K. 793. H.K. 793: vol. 97, 412a.3–4. The H.K. recension reads . . . *skye ba nyid na skye ba med*; the *Moonbeams* citation (*MB* VVI 321.16) . . . *skye tsam nyid na skye ba med.*
967. H.K. 378a: vol. 79, 352b.1–2.
968. H.K. 378b: vol. 79, 364.1.
969. H.K. 378b: vol. 79, 364b.2.
970. H.K. 378a: vol. 79, 348a.4–6.
971. *Dohā for the Queen.* D 2264: vol. 52, 32a.2–3. The Dg.T. recension reads . . . *rig par byed pa'i skyes bu mchog* . . . ; the *Moonbeams* citation (*MB* VVI 322.10) reads . . . *rig par byed pa'i ye shes mchog* . . .
972. *Fundamental Treatise on the Middle Way.* D 3824: vol. 96, 17a.1–2.
973. *Nirvikalpaprakaraṇa*, *rNam par mi rtog pa'i rab tu byed pa.* Toh. 2279. D 2279: vol. 52, 133a.6–7.
974. *Treasury of Dohā.* D 2280: vol. 52, 134b.5.
975. *Treasury of Dohā* (*Dohakoṣa*, *Do ha mdzod*). Toh. 2281. D 2281: vol. 52, 136a.5. The Dg.T. recension reads *phung po khams dang skye mched dbang po rnams/ lhan cig skye pa'i rang bzhin las/ ma lus de las byung zhing de ru thim*; the *Moonbeams* citation (*MB* VVI 323.5–6) reads *phung po khams dang skye mched rnams/ phyag rgya chen po'i rang bzhin las/ ma lus der byung de ru thim.* The *Moonbeams* citation is identical to the one in the Eight Dohā Treasures, 23.5.
976. Nāropa's *Summary Verses on Mahāmudrā*, 47.7. Maitrīpa's *Summary Verses on Mahāmudrā*, 46.3.
977. Nāropa's *Summary Verses on Mahāmudrā*, 48.2. Maitrīpa's *Summary Verses on Mahāmudrā*, 46.6.

978. Source not found.

979. *Seeing Is Meaningful: The Biography of the Translator Marpa Lotsāwa* (*sGra sgyur mar pa lo tsA'i rnam thar mthong ba don ldan*). Collected Works of Marpa Lotsāwa, vol. 1, 197.

980. *Biography and Songs of the Great Lord of Yogins, Milarepa* (*rNal 'byor gyi dbang phyug chen po mi la ras pa'i rnam mgur*) by Tsang Nyön Heruka. mTsho sngon mi rigs dpe skrun khang, 465.

981. *The Flag of Renown: The Biography of Gampopa*, 118. The Collected Works text reads . . . *btsir gyis bzung*; the *Moonbeams* citation (*MB* VVI 324.4) reads . . . *tsir gyis bzung.* The Collected Works seems to be accurate because this phrase is repeated in a series of parallel verses.

982. *MB* VVI (325.12): *rig pas* should be *rigs pa.* See *MB* DLG (218.4).

983. *MB* VVI (326.13): *sgom* should be *sgo ma.* See *MB* DLG (219.2).

984. Source unidentified.

985. Citation not found in a text by Nāgārjuna. It is found (unattributed) in Haribhadra's *Illumination of the "Ornament for Clear Realization,"* (D 3791: vol. 85, 314b.1–314b.2); his *Commentary on the "Ornament for Clear Realization"* (D 3793: vol. 86, 130a.6–7); and Bodhibhadra's *Commentary on the "Compendium on the Heart of Wisdom"* (D 3852: vol. 97, 33b.3–4). On p. 241 the same citation is attributed to Āryadeva.

986. *Prajñāpāramitāhṛdaya, Shes rab snying po.* Toh. 21, H.K. 26. H.K. 26: vol. 34, 259b.7–260a.1.

987. Source not found.

988. H.K. 129: vol. 55, 134a.5.

989. H.K. 129: vol. 55, 134a.6–7.

990. H.K. 129: vol. 55, 134b.2.

991. *Garland of Renown: A Commentary on the Mahāyāna Sūtra "King of Samādhi"* (*Sarvadharmasvabhāvasamatāvipañcitasamādhirāja-nāma-mahāyānasūtraṭīkākīrtimālā, Chos thams cad kyi rang bzhin mnyam pa nyid rnam par spros pa'i ting nge 'dzin kyi rgyal po zhes bya ba theg pa chen po'i mdo'i 'grel pa grags pa'i phreng ba*). Toh 4010. D 4010: vol. 117, 80b.3–4.

992. D 4010: vol. 117, 80b.7.

993. H.K. 129: vol. 55, 133b.3–4.

994. H.K. 378a: vol. 79, 348a.4–6.

995. H.K. 379: vol. 79, 418a.3. See note 188 for textual differences.

996. H.K. 396: vol. 81, 374b.1–3. The H.K. recension reads . . . *sna tshogs ro ni za ba dang/ . . . rnal 'byor pa'i/. . . skye bar 'gyur/ 'di ni gnyis su med par brjod/ 'di ni byang chub* . . . ; the *Moonbeams* citation (*MB* VVI 328.16–18) reads . . . *sna tshogs ro ni myang dang/ . . . rnal 'byor pas/. . . skye bar 'gyur/ 'di ni byang chub* . . . *MB* VVI (328.16): *sna tshogs de* should be *sna tshogs ro.* See *MB* DLG (220.6).

997. *Lhan cig skyes pa bsam gyis mi khyab pa'i rgyud.* Citation and text not found in the Kangyur. It is found in Jikten Sumgön's *Ornament for the Illumination of Wisdom*, 489.6–490.1. The *Ornament for the Illumination of Wisdom* citation reads . . . *'di*

ni snang sems dbyer med lhan ci skyes; the *Moonbeams* citation (329.4) reads . . . *de phyir snang sems dbyer med lhan ci skyes.*

998. *Dohā for the Queen.* D 2264: vol. 52, 29a.7–29b.1. The Dg.T. recension reads . . . *ro gcig* . . . ; the *Moonbeams* citation (329.7) reads . . . *ro nyid* . . . The translation follows the Dg.T. recension. *MB* VVI (329.9) *yin pas* should be *yin par*. See *MB* DLG (221.2).

999. *Treasury of Dohā: Instructions on Mahāmudrā.* D 2273: vol. 52, 123.3–4. The Dg.T. recension reads . . . *mtha' bral dbus mar* . . . ; the *Moonbeams* citation (*MB* VVI 329.14) reads . . . *mtha' bral dbus med* . . .

1000. *Treasury of Dohā.* D 2280: vol. 52, 134b.1.

1001. *Treasury of Dohā.* D 2281: vol. 52, 136a.5. The Dg.T. recension reads *phung po khams dang skye mched dbang po rnams/ lhan cig skye pa'i rang bzhin las/ ma lus de las byung zhing de ru thim*; the Moonbeams citation (MB VVI 323.5–6) reads *phung po khams dang skye mched rnams/ phyag rgya chen po'i rang bzhin las/ ma lus der byung de ru thim.* The *Moonbeams* citation is identical to the one in the Eight Dohā Treasures, 23.5.

1002. *Summary of the View.* D 2304: vol. 52, 244a.6–7.

1003. Nāropa's *Summary Verses on Mahāmudrā*, 48.2. Maitrīpa's *Summary Verses on Mahāmudrā*, 46.6. Both the DNZ and TsRP recensions read . . . *chos kyi dbyings*; the *Moonbeams* citation (*MB* VVI 330.7) reads . . . *chos kyi sku.*

1004. Nāropa's *Summary Verses on Mahāmudrā*, 47.4–5. Maitrīpa's *Summary Verses on Mahāmudrā*, 45.5–6. The DNZ (Nāropa) recension and *Moonbeams* citation (*MB* VVI 330.8) read . . . *mthong rtogs na* . . . ; the TsRP (Maitrīpa) recension reads . . . *mngon rtogs na* . . .

1005. Citation not found in a text attributed to Maitrīpa. It is found in Saraha's *Dohā Song on View, Meditation, Conduct, and Fruition.* D 2345: vol. 53, 3b.7. The Dg.T. recension reads . . . *tug phrad tsam gyis* . . . ; the *Moonbeams* citation (*MB* VVI 330.12) reads . . . *thug phrad tsam gyi* . . . *MB* VVI (330.12): *gyi* should be *gyis*. See *MB* VVI (390.13 and 436.3); and the Dg.T. recension.

1006. *Seeing Is Meaningful: The Biography of the Translator Marpa Lotsāwa*, 197.

1007. *Biography and Songs of the Great Lord of Yogins, Milarepa*, 465.

1008. *The Flag of Renown: The Biography of Gampopa*, 118.

1009. *Commentary on Bodhicitta.* D 1800: vol. 35, 41a.3. For textual differences, see note 465.

1010. H.K. 129: vol. 55, 44a.7–44b.1.

1011. *MB* VVI (333.7): *stongs po* should be *stengs po.* See *MB* DLG (223.3) and *MB* TsRP (451.5).

1012. D 4158: vol. 172, 115b.3.

1013. D 3871: vol. 105, 32b.4–5.

1014. *Core of Mahāmudrā: The Instructions on the Ultimate Essence*, 8a. The Collected Works edition reads . . . *chos kyi gnas lugs ma gos ba yin*; the *Moonbeams* citation (*MB* VVI 335.3) reads . . . *chos kyi gnad ma gos ba yin.*

1015. *Uncommon Amṛta of Speech*, 7b.

1016. In Gampopa's Collected Works, see *Abundant Auspiciousness: A Collection of Dharma Lectures* (7b); *Core of Mahāmudrā: The Instructions on the Ultimate Essence* (10a); *Compendium on the Meditation Topics of Sūtra and Mantra* (*mDo sngags kyi sgom don bsdus pa*) (text 28/sa, 10a); and *Presentation of the Three Trainings* (*bsLab gsum rnam gzhag*) (text 30/A, 10b). *MB* VVI (335.12): *snang lam nges pa* should be *snang la ma nges pa.* See *MB* DLG (225.1).

1017. *Fundamental Treatise on the Middle Way.* D 3824: vol. 96, 8a.6–7.

1018. *Fundamental Treatise on the Middle Way.* D 3824: vol. 96, 15a.2.

1019. *Precious Garland.* D 4158: vol. 172, 109a.2–3. The Dg.T. recension reads *med pa pa ni ngan 'gror 'gro*; the *Moonbeams* citation (*MB* VVI 336.5) reads *med pa po ni ngan 'gror 'gro.*

1020. *Analysis of the Three Vows*, 59.11–14.

1021. *Analysis of the Three Vows*, 59.21–60.1.

1022. *MB* VVI (337.1): *smra med* should be *smra mod.* See *MB* DLG (226.1).

1023. H.K. 378b: vol. 79, 355a.4–6.

1024. D 3917: vol. 110, 62b.5–6.

1025. *Analysis of the Three Vows*, 61.14–18. The bracketed word is from Sakya Paṇḍita's own annotations (*rang mchan*).

1026. *De kho na nyid rab tu mi gnas pa'i rgyud.* Citation and text not found in the Kangyur. The citation is found (attributed to the *Tantra of Nonabiding Suchness*) in Gampopa's *Sunrays of Scriptural Citations*, 6b–7a.

1027. *Treasury of Dohā: Instructions on Mahāmudrā.* D 2273: vol. 52, 123a.7–123b.1. The Dg.T. recension reads . . . *ma bzung ma btang rang dga' nyid du zhog*; the *Moonbeams* citation (*MB* VVI 341.18) reads . . . *ma bzung ma btang rang ga nyid du zhog.*

1028. In the *Heart of the Realization of the Eighty-Four Siddhas* (*Caturaśītisiddhasambodhihṛdaya, Grub thob brgyad cu rtsa bzhi'i rtogs pa'i snying po*) by *Vīraprabhāsvara/Vīraprakāśa (Toh. 2292; D 2292: vol. 52, 156a.4–5); and in *Rosary of Golden Bindus: The Esoteric Instructions of Experiences Expressed in Vajra Songs by Forty Yogin-Siddhas During Gaṇacakra in Glorious Oḍḍiyāna* (*dPal u rgyan du tshogs 'khor byas pa'i dus su rnal 'byor pa grub pa thob pa bzhi bcus rdo rje'i mgur bzhengs pa nyams kyi man ngag thig le gser gyi phreng ba*) by forty mahāsiddhas (Toh. 2449; D 2449: vol. 53, 83a.3–4).

The Dg.T. 2292 recension reads . . . *btags pa* . . . *bsgom dang bsgom med gnyug ma'i ngang* . . . The Dg.T. 2449 recension reads . . . *bde chen rgyun mi chad/* . . . *don med gyeng ba'i rgyu/ sgom du med pas* . . . The *Moonbeams* citation (342.3–4) recension reads . . . *bde ba rgyun mi chad/ brtags pa* . . . *bsgom du med pa gnyug ma'i ngang*. . .

The *Moonbeams* citation is almost identical to one (attributed to Kuddāla/Tog rtse ba) found in Gampopa's *Pointing Out the Ultimacy of Thoughts* (*rNam rtog don dam gyi ngo sprod*). Collected Works of Gampopa, text 26/la, 11a. The Collected works citation reads . . . *byas pa thams cad don med* . . . ; the *Moonbeams* citation reads . . . *brtags pa thams cad don med* . . .

1029. Source not found.

1030. *Revealing the Hidden Characteristics of Mind* (*Sems kyi mtshan nyid gab pa mngon du phyung ba*). Collected Works of Gampopa, text 14/pha, 4a.
1031. *Tshogs chos chen po*, 13b.
1032. See *Tshogs chos chen po*, 13b–15a.
1033. *Treasury of the Ultimate Essence: The Stages of the Four Yogas of Mahāmudrā* (*Phyag rgya chen po rnal 'byor bzhi'i rim pa snying po don gyi gter mdzod*). TsRP, vol. 4, 133.1–2.
1034. *Pointing Out the Root of Mahāmudrā*, 6b.
1035. *Esoteric Instructions on the Twofold Abiding State and Esoteric Instructions on Twofold Armor*, 18a–18b.
1036. *Treasury of the Ultimate Essence*, 132.6–133.1. The phrase "being just as you are" (*ang so re ba*) is a colloquial-sounding expression that might also be translated as "completely fresh." Thanks to Ringu Tulku Rinpoche and Gerardo Abboud and Choegyal Rinpoche for help understanding this.
1037. *Treasury of the Ultimate Essence*, 133.6–134.1.
1038. *Revealing the Hidden Characteristics of Mind*, 2b.
1039. Source not found.
1040. Source not found.
1041. *The Flag of Renown: The Biography of Gampopa*, 110.
1042. D 401: vol. 79, 34a.2–3. The Dg.K. recension reads *rang rig stong pa 'od gsal la/ bsgom pas nyes pa ma yin te/ ma bsgom pas kyang nyes pa min/ . . . med pa 'di*; the *Moonbeams* citation (*MB* VVI 347.6–9) reads *rang bzhin stong pa 'od gsal la/ bsgom pas rnyed pa ma yin te/ ma bsgom pas kyang rnyed pa min/. . med pa pa'o.*
1043. Citation not found in the Tengyur. It is found (attributed to Ritrö Wangchuk) in Gampopa's *Ornament of Precious Liberation*, 105a.
1044. *sGom don grub pa.* Citation and text not found in the Kangyur. The citation is found (attributed to the *Accomplishment of the Purpose of Meditation*) in Gampopa's *Sunrays of Scriptural Citations*, 18a.
1045. *Pointing Out the Root of Mahāmudrā*, 5a.
1046. Source not found.
1047. *Pointing Out the Root of Mahāmudrā*, 4a.
1048. *Dohā for the Queen.* D 2264: vol. 52, 30a.1–2. The Dg.T. recension reads . . . *'khor ba'i bde ba dag la reg pa nyid kyis ching*; the *Moonbeams* citation (*MB* VVI 351.12) reads . . . *'khor ba'i bde ba dag la reg pa nyid kyis ching.*
1049. Source not found.
1050. *Dohā for the Queen.* D 2264: vol. 52, 30a.2–3.
1051. *Ganges Mahāmudrā.* D 2303: vol. 52, 243a.2–3.
1052. *Lamp That Summarizes Conduct.* D 3960: vol. 111, 313a.5. The Dg.T. recension reads *spyir na mnyam gzhag* . . . ; the *Moonbeams* citation (*MB* VVI 352.10) reads *gcig tu mnyam gzhag* . . . The *Moonbeams* citation is identical to one found in Gampopa's *Sunrays of Scriptural Citations*, 23a.
1053. *Biography and Songs of the Great Lord of Yogins, Milarepa*, 656.
1054. *Biography and Songs of the Great Lord of Yogins, Milarepa*, 657.

1055. *Synopsis of the Pāramitās.* D 3944: vol. 111, 229a.4. The Dg.T. recension reads... *zhing ngal bso na/ gtsubs pas me phyin me 'gyur te* ... ; the *Moonbeams* citation (*MB* VVI 353.2–3) reads... *shing ngal gsos na/ gtsubs pas me phyin mi 'gyur te*...

1056. Toh. 3786. D 3786: vol. 80, 8b.7–9a.1. The Dg.T. recension reads *nges 'byed yan lag dang mthong ba'i/ lam dang sgom pa'i lam nyid la/... 'jal dang nges rtog sgom pa'i lam*; the *Moonbeams* citation (*MB* VVI 353.9) reads *nges 'byed yan lag dang mthong ba yi/ lam dang goms pa'i lam dag la/... mjal dang nges rtog sgom pa'i lam.* The translation follows the Dg.T. recension.

1057. Source unidentified.

1058. D 3871: vol. 105, 11a.3–4. The Dg.T. recension reads... *thams cad 'bad pas srungs shig ces/ bdag ni de ltar thal mo sbyor*; the *Moonbeams* citation (*MB* VVI 353.17–18) reads... *srog la bab kyang srungs shig ces/ bdag ni de skad 'doms par byed.*

1059. H.K. 91: vol. 40, 395b.5–7. The H.K. recension reads *yang dag pa'i dran pa gang gis nyon mongs pa thams cad kyi skabs mi 'byed pa dang/ dran pa gang gis bdud kyi las thams cad kyi skabs mi 'byed pa dang/ dran pa gang gis lam gol ba dang/ lam ngan par mi ltung ba dang/ dran pa bsgom pa lta bur gyur pa gang gis sems dang sems las byung ba'i chos mi dge ba thams cad kyi skabs mi 'byed pa ste/* .... The *Moonbeams* citation (*MB* VVI 354.2–6) reads *de la dran pa gang gis nyon mongs pa thams cad 'byung bar mi 'gyur ba dang/ dran pa gang gis bdud kyi las thams cad kyi skabs mi 'byed pa dang/ dran pa gang gis lam ngan pa dang lam gol bar mi 'gro ba dang/ dran pa sgo lta bur dag gis sems dang sems las byung ba'i mi dge ba thams cad kyi skabs mi 'byed pa ste/*...

1060. Citation not found in the *Compendium of Dharma Sūtra.* It is found in the *Sūtra of the Teaching of Akṣayamati.* See H.K. 176: vol. 60, 254a.2–4.

1061. Citation not found in the *Sūtra of the Questions of Akṣayamati* (*Akṣayamatiparipṛcchāsūtra, bLo gros mi zad pas zhus pa'i mdo*). Toh. 89, H.K. 89. It is found in the *Sūtra of the Teaching of Akṣayamati.* See H.K. 176: vol. 60, 256b.7–257a.2.

1062. H.K. 239: vol. 65, 70a.5–70b.2. The H.K. recension reads... *mi bskyod pa drang pa... gting dang 'gram mi rtogs pa*... ; the *Moonbeams* citation (*MB* VVI 355.6) reads... *mi bskyod pa dran pa... gting dang mtha' mi rtogs pa*...

1063. D 3846: vol. 97, 13a.4. The Dg.T. recension reads... *slar yang sems skye min des na/... don la log pa kho na byung*; the *Moonbeams* citation (*MB* VVI 355.10–11) reads ... *slar yang sems kyis min nges na/ ... don la rtog pa kho na byung.* The translation follows the Dg.T. recension.

1064. *Commentary on Valid Cognition.* D 4210: vol. 174, 137b.2. The Dg.T. recension reads... *dngos po rnams ni*... ; the *Moonbeams* citation (355.13–14) reads... *dbang po rnams ni*... The translation follows the Dg.T. recension.

1065. D 4049: vol. 134, 48b.3.

1066. D 3871: vol. 105, 11b.2. *MB* VVI (356.3): *bsdud pa'i don* should be *bsrung pa'i don.* See *MB* VVI (45.11) and (232.20).

1067. D 3871: vol. 105, 14b.1–2.

1068. D 3871: vol. 105, 11a.4–6.

1069. H.K. 47: vol. 35, 272a.6–7.

1070. H.K. 47: vol. 35, 272b.2. The H.K. recension reads *tshul bzhin ma yin pa yid la byed pa rgyu ba . . . thams cad kyi rgyu ba med . . .* ; the *Moonbeams* citation (*MB* VVI 357.5–6) reads *tshul bzhin ma yin pa'i rnam par rtog pa rgyu ba . . . thams cad kyi rnam par rtog pa rgyu ba med . . .*

1071. Citation not found in the Kangyur. It is found (attributed to the *Moon Lamp Sūtra*) in Śāntideva's *Compendium of Training*. D 3940: vol. 111, 191b.3–4.

1072. D 4182: vol. 173, 41a.5–7.

1073. D 4182: vol. 173, 43a.5–6. the Dg.T. recension reads . . . *lus rtog* . . . ; the *Moonbeams* citation (*MB* VVI 10) reads . . . *lus gtogs* . . . The translation follows the Dg.T. recension.

1074. *Replies to the Exalted Gomtsul's Questions*, 8a.

1075. *Precious Sash* (*Rin po che'i ska rags*). Collected Works of Pakmo Drupa, vol. 3/ga, text 6. The Collected Works edition reads *dran pa'i mi tshe 'di ma byas na/ . . . ye shes gyi ling 'di 'chor dogs yod*; the *Moonbeams* citation (*MB* VVI 359.1–3) reads *dran pa'i mal tshe 'di ma byas na/ . . . ye shes kyi nor bu shor dogs yod.* The translation follows the Collected Works edition.

1076. Exact citation not found in the Collected Works of Jikten Sumgön. Lines similar to the first two lines of the *Moonbeams* citation are found in his *Blazing Victory Banner: The Precious Stages of the Path of the Victors' Children* (*rGyal sras rnams kyi lam rim rin po che 'bar ba'i rgyal mtshan*) (vol. 1, 231.4). They read *dus gsum rgyal ba'i gzhung lam de rgyun chad med pa'i dran pas gzung . . . dran pa rgyun chad med pa yin.*

Lines similar to the second two lines of the *Moonbeams* citation are found in his *Genuine Dedication That Is the Victory Banner for the Avataṃsaka* (*'Phags pa sangs rgyas phal po che rdo rje rgyal mtshan gyi bsngo ba dam pa*) (vol. 4, 235.1). They read *dran pa rgyun chad ma shes na/ lus ngag tab tab kha na med.* The *Moonbeams* citation (*MB* VVI 359.5–8) reads *dus gsum sangs rgyas kyi gzhung lam de/ dus rgyun chad med pa'i dran pa yin/ dran pa yengs med ma shes na/ lus ngag tab tab kyi kha na med.*

The exact citation is found in other works within the Drikung Kagyu tradition, such as the first Drikung Chungtsang Rigzin Chödrak's *Illumination of the Sun: Elucidating the Explanation of the Single Intent of the Genuine Dharma* (*Dam pa'i chos dgongs pa gcig pa'i rnam bshad lung don gsal byed legs bshad nyi ma'i snang ba*). See BDRC W22082:003:0001 (work:volume:text).

1077. *MB* VI (359.16): *dran pa'i* should be *dran pa'am.* See *MB* DLG (241.2).

1078. H.K. 153: vol. 58, 33b.2. *MB* VVI (360.19): *sngon* should be *ston.* See *MB* DLG (242.1).

1079. *Buddhasaṅgītisūtra*, *'Phags pa sangs rgyas bgro ba.* Toh. 228, H.K. 229. H.K. 229: vol. 63, 335b.2–3. The H.K. recension reads *de la 'jam dpal gzhon nur gyur pa'i dran pa nyer bar gzhag pa ni/ 'di yin te/ 'di lta ste/ . . .* ; the *Moonbeams* citation (*MB* VVI 360.20) reads *gsol pa/ 'jam dpal/ dran pa nye bar bzhag pa la gnas pa ji lta bu lags/ smra ba/ . . .*

Note that although *MB* cites the text as *'Phags pa sangs rgyas 'gro ba*, there is no text with that title in the Kangyur.

1080. H.K. 229: vol. 63, 335b.5. The H.K. recension reads *dran pa med cing yid la byed pa med pa ni/ 'jam dpal gyi dran pa nyer bar 'jog pa yin no*; the *Moonbeams* citation (*MB* VVI 361.2) reads *dran med yid la byed med pa'i/ sangs rgyas rjes su dran pa sgom.*

1081. *Avikalpapraveśadhāraṇī, rNam par mi rtog par 'jug pa'i gzungs*. Toh. 142, H.K. 144. Citation not found in this text or the Kangyur. It is found (attributed to the *Dhāraṇī: Access to the Nonconceptual*) in Maitrīpa's *Teaching on Mental Nonengagement* (*Amanasikāroddeśa, Yid la mi byed pa ston pa*). Toh. 2249. See D 2249: vol. 51, 139b.2–3.

1082. D 3915: vol. 110, 34a.2–3. The Dg.T. recension reads . . . *mi dmigs pa gang yin de/ der yid* . . . ; the *Moonbeams* citation (*MB* VVI 361.17) reads . . . *mi dmigs pa gang yin der yid* . . .

1083. *Dohā for the People.* D 2224: vol. 51, 72a.5–6.

1084. *Treasury of Dohā: Instructions on Mahāmudrā.* D 2273: vol. 52, 122b.7.

1085. D 4036: vol. 128, 145a.6.

1086. D 3917: vol. 110, 62a.4–6.

1087. D 3917: vol. 110, 62b.6–63a.2. The Dg.T. recension reads . . . *dam pa'i chos la dran pa med pa* . . . *don dam par na dus gsum du chos skyes pa gang yang ma mthong ba de'i tshe ji ltar na dran pa dang/ yid la nyed par bya/ don dam par na dus gsum med pa'i phyir mong ba med pa gang yin pa de ji ltar dran par bya/ yid la byed par bya/ de'i phyir de spros pa thams cad nyer bar zhi bas rnam par mi rtog pa'i ye shes la zhugs pa yin no/ de la zhugs pas* . . . The *Moonbeams* citation (*MB* VVI 362.17–19) reads . . . *dam pa'i chos las dran pa med pa* . . . *don dam na dus gsum du chos skyes pa gang yang dran pa ma mthong ba de'i tshe ji ltar dran pa med pa dang yid la byed pa med pa la zhugs pa yin no/ de la zhugs pas* . . .

1088. D 3929: vol. 110, 96a.1–2.

1089. *Consummate Sublime Path of Mahāmudrā.* DNZ, 450.3–4, and TsRP, 89.4–90.1. The DNZ recension reads . . . *gsal stong ma 'gags sal le ba/ sing nge ye re 'dug pa de* . . . ; the *Moonbeams* citation (*MB* VVI 364.11–12) and TsRP read . . . *gsal stong ma 'gags mtha' dbus med/ sing nge ye re gnas pa de* . . .

1090. *MB* VVI (365.12): *'go* should be *mgo*. See *MB* DLG (246.1).

1091. This and the following two related sayings are found in six places in Gampopa's Collected Works: *Abundant Auspiciousness: A Collection of Dharma Lectures* (12a), *Abundant Virtue: A Collection of Dharma Lectures* (13a), *Replies to Dusum Khyenpa's Questions* (50a), *Core of Mahāmudrā: The Instructions on the Ultimate Essence* (11a), *Pointing Out the Essence: An Ultimate Treasury* (6a), and *Synopsis of the Meditations of Sūtra and Mantra* (*mDo sngags kyi sgom don bsdus pa*) (text 28/sa, 8b).

1092. See the above note.

1093. Ibid.

1094. This and the following four analogies are found in *Replies to the Exalted Pakmo Drupa's Questions*, 8a.

1095. *Earlier Authoritative Text / Truly Valid Words.* DNZ, vol. 7, 69.7. (Not found in the Tengyur recension.) The DNZ recension reads *mi mno mi bsam mi dpyad cing/ mi bsgoms mi sem rang babs bzhag;* the *Moonbeams* citation (367.5–6) reads *mi mno mi bsam mi sem zhing/ mi sgom mi dpyad rang bzhin bzhag.* The *Moonbeams* citation is similar to one found in Gampopa's *Ornament of Precious Liberation,* 105a, which reads *mi mno mi bsam mi shes shing/ mi sgom mi dpyad rang sar bzhag.*

1096. D 2224: vol. 51, 74a.2–3. The Dg.T. recension reads . . . *tshul du gnas par bya*; the *Moonbeams* citation (*MB* VVI 223.4) reads . . . *tshul du bzhag par bya.*

1097. *Dohā for the Queen.* D 2264: vol. 52, 30a.5–6.

1098. *Dohā for the People.* D 2224: vol. 51, 71b.6.

1099. *Treasury of Dohā: Instructions on Mahāmudrā.* D 2273: vol. 52, 123b.2. The Dg.T. recension reads . . . *yid la bya ba med cing ma bral . . . tha snyad gdags*; the *Moonbeams* citation (*MB* VVI 368.2) reads . . . *yid la byar med mtha' bral . . . tha snyad bzhag.*

1100. *Dohā for the Queen.* D 2264: vol. 52, 29b.4–5.

1101. *Dohā for the Queen.* D 2264: vol. 52, 30a.7.

1102. *Treasury of Dohā: Instructions on Mahāmudrā.* D 2273: vol. 52, 123b.1–2.

1103. *Treasury of Dohā.* D 2280: vol. 52, 135a.3. The Dg.T. recension reads *sems kyis chos kyi dbyings la 'di zhes med . . .* ; the *Moonbeams* citation (*MB* VVI 368.18) reads *sems kyi chos nyid klong la 'di yin med . . .*

1104. *Dohā for the Queen.* D 2264: vol. 52, 29a.3. See note 457 for textual differences.

1105. *Dohā for the King.* D 2263: vol. 52, 27b.6–7.

1106. *Dohā for the Queen.* D 2264: vol. 5·, 33a.5.

1107. *Treasury of Dohā: Instructions on Mahāmudrā.* D 2273: vol. 52, 122b.4. The Dg.T. recension reads *btags pa'i sems . . .* ; the *Moonbeams* citation (*MB* VVI 369.15) reads *brtags pa'i sems . . .*

1108. *Treasury of Dohā.* D 2280: vol. 52, 134a.2–3. The Dg.T. recension reads *rang bzhin spros med . . .* ; the *Moonbeams* citation (*MB* VVI 369.17) reads *rang bzhin brjod med . . .*

1109. *Dohā for the Queen.* D 2264: vol. 52, 33a.5–6. *MB* VVI (370.4) *ngang la gnas* should be *rang la gnas.* See *MB* DLG (248.7).

1110. *Dohā for the People.* D 2224: vol. 51, 71b.7. The Dg.T. recension reads . . . *bdag gi de nyid bde . . .* ; the *Moonbeams* citation (*MB* VVI 370.6) reads . . . *bdag nyid bde . . .*

1111. *Treasury of Dohā: Instructions on Mahāmudrā.* D 2273: vol. 52, 123b.1. The Dg.T. recension reads . . . *ma bzung ma btang rang dga' nyid du zhog*; the *Moonbeams* citation (*MB* VVI 370.9) reads . . . *ma bzung ma btang rang ga nyid du zhog.*

1112. *Treasury of Dohā.* D 2280: vol. 52, 135b.1–2. The Dg.T. recension reads . . . *rang lus ci bder . . .* ; the *Moonbeams* citation (*MB* VVI 370.13) . . . *rang lugs ci bder . . .* *MB* VVI (370.12): *'gos* should be *'gog.* See *MB* DLG (249.1).

1113. *Summary Verses on Mahāmudrā,* 45.6

1114. Source not found.

1115. 13b.

1116. *Uncommon Amṛta of Speech,* 17b.

1117. *Consummate Sublime Path of Mahāmudrā.* DNZ, 441.2–3. The DNZ recension reads *shes pa lhod kyis glod tsam na . . . dkyil ltar gnas . . .*; the *Moonbeams* citation (*MB* VVI 371.15–17) reads *shes pa lhod kyis glod pa'i dus . . . dkyil ltar 'char . . .*

1118. *Dohā for the People.* D 2224: vol. 51, 73a.4.

1119. *Dohā for the People.* D 2224: vol. 51, 72b.5–6.

1120. *Ganges Mahāmudrā.* D 2303: vol. 52, 243b.2.

1121. *Ganges Mahāmudrā.* D 2303: vol. 52, 243b.3–4.

1122. *Dohā for the People.* D 2224: vol. 51, 72b.2. The Dg.T. recension reads . . . *man ngag mthong ba . . .*; the *Moonbeams* citation (*MB* VVI 373.4) reads . . . *man ngag thob pa . . .*

1123. *Dohā for the Queen.* D 2264: vol. 52, 32b.6.

1124. *Treasury of Dohā: Instructions on Mahāmudrā.* D 2273: vol. 52, 122b.7.

1125. *Treasury of Dohā.* D 2280: vol. 52, 134a5–6.

1126. *Dohā for the People.* D 2224: vol. 51, 73a.5. The Dg.T. recension reads *thong bar gyur . . . go bzlog*; the *Moonbeams* citation (229.18) reads *thongs bar gyur . . . go log.*

1127. *Dohā for the People.* D 2224: vol. 51, 71b.2. The Dg.T. recension reads . . . *yod pa de yang . . .*; the *Moonbeams* citation (*MB* VVI 374.5) reads . . . *yod na de yang . . .*

1128. *Dohā for the People.* D 2224: vol. 51, 72a.5–6.

1129. Exact source unidentified. See *Uncommon Amṛta of Speech*, 17b.

1130. *Treasury of Dohā: Instructions on Mahāmudrā.* D 2273: vol. 52, 123a.7–123b.1.

1131. *Treasury of Dohā: Instructions on Mahāmudrā.* D 2273: vol. 52, 123b.3.

1132. Citation not found in a text attributed to Maitrīpa. It is found in Saraha's *Dohā Song on View, Meditation, Conduct, and Fruition.* D 2345: vol. 53, 3b.2.

1133. *Summary Verses on Mahāmudrā*, 46.4–5.

1134. Citation not found in the Tengyur. It is found (attributed to Nāgārjuna) in Gampopa's *Sunrays of Scriptural Citations*, 18a.

1135. *Sems nyid ngal gso.* Also known as *Finding Ease in Mind-Itself: The Esoteric Instructions Taught to the Mahāsiddha Mitrayogin by the Noble Avalokiteśvara* (*'Phags pa spyan ras gzigs kyis grub chen mi tra dzo ki la gsungs pa'i rang gi sems nyid ngal gso ba'i man ngag*) by Gelong Pal. DNZ, vol. 16, 500.1–2. It is also cited in Gampopa's *Ornament of Precious Liberation*, 105a.

1136. *Uncommon Amṛta of Speech*, 12a.

1137. *Phyag rgya chen po yi ge bzhi pa'i gdams pa* by Milarepa. DNZ, vol. 8, 42.3–4. The DNZ recension reads . . . *nyi zla sprin . . .*, *mnyam par bzhag* in each instance, and lists *bu chung lha khang blta ba bzhin* before *chu'i rba rlabs bzhin*; the *Moonbeams* citation (*MB* VVI 376.5–10) reads . . . *nyi ma sprin . . .*, only *bzhag* in each instance, and lists *chu'i rba rlabs bzhin* before *bu chung lha khang blta ba bzhin.*

1138. Source(s) not found.

1139. This statement is found in Gampopa's Collected Works in five texts: *Abundant Auspiciousness: A Collection of Dharma Lectures* (4b); *Replies to Dusum Khyenpa's Questions* (30a); *Replies to the Exalted Pakmo Drupa's Questions* (10a); *Core of Mahāmudrā: The Instructions on the Ultimate Essence* (6a); and *Esoteric Instructions on the Twofold Abiding State and Esoteric Instructions on Twofold Armor* (21a). There are some slight word variations, mainly between the use of *shes pa* and *rig pa.*

1140. This statement is found in Gampopa's Collected Works in five texts: *Abundant Auspiciousness: A Collection of Dharma Lectures* (4b); *Replies to Dusum Khyenpa's Questions* (30a); *Replies to the Exalted Pakmo Drupa's Questions* (6a); *Core of Mahāmudrā: The Instructions on the Ultimate Essence* (6b); and *Pointing out the Ultimacy of Thoughts* (3b–4a).
1141. *Three Cycles of Illumination* (*gSal ba skor gsum*). DNZ, vol. 7, 115.2–3.
1142. *Prajñāpāramitā in Eight Thousand Lines*. H.K. 11: vol. 29, 266a.2. The H.K. recension read . . . *chos thams cad mi sgom pa lags so*; *the Moonbeams* citation (*MB* VVI 378.13) reads . . . *chos ci yang mi sgom pa lags so*.
1143. H.K. 416a: vol. 82, 438b.6
1144. Citation not found in the *Vajra Pañjarā*. It is found in the *Sampuṭa*. See H.K. 396: vol. 81, 373b.3–4.
1145. *Dohā for the People*. D 2224: vol. 51, 71b.2. The Dg.T. recension reads . . . *yod pa de yang* . . . ; the Moonbeams citation (*MB* VVI 378.21) reads . . . *yod na de yang* . . .
1146. *Dohā for the Queen*. D 2264: vol. 52, 33a.4.
1147. *Dohā for the People*. D 2224: vol. 51, 75a.2–3.
1148. *Treasury of Dohā: Instructions on Mahāmudrā*. D 2273: vol. 52, 123b.3.
1149. *Treasury of Dohā*. D 2280: vol. 52, 135a.6. The Dg.T. recension reads . . . *don la goms* . . . ; the *Moonbeams* citation (*MB* VVI 379.11) reads . . . *don la dmigs* . . .
1150. *Ganges Mahāmudrā*. D 2303: vol. 52, 243b.3. See note 713 for textual differences.
1151. *Summary Verses on Mahāmudrā*, 46.4–5.
1152. *Dohā for the Queen*. D 2264: vol. 52, 29b.1–2.
1153. *Treasury of Dohā: Instructions on Mahāmudrā*. D 2273: vol. 52, 123a.1.
1154. *Treasury of Dohā*. D 2280: vol. 52, 135a.3.
1155. *Ganges Mahāmudrā*. D 2303: vol. 52, 243.5.
1156. *Summary Verses on Mahāmudrā*, 46.4.
1157. *Dohā for the People*. D 2224: vol. 51, 76b.3–4.
1158. *Dohā for the People*. D 2224: vol. 51, 72b.6.
1159. *Treasury of Dohā*. D 2280: vol. 52, 135a.2–3. The Dg.T. recension reads . . . *yid kyi ri bo* . . . ; The *Moonbeams* citation (*MB* VVI 382.2) reads . . . *yid kyi ngo bo* . . .
1160. *Treasury of Dohā*. D 2280: vol. 52, 135a.3–4. The Dg.T. recension reads . . . *yid la byed pa na/* . . . *shin tu yengs pa'o*; the *Moonbeams* citation (*MB* VVI 382.5–6) reads . . . *yid la byed pa ni/* . . . *shin tu ring ba'o.*
1161. Citation not found in a text by either the Śavara (Saraha) or Śavaripa. It is found (unattributed) in Gampopa's *Revealing the Hidden Characteristics of Mind*, 4b–5.
1162. H.K. 17: vol. 34, 199a.1–3.
1163. H.K. 396: vol. 81, 481.4.
1164. D 1800: vol. 35, 40a.6–7. The Dg.T. recension reads *sems la dmigs pa med pa yi/ gnas pa nam mkha'i mtshan nyid yin/ de dag stong nyid bsgom pa ni/ nam mkha' bsgom par bzhed pa yin*; the *Moonbeams* citation (*MB* VVI 384.5–6) reads *dmigs pa dang ni bral ba'i sems/ nam mkha'i mtshan nyid la gnas te/ nam mkha' sgom par*

byed pa ni/ stong pa nyid ni sgom par bzhed. The *Moonbeams* citation is identical to the one in Gampopa's *Sunrays of Scriptural Citations*, 20a.

1165. D 1118: vol. 1, 65a.6. The Dg.T. recension reads *rang bzhin med pa nyid*; the *Moonbeams* citation (*MB* VVI 384.9) reads *rang bzhin med nyid las.*

1166. D 3871: vol. 105, 32a.4.

1167. *Lamp That Summarizes Conduct.* D 3960: vol. 111, 313a.5. The Dg.T. recension reads *chos nyid spros pa dang bral ba*; the *Moonbeams* citation (*MB* VVI 384.14) reads *chos dbyings spros dang bral ba la.*

1168. *The Flag of Renown: The Biography of Gampopa*, 118.

1169. *Verses on the Four Yogas Requested by Geshe Nyang Gom.* The Collected Works of Pakmo Drupa edition reads . . . *bzhag sar steng dang* . . . ; the *Moonbeams* citation (*MB* VVI 385.12) reads . . . *bzhag sar stengs dang* . . .

I take the *Moonbeams* citation to be correct, with *stengs* ("stagnant") being cognate with *lteng* ("stupor"). This is supported by Pakmo Drupa's *Short Notes on the Four Yogas* (*rNal 'byor bzhi'i zin bris chung ngu*) (Collected Works of Pakmo Drupa, vol. 4/nga, text 10.80), where it says *de yang gzhag sar ma ltengs pa/ gtang sar ma 'khyams pa zhig dgos/ gzhag sar ltengs na bying ba yin pas shes pa g.yer thon par bya/ btang sar 'khyams na rgod pa yin pas skyes sbyor sbyar la.*

Also Götsangpa's explanation of two faults in meditation, *ltengs 'kyams* ("stagnation and wandering"), uses the phrase *bzhag sar ltengs pa ni*, and provides explanation. See his *Commentary on Mahāmudrā, Connate Union* (*Phyag rgya chen po lhan cig skyes sbyor gyi khrid*). Collected Works of Götsangpa, vol. 5/ca, text 8.

1170. Sakya Paṇḍita's *Letter to the Buddhas and Bodhisattvas of the Ten Directions*, 7a.2–3.

1171. *Collected Songs of the Glorious, Unequalled, Victor Götsangpa* (*dPal mnyam med rgyal ba rgod tshang pa'i mgur 'bum chen mo*) (Collected Works of Götsangpa, vol. 6/cha, text 1); and *Lamp Illuminating the Jeweled Commentary Containing a Treasury of Precious Instructions* (*gDams pa rin po che za ma tog bkod pa'i 'grel pa rin chen gsal ba'i sgron me*) (Collected Works of Götsangpa, vol. 4/nga, text 14).

1172. Source not found.

1173. D 3871: vol. 105, 31b.6–7. The Dg.T. recension reads . . . *rtog pa bzlog bya yin*; the *Moonbeams* citation (*MB* VVI 387.11) reads. . . *rtog pa dgag bya yin.*

1174. *MB* VVI (387.14): *'gro zhing yin* should be *'gro zhing yan*. See *MB* DLG (259.7) and *MB* TsRP (529.1).

1175. *Collected Songs of the Glorious, Unequalled, Victor Götsangpa* and *Lamp Illuminating the Jeweled Commentary Containing a Treasury of Precious Instructions.*

1176. *Dohā for the Queen.* D 2264: vol. 52, 29a.3–4. The Dg.T. recension reads . . . *de yis mi mthun bral*; the *Moonbeams* citation (*MB* VVI 389.10) reads . . . *de yi rang bzhin bral.*

1177. *Dohā for the Queen.* D 2264: vol. 52, 31a.1–2. The Dg.T. recension reads . . . *snang ba'i rang bzhin* . . . ; the *Moonbeams* citation (*MB* VVI 389.11) reads . . . *snang ba'i de bzhin* . . .

1178. *Treasury of Dohā: Instructions on Mahāmudrā.* D 2273: vol. 52, 123a.4–5.

1179. *Treasury of Dohā.* D 2280: vol. 52, 134a.5.
1180. See *A Major Collection of Dharma Lectures* (6a), *Pointing out the Ultimacy of Thoughts* (1a), *Presentation of the Three Trainings* (4a–4b), and *Esoteric Instructions on the Twofold Abiding State and Esoteric Instructions on Twofold Armor* (16a). Note that in some instances the third point is seemingly misspelled as *me sprul.*
1181. *Dohā for the People.* D 2224: vol. 51, 72a.3.
1182. *Dohā for the People.* D 2224: vol. 51, 74b.7.
1183. Citation not found in a text attributed to Maitrīpa. It is found in Saraha's *Dohā Song on View, Meditation, Conduct, and Fruition.* See D 2345: vol. 53, 3b.7. *MB* VVI (390.12): *ngo bo 'di thug* should be *ngo bo 'di/ thug.* See *MB* DLG (261.7).
1184. *Dohā for the People.* D 2224: vol. 51, 74b.5.
1185. *Treasury of Dohā: Instructions on Mahāmudrā.* D 2273: vol. 52, 123a.6–7. The Dg.T. recension reads . . . *bstan pa'i rjes bcad kyang*; the *Moonbeams* citation (*MB* VVI 391.6) reads . . . *rtog pa'i rjes bcad kyang.*
1186. *Dohā for the People.* D 2224: vol. 51, 75a.2. The Dg.T. recension reads *nags la mched pa'i lce . . . sems kyi rtsa ba stong pa . . .* ; the *Moonbeams* citation (*MB* VVI 391.14–16) reads *ji ltar nags la mched pa'i me lce . . . khyod kyi rtsa ba stong pa . . .* The translation follows the Dg.T. recension.
1187. *Summary Verses on Mahāmudrā*, 46.3.
1188. *Summary Verses on Mahāmudrā*, 46.6.
1189. *MB* VVI (393.2): *rtog pa skye* should be *rtogs pa skye.* See *MB* DLG (263.3).
1190. *Connate Union.* Collected Works of Pakmo Drupa, vol. 4/nga, text 10.1.
1191. H.K. 17: vol. 34, 190a.6–7.
1192. H.K. 129: vol. 55, 42b.4–5.
1193. H.K. 129: vol. 55, 43a.2–3. The H.K. recension reads . . . *rta dang glang po'i shing rta . . .* ; the *Moonbeams* citation (*MB* VVI 395.5) reads . . . *rta dang glang po shing rta . . .*
1194. *Treasury of Dohā: Instructions on Mahāmudrā.* D 2273: vol. 52, 124a.1–2. The Dg.T. recension reads . . . *chags thogs bral bas dka' zhing skye med pa/ sgyu ma mkhas pa . . .* ; the *Moonbeams* citation (*MB* VVI 396.3–4) reads . . . *chags thogs bral bas dga' zhing skyo med pas/ sgyu ma mkhan po . . .* The three reference points (*dmigs pa gsum*) are probably object of action, action, and doer of the action.
1195. *Treasury of Dohā: Instructions on Mahāmudrā.* D 2273: vol. 52, 123a.3–4. *MB* VVI (396.6): *dngos go* should be *dngos po.* See *MB* DLG (265.5).
1196. D 1800: vol. 35, 41b.4–5.
1197. *Instructions to Parpuwa: Summary of the Glorious Saraha's Five Types of Noncontrivance in Mahāmudrā* (*dPal sa ra ha'i phyag chen ma bcos rnam lnga'i bsdus don par phu ba la gdams pa*). Collected Works of Jikten Sumgön, vol. 1, 449.1–4.
1198. *Replies to the Exalted Gomtsul's Questions*, 8a. *MB* VVI (399.8): *rnam rtog yong* should be *rnam rtog yod.* See *MB* DLG (268.3), *MB* VVI (493.7), and Collected Works of Gampopa edition.
1199. *Revealing the Hidden Characteristics of Mind*, 5b. *MB* VVI (399.8): *yong* should be *yod.* See *MB* DLG (268.3) and *MB* VVI (499.7).

1200. *Replies to Yogin Chöyung's Questions*, 3a.

1201. *Heart Advice to Keep in Mind: Replies to Students' Questions About What to Do* (*sLob mas ji lta bya'i dris lan snying gtam blo bzhag*). Collected Works of Jikten Sumgön, vol. 3, 411.5–412.1.

1202. *Replies to the Exalted Gomtsul's Questions*, 1a–b.

1203. H.K. 17: vol. 34, 190a.3. the H.K. recension reads *bdag ni . . .* ; the *Moonbeams* citation (*MB* VVI 401.2) reads *'di ni . . .*

1204. *Treasury of Dohā: Instructions on Mahāmudrā*. D 2273: vol. 52, 123a.1–2.

1205. *MB* VVI (404.11): *mnyan* should probably be *ma nyan*. See *MB* TsRP (555.3), *MB* RD (346.17), and *MB* DK (648.2). The translation follows this reading.

1206. *Dohā for the Queen*. D 2264: vol. 52, 29a.4–5. The Dg.T. recension reads *dngos med rtog pa de bas shin tu blun 'gyur zhes*; the *Moonbeams* citation (404.16–17) reads *dngos med 'dzin pa de bas kyang ni blun*.

1207. *Fundamental Treatise on the Middle Way*. D 3824: vol. 96, 15a.2.

1208. *Precious Garland*. D 4158: vol. 172, 109a.2–3. The Dg.T. recension reads *med pa pa ni ngan 'gror 'gro*; the *Moonbeams* citation (*MB* VVI 405.2) reads *med pa po ni ngan 'gror 'gro*.

1209. *The Flag of Renown: The Biography of Gampopa*, 122.

1210. D 3824: vol. 96, 15a.6–7.

1211. D 1800: vol. 35, 41a.1.

1212. *Dohā for the Queen*. D 2264: vol. 52, 29a.6–7. The Dg.T. recension reads . . . *go gcig pa'i/ . . . 'di ni yin gyi yid la dris*; the *Moonbeams* citation (405.20–406.1) reads . . . *ro gcig pa'i/ . . . 'di ni yid kyis yid la dris*. The T. PD. (26.1021) notes that the Peking and Narthang Tengyurs read *ro* (not *go*). The Tibetan commentators Karma Tinle (128) and Parpuwa Lodrö Seng-ge (155) explain the lines following a reading that accords with the *Moonbeams* citation.

1213. *Dohā for the Queen*. D 2264: vol. 52, 32b.6.

1214. *Dohā for the Queen*. D 2264: vol. 52, 33a.5–6.

1215. Citation not found in a text by Āryadeva. It is found (unattributed) in Haribhadra's *Commentary on the "Ornament for Clear Realization"* (D 3793: vol. 86, 130a.6), and three other texts in the Tengyur.

1216. *The Flag of Renown: The Biography of Gampopa*, 110.

1217. H.K. 378a: vol. 79, 352a.1.

1218. H.K. 378b: vol. 79, 364b.2.

1219. *Fundamental Treatise on the Middle Way*. D 3824: vol. 96, 17a.1–2.

1220. *Summary Verses on Mahāmudrā*, 46.3.

1221. *Treasury of Dohā*. D 2280: vol. 52, 134b.1–2.

1222. *Treasury of Dohā: Instructions on Mahāmudrā*. D 2273: vol. 52, 122b.3.

1223. *Summary Verses on Mahāmudrā*, 45.5–6.

1224. *Esoteric Instructions: Illuminating Mahāmudrā*, 4b.

1225. *Letter on the Way of Being of the Reflexive Awareness of the Phenomena of Saṃsāra and Nirvāṇa* (*'Khor 'das gnyis kyi chos rang rig 'dug lugs kyi springs yig*). Collected Works of Jikten Sumgön, vol. 3, 199.2–3.

1226. *Letter to the Buddhas and Bodhisattvas of the Ten Directions*, 7a.3–5.

1227. *Summary Verses on Mahāmudrā*, 46.6.
1228. D 4020: vol. 123, 6b.6.
1229. D 3871: vol. 105, 33a.1. The Dg.T. recension reads ... *de ni ji ltar sgom mi byed*; the *Moonbeams* citation (*MB* VVI 409.10) reads ... *stong pa nyid ni bsgom par bya.*
1230. *Analysis of the Three Vows*, 59.11–12.
1231. *MB* VVI (410.21): *rig mthong* should be *reg mthong.* See *MB* DLG (277.1) and *MB* TsRP (564.4).
1232. Source unidentified. *MB* VVI (411.19): *du* should be *ngu.* See *MB* DLG (277.5).
1233. *Presentation of the Three Trainings*, 3b.
1234. *Synopsis of the Meditations of Sūtra and Mantra*, 10a. The Collected Works edition reads *srog dhU tir tshud pa'i stobs kyis/ rtags lnga dang phan yon brgyad la sogs pa yon tan mang du 'byung ngo/ de lta bu'i lus sems bde ba ci nying yang zhi gnas yang yin te/ 'ong kyang rtags lnga dang phan yon brgyad po de zhi gnas dang/ lha mthong zung du 'brel ba las 'byung ste/ dmigs pa phra mo zin pa'i gnas pa lteng lteng la mi 'byung ngo.* The *Moonbeams* (*MB* VVI 412.10–12) citation reads *rlung dhU tir tshud pa'i stobs kyis rtags lnga dang phan yon brgyad la sogs pa'i rtags de rnams zhi gnas dang lha mthong zung du 'brel bar bsgoms pa las 'byung gi/ dmigs pa phra mo zin pa'i gnas pa ltam ltem la mi 'byung ngo.*
1235. *Presentation of the Three Trainings*, text 30/AA, 3b. The Collected Works edition reads ... *kha na tson ne snyam byed pa'o/ spar mos bcang du 'dod* ... ; the *Moonbeams* (412.16) citation reads ... *kha na tse ne snyam byed pa sngar mos bcad du 'dod* ... The translation follows the Collected Works edition.
1236. *Dohā for the Queen.* D 2264: vol. 52, 33a.4–5.
1237. *Dohā for the Queen.* D 2264: vol. 52, 29b.2–3. The Dg.T. recension has the *Moonbeams* citation's third line as the second line, and its second line as third.
1238. *Dohā for the People.* D 2224: vol. 51, 75a.2–3.
1239. *Treasury of Dohā.* D 2280: vol. 52, 135a.6. The Dg.T. recension reads ... *don la goms* ... ; the *Moonbeams* citation (*MB* VVI 414.3) reads ... *don la dmigs* ...
1240. *A Major Collection of Dharma Lectures*, text 8/nya, 16a. *MB* VVI (414.16): *rlung gi* should be *rlung gis.* See *MB* DLG (279.6).
1241. *Verses on the Four Yogas Requested by Geshe Nyang Gom.*
1242. Source not found.
1243. Source not found.
1244. *Verses on the Four Yogas Requested by Geshe Nyang Gom.*
1245. *Treasury of the Ultimate Essence*, 139.5–6.
1246. *Abundant Auspiciousness: A Collection of Dharma Lectures*, 7b.
1247. D 4089: vol. 140, 2a.2.
1248. D 4090: vol. 140, 28b.3–4.
1249. D 3871: vol. 105, 32b.4–5.
1250. H.K. 129: vol. 55, 44a.7–44b.1. The H.K. recension reads ... *de ni nyon mongs phyir yang rab tu ldang/ lhag spyod kyis ni* ... ; the *Moonbeams* citation (*MB* VVI 418.19) reads ... *de ni phyir zhing nyon mongs rab 'khrug ste/ lhag spyod kyi ni* ... See also note 784.

1251. *Commentary on Valid Cognition*. D 4210: vol. 174, 116a.1–2.
1252. *Analysis of the Three Vows*, 59.11–14.
1253. Source not found.
1254. *Esoteric Instructions: Illuminating Mahāmudrā*, 4a. This song is also found in *The Flag of Renown: The Biography of Gampopa*, 121.
1255. *Abundant Auspiciousness: A Collection of Dharma Lectures*, 7b.
1256. *Esoteric Instructions: Illuminating Mahāmudrā*, 4b. An almost identical passage is found in *Replies to Dusum Khyenpa's Questions*, 48b–49a.
1257. *The Grand Collection of Dharma Lectures*, 44b–45a. Śrīghoṣa's *Lamp for the True View* (*lTa ba yang dag sgron pa*). Toh. 4447. D 4447: vol. 212, 384a.6. The Dg.T. recension reads *btang snyoms chen por ma bcos ngang bzhag na/ tha snyad tsam du'ang bsgom zhes de la bya*; the Collected Works and *Moonbeams* citations (*MB* VVI 422.1–2) read *btang snyoms tsam du ma bcos ngang bzhag na/ tha snyad tsam du sgom zhes de la brjod. MB* VVI (422.1): *dang* should be *ngang*. See *MB* DLG (284.7).
1258. *Abundant Auspiciousness: A Collection of Dharma Lectures*, 7b.
1259. *Vajra Song of Vajrāsana* (*Vajrāsanavajragīti, rDo rje gdan gyi rdo rje'i glu*). Toh. 1494. D 1494: vol. 22, 209a.1–2. The Dg.T. recension reads *nges sbyangs bag chags* . . . ; the *Moonbeams* citation (422.10) reads *nges 'byung bag chags* . . . Since Atīśa's commentary on this text, *Commentary on the "Vajra Song of Vajrāsana"* (*Vajrāsanavajragītivṛtti, rDo rje gdan gyi rdo rje'i glu'i 'grel pa*) (Toh. 1495; D 1494: vol. 22, 214a.4), reads *nges sbyangs bag chags* . . . , the translation follows the Dg.T. recension.
1260. *A Major Collection of Dharma Lectures*, 12a.
1261. *A Major Collection of Dharma Lectures*, 12a.
1262. This statement is found in Gampopa's Collected Works in five texts: *Abundant Auspiciousness: A Collection of Dharma Lectures* (4b); *Replies to Dusum Khyenpa's Questions* (30a); *Replies to the Exalted Pakmo Drupa's Questions* (10a); *Core of Mahāmudrā: The Instructions on the Ultimate Essence* (6a); and *Esoteric Instructions on the Twofold Abiding State and Esoteric Instructions on Twofold Armor* (21a). There are some slight word variations, mainly between the use of *shes pa* and *rig pa*.
1263. This statement is found in Gampopa's Collected Works in five texts: *Abundant Auspiciousness: A Collection of Dharma Lectures* (4b); *Replies to Dusum Khyenpa's Questions* (30a); *Replies to the Exalted Pakmo Drupa's Questions* (6a); *Core of Mahāmudrā: The Instructions on the Ultimate Essence* (6b); and *Pointing Out the Ultimacy of Thoughts* (3b–4a).

The same citation is found in *Moonbeams* (*MB* VVI 377.1 and 475.8), where it reads *de yang gsal sing nge ba* . . . and *gsal sing nge ba* . . . , which is how this citation appears in the five instances in Gampopa's Collected Works, not as found in *MB* VVI (423.3–4): *de yang rig pa gsal sing nge ba* . . . ; therefore the translation follows all the other instances.
1264. *A Major Collection of Dharma*, 12a–b.

1265. Source unidentified.
1266. Sakya Paṇḍita's *Letter to the Buddhas and Bodhisattvas of the Ten Directions*, 7a.3.
1267. *Analysis of the Three Vows*, 85. About the citation from the prajñāpāramitā sūtras, Rhoton, *Clear Differentiation*, 193n78, provides this information:

> Gorampa, *DSNSh*, fol. 140b, quotes from the *Aṣṭasāhasrikā Prajñāpāramitā*: "Thus, Subhūti, a bodhisattva, a great being, does not think, 'I should directly realize emptiness that is endowed with excellence in every way.' He does not think, 'I should become thoroughly familiar with it.' He does not think, 'Now is the time to confront it.'"

1268. Reference not found.
1269. *The Flag of Renown: The Biography of Gampopa*, 76. *MB* VVI (426.3): *gi ston pa* should be *ge ston pa*. See *MB* DLG (287.7).
1270. *Uncommon Amṛta of Speech*, 9b.
1271. H.K. 462: vol. 86, 340b.4–5.
1272. H.K. 462: vol. 86, 340b.5–7. The H.K. recension reads . . . *yi ga 'chus/ . . . rims nad ni/ grang rlung . . .* ; the *Moonbeams* citation (*MB* VVI 426.8–9) reads . . . *yi ga 'chu/ . . . rims rnams ni/ rlung grang . . .*
1273. *MB* VVI (428.6): *sgros pa bcad pa* should be *spros pa bcad pa*. See *MB* DLG (289.5).
1274. *Ganges Mahāmudrā*. D 2303: vol. 52, 243b.3. See note 713 for textual differences.
1275. *Dohā for the People*. D 2224: vol. 51, 72b.2. The Dg.T. recension reads . . . *man ngag mthong ba . . .* ; the *Moonbeams* citation (*MB* VVI 428.11) reads . . . *man ngag thob pa . . .*
1276. *Dohā for the People*. D 2224: vol. 51, 73b.6.
1277. *Treasury of Dohā: Instructions on Mahāmudrā*. D 2273: vol. 52, 123b.2. The Dg.T. recension reads . . . *yid la bya ba med cing ma bral . . .* ; the *Moonbeams* citation (*MB* VVI 428.16) reads . . . *yid la byar med mtha' bral . . .*
1278. *Ganges Mahāmudrā*. D 2303: vol. 52, 243b.4.
1279. *Summary Verses on Mahāmudrā*, 45.4. It is also found in Gampopa's *Sunrays of Scriptural Citations*, 14a.
1280. Collected Works of Gampopa, text 14/pha. This text is mentioned by name in Tashi Namgyal's biography in the context of Tashi Namgyal's realization of Gampopa's teachings. See p lxix.
1281. Source not found.
1282. *Dohā for the People*. D 2224: vol. 51, 71b.4–5.
1283. *Treasury of Dohā: Instructions on Mahāmudrā*. D 2273: vol. 52, 122a.1–3. In the Dg.T. recension *ji ltar dngos dang dngos med snang stong dang* precedes *rgyu dang mi rgyu g.yo dang mi g.yo ba*, and it reads . . . *mtshan pa'i yul . . .* ; the *Moonbeams* citation (*MB* VVI 431.8) reads . . . *mtshon pa'i yul . . .*
1284. *Treasury of Dohā*. D 2280: vol. 52, 134a.6–7.
1285. *Ganges Mahāmudrā*. D 2303: vol. 52, 243b.1–3. The Dg.T. recension reads *dper na nam mkha' stong par rab rtags kyang/ . . . brjod par 'di 'dra grub ces brtags gzhi*

med/ de ltar sems kyi rang bzhin nam mkha' 'dra; the *Moonbeams* citation (*MB* VVI (432.4–8) reads *dper na nam mkha' stong par tha snyad rab rtags kyang/ . . . 'di 'drar grub ces ces tha snyad gdags gzhi med/ de ltar sems kyi rang bzhin gdod nas nam mkha' 'dra.*

1286. *Treasury of Dohā: Instructions on Mahāmudrā.* D 2273: vol. 52, 122b.1–2. *MB* VVI (432.15): *med pas* should probably be *med pa.* See *MB* VVI (272.1) and the Dg.T. recension.

1287. *Treasury of Dohā: Instructions on Mahāmudrā.* D 2273: vol. 52, 124a.2.

1288. Source not found.

1289. *Song of Realizing Fivefold Mahāmudrā* (*Phyag rgya chen po lnga ldan rtogs pa'i mgur*). Collected Works of Jikten Sumgön, vol. 10, 97.2–3.

1290. D 2264: vol. 52, 31b.6–7. The Dg.T. recension reads . . . *thams cad ro gcig par/ ston par* . . . ; the *Moonbeams* citation (433.13–14) reads . . . *thams cad don gcig par/ rtogs par* . . . The translation follows the Dg.T. recension in reading *ro gcig*, which is also found in Karma Tinle's *Mirror That Reveals the Liberation of Mind: The Middle-Length Commentary on the Queen's Dohā*, 170.

1291. *Dohā for the People.* D 2224: vol. 51, 75a.2. The Dg.T. recension reads . . . *sems kyi rtsa ba stong pa* . . . ; the *Moonbeams* citation (*MB* VVI 435.5) reads . . . *khyod kyi rtsa ba stong pa* . . . The translation follows the Dg.T. recension. *MB* VVI (435.5): *kyis* should be *kyi.* See *MB* VVI 391.16.

1292. *Treasury of Dohā: Instructions on Mahāmudrā.* D 2273: vol. 52, 123a.4–5.

1293. *Treasury of Dohā.* D 2280: vol. 52, 134a.7.

1294. *Ganges Mahāmudrā.* D 2303: vol. 52, 243a.6–7. The Dg.T. recension reads *dper na sa rlung sprin ni nam mkhar dengs/ gar yang song med gar yang gnas pa med/* . . . The *Moonbeams* citation (*MB* VVI 435.15–16) reads *dper na khug sna sprin rnams nam mkha'i khams su dengs/ gar yang song ba med cing gang du'ang gnas pa med/* . . .

1295. Source not found.

1296. Citation not found in a text attributed to Maitrīpa. It is found in Saraha's *Dohā Song on View, Meditation, Conduct, and Fruition.* D 2345: vol. 53, 3b.7.

1297. *Dohā for the Queen.* D 2264: vol. 52, 29b.4–5.

1298. *Dohā for the Queen.* D 2264: vol. 52, 30a.7.

1299. *Dohā for the People.* D 2224: vol. 51, 72a.3.

1300. *Treasury of Dohā: Instructions on Mahāmudrā.* D 2273: vol. 52, 123b.1–2.

1301. *Treasury of Dohā.* D 2280: vol. 52, 135a.3. The Dg.T. recension reads *sems kyis chos kyi dbyings la 'di zhes med* . . . ; the *Moonbeams* citation (*MB* VVI 368.18) reads *sems kyi chos nyid klong la 'di yin med* . . .

1302. *Treasury of Dohā.* D 2280: vol. 52, 135b.5–6.

1303. *MB* VVI (439.3) and *MB* TsRP (606.3): *rtog par bya* should probably be *rtogs par bya.* See *MB* DLG (296.7).

1304. *MB* VVI (439.11) (and *MB* DLG, 297.2): *du ma re* should be *dum re.* See *MB* TsRP (606.6).

1305. *MB* VVI (439.13): *'chags* should be *'chag.* See *MB* DLG (297.3).

1306. *Dohā for the Queen.* D 2264: vol. 52, 32b.6.

1307. *Dohā for the Queen.* D 2264: vol. 52, 30b.2.
1308. *Dohā for the Queen.* D 2264: vol. 52, 33b.1.
1309. *Dohā for the People.* D 2224: vol. 51, 72b.6.
1310. *Dohā for the People.* D 2224: vol. 51, 74a.4.
1311. *Dohā for the People.* D 2224: vol. 51, 73b.6–7.
1312. *Treasury of Dohā: Instructions on Mahāmudrā.* D 2273: vol. 52, 123a.3.
1313. *Treasury of Dohā: Instructions on Mahāmudrā.* D 2273: vol. 52, 123b.4–5. The Dg.T. recension reads . . . *ngas ni chos kun ma btang bas/* . . . ; the *Moonbeams* citation (*MB* VVI 442.3) reads . . . *ngas ni chos kun ma bzung ma btang bas/* . . .
1314. *Treasury of Dohā.* D 2280: vol. 52, 134b.3–5.
1315. *Treasury of Dohā.* D 2280: vol. 52, 134b.6–7.
1316. *Treasury of Dohā.* D 2280: vol. 52, 135b.1–2. The Dg.T. recension reads . . . *rang lus ci bder* . . . ; the *Moonbeams* citation (*MB* VVI 442.18) . . . *rang lugs ci bder* . . .

    The *MB* VVI citation (442.16) here reads *don dam rnal ma chos nyid* . . . However *MB* VVI (370.11) and the Dg.T. recension read *don dam rnal ma chags med* . . . The translation follows the latter.
1317. Source not found.
1318. Source not found.
1319. Source not found.
1320. *Revealing the Hidden Characteristics of Mind*, 3a.
1321. *Revealing the Hidden Characteristics of Mind*, 3b.
1322. *Revealing the Hidden Characteristics of Mind*, 4a.
1323. *Revealing the Hidden Characteristics of Mind*, 4a.
1324. *Revealing the Hidden Characteristics of Mind*, 5b.
1325. Collected Works of Gampopa, text 14/pha.
1326. *Consummate Sublime Path of Mahāmudrā.* DNZ, 440.5–6, and TsRP, 70.6 and 71.1–2. The DNZ and TsRP recensions read . . . *'di bya'i tig po mi dgos so* [two intervening lines] and reverses the next two lines with its first one reading: *nam dran 'drogs la glod la zhog.* The *Moonbeams* citation (*MB* VVI 445.7–8) reads . . . *'di bya'i tig tig mi 'dog gi/* . . . *nam dran dus su glod la zhog.* Note that the TsRP recension agrees with the *MB* recension in its reading of the last line. *MB* VVI (445.7): *mi 'dog gi* probably should be *mi bdog gi* in keeping with *MB* DLG (300.5), although *MB* TsRP (614.1) also reads *mi 'dog gi.*
1327. *Treasury of Dohā: Instructions on Mahāmudrā.* D 2273: vol. 52, 123b.3–4.
1328. *Replies to Yogin Chöyung's Questions*, 3b–4a.
1329. *Replies to the Exalted Gomtsul's Questions*, 7b.
1330. *Revealing the Hidden Characteristics of Mind*, 3a.
1331. *Revealing the Hidden Characteristics of Mind*, 5b.
1332. H.K. 378a: vol. 79, 342.6–7.
1333. H.K. 378b: vol. 79, 355.4.
1334. *MB* VVI (451.11): *yang ba'i* should be *ya nga ba'i.* See *MB* DLG (305.4).
1335. This passage is drawn virtually verbatim from *A Major Collection of Dharma Lectures* (9b) and *Replies to the Exalted Gomtsul's Questions* (19b).

1336. *A Major Collection of Dharma Lectures* (18b) and *Replies to the Exalted Gomtsul's Questions* (10a).

1337. *Consummate Sublime Path of Mahāmudrā.* DNZ, 438.3.

1338. Citation not in *Vairocanābhisambodhi.* It is found in the *Sampuṭa Tantra* (H.K. 396: vol. 81, 481a.4), *Ornament of the Vajra Heart* (H.K. 788: vol. 96, 440a.6), and *Māyājāla* (*sGyu 'phrul drva ba*) (Toh. 466; H.K. 431, H.K. 431: vol. 83, 341b.3). The same two lines are found on p. 275 attributed to the *Sampuṭa*. However, the *Moonbeams* citation here (*MB* VVI 453.9–10) could also be drawn from Rangjung Dorje's *Collection on Equal Taste* (*Ro snyoms sgang 'dril*) (Collected Works of Rangjung Dorje, vol. 11/A, 131.1–2), since both attribute the citation to the *Vairocanābhisambodhi* and read *rnam rtog ma rig chen po ste . . .*

The H.K. recension of the *Sampuṭa Tantra* reads *rnam rtog gti mug chen po ste . . .* ; and the H.K. recensions of the *Ornament of the Vajra Heart* and *Māyājāla* read *rnam rtog rmongs pa chen po ste . . .*

The same citation is found in Gampopa's *Uncommon Amṛta of Speech* (14a) and *Sunrays of Scriptural Citations* (8b), attributed to the *Sampuṭa Tantra.* It reads *rnam rtog ma rig chen po ste . . .*

1339. H.K. 378b: vol. 79, 357a.5.

1340. Source not found.

1341. Nāropa's *Summary Verses on Mahāmudrā*, 48.2. Maitrīpa's *Summary Verses on Mahāmudrā*, 46.6.

1342. Source not found.

1343. Source not found.

1344. *gZer rnam pa lnga'i man ngag.* Text not found.

1345. H.K. 378b: vol. 79, 357.5–6.

1346. *A Major Collection of Dharma Lectures*, 5b.

1347. Source not found.

1348. *Replies to the Exalted Gomtsul's Questions*, 8b.

1349. *Collected Songs of the Glorious, Unequalled, Victor Götsangpa* and *Lamp Illuminating the Jeweled Commentary Containing a Treasury of Precious Instructions.*

1350. *Collected Songs of the Glorious, Unequalled, Victor Götsangpa* and *Lamp Illuminating the Jeweled Commentary Containing a Treasury of Precious Instructions.*

1351. H.K. 378b: vol. 79, 357.6–7.

1352. H.K. 396: vol. 81, 365b.2–3. The H.K. recension reads *gti mug dag pas gti mug ste/ zhe sdang dag pas zhe sdang nyid/ 'dod chags dag pas 'dod chags te/ nga rgyal rnam dag nga rgyal che/ phrag dog dag pas phrag dog snyed/ thams cad rnam dag rdor 'dzin mgon.* The *Moonbeams* citation (*MB* VVI 459.7–9) may be drawn from Rangjung Dorje's *Collection on Equal Taste* (136.3–4), both of which read: *chags pas chags pa 'dag par byed/ zhe sdang gis ni zhe sdang sbyongs/ gti mug gis ni gti mug sbyong/ nga rgyal gyis ni nga rgyal sbyong/ phrag dog gis ni phrag dog sbyong/ rdo rje 'dzin sogs thams cad sbyang.*

1353. H.K. 396: vol. 81, 365b.3–4. The H.K. recension reads *nyon mongs lnga ni mnyam par 'gyur/ de ltar rigs ni lnga rnams dang/ ye shes lnga dang sangs rgyas lnga*; the

Moonbeams citation (*MB* VVI 459.15–17) reads *ye shes nyon mongs mnyam par 'gro/ de dag rigs ni lnga nyid de/ ye shes lnga dang sangs rgyas lnga.*

1354. H.K. 378b: vol. 79, 357.7.

1355. *Dohā for the People.* D 2224: vol. 51, 74a.7–74b.1.

1356. *Dohā for the King.* D 2263: vol. 52, 27a.7–27b.1.

1357. *Summary Verses on Mahāmudrā*, 46.3.

1358. Source unidentified.

1359. Citation not found in the Tengyur. It is found (attributed to Nāropa) in Gampopa's *Treatise Containing a Garland of Amṛta-Advice and [the Means for] Annihilating the Four Demons*, 10b.

1360. *Biography and Songs of the Great Lord of Yogins, Milarepa*, 241.

1361. *Biography and Songs of the Great Lord of Yogins, Milarepa*, 232.

1362. One possible source for this statement may be Gampopa's *Treatise Containing a Garland of Amṛta-Advice and [the Means for] Annihilating the Four Demons*, 10a.

1363. *Treatise Containing a Garland of Amṛta-Advice and [the Means for] Annihilating the Four Demons*, 9a–11b, particularly 10a–11a.

1364. *Treatise Containing a Garland of Amṛta-Advice and [the Means for] Annihilating the Four Demons*, 10b.

1365. *The Grand Collection of Dharma Lectures*, 6a–6b.

1366. *Precious Garland.* D 4158: vol. 172, 113b.1–2.

1367. H.K. 378a: vol. 79, 352.3.

1368. H.K. 379: vol. 79, 416a.6. The H.K. recension reads *stong pa snying rje tha dad med . . .* ; the *Moonbeams* citation (*MB* VVI 465.18–19) reads *stong nyid snying rje dbyer med pa . . .*

1369. H.K. 396: vol. 81, 373b.7–374a.1. The H.K. recension reads . . . *thams cad don byed snying rje ste*; the *Moonbeams* citation (*MB* VVI 466.2) reads . . . *sems can don byed snying rje ste.*

1370. *Dohā for the People.* D 2224: vol. 51, 71b.1.

1371. *Treasury of Dohā: Instructions on Mahāmudrā.* D 2273: vol. 52, 123b.7–124a.1.

1372. See *A Major Collection of Dharma Lectures* (5a) and *Core of Mahāmudrā: The Instructions on the Ultimate Essence* (10b).

1373. *MB* VVI (468.9): I am reading *ma chugs pa* as *ma 'chugs pa*, following *MB* RD (400.8), which seems to be a correction of *ma chugs pa* found in *MB* DLG (317.3) and *MB* TsRP (649.4).

1374. *MB* VVI (468.19): *nang bcos* should be *nad bcos.* See *MB* DLG (317.6).

1375. *Laghusaṃvara* (*sDom pa chung ngu*), also known as the *Cakrasaṃvara Root Tantra* (*bDe mchog rtsa rgyud*). Toh. 368, H.K. 384. H.K. 384: vol. 80, 130b.2.

1376. This famous quotation is usually attributed to the *Name-Chanting of Mañjuśrī*, although in the H.K. recension the first line is not found.

In the Tengyur commentaries on the *Name-Chanting of Mañjuśrī*, Ḍombi Heruka's *Commentary on the "Name-Chanting of Mañjuśrī"* (**Nāmasaṃgītivṛtti*, *'Jam dpal gyi mtshan yang dag par brjod pa'i 'grel pa*) (Toh. 2542; D 2542: vol. 64, 268b.4–268b.5) contains the same citation as is found in *Moonbeams* (*MB*

VVI 470.14–15): *skad cig gcig* [or *cig*] *gis bye brag phyed/ skad cig gcig gis rdzogs sangs rgyas.*

In the H.K. recension of *Name-Chanting of Mañjuśrī* (H.K. 369: vol. 79, 10b.2) the corresponding lines read *skad cig thams cad rnam sgom pa/ skad cig gcig mngon rdzogs sangs rgyas.*

1377. *The Flag of Renown: The Biography of Gampopa*, 151–52.

1378. *Questions and Answers with Instructions on the Four Yogas* (*Zhu lan rnal 'byor bzhi'i gdams pa dang bcas pa*). Collected Works of Tsangpa Gyare Yeshe Dorje, 584.6–585.1.

1379. *MB* VVI (475.2): *rags rims* should be *rags rim*. See *MB* DLG (321.2).

1380. This statement is found in Gampopa's Collected Works in five texts: *Abundant Auspiciousness: A Collection of Dharma Lectures* (4b); *Replies to Dusum Khyenpa's Questions* (30a); *Replies to the Exalted Pakmo Drupa's Questions* (6a); *Core of Mahāmudrā: The Instructions on the Ultimate Essence* (6b); and *Pointing Out the Ultimacy of Thoughts* (3b–4a).

1381. *Replies to the Exalted Pakmo Drupa's Questions*, 3b. The Collected Works edition reads *nyams dang rtogs pa gnyis la khyad ci tsam bdog zhus pas/ nyams ni blo'i cha las ma 'das pa yin te/ dper na sprin gseb kyi nyi ma dang 'dra/ bde gsal mi rtog pa gsum/ res mtho res dma' ba gnas pa 'ong ba yin pas/ 'di la ma zhen par bskyangs pas blo'i dri ma dvangs nas rtogs pa gdod 'char gsung/ rtogs pa ni snang sems gnyis med du blo yi steng nas rtogs pa/ 'od gsal ngang nas rgyun chad med pas bsgom bya sgom byed dang bral ba'i dus su rtogs thob dus mnyam du 'char ba la zer ba yin gsung.*

The *Moonbeams* citation (*MB* VVI 475.11–16) reads *nyams dang rtogs pa gnyis la khyad ci yod zhus pas/ nyams ni blo'i yul las ma 'das par yod pa yin te/ dper na sprin gseb kyi nyi ma dang 'dra bas bde gsal ba mi rtog pa gsum res mtho res dma' ba res gnas pa 'ong ba la/ de la ma zhen par bskyangs pas blo'i dri ma dag nas rtogs pa gzod 'char rtogs pa ni snang sems gnyis med du blo'i gting nas 'od gsal gyi ngang la rgyun chad med pas bsgom bya sgom byed dang bral ba'i dus su rtogs thob dus gcig tu 'char ba la zer ba yin.* The bracketed words "are realized" in the translation are from the Collected Works edition.

1382. *Analysis of the Three Vows*, 87.11–19. Gorampa Sönam Seng-ge in his *Commentary on "Analysis of the Three Vows"* (*sDom pa gsum gyi rab tu dbye ba'i rnam bshad rgyal ba'i gsung rab gyi dgongs pa gsal ba*) (International Buddhist Academy, digital text, 222) comments that Ling Repa and others are the ones who say, "Experience is inferior, understanding is middling, and realization is best."

1383. *Analysis of the Three Vows*, 87.21–22. Although the *Moonbeams* citations read *rtog pa gsal . . .* in the *Analysis of the Three Vows* this line reads *rtogs pa gsal . . .* The translation follows *Moonbeams* in order to be in keeping with Dakpo Tashi Namgyal's rebuttal.

1384. H.K. 110: vol. 51, 137a.6–137b.2.

1385. H.K. 110: vol. 51, 137b.2–6. The H.K. recension reads . . . *mngon par zhen pas bsgos pa . . .* ; the *Moonbeams* citation (*MB* VVI 477.18) reads . . . *mngon par zhen pas bgos pa . . .* The translation follows the H.K. recension.

1386. H.K. 110: vol. 51, 137b.6–138a.4.

1387. H.K. 110: vol. 51, 138b.4–7. The H.K. recension reads... *zhes yang dag par mthong nas 'phags pa so so rang gi ye she kyis rtogs pa'i yul la mngon par mos so/*; the *Moonbeams* citation (*MB* VVI 478.20–21) reads... *zhes yang dag par mthong ba'i byang chub sems dpa'/.*

1388. H.K. 110: vol. 51, 138a.4–5. The first part of the citation found in *Moonbeams* (*MB* VVI 479.2–3) (*blo gros chen po/ ji ltar na byang chub sems dpa' sems dpa' chen po 'phags pa so so rang gi ye shes khong du chud par mos pa yin zhe na/ 'di lta ste*) is not found in the H.K. recension. The text that follows in *Moonbeams* is included under the explanation of the second quality (dharma) in the H.K. recension. The *Moonbeams* citation is identical to one found in Gö Lotsāwa's *Mirror Illuminating Suchness: A Commentary on the "Highest Continuum,"* 65.13–16. For information on this and comparisons between the Tibetan translations of the *Descent into Laṅkā* from the Sanskrit and from the Chinese, see Mathes, *Direct Path to the Buddha Within*, 530–31n1589.

1389. H.K. 110: vol. 51, 270a.1–3. See note 469 for textual differences.

1390. See first *Stages of Meditation* (D 3915: vol. 110, 33a.3–33b.6) and *Instructions on Prajñāpāramitā* (D 4079: vol. 138, 161a.5–161b.7).

1391. *Alikaliguhyatsindhapanibhayumahātantranāma, gSang ba bsam gyis mi khyab pas dpa' sems gsang ba bsam gyis mi khyab pa chu klung chen po'i rgyud.* Text and citation not found in the Kangyur. This text is probably authored by Padampa Sangye and the citation is found in Dingri Volumes / The Volumes of the Root Teachings of the Sacred Dharma Pacification of Suffering, and the Subsidiary, Severance of Evil Object (*Dam chos sdug bsngal zhi byed rtsa ba'i chos sde dang / yan lag bdud kyi gcod yul gyi glegs bam*), vol. 1/ka, 42.5–43.3.

The Dingri Volumes recension reads... *mi g.yo rtse gcig dvangs ma'i shes pa gsal/ rang rig ye shes khong nas sad par byed/ bzod pa brtan pos ngan song sdug bsngal spong/ gnyis pa . . . ting 'dzin rtsal du 'char/ drod thob nas ni skye la dbang ba yin/ gsum pa... gzhan don mdzad/ rtse mo thob nas 'phel ba rgyun chad med/ bzhi pa... zhing khams mthong/ ma brtsal lhun grub chos mchog chen po'i ngang.*

The *Moonbeams* citation (479.14–480.2) reads... *rtse gcig mi g.yo dvangs ma'i shes pa gsal/ rang rig ye shes khong nas sad par byed/ drod thob nas ni skye la dbang ba yin/ gnyis pa . . . ting 'dzin rtsal du 'char/ rtse mo thob nas 'phel ba rgyun mi chad / gsum pa... gzhan don mdzad/ bzod pa brtan pas ngan song sdug bsngal sel/ bzhi pa . . . zhing khams dpag med thob/ . . . ma btsal lhun grub chos mchog chen po'i ngang.*

1392. H.K. 378a: vol. 79, 348.6

1393. H.K. 378a: vol. 79, 341a.4–5.

1394. H.K. 378b: vol. 79, 372b.2.

1395. H.K. 378a: vol. 79, 348a.1.

1396. H.K. 378a: vol. 79, 341.6.

1397. *Dohā for the People.* D 2224: vol. 51, 74a.2–3.

1398. *Dohā for the People.* D 2224: vol. 51, 72b.2.

1399. *Dohā for the People.* D 2224: vol. 51, 73a.2.
1400. *Dohā for the People.* D 2224: vol. 51, 71b.6.
1401. This is drawn from Yang Gönpa's *Treasury of the Ultimate Essence* (and possibly other sources). There are three consulted editions of Yang Gönpa's *Treasury of the Ultimate Essence.* The TsRP edition (3a.5–3b.1) reads the same as *Moonbeams* (*MB* VVI 480.20): "the terminology is also used explicitly in the tantras" (*rgyud sde rnams nas tha snyad dngos su gsungs pa'ang yod*). (All consulted editions of *Moonbeams* concur.)

However, two other editions of Yang Gönpa's *Treasury of the Ultimate Essence* (Drikung Kagyu Great Treasury of Dharma, vol. 48: 78.4; and Collected Works of Yang Gönpa, vol. 1, 2b.2) state the opposite: "the terminology of the four yogas is not used explicitly in the tantras" (*rnal 'byor bzhi'i chos skad 'di rnams rgyud sde rnams nas tha snyad dngos su gsungs pa ni med*). All the editions of *Treasury of the Ultimate Essence* continue with "the features [of the four yogas] are found [in the tantras] exactly in that way" (*don ji lta ba bzhin du bzhugs*) and then say "they are a special quality, or dharma, that is not in contradiction with the tantras" (*des na rgyud sde dang 'gal ba med pa'i khyad par gyi chos*), concluding with "they are a dharma of realization of Dakpo Rinpoche" (*dvags po rin po che'i rtogs chos yin*).

It seems likely that the editions of Yang Gönpa's *Treasury of the Ultimate Essence* that read "the terminology of the four yogas is not used explicitly in the tantras" (*rgyud sde rnams nas tha snyad dngos su gsungs pa ni med*) are correct.
1402. In Yang Gönpa's *Treasury of the Ultimate Essence*, 144.1–2.
1403. *Core of Mahāmudrā: The Instructions on the Ultimate Essence*, 6a.
1404. *Condensed Verses on the Four Yogas* (*rNal 'byor bzhi'i tshigs bcad ma chung ba*). Collected Works of Pakmo Drupa, vol. 4/nga, text 10.9.
1405. *Consummate Sublime Path of Mahāmudrā.* DNZ, 450.3–4, and TsRP, 89.4–6. The DNZ recension reads . . . *gsal stong ma 'gags sal le ba/ sing nge ye re 'dug pa de* . . . ; the *Moonbeams* citation (*MB* VVI 482.15) and the TsRP recension read . . . *gsal stong ma 'gags mtha' dbus med/ sing nge ye re gnas pa de* . . .
1406. *Condensed Verses on the Four Yogas.*
1407. *Consummate Sublime Path of Mahāmudrā.* DNZ, 450.4–5.
1408. *Condensed Verses on the Four Yogas. MB* VVI (483.13): *spros bral spros bral* should read *spros dang spros bral.* See *MB* VVI (509.8) and Collected Works of Pakmo Drupa edition.
1409. *Consummate Sublime Path of Mahāmudrā.* DNZ, 450.6–7.
1410. *Condensed Verses on the Four Yogas.*
1411. *Consummate Sublime Path of Mahāmudrā.* DNZ, 451.2–3.
1412. In Yang Gönpa's *Treasury of the Ultimate Essence*, 144.2–3.
1413. *Uncommon Amṛta of Speech*, 18b.
1414. In Yang Gönpa's *Treasury of the Ultimate Essence*, 144.4–5. The *Treasury of the Ultimate Essence* recension reads . . . *stong rdzis khyer/* . . . *sba la g.yengs/* . . . *sprin gyis bkag*; the *Moonbeams* citation (*MB* VVI 486.1–2) reads . . . *stong rtsis khyer/* . . . *rba la g.yengs/* . . . *sprin gyis bkab.*

1415. In Yang Gönpa's *Treasury of the Ultimate Essence*, 144.5–6. The *Treasury of the Ultimate Essence* recension reads . . . *'thas su skye/ . . . sgyu mar skye/ . . . stong par skye/ . . . snying rjer skye*; the *Moonbeams* citation (*MB* VVI 16–17) reads . . . *'thas/ . . . sgyu ma / . . . stong pa / . . . snying rje.*
1416. H.K. 17: vol. 34, 203a.4–5.
1417. *Dohā for the People.* D 2224: vol. 51, 76b.6–7. *MB* VVI (487.12): *yid* should be *ming.* See *MB* DLG (331.7) and D 2224: vol. 51, 76b.6.
1418. *Questions and Answers with Instructions on the Four Yogas*, 582.2–3.
1419. In Yang Gönpa's *Treasury of the Ultimate Essence*, 144.6–145.1.
1420. In Yang Gönpa's *Treasury of the Ultimate Essence*, 144.1–3.
1421. In Yang Gönpa's *Treasury of the Ultimate Essence*, 145.3–5. The *Treasury of the Ultimate Essence* recension reads *rtse gcig man chad la mnyam rjes mtshan nyid pa med/ rang sa'i mnyam rjes yod/ de'i don gyis rjes snang 'ba' zhig yin/ spros bral gyi dus su mnyam rjes shags kyis dbye/ . . .* ; the *Moonbeams* citation (*MB* VVI 489.1–2) reads *rtse gcig rang sa'i mnyam rje yod/ spros bral mnyam rjes so sor byed/ . . .*
1422. *Consummate Sublime Path of Mahāmudrā.* DNZ, 451.1–2.
1423. *Consummate Sublime Path of Mahāmudrā.* TsRP, vol. 4, 91.1–3. (Not found in DNZ.)
1424. In Yang Gönpa's *Treasury of the Ultimate Essence*, 145.5–6.
1425. *Uncommon Amṛta of Speech*, 18a.
1426. *Questions and Answers with Instructions on the Four Yogas*, 581.6–582.2. The Collected Works edition reads . . . *phal cher bsgom med btang bar yod*; the *Moonbeams* citation (*MB* VVI 491.8) reads . . . *phal cher sgom med btags par song.* The Collected Works also contains an interlinear note to this line: "Since the mind has nothing to meditate on, it is also said to be "nonmeditation" (*sems la bsgom rgyu med pas bsgom med du 'dod pa yang yod*).
1427. *Questions and Answers with Instructions on the Four Yogas*, 582.3–583.1. The Collected Works edition reads . . . *snying rje 'char thang yin/ . . . 'greng log spyi btsug . . .* ; the *Moonbeams* citation (*MB* VVI 491.15–16) reads . . . *snying rje char thang yin/ . . . 'dre log spyi btsug . . .* The translation follows the Collected Works in reading *'char.*
1428. *Treasury of the Ultimate Essence*, 146.1–3.
1429. *Treasury of the Ultimate Essence*, 146.3–4.
1430. *Treasury of the Ultimate Essence*, 146.5–6.
1431. Source unidentified.
1432. D 4158: vol. 172, 108a.5–6.
1433. *Revealing the Hidden Characteristics of Mind*, 5b.
1434. *The Grand Collection of Dharma Lectures*, 45b.
1435. *Highest Continuum.* D 4024: vol. 123, 57b.3. The Dg.T. recension reads *'phags pas 'chi dang na ba dang . . .* ; the *Moonbeams* citation (*MB* VVI 493.18) reads *'phags pas na dang 'chi ba dang . . .*
1436. D 3871: vol. 105, 32a.3.
1437. D 3871: vol. 105, 32a.2–3. *MB* VVI (494.6): *shes byed la* should be *shes bya la.* See *MB* DLG (337.2) and Dg.T. (32a.2).

1438. *MB* VVI (497.2) and *MB* TsRP (696.5) read *ngo shes*. *MB* DLG (339.5) reads *go shes*, which matches more closely to the point being refuted, and, therefore, has been followed in the translation. *MB* RD (426) reads *nges shes*.

1439. In Yang Gönpa's *Treasury of the Ultimate Essence*, 144.2.

1440. Source not found.

1441. *MB* VVI (497.15): *mnyam rjes rang* should be *mnyam rjes dang*. See *MB* DLG (340.2).

1442. *MB* VVI (498.3–4): *'char sgo 'gags pas na* should be *'char sgo ma 'gags pas na*. See *MB* DLG (340.4).

1443. *MB* VVI (502.2): *'chor 'dod* should be *phyor 'dod*. See *MB* DLG (343.6) and *MB* TsRP (705.3).

1444. This statement is found in Gampopa's Collected Works in five texts: *Abundant Auspiciousness: A Collection of Dharma Lectures* (4b); *Replies to Dusum Khyenpa's Questions* (30a); *Replies to the Exalted Pakmo Drupa's Questions* (10a); *Core of Mahāmudrā: The Instructions on the Ultimate Essence* (6a); and *Esoteric Instructions on the Twofold Abiding State and Esoteric Instructions on Twofold Armor* (21a). There are some slight word variations, mainly between the use of *shes pa* and *rig pa*.

1445. *Questions and Answers with Instructions on the Four Yogas*, 581.2.

1446. *Esoteric Instructions: Illuminating Mahāmudrā*, 4a. This song is also found in *The Flag of Renown: The Biography of Gampopa*, 121.

1447. *Instructions to Parpuwa: Summary of the Glorious Saraha's Five Types of Noncontrivance in Mahāmudrā*, 449.1–2.

1448. D 2224: vol. 51, 71b.2. The Dg.T. recension reads . . . *yod pa de yang* . . . ; the *Moonbeams* citation (*MB* VVI 503.2) reads . . . *yod na de yang* . . .

1449. *Esoteric Instructions: Illuminating Mahāmudrā*, 4a. This song is also found in *The Flag of Renown: The Biography of Gampopa*, 121. The *Moonbeams* citation accords with *The Flag of Renown* in reading *gnyis 'dzin can gyi sgom chen . . . don ma yin*; *Esoteric Instructions: Illuminating Mahāmudrā* reads *gnyis 'dzin ma bral sgom chen . . . don ma mthong*.

1450. D 3824: vol. 96, 1b.2–3. The Dg.T. recension reads . . . *nyer zhi zhi bstan pa*; the *Moonbeams* citation (*MB* VVI 503.13–14) reads . . . *nyer zhi zhi ldan pa*. The cited lines are part of the opening homage, which reads in full (here the translation follows the Dg.T. recension):

> Whatever is dependently arisen has
> neither cessation nor origination,
> neither annihilation nor permanence,
> neither coming nor going,
> neither discreteness nor the sameness:
> elaborations are pacified.
> Homage to the perfect Buddha, the best of orators,
> whose teaching is of peace.

1451. This line is found on p. 275 where it is attributed to the *Play in Full*. See H.K. 96: vol. 48, 305b.7 and note 952 for textual differences.

1452. D 4024: vol. 123, 57b.1.

1453. *Replies to the Exalted Pakmo Drupa's Questions*, 9b.

1454. *Questions and Answers with Instructions on the Four Yogas*, 581.2. The Collected Works edition does not have the line *spros bral dus su song tsam na*, which is found in the *Moonbeams* citation (*MB* VVI 508.2–3).

1455. Source not found.

1456. *Dohā for the Queen*. D 2264: vol. 52, 31b.6–7. The Dg.T. recension reads . . . *thams cad ro gcig par/ ston par* . . . ; the *Moonbeams* citation (508.19–20) reads . . . *thams cad don gcig par/ rtogs par* . . . The translation follows the Dg.T. recension in reading *ro gcig*, which is also found in Karma Tinle's *Mirror That Reveals the Liberation of Mind: The Middle-Length Commentary on the Queen's Dohā*, 170.

1457. *Treasury of Dohā: Instructions on Mahāmudrā*. D 2273: vol. 52, 123a.4–5.

1458. *Condensed Verses on the Four Yogas.*

1459. Although all consulted editions of *Moonbeams* read *nges shes kyi khris yod pa*, Dakpo Tashi Namgyal's *Clarifying the Suchness of the Innate State* (73.5) has the same phrase with one word difference: *nges shes kyi 'khris yod pa*. Later in this section, *Moonbeams* (*MB* VVI 510.13) reads *gnyen po'i khris dang ma bral*, and a corresponding section in *Clarifying the Suchness of the Innate State* (73.14) reads *gnyen po'i 'khris dang ma bral*. I am assuming misprints in *Moonbeams* and am following *Clarifying the Suchness of the Innate State* in reading *'khris*.

1460. In the *Thunderbolt of Instructions on Mahāmudrā and Collection of Songs* (*Phyag rgya chen po'i man ngag thog babs dang mgur 'bum*). Collected Works of Gampopa, text 20/wa. The Collected Works edition reads . . . *dkar po'i chos rnams mi gcog 'tshal/* . . . *thabs kyi zhabs tog mi gcog 'tshal/* . . . *sems nyong mongs kha yan* . . . ; the *Moonbeams* citation (*MB* VVI 512.19–513.3) reads . . . *dkar po'i chos rnams mi cog 'tshal/* . . . *thabs kyi zhabs tog mi bcag 'tshal/* . . . *nyong mongs kha yan* . . .

1461. *MB* VVI (513.12): *rtogs* should be *rtog*. See *MB* DLG (353.3).

1462. Drawn almost verbatim from Pakmo Drupa's *Long Four Yogas* (*rNal 'byor bzhi chen mo*) (Collected Works of Pakmo Drupa, vol. 4/nga, text 10.5, 347.1–348.1); and Jikten Sumgön's *Longer Instructions on the Four Yogas* (*rNal 'byor bzhi'i zhal gdams chen mo*) (Collected Works of Jikten Sumgön, vol. 7, 237.4–238.4).

1463. *Replies to the Exalted Pakmo Drupa's Questions*, 9b.

1464. *Questions and Answers with Instructions on the Four Yogas*, 581.2–3.

1465. Source not found.

1466. This citation is found in the *Guhyasamāja Tantra*. H.K. 416a: vol. 82, 438b.6. While it is not found in the *Kālacakra Tantra* or the *Summary of the [Kālacakra] Initiation*, it is in Nāropa's *Commentary on "The Summary of the [Kālacakra] Initiation": Compendium of the Ultimate* (D 1351: vol. 13, 254a.1–2) where it is attributed to the *Guhyasamāja Tantra*.

1467. *Dohā for the Queen*. D 2264: vol. 52, 29b.4–5. *MB* VVI (514.18): *yong* should be *yod*. See *MB* VVI (368.7 and 437.16).

1468. *Treasury of Dohā: Instructions on Mahāmudrā*. D 2273: vol. 52, 123b.1–2.

1469. *Consummate Sublime Path of Mahāmudrā*. DNZ, 451.2.

1470. *MB* VVI (516.1) and *MB* TsRP (729.5): *gnyis* should probably be *nyid*. See *MB* DLG (355.3).

1471. *Questions and Answers with Instructions on the Four Yogas*, 582.1.

1472. In Yang Gönpa's *Treasury of the Ultimate Essence*, 182.6–183.2.

1473. According to the *Blue Annals*, these are Jikten Sumgön, Bandha Pukpa ('Ban dha phug pa), Chöje Dum (Chos rje lDum), and Chöje Dum (Chos rje gDum), also called the "four sons of instructions" (*gdams pa'i bu bzhi*). See Roerich, *Blue Annals*, 563.

1474. *Replies to the Exalted Pakmo Drupa's Questions*, 9b.

1475. *Questions and Answers with Instructions on the Four Yogas*, 581.4–5.

1476. Source not found.

1477. *MB* VVI (520.2) and *MB* TsRP (736.4): *cir* should be *spyir*. See *MB* DLG (358.6).

1478. D 4158: vol. 172, 108a.5–6.

1479. D 4210: vol. 174, 116a.1.

1480. D 3871: vol. 105, 28b.5–6.

1481. *Dohā for the People*. D 2224: vol. 51, 75a.2–3.

1482. *Dohā for the Queen*. D 2264: vol. 52, 29a.4–5. The Dg.T. recension reads *dngos por rtogs pa phyugs dang 'dra bar brjod/ dngos med rtog pa de bas shin tu blun 'gyur zhes*; the *Moonbeams* citation (521.12–13) reads *dngos por 'dzin pa phyugs dang 'dra bar ste/ dngos med 'dzin pa de bas kyang ni blun*.

1483. *Dohā for the Queen*. D 2224: vol. 51, 71b.2. The Dg.T. recension reads ... *yod pa de yang* ... ; the *Moonbeams* citation (*MB* VVI 521.14) reads ... *yod na de yang* ...

1484. *Revealing the Hidden Characteristics of Mind*, 4b.

1485. *Revealing the Hidden Characteristics of Mind*, 4b.

1486. *Revealing the Hidden Characteristics of Mind*, 5a.

1487. *Revealing the Hidden Characteristics of Mind*, 2b. *MB* VVI (522.7): *spangs* should be *sbags*. See *MB* DLG (360.5) and Collected Works of Gampopa edition.

1488. *Revealing the Hidden Characteristics of Mind*, 5b.

1489. D 3824: vol. 96, 10b.7–11a.1. *MB* VVI (522.16): *mnyam* should be *snyam*. See Dg.T. recension and *MB* VVI (88.17).

1490. *Consummate Sublime Path of Mahāmudrā*. DNZ, 456.3.

1491. *Madhyamakāvatārabhāṣya*, *dBu ma 'jug 'grel / dBu ma la 'jug pa'i bshad pa* by Candrakīrti. Toh. 3862. D 3862: vol. 102, 224a.4 and 230b.6. In the Dg.T. recension the first phrase of the *Moonbeams* citation (*de ni shes pa'i rang bzhin yin pa nyid kyis*) is found on 230b.6 and the second part reads *rang gi ngo bo'i khyad par gyis byas pa'i dbye ba ni yod pa ma yin no/ ji skad du/ ji ltar bar snang* ... ; the *Moonbeams* citation (523.11–13) reads ... *rang gi ngo bo'i sgo nas dbye ba bya bar mi nus te / ji ltar bar snang* ...

The *Sūtra on the Ten Bhūmis* citation: H.K. 94: vol. 43/03, 78b.4–5. The H.K. recension reads *ji ltar bar snang gnas kyi bya yi rjes/ shin tu smra dka' bstan par mi nus pa/ de ltar bde gshegs sras kyi sa rnams kyang/ yid dang sems kyi yul gyis shes mi nus*; the *Moonbeams* citation (523.12–14) reads *ji ltar bar snang bya rjes mkhas rnams kyis/ brjod par nus ma yin shing mi mthong ba/ de bzhin rgyal ba'i sras kyi sa kun yang/ brjod mi nus na mnyan par ga la nus.*

The *Moonbeams* citation of the *Commentary on the "Entrance to the Middle Way"* is identical to the one found in Gö Lotsāwa's *Mirror Illuminating Suchness: A Commentary on the "Highest Continuum,"* 73.10–12.

1492. *Abhisamayālaṃkāra-nāma-prajñāpāramitopadeśaśāstravṛtti, 'Grel pa don gsal / Shes rab kyi pha rol tu phyin pa'i man ngag gi bstan bcos mngon par rtogs pa'i rgyan zhes bya ba'i 'grel pa* by Haribhadra. Toh. 3793. D 3793: vol. 86, 85a.4–5. *MB* VVI (523.16): *lam gyi mngon sum* should be *lam gyis mngon sum*. See *MB* DLG (361.6) and the Dg.T. recension.

1493. *Consummate Sublime Path of Mahāmudrā*. DNZ, 456.3–4. *MB* VVI (524.1): *lhag gi* should be *lhag gis*. See DNZ (456.3) and TsRP (103.2) recensions.

1494. *Questions and Answers with Instructions on the Four Yogas*, 583.4–6.

1495. Source not found.

1496. *MB* VVI (526.3): *mkhyen ldan rnam kyi* should be *mkhyen ldan rnam kyis*. See *MB* DLG (363.7).

1497. *Analysis of the Three Vows*, 88.4–7. *MB* VVI (526.11): *sangs rgyas so* should be *sangs rgyas sa*. See *MB* DLG (364.3) and *Analysis of the Three Vows*. Sakya Paṇḍita's notes state that the proponents of this schema are those who accept the oral instructions of Kor Nirupa. For some information on Kor Nirupa, see Roberts, *Mahāmudrā and Related Instructions*, 11; and Schaeffer, *Dreaming the Great Brahmin*, 66–67.

1498. *Analysis of the Three Vows*, 89.3.

1499. *Analysis of the Three Vows*, 63.16–18.

1500. *MB* VVI (526.19): *thob pa las* should be *thob pa la sa*. See *MB* DLG (364.5).

1501. *MB* VVI (527.7): *thob pa las* should probably be *thob pa la sa*. See *MB* DLG (365.1).

1502. See H.K. 94: vol. 43/03, 94a.1–3. *Moonbeams* paraphrases the H.K. recension and seems to be drawn from Gö Lotsāwa's *Mirror Illuminating Suchness: A Commentary on the "Highest Continuum,"* 74.3–5.

1503. *MB* VVI (527.15): *rdzun rig* should be *rdzun rib*. See *MB* DLG (365.3).

1504. This may be in reference to statements by Zhang Rinpoche in his *Consummate Sublime Path of Mahāmudrā*. See TsRP, 91.6–92.1; and Roberts, *Mahāmudrā and Related Instructions*, 114.

1505. *Analysis of the Three Vows*, 62.22–63.1.

1506. *Caturdevī-paripṛcchā, Lha mo bzhis yongs su zhus pa*. Toh. 446, H.K. 420. H.K. 420: vol. 83, 189a.1–2. The commentaries on this tantra by Smṛtijñānakīrti and Jñānagarbha explain that "karmic body" (*las kyi lus*) means the body of the latent tendencies of the virtuous karma of meditating on your body as the maṇḍala of the deities. "A similar body will manifest" means yogins and yoginīs will achieve the maṇḍala of body, which is the attainment of nonabiding nirvāṇa.

See Smṛtijñānakīrti's *Commentary on "Questions of the Four Goddesses"* (*Caturdevatāparipṛcchāvyākhyāna-upadeśapauṣṭika, Lha mo bzhis yongs su zhus pa'i rnam par bshad pa man ngag rgyas pa*) (Toh. 1915; D 1915: vol. 45, 230b.4–6);

and Jñānagarbha's *Commentary on "Questions of the Four Goddesses"* (*Caturdevatāparipṛcchāṭīkā, Lha mo bzhis yongs su zhus pa'i rnam par bshad pa*) (Toh. 1916; D 1916: vol. 45, 255a.4–7).

1507. H 396: vol. 81, 357a.3.

1508. *Consummate Sublime Path of Mahāmudrā.* The *Moonbeams* citation accords with the TsRP, 103.5–104.1. In the DNZ, the first three lines of the *Moonbeams* citation are on 456.4–5 and the last five on 455.3–4.

1509. *Questions and Answers with Instructions on the Four Yogas,* 583.6–584.2. The Collected Works edition reads . . . *yon tan bshad tshod bstan bstun gnyis* . . . ; the *Moonbeams* citation (*MB* VVI 528.16) reads . . . *yon tan bshad tshod bstan thub gnyis* . . .

1510. *Letter to a Friend.* D 4182: vol. 173, 43a.6.

1511. Although all the consulted editions of *DDI* read *'char ba'i zhi gnas skyon med de bzhin yang rgyud la skye,* since a corresponding section in *Pointing Out the Dharmakāya* (*Chos sku mdzub tshugs*) (363.1) has *'char bas 'di bzhin rgyud la skyes,* it is assumed that the text in *DDI* should be *'char bas.*

1512. *DDI* RD (316.9–10): *cang med gcig tu smra mi shes pa zhig 'dug gnas pa'i ngo bo de'ang shes pa nag thos me ba zhig 'dug gam gnas pa'i ngang* should be *cang med gcig 'dug gam gnas pa'i ngang.* See *DDI* PP (390.5).

1513. *DDI* RD (319.3): reading *sems de'ang 'dzin med gsal med du shig ge ba* as *sems de'ang 'dzin med gal med du shig ge ba* following *NG* RD (188.1).

1514. *DDI* RD (323.10): *med re ba* should be *mer re ba.* See *DDI* PP (398.5).

1515. *DDI* RD (326.7): *bros* should be *blos.* See *DDI* PP (401.7).

1516. *Chos sku mdzub tshugs* by the Ninth Karmapa, Wangchuk Dorje.

1517. Although the consulted editions of *DDI* read *stong nyid lam shor,* it should be *stong nyid gnyen por shor ba.*

1518. Although the text does not refer to any section here as part 4, "The Five Difficult Passages" are probably part 4 and "Hindrances" are part 5.

1519. This probably refers to the tradition of Pakmo Drupa continued on at his monastery, Densatil, possibly directly linked to Chen-nga Drakpa Jungnay (sPyan snga Grags pa 'byung gnas) (1175–1255), the disciple of Jikten Gönpo who succeeded Pakmo Drupa as abbot of Densatil.

1520. This closing phrase "śubham astu sarva-jagatām" means "May the whole world be pure/prosperous/fortunate," "May there be auspiciousness throughout the whole world."

Glossary

appearing yet not ascertained (*snang la ma nges pa*). This term refers to when objects appear to the mind and, although it experiences, or perceives, them, the mind does not ascertain or recognize them. It is a category of direct cognition or awareness (*mngon sum*), demonstrating that not all direct cognition recognizes its object. Although, as direct cognition, it is an unmistaken and nonconceptual state of mind, because it may be focused elsewhere or is very brief, there is no ascertainment. A common example is when walking down a busy street and focused on a conversation with someone else, we do not identify the other people walking by. We have had direct cognition of others passing by and are not mistaken about that but we have no certainty about who they were.

arhats with twofold liberation (*gnyis ka'i cha las rnam par grol ba'i dgra bcom pa*). Arhats who are liberated from both the afflictive obscurations (*nyon sgrib*) and the obscurations to absorption (*snyoms 'jug gi sgrib pa*).

ascertainment of simultaneous observation (*lhan cig dmigs nges*). Reasoning used in the Yogācāra system to prove that the perceiving subject and its object are not different. When an object appears to the visual consciousness, its appearance and the perception of it occur simultaneously. There is no visual object that is not appearing to a visual consciousness and no visual consciousness that is not observing an object.

avadhūti (*kun 'dar ma*). The central channel of the subtle body. Often simply transliterated in Tibetan; when translated, it is either *kun 'dar ma* ("all-shaking," "all-vibrating," "all-encompassing," possibly "ascetic") or *kun spang ma* ("all-abandoning," possibly "renunciant"). Ngo-tro Rabjampa in his *Precious Jeweled Garland of Eloquence* (194.6) explains: "It is called avadhūti because it is the path that abandons the two extremes.... It is "all-shaking" because it is [where] the white elements fall."

Barawa Gyaltsen Palzang ('Ba' ra ba rgyal mtshan dpal bzang). 1310–1391. Drukpa Kagyu master and incarnation of Yang Gönpa.

Barom Kagyu ('Ba' rom bka' brgyud). Originates from Gampopa's student Barompa Darma Wangchuk ('Ba' rom pa dar ma dbang phyug) (1127–1199/1200).

bhūmi of beginners (*las dang po'i sa*). The three levels of the path of accumulation.

caṇḍālī (*gtum mo*). In the Kagyu tradition, one of the six dharmas (*chos drug*) of Nāropa. A meditation technique based on the subtle body's channels, winds, and bindus that invokes the realization of bliss-emptiness.

causal condition (*rgyu'i rkyen*). That which assists the arising of its specific result.

channels, winds, and bodhicittas (*rtsa rlung byang chub kyi sems*). The three elements of the subtle body, which correspond to body, speech, and mind. Bodhicittas, in this context, are bindus (*thig le*).

Chegompa (lCe sgom pa / lCe sgom shes rab rdo rje). ca. 1140/50–1220. Chegom Sherab Dorje was a Kadampa teacher, best known for his texts called the Set of Three Heaps (sPung pa rnam gsum). He was a student of Jangchub Nangwa (a student of Potowa) and also associated with the Tropu Kagyu.

Collection of Reasonings (Rigs tshogs). Five texts by Nāgārjuna: *Fundamental Treatise on the Middle Way* (*Prajñā-nāma-mūlamadhyamakakārikā, dBu ma rtsa ba'i tshig le'ur byas pa shes rab*), *Rebuttal of Objections* (*Vigrahavyāvartanīkārikā, rTsod pa bzlog pa'i tshig le'ur byas pa*), *Seventy Verses on Emptiness* (*Śūnyatāsaptati, sTong nyid bdun cu pa*), *Sixty Verses on Reasoning* (*Yukiṣaṣṭīkā, Rigs pa drug cu ba*), and *Thorough Grinding* (*Vaidalya-sūtra, Zhib mo rnam 'thag*). Some lists include a sixth, the *Precious Garland* (*Ratnāvalī, Rin chen phreng ba*).

contamination (*grib*). Caused by contact with "impure" or negative people or their possessions. Could also be translated as "negative influences."

definite goodness (*nges legs*). Lasting happiness: the states of liberation and omniscience.

Dharma Cycle on Amanasikāra [Non-Attention] (A ma na si'i chos skor). See twenty-four texts in the Dharma Cycle on Amanasikāra [Nonattention] in the Glossary of Enumerations.

dohā (*do ha*). The name of the dominant poetic meter of Apabhraṃśa, a late Middle Indo-Aryan dialect. The term, which is Apabhraṃśa (though may be derived from Sanskrit terms for couplets), has come to be used for the spiritual songs composed in its meter.

Dohā Trilogy (Do ha skor gsum). See Glossary of Enumerations.

dominant condition (*bdag rkyen*). That which primarily produces its specific result by its own power.

Dorje Sherab (rDo rje shes rab). ca. 12th century. Student of both Jikten Sumgön and his student Sherab Jungnay.

downward-expelling winds (*thur sel gyi rlung*). One of five root winds. It is associated with the earth element and resides in the lower part of the madhyamā channel. Its function is to retain the quintessences of feces, urine, semen, and blood, and to expel their dregs.

Drikung Kagyu ('Bri gung bka' brgyud). Originates from Pakmo Drupa's student Jikten Sumgön.

Drukpa Kagyu ('Brug pa bka' brgyud). Originates from Pakmo Drupa's student Ling Repa.

emptiness endowed with the most sublime of manifestations (*rnam kun mchog ldan gyi stong nyid*). Dak Rampa in his *Ornament for Liberating the Mind* says, "'Endowed with the most sublime of manifestations' is explained in two ways. In the Pāramitāyāna it means to be endowed with the most sublime of the manifestations of method: generosity and the other [pāramitās]. The *Kālacakra Tantra* and other texts teach that it means that all the manifestations of knowable objects are clarity."

engagement through belief (*mos spyod*). This refers, broadly speaking, to the first two paths (the paths of accumulation and preparation), though, in some cases, it refers only to the path of preparation.

fire-coinciding wind (*me mnyam rlung*). One of five root winds. It is associated with the wind element, and it resides in a channel at the heart and enters the stomach. Its function is to digest food and drink, to separate quintessences (*dvangs ma*) from dregs (*snyigs ma*), and to distribute the quintessences throughout the body.

generally characterized (*spyi'i mtshan pa*). Generally characterized phenomena, or universals, are the general conceptual category of objects, contrasted with a specifically characterized phenomenon, or particular.

ghaṭikā (or *nāḍī*, *chu tshod*, "water-measure"). A time period equivalent to 360 breaths, or twenty-four minutes. It was measured by one of two types of ancient Indian water clocks (an outflow type or floating-bowl type). There are sixty ghaṭikās in one solar day.

Gomchung (sGom chung shes rab byang chub). 1130–1173. Gampopa's youngest nephew and brother of Gomtsul; third throne-holder of Daklha Gampo monastery.

Gomtsul (sGom tshul / sGom po tshul khrims snying po). 1116–1169. Gampopa's eldest nephew and second throne-holder of Daklha Gampo monastery.

gotra (*rigs*). The potential, or affinity, for awakening that all beings possess.

Götsangpa (rGod tshang pa). 1189–1258. Student of Tsangpa Gyare, founder of the Upper Druk tradition. His best-known students are Yang Gönpa and Orgyenpa.

happy states (*bde 'gro*). The three higher states of gods, demigods, and humans.

Heshang Moheyan (Hva shang ma hA ya na). The Chinese monk (heshang or upādhyāya) who, according to Tibetan sources, propounded a doctrine of "instantaneous awakening" and, after being defeated in debate with the Indian master Kamalaśīla, was banished from Tibet. Chinese sources dispute this account.

immediate condition (*de ma thag rkyen*). That which primarily produces mere clear and aware consciousness.

isolate (*ldog pa*). An isolate (or reverse, distinguisher) is a conceptual object and refers to the conceptual process of isolation or elimination, which operates whenever we think of something. For example, when we think "impermanent phenomena," we conceptually exclude or eliminate everything that is not an impermanent phenomenon, and we isolate the notion of "impermanent phenomena."

Jikten Sumgön ('Jig rten gsum mgon). 1143–1217. Student of Pakmo Drupa, founder of the Drikung Kagyu lineage, propounder of the Single Intent (dGongs gcig) teachings.

Kadam (bKa gdams). Tradition of teachings originating in Tibet with Atīśa, whose popularity led to it being gradually absorbed into the other main Tibetan religious traditions, Kagyu, Sakya, and Geluk being the primary ones with the latter sometimes referred to as New Kadampa.

Karma Kagyu (Karma bka' brgyud). Originates from Gampopa's student the First Karmapa, Dusum Khyenpa (Dus gsum mkhyen pa) (1110–1193).

Könchok Yenlak (dKon mchog yan lag). The Fifth Shamarpa (1525–1583), who was a student of the Eighth Karmapa, Mikyö Dorje, and teacher of the Ninth Karmapa, Wangchuk Dorje.

kusāli (*ku su lu / ku su li / ku sa li*). Probably derived from the Sanskrit *kuśali* or *kuśala*, "possessor of virtue." It is used in Tibetan to refer to someone who practices in a simple, experiential way, often someone without a scholarly background. It also in some contexts can refer to a beggar or simple hermit.

kusāli, offerings and generosity of a (*ku su lu'i mchod spyin*). An imagined offering of one's own body as is done in the practice of Chö (gCod). Kusālis, or beggars, lack possessions so they make offerings of their own body.

life-force wind (*srog 'dzin rlung*). One of five root winds. It is associated with the space element and resides in the madhyamā channel. Its function is to provide a sense of self and memories (and mindfulness).

Ling Repa (gLing ras pa). 1128–1188. Student of Pakmo Drupa and teacher of Tsangpa Gyare; the founder of the Drukpa Kagyu lineage.

longer and shorter dohā texts (*do ha'i gzung che chung*). Some consider this to refer to Saraha's Dohā Trilogy and the Eightfold Treasury of Shorter Dohās. Others regard it as referring to Saraha's *Dohā for the People* and *Dohā for the King*.

madhyamā (*dbu ma*). The central channel of the subtle body. Also called avadhūti (*kun 'dar ma*).

Martsang Kagyu (sMar tshang bka' brgyud). Founded by Pakmo Drupa's student Marpa Sherab Yeshe (sMar pa shes rab ye shes) (1135–1203).

misinterpretations/superimpositions (*sgro 'dogs*). To take something to exist in a way that it does not, as in ascribing true existence to something that does not truly exist.

negative states (*ngan 'gro*). The three lower states of the hell-beings, hungry ghosts, and animals.

nonanalytical cessations (*so sor brtags pa ma yin pa'i 'gog pa*). Nonanalytical cessations, or cessations not resulting from knowledge, are temporary absences of mental afflictions owing to the incompleteness of the necessary conditions. For example, when one concentrates intently on a specific task, one does not feel tired, but feelings of tiredness will return.

nonimplicative negation (*med dgag*). A negation that does not indicate or imply anything in place of its object of negation. The other main type of negation used in Indo-Tibetan debate is an implicative negation (*ma yin dgag*), which implies or affirms something in place of the object of negation.

nonreturners who physically actualize [nirvāṇa] (***phyir mi 'ong lus mngon byed***). One of four main categories of Abiders in the Result of a Nonreturner (Phyir mi 'ong ba'i 'bras gnas).

object condition (***dmigs pa'i rkyen***). That which primarily produces a consciousness with the aspect of itself as its specific result.

Pakmo Drupa (Phag mo gru pa). 1110–1170. Student of Gampopa; founder of the Pakdru Kagyu lineage, one of the four main Kagyu traditions. Eight of his students were the initiators of the eight Kagyu sub-schools: Drikung, Drukpa, Taklung, Martsang, Yelpa, Yasang, Tropu, and Shukseb.

pāṇīpala (***chu srang,*** **"water weights").** The period of time it takes to breathe in and out six times. Sixty pāṇīpalas make up one ghaṭikā. One pāṇīpala is equivalent to twenty-four seconds.

path of method (***thabs lam***). In the Kagyu tradition, this is the completion stage practices of the six dharmas of Nāropa: caṇḍālī (*gtum mo*), illusory body (*sgyu lus*), dream (*rmi lam*), luminosity (*'od gsal*), transference (*'pho ba*), and *bardo* (*bar do*).

pervading wind (***khyab byed rlung***). One of five root winds. It is associated with the water element, and it resides in a channel at the heart and connects with the right, rasanā, channel. Its function is to provide physical strength, particularly in the limbs.

Pinnacle of Existence (Srid pa'i rtse mo). Another name for Neither Discrimination nor Nondiscrimination ('Du shes med min gyi skye mched), the fourth and final sphere of the formless realm.

poṣadha (***gso sbyong,*** **"purification-renewal").** In some contexts, this refers to eight vows, which include celibacy, taken for one day. In other contexts, *poṣadha* is the monastic confession ceremony.

postmeditative attainment (***rjes thob***). The period following meditative equipoise. Although often translated simply as "postmeditation," it refers to the level of realization of emptiness that is attained when emerging from meditative equipoise. This is then applied to seeing the illusionlike nature of all appearances and experiences while cultivating the six pāramitās. True meditative equipoise and postmeditative attainment do not occur until the attainment of the first bhūmi in the Pāramitā path or freedom from elaborations in the Mahāmudrā path.

qualitative aspect [of phenomena] (***ji snyed yod par gyur pa***). A term meaning "as much as there is," and signifying all conventional phenomena.

quantitative aspect [of phenomena] (***ji lta ba bzhin du gyur pa***). The ultimate aspect of phenomena, their dharmatā.

Rangjung Dorje (Rang byung rdo rje). 1284–1339. The Third Karmapa and author of *The Profound Inner Principles* (*Zab mo nang don*), *Mahāmudrā Aspiration Prayer* (*Phyag chen smon lam*), and other philosophical works.

reasons having the three modes (*tshul gsum pa can gyi rtags*). In Buddhist logic, three modes (or criteria) (*tshul gsum*) are examined to determine whether a reason is valid or not: the subject property, the positive entailment, and the negative entailment. These are concerned with the reason's relationship to the subject and to the predicate. If they are determined to be correct, the reason is a valid means to establish what is to be proven.

repa (*ras pa*). Repas, or "cotton-clad ones," are meditators who, owing to their mastery of caṇḍālī, wear cotton clothing.

rock crushing / pulverizing bones (*rdo rus 'phrod pa / thug pa*). Tibetan dictionaries explain that the phrase means perseverance or effort, which is needed when one pulverizes bones. The annotation in the *Blue Annals*, presumably from Gendün Chöpel, says: "a famous saying often quoted in religious texts, meaning that if one wishes to eat the marrow of the bone, one should crush the bone with a stone. In meditation there is need of a direct contact between the Mind and the Doctrine." (Roerich, *Blue Annals*, 944).

root winds (*rtsa ba'i rlung*). There are five root winds (*vāyu*, *rlung*): life-force (*prāṇa*, *srog*), downward-expelling (*apāna*, *thur sel*), upward-moving (*udāna*, *gyen rgyu*), fire-coinciding (*samāna*, *me mnyam / me dang mnyam par gnas pa*), and pervading (*vyāna*, *khyab byed*).

Saraha senior and junior (Sa ra ha che chung). The Great Brahmin Saraha is the senior Saraha, and his student Śavaripa is the junior Saraha.

secondary winds (*yan lag gi rlung*). There are five secondary winds: *nāga* (*klu*), tortoise (*kūrma*, *rus sbal*), lizard (*kṛkara*, *rtsangs pa*), *devadatta* (*lha sbyin*), and *dhanaṃjaya* (*nor las rgyal*). Their primary functions are related to the five senses. (Note that the Sanskrit *kṛkara/kṛkala* is "partridge," whereas the Tibetan *rtsangs pa* is "lizard.")

self-liberating / free in itself (*rang grol*). A phrase meaning to be free in and of itself: being free in itself, it "frees" itself only by means of itself. Its nature is one of freedom or liberation. There is neither something to be liberated nor any agent doing the liberating. It could also be translated as "intrinsically liberated/free." It is translated elsewhere variously as "self-releasing," "self-subsiding," or "natural release."

Serdingpa (gSer sdings pa). Probably Serdingpa Zhön-nu Ö (gSer sdings pa gzhon nu 'od). ca. 1100. A teacher in the Guhyasamāja transmission.

Shukseb Kagyu (Shug gseb bka' brgyud). Originates from Pakmo Drupa's student Gyer-gom Tsultrim Seng-ge (Gyer sgom tshul khrims seng ge) (1144–1204).

Sönam Lhundrup (bSod nams lhun grub). 1488–1552. Sixteenth throne-holder of Daklha Gampo monastery, uncle of Dakpo Tashi Namgyal, and author of *The Flag of Renown*: *The Biography of Gampopa.*

specifically characterized (*rang mtshan pa*). In a technical philosophical sense, a specifically characterized phenomenon, or particular, is a concrete phenomenon that has its own specific, unique characteristics, contrasted with generally characterized phenomena, or universals. The term is also used in *Moonbeams* in a less technical way, such as in referring to our normal, unrecognized thoughts with the phrase "usual thoughts" (*rnam rtog rang mtshan pa*).

spontaneous existence (*lhun gyis grub pa*). A term pointing to the fact that all that is empty is also apparent and has always been that way. Also translated elsewhere as "spontaneous presence," "natural presence."

stable karma (*mi g.yo ba'i las*). Stable karma (or unmoving karma) is the special mental state of the main absorptions of the four meditative concentrations and four formless states. Its maturation does not occur, or move to, anywhere but its originating states, which are the form and formless realms.

substantial cause (*nyer bar len pa'i rgyu*). That which primarily produces the continuum of its own substance as its specific result.

supercognitive abilities (*mngon par shes pa*). Usually listed as the following five: magical powers (*rdzu 'phrul*), divine eye (*lha'i mig*), divine ear (*lha'i rna*), recollection of previous lives (*sngon gnas rjes dran*), and knowledge of others' minds (*gzhan sems shes pa*).

Taklung Kagyu (sTag lung bka' brgyud). Founded by Pakmo Drupa's student Taklung Tangpa Tashi Pal (sTag lung thang pa bkra shis dpal) (1142–1209/1210).

tīrthikas (*mu stegs pa*, "forders"). A term used for non-Buddhist spiritual practitioners in India. Jamgön Kongtrul (*TOK*, vol. 2, 335) explains that it means that they remain at the edge (*mu*) of, or on a rung (*stegs*) to, liberation; that is, they approach liberation, but they are not on the path to the true nirvāṇa.

transparency (*zang thal*). A term that means "unobstructed," "transparent," and "omnipresent" or "all-pervasive." It is also translated elsewhere as "penetrating" or "all-penetrating," as well as many other ways.

Tropu Kagyu (Khro phu bka' brgyud). Originates from Pakmo Drupa's student Gyaltsa Rinchen Gön (rGyal tsha rin chen mgon) (1118–1195).

trulkhor (*yantra*, *'phrul 'khor*). Yogic exercises, usually associated with caṇḍālī meditation.

tsa-tsa (*tsha tsha*). Small clay images of deities or stūpas made from a mold or with a stamp.

Tsalpa Kagyu (Tshal pa bka' brgyud). Originates from Zhang Tsöndru Drakpa.

Tsang Nyön Heruka (gTsang smyon he ru ka). 1452–1507. Author of the *Biography and Songs of the Great Lord of Yogins, Milarepa*, and *Seeing Is Meaningful: The Biography of the Translator Marpa Lotsāwa*.

Tsangpa Gyare (gTsang pa rgya ras). 1161–1211. Student of Ling Repa and founder of Druk monastery ('Brug dgon). He extracted teachings on "Equal Taste" (Ro snyom) hidden by Rechungpa. His two most well-known students are Götsangpa and Lorepa, founders of the Upper Druk and Lower Druk, respectively.

Tsongkhapa (Tsong kha pa). 1357–1419. Founder of the Geluk school and author of the *Great Treatise on the Stages of the Path to Awakening* and many other famous works.

Udraka (Lhag spyod). Udraka Rāmaputra was one of two teachers from whom the Buddha received instructions. Udraka taught a meditation system that led to the state of Neither Discrimination nor Nondiscrimination, the fourth sphere of the formless realm. After achieving that and realizing it was not liberation from saṃsāra, the Buddha set out on his own to achieve awakening.

upāsaka (*dge bsnyen*). A lay person observing vows of individual liberation (*prātimokṣa, so sor thar pa*).

upward-moving wind (*gyen rgyu'i rlung*). One of five root winds. It is associated with the fire element and resides in a channel at the heart. Its function is to perform activities related to the throat (such as swallowing) and the physical and verbal expressions used during the performing arts.

vase-breathing (*kumbhaka, bum can*). A form of breath retention usually involving four parts: inhaling (*brngub*), filling (*gang*), dispersing (*gzhil*), and releasing like an arrow (*mda' ltar 'phang ba*).

Yabzang Kagyu (g.Ya' bzang bka' brgyud). Originates from Pakmo Drupa's student Yabzang Chöje Chökyi Monlam (g.Ya' bzang chos rje chos kyi smon lam) (1169–1223).

Yang Gönpa (Yang dgon pa). 1213–1258. Student of Götsangpa, Drikung Chennga Drakpa Jungnay (the fourth throne-holder of Drikung Til monastery), and the Sakya masters Kodrakpa Sönam Gyaltsen and Sakya Paṇḍita.

Yelpa Kagyu (Yel pa bka' brgyud). Originates from Pakmo Drupa's student Yelpa Yeshe Tsek (Yel pa ye shes brtsegs) (1134–1194).

Zhang / Zhang Tsöndru Drakpa (Zhang / Zhang brtson 'grus grags pa). 1123–1193. Student of Gampopa's nephew Gomtsul and initiator of the Tsalpa Kagyu tradition, sometimes also called Zhang Kagyu (Zhang bka' brgyud).

Glossary of Enumerations

2

two categorizations of śamatha in terms of its nature (*zhi gnas kyi dbye ba la ngo bo'i sgo nas phye na gnyis*). Mundane śamatha (*'jig rten pa'i zhi gnas*) and transmundane śamatha (*'jig rten las 'das pa'i zhi gnas*).

two great chariot-systems (*shing rta chen po rnam pa gnyis*). The system of profound view (*zab mo lta ba'i srol*) founded by Nāgārjuna and the system of vast conduct (*rgya chen spyod pa'i srol*) founded by Asaṅga.

two processes (*rim gnyis*). The generation (*utpattikrama, bskyed rim*) and perfection processes (*utpannakrama/niṣpannakrama/sampannakrama, rdzogs rim*). Also translated elsewhere as "creation stage" and "completion stage."

two types of connateness (*lhan skyes gnyis*). Natural connateness (*rang bzhin lhan skyes*) and the connateness of melting bliss (*zhu bde lhan skyes*), or the connateness of mind-itself (*sems nyid lhan cig skyes pa*) and the connateness of appearances (*snang ba lhan cig skyes pa*).

two types of mindfulness (*dran pa gnyis*). Mindfulness that leads to mindfulness (*dran pa 'dren par byed pa'i dran pa*) and mindfulness that focuses on mindfulness (*dran pa la dmigs pa'i dran pa*), or mindfulness involving effort (*rtsol bcas kyi dran pa*) and effortless mindfulness (*rtsol med kyi dran pa*).

two types of objects of meditation for purifying mental afflictions (*nyon mongs rnam sbyong gi dmigs pa gnyis*). Calmness and coarseness (*zhi rags*) and the four truths (*bden pa bzhi*).

3

Dohā Trilogy (Do ha skor gsum). Three texts by Saraha: *Dohā for the King* (*rGyal po do ha*), also known as *Treasury of Dohā: Songs on Conduct* (*Dohakoṣa-nāma-caryāgīti, Do ha mdzod ces bya ba spyod pa'i glu*); *Dohā for the Queen* (*bTsun mo Do ha*), also known as *Song of an Inexhaustible Treasure of Instruction* (*Dohākoṣopadeśagīti, Mi zad pa'i gter mdzod man ngag gi glu*); and *Dohā for the People* (*dMangs do ha*), also known as *Song That Is a Treasury of Dohās* (*Doha-koṣagīti, Do ha mdzod kyi glu*).

three attachments (*zhen pa gsum*). Attachment to one's sense of self (*bdag tu zhen pa*), attachment to possessions (*longs spyod la zhen pa*), and attachment to samādhi (*ting nge 'dzin la zhen pa*).

three categorizations of śamatha in terms of its functions (*zhi gnas kyi dbye ba la byed las kyi sgo na phye na gsum*). *Moonbeams* only lists the first: the śamatha of resting at ease in the present life (*mthong chos la bde bar gnas pa'i* *zhi gnas*). This may be a reference to a threefold categorization of meditative concentration, the first of which is the meditative concentration of resting at ease in the present life (*mthong chos bder gnas kyi bsam gtan*). According to the *TOK*, the other two meditative concentrations are the meditative concentration aimed at acquiring good qualities (*yon tan sgrub pa'i bsam gtan*) and the meditative concentration of working for the welfare of others (*sems can gyi don la dmigs pa'i bsam gtan*). According to the *Dharmasaṅgraha-Kośaḥ*, the second is the meditative concentration aimed at acquiring supercognitive abilities (*mngon par shes pa mngon par sgrub pa'i bsam gtan*). See Kongtrul, *Treasury of Knowledge: Buddhist Ethics*, 202; and Negi, *Dharmasaṅgraha-Kośaḥ*, 401–402.

three conditions (*rkyen gsum*). In this context: bliss (*bde*), clarity (*gsal*), and nonconceptuality (*mi rtog pa*). See Kongtrul, *Treasury of Knowledge: Book Esoteric Instructions*, 221. The three conditions are enumerated differently in other contexts.

three divisions of the Secret Mantrayāna (*gsang sngags kyi theg pa phye ba gsum*). The path of blessings (*byin rlabs kyi lam*), path of reviving (*dbugs dbyung gi lam*), and path of direct cognition (*mngon sum gyi lam*), according to some of the Symbolic Transmission of Mahāmudrā Cycle (Phyag chen brda brgyud kyi skor).

three doors of vipaśyanā (*lhag mthong gi sgo gsum*). Vipaśyanā that engages with just characteristics (*mtshan ma tsam gyi rjes su zhugs pa'i lhag mthong*), vipaśyanā that engages with thorough investigation (*yongs su btsal ba'i rjes su zhugs pa'i lhag mthong*), and vipaśyanā that engages with the discernment of the thorough investigation (*yongs su btsal ba la so sor rtog pa'i rjes su zhugs pa'i lhag mthong*). (*Śrāvakabhūmi*, Dg.T. 134a.4–5.)

three paths (*lam gsum*). According to Gampopa's teachings, there are three ways to categorize the path as threefold. First: the path that utilizes inferential cognition (*rjes dpag lam du byed pa*), the path that utilizes blessings (*byin rlabs lam du byed pa*), and the path that utilizes direct cognition (*mngon sum lam du byed pa*). Second: the path that abandons the bases (*gzhi spong ba'i lam*), the path that transforms the bases (*gzhi bsgyur ba'i lam*), and the path that recognizes the bases (*gzhi shes pa'i lam*). Third: the paths of the Pāramitās (Pha rol tu phyin pa), Secret Mantra (gSang sngags), and Mahāmudrā (Phyag rgya chen po).

three planes (*sa gsum*). Below the earth (*sa 'og*), on the earth (*sa steng*), and above the earth (*sa bla*).

three pure bhūmis (*dag pa'i sa gsum*). The eighth, ninth, and tenth bhūmis.

three reference points (*dmigs pa gsum*). Equivalent to the three spheres (*'khor lo gsum*) of agent, action, and object of the action.

three representations (*rten gsum*). Statues, texts, and stūpas, representing awakened body, speech, and mind.

three seals (*rgya gsum*). Maturation sealing the body (*rnam smin lus rgya*), latent tendencies sealing appearances (*bag chags snang rgya*), and consciousnesses sealing the mind (*rnam shes sems rgya*).

three types of conduct (*spyod pa gsum*). Elaborate conduct (*spros bcas*), unelaborate conduct (*spros med*), and very unelaborate conduct (*shin tu spros med khyi spyod pa*); or secret conduct (*gsang spyod*), conduct of discipline (*brtul zhugs kyi spyod pa*), and conduct that is victorious in all directions (*phyogs las rnam rgyal gyi spyod pa*).

three types of connateness (*lhan skyes gsum*). Natural connateness (*rang bzhin lhan skyes*), the connateness of melting bliss (*zhu bde lhan skyes*), and the connateness of bliss-emptiness (*bde stong lhan skyes*); or the connateness of mind-itself (*sems nyid lhan cig skyes pa*), the connateness of appearances (*snang ba lhan cig skyes pa*), and the connateness of thoughts (*rnam rtog lhan cig skyes pa*).

three types of faith (*dad pa gsum*). Inspired faith (*dang ba'i dad pa*), aspiring faith (*'dod pa'i dad pa*), and trusting faith (*yid ches pa'i dad pa*).

three types of laziness (*le lo gsum*). *Moonbeams* lists [self-]reproach (*smad pa*), idleness (*snyom las*), and discouragement (*sgyid lug pa*). *GTCD* lists the laziness of being attached to negative actions (*bya ba ngan zhen gyi le lo*), the laziness of discouragement (*sgyid lugs pa'i le lo*), and the laziness of self-contempt (*rang la brnyas pa'i le lo*).

three types of suffering (*sdug bsngal gsum*). Suffering related to sufferings (*sdug bsngal gyi sdug bsngal*), suffering related to changes (*'gyur ba'i sdug bsngal*), and suffering related to conditioned existence (*'du byed kyi sdug bsngal*).

three types of vipaśyanā (*lhag mthong gi dbye ba gsum*). One categorization is the vipaśyanā that arises from characteristics (*mtshan ma las byung ba*), the vipaśyanā that arises from thorough investigation (*yongs su 'tshol ba las byung ba*), and the vipaśyanā that arises from discernment (*so sor rtog pa las byung ba*). Another categorization is mundane vipaśyanā (*'jig rten pa'i lhag mthong*), a lesser type of supramundane vipaśyanā (*'jig rten las 'das pa dman pa'i lhag mthong*), and Mahāyāna vipaśyanā (*theg chen pa'i lhag mthong*).

three ways thoughts are incorporated into the path (*rtog pa lam du byed tshul gsum*). As the impact of meeting (*phrad 'joms*), as the aftereffect (*phyi bsnyag*), and as nonexistent fantasies (*med sprul*).

three yānas (*theg pa gsum*). A categorization attributed to the Secret Conduct Collection (gSang spyod kyi skor): Philosophical Pāramitāyāna (mTshan nyid par phyin theg pa), Secret Mantra Vajrayāna (gSang sngags rdo rje'i theg pa), and the Yāna of the Unsurpassed Essence (bLa med snying po'i theg pa).

threefold classification of connateness (*lhan skyes gsum*). Ground, path, and fruition connateness (*gzhi lam 'bras bu'i lhan skyes*).

4

four causes (*rgyu bzhi*) [of mental afflictions]. Ignorance (*mi shes pa*), excessive mental afflictions (*nyong mongs mang ba*), carelessness (*bag med pa*), and lack of respect (*ma gus pa*).

four conditions (*rkyen bzhi*). Causal (*rgyu rkyen*), dominant (*bdag rkyen*), object (*dmigs rkyen*), and immediate (*de ma thag rkyen*) conditions.

four daily activities (*spyod lam rnam bzhi*). Walking (*'chag pa*), standing (*'greng ba*), sitting (*'dug pa*), and sleeping (*nyal ba*); or eating (*za*), sitting (*'dug*), moving (*'gro*), and sleeping (*nyal*).

four deviations in relation to emptiness (*stong nyid la shor sa bzhi*). Deviating from, or in relation to, emptiness as the basic nature of knowable objects (*stong nyid shes bya'i gshis la shor ba*), deviating from emptiness as the path (*stong nyid lam du shor ba*), deviating from emptiness as the remedy (*stong nyid gnyen por shor ba*), and deviating from emptiness as the seal (*stong nyid rgyas 'debs su shor ba*).

four feet of miraculous powers (*rdzu 'phrul rkang bzhi*). The samādhis of intention (*'dun pa*), diligence (*brtson 'grus*), mind (*sems*), and analysis (*dpyod pa*).

four joys (*dga' ba bzhi*). Joy (*ānanda, dga' ba*), supreme joy (*paramānanda, mchog dga'*), joy-without-joy / special joy (*viramānanda, dga' bral gyi dga' ba / khyad dga'*), and connate joy (*sahajānanda, lhan cig skyes pa'i dga' ba*).

four methods for resting (*bzhag thabs bzhi*). Remain relaxed (*glod la bzhag pa*), rest in freshness (*so mar bzhag pa*), rest freely (*rang gar bzhag pa*), and rest loosely (*lhug par bzhag pa*).

four objects of meditation shared by śamatha and vipaśyanā (*zhi lhag thun mongs pa'i dmigs pa bzhi*). Universal objects of meditation (*khyab pa'i dmigs pa*), objects of meditation for purifying previous behavior (*spyad pa rnam sbyong gi dmigs pa*), objects of meditation for expertise (*mkhas pa'i dmigs pa*), and objects of meditation for purifying mental afflictions (*nyon mongs rnam sbyong gi dmigs pa*).

four powers (*stobs bzhi*). The practice of repudiation (*rnam par sun 'byin pa kun tu spyod pa*), the application of remedies (*gnyen po kun tu spyod pa*), turning away from wrong doing (*nyes pa pas zlog pa*), and the power of reliance (*rten gyi stobs*).

four remedies for laziness (*le lo'i gnyer po bzhi*). Faith (*dad pa*), motivation (*'dun pa*), exertion (*rtsol ba*), and suppleness (*shin sbyangs*). Also referred to as four applications (*'du byed bzhi*).

four rituals for generation (*bskyed chog bzhi*). Four ways of generating oneself as a deity: the fivefold awakening (*abhisaṃbodhi, mngon par byang chub pa lnga*), four vajras (*rdo rje bzhi*), threefold vajra ritual (*rdo rje'i chog gsum*), and complete in the moment of recollection (*skad cig dran rdzogs*).

four spheres / four spheres of the formless realms (*skye mched bzhi / gzugs med skye mched mu bzhi*). The sphere of Limitless Space (Nam mkha' mtha' yas skye mched), the sphere of Limitless Consciousness (rNam shes mtha' yas skye mched), the sphere of Nothingness (Ci yang med pa'i mtha' yas skye mched), and the sphere of Neither Discrimination nor Nondiscrimination ('Du shes med min gyi skye mched). Also called four formless states (*gzugs med pa'i srid pa bzhi*).

Four Syllables of Mahāmudrā (Phyag rgya chen po yi ge bzhi pa) Four instructions Marpa received related to the four syllables of mahāmudrā. They cut through a base or root of mind (*sems kyi gzhi rtsa bcad*), are techniques for resting the mind (*sems kyi bzhag thabs bstan*), eliminate mental strayings (*sems kyi go las spong*), and integrate everything into the path within the mind (*sems kyi lam khyer*). These instructions are found at the end of Marpa's *Vajra Song of the Meaning of the Four Syllables* and in Milarepa's *Instructions on the Four Syllables of Mahāmudrā.*

four types of attention (*yid byed / yid la byed pa bzhi*). Attention that is tightly focused (*bsgrim te 'jug pa*), attention that engages intermittently (*chad cing 'jug pa*), attention that engages uninterruptedly (*chad pa med par 'jug pa*), and attention that engages spontaneously (*lhun grub kyi 'jug pa*).

four types of conduct (*spyod pa bzhi*). *Moonbeams* has two lists. First: excellent conduct (*kun bzang gi spyod pa*), secret, or hidden, conduct (*gsang spyod sbas pa'i spyod pa*), conduct of discipline with awareness (*rig pa brtul zhugs kyi spyod pa*), and conduct that is victorious in all directions (*phyogs las rnam rgyal gyi spyod pa*). Second: conduct for beginners (*las dang po pa'i spyod pa*), conduct of mastering wisdom (*ye shes la dbang ba'i spyod pa*), conduct of greatly mastering wisdom (*ye shes la cher dbang ba'i spyod pa*), and conduct of liberation (*rnam grol gyi spyod pa*). *Dispelling the Darkness of Ignorance* lists excellent conduct (*kun bzang gi spyod pa*), secret conduct (*gsang spyod*), group conduct (*tshogs spyod pa*), and conduct that is victorious in all directions (*phyogs las rnam rgyal gyi spyod pa*). There are other lists elsewhere.

four types of mindfulness (*dran pa bzhi*). Mindfulness that solidifies (*a 'thas kyi dran pa*) or enforced mindfulness (*'jur dran*), mindfulness applied to emptiness (*stong nyid kyi bzung dran*) or the mindfulness that recognizes (*ngo shes kyi dran pa*), true mindfulness (*yang dag gi dran pa*) or mindfulness of unification (*zung 'jug gi dran pa*), and mindfulness that is free from or transcends the intellect (*blo bral lam blo 'das kyi dran pa*).

four types of universal objects of meditation (*khyab pa'i dmigs pa bzhi*). Conceptual representations (*rnam par rtog pa dang bcas pa'i gzugs brnyan*), nonconceptual representations (*rnam par mi rtog pa'i gzugs brnyan*), limits of existence (*dngos po'i mtha'*), and accomplishment of purpose (*dgos pa yongs su grub pa*).

four types of vipaśyanā (*lhag mthong gi dbye ba bzhi*). The differentiation of phenomena (*chos rnam par 'byed par byed pa*), thorough differentiation (*rab tu rnam par 'byed par byed pa*), complete discernment (*yongs su rtogs par byed pa*), and complete analysis (*yongs su dpyod par byed pa*).

four ways of gathering [disciples] (*bsdu pa'i dngos po bzhi*). Being generous with the dharma and material goods, speaking pleasantly, conducting oneself in a meaningful way, and being consistent with the point [of the teachings].

four yogic techniques (*sbyor ba bzhi*). Inhaling (*rngub pa*), filling (*dgang ba*), dispersing (*gzhil ba*), and releasing like an arrow (*mda' ltar 'phang ba*).

5

five buddhas (*sangs rgyas lnga*). Vairocana (rNam par snang mdzad), Ratnasambhava (Rin chen 'byung gnas), Amitābha ('Od dpag med), Amoghasiddhi (Don yon grub pa), and Akṣobhya (Mi bskyod pa).

five components of both siddhanta and karaṇa (*byed grub gyi lnga bsdus*). Weekdays (*res gza'*), lunar days (*tshes zhag*), lunar mansions (*rgyu skar*), yogas (*sbyor ba*), and karaṇas (*byed pa*).

Five Dharma Treatises of Maitreya (Byams chos sde lnga). *Ornament of Clear Realization* (*Abhisamayālaṃkāra, mNgon rtogs rgyan*), *Ornament for the Mahāyāna Sūtras* (*Mahāyānasūtrālaṃkāra, Theg pa chen po mdo sde rgyan*), *Differentiation of the Middle and the Extremes* (*Madhyāntavibhāga, dBus mtha' rnam 'byed*), *Differentiation of Phenomena and Their Nature* (*Dharmadharmatāvibhāga, Chos dang chos nyid rnam 'byed*), and *Highest Continuum* (*Mahāyānottaratantraśāstra, Theg pa chen po rgyud bla ma'i bstan bcos*).

five distractions (*rnam g.yeng lnga*). Distractions of attention (*yid la byed pa'i rnam par g.yengs ba*), external mental distractions (*phyi rol du sems rnam par g.yengs ba*), internal distractions (*nang du rnam par g.yengs ba*), distractions related to characteristics (*mtshan ma'i rnam par g.yengs ba*), and distractions related to negative propensities (*gnas ngan len gyi rnam par g.yengs ba*).

Five Divisions of the *Yogācāryābhūmi* (Sa sde lnga). (1) *Yogācāryābhūmi* (*rNal 'byor spyod pa'i sa*), *Yogācāryābhūmi-śrāvakabhūmi* (*rNal 'byor spyod pa'i sa las nyan thos kyi sa*), and *Yogācāryābhūmi-bodhisattvabhūmi* (*rNal 'byor spyod pa'i sa las byang chub sems dpa'i sa*), (2) *Yogācāryābhūmi viniścayasaṃgraha* (*rNal 'byor spyod pa'i sa rnam par gtan la dbab pa bsdu ba*), (3) *Yogācāryābhūmi vastusaṃgraha* (*rNal 'byor spyod pa'i sa las gzhi bsdu ba*) and *Yogācāryābhūmi vinayasaṃgraha* (*rNal 'byor spyod pa'i sa las 'dul ba bsdu ba*), (4) *Yogācāryābhūmi paryayasaṃgraha* (*rNal 'byor spyod pa'i sa las rnam grangs bsdu ba*), and (5) *Yogācāryābhūmi vivaraṇasaṃgraha* (*rNal 'byor spyod pa'i sa las rnam par bshad pa bsdu ba*). Toh. 4035–43.

five excellences (*phun sum tshogs pa lnga*). Teacher, retinue, place, teaching, and time.

five eyes (*spyan lnga*). Flesh eye (*sha'i spyan*), divine eye (*lha'i spyan*), eye of prajñā (*shes rab kyi spyan*), eye of dharma (*chos kyi spyan*), and eye of wisdom (*ye shes kyi spyan*).

five faults (*nyes pa lnga*). Laziness (*le lo*), forgetfulness (*brjed nges*), dullness (*bying ba*), agitation (*rgod pa*), lack of application (*'du mi byed pa*) or lack of exertion (*mi rtsol ba*), and [excessive] application (*'du byed sems pa*).

five obscurations (*sgrib pa lnga*). Agitation (*rgod pa*), remorse (*'gyod pa*), sluggishness (*rmugs pa*), drowsiness (*gnyid*), doubt (*the tshom*), pleasure-seeking (*'dod pa la 'dun pa*), and malice (*gnod sems*).

five paths (*lam lnga*). Paths of accumulation (*tshogs lam*), preparation (*sbyor lam*), seeing (*mthong lam*), meditation (*sgom lam*), and perfection (*mthar phyin pa'i lam*).

five planets (***gza' lnga***). Mars (Kuhja/Aṅgāraka, Mig dmar; Maṅgala, bKra shis), Mercury (Budha, Lhag pa), Jupiter (Bṛhaspati, Phur bu), Venus (Śukra, Pa sangs), and Saturn (Śanaiścara/Śanina, sPen pa).

five qualities conducive to liberation (***thar pa cha thun gyi chos lnga***). Ethical conduct of ordinary beings (*so so skye bo'i tshul khrims*), control of the senses (*dbang po'i sgo sdom pa*), alert behavior (*shes bzhin du spyod pa*), moderation of food (*zas kyi tshod rig pa*), exertion in yoga during the first and last periods [of the night] without sleeping (*nam gyi cha stod dang cha smad la mi nyal bar rnal 'byor la brtson pa*).

five signs (***rtags lnga***). Smoke, mirage, fireflies, candle flames, and a cloudless sky.

five skandhas (***phung po lnga***). Forms, feelings, discriminations, formative forces, and consciousnesses.

five topics (***chos lnga***). Names (*ming*), characteristics (*mtshan ma*), concepts (*rnam rtog*), thusness (*de bzhin nyid*), and nonconceptual wisdom (*mi rtog ye shes*).

five types of objects of meditation for expertise (***mkhas pa'i dmigs pa lnga***). Expertise in the skandhas (*phung po pa mkhas pa*), expertise in the dhātus (*khams la mkhas pa*), expertise in the āyatanas (*skye mched la mkhas pa*), expertise in dependent origination (*rten 'brel la la mkhas pa*), expertise in what is the case and what is not the case (*gnas dang gnas ma yin pa la mkhas pa*).

five types of objects of meditation for purifying previous behavior (***spyad pa rnam sbyong gi dmigs pa lnga***). Ugliness (*mi sdug pa*), kindness (*byams pa*), dependent origination (*rten 'brel*), differentiation of dhātus (*khams kyi rab dbye*), and inhalation and exhalation of breath (*dbugs 'byung rngub*).

five wisdoms (***ye shes lnga***). Mirrorlike wisdom (*me long lta bu'i ye shes*), wisdom of equality (*mnyam pa nyid kyi ye shes*), discriminating wisdom (*so sor rtog pa'i ye shes*), all-accomplishing, or wisdom that accomplishes all activities (*bya ba grub pa'i ye shes*), and dharmadhātu wisdom (*chos kyi dbyings kyi ye shes*).

Fivefold Mahāmudrā (Phyag rgya chen po lnga ldan). Bodhicitta, yidam deities, guru yoga, sequential meditations on mahāmudrā, and concluding dedications.

6

six categories of the basis (***gzhi rab tu dbye ba drug***). Meaning (*don*), entities (*dngos po*), characteristics (*mtshan nyid*), qualities (*phyogs*), time (*dus*), and reasonings (*rigs pa*).

six dhātus (***khams drug***). Earth, water, fire, wind, space, and consciousness.

six dharmas (***chos drug***). Caṇḍālī (*gtum mo*), illusory body (*sgyu lus*), dream (*rmi lam*), luminosity (*'od gsal*), transference (*'pho ba*), and bardo (*bar do*).

six internal āyatanas (***nang gi skye mched drug***). The visual, auditory, olfactory, gustatory, bodily, and mental faculties.

six external āyatanas (***phyi'i skye mched drug***) Forms, sounds, smells, tastes, tangible objects, and phenomena.

six strengths (***stobs drug***). Hearing (*thos pa*), reflection (*bsam pa*), mindfulness (*dran pa*), alertness (*shes bzhin*), diligence (*brtson 'grus*), and familiarization ('*dris pa*).

six types of attention (*yid byed drug*). Attention that cognizes meaning (*don so sor rig pa*), attention that comes from conviction (*mos pa las byung ba*), attention that isolates (*rab tu dban pa*), attention that consolidates joy (*dga' ba sdud pa*), attention that analyzes (*dpyod pa*), and attention that completes the practice (*sbyor ba mthar thug pa*).

six ways of resting (*bzhag thabs drug*). Do not reflect (*mi mno*), do not think (*mi bsam*), do not speculate (*mi sem*), do not meditate (*mi sgom*), do not analyze (*mi dpyad*), and rest naturally (*rang bzhin bzhag*).

Sixfold Essence Cycle (sNying po skor drug). According to *Butön's Record of Teachings Received* (*Bu ston gsan yig*, 115.7–116.1) and Indian Mahāmudrā Texts (*Phyag chen rgya gzhung*) compiled by Chödrak Gyatso, these are (1) Āryadeva's **Cittāvaraṇaviśodhana* (*Sems kyi sgrib sbyong*) (Toh. 1804), (2) Saraha's *Dohā for the People* (*Dohakoṣagīti, dMangs do ha / Do ha mdzod kyi glu*) (Toh. 2224), (3) Nāgārjunagarbha's *Caturmudrā* (*Phyag rgya bzhi pa*) (Toh. 2225), (4) *Devacandra's **Prajñājñānaprakāśa* (*Shes rab ye shes gsal ba*) (Toh. 2226), (5) Sahajavajra's *Sthitisamuccaya* (*gNas pa bsdus pa*) (Toh. 2227), and (6) Koṭali/Kuddālī's *Acintyakramopadeśa* (*bSam mi khyab pa'i rim pa'i man ngag*) (Toh. 2228). Note that Pema Karpo (*Vault of the Victors*, 28) omits 4 and 5 from the above list and instead includes Saraha's *Svādhiṣṭhānakrama* (*Rang byin gyis brlab pa'i rim pa*) (Toh. 2275) and *Tattvopadeśaśikharadohagīti* (*De kho na nyid kyi man ngag rtse mo do ha'i glu*) (2276).

sixfold recollection (*rjes su dran pa drug*). Recollection of the buddhas (*sangs rgyas*), dharma (*chos*), saṅgha (*dge 'dun*), ethical conduct (*tshul khrims*), generosity (*gtong ba*), and deities (*lha*).

7

Seven Siddhi Texts / Seven Mahāmudrā Siddhi Texts (Grub pa sde bdun / Phyag rgya chen po grub pa sde bdun). According to *Butön's Record of Teachings Received* (115.4–7): (1) Padmavajra's *Guhyasiddhi / Sakalatantrasambhavasaṃcodanī-śrīguhyasiddhi* (*rGyud ma lus pa'i don dam pa'i don nges par skul bar byed pa dpal gsang ba grub pa*) (Toh. 2217), (2) Anaṅgavajra's *Prajñopāyaviniścayasiddhi* (*Thabs dang shes rab rnam par gtan la dbab pa sgrub pa*) (Toh. 2218), (3) Indrabhūti's *Jñānasiddhi-nāma-sādhana* (*Ye shes grub pa zhes bya ba'i sgrub pa'i thabs*) (Toh. 2219), (4) Lakṣmīṃkarā's *Advayasiddhisādhana* (*gNyis su med par grub pa'i sgrub thabs*) (Toh. 2220), (5) Sahajayoginī Cito's *Vyaktabhāvānugatatattvasiddhi* (*dNgos po gsal ba'i rjes su 'gro ba'i de kho na nyid grub pa*) (Toh. 2222), (6) Ḍombi Heruka's *Sahajasiddhi* (*Lhan cig skyes pa grub pa*) (Toh. 2223), and (7) Dārika's *Śrī-uḍḍiyānavinirgataguhyamahāguhya-tattvopadeśa*) (*dPal o rgyan nas byung ba gsang ba'i gsang ba chen po de kho na nyid kyi man ngag*) (Toh. 2221). The same list is found in the *BA* (Roerich 1949, 856), but Pema Karpo's list (*Vault of the Victors*, 7) includes more than seven texts.

sevenfold service (*yan lag bdun pa*). Homage, offerings, requesting [dharma teachings], supplicating [not to pass into nirvāṇa], confession, rejoicing, and dedication.

8

eight applications (*'du byed*). Faith (*dad pa*), motivation (*'dun pa*), exertion (*rtsol ba*), suppleness (*shin sbyang*), mindfulness (*dran pa*), alertness (*shes bzhin*), applied intention (*'du byed pa'i sems*), and the equanimity of remaining in the natural state (*rnal du dbab pa'i btang snyoms*).

eight benefits (*phan yon brgyad*). This may be the same as the eight excellent qualities (*yon tan brgyad*) that are signs of meditative experience during caṇḍālī: "The excellent quality of earth is that your body is majestic and dignified. The excellent quality of water is that your body is shiny. The excellent quality of fire is that your [body] glows. [The excellent quality] of wind is that your body is light. [The excellent quality] of the moon is that others do not see your shadow. [The excellent quality] of the sun is that your form is invisible. The excellent quality of space is that, throughout the day and night, your eyes are always open, like an autumn sky." From Marpa's *Stream of Amṛta* (*bDud rtsi'i chu rgyun*) as cited in *TOK*, vol. 3, 345. See Kongtrul, *Treasury of Knowledge: Esoteric Instructions*, 172.

eight cold hells (*grang ba'i dmyal ba brgyad*). Blisters (*chu bur can*), bursting blisters (*cu bur rdo ba can*), chattering teeth (*so tham tham pa*), moaning/crying "*kyi-hu*" (*kyi hud 'don pa*), saying "*a-chu*" (*a chu zer ba*), utpala-like cracks (*utpala ltar gas pa*), lotus-like cracks (*padma ltar gas pa*), and giant lotus-like cracks (*padma chen po ltar gas pa*).

eight hot hells (*tsha ba'i dmyal ba brgyad*). Reviving (*yang sos*), black line (*thig nag*), crushed together (*bsdus 'joms*), crying (*ngu 'bod*), great crying (*ngu 'bod chen po*), hot (*tsha ba*), very hot (*rab tu tsha ba*), and interminable (*mnar med*).

eight liberations (*rnam thar brgyad*). The liberation of the embodied looking at forms, the liberation of those without inner forms looking at forms, and the liberation of [ideas about] beauty, the liberation of the sphere of Limitless Space, the liberation of the sphere of Limitless Consciousness, the liberation of the sphere of Nothingness, the liberation of the sphere of Neither Discrimination nor Nondiscrimination, and the liberation of the equipoise of cessation.

eight worldly qualities/values (*'jig rten chos brgyad*). To feel happy over slight advantages or sadness over the disadvantages that arise through: personal gain or the lack of it, hearing pleasant words or not, being praised or denigrated, and having happiness or unhappiness.

Eightfold Treasury of Shorter Dohās / Eight Dohā Treasures (Do chung mdzod brgyad / Do ha mdzod brgyad). (1) Saraha's *Treasury of Dohā: Instructions on Mahāmudrā* (*Dohakoṣa-nāma-mahāmudropadeśa, Do ha mdzod ces bya ba phyag rgya chen po'i man ngag*) (Toh. 2273), (2) Virūpa's *Treasury of Dohā* (*Dohakoṣa, Do ha mdzod*) (Toh. 2280), (3) Tilopa's *Treasury of Dohā* (*Dohakoṣa, Do ha mdzod*) (Toh. 2281), (4) Kṛṣṇavajra/Kāṅha's *Treasury of*

Dohā (*Dohakoṣa, Do ha mdzod*) (Toh. 2301), (5) Tilopa's *Ganges Mahāmudrā* (*Phyag chen gang ga' ma / Mahāmudropadeśa, Phyag rgya chen po'i man ngag*) (Toh. 2303), (6) Saraha's *Dohā Song on View, Meditation, Conduct, and Fruition* (*Bhāvanādṛṣṭicaryāphaladohagītikā, lTa bsgom spyod pa 'bras bu'i do ha'i glu*) (Toh. 2345), (7) Nāropa's *Summary of the View* (*Dṛṣtisaṃkṣipta, lTa ba mdor bsdus pa*) (Toh. 2304), and (8) Maitrīpa's (or sometimes unattributed) *Summary Verses for Mahāmudrā* (*Phyag rgya chen po'i tshig bsdus pa*).

9

nine mental states / nine mental states of resting (*sems rnam pa dgu / sems gnas pa rnam pa dgu*). *Moonbeams* provides three almost identical lists. (1) From Vasubandhu's *Explanation of the "Ornament for the Mahāyāna Sūtras"*: settling the mind (*sems 'jog par byed pa*), constant settling (*kun tu 'jog par byed pa*), definite settling (*nges par 'jog par byed pa*), increased settling (*nye bar 'jog par byed pa*), taming (*'dul bar byed pa*), pacification (*zhi bar byed pa*), thorough pacification (*nye bar zhi bar byed pa*), creating a single continuum (*rgyud gcig tu byed pa*), and equipoise (*mnyam par 'jog par byed pa*). (2) From Asaṅga's *Compendium of Abhidharma*: settling the mind (*sems 'jog pa*), continuous settling (*rgyun tu 'jog pa*), renewed settling (*blan te 'jog pa*), increased settling (*nye bar 'jog pa*), taming (*'dul ba*), pacification (*zhi ba*), full pacification (*rnam par zhi bar byed pa*), one-pointedness (*rtse gcig tu byed pa*), and equipoise (*mnyam par 'jog pa*). (3) From Asaṅga's *Śrāvakabhūmi:* settling (*'jog par byed pa*), correct settling (*yang dag par 'jog par byed pa*), resetting (*bsdus te 'jog par byed pa*), increased settling (*nye bar 'jog par byed pa*), taming (*'dul bar byed pa*), pacification (*zhi bar byed pa*), thorough pacification (*nye bar zhi bar byed pa*), creating a single continuum (*rgyud gcig tu byed pa*), and engagement in samādhi (*ting nge 'dzin du byed pa*).

10

ten bhūmis (*sa bcu*, "ten levels," or "ten grounds"). (1) Very Joyful (Rab tu dga' ba), (2) Stainless (Dri ma med pa), (3) Illuminating ('Od byed pa), (4) Radiant ('Od 'phro ba), (5) Difficult to Overcome (sByang dka' ba), (6) Manifest (mNgon du gyur pa), (7) Gone Afar (Ring du song ba), (8) Immovable (Mi g.yo ba), (9) Excellent Intelligence (Legs pa'i blo gros), and (10) Cloud of Dharma (Chos kyi sprin).

ten dharma activities (*chos spyod bcu*). Writing [the scriptures] (*yi ge 'bri ba*), making offerings (*mchod pa 'bul ba*), being generous (*sbyin pa gtong ba*), listening to the dharma (*chos nyan pa*), memorizing [the dharma] (*'dzin pa*), reading [the dharma] (*klog pa*), explaining [the dharma] (*'chad pa*), reciting [the dharma] (*kha ton bya ba*), contemplating the meaning of the dharma (*chos kyi don sems pa*), and meditating on the meaning of the dharma (*chos kyi don sgom pa*).

ten points for training (*bslab pa'i gnas bcu*). According to Jamgön Kongtrul in his *Revealing the Indestructible Vajra Secrets*, this is either the ten precepts for shrāmaṇas or the avoidance of the ten unvirtuous actions.

ten signs (*rtags bcu*). Ngo-tro Rabjampa in his *Precious Jeweled Garland of Eloquence* lists smoke, mirage, fireflies, sky, candle flames, the moon, sun, blazing, bindus, and rainbows. Other enumerations are found.

ten unvirtuous actions (*mi dge ba bcu*). Divided into three of body, four of speech, and three of mind. The three of body are to kill, steal, and engage in sexual misconduct. The four of speech are to lie, speak divisively, use harsh language, and engage in useless talk. The three of mind are to covet the possessions of others, have a malicious attitude, and hold wrong views.

11

eleven types of attentiveness (*yid la byed pa bcu gcig pa*). That which involves conceptuality and analysis (*rtog pa dang bcas shing dpyod pa dang bcas pa*), that which is mere analysis without conceptuality (*rtog pa med la dpyod pa tsam*), that which involves neither conceptuality nor analysis (*rtog pa yang med dpyod pa yang med pa*), attentiveness to śamatha (*zhi gnas yid la byed pa*), attentiveness to vipaśyanā (*lhag mthong yid la byed pa*), attentiveness to their unification (*zung du 'brel ba yid la byed pa*), attentiveness with the characteristics of concentration (*rab tu 'dzin pa'i rgyu mtshan yid la byed pa*), attentiveness with the characteristics of śamatha (*zhi gnas kyi rgyu mtshan yid la byed pa*), attentiveness with the characteristics of equanimity (*btang snyoms kyi rgyu mtshan yid la byed pa*), constant attentiveness (*rtag tu bya ba yid la byed pa*), and devoted attentiveness (*gus par bya ba yid la byed pa*).

12

twelve āyatanas (*skye mched bcu gnyis*). The six sense faculties and their six objects.

twelve bhūmis (*sa bcu gnyis*). The bhūmi of engagement through belief, the ten bhūmis, and the bhūmi of buddhahood.

twelve links of dependent origination (*rten 'brel bcu gnyis*). Ignorance (*ma rig pa*), karmic formative forces (*'du byed kyi las*), consciousnesses (*rnam shes*), names and forms (*ming gzugs*), six sense spheres (*skye mched, āyatana*), contact (*reg pa*), feelings (*tshor ba*), craving (*sred pa*), grasping (*len pa*), existence (*srid pa*), birth (*skye ba*), and aging and death (*rga shi*).

twelve sets of one hundred excellent qualities (*yon tan brgya phrag bcu gnyis*). The excellent qualities attained on the first bhūmi and multiplied on the subsequent bhūmis by factors of ten. Bodhisattvas on the first bhūmi are able to (1) see one hundred buddhas in an instant, (2) know that they are being blessed by those buddhas, (3) send out one hundred emanations, (4) travel to one hundred buddha realms, (5) see past and future births throughout one hundred aeons, (6) be absorbed in and arise from one hundred types of samādhi, (7) mature one hundred beings, (8) shake one hundred buddha realms, (9) illuminate one hundred buddha realms, (10) open one hundred entrances to the dharma, (11) display one hundred forms of their own bodies, and (12) surround each of those forms with one hundred bodhisattvas.

16

sixteen aspects of the four truths (*bden pa bzhi'i rnam pa bcu drug*). Each of the four truths, or realities, has four general characteristics, or aspects. The four aspects of the truth of suffering are that it is impermanent (*mi rtag*), suffering (*sdug bsngal*), empty (*stong pa*), and without self-entity (*bdag med pa*). The four aspects of the origins [of suffering] are that they are causes (*rgyu*), origins (*kun 'byung*), strong producers (*rab skye*), and conditions (*rkyen*). The four aspects of cessation are that it is cessation (*'gog pa*), peace (*zhi ba*), perfection (*gya nom*), and definite release (*nges 'byung*). The four aspects of the path are that it is a path (*lam*), suitable (*rigs pa*), effective (*sgrub pa*), and what brings definite release from saṃsāra (*nges par 'byin pa*).

18

eighteen dhātus (*khams bco brgyad*). The six objects of perception, six sense faculties, and six consciousnesses.

24

twenty-four texts in the Dharma Cycle on Amanasikāra [Nonattention] (A ma na si'i chos skor nyer bzhi). *Moonbeams* refers to twenty-four texts; other lists have twenty-five by counting two separately, which are in fact two different Tibetan translations of the same text, *Prīṇapañcaka* (Toh. 2237 and Toh. 2246). All are authored by Maitrīpa. (1) *Kudṛṣṭinirghāta/ Kudṛṣṭinirghātana* (*lTa ba ngan pa sel ba*) (Toh. 2229), (2) *Madhyamaṣaṭka* (*dBu ma drug pa*) (Toh. 2230), (3) *Kudṛṣṭinirghātaṭīkā/Kudṛṣṭinirghātacintā/ Kudṛṣṭinirghātavākyaṭippinikā* (*lTa ba ngan sel gyi dka' 'grel*) (Toh. 2231), (4) *Sahajaṣaṭaka* (*Lhan cig skyes pa drug pa*) (Toh. 2232), (5) *Svapnanirdeśa/ Svapnanirukti* (*rMi lam nges par bstan pa*) (Toh. 2233), (6) *Māyānirukti* (*sGyu ma nges par bstan pa*) (Toh. 2234), (7) *Aprasahaprakāśa/Apratiṣṭhānaprakāśa* (*Rab tu mi gnas pa gsal bar bstan pa*) (Toh. 2235), (8) *Tattvadaśaka* (*De kho na nyid bcu pa*) (Toh. 2236), (9) *Yuganaddhaprakāśa* (*Zung du 'jug pa rab tu gsal bar bstan pa*) (Toh. 2237), (10) *Prīṇapañcaka/Premapañcaka* (*dGa' bcugs lnga pa*) and *Prajñopāyadayāpañcaka/Prajñopāyakrīḍāpañca/Premapañcaka* (*Thabs dang shes rab rtse pa lnga pa*) (Toh. 2237b and Toh. 2246), (11) *Nirbhedapañcaka/Nirvedhapañcaka* (*Mi phyed pa lnga pa*) (Toh. 2238), (12) *Mahāsukhaprakāśa* (*bDe ba chen po gsal ba*) (Toh. 2239), (13) *Tattvaratnāvalī* (*De kho na nyid rin po che'i phreng ba*) (Toh. 2240), (14) *Tattvaprakāśa* (*De kho na nyid rab tu bstan pa*) (Toh. 2241), (15) *Tathāgatapañcamudrāvivaraṇa/ Pañcatathāgatamudrāvivaraṇa* (*De bzhin gshegs pa lnga'i phyag rgya rnam par bshad pa*) (Toh. 2242), (16) *Sekakāyasaṃgraha/Sekatāparyasaṃgraha* (*dBang* *gi dgos pa mdor bsdus pa*) (Toh. 2243), (17) *Saṃkṣiptasekaprakriyā* (*dBang gi bya ba mdor bsdus pa*) (Toh. 2244), (18) *Pañcasvabhāva/Pañcākāra* (*Rang bzhin lnga pa*) (Toh. 2245), (19) **Dohānidhināmatattvopadeśa* (*Do ha ni zhes bya ba de kho na nyid kyi man ngag*) (Toh. 2247), (20) *Mahāyānaviṃśati/Mahāyānaviṃśika* (*Theg pa chen po nyi shu pa*) (Toh. 2248), (21) *Amanasikāroddeśa/Amanasikārādhāra* (*Yid la mi byed pa ston pa*) (Toh. 2249), (22) *Tattvamahāyānaviṃśati/Tattvaviṃśika* (*De kho na nyid theg pa chen po nyi shu pa*) (Toh. 2250), and (23) *Sekanirdeśa* (*dBang bskur ba nges par bstan pa*) (Toh. 2252), and (24) *Upadeśaparama* (*Shes pa spro bsdu mi byed par 'jog pa'i man ngag*) (Toh. 2251). Alternate lists are found. See Mathes, *Fine Blend*, 4–6.

Translation Equivalents

For terms not found here, consult the Glossary or the Glossary of Enumerations. Since many words require contextual translations, all ways that a given Tibetan word has been translated may not be provided; the less common ones are in parentheses. The English translation terms are also specific to this text and mahāmudrā literature in general; the same Tibetan words might be translated differently in other literary genres.

English / Sanskrit	Tibetan
abiding mode, the way things actually are	*gnas tshul*
abiding state	*gnas lugs*
abiding-state mahāmudrā	*gnas lugs phyag chen*
absence of self/self-entity	*bdag med*
absorptions	*snyoms 'jug*
abstract idea	*don spyi*
abstract image	*rnam spyi / spyi'i rnam pa*
achievement of mastery	*rtsal rdzogs*
activating the mind, mind becoming [overly] active	*sems mngon par 'du byed pa*
active application, to actively apply	*mngon par 'du byed pa*
actual lineage	*don brgyud*
actual luminosity	*don gyi 'od gsal*
actual realizations	*rtogs pa dngos gzhi*
actual view	*lta ba dngos gzhi*

English / Sanskrit	Tibetan
actual, actuality, fact, principle, referent, point, meaning, nature, topic, object (state, what is true, ultimate, reality, true point, subject, intent, aim, import, situation, matter, what signifies)	*don*
adulterate (corrupt, spoil, distort, alter)	*bslad pa*
afflictive obscurations	*nyon mongs kyi sgrib pa*
agitation	*rgod pa*
Ajita	Ma pham pa
Akaniṣṭha	'Og min
alarm, concern, anxiety (uncertainty, uneasiness)	*'khu phrig*
ālaya	*kun gzhi*
alteration	*bcas bcos*
alertness	*shes bzhin*
ambition, expectation, preoccupation	*zhe 'dod / sems kyi zhe 'dod*
Amitāyus	Tshe dpag med
amorphous	*bkrag med lta bu*
analytical emptiness	*dpyad stong / dpyad pa'i stong nyid*
analytical meditation	*dpyad sgom*
analytical mind	*brtag dpyad kyi blo*
appearance, to appear, be visible, illuminate (illumination, light)	*snang ba*
appearing object	*yul snang*
application, [excessive] application, active application, applied intention, mental formations (mental applications, mental fabrications)	*'du byed pa, 'du byed sems pa, 'du byed pa'i sems, yid 'du byed, yid 'du byed pa'i sems pa, blo yi 'du byed*
applications that eliminate [faults]	*spong ba'i 'du byed*

ENGLISH / SANSKRIT	TIBETAN
applied mindfulness	*bzung dran*
apprehension of characteristics (perceived characteristics, characterization processes)	*mtshan 'dzin*
apprehension of characteristics that are taken to be real	*bden zhen gyi mtshan 'dzin*
appropriated [skandhas]	*nye bar len pa*
approximation	*rjes mthun pa*
arising, abiding, ceasing	*skye gnas 'gag*
ascertainment, certainty, to ascertain, determine, be certain	*nges pa*
assumption	*yid dpyod*
asura	*lha ma yin*
attention, attentiveness, to be attentive, to attend, bring to mind, engage mentally, take to mind (mental activities, formulation)	*yid byed / yid la byed pa*
attitude and behavior (thought and deed, contemplate and engage)	*bsam sbyor*
authentic, true	*mtshan nyid pa*
Avalokiteśvara	sPyan ras gzigs
awareness, be aware, recognize (cognize, know, understand)	*rig pa*
balanced	*cha snyoms pa / snyoms pa*
basic abiding state, abiding state of the basic nature	*gshis kyi gnas lugs*
basic nature	*gshis, rang gshis*
basic state	*gshis babs, gshis lugs*
be mindful (apply mindfulness, maintain awareness, concentrate with mindfulness, focus with mindfulness)	*dran 'dzin/zin, dran pas bzung/'dzin/zin*

English / Sanskrit	Tibetan
belief in a self, clinging to a self (sense of self)	*bdag 'dzin*
bewilderment, stupidity	*gti mug*
Bhairava	'Jigs byed
Bhaiṣajyaguru	sMan bla / Sangs rgyas sman bla
bhūta	*'byung po*
blank, open	*had de chod de ba*
bliss, pleasure, serenity (comfort, be comfortable, happiness)	*bde ba*
breakthrough	*la bzla ba*
breath control (prāṇāyāma)	*srog rtsol*
breath yoga	*rlung sbyor*
breath, wind	*rlung*
brilliance (sparkling, vibrant, vivid)	*dvangs*
brilliant, clearly, vivid	*lam me*
bring proficiency (refinement, to perfect the display)	*rtsal sbyong ba*
buoyant	*'bol le*
bypassing way of development (nonlinear way)	*thod rgal ba'i skye tshul, thod rgal du skye ba*
calmness, peace, to subside, pacify	*zhi ba*
carelessly (in an oblivious way)	*byung rgyal du*
causes and results that are of similar types and connected	*rgyu 'bras rigs 'dra mtshungs shing 'brel ba*
certainty in grasping emptiness	*stong 'dzin nges shes*
certainty, conviction	*nges shes*
Cakrasaṃvara	bDe mchog / 'Khor lo bde mchog

ENGLISH / SANSKRIT	TIBETAN
Caṇḍa	gTum chung
Candraprabha Kumāra	Zla 'od gzhon nu
characteristic, definition	*mtshan nyid*
characteristic, sign, characterization, symbol, quality	*mtshan ma*
Cittavajra	Thugs kyi rdo rje
clarity, clear	*gsal ba*
cling, grasp, hold, perceive, believe, maintain, adhere, retain (perception, notion, belief, concentration, conceptualization)	*'dzin pa*
cognition	*rnam par rig pa*
cognitive obscurations	*shes bya'i sgrib pa*
cognizable	*nam par rig byed*
collapse of the distinction	*bar lag 'gyel ba*
common locus	*gzhi mthun*
complete analysis	*yongs su dpyod pa*
complete discernment	*yongs su rtog pa*
concentrate, concentration (hold the mind)	*sems gzung ba/'dzin pa*
conceptual images	*rnam par rtog pa'i rnam pa can*
conceptual representations	*rnam par rtog pa dang bcas pa'i gzugs brnyan*
conclude, reach a decision, reach a conclusion	*thag chod pa*
conditions, situations, circumstances	*rkyen*
conduct, behavior	*spyod pa*
confusion	*rmongs pa*
connate, connateness, connate state	*lhan cig skyes pa*

English / Sanskrit	Tibetan
conscientiousness	*bag yod*
continuity of training, possessing the	*sbyangs pa'i 'phro can*
contrivance or tampering, to alter or manipulate	*bcos bslad*
contrived (alterations, artifice, corrections, alter, fix)	*bcos pa*
conventional, conventionalities	*kun rdzob*
conviction, dedication, aspiration (intention)	*mos pa*
correct attention	*yang dag par yid la byed* pa
correct cognition	*yang dag pa'i shes pa*
correct discernment	*yang dag par rtog pa / yang dag par so sor rtog pa*
correct view	*yang dag pa'i lta ba*
crisp	*sem me ba*
crisp, vividly	*ye re*
critical investigation	*dpyad gzhig*
cultivate, meditate (contemplate)	*bsgoms pa, sgom pa, bsgom pa, sgoms*
Daṇḍa	Beng
dankness	*rlan pa*
dazed dazed (torpor)	*'thongs pa* *'thibs pa*
dazzling	*gsal gsal po*
deficiency, disadvantage, problem	*nyes dmigs*
definite goodness	*nges legs*
definitive meaning	*nges don*
delusion, to be deluded, be mistaken	*'khrul pa*

ENGLISH / SANSKRIT	TIBETAN
demons	*dre*
denial	*skur 'debs*
dependent origination, interdependence, dependent arisings, dependently originated, interdependent connections (interdependent display)	*rten 'brel*
destroy (let go, disrupt)	*bshig, 'jig pa, bshig pa, shig*
determination to be released	*nges 'byung*
determine (establish)	*gtan la phab pa/'bebs pa/dbab pa*
develop assurance, feel certain, experience confidence	*phrig tshud pa*
deviate (lose, slip away, vanish, fade, lapse, dissipate)	*shor ba, 'chor ba, 'chor ba*
deviations	*shor sa*
dharma to be realized	*rtogs chos*
dharmatā, the way of things	*chos nyid*
dharmin	*chos can*
differentiation	*rnam par 'byed pa*
direct cause	*dngos rgyu*
discern, examine (imagine, conceptualize)	*brtags pa, rtog pa, brtag pa, rtogs*
discerning prajñā	*so sor rtog pa'i shes rab*
discernment and analysis, examine and analyze (analysis, conceptuality and analysis)	*rtog dpyod*
discernment, to discern	*so sor rtog pa*
discouragement	*sgyid lug pa*
discrimination (perception, awareness, notions)	*'du shes*

English / Sanskrit	Tibetan
discursiveness, scatteredness, proliferations, to be active (busyness, to stray, pursue, project)	*'phros pa, 'phro ba, 'phro ba*
disillusioned [with saṃsāra]	*yid 'byung*
distracted, wander, waver	*yengs pa, yeng ba, yengs ba*
distraction	*g.yeng ba*
dormant tendencies	*bag nyal / bag la nyal*
drowsiness, sleep	*gnyid*
dullness	*bying ba*
earth-lords	*sa bdag*
effort, exertion	*rtsol ba*
elaborations, conceptual elaborations	*spros pa*
Eleven-Faced [Avalokiteśvara]	bCu gcig zhal [sPyan ras gzigs]
emptiness imbued with the heart of compassion	*stong nyid snying rje'i snying po can*
emptiness of nature, empty of any nature (natural emptiness)	*rang bzhin stong nyid*
emptiness of the inanimate	*bems po'i stong pa*
emptiness that is a nothingness	*cang med stong pa*
emptiness that is nonexistence	*med pa'i stong pa*
empty appearances, appearance-emptiness	*snang stong*
empty clarity, clarity-emptiness	*gsal stong*
empty of inherent nature, empty of nature	*rang bzhin gyis stong nyid*
empty of reality	*bden stong*
energize	*hur 'byin pa*
energy or light touch of the mindfulness	*dran pa'i rtsi'am shugs*

English / Sanskrit	Tibetan
enforced mindfulness	*'jur dran*
entities, things (existent thing)	*dngos po*
epitome, principle, embodiment (nature, essence)	*bdag nyid*
equal taste	*ro mnyam*
equality	*mnyam nyid*
equanimity (indifference)	*btang snyoms*
equivalents, identical	*don gcig*
esoteric instructions	*man ngag*
essence (heart, core)	*snying po*
essence (nature)	*ngo bo*
essence (nature, very essence, essential nature, inherent nature, inherently real)	*ngo bo nyid*
essential points for the body	*lus gnad*
ethical conduct	*tshul khrims*
evil spirits	*btsan*
excellent qualities, virtues	*yon tan*
exclusion	*rnam par bcad pa/gcod pa*
expanse	*dbyings*
experience	*nyams*
experiences intrinsic to realization	*rtogs pa'i rang nyams*
experiences intrinsic to the essence	*ngo bo'i rang nyams*
experiences [of things] as illusionlike	*sgyu ma lta bu'i nyams myong*
experiential term	*nyams myong gi skad*
expression, term, terminology, label	*tha snyad*

ENGLISH / SANSKRIT	TIBETAN
expressions, manifestations	*rnam 'gyur*
expressive power	*rtsal*
externally oriented aspect	*kha phyir blta ba'i rnam pa*
fabrication (to manipulate, tamper with)	*bzo bcos*
familiarize, habituate	*'dris pa, goms pa*
faults (what is unwholesome, problems, wrongdoings)	*nyes pa*
fixation, to fixate, believe (attachment)	*zhen pa*
fixedly, directly	*ce re*
fleeting, adventitious	*glo bur*
flexibility	*las su rung ba*
focal support	*dmigs rten*
focus	*gtod pa*
foundation of mindfulness	*dran pa nyer bar bzhag pa*
four possibilities	*mu bzhi*
Four-Armed One	Phyag bzhi pa
free rein, run free	*kha yan*
freely	*khrol le*
freely, regular, normal, ordinary (just as you are, in the usual sense)	*rang ga / rang ga ma*
freshness	*so ma*
fundamental deviation	*ye shor*
fundamental state	*yin lugs*
fuzzy	*'jam nyal le ba*
gandharva	*dri za*

ENGLISH / SANSKRIT	TIBETAN
gaze vacantly	*ha re lta*
general-meaning luminosity	*spyi don gyi 'od gsal*
glazed	*thom me*
governing principle	*khyab bdag*
grasping at / clinging to emptiness (hold onto something as being empty)	*stong 'dzin*
grounded in experience	*nyams 'og tu tshud / 'dzud pa*
Guhyapati	gSang ba'i bdag po
Guhyasamāja	gSang ba 'dus pa
Guṇālaṃkāra	Yon tan gyis brgyan pa
hazy, vague	*ban bun*
heroic-stride samādhi	*dpa' bar 'gro ba'i ting 'dzin*
Hevajra	dGyes rdor
hindering spirits	*bgegs*
hungry ghost (preta)	*yi dvags*
identical in essence, one essence but discrete isolates	*ngo bo gcig la ldog pa tha dad pa*
identify, identification, recognize	*ngos bzung ba/'dzin pa/gzung ba*
idleness	*snyom las*
illustrative luminosity	*dpe'i 'od gsal*
impressions and sensations	*byung tshor*
inclusions, [positive]	*yongs gcod*
incorporate into the path (take as the path)	*lam du slongs pa*
independent, stand on its own	*rang rkya thub pa*
inferential rational cognition	*rigs shes rjes dpag*

English / Sanskrit	Tibetan
innate quality, innately	*rang chas / rang chas su*
inspiration, enthusiasm	*spro ba*
instantiation	*mtshan gzhi*
instruction manual	*khrid gzhung/yig*
instructional tradition	*khrid srol*
instructions on the essence	*snying po'i gdams pa*
instructions on the ultimate	*don gyi gdams pa*
instructions on the ultimate essence	*snying po don gyi gdams pa*
instructions, oral instructions (advice)	*gzhal gdams*
instructions, oral instructions, key instructions	*gdams ngag*
integrate into the path	*lam khyer / lam du khyer ba*
intellectual constructs, to be intellectually created, intellectually fabricated (fabrication, mentally fabricated)	*blos byas*
intellectual elaborations	*blo spros pa*
intellectual object, mental object	*blo yul*
intellectualization	*blo'i 'dzin stangs*
intellectually meditating	*blos bsgoms*
intense, awake	*hu re*
intent upon, to strive, seek, aim for, intention to pursue, motivation to strive, pursue what will benefit	*don du gnyer ba / don gnyer*
intentionally ambiguous	*dgongs pa can*
internally oriented aspect	*kha nang du blta ba'i rnam pa*
interrupt	*shigs kyis bshig / shigs bshig*
intrinsic experiences	*rang nyams*

English / Sanskrit	Tibetan
intrinsic state, intrinsic	*gnyug ma*
intuitive reflexive awareness	*so so rang rig*
investigate, seek, pursue (inquire, explore, discover)	*btsal ba, 'tshal ba, btsal ba, 'tshol*
isolate	*ldog pa*
jaded, complacent	*dred po*
Jīvaka	'Tsho byed
Kālacakra	Dus 'khor
karma, action, function	*las*
karmically destined	*las can*
keenly aware and vividly clear	*rig rig tur tur po*
key point	*mtshang*
key point, vital point, essential point	*gnad*
knowable objects, objects of knowledge	*shes bya*
lack any nature	*rang bzhin med pa*
lack of application	*'du mi byed pa*
lambs linked together, in a line [like]	*lu gu brgyud*
latent tendencies	*bag chag*
let go and relax	*lhod kyis glod*
let go, set free	*shigs gyis btong*
lethargic	*snyom me ba, nyogs pa*
level, bhūmi	*sa*
liberate, free, unravel	*grol ba*
lift up, uplift, rouse	*gzengs bstod*
light touch of mindfulness, hold with	*dran pa'i rtsis zin du bskyang ba*

English / Sanskrit	Tibetan
listening, study	*thos pa*
logicians	*rtog ge ba*
look, look to see (examine)	*bltas, lta ba, blta ba*
lookout	*bya ra*
loose, relaxed	*lhod de*
loosen up, relax (be at ease, let go, set free, release)	*glod pa*
lord	*dbang phyug*
lure of appearances, seductiveness of appearances	*snang shas*
Madhyadeśa	Yul dbus
main practices, actual stage (actual state)	*dngos gzhi*
male spirit	*pho gdon*
manifestation	*rnam pa, 'char sgo*
Mañjuśrī	'Jam dpal
master (perfect)	*klong du gyur pa*
mastery	*rang dbang*
meditative equipoise, equipoise	*mnyam gzhag*
meditative experiences, visions	*nyams snang*
mental flexibility	*sems las su rung ba*
mental formulations, something intellectually manufactured	*yid byed kyi blos*
mental stillness, mental resting	*sems gnas pa*
mind (mentation, cognition, mindset)	*yid*
mind-itself	*sems nyid*
mind, intellect (mentality, mindset)	*blo*

ENGLISH / SANSKRIT	TIBETAN
"mine," what belongs to a self, what is mine	*bdag gi ba / bdag gir*
"minder"	*gnyer kha*
mindfulness (recollection, awareness)	*dran pa*
mindfulness of the object of mindfulness	*dran rgyu'i dran pa*
misinterpretations, superimpositions, exaggerated conjecture	*sgro 'dogs*
mistaken consciousness	*'khrul shes, log shes*
mode of abiding	*tshul lugs*
mode of arising	*'char lugs*
mode of being, way of being	*yin tshul*
modes of inquiry	*'tshol lugs*
moments, momentary, flashes	*yud de / yud de ba*
monastic	*rab byung*
motivation, resolve	*'dun pa*
movement	*'gyu ba*
Munīndra	Thub pa'i dbang po
nāga	*klu*
naked, stark (clear vivid)	*lhang nge / lhang nge ba*
naked, stripped down	*rjen ne*
nakedly, directly	*cer gyis*
natural brilliance	*rang dvangs*
natural condition, just as they are, in its own state (natural state, own nature, natural way)	*rang lugs*
natural expression, own expressive power	*rang rtsal*
natural mind	*rang bzhin gyi shes pa*

English / Sanskrit	Tibetan
natural outflow	*rgyu mthun*
natural state	*rang bzhin gnas*
natural, natural state	*rnal ma*
naturally occurring mindfulness	*shugs 'byung gi dran pa*
naturally settled (natural state)	*rang babs*
nature	*rang bzhin*
nature of mind	*sems don*
neither one nor many	*gcig du bral*
neutral state of indifference	*lung ma bstan btang snyoms*
nihilistic view	*chad lta*
no fluctuation	*'phel 'grib med pa*
no fuss, no caretaking	*gnyer med*
no sense of ownership	*bdag po med pa*
nonattention, not be attentive, mind not attending, not engaging mentally, mind is unengaged, mind not doing anything	*yid la mi byed pa*
nonconceptuality	*rtog med*
nonelaboration, devoid of elaborations, unelaborate	*spros med / spros pa med pa*
nonmindfulness (unmindful, lack of mindfulness, no mindfulness)	*dran med*
nonobservation, not observed	*mi dmigs pa*
normal	*rang kha ma, rang kha ba*
not truly exist	*bden par mi 'grub pa*
object for practice	*bsgrub bya'i don*
object of engagement	*'jug yul*

English / Sanskrit	Tibetan
object of meditation (what is to be meditated upon)	*sgom bya*
object of meditation, object, focus, observe (aim, reference point, meditation techniques, techniques)	*dmigs pa*
objectively existent, exist objectively	*rang mtshan du grub pa*
objects and perceiving subjects	*yul yul can / yul dang yul can*
one thing can arise as many	*gcig la du mar snang ba*
one-dimensional emptiness	*stong pa phyogs gcig pa*
one, identical, same, single unit	*gcig*
open	*a chad de*
open, fluid, openness (evenly)	*phyal le ba*
open, spaciousness	*had de*
openness	*chad de*
operative [or sense] consciousnesses	*'jug shes*
ordinary mind	*tha mal gyi shes pa*
origin, abiding, and departure	*byung gnas 'gro*
original mind	*dang po'i shes pa*
overpowering	*zil gnon / zil gyis mnan*
path of a single stride	*lam gcig chod*
path of logic	*rtog ge'i lam*
path of the essence	*snying po'i lam*
perception, cognitive process, apprehension	*'dzin stangs*
percepts and perceivers, something perceived and a perceiver	*gzung 'dzin*
phenomena	*chos can*

ENGLISH / SANSKRIT	TIBETAN
phenomena, dharma, quality, topic (dharma topic)	*chos*
physical flexibility	*lus las su rung ba*
play (display)	*rol pa*
postmeditative appearances	*rjes snang*
postmeditative attainment	*rjes thob*
postmeditative attainment [of seeing things] as illusionlike	*sgyu ma lta bu'i rjes thob*
postmeditative mind/mental states, mental states of/during postmeditative attainment	*rjes shes*
practice (bring into experience)	*nyams su len pa*
practice lineage	*sgrub brgyud*
practice tradition	*sgrub lugs*
practice, preparation (yogic techniques, preparatory practices)	*sbyor ba*
practice, rely upon, foster, cultivate (resort to, turn to, study with, train with, apprentice, serve, attend to, consult with, tend)	*bsten pa*
prajñā	*shes rab*
preparatory stage	*nyer bsdogs*
presume, assume, be conceited	*rlom pa*
primordial, open emptiness	*ye stong phyal ba*
problem, fault, failing, flaw	*skyon*
proficient, skilled, to master	*rang byan tshud pa*
projection, display	*rnam 'phrul*
provisional meaning	*drang don*
pure emptiness, utterly empty	*stong sang nge ba*

ENGLISH / SANSKRIT	TIBETAN
pure perception	*dag snang*
qualitativeness and quantitativeness	*ji lta ji snyed kyi don*
quiet	*lhan ne*
quiet, expansive	*cham me*
quietly, comfortably, with ease (gently, wholly, completely, easily)	*cham gyis / cham cham*
radiance	*'od / 'od zer, gdangs*
radiance (radiant light)	*'od kyi snang ba*
radiant	*tse ne, wal le*
radiant, sparkling	*mdangs*
rākṣasī	*srin mo*
random experience	*nyams byung rgyal*
rational analysis	*rigs pas dpyad pa*
Ratnamati	bLo gros rin chen
real, usual, objectively existent (actual, objectively real things, specifically characterized)	*rang mtshan pa*
realize (understand, recognize, know)	*rtogs pa*
recall, clarify	*gsal 'debs pa*
recognition of [mind] itself (recognize, recognition)	*rang ngo shes*
recognize	*ngo shes pa*
recognize [what is pointed out]	*ngo 'phrod pa*
recollections and thoughts, memories and thoughts	*dran rtog*
reflexive awareness	*rang rig*
reflexively aware (aware of itself by itself)	*rang gis rang rig*

English / Sanskrit	Tibetan
reflexively aware cognition	*rang gis rig pa'i shes pa*
reflexively aware wisdom	*rang gis rig pa'i ye shes*
reflexively clear (itself clear)	*rang gsal ba*
reification (clinging to reality)	*bden 'dzin*
reify, grasp at existence, reification	*dngos 'dzin*
relaxed, loose	*lhug pa*
released bliss that is changeable	*'pho 'gyur dang bcas pa'i 'dzag bde*
renunciate	*bya btang*
reparation and restoration [liturgies]	*bskang gso*
representations	*gzugs brnyan*
rest, settle	*'jog pa, gnas pa*
rest/remain in equipoise, rest evenly	*mnyam par bzhag pa/'jog pa/gzhag pa/zhog*
resting meditation	*'jog sgom*
rigid	*dur dur po / dur drags pa*
ritual permissions	*dbang rjes gnang*
routine, habitual state, regular, bad habit	*lang can*
samādhi	*ting nge 'dzin*
samādhi of a majestic lion	*seng ge rnam par bsgyings pa'i ting 'dzin*
same or different	*gcig tha dad*
Sarvavid Vairocana	Kun rig rNam par snang mdzad
scorn, ignore, deny, have contempt (downplay, care nothing for, look down upon, dismiss)	*khyad du bsad pa/gsod pa/gsad pa*
scriptural tradition	*gzhung lugs*
seeing mind	*sems mthong ba*

English / Sanskrit	Tibetan
self of persons, personal self	*gang zag gi bdag*
self-entity of phenomena	*chos kyi bdag*
self-luminous	*rang 'od*
self-pacified, be pacified in and of themselves	*rang zhi*
self-radiance	*rang mdangs*
self, self-entity	*bdag*
serene	*mer re*
settle, rest (establish)	*bzhag pa, 'jog pa, gzhag pa, zhog*
Śankhapālo	Dung skyong
sharp	*hrig ge*
sharp, intense, strong	*ngar*
sharp, vivid	*sa le*
sheer openness	*yal le chad de*
Siddharājñī	Grub pa'i rgyal mo
single unit or a plurality	*gcig du ma*
six modes of consciousness	*tshogs drug / rnam shes tshogs drug*
Six-Armed One	Phyag drug pa
Sixteen Suchnesses	De nyid bcu drug
slack	*lhod po*
slackness	*zhum pa*
sluggishness	*rmugs pa*
solid, solidity, solidification	*a 'thas*
"something" about which you think, what is thought of, "something" thought of	*snyam pa'i skad de ba / de skad snyam*
something known	*shes rgyu*

English / Sanskrit	Tibetan
something luminous	*'od gsal rgyu*
something nominal	*btags pa ba*
spacious	*gu yangs*
sparkling bliss, suffused with bliss	*bde lham me*
sphere of experience, experiential sphere, province, sphere, domain	*spyod yul*
spirits	*gdon*
spiritual practices	*dge sbyor*
spontaneously existent, spontaneous existence	*lhun grub / lhun gyis grub pa*
stabilizing the settled mind	*sems zin pa brtan par byed pa*
stage of union	*zung 'jug gi rim pa*
stages of instruction	*khrid rim*
stages of meditation, way to cultivate, meditation process (meditation manual, texts on the stages of meditation, meditation systems)	*sgom rim*
stages of the path, graduated path	*lam rim*
stagnant, stagnant state	*steng po*
stagnate	*mthug po*
stillness, resting, abide (maintain, sustain, to be present)	*gnas pa*
straying (place/points to go astray)	*gol sa*
Subhaginī	sKal pa bzang mo
subversive meditation	*bzlog sgom, ldog sgom*
suchness (tattva)	*de kho na nyid*
sudden	*thol le ba*
Sukhanātha	bDe ba'i mgon po

ENGLISH / SANSKRIT	TIBETAN
summoning meditation	*'gugs sgom*
superior states of mind	*lhag pa'i sems*
suppleness	*shin sbyangs / shin tu sbyangs pa*
sustain, nurture, practice, cultivate, continue (continue to practice, continue to meditate, apply)	*bskyangs ba, skyong ba, bskyang ba, skyongs*
Sūtra-oriented	*mdo phyogs*
take as the path (incorporate into the path)	*lam du byed pa*
talk of emptiness (jargon of emptiness)	*stong skad*
Tārā	sGrol ma
techniques for resting, methods for resting, ways of resting	*bzhag thabs*
temporary deviation	*'phral shor*
terms and referents	*sgra don*
the view of [or belief in] the perishing [collection, that is, the skandhas]	*'jig lta / 'jig tshogs la lta ba*
theoretical understanding, object of understanding, intellectual understanding	*go yul*
things characterized by illumination, [things with] illuminating characteristics (quality of illumination)	*snang ba'i mtshan ma*
thorough differentiation	*rab tu rnam par 'byed pa*
thorough investigation	*yongs su btsal ba / 'tshol ba*
those without cognitive discrimination	*'dus shes med pa po*
thought in the usual sense, regular thoughts	*rnam rtog rang mtshan pa*
thought, conceptuality (ideas, notions)	*rnam rtog*
thoughts that [reflect] their inherent nature	*ngo bo nyid kyi rnam rtog*
thusness (tathātā)	*de bzhin nyid*

ENGLISH / SANSKRIT	TIBETAN
tighten, be taut (be attentive, tightly focused)	*bsgrims pa, sgrim pa, bsgrim pa, sgrims*
total emptiness	*thams cad stong pa*
totalities	*zad pa*
tranquil	*tshom me*
transmundane, transcendent	*'jig rten las 'das pa*
transparent	*zang thal*
true and correct, what is true, just as it is	*yang dag pa ji lta ba*
true dharma	*yang dag pa'i chos*
true essence	*yang dag pa'i ngo bo nyid*
true mindfulness	*yang dag pa'i dran pa*
true nature	*yang dag don / yang dag pa'i don*
true object of meditation	*yang dag pa'i sgom don*
true view	*lta ba ji lta ba*
true vipaśyanā	*yang dag pa'i lhag mthong*
true wisdom	*yang dag pa'i ye shes*
true, correct, real, authentic (accurate)	*yang dag pa*
turbidity	*rnyog pa*
turbulent, disturbed	*'tshub pa / 'tshub be ba*
Ucaryā Vajrapāṇi	U tsaryA phyag rdor
ultimate essence	*snying po'i don*
ultimate-essence mahāmudrā	*snying po don gyi phyag chen*
unborn, nonarising	*skye med*
unconstrained	*shig ge ba*

English / Sanskrit	Tibetan
uncontrived, noncontrivance (unaltered, non-modification, not modifying, not tampering)	*ma bcos pa*
undercurrents	*'og 'gyus*
unification	*bzung 'jug / bzung du 'jug pa*
universal excellence	*kun tu bzang po*
unsettling circumstances	*rkyen snang*
unspecified (neutral)	*lung ma bstan pa*
vacant, blank	*had po*
vague	*wal po*
Vaiśravaṇa	rNam sras
Vajrapāṇi	Phyag na rdo rje
Vajrāsana	rDo rje gdan
Vajravārāhī	rDo rje phag mo
Vajravidāraṇā	rNam 'joms
vanish on their own	*rang log*
vanish, free	*shigs se*
vibrancy	*sang nge*
vibrant, vivid, sparkling	*sing nge*
view, to look	*lta ba*
Vimalaprabhā	'Og dri ma med pa
visual impairment (blurriness)	*rab rib*
vivid	*gsal lam, gsal le, lhang lhang*
vivid appearances	*gsal snang*
vivid brilliance	*bkra rig rig pa*
void	*stong stong po*

English / Sanskrit	Tibetan
wakeful state	*grung sang nge*
wander, move, waver	*g.yo ba*
way of being	*'dug tshul, 'dug lugs*
way things appear, mode of appearance	*snang tshul*
ways of looking	*blta lugs*
weary, disenchanted, disillusioned	*skyo ba, yid 'byung ba*
what is concordant	*cha mthun pa*
wisdom	*ye shes*
without any compartmentalization	*grva ma nyams/chag*
yakṣa	*gnod sbyin*
[yogic] discipline	*rtul zhugs*

Tibetan Transliterations

Phonetic Spelling	Wylie Transliteration
Bab-rom	'Bab rom
Barawa	'Ba' ra ba
bardo	*bar do*
Barom Dza De'u	'Ba' rom rdza de'u
Barom Kagyu	'Ba' rom bKa' brgyud
Barom Ka-zhi-druk	'Ba' rom Ka bzhi drug
Barompa	'Ba' rom pa
Butön	Bu ston
Chegompa	lCe sgom pa
Chen-nga Rinchen Den	sPyan snga Rin chen ldan
Chen-nga Tup-wang Tenzin	sPyan snga Thub dbang bstan 'dzin
Chö Gowa	Chos sgo ba
Chödrak Gyatso	Chos grags rgya mtsho
Chödrak Yeshe	Chos grags ye shes
Chöje Cham Gönpa	Chos rje Cham dgon pa
Chöje Khyung-tsangpa	Chos rje Khyung tshang ba
Chöje Machen	Chos rje Ma chen
Chöje Ngokpa	Chos rje rNgog pa
Chöje Rabjampa	Chos rje Rab 'byams pa
Chöje Rupa Samten Gyatso	Chos rje Ru pa bsam gtan rgya mtsho

Phonetic Spelling	Wylie Transliteration
Chöje Tashi Tinle	Chos rje bKra bshis phrin las
Chuzang Loppön	Chu bzang sLob dpon
Dagön	Zla dgon
Dak Rampa	Dvags rams pa
Daklha Gampo	Dvags lha sgam po
Dakpo Lhaje	Dvags po lha rje
Dakpo Paṇchen Tashi Namgyal	Dvags po paN chen bKra shis rnam rgyal
Dakpo Tashi Namgyal	Dvags po bKra shis rnam rgyal
Daktong Gyalpo	Dvags stong rgyal po
Darma Wangchuk	Dar ma dbang phyug
Datong Chewa	mDa' stong mche ba
Dechen Lingpa	bDe chen gling pa
Dedak Chenmo Chöwang	sDe bdag chen mo chos dbang
Densatil	gDan sa mthil
Deteng	bDe stengs
Deteng Tulku Tashi Gyatso	bDe stengs sprul sku bKra shis rgya mtsho
Dönyö Gyatso	Don yon rgya mtsho
Dorje Sherab	rDo rje shes rab
Drak-long	Brag long
Dre-drang Chumik Nakpo	Dred 'brang chu mig nag po
Drikung Chen-nga Drakpa Jungnay	'Bri gung spyan snga Grags pa 'byung gnas
Drikung Chungtsang Rigzin Chödrak	'Bri gung Chung tshang Rig 'dzin chos kyi grags pa
Drikung Kagyu	'Bri gung bKa' brgyud
Drikung Khang-tok	'Bri gung khang thog

Phonetic Spelling	Wylie Transliteration
Drö	sGros
Drom Tönpa	'Brom ston pa
Drukpa Kagyu	'Brug pa bKa' brgyud
Drum Tsa-nyin Sibwa	Byang brum tsha nyin srib ba
Drung Rabjampa Tashi Palzang	Drung rab 'jams pa bKra shis dpal bzang
Drungpa Namkha Dorje	Drung pa Nam mkha' rdo rje
Drupwang Mipam Tashi Lodrö	Grub dbang mi pham bkra shis blo gros
Dusum Khyenpa	Dus gsum mkhyen pa
Dzare	rDza ras
Dzi-go Chö-yak	rDzis mgo mchod g.yag
dzog-chen	rdzogs chen
Gampo Chöje Sönam Lhundrup	sGam po chos rje bSod nams lhun grub
Gampopa	sGam po pa
Gelong Pal	dGe slong dpal
Geluk	dGe lugs
Gö Lotsāwa	'Gos lo tsā ba
Go-lek	mGo legs
Gomchung	sGom chung
Gomde Tse	sGom bde rtse
Gomtsul	sGom tshul
Gorampa Sönam Seng-ge	Go rams pa bSod nams seng ge
Götsangpa	rGod tshang pa
Gungtang	Gung thang
Guru Teng	Gu ru steng

Phonetic Spelling	Wylie Transliteration
Gyal	rGyal
Gyatön Namkha Lekpa	rGya ston Nam mkha' legs pa
Gyatönpa	rGya ston pa
Gyer-gom Tsultrim Seng-ge	Gyer sgom tshul khrims seng ge
Hor	Hor
Hor-pön Tarpa Bum	Hor dpon Thar pa 'bum
Jamgön Kongtrul Lodrö Taye	'Jam mgon kong sprul bLo gros mtha' yas
Jamyang Shepa	'Jam dbyangs bzhad pa
Jangchub Nangwa	Byang chub snang ba
Je Rinpoche	rJe rin po che
Jetsun	rJe btsun
Jikme Lingpa	'Jigs med gling pa
Jikten Sumgön	'Jig rten gsum mgon
Jorpu	sByor phu
Ka-chen Tashi Lekpa	bKa' chen bkra shis legs pa
Ka-zhipa	Ka bzhi pa
Khachö Wangpo	mKha' spyod dbang po
Kadam	bKa gdams
Kagyu	bKa' brgyud
Kangyur	bKa' 'gyur
Kar	Kar
Karma Kagyu	Kar ma bKa' brgyud
Karma Tashi Chöpel	Karma bkra shis chos 'phel
Karma Tinle	Karma phrin las

PHONETIC SPELLING	WYLIE TRANSLITERATION
Karmapa	Karma pa
Kham	Khams
Khampa Dor-gyal	Khams pa rDor rgyal
Khamtrul Kunga Tenzin	Khams sprul Kun dga' bstan 'dzin
Khenchen Shākya Zangpo	mKhan chen ShAkya bzang po
Khenpo Jang Rampa	mKhan po Byang ram pa
Khenpo Shenga	mKhan po gZhan dga'
Khyentse Wangpo	mKhyen brtse'i dbang po
Kodrakpa Sönam Gyaltsen	Ko brag pa bSod nams rgyal mtshan
Könchok Yenlak	dKon mchog yan lag
Kunga Rinchen	Kun dga' rin chen
Kyol Zam Dong	sKyol zam gdong
La-dingwa	bLa sdings ba
Lama Nyima Drakpa	bLa ma Nyi ma grags pa
Lama Sangye Drumpa	bLa ma Sangs rgyas bhrum pa
Lama Zhang	bLa ma Zhang
Lay-tö	Las stod
Len-me Gyalwa	rLan smad rgyal ba
Lhasung	Lha srung
Lho Layakpa Jangchub Ngödrup	Lho la yag pa Byang chub dngos grub
Lhodrak Ku-kye	Lho brag sku skye
Ling Repa	gLing ras pa
Loppön Chöpel Tashi	sLob dpon Chos dpal bkra shis
Loppön Tubten Palbar	sLob dpon Thub bstan dpal 'bar

Phonetic Spelling	Wylie Transliteration
Mar-yulway Gyalse Chöje	Mar yul ba'i rgyal sras chos rje
Markham	dMar khams
Marpa	Mar pa
Martsang Kagyu	sMar tshang bKa' brgyud
Mikyö Dorje	Mi bskyod rdo rje
Milarepa	Mi la ras pa
Mipam	Mi pham
Mipam Chöwang	Mi pham chos dbang
Nālendra	NA lan dra
Nam-tser Kha	gNam tsher kha
Namtso'i Donang	Nam mtsho'i do nang
Nang	Nang
Nangchen Seng-ge Gyaltsen	Nang chen Seng ge rgyal mtshan
Nangdo	Nang do
Ngo-tro Rabjampa	Ngo khro rab 'byams pa
Ngu-gang Khyungpo	sNgu sgang khyung po
Norbu Gyenpa	Nor bu rgyan pa
Nyedo	rNyed rdo
Nyi Triru	Nyi khri ru
Nyima Drakpa	Nyi ma grags pa
Nyingma	rNying ma
Nyukla Lekshe Ling	sNyug la legs bshad gling
nyungne	*smyung gnas*
Orgyenpa	O rgyan pa

Phonetic Spelling	Wylie Transliteration
Pakdru	Phag gru
Pakmo	Phag mo
Pakmo Drupa	Phag mo gru pa
Pang Karwa Tashi Chöjor	sPang dkar ba bKra shis chos 'byor
Pang Melong	sPang me long
Parpuwa Lodrö Seng-ge	Par phu ba bLo gros seng ge
Pema Karpo	dPadma dkar po
Pö-sang Sum-do	sPod gsang gsum mdo
Pön Karma Pal	dPon Karma dpal
Potowa	Po to ba
Rangjung Dorje	Rang byung rdo rje
Rechungpa	Ras chung pa
Ri-zhol	Ri zhol
Rigdzin Drolma	Rig 'dzin sgrol ma
Rigdzin Gödem	Rig 'dzin rgod ldem
Rigzin Chödrak	Rig 'dzin chos grags
Rinchen Puntsok	Rin chen phun tshogs
Ritil	Ri mthil
Ritrö Wangchuk	Ri khrod dbang phyug
Rongtön Sheja Kunzik	Rong ston Shes bya kun rig
Sakya	Sa skya
Sakya Paṇḍita	Sa skya PaNDi ta
Sal-tong Shogom	gSal stong sho/shvo sgom
Samdey Lama Rabjam Mrawa Samten Kunga	bSam sde bla ma rab 'byams smra ba bSam gtan kun dga'

Phonetic Spelling	Wylie Transliteration
Samye	bSam yas
Sangye Lingpa	Sangs rgyas gling pa
Segul	bSe mgul
Serdingpa	gSer sdings pa
Serdok Chöje Drakpa	gSer mdog Chos rje grags pa
Shākya Chokden	ShAkya mchog ldan
Shākya Gelong Zangpo	ShAkya'i dge slong bZang po
Shangpa Kagyu	Shangs pa bKa' brgyud
Sherab Namgyal	Shes rab rnam rgyal
Shukseb Kagyu	Shug gseb bKa' brgyud
Sönam Gyatso	bSod nams rgya mtsho
Sönam Lhundrup	bSod nams lhun grub
Taklung Kagyu	sTag lung bKa' brgyud
Taklung Zim-jilpa	sTag lung gZims spyil pa
Tana	rTa rna
Tana Gelong	rTa rna dge slong
Tashi Do	bKra shis do
Tashi Namgyal Chokyi Palzangpo	bKra shis rnam rgyal chos kyi dpal bzang po
Tel	Thel
Tengyur	bsTan 'gyur
Thrangu Rinpoche	Khra 'gu rin po che
Til	mThil
Tri Rinpoche Tashi Kundrak	Khri rin po che bKra shis kun grags
Trisong De-tsen	khri srong lde btsan

Phonetic Spelling	Wylie Transliteration
Tro-gyal Bum	Khro rgyal 'bum
Tropu Kagyu	Khro phu bKa' brgyud
trulkhor	*'phrul 'khor*
Tsalpa Kagyu	Tshal pa bKa' brgyud
Tsang	gTsang
Tsang Nyön Heruka	gTsang smyon he ru ka
Tsang-sar Go Shri	Tsang sar go shri
Tsangpa Gyare Yeshe Dorje	gTsang pa rgya ras ye shes rdo rje
Tsewa	rTse ba
Tsongkhapa	Tsong kha pa
tulku/tülku	*sprul sku*
Tulku Sönam Gyatso	sPrul sku bSod nams rgya mtsho
Tulku Sönam Rinchen	sPrul sku bSod nams rin chen
Tulku Tashi Tinle	sPrul sku bKra shis phrin las
Tulku Tinle Namgyal	sPrul sku Phrin las rnam rgyal
Tup-wang Tenzin	Thub dbang bstan 'dzin
U	dbUs
U-se	dbU se
Uru	dbU ru
Wangchuk Dorje	dBang phyug rdo rje
Wangchuk Gyaltsen	dBang phyug rgyal mtshan
Wolwawa	Wol wa ba
Yang Gönpa	Yang dgon pa
Yangri	Yang ri

Phonetic Spelling	Wylie Transliteration
Yasang Kagyu	g.Ya' bzang bKa' brgyud
Yelpa Kagyu	Yel pa bKa' brgyud
Yelpa Yeshe Tsekpa	Yel pa Ye shes brtsegs pa
Yong-dzin Sönam Chöpal	Yongs 'dzin bSod nams chos 'phel
Zang-lung	Zang lung
Zhab-de Önpo	Zhabs bde dbon po
Zhal-kor Bumpa	Zhal skor 'bum pa
Zhal-nga Önpo Gendün Seng-ge	Zhal snga dbon po dGe 'dun seng ge
Zhang Rinpoche Tsön-dru Drakpa	Zhang rin po che brTson 'grus grags pa
Zhigpo Lingpa	Zhig po ling pa
Zhokha Or	Zho kha 'or
Zhol-teng Sarma	Zhol stengs/steng gsar ma
Zur	Zur
Zurmang Chöje Padma Gyalpo	Zur mang Chos rje Padma rgyal po

Bibliography

Works Cited in *Moonbeams*

Canonical Scriptures

Abhidhāna-uttaratantra (*mNgon par brjod pa'i rgyud bla ma*), also known as *Avadāna-stotra-tantra* (*Nges par brjod pa'i rgyud*). Toh. 369, H.K. 385.

Accomplishment of the Purpose of Meditation (*sGom don grub pa*). Not found in the Kangyur. Cited in Gampopa's *Sunrays of Scriptural Citations.*

Account of the Noble Deeds of Avalokiteśvara (*sPyan ras gzigs kyi rtogs brjod*). In the *Compendium of Dharma Sūtra.*

Avataṃsaka (*Avataṃsakasūtra, Phal po che / Phal po che'i mdo / Sangs rgyas phal chen / Sangs rgyas phal po che zhes bya ba shin tu rgyas pa chen po'i mdo*). Toh. 44, H.K. 94.

Bodhisattva's Piṭaka (*Bodhisattvapiṭakasūtra, Byang chub sems dpa'i sde snod*). Toh. 56, H.K. 56.

Buddha-kapāla (*Buddhakapālatantra, Sangs rgyas thod pa*). Toh. 424, H.K. 400.

Buddhasamāyoga (*Sarvabuddha-samāyogaḍākinī-jālasaṁvara-nāma-uttaratantra, Sangs rgyas mnyam sbyor / Sangs rgyas thams cad dang mnyam par sbyor ba mkha' 'gro ma sgyu ma bde ba'i mchog ces bya ba'i rgyud bla ma*). Toh. 366, H.K. 376.

Caturpīṭha (*Caturpīṭha-mahāyoginī-tantrarāja, rNal 'byor ma'i rgyud kyi rgyal po chen po dpal gdan bzhi pa*). Toh. 428, H.K. 404.

Compendium of Dharma Sūtra (*Dharmasaṃgītisūtra, Chos yang dag par sdud pa'i mdo*). Toh. 238, H.K. 239.

Descent into Laṅkā Sūtra (*Laṅkāvatārasūtra, Lang kar gshegs pa'i mdo*). Toh. 107, H.K. 110.

Dhāraṇī: Access to the Nonconceptual (*Avikalpapraveśadhāraṇī, rNam par mi rtog par 'jug pa'i gzungs*). Toh. 142, H.K. 144.

Discourse for Kāśyapa. (*Kāśyapa-parivarta-sūtra, 'Od srung gi le'u zhes bya ba'i mdo*). Toh. 87, H.K. 87.

Excellent Siddhi Tantra (*Susiddhikara-mahātantra-sādhanopāyika-paṭala, Legs grub / Legs par grub par byed pa'i rgyud chen po las sgrub pa'i thabs rim par phye ba*). Toh. 807, H.K. 764.

Gaṇḍavyūha (*sDong po bkod pa*). Chapter 45 of the *Avataṃsaka.* Toh. 44, H.K. 94.

Guhyasamāja Tantra (*Sarvatathāgatakāyavākcittarahasyaguhyasamājanāmamahākalparāja, gSang 'dus / De bzhin gshegs pa thams cad kyi sku gsung thugs kyi gsang chen gsang ba 'dus pa zhes bya ba brtag pa'i rgyal po chen po*). Toh. 442, H.K. 416a.

Heap of Jewels (Ratnakūṭa, dKon mchog brtsegs pa). Toh. 45–93.

Heart of Wisdom Tantra (*Jñānagarbha, Ye shes snying po*). Toh. 421, H.K. 381.

Heart Sūtra (*Prajñāpāramitāhṛdaya, Shes rab snying po / bCom ldan 'das ma shes rab kyi pha rol tu phyin pa'i snying po*). Toh. 21, H.K. 26.

Hevajra Tantra / Two-Part Hevajra Tantra / The King of Tantras, Called the Glorious Hevajra (*Hevajra-tantra-rāja-nāma, dPal brtag pa gnyis pa / Kye'i rdo rje zhes bya ba rgyud kyi rgyal po* (Part I) and *Kye'i rdo rje mkha' 'gro ma dra ba'i sdom pa'i rgyud kyi rgyal po* (Part II)). Toh. 417 and 418, H 378a and H 378b.

Instructions on the Mahāyāna (*Mahāyānopadeśasūtra, Theg pa chen po'i man ngag gi mdo*). Toh. 169, H.K. 170.

Jewel Cloud Sūtra (*Ratnameghasūtra, dKon mchog sprin gyi mdo*). Toh. 231, H.K. 232.

Kālacakra Tantra / [Kālacakra] Laghutantra / Glorious Kālacakra, King of Tantras: Issued from the Supreme, Original Buddha (by Mañjuśrī Yashas) (*Laghutantra / Laghukālacakra / Paramādibuddhoddhṛta-śrīkālacakra-nāma-tantrarāja, bsDus pa'i rgyud / Dus 'khor nyung ngu / mChog gi dang po'i sangs rgyas las phyung ba rgyud kyi rgyal po dpal dus kyi 'khor lo*). Toh. 362/1346.

King of Samādhi Sūtra / King of Samādhi, Which Elaborates on the Equality That Is the Nature of Phenomena (*Samādhirāja-sūtra / Ārya-sarvadharma-svabhāva-samatā-vipañcita-samādhirāja-nāma-mahāyāna-sūtra, Ting nge 'dzin gyi rgyal po'i mdo / 'Phags pa chos thams cad kyi rang bzhin mnyam pa nyid rnam par spros pa ting nge 'dzin gyi rgyal po zhes bya ba theg pa chen po'i mdo*). Toh. 127, H.K. 129.

King of the Tantras of Secret Amṛta (*Amṛta-guhyatantrarāja, gSang ba bdud rtsi rgyal po'i rgyud / gSang ba bdud rtsi'i rgyud kyi rgyal po*). Toh. 401, not in H.K.

Laghusaṃvara (*sDom pa chung ngu*), also known as the *Cakrasaṃvara Root Tantra* (*bDe mchog rtsa rgyud*). Toh. 368, H.K. 384.

Mahāmudrā-tilaka (*Mahāmudrā-tilakaṃ, Phyag rgya chen po'i thig le*). Toh. 420, H.K. 380.

Mañjuśrī Root Tantra (*Mañjuśrīmūlatantra, 'Jam dpal gyi rtsa ba'i rgyud*). Toh. 543, H.K. 501.

Moon Lamp Sūtra (*Zla ba sgron me'i mdo*). See *King of Samādhi Sūtra.*

Name-Chanting of Mañjuśrī (*Mañjuśrī-nāmasaṁgīti / Mañjuśrījñānasattvasya-paramārtha-nāmasaṃgīti, 'Jam dpal mtshan brjod / 'Jam dpa'i don dam pa'i mtshan yang dag par brjod pa*). Toh. 360, H.K. 369.

Nīvaraṇaviṣkambhin's Praise of the Bhagavān (*sGrib pa rnam sel gyis bcom ldan 'das la bstod pa*). Not found in the Kangyur.

Ornament of the Light of Wisdom (*Jñānālokālaṃkāra / Sarvabuddhaviṣayāvatāra-jñānālokālaṃkārasūtra, Ye shes snang ba rgyan / Sangs rgyas thams cad kyi yul la 'jug pa'i ye shes snang ba'i rgyan*). Toh. 100, H.K. 103.

Ornament of the Vajra Heart (*Vajrahṛdaya-alaṃkāra-tantra, rDo rje snying po rgyan gyi rgyud*). Toh. 451, H.K. 788.

Play in Full (*Lalitavistara, rGya cher rol pa*). Toh. 95, H.K. 96.

Play of Mañjuśrī Sūtra (*Mañjuśrīvikrīḍitasūtra, 'Jam dpal rnam par rol pa'i mdo*). Toh. 96, H.K. 97.

Prajñāpāramitā in Eight Thousand Lines (*Aṣṭasāhasrikāprajñāpāramitā, brGyad stong pa / Shes rab kyi pha rol tu phyin pa brgyad stong pa*). Toh. 12, H.K. 11.

Prajñāpāramitā in Eighteen Thousand Lines (*Aṣṭādaśasāhasrikā-prajñāpāramitā, Shes rab kyi pha rol tu phyin pa khri brgyad stong pa*). Toh. 10, H.K. 12.

Prajñāpāramitā in One Hundred Thousand Lines (*Śatasāhasrikā-prajñāpāramitā, Shes rab kyi pha rol tu phyin pa stong phrag brgya pa*). Toh. 8, H.K. 9.

Prajñāpāramitā in Seven Hundred Lines (*Saptaśatikānāmaprajñāpāramitā, Sher phyin bdun brgya pa / Shes rab kyi pha rol tu phyin pa bdun brgya pa)*. Toh. 24, H.K. 15.

Prajñāpāramitā in Ten Thousand Lines (*Daśasāhasrikā-prajñāpāramitā, Shes rab kyi pha rol tu phyin pa khri pa*). Toh. 11, H.K. 13.

Prajñāpāramitā in Twenty-Five Thousand Lines (*Pañcaviṃśatisāhasrikā-prajñāpāramitā, Shes rab kyi pha rol tu phyin pa stong phrag nyi shu lnga pa*). Toh. 9, H.K. 10.

Precious Torch Dhāraṇī (*Ratnolkādhāraṇīsūtra, dKon mchog ta la la'i gzungs*). Toh. 145/847, H.K. 100.

Questions of the Four Goddesses. (*Caturdevī-paripṛcchā, Lha mo bzhis yongs su zhus pa*). Toh. 446, H.K. 420.

Samputa (*Samputa-nāma-mahātantra, Yang dag par sbyor ba zhes bya ba'i rgyud*). Toh. 381, H.K. 396.

Saṃvarodaya (*Saṃvarodaya / Mahāsaṃvarodaya-nāma-tantrarāja, bDe mchog 'byung ba / sDom 'byung / bDe mchog 'byung ba zhes bya ba'i rgyud kyi rgyal po chen po*). Toh. 373, H.K. 389.

Secret Tilaka of the Moon (*Candraguhyatilaka, Zla gsang thig le*). Toh. 477, H.K. 446.

Secret Vajra Ḍāka Tantra (*Vajraḍāka-guhyatantrarāja, rDo rje mkha' 'gro gsang ba'i rgyud kyi rgyal po*). Toh. 399, not in H.K.

Spacelike Samādhi Sūtra (*Nam mkha lta bu'i ting nge 'dzin gyi mdo*). Not found in the Kangyur. Cited in Gampopa's *Sunrays of Scriptural Citations.*

Summary of the [Kālacakra] Initiation (*Sekoddeśa, dBang mdor bstan pa*). Toh. 361, H.K. 370.

Sūtra on the Buddha's Deliberations (*Buddhasaṅgītisūtra, 'Phags pa sangs rgyas bgro ba'i mdo*). Toh. 228, H.K. 229.

Sūtra of the Chapter on the Thirty-Three (*Trayastriṃśatparivartasūtra, Sum cu rtsa gsum pa'i le'u*). Toh. 223, H.K. 224.

Sūtra on Cultivating Faith in the Mahāyāna (*Mahāyānaprasādaprabhāvanasūtra, Theg chen la dad pa'i mdo*). Toh. 144, H.K. 146.

Sūtra on Ethical Conduct (*Śīlasaṃyuktasūtra, Tshul khrims dang ldan pa'i mdo / Tshul khrims yang dag par ldan pa'i mdo*). Toh. 303, H.K. 306.

Sūtra of Expanding Realization (*rTogs pa rgyas pa'i mdo/ rTogs pa chen po yongs su rgyas pa'i mdo*). Toh. 265, H.K. 267.

Sūtra of Fragments (*mDo sil bu*). Not found in the Kangyur. Cited in Gampopa's *Ornament of Precious Liberation.*

Sūtra of Genuine Samādhi (*Ting 'dzin dam pa'i mdo*). Possibly *Sūtra of the Supreme, Genuine Samadhi* (*Samādhi-agrottama, Ting nge 'dzin mchog dam pa*). Toh. 137, H.K. 139. Cited in Gampopa's *Sunrays of Scriptural Citations.*

Sūtra of the Good Eon (*Bhadrakalpikasūtra, bsKal bzang/ bsKal pa bzang po pa*). Toh. 94, not in H.K.

Sūtra of the Great Uṣṇīṣa (*Mahoṣṇīṣa / *Bhagavato mahoṣṇīṣa tathāgata-guhya-sādhanārtha-prāptihetu-sarvabodhisattvacaryāśūramgame-daśasahasraparivartte daśama-parivartta, gTsug tor chen po'i mdo / bCom ldan 'das kyi gtsug tor chen po de bzhin gshegs pa'i gsang ba sgrub pa'i don mngon par thob pa'i rgyu byang chub sems dpa' thams cad kyi spyod pa dpa' bar 'gro ba'i mdo le'u stong phrag bcu pa las le'u bcu pa*). Toh. 236, H.K. 237.

Sūtra on Holding the Genuine Dharma (*Dam pa'i chos yongs su 'dzin pa'i mdo*). Not found in the Kangyur. Cited in Gampopa's *Sunrays of Scriptural Citations.*

Sūtra on the Inconceivable Secret Teachings of the Tathāgatas (*Tathāgatācintya-guhyanirdeśa, De bzhin gshegs pa gsang ba'i mdo / De bzhin gshegs pa'i gsang ba bsam gyis mi khyab pa bstan pa'i mdo*). Toh. 47, H.K. 47.

Sūtra of the King of the Genuine Dharma (*Saddharmarājasūtra, Chos kyi rgyal po'i mdo/ Dam pa'i chos kyi rgyal po'i mdo*). Toh. 243, H.K. 244.

Sūtra on Maitreya's Setting Forth (*Maitreyaprasthānasūtra, Byams pa 'jug pa'i mdo*). Toh. 198, H.K. 199.

Sūtra on Not Moving from Dharmatā / Sūtra on the Light of All Individual Things Not Moving from Dharmatā, Emptiness (*Dharmatā-svabhāva-śūnyatācala-pratisarvāloka-sūtra, Chos nyid mi g.yo ba'i mdo / Chos nyid rang gi g.yo bar tha dad par thams cad la snang ba'i mdo*). Toh. 128, H.K. 130.

Sūtra of Precious Space (*Nam mkha' rin po che'i mdo*). Not found in the Kangyur. Cited in Gampopa's *Ornament of Precious Liberation.*

Sūtra of the Questions of Akṣayamati (*Akṣayamatiparipṛcchāsūtra, bLo gros mi zad pas zhus pa'i mdo*). Toh. 89, H.K. 89.

Sūtra of the Questions of Bhadrapāla (*Bhadrapālaparipṛcchāsūtra, bZang skyong gis zhus pa'i mdo*). See *Sūtra on the Samādhi in Which the Buddhas of the Present All Stand Before One.*

Sūtra of the Questions of Brahmaviśeṣacintin (*Brahmaviśeṣacintiparipṛcchā, Khyad par sems kyis zhus pa'i mdo / Tshangs pa khyad par sems kyis zhus pa'i mdo*). Toh. 160, H.K. 161.

Sūtra of the Questions of Gaganagañja (*Gaganagañjaparipṛcchāsūtra, Nam mkha' mdzod kyis zhus pa*). Toh. 148, H.K. 149.

Sūtra of the Questions of the Girl Ratna. See *Instructions on the Mahāyāna.*

Sūtra of the Questions of Kāshyapa (*'Od srungs kyis zhus pa*). See *Discourse for Kāshyapa.*

Sūtra of the Questions of Maitreya (*Maitreya-paripṛcchā, Byams zhus kyi mdo*). Toh. 85, H.K. 85. Cited in Gampopa's *Sunrays of Scriptural Citations.*

Sūtra of the Questions of Rāṣṭrapāla (*Rāṣṭrapālaparipṛcchāsūtra, Yul 'khor skyong gis zhus pa'i mdo*). Toh. 62, H.K. 62.

Sūtra of the Questions of Ratnachūḍa (*Ratnacūḍaparipṛcchāsūtra, gTsug na rin po ches zhus pa'i mdo*). Toh. 91, H.K. 91.

Sūtra of the Questions of Revatī (*Nam grus zhus pa'i mdo*). Not found in the Kangyur.

Sūtra of the Questions of Sāgaramati (*Sāgaramati-paripṛcchā-nāma-mahāyāna-sūtra, bLo gros rgya mtshos zhus pa zhes bya ba theg pa chen poi mdo*). Toh. 152, H.K. 153.

Sūtra of the Questions of Subāhu (*Subāhu-paripṛcchā-nāma-mahāyāna-sūtra, Lag bzangs kyis zhus pa zhes bya ba theg pa chen po'i mdo*). Toh 70, H.K. 70.

Sūtra of the Questions of Upāli (*Upāli-paripṛcchāsutra, Nye bar 'khor gyis zhus pa'i mdo*). Toh. 68, H.K. 68.

Sūtra of the Questions of Vīradatta (*Vīradattaparipṛcchāsutra, dPas byin gyis zhus pa'i mdo*). Toh. 72, H.K. 72.

Sūtra Revealing Suchness (*De kho na nyid bstan pa'i mdo*). Not found in the Kangyur. Cited in Gampopa's *Sunrays of Scriptural Citations.*

Sūtra on the Samādhi in Which the Buddhas of the Present All Stand Before One (*Pratyutpannabuddhasaṃmukhāvasthitasamādhisūtra, Da ltar gyi sangs rgyas mngon sum du bzhugs pa'i ting nge 'dzin gyi mdo*). Toh 133, H.K. 135. Also called *Sūtra of the Questions of Bhadrapāla* (*Bhadrapālaparipṛcchāsūtra, bZang skyong gis zhus pa'i mdo*).

Sūtra of the Teaching of Akṣayamati (*Akṣayamatinirdeśasūtra, bLo gros mi zad pas bstan pa'i mdo*). Toh. 175, H.K. 176.

Sūtra Teaching Four Qualities (*Caturdharmanirdeśa, Chos bzhi bstan pa'i mdo*). Toh. 249, H.K. 250.

Sūtra Teaching Great Compassion (*Tathāgatamahākaruṇānirdeśasūtra, sNying rje chen po bstan pa'i mdo / De bzhin gshegs pa'i snying rje chen po nges par bstan pa*). Toh. 147, H.K. 148.

Sūtra Teaching the Undifferentiable Nature of the Dharmadhātu (*Dharmadhātu-prakṛti-asaṃbheda-nirdeśa, Chos kyi dbyings kyi rang bzhin dbyer med pa bstan pa'i mdo*). Toh 52, H.K. 52.

Sūtra on the Ten Bhūmis (*Daśabhūmikasūtra, Sa bcu pa'i mdo*). Chapter 31 of the *Avataṃsaka.* Toh. 44, H.K. 94.

Sūtra of the Ten Wheels of Kṣitigarbha (*Daśacakrakṣitigarbha, Sa'i snying po'i 'khor lo bcu pa*). Toh. 239, H.K. 240.

Sūtra on the Wisdom Mudra (*Tathāgatajñānamudrāsamādhisūtra, Ye shes phyag rgya'i mdo / De bzhin gshegs pa'i ye shes kyi phyag rgya'i ting nge 'dzin gyi mdo*). Toh. 131, H.K. 133.

Tantra of the Great River of the Inconceivable Secrets of Ālikāli (*Alikaliguhyatsin-dhapanibhayumahātantranāma, gSang ba bsam gyis mi khyab pa'i rgyud / A li kA li gsang ba bsam gyis mi khyab pa chu klung chen po'i rgyud*). Not found in the Kangyur. Probably authored by Padampa Sangye. Dingri Volumes / The Volumes of the Root Teachings of the Sacred Dharma Pacification of Suffering, and the Subsidiary, Severance of Evil Object (*Dam chos sdug bsngal zhi byed rtsa ba'i chos sde dang / yan lag bdud kyi gcod yul gyi glegs bam*). Vol. 1/ka. New Delhi: Dingri langkor tsuglag khang, 2013.

Tantra of the Inconceivable Connateness (*Lhan cig skyes pa bsam gyis mi khyab pa'i rgyud*). Not found in the Kangyur.

Tantra of the Inconceivable Secrets (*Cakrasaṃvara-guhyācinta, gSang ba bsam gyis mi khyab pa'i rgyud / 'Khor lo sdom pa gsang ba bsam gyis mi khyab pa'i rgyud*). Toh. 385, not in H.K.

Tantra of Nonabiding (*Rab tu mi gnas pa'i rgyud*). Not found in the Kangyur. Cited in Gampopa's *Ornament of Precious Liberation.*

Tantra of Nonabiding Mahāmudrā (*Phyag rgya chen po rab tu mi gnas pa'i rgyud*). Not found in the Kangyur.

Tantra of Nonabiding Suchness (*De kho na nyid rab tu mi gnas pa'i rgyud*). Not found in the Kangyur. Cited in Gampopa's *Sunrays of Scriptural Citations.*

Tantra Prophesying the Intent (*Sandhivyākaraṇa-tantra, dGongs pa lung bsten pa'i mdo / dGongs pa lung bsten pa'i rgyud*). Toh. 444, H.K. 418.

Tantra of the Questions of Subāhu (*Subāhu-paripṛcchā-nāma-tantra, dPung bzang gis zhus pa zhes bya ba'i rgyud*). Toh. 805, H.K. 761.

Tantra on the Unsullied (*Anāvila-tantrarājā, rNyog pa med pa / rGyud kyi rgyal po rnyog pa med pa*). Toh. 414, H.K. 399.

Teaching on the Armor Array (*Varmavyūhanirdeśasūtra, Go cha'i bkod pa bstan pa*). Toh. 51, H.K. 51.

Teaching on How All Phenomena Are Without Any Origin (*Sarvadharmāpravṛtti-nirdeśa, Chos thams cad 'byung ba med par bstan pa*). Toh. 180, H.K. 181.

Ten Dharmas Sūtra (*Daśadharmakasūtra, Chos bcu pa'i mdo*). Toh. 53, H.K. 53.

Two-Part [Hevajra Tantra]. See *Hevajra Tantra.*

Unraveling the Intent (*Saṃdhinirmocanasūtra, dGongs pa nges 'grel / mDo dgongs 'grel*). Toh. 106, H.K. 109.

Vairocanābhisambodhi (*Mahāvairocanābhisambodhi, rNam snang mngon byang / rNam par snang mdzad chen po mngon par rdzogs par byang chub pa*). Toh. 494, H.K. 462.

Vajramālā (*Vajramālābhidhānamahāyogatantra-sarvatantrahṛdaya-rahasyavibhaṅga, rDo rje phreng ba / rNal 'byor chen po'i rgyud dpal rdo rje phreng ba mngon par brjod pa rgyud thams cad kyi snying po gsang ba rnam par phye ba*). Toh. 445, H.K. 417.

Vajra Ḍāka (*Vajraḍāka-nāma-mahātantrarāja, rDo rje mkha' 'gro / rGyud kyi rgyal po chen po dpal rdo rje mka' 'gro*). Toh. 370, H 386.

Vajra Pañjarā (*Vajrapañjarā / Ārya-ḍākinī-vajrapañjarā-mahātantrarāja-kalpa-nāma, rDo rje gur / 'Phags pa mkha' 'gro ma rdo rje gur zhes bya ba'i rgyud kyi rgyal po chen po'i brtag pa*). Toh. 419, H.K. 379.

Vajra Samādhi Sūtra (*rDo rje ting nge 'dzin gyi mdo*). Not found in the Kangyur. Cited in Gampopa's *Sunrays of Scriptural Citations.*

Verses That Summarize the Prajñāpāramitā Sūtras (*Prajñāpāramitā-saṃcayagāthā, sDud pa / 'Phags pa mdo sdud pa tshigs su bcad pa / Shes rab kyi pha rol tu phyin pa sdud pa*). Toh. 13, H.K. 17.

White Lotus of Great Compassion (*Mahākaruṇāpuṇḍarīka, sNying rje chen po'i padma dkar po*). Toh. 111, H.K. 114.

Wisdom at the Moment of Death (*Ātyayajñāna, 'Da' ka ye shes*). Toh. 122, H.K. 124.

Wisdom Tilaka (*Jñānatilaka-yoginī-tantrarājā-paramamahādbhutaṃ, Ye shes thig le rnal 'byor ma'i rgyud kyi rgyal po chen po mchog tu rmad du byung ba*). Toh. 422, H.K. 382.

Canonical Treatises

Abhayākaragupta. *Commentary on the "Buddhakapāla" / Abhayākara's Source Commentary: A Detailed Explanation of the "Buddhakapāla, King of Tantras"* (*Buddhakapālamahātantrarājaṭīkā-abhayapāddhati, Sangs rgyas thod pa'i 'grel pa / Sangs rgyas thod pa'i rgyud kyi rgyal po chen po'i rgya cher 'grel pa 'jigs pa med pa'i gzhung 'grel*). Toh. 1654.

——. *Kernels of Esoteric instructions* (*Upadeśa-mañjari / Saṃpuṭatantrarāja-ṭīkāmnāyamañjarī, Man snye / Man ngag snye ma / Yang dag par sbyor ba'i rgyud kyi rgyal po'i rgya cher 'grel pa man ngag gi snye ma*). Toh. 1198.

Ācārya Śūra. See Aśvaghoṣa.

Alaṃkakalaśa. *Commentary on the Profound Meaning: Detailed Explanation of the "Glorious Vajramālā," a Mahāyoga Tantra* (*Śrīvajramālāmahāyogatantraṭīkāgaṃbhīrārthadīpikā, rNal 'byor chen po'i rgyud dpal rdo rje phreng ba'i rgya cher 'grel pa zab mo'i don gyi 'grel pa*). Toh. 1795.

Amītavajra. *Illuminating the Suchness of Connate Cakrasaṃvara* (*Cakrasaṃvarasahajatattvāloka, dPal 'khor lo sdom pa'i lhan cig skyes pa'i de kho na nyid snang ba*). Toh. 1504.

Āryadeva. *Discussion of Nonconceptuality* (*Nirvikalpaprakaraṇa, rNam par mi rtog pa'i rab tu byed pa*). Toh. 2279.

——. *Four Hundred Verses* (*Catuḥśatakaśāstra, bZhi brgya pa / bsTan bcos bzhi brgya pa*). Toh. 3846.

——. *Lamp That Summarizes Conduct* (*Caryāmelāpakapradīpa, sPyod bsdus / sPyod pa bsdus pa'i sgron ma*). Toh. 1803.

Āryaśūra. *Synopsis of the Pāramitās* (*Pāramitāsamāsa, Phar phyin bsdus pa / Sher phyin bsdus pa / Pha rol tu phyin pa bsdus pa*). Toh. 3944.

Asaṅga. *Bodhisattvabhūmi* (*Byang chub sems dpa'i sa*). Toh. 4037.

——. *Compendium of Abhidharma* (*Abhidharmasamuccaya, Kun las btus / Chos mngon pa kun las btus pa*). Toh. 4049.

——. *Śrāvakabhūmi* (*Śrāvakabhūmi, Nyan thos kyi sa*). Toh. 4036.

——. *Yogācāryābhūmi* (*Yogācāryābhūmi, Sa'i dngos gzhi / rNal 'byor spyod pa'i sa las dngos gzhi'i sa mang po*). Toh 4035.

Aśvaghoṣa/Bhavideva/Mātṛheṭa/Ācārya Śūra (or Āchārya Vīra). *Compendium of Root Downfalls in the Vajrayāna* (*Vajrayānamūlāpattisaṃgraha, rDo rje theg pa rtsa ba'i ltung ba bsdus pa*). Toh. 2478.

——. *Fifty Verses for the Guru* (*Gurupañcāśikā, bLa ma lnga bcu pa*). Toh. 3721.

——. *Varṇārhavarṇe* (*Varṇārhavarṇe bhagavato buddhasya stotre śakyastava, Sangs rgyas bcom ldan 'das la bstod pa bsngags par 'os pa bsngags pa las bstod par mi nus par bstod pa*). Toh. 1138.

Atīśa. *Detailed Explanation of the Root Downfalls* (*Mūlāpattiṭīkā, rTsa ba'i ltung ba'i rgya cher 'grel pa*). Toh. 2487.

——. *Entrance to the Two Truths* (*Satyadvayāvatāra, bDen pa gnyis la 'jug pa*). Toh. 3902.

——. *Instructions on Madhyamaka* (*Madhyamakopadeśa, dbU ma'i man ngag*). Toh. 3929.

——. *Lamp for the Path of Awakening* (*Bodhipathapradīpa, Byang chub lam sgron*). Toh. 3947/4465.

——. *Lamp That Summarizes Conduct* (*Caryāsaṃgrahapradīpa, sPyod pa bsdus pa'i sgron ma*). Toh. 3960.

——. *Song of the View of Dharmadhātu* (*Dharmadhātudarśanagīti, Chos kyi dbyings lta ba'i glu*) Toh. 2314.

——. *Vajra Song of Vajrāsana* (*Vajrāsanavajragīti, rDo rje gdan gyi rdo rje'i glu*). Toh. 1494.

Bhāvaviveka. *Heart of the Middle Way* (*Madhyamakahṛdayakārikā, dBu ma'i snying po'i tshig le'ur byas pa*). Toh. 3855.

Bhavideva. See Aśvaghoṣa.

Bhekuni. *Sun and Moon Sādhana* (*Kālacakropadeśa-sūryacandrasādhana, Dus kyi 'khor lo'i gdams ngag nyi ma zla ba bsgrub pa*). Toh. 1369.

Bodhibhadra. *A Work on the Requisites for Samādhi* (*Samādhisambhāraparivarta, Ting nge 'dzin gyi tshogs kyi le'u*). Toh. 3924.

Buddhaśrījñānapāda. *Oral Teachings of Mañjuśrī* (*'Jam dpal zhal lung*). Also known as *Oral Teachings: Meditation on the Suchness of the Two Stages* (*Dvikramatattvabhāvanā-nāma-mukhāgama, Rim pa gnyis pa'i de kho na nyid bsgom pa zhes bya ba zhal gyi lung*). Toh 1853.

Candragomin. *Praise of Confession* (*Deśanāstava, bShags pa'i bstod pa*). Toh. 1159.

Candrakīrti. *Commentary on the "Entrance to the Middle Way"* (*Madhyamakāvatārabhāṣya, dBu ma 'jug 'grel / dBu ma la 'jug pa'i bshad pa*). Toh. 3862.

——. *Commentary on the "Four Hundred Verses"* (*Bodhisattvayogacarācatuḥśatakaṭīkā, bZhi brgya pa'i rgya cher 'grel pa / Byang chub sems dpa'i rnal 'byor spyod pa bzhi brgya pa'i rgya cher 'grel pa*). Toh. 3865.

——. *Entrance to the Middle Way* (*Madhyamakāvatāra, dBu ma la 'jug pa*). Toh. 3861.

——. *Illuminating Lamp* (*Pradīpoddyotana-nāma-ṭīkā, sGron gsal / sGron ma gsal bar byed pa zhes bya ba'i rgya cher bshad pa*). Toh. 1785.

——. *Lucid Words* (*Mūlamadhyamakavṛttiprasannapadā, dBu ma'i rtsa ba'i 'grel pa tshig gsal ba, by Candrakīrti*). Toh. 3860.

Dharmakīrti. *Commentary on Valid Cognition* (*Pramāṇavārttikakārikā, rNam 'grel / Tshad ma rnam 'grel gyi tshig le'ur byas pa*). Toh. 4210.

Dharmatrāta. *Collection of Meaningful Expressions* (*Udānavarga, Ched du brjod pa'i tshoms*). Toh. 326, H.K. 330.

Dignāga. *Compendium of Valid Cognition* (*Pramāṇasamuccaya, Tshad ma kun las btus pa zhes bya ba'i rab tu byed pa*). Toh 4203.

——. *Entrance to Yoga* (*Yogāvatāra, rNal 'byor la 'jug pa*). Toh. 4074.

Ḍombi Heruka. *Accomplishment of the Connate* (*Sahajasiddhi, Lhan cig skyes pa grub pa*). Toh. 2223.

Eight Dohā Treasures: Texts Elucidating the Esoteric Instructions of Mahāmudrā (Do ha mdzod brgyad ces bya ba phyag rgya chen po'i man ngag gsal bar ston pa'i gzhung). TsRP, vol. 4, 1–47. Darjeeling: Kargyu Sungrab Nyamso Khang, 1978–1985.

Gambhīravajra. *Great, Wondrous Clarification of the Glorious Profound Principles* (*Śrīguhyārthaprakāśamahādbhūta, dPal zab mo'i don gsal ba rmad du byung ba chen po*). Toh. 1200.

Haribhadra. *Commentary on the "Ornament for Clear Realization"* (*Abhisamayālaṃkāra-nāma-prajñāpāramitopadeśaśāstravṛtti, 'Grel pa don gsal / Shes rab kyi pha rol tu phyin pa'i man ngag gi bstan bcos mngon par rtogs pa'i rgyan zhes bya ba'i 'grel pa*). Toh. 3793.

Indrabhūti. *Sādhana for the Siddhi of Wisdom* (*Jñānasiddhi-nāma-sādhanopāyikā, Ye shes grub pa zhes bya ba'i sgrub pa'i thabs*). Toh 2219.

Jñānagarbha. *Commentary on the "Differentiation of the Two Truths"/ Autocommentary on the "Two Truths"* (**Satyadvaya-vibhaṅga-vṛtti, bDen gnyis rang 'grel / bDen gnyis rnam par 'byed pa'i 'grel pa*). Toh. 3882.

——. *Explanation of Just the Maitreya Chapter from "Unraveling the Intent"* (**Saṃdhinirmocanasūtre-āryamaitreyakevalaparivartabhāṣya, dGongs pa nges par grel pa'i mdo las 'phags pa byams pa'i le'u nyi tshe bshad pa*). Toh. 4033.

Jñānakīrti. *Entrance to Suchness* (*Tattvāvatārākhyasakalasugatavacastātparyavyākhyāprakaraṇa, De kho na nyid la 'jug pa zhes bya ba bde bar gshegs pa'i bka' ma lus pa mdor bsdus te bshad pa'i rab tu byed pa*). Toh. 3709.

Jñānaparama. *Secret Suchness: Commentary on the Difficult Points of the "Wisdom Tilaka Tantra"* (*Jñānatilakapañjikāguhyatattva, Ye shes thig le'i dka' 'grel gsang ba'i de kho na nyid*). Toh. 120.

Kālacakramahāpāda. *Padmani: Commentary on the Difficult Points* (*Padmanināma-pañjikā, Padma can zhes bya ba'i dka' 'grel*). Toh. 1350.

Kamalaśīla. *Commentary on the "Dhāraṇī of Entering Nonconceptuality"* (*Avikalpapraveśadhāraṇīṭīkā, rNam par mi rtog par 'jug pa'i gzungs kyi rgya cher 'grel pa*). Toh. 4000.

——. *Entering Yoga Meditation* (*Yogabhāvanāvatāra, rNal 'byor bsgom pa la 'jug pa*). Toh. 3918.

——. *Stages of Meditation* (*Bhāvanākrama, dBu ma'i sgom pa'i rim pa*). Toh. 3915–7.

Kuddāla. In *Heart of the Realization of the Eighty-Four Siddhas* (*Caturaśītisiddhasambodhihṛdaya, Grub thob brgyad cu rtsa bzhi'i rtogs pa'i snying po*) by *Vīraprabhāsvara/Vīraprakāśa. Toh. 2292. Also in *Rosary of Golden Bindus: The Esoteric Instructions of Experiences Expressed in Vajra Songs by Forty Yogin-Siddhas During Gaṇacakra in Glorious Oḍḍiyāna* (*dPal u rgyan du tshogs 'khor byas pa'i* *dus su rnal 'byor pa grub pa thob pa bzhi bcus rdo rje'i mgur bzhengs pa nyams kyi man ngag thig le gser gyi phreng ba*) by forty mahāsiddhas. Toh. 2449.

Lakṣmī. *Source Commentary on the "Accomplishment of the Connate"* (*Sahajasiddhipaddhati, Lhan cig skyes grub kyi gzhung 'grel*). Toh. 2261.

Maitreya. *Determining the Four Mudrās* (*Caturmudrāniścaya, Phyag rgya bzhi gtan la dbab pa*). Toh. 2225.

———. *Differentiation of the Middle and the Extremes* (*Madhyāntavibhāga, dBus mtha' rnam 'byed*). Toh. 4021.

———. *Highest Continuum / The Mahāyāna Treatise of the Highest Continuum* (*Mahāyānottaratantraśāstra, Theg pa chen po rgyud bla ma'i bstan bcos*). Toh. 4024.

———. *Ornament for the Mahāyāna Sūtras* (*Mahāyānasūtrālaṃkāra, Theg pa chen po mdo sde'i rgyan*). Toh. 4020.

———. *Ornament of Clear Realization* (*Abhisamayālaṃkāra, mNgon rtogs rgyan*). Toh. 3786.

Maitrīpa (also known as Advayavajra and Advaya Avadhūta). *Extensive Commentary That Reveals the Intrinsic Thusness of the "Song That Is a Treasury of Dohās"* (*Dohanidhikoṣaparipūrṇagīti-nāma-nijatattvaprakāśatīkā, Mi zad ba'i gter mdzod yongs su gang ba'i glu zhes bya ba gnyug ma'i de nyid rab tu ston pa'i rgya cher bshad pa*). Toh. 2257.

———. *Summary Verses on Mahāmudrā* (*Mahāmudrāsañcamitha* [sic], *Phyag rgya chen po'i tshig bsdus pa*). TsRP, vol. 4, 45–47. Darjeeling: Kargyu Sungrab Nyamso Khang, 1978–1985.

———. *Ten Verses on Suchness* (*Tattvadaśaka, De kho na nyid bcu pa*). Toh. 2236.

Mañjuśrīkīrti. *Garland of Renown: A Commentary on the Mahāyāna Sūtra "King of Samādhi"* (*Sarvadharmasvabhāvasamatāvipañcitasamādhirāja-nāma-mahāyānasūtraṭīkākīrtimālā, Chos thams cad kyi rang bzhin mnyam pa nyid rnam par spros pa'i ting nge 'dzin kyi rgyal po zhes bya ba theg pa chen po'i mdo'i 'grel pa grags pa'i phreng ba*). Toh 4010.

———. *Ornament of the Heart* (*Sarvaguhyavidhigarbhālaṃkāra-nāma, sNying po rgyan / gSang ba thams cad kyi spyi'i cho ga'i snying po rgyan*). Toh. 2490.

Nāgārjuna. *Commentary on Bodhicitta* (*Bodhicittavivaraṇa, Byang chub sems 'grel*). Toh. 1800.

———. *Delineating the Four Empowerments* (*Sekacatuḥprakaraṇa, dBang bzhi pa'i rab tu byed pa*). Toh. 1799.

———. *Five Stages* (*Pañcakrama, Rim pa lnga pa*). Toh. 1802.

———. *Fundamental Treatise on the Middle Way* (*Prajñā-nāma-mūlamadhyamakakārikā, rTsa sher / dBu ma rtsa ba'i tshig le'ur byas pa shes rab ces bya ba*). Toh. 3824.

———. *Letter to a Friend.* (*Suhṛllekha, bShes pa'i spring yig*). Toh. 4496.

———. *Praises of the Dharmadhātu.* (*Dharmadhātustava, Chos dbyings bstod pa*). Toh. 1118.

———. *Precious Garland / Precious Garland of Advice for the King.* (*Ratnāvalī / Rāja-*

parikathāratnāvalī, Rin chen phreng ba / rGyal po la gtam bya ba rin po che'i phreng ba). Toh. 4158.

Narendrakīrti. *Synopsis of Our View Asserted by Mañjuśrī* (*Pradarśanānumatoddeśaparīkṣā / Āryamañjuśrīpradarśana, Rang gi lta ba'i 'dod pa mdor bstan pa yongs su brtag pa / 'Phags pa 'jam dpal gyi rang gi lta ba*). P 4610, N 3400.

Nāropa. *Authoritative Text in Verse on the Six Dharmas: Instructions of the Mahāsiddha Nāropa* (*Grub chen na ro pa'i gdams ngag chos drug skor gyi bka' dpe tshigs su bcad pa*). DNZ, vol. 7, 95–106. Delhi: Shechen Publications, 1998.

———. *Clarifying Wisdom*. (*Ye shes gsal byed*). Not found.

———. *Latter Authoritative Text* (*Pravacanottaropamā, bKa' dpe phyi ma*). Toh. 2332.

———. *Summary of the View* (*Dṛṣtisaṃkṣipta, lTa ba mdor bsdus pa*). Toh 2304.

———. *Summary Verses on Mahāmudrā* (*Mahāmudrapādaṃetha* [sic] or *Mahāmudrāsañcamitha* [sic], *Phyag rgya chen po'i tshig bsdus pa*). DNZ, vol. 7, 47–48. Delhi: Shechen Publications, 1998. Also DNZ, vol. 8, 216–19. Delhi: Shechen Publications, 1998. Also in Indian Mahāmudrā Texts (Phyag chen rgya gzhung), vol. 2, 329b–30b. Derge: dPal spungs dgon pa.

———. *Vajra Song Summarizing the Six Dharmas: Instructions by the Great Scholar-Siddha Nāropa for the Lord of Yogins Marpa Lotsāwa* (*mKhas grub chen po nA ro tA pas rnal 'byor gyi dbang phyug mar pa lo tsA la gdams pa'i chos drug dril ba rdo rje'i mgur*). DNZ, vol. 7, 108–9. Delhi: Shechen Publications, 1998.

Nāropa/Yashobhadra. *Commentary on the Difficult Points: Summarizing the Essence of the Vajra Words* (*Vajrapādasāra-saṃgraha-pañjikā, rDo rje'i tshig gi snying po bsdus pa'i dka' 'grel*). Toh. 1186.

Padmavajra. *Secret Siddhis* (*Guhyasiddhi / Sakalatantrasambhavasaṃcodanī-śrīguhyasiddhi, gSang ba grub pa / rGyud ma lus pa'i don nges par skul bar byed pa*). Toh. 2217.

*Pramuditāvajra. *Commentary on the "Sarvabuddha-samayoga"* (*Sarvabuddhasamayogaḍākinīmāyāśambaravṛttisamayogālaṃkāra, Sangs rgyas mnyam sbyor gyi 'grel pa / Sangs rgyas thams cad dang mnyam par sbyor ba mkha' 'gro ma sgyu ma bde mchog gi 'grel pa mnyam sbyor gyi rgyan*). Toh. 1660.

Puṇḍarīka. *Stainless Light* (*Vimalaprabhā / Vimalaprabhā-nāma-mūlatantrānusāriṇī-dvādaśasāhasrikā-laghu-kālacakra-tantrarāja-ṭīkā, Dri ma med pa'i 'od / bsDus pa'i rgyud kyi rgyal po dus kyi 'khor lo'i 'grel bshad rtsa ba'i rgyud kyi rjes su 'jug pa stong phrag bcu gnyis pa dri ma med pa'i 'od ces bya ba*). Toh. 845 and Toh. 1347.

Rāmapāla. *Commentary on the Difficult Points of "Ascertaining Abhiṣekas"* (*Sekanirdeśapañjikā, dBang bskur ba nges par bstan pa'i dka' 'grel*). Toh. 2253.

Ratnākaraśānti. *Handful of Flowers: Explanation of the "Guhyasamāja"* (*Kusumāñjaliguhyasamājanibandha, gSang ba 'dus pa'i bshad sbyar snyim pa'i me tog*). Toh. 1851.

———. *Instructions on Prajñāpāramitā* (*Prajñāpāramitopadeśa, Sher phyin gyi man ngag/ Shes rab kyi pha rol tu phyin pa'i man ngag*). Toh. 4079.

Sahajavajra. *Extensive Commentary on the "Ten Verses on Suchness"* (*Tattvadaśakaṭīkā, De kho na nyid bcu pa'i rgya cher 'grel pa*). Toh. 2254.

Śāntideva. *Entrance to the Bodhisattva's Way of Life* (*Bodhicaryāvatāra, sPyod 'jug / Byang chub sems dpa'i spyod pa la 'jug pa*). Toh. 3871.

Saraha. *Commentary on the Difficult Points of the "Buddha-kapāla Tantra"* (*Buddhakapālatantrasya pañjikājñānavatī, Sangs rgyas thod pa'i rgyud kyi dka' 'grel ye shes ldan pa*). Toh. 1652.

———. *Dohā for the King* (*rGyal po do ha*). Also known as *Treasury of Dohā: Songs on Conduct* (*Dohakoṣa-nāma-caryāgīti, Do ha mdzod ces bya ba spyod pa'i glu*). Toh. 2263.

———. *Dohā for the People* (*dMangs do ha*). Also known as *Song That Is a Treasury of Dohās* (*Dohakoṣagīti, Do ha mdzod kyi glu*). Toh. 2224.

———. *Dohā for the Queen* (*bTsun mo do ha*). Also known as *Song of an Inexhaustible Treasure of Instruction* (*Dohākoṣopadeśagīti, Mi zad pa'i gter mdzod man ngag gi glu*). Toh. 2264.

———. *Dohā Song on View, Meditation, Conduct, and Fruition* (*Bhāvanādṛṣṭicaryāphaladohagītikā, lTa bsgom spyod pa 'bras bu'i do ha'i glu*). Toh. 2345.

———. *Treasury of Dohā: Instructions on Mahāmudrā* (*Dohakoṣa-nāma-mahāmudropadeśa, Do ha mdzod ces bya ba phyag rgya chen po'i man ngag*). Toh. 2273.

Śavara, the. See Saraha.

Śrīghoṣa. *Lamp for the True View* (*lTa ba yang dag sgron pa*). Toh. 4447.

Sthiramati. *A Detailed Commentary on "The Explanation of the Five Skandhas"* (*Pañcaskandhaprakaraṇavaibhāṣyā, Phung po lnga'i rab tu byed pa bye brag tu bshad pa*). Toh. 4066.

———. *Subcommentary on the "Differentiation of the Middle and the Extremes"* (*Madhyāntavibhāga-ṭīkā, dBus dang mtha' rnam par 'byed pa'i 'grel bshad*). Toh. 4032.

Tilopa. *Earlier Authoritative Text / Truly Valid Words: The Esoteric Instructions of the Ḍākinīs* (*Ājñāsaṁyakpramāṇa-nāma-ḍākinyupadeśa / Āhapramāṇasaṁyagnāma-ḍākinyupadeśa, bKa' dpe snga ma / bKa' yang dag pa'i tshad ma shes bya ba mkha' 'gro ma'i man ngag*). Toh. 2331. DNZ, vol. 7, 69–89. Delhi: Shechen Publications, 1998.

———. *Ganges Mahāmudrā* (*Phyag chen gang gA ma*). Also known as the *Esoteric Instructions on Mahāmudrā* (*Mahāmudropadeśa, Phyag rgya chen po'i man ngag*). Toh. 2303.

———. *Teachings of the Formless Vajra Ḍākinīs* (*Vajraḍākiniṣkāyadharma, rDo rje mkha' 'gro lus med pa'i chos*). Toh. 1527.

———. *Treasury of Dohā* (*Dohakoṣa, Do ha mdzod*). Toh. 2281. Also TsRP, vol. 4, 23–25. Darjeeling: Kargyu Sungrab Nyamso Khang, 1978–1985.

Vajragarbha. *Commentary That Summarizes the "Hevajra Tantra"* (*Hevajra-piṇḍārthaṭīkā, Kye'i rdo rje bsdus pa'i don gyi rgya cher 'grel pa / rDo rje snying 'grel*). Toh. 1180.

Vasubandhu. *Explanation of the "Ornament for the Mahāyāna Sūtras"* (*Sūtrālaṃkārabhāṣya, mDo sde rgyan gyi 'grel pa / mDo sde'i rgyan gyi bshad pa*). Toh. 4026.

——. *Explanation of the "Treasury of Abhidharma"* (*Abhidharmakośa-bhāṣya, mDzod kyi rang 'grel / Chos mngon pa'i mdzod kyi bshad pa*). Toh. 4090.

——. *Treasury of Abhidharma* (*Abhidharmakośakārikā, Chos mngon pa'i mdzod kyi tshig le'ur byas pa*). Toh. 4089.

Virūpa. *Treasury of Dohā* (*Dohakoṣa, Do ha mdzod*). Toh. 2280.

Vitapāda. *Seven Yogas / Seven Yogas: A Treatise on the Four Empowerments* (*Yogasaptanāmacaturabhiṣekhaprakaraṇa, sByor ba bdun pa zhes bya ba dbang bzhi'i rab to byed pa*). Toh 1875.

Tibetan and Chinese Works

Gampopa. *Abundant Auspiciousness: A Collection of Dharma Lectures* (*Tshogs chos bkra shis phun tshogs*). Collected Works of Gampopa, text 4/nga. Lekshey Ling Publications.

——. *Abundant Virtue: A Collection of Dharma Lectures* (*Tshogs chos yon tan phun tshogs*). Collected Works of Gampopa, text 6/cha. Lekshey Ling Publications.

——. *Compendium on the Meditation Topics of Sūtra and Mantra* (*mDo sngags kyi sgom don bsdus pa*). Collected Works of Gampopa, text 28/sha. Lekshey Ling Publications.

——. *Core of Mahāmudrā: The Instructions on the Ultimate Essence* (*sNying po don gyi gdams pa phyag rgya chen po'i 'bum tig*). Collected Works of Gampopa, text 23/'a. Lekshey Ling Publications.

——. *Esoteric Instructions on the Five Nails* (*gZer rnam pa lnga'i man ngag*). Not found.

——. *Esoteric Instructions: Illuminating Mahāmudrā* (*Phyag rgya chen po gsal byed kyi man ngag*). Collected Works of Gampopa, text 21/zha. Lekshey Ling Publications.

——. *Esoteric Instructions on the Twofold Abiding State and Esoteric Instructions on Twofold Armor* (*gNas lugs gnyis kyi man ngag dang go cha gnyis kyi man ngag*). Collected Works of Gampopa, text 31/ki. Lekshey Ling Publications.

——. *The Grand Collection of Dharma Lectures* (*Tshogs chos legs mdzes ma*). Collected Works of Gampopa, text 5/ca. Lekshey Ling Publications.

——. *A Major Collection of Dharma Lectures* (*Tshogs chos chen po*). Collected Works of Gampopa, text 8/nya. Lekshey Ling Publications.

——. *Pointing Out the Essence: An Ultimate Treasury* (*sNying po'i ngo sprod don dam gter mdzod*). Collected Works of Gampopa, text 25/ra. Lekshey Ling Publications.

——. *Pointing Out the Root of Mahāmudrā* (*Phyag rgya chen po'i rtsa ba la ngo sprad pa zhes kyang bya / sNang ba lam 'khyer gyi rtogs pa cig chog ces kyang bya/ phyag rgya chen po gnyug ma mi 'gyur shes kyang bya ba*). Collected Works of Gampopa, text 24/ya. Lekshey Ling Publications.

——. *Pointing Out the Ultimacy of Thoughts* (*rNam rtog don dam gyi ngo sprod*). Collected Works of Gampopa, text 26/la. Lekshey Ling Publications.

——. *Presentation of the Three Trainings* (*bsLab gsum rnam gzhag*). Collected Works of Gampopa, text 30/A. Lekshey Ling Publications.

——. *Replies to Dusum Khyenpa's Questions* (*Du gsum mkhyen pa'i zhus len*). Collected Works of Gampopa, text 10/tha. Lekshey Ling Publications.

——. *Replies to the Exalted Gomtsul's Questions* (*rJe sgom tshul gyi zhus len*). Collected Works of Gampopa, text 9/ta. Lekshey Ling Publications.

——. *Replies to the Exalted Pakmo Drupa's Questions* (*rJe phag mo gru pa'i zhus len*). Collected Works of Gampopa, text 11/da. Lekshey Ling Publications.

——. *Replies to Yogin Chöyung's Questions* (*rNal 'byor chos g.yung gi zhus lan*). Collected Works of Gampopa, text 12/na. Lekshey Ling Publications.

——. *Revealing the Hidden Characteristics of Mind* (*Sems kyi mtshan nyid gab pa mngon du phyung ba*). Collected Works of Gampopa, text 14/pha. Lekshey Ling Publications.

——. *A String of Pearls: A Collection of Dharma Instructions* (*Khrid chos mu tig tsar la brgyus pa*). Collected Works of Gampopa, text 13/pa. Lekshey Ling Publications.

——. *Synopsis of the Meditations of Sūtra and Mantra* (*mDo sngags kyi sgom don bsdus pa*). Collected Works of Gampopa, text 28/sa. Lekshey Ling Publications.

——. *Thunderbolt of Instructions on Mahāmudrā and Collection of Songs* (*Phyag rgya chen po'i man ngag thog babs dang mgur 'bum*). Collected Works of Gampopa, text 20/wa. Lekshey Ling Publications.

——. *Treatise Containing a Garland of Amṛta-Advice and [the Means for] Annihilating the Four Demons* (*bsTan bcos gros 'debs bdud rtsi'i phreng ba dang 'dre bzhi rtsad gcod*). Collected Works of Gampopa, text 33/gi. Lekshey Ling Publications.

——. *Uncommon Amṛta of Speech* (*Zhal gyi bdud rtsi thun mong ma yin pa*). Collected Works of Gampopa, text 19/dza. Lekshey Ling Publications.

Gelong Pal. *Finding Ease in Mind-Itself / Finding Ease in Mind-Itself: The Esoteric Instructions Taught to the Mahāsiddha Mitrayogin by the Noble Avalokiteśvara* (*Sems nyid ngal gsor / 'Phags pa spyan ras gzigs kyis grub chen mi tra dzo ki la gsungs pa'i rang gi sems nyid ngal gso ba'i man ngag*). DNZ, vol. 16, 497–523. Delhi: Shechen Publications, 1998.

Götsangpa. *Collected Songs of the Glorious, Unequalled, Victor Götsangpa* (*dPal mnyam med rgyal ba rgod tshang pa'i mgur 'bum chen mo*). Collected Works of Götsangpa, vol. 6/cha, text 1. Khenpo Shedrup Collections. Kathmandu: Khenpo Shedup Tenzin and Lama Thinley Namgyal, 2017.

——. *Commentary on Mahāmudrā, Connate Union* (*Phyag rgya chen po lhan cig skyes sbyor gyi khrid*). Collected Works of Götsangpa, vol. 5/ca, text 8. Kathmandu: Khenpo Shedup Tenzin and Lama Thinley Namgyal, 2017.

——. *Lamp Illuminating the Jeweled Commentary Containing a Treasury of Precious Instructions* (*gDams pa rin po che za ma tog bkod pa'i 'grel pa rin chen gsal ba'i sgron me*). Collected Works of Götsangpa, vol. 4/nga, text 14. Kathmandu: Khenpo Shedup Tenzin and Lama Thinley Namgyal, 2017.

Heshang Mahāyāna. *Drawn from Eighty Sūtras* (*mDo sde brgyad bcu khungs*). International Dunhuang Project. IOL Tib J 705. http://idp.bl.uk/database/oo_scroll_h.a4d?uid=5206105613;bst=1;recnum=23191;index=1;img=1.

Jikten Sumgön. *Background Teachings on the Ten Instructions That Resemble a Mighty King* (*dBang gi rgyal po lta bu'i gdams pa bcu chos kyi rgyab chos*). Collected Works of Jikten Sumgön, vol. 8, 349–57. Delhi: Drikung Kagyu Ratna Shri Sungrab Nyamso Khang, 2001.

——. *Heart Advice to Keep in Mind: Replies to Students' Questions About What to Do* (*sLob mas ji lta bya'i dris lan snying gtam blo bzhag*). Collected Works of Jikten Sumgön, vol. 3, 405–13. Delhi: Drikung Kagyu Ratna Shri Sungrab Nyamso Khang, 2001.

——. *Instructions to Parpuwa: Summary of the Glorious Saraha's Five Types of Noncontrivance in Mahāmudrā* (*dPal sa ra ha'i phyag chen ma bcos rnam lnga'i bsdus don par phu ba la gdams pa*). Collected Works of Jikten Sumgön, vol. 1, 448–49. Delhi: Drikung Kagyu Ratna Shri Sungrab Nyamso Khang, 2001.

——. *Letter on the Way of Being of the Reflexive Awareness of the Phenomena of Saṃsāra and Nirvāṇa* (*'Khor 'das gnyis kyi chos rang rig 'dug lugs kyi springs yig*). Collected Works of Jikten Sumgön, vol. 3, 196–200. Delhi: Drikung Kagyu Ratna Shri Sungrab Nyamso Khang, 2001.

——. *Song of Realizing Fivefold Mahāmudrā* (*Phyag rgya chen po lnga ldan rtogs pa'i mgur*). Collected Works of Jikten Sumgön, vol. 10, 96–97. Delhi: Drikung Kagyu Ratna Shri Sungrab Nyamso Khang, 2001.

Marpa. See Tsang Nyön Heruka. *Seeing Is Meaningful: The Biography of the Translator Marpa Lotsāwa.*

Milarepa. *Instructions on the Four Syllables of Mahāmudrā* (*Phyag rgya chen po yi ge bzhi pa'i gdams pa*). DNZ, vol. 8, 39–44. Delhi: Shechen Publications, 1998.

——. *Three Cycles of Illumination* (*gSal ba skor gsum*). DNZ, vol. 7, 109–20. Delhi: Shechen Publications, 1998.

——. See Tsang Nyön Heruka. *Biography and Songs of the Great Lord of Yogins, Milarepa.*

Pakmo Drupa. *Condensed Verses on the Four Yogas* (*rNal 'byor bzhi'i tshigs bcad ma chung ba*). Collected Works of Pakmo Drupa, vol. 4/nga, text 10.10. Kathmandu: Khenpo Shedup Tenzin and Lama Thinley Namgyal, 2003.

——. *Connate Union* (*Lhan cig skyes sbyor*). Collected Works of Pakmo Drupa, vol. 4/nga, text 10.1. Kathmandu: Khenpo Shedup Tenzin and Lama Thinley Namgyal, 2003.

——. *Precious Banner: The Meditations on the Three [Levels of Each of the] Four Yogas* (*rNal 'byor bzhi gsum sgom rin chen rgyal mtshan*). Collected Works of Pakmo Drupa, vol. 4/nga, text 10.11. Kathmandu: Khenpo Shedup Tenzin and Lama Thinley Namgyal, 2003.

——. *Precious Sash* (*Rin po che'i ska rags*). Collected Works of Pakmo Drupa, vol. 3/ga, text 6. Kathmandu: Khenpo Shedup Tenzin and Lama Thinley Namgyal, 2003.

——. *Verses on the Four Yogas Requested by Geshe Nyang Gom* (*rNal 'byor bzhi'i tshigs *bcad ma dge bshes nyang sgom gyis zhus pa*). Collected Works of Pakmo Drupa, vol. 4/nga, text 10.9. Kathmandu: Khenpo Shedup Tenzin and Lama Thinley Namgyal, 2003.

Rangjung Dorje. *The Profound Inner Principles* (*Zab mo nang gi don*). Collected Works of Rangjung Dorje, vol. 7/ja: 308–60. Lhasa: dPal brtsegs bod yig dpe rnying zhib 'jug khang, 2006.

Sakya Paṇḍita. *Analysis of the Three Vows* (*sDom pa gsum gyi rab tu dbye ba'i bstan bcos*). Sakya Collected Teachings, vol. 12a: 1–127. Beijing: Mi rigs dpe skrun khang, 2004.

———. *Clarifying the Sage's Intent* (*Thub dgongs / Thub pa'i' dgongs pa rab tu gsal ba*). Sarnath, Varanasi: Sakya Students' Union, 2005.

———. *Letter to the Buddhas and Bodhisattvas of the Ten Directions* (*Phyogs bcu'i sangs rgyas dang byang chub sems pa thams cad la phul ba'i yi ge*). Sakya Collected Works, vol. 12: 127–58. Kathmandu: Sachen International, 2006.

Serdingpa. *Lamp for the Yānas* (*Theg sgron*). Not found.

Sönam Lhundrup. *The Flag of Renown: The Biography of Gampopa* (*Chos kyi rje dpal ldan sgam po pa chen po'i rnam par thar pa yid bzhin gyi nor bu rin po che kun khyab snyan pa'i ba dan thar pa rin po che'i rgyan gyi mchog*). Collected Works of Gampopa, text 3/ga.

Tsang Nyön Heruka. *Biography and Songs of the Great Lord of Yogins, Milarepa* (*rNal 'byor gyi dbang phyug chen po mi la ras pa'i rnam mgur*). Ziling: mTsho sngon mi rigs dpe skrun khang, 1989.

———. *Seeing Is Meaningful: The Biography of the Translator Marpa Lotsāwa* (*sGra sgyur mar pa lo tsA'i rnam thar mthong ba don ldan*). Collected Works of Marpa Lotsāwa, vol. 1, 169–330. Beijing: Krung go'i bod rig pa dpe skrun khang, 2011.

Tsangpa Gyare. *Questions and Answers with Instructions on the Four Yogas* (*Zhu lan rnal 'byor bzhi'i gdams pa dang bcas pa*). Collected Works of Tsangpa Gyare Yeshe Dorje, 581–94. Kathmandu: Khenpo Shedup Tenzin and Lama Thinley Namgyal, 1998.

Yang Gönpa. *Treasury of the Ultimate Essence: The Stages of the Four Yogas of Mahāmudrā* (*Phyag rgya chen po rnal 'byor bzhi'i rim pa snying po don gyi gter mdzod*). TsRP, vol. 4, 119–84. Darjeeling: Kargyu Sungrab Nyamso Khang, 1978–1985. Also as *sNying po don gyi gter mdzod rnal 'byor bzhi gsum bcu gnyis*. Drikung Kagyu Great Treasury of Dharma, vol. 48, 71–116. Lhasa: n.p., 2004. BDRC W00JW501203. Also as *Ri chos kyi rnal 'byor bzhi pa phyag rgya chen po snying po don gyi gter mdzod*. Collected Works of Yang Gönpa, vol. 1, 241–78. Tango, Thimphu, Bhutan: Tango Monastic Community, 1982.

Zhang Rinpoche. *Consummate Sublime Path of Mahāmudrā Composed by the Unborn Zhang Rinpoche* (*sKye med zhang rin po ches mdzad pa'i phyag rgya chen po'i lam mchog mthar thug*). DNZ, vol. 8, 429–62. Delhi: Shechen Publications, 1998. Also TsRP, vol. 4, 49–117. Darjeeling: Kargyu Sungrab Nyamso Khang, 1978–1985.

Works Consulted by the Translator

Canonical Scriptures and Treatises

Abhayākaragupta. *Moonlight: Commentary on the Thought of the "Five Stages"* (*Pañcakramamataṭīkācandraprabhā, Rim pa lnga pa'i dgongs 'grel zla ba'i 'od zer*). Toh. 1831.

Account of the Noble Deeds of Puṇyabala (*Puṇyabala-avadāna, bSod nams kyi stobs kyi rtogs pa brjod pa*). Toh. 347, H.K. 355.

Advayavajra. *Explanation on Difficult Points in the "Dohā Treasury."* (*Dohakoṣapañjikā, Do ha mdzod kyi dka' 'grel*). Toh. 2256.

Ānandagarbha. *Ritual for the Maṇḍala of Prajñāpāramitā* (*Prajñāpāramitāmaṇḍalopāyikā, Shes rab kyi pha rol tu phyin pa'i dkyil 'khor gyi cho ga*). Toh. 2644.

Anupamarakṣita. *Six-Branch Yoga* (*Ṣaḍaṅgayoga, sByor ba yan lag drug pa*). Toh. 1387.

Asaṅga. **Yogācāryābhūmi vastusaṃgrahaṇī* (*rNal 'byor spyod pa'i sa las gzhi bsdu ba*). Toh. 4039.

Atīśa. *Commentary on the "Vajra Song of Vajrāsana"* (*Vajrāsanavajragītivṛtti, rDo rje gdan gyi rdo rje'i glu'i 'grel pa*). Toh. 1495.

———. *Teaching on Refuge* (*Śaraṇagamanadeśanā, sKyabs su 'gro ba bstan pa*). Toh. 3953.

Avadhūtipa. *Explanation of the Difficult Points of the Tantra of the Six-Branch Yoga, the Kālacakra Esoteric Instructions* (*Kālacakropadeśayogaṣaḍaṅgatantrapañjikā, Dus kyi 'khor lo'i man ngag sbyor ba yan lag drug gi rgyud kyi dka' 'grel*). Toh. 1373.

———. *Explanation of the "Song That Is the Ultimate Essence of the Treasury of Dohās"* (*Dohakoṣahṛdayārthagītāṭīkā, Do ha mdzod kyi snying po don gyi glu'i 'grel pa*). Toh. 2268.

Basis of the Minor Vinaya (*Vinaya-kṣudraka-vastu, 'Dul ba phran tshegs kyi gzhi*). Toh. 6, H.K. 6.

Bhavabhadra. *Commentary on "The King of Tantras, the Glorious Vajra Ḍāka"* (*Vajraḍāka-nāma-mahātantrarājasyavṛtti, rGyud kyi rgyal po chen po dpal rdo rje mkha' 'gro zhes bya ba'i rnam par bshad pa*). Toh. 1415.

———. *Reasons for Recollection: Commentary on the "Caturpīṭha"* (*Catuḥpīṭhatantrarājasya ṭīkāsmṛtinibandha, rGyud kyi rgyal po dpal gdan bzhi pa'i 'grel pa dran pa'i rgyu mtshan*). Toh. 1607.

Bhavapa. *Ritual for the Great Uniting with the Great Chief of Yakṣas, Blue-Clad Vajrapāṇi* (*Mahāyakṣasenāpatinīlāmbāradharavajrapāṇimahāgaṇavidhi, gNod sbyin gyi sde dpon chen po lag na rdo rje gos sngon po can gyi sbyor ka chen po'i cho ga*). Toh. 2174.

Bhāvaviveka. *Blaze of Reasoning / Blaze of Reasoning: Commentary on the "Heart of the Middle Way"* (*Tarkajvālā / Madhyamakahṛdayavṛttitarkajvālā, rTog ge 'bar ba/ dBu ma'i snying po'i 'grel pa rtog ge 'bar ba*). Toh. 3856.

——. *Precious Lamp of Madhyamaka* (*Madhyamakaratnapradīpa*, *dbU ma rin po che'i sgron ma*). Toh. 3854.

Bodhibhadra. *Commentary on the "Compendium on the Heart of Wisdom"* (*Jñāna-sārasamuccaya-nāma-nibandhana*, *Ye shes snying po kun las btus pa zhes bya ba'i bshad sbyar*). Toh. 3852.

Buddhaguhya. *Entrance to the Meaning of the Tantras.* (*Tantrārthāvatāra*, *rGyud kyi don la 'jug pa*). Toh. 2501.

Buddhaśrījñānapāda. *Commentary on the Difficult Points of the "[Verses that] Summarize [the Prajñāpāramitā Sūtras]"* (*Saṃcayagāthāpañjikā*, *sDud pa tshigs su bcad pa'i dka' 'grel*). Toh. 3798.

Descent into Laṅkā Sūtra: The Chapter on the Essence of the Speech of All Buddhas (*Lang kar gshegs pa'i mdo las sangs rgyas thams cad kyi gsung gi snying po'i le'u*). Toh. 108, H.K. 111.

Ḍombi Heruka. *Commentary on the "Name-Chanting of Mañjuśrī"* (**Nāmasaṃgītivṛtti*, *'Jam dpal gyi mtshan yang dag par brjod pa'i 'grel pa*). Toh. 2542.

Haribhadra. *Illumination of the "Ornament for Clear Realization"* (*Āṣṭasāhasrikāprajñāpāramitāvyākhyānābhisamayālaṃkārāloka*, *Shes rab kyi pha rol tu phyin pa brgyad stong pa'i bshad pa mngon par rtogs pa'i rgyan gyi snang ba*). Toh. 3791.

Indrabhūti. *Accomplishment of the Connate* (*Sahajasiddhi*, *Lhan cig skyes grub*). Toh. 2260.

Jinadatta. *Commentary on the Difficult Points of the "Guhyasamāja Tantra"* (*Guhyasamājatantrapañjikā*, *dPal gsang ba 'dus pa'i rgyud kyi dka' 'grel*). Toh. 1847.

Jñānagarbha. *Commentary on "Questions of the Four Goddesses"* (*Caturdevatāparipṛcchāṭīkā*, *Lha mo bzhis yongs su zhus pa'i rnam par bshad pa*). Toh. 1916.

Jñānaśrībhadra. *Commentary on the "Descent into Laṅkā"* (*Laṅkāvatāra-vṛtti*, *Lang kar gshegs pa'i 'grel pa*). Toh. 4018.

Jñānavajra/Advayajñānavajra. *Ornament for the Heart of the Tathāgatas: A Commentary on the Mahāyāna Sūtra "Descent into Laṅkā"* (*Laṅkāvatāra-nāma-mahāyānasūtra-vṛtti-tathāgata-hṛdayālaṃkāra*, *Lang kar gshegs pa zhes bya ba theg pa chen po'i mdo'i 'grel pa de bzhin gshegs pa'i snying po'i rgyan*). Toh. 4019.

Kalyāṇavarman. *Explanation of the "Caturpīṭha"* (*Catuḥpīṭhaṭīkā*, *gDan bzhi pa'i rnam par bshad pa*). Toh. 1608.

Kamalaśīla. *Fifty Kārika* (*Śramaṇapañcāśatkārikāpadābhismaraṇa*, *Kā ri kā lnga bcu / dGe sbyong gi kā ri kā lnga bcu pa'i tshig gi brjed byang du byas pa*). Dg.T. 4128.

——. *Illumination of Madhyamaka* (*Madhyamakāloka*, *dbU ma snang ba*). Toh. 3887.

Kambala. *Garland of Light* (*Ālokamālaprakaraṇa*, *sNang ba'i phreng ba*). Toh. 3895.

Kurukullātārā, Mañjuśrī, Avalokiteśvara, Vajrapāṇi, Yamāri, Khasarpaṇa, Nivaraṇaviṣkambin, Svayambhūrājñī, Mārīchīdevī, Samantabhadra, Vajravārāhī, and Acala. *Symbolic Transmission of Mahāmudrā* (*Mahāmudrābhigīti*, *Phyag rgya chen po brda'i brgyud pa*). Toh. 2439. (Authorship also attributed to Padampa Sangye.)

Lakṣmī / Kaśmiri Mahākauśalya Lakṣmī. *Elucidation of the Meaning That Explains the "Five Stages"* (**Pañcakramaṭīkā-kramārtha-prakāśikā, Rim pa lnga'i 'grel pa'i don gsal bar byed pa*). Toh. 1842.

Lu'i Gyaltsen. *Explanation of "Unraveling the Intent"* (*Āryasaṃdhinirmocanasūtra-vyākhyāna, 'Phags pa dgongs pa nges par 'grel pa'i mdo'i rnam par bshad pa*). Toh. 4358.

Mahāparinirvāṇa Sūtra (*Mahāparinirvāṇa-mahāsūtra, Yongs su mya ngan las 'das pa chen po'i mdo*). Toh. 119, H.K. 368.

Maitrīpa. *Teaching on Mental Non-Engagement* (*Amanasikāroddeśa, Yid la mi byed pa ston pa*). Toh. 2249.

Māyājāla (*sGyu 'phrul drva ba*). Toh. 466, H.K. 431.

Nāgabodhi. *Elucidation of the Meaning of the "Five Stages"* (*Pañcakramārthabhā-skaraṇa, Rim pa lnga'i don gsal bar byed pa*). Toh. 1833.

—— or Pseudo-Nāgabodhi. *Garland of Jewels: Explanation of the "Five Stages"* (*Pañcakramaṭīkā-maṇimālā, Rim pa lnga pa'i bshad pa nor bu'i phreng ba*). Toh. 1840. (Author unidentified in Toh.)

Nāgārjuna (or Rāhulabhadra). *Praises of Prajñāpāramitā* (*Prajñāpāramitāstotra, Shes rab kyi pha rol tu phyin ma'i bstod pa*). Toh. 1127.

Nāgārjuna. *Stages of Meditation* (*Bhāvanākrama, bsGom pa'i rim pa*). Toh. 3908.

Nāropa. *Commentary on "The Summary of the [Kālacakra] Initiation": Compendium of the Ultimate* (*Paramārthasaṃgrahanāmasekoddeśaṭīkā, dBang mdor bstan pa'i 'grel bshad don dam pa bsdus pa*). Toh. 1351.

Prajñākaramati. *Explanation of the Difficult Points of the "Entrance to the Bodhisattva's Way of Life"* (*Bodhicaryāvatārapañjikā, Byang chub kyi spyod pa la 'jug pa'i dka' 'grel*). Toh. 3872.

Ratnakīrti. *Praises to the Deities of the Four Yogas* (*Yogacaturdevastotra, sByor ba bzhi'i lha la bstod pa*). Toh. 1170.

Saṃvarabhadra. *Maṇḍala* (**Maṇḍala-nāma, Maṇḍala bzhugs*). Toh. 2121.

Śāntideva. *Compendium of Training* (*Śikṣāsamuccaya, bsLab pa kun las btus pa*). Toh. 3940.

Smṛtijñānakīrti. *Commentary on "Questions of the Four Goddesses"* (*Caturdevatāpa-ripṛcchāvyākhyāna-upadeśapauṣṭika, Lha mo bzhis yongs su zhus pa'i rnam par bshad pa man ngag rgyas pa*). Toh. 1915.

——. *[Eight] Concordant Topics of the Major [Prajñā]pāramitā Scriptures / Teaching on the Eight Clear Realizations as the Concordant Topics of the [Prajñāpāramitā Sūtras in] 100,000, 25,000, and 18,000 [Lines]* (*Prajñāpāramitāmātṛkā-śatasā hasrikābṛhacchāsanapañcaviṃśatisāhasrikāmadhyaśāsanāṣṭādaśasāhasrikā-laghuśāsanāṣṭasamānārthaśāsana, Phar phyin lung chen don mthun / 'Bum dang nyi khri lnga stong pa dang khri brgyad stong pa gsum don mthun par mngon rtogs brgyad du bstan pa).* Toh. 3789.

——. *Explanation of the "Commentary on Bodhicitta"* (*Bodhicittavivaraṇaṭīkā, Byang chub sems kyi 'grel pa'i rnam par bshad pa*). Toh. 1829.

Śrīghoṣa. *Lamp Eliminating the Darkness of Extremes* (n/a, *mTha'i mun sel sgron pa*). Toh. 4448.

Sthiramati. *Extensive Commentary on the "Kāśyapa Chapter" (Kāśyapaparivartaṭīkā, 'Od srungs kyi le'u rgya cher 'grel pa)*. Toh. 4009.

Sūtra on Obtaining the Roots of Virtue (Kuśalamūlasaṃparigraha, dGe ba'i rtsa ba yongs su 'dzin pa'i mdo). Toh. 101, H.K. 104.

Sūtra That Gathers All Intentions (Sarvatathāgata-citta-jñāna-guhyārtha-garbha-vyūha-vajra-tantra-siddhi-yogāgama-samāja-sarvavidyāsūtra-mahāyānābhisamaya-dharmaparyāya-vivyūha, mDo dgongs pa 'dus pa / De bzhin gshegs pa thams cad kyi thugs gsang ba'i ye shes don gyi snying po rdo rje bkod pa'i rgyud rnal 'byor grub pa'i lung kun 'dus rig pa'i mdo theg pa chen po mngon par rtogs pa chos kyi rnam grangs rnam par bkod pa zhes bya ba'i mdo). Toh. 829, H.K. 793.

Tilopa. *Esoteric Instructions on the Six Dharmas (Ṣaḍdharmopadeśa, Chos drug gi man ngag)*. Toh. 2330.

Vajrapāṇi. *Commentary That Summarizes the Meaning of the "Laghutantra" (Lakṣābhidhānāduddhṛtalaghutantrapiṇḍārthavivaraṇa, mNgon par brjod pa 'bum pa las phyung ba nyung ngu'i rgyud kyi bsdus pa'i don rnam par bshad pa)*. Toh. 1402.

Vimalamitra. *Import of Instantaneous, Nonconceptual Meditation (*Sakṛtprāveśikanirvikalpabhāvanārtha, Cig car 'jug pa rnam par mi rtog pa'i bsgom don)*. Toh. 3910.

Vinītadeva. *Three Hundred Stanzas. (Triśatakārikāvyākhyāna, Sum brgya pa / dGe tshul gyi tshig le'ur byas pa sum brgya pa'i rnam par bshad pa)*. Dg.T. 4126.

Wonch'uk. *Extensive Commentary on "Unraveling the Intent" (Gambhīrasaṃdhinirmocanasūtraṭīkā, dGongs pa zab mo nges par 'grel pa'i mdo rgya cher 'grel pa)*. Toh. 4016.

Yaśobhadra. *Difficult Points That Condense the Essence of the Vajra Lines (Vajrapadasārasaṃgrahapañjikā, rDo rje'i tshig gi snying po bsdus pa'i dka' 'grel)*. Toh. 1186.

Tibetan

Butön. *Butön's Record of Teachings Received (Bu ston gsan yig / bLa ma dam pa rnams kyis rjes su gzung ba'i tshul bka' drin rjes su dran par byed pa)*. In Collected Works of Butön, vol. la, 1–142. New Delhi: International Academy of Indian Culture, 1971.

Chegompa. *Heap of Precious Esoteric Instructions (Man ngag rin po che spungs pa)*. Sarnath: Mongolian Lama Guru Deva, 1971.

Chödrak Gyatso, comp. Indian Mahāmudrā Texts (Phyag chen rgya gzhung). 3 volumes. mDo khams sde dge: dPal spungs dgon pa, n.d. Also Nges don phyag rgya chen po'i khrid mdzod, vols. oṃ, āḥ, and hūṃ. New Delhi: rTsib ri par khang, 1997.

Chödrak Yeshe. *Elucidating the Word-Meaning: An Explanation of the "Commentary on Bodhicitta" (Byang chub sems 'grel gyi rnam par bshad pa tshig don gsal ba)*. In Collected Works of Chödrak Yeshe, vol. 2: 651–88. Beijing: Krung go'i bod rig pa dpe skrun khang, 2009.

Dak Rampa. *The Ornament for Liberating the Mind / The Ornament Illuminating the Liberation of the Mind: A Commentary on "The Profound Inner Principles," Glorious Vajra Words* (*Zab mo nang don sems kyi rnam par thar pa'i rgyan / dPal rdo rje'i tshig zab mo nang gi don gyi 'grel bshad sems kyi rnam par thar pa gsal bar byed pa'i rgyan*). Seattle: Nitartha *international* Publications, 2005.

Dakpo Tashi Namgyal. *Clarifying the Suchness of the Great Secret: A Major Instruction Manual on the Profound Path of the Six Dharmas* (*Zab lam chos drug gi khrid yig chen mo gsang chen gyi de nyid gsal ba*). In DNZ, vol. 8, 253–344. New Delhi: Shechen Publications, 1999.

———. *Clarifying the Suchness of the Innate State: A Major Instruction Manual on the Definitive Meaning, Mahāmudrā* (*gNyug ma'i de nyid gsal ba / Nges don phyag rgya chen po'i khrid yig chen mo gnyug ma'i de nyid gsal ba*). Rigpe Dorje Practice Series, vol. 11, 29–81. Kalimpong: Rigpe Dorje Publications, 2010.

Drikung Chungtsang Rigzin Chödrak. *Illumination of the Sun: Elucidating the Explanation of the Single Intent of the Genuine Dharma* (*Dam pa'i chos dgongs pa gcig pa'i rnam bshad lung don gsal byed legs bshad nyi ma'i snang ba*). In Collected Works of Rigzin Chödrak, vol. 3, 1–382. Kulhan: Drikung Kagyu Institute, 1999. BDRC W22082.

Gampopa. *Ornament of Precious Liberation* (*Thar pa rin po che'i rgyan*). In Collected Works of Gampopa, text 38/nyi. Lekshey Ling Publications.

———. *Sunrays of Scriptural Citations* (*bsTan chos lung gi nyi 'od*). Collected Works of Gampopa, text 37/ji. Lekshey Ling Publications.

Gö Lotsāwa. *Blue Annals* (*Deb ther sngon po*). Sarnath: Vajra Vidya Institute Library, 2002.

———. *Mirror Illuminating Suchness: A Commentary on the "Highest Continuum"* (*rGyud bla ma'i 'grel bshad de kho na nyid rab tu gsal ba'i me long*). Stuttgart: Franz Steiner Verlag, 2003.

Gorampa Sönam Seng-ge. Collected Works of Gorampa Sönam Seng-ge. sDe dge rdzong: rDzong sar khams bye'i slob gling, 2004.

———. *Commentary on "Analysis of the Three Vows"* (*sDom pa gsum gyi rab tu dbye ba'i rnam bshad rgyal ba'i gsung rab gyi dgongs pa gsal ba*). Digital text. International Buddhist Academy, 2015. http://www.sakyalibrary.com/library/Collection/76334317-a466-4e6f-9a5d-e538015afb4c?topicId=270169f8-166f-476a-aa5e-b1bcc481fc5d.

Great Tibetan-Chinese Dictionary (*Bod rgya tshig mdzod chen mo*). Edited by Zhang Yisun et al. 3 volumes. Beijing: Mi rigs dpe skrun khang, 1985.

Jamyang Shepa et al. (*Lam rim mchan bzhi sbrags rna / mNyam med rje btsun tsong kha pa chen pos mdzad pa'i byang chub lam rim chen mo'i dka' ba'i gnad rnams mchan bu bzhi'i sgo nas legs par bshad pa theg chen lam gyi gsal sgron*). New Delhi: Chophel Lekden, 1972.

Jikten Sumgön. *Blazing Victory Banner: The Precious Stages of the Path of the Victors' Children* (*rGyal sras rnams kyi lam rim rin po che 'bar ba'i rgyal mtshan*). In Collected Works of Jikten Sumgön, vol. 1, 226–80. Delhi: Drikung Kagyu Ratna Shri Sungrab Nyamso Khang, 2001.

———. *Essential Points of the Instructions on the Four Yogas* (*rNal 'byor bzhi'i zhal *gdams gnad kyi nying khu*). In Collected Works of Jikten Sumgön, vol. 7, 193–97. Delhi: Drikung Kagyu Ratna Shri Sungrab Nyamso Khang, 2001.

———. *Genuine Dedication That Is the Victory Banner for the Avataṃsaka* (*'Phags pa sangs rgyas phal po che rdo rje rgyal mtshan gyi bsngo ba dam pa*). In Collected Works of Jikten Sumgön, vol. 4, 370. Delhi: Drikung Kagyu Ratna Shri Sungrab Nyamso Khang, 2001.

———. *Instructions on the Four Yogas* (*rNal 'byor bzhi'i zhal gdams*). In Collected Works of Jikten Sumgön, vol. 7, 197–205. Delhi: Drikung Kagyu Ratna Shri Sungrab Nyamso Khang, 2001.

———. *Longer Instructions on the Four Yogas* (*rNal 'byor bzhi'i zhal gdams chen mo*). In Collected Works of Jikten Sumgön, vol. 7, 205–42. Delhi: Drikung Kagyu Ratna Shri Sungrab Nyamso Khang, 2001.

———. *Ornament for the Illumination of Wisdom That Dispels the Darkness of Ignorance: Pointing Out Connate Union* (*Phyag rgya chen po lhan gcig skyes sbyor gyi ngo sprod ma rig mun sel ye shes snang ba'i rgyan*). In Collected Works of Jikten Sumgön, vol. 9: 477–534. Delhi: Drikung Kagyu Ratna Shri Sungrab Nyamso Khang, 2001.

Karma Tashi Chöpel. *Earrings of the Accomplishments [of] the Practice Lineage: A Summary Catalog and Index [Showing] How the Three Volumes of Indian Mahāmudrā Texts on the Abiding State Were Arranged as a Literary Source* (*gNas lugs phyag rgya chen po'i rgya gzhung glegs bam gsum yi ge'i 'byung gnas su ji ltar bkod pa'i dkar chag bzhugs byang mdor bsdus pa sgrub brgyud grub pa'i rna rgyan*). In Indian Mahāmudrā Texts, vol. 1, 1–98. Khreng tu'u: Si khron mi rigs dpe skrun khang, 2008.

Karma Tinle. *Mirror That Reveals the Liberation of Mind: The Exposition of the Word Meaning of the Dohā Trilogy* (*Do ha skor gsum gyi tshig don gyi rnam bshad sems kyi rnam thar ston pa'i me long*). Sarnath: Vajra Vidya Institute Library, 2009.

Khamtrul Kunga Tenzin. *Unsurpassable Complete Path: Commentary on the Main Practice of Connate Mahāmudrā* (*Phyag rgya chen po lhan cig skyes sbyor gyi dngos gzhi'i khrid yig zab don rgya mtsho'i lam tshang bla na med pa*). Tashijong, Palampur, H.P.: Sungrab Nyamso Gyunphel Parkhang, Tibetan Craft Community, 1974.

Khenpo Shenga. *Annotations on the "Entrance to the Bodhisattva's Way of Life"* (*Byang chub sems dpa'i spyod pa la 'jug pa'i mchan 'grel*). Khreng tu'u: Si khron mi rigs dpe skrun khang, 2006.

———. *Annotations on the "Fundamental Treatise on the Middle Way"* (*dBu ma rtsa ba tshig le'ur byas pa shes rab ces bay ba'i mchan 'grel*). Khreng tu'u: Si khron mi rigs dpe skrun khang, 2006.

Khyentse Wangpo. *A Concise Summary Explaining "Finding Ease in Mind-Itself: The Mahāmudrā Taught to the Mahāsiddha Mitrayogin by the Noble Avalokiteśvara"* (*'Phags pa spyan ras gzigs kyis grub chen mi tra dzo ki la gsungs pa'i phyag rgya chen po sems nyid ngal gso'i gzhung 'grel snying po bsdus pa*). In DNZ, vol. 16, 525–52. Delhi: Shechen Publications, 1998.

Kongtrul Lodrö Taye, Jamgön. *Revealing the Indestructible Vajra Secrets: An Elu-*

cidation of the Word-Meaning of the "Two-Part King of Tantras, the Glorious Hevajra" (gZhom med rdo rje'i gsang ba 'byed pa / dPal dgyes pa rdo rje'i rgyud kyi rgyal po brtag pa gnyis pa'i tshig don rnam par 'grol ba gzhom med rdo rje'i gsang ba 'byed pa). Seattle: Nitartha *international* Publications, 2005.

Lho Layakpa Jangchub Ngödrup. *Ornament That Clarifies the Heart: A Commentary on the "Text Known as the Four Dharmas of Dakpo" (Dvags po'i chos bzhir grags pa'i gzhung gi 'grel pa snying po gsal ba'i rgyan)*. In bLo gros mtha' yas pa'i mdzod. Rigpe Dorje Institute Series, vol. 3. 52–392. Kathmandu: Rigpe Dorje Publications, 2008.

Marpa Lotsāwa. *Vajra Song of the Meaning of the Four Syllables: Instructions on the Essence, the Mahāmudrā of Non-Attention as Heard by the Master Marpa Lotsāwa from the Glorious Saraha (mNga' bdag mar pa lo tsA bas dpal sa ra ha las gsan pa'i phyag rgya chen po yid la mi byed pa snying po don gyi gdams ngag yi ge bzhi pa'i don rdo rje'i mgur du bzhengs pa)*. In DNZ, vol. 7, 63–66. Delhi: Shechen Publications, 1998.

Mikyö Dorje, comp. *Ocean of Kagyu Songs* (or *Rain of Wisdom*) (*bKa' brgyud mgur mtsho*). Rumtek: Karma chos sgar, 1972.

Mipam Gyatso. *Feast of Nectar: Commentary on the "Ornament for the Sūtras" (mDo sde rgyan gyi rnam bshad bdud rtsi'i dga' ston)*. Rigpe Dorje Practice Series, volume 11. Kalimpong: Rigpe Dorje Publications, 2009.

Negi, J. S. *Dharmasaṅgraha-Kośaḥ (Chos bsdus pa'i tshig mdzod)*. Sarnath: Central Institute of Higher Tibetan Studies, 2006.

Ngo-tro Rabjampa. *Precious Jeweled Garland of Eloquence That Clarifies the Word-Meaning of "A Systematic Presentation of 'The Profound Inner Principles'" Treatise (Zab mo nang gi don rnam par bshad pa'i bstan bcos kyi tshig don gsal bar byed pa'i legs bshad nor bu rin po che'i phreng ba)*. In Collected Works of Rangjung Dorje, vol. 3/hūṃ: 1–673. Lhasa: dPal brtsegs bod yig dpe rnying zhib 'jug khang, 2006.

Norbu Gyenpa. *Great Treasure for the Faithful: Description of the Wonders of Daklha Gampo (Dvags lha sgam po'i ngo mtshar gyi bkod pa dad pa'i gter chen)*. Drikung Kagyu Great Treasury of Dharma, vol. 75: 369–460. Lhasa, 2004. BDRC W00JW501203. Also n.p., n.d. BDRC W00EGS1016798.

Pakmo Drupa. *Brief Notes on the Four Yogas (rNal 'byor bzhi'i zin bris chung ngu)*. In Collected Works of Pakmo Drupa, vol. 4/nga, text 10.8. Kathmandu: Khenpo Shedup Tenzin and Lama Thinley Namgyal, 2003.

———. *Long Four Yogas (rNal 'byor bzhi chen mo)*. In Collected Works of Pakmo Drupa, vol. 4/nga, text 10.5. Kathmandu: Khenpo Shedup Tenzin and Lama Thinley Namgyal, 2003.

———. *Medium Four Yogas (rNal 'byor bzhi 'bring po)*. In Collected Works of Pakmo Drupa, vol. 4/nga, text 10.6. Kathmandu: Khenpo Shedup Tenzin and Lama Thinley Namgyal, 2003.

———. *Short Four Yogas (rNal 'byor bzhi chung ngu)*. In Collected Works of Pakmo Drupa, vol. 4/nga, text 10.7. Kathmandu: Khenpo Shedup Tenzin and Lama Thinley Namgyal, 2003.

———. *Short Notes on the Four Yogas (rNal 'byor bzhi'i zin bris chung ngu)*. In Collected Works of Pakmo Drupa, vol. 4/nga, text 10.8. Kathmandu: Khenpo Shedup Tenzin and Lama Thinley Namgyal, 2003.

———. *Three [Sets of] the Four Yogas Meditation Composed by Rinchen Gyaltsen* (*rNal 'byor bzhi gsum sgom rin chen rgyal mtshan la mdzad pa*). In Collected Works of Pakmo Drupa, vol. 4/nga, text 10.11. Kathmandu: Khenpo Shedup Tenzin and Lama Thinley Namgyal, 2003.

Parpuwa Lodrö Seng-ge. *Determining the Pith: A Commentary on the "Dohā for the Queen."* (*bTsun mo do ha'i 'grel bshad snying po rnam par nges pa*). In A Collection of Three Famous Tibetan Commentators' Works on the Threefold Cycle of Dohās of Saraha, 147–206. Sarnath: Vajra Vidya Institute Library, 2011.

Pema Karpo. *Vault of the Victors: An Explanation of the Esoteric Instructions on Mahāmudrā* (*Phag rgya chen po'i man ngag gi bshad sbyar rgyal ba'i gan mdzod*). Sarnath: Vajra Vidya Institute Library, 2005.

Rangjung Dorje. *Collection on Equal Taste* (*Ro snyoms sgang 'dril*), In Collected Works of Rangjung Dorje, vol. 11/A: 129–58. Lhasa: dPal brtsegs bod yig dpe rnying zhib 'jug khang, 2006.

———. *Mahāmudrā: Connate Union* (*Phyag chen lhan cig skyes sbyor*). In DNZ, vol. 9, 1–16. Delhi: Shechen Publications, 1998.

———. *Molten Gold of the Six Dharmas* (*Chos drug gser zhun ma*). In DNZ, vol. 9, 17–37. Delhi: Shechen Publications, 1998.

———. *Nondual Wind-Mind* (*rLung sems gnyis med*). In DNZ, vol. 9, 167–73. Delhi: Shechen Publications, 1998.

———. *Pointing Out the Three Kāyas* (*sKu gsum ngo sprod*). In Collected Works of Rangjung Dorje, vol. 11/A, 1–19. Lhasa: dPal brtsegs bod yig dpe rnying zhib 'jug khang, 2006.

Rongtön Sheja Kunrik. *Drumroll of the Gods: A Commentary on the Final "Stages of Meditation"* (*sGom rim tha ma'i 'grel pa lha'i rnga sgra*). sKye dgu mdo: Gangs ljongs rig rgyan gsung rab par khang, 2004.

———. *Moonlight of Key Points: A Commentary on the Middle "Stages of Meditation"* (*sGom rim bar pa'i 'grel pa gnad kyi zla zer*). Kathmandu: Sa skya rgyal yongs gsung rab slob gnyer khang, 1999.

———. *Ornament That Illuminates Śamatha and Vipaśyanā: A Commentary on the First "Stages of Meditation"* (*sGom rim dang po'i 'grel pa zhi lhag gsal bar byed pa'i rgyan*). sKye dgu mdo: Gangs ljongs rig rgyan gsung rab par khang, 2004.

Sakya Paṇḍita. *Letter to the Holy Beings* (*sKyes bu dam pa rnams la spring ba'i yi ge*). In Sakya Collected Works, vol. 12: 159–72. Kathmandu: Sachen International, 2006.

———. *Replies to the Questions of Tok-den Gyalpo* (*rTogs ldan rgyal po'i dris lan*). Mes po'i shul bzhag, vol. 1: 405–11. Beijing: Krung go'i bod rig pa dpe skrun khang, 2007.

Shākya Chokden. *Extracting the Heart of Madhyamaka: An Explanation of the "Commentary on Ultimate Bodhicitta"* (*Don dam byang chub sems 'grel gyi bshad pa dbu ma'i snying po bsdus pa*). In Collected Works of Serdok Paṇchen Shākya Chokden, vol. 7: 348–94. Thimphu, Bhutan: Kunzang Tobgey, 1975.

Shākya Gelong Zangpo. *An Abbreviated Biography of Dakpo Tashi Namgyal, Dharma King of the Three Realms, Emanation of the Great, Incomparable Gampopa* (*mNyam med sgam po pa chen po'i rnam rol khams gsum chos kyi rgyal po dvags po bkra shis rnam par rgyal ba'i rnam thar mdor bsdus*). In Phyag rgya chen po'i sgom rim gsal bar byed pa legs bshad zla ba'i 'od zer, iii–xxxiv. Delhi: Drikung Kagyu Publications, 2004. Also in dPal kye rdo rje zhes bya ba'i rgyud kyi rgyal po'i 'grel pa legs bshad nyi ma'i 'od zer, iii–xxxiv. Delhi: Drikung Kagyu Publications, 2004.

———. *Garland of Vaiḍūrya: An Account of the Holy Hereditary Throne-Holders of the Glorious Gampopa, Regent of the Teacher in This Snowy Land* (*Gangs can 'dir ston pa'i rgyal tshab dpal sgam po pa'i khri gdung dzin pa'i dam pa rnams kyi gtam Bai durya'i phreng ba*). Probable Daklha Gampo edition. n.p, n.d. BDRC W00EGS1016800. Also in Drikung Kagyu Great Treasury of Dharma, vol. 76: 341–585. Lhasa, 2004. BDRC W00JW501203. Also in Sørensen, Per K. and Sonam Dolma, eds. *Rare Texts from Tibet: Seven Sources for the Ecclesiastic History of Medieval Tibet*, 191–247. Lumbini International Research Institute Series. Lumbini: Lumbini International Research Institute, 2007.

Tāranātha. *Hundreds of Light Rays: An Addendum to Tongwa Dönden's "Vajrayoginī Commentary"* (*rDo rje'i rnal 'byor gyi 'khrid yig mthong ba don ldan gyi lhan thabs 'od brgya 'bar ba*). Collected Works of Tāranātha, vol. 7. Beijing: Krung go'i bod rig pa dpe skrun khang, 2008.

Thrangu Rinpoche. *Essential Instructions: A Word-Commentary on the "Entrance to the Bodhisattva's Way of Life"/ Essential Instructions: Word-Commentary on the Ocean of Mahāyāna Dharma: A Commentary on the "Entrance to the Bodhisattva's Way of Life"* (*sPyod 'jug tshig 'grel gces btus / Byang chub sems dpa'i spyod pa la 'jug pa'i rnam bshad theg chen chos kyi rgya mtsho'i tshig 'grel gces btus*). Sarnath: Vajra Vidya Institute Library, 2007.

Tsangpa Gyare. *Instructions on the Four Yogas Bestowed on Tuk-kyi Dorje* (*rNal 'byor bzhi'i zhal gdams thugs kyi rdo rje la gnang ba*). In Collected Works of Tsangpa Gyare Yeshe Dorje, 547–62. Kathmandu: Khenpo Shedup Tenzin and Lama Thinley Namgyal, 1998.

———. *Instructions on the Four Yogas Composed by the Dharma Lord Protector of Beings [Tsangpa Gyare]* (*rNal 'byor bzhi'i zhal gdams chos rje 'gro mgon gyis mdzad pa*). In Collected Works of Tsangpa Gyare Yeshe Dorje, 537–46. Kathmandu: Khenpo Shedup Tenzin and Lama Thinley Namgyal, 1998.

Tsongkhapa. *Condensed Points of the Stages of the Path* (*Lam rim chung ngu / Lam rim nyams mgur / Byang chub lam gyi rim pa'i nyams len gyi rnam gzhag mdor bsdus te brjed byang*). In Tsongkhapa's Collected Works, vol. 3: 138–44. New Delhi: Ngawang Gelek Demo, 1975.

———. *Great Treatise on the Stages of the Path to Awakening* (*Byang chub lam rim che ba / sKyes bu gsum gyi nyams su blang ba'i rim pa thams cad tshang bar ston pa'i byang chub lam gyi rim pa*). Delhi: Tibetan Cultural and Religious Publication Centre, 2004.

Wangchuk Dorje, Ninth Karmapa. *Feast for the Fortunate: An Easy Way into the*

"Chariot of the Dakpo Siddhas," A Commentary on the "Entrance [to the Middle Way]" ('Jug ṭikā dvags brgyud grub pa'i shing rta bde bar 'dren byed skal bzang dga' ston). Sarnath: Vajra Vidya Institute Library, 2003.

——. *Ocean of Definitive Meaning (Nges don rgya mtsho / Lhan cig skyes sbyor gyi zab khrid nges don rgya mtsho'i snying po phrin las 'od 'phro)*. Rigpe Dorje Practice Series, vol. 2, 53–301. Kalimpong: Rigpe Dorje Publications, 2010.

——. *Pointing Out the Dharmakāya (Chos sku mdzub tshugs / Phyag rgya chen po lhan cig skyes sbyor gyi khrid zin bris snying po gsal ba'i sgron me bdud rtsi'i nying khu chos sku mdzub tshugs su ngo sprod pa)*. Rigpe Dorje Practice Series, vol. 2, 343–76. Kalimpong: Rigpe Dorje Publications, 2010.

——. *Youthful Play: An Explanation of the "Treasury of Abhidharma" (mNgon par mdzod kyi rnam bshad gzhon nu rnam rol / Chos mngon pa mdzod kyi rnam par bshad pa chos mngon rgya mtsho'i snying po mkhyen rtse'i zhal lung gzhon nu rnam rol legs bshad chos mig rnam 'byed grub bde'i shing rta zhes bya ba bzhugs so)*. Sarnath: Vajra Vidya Library, 2003.

Wangchuk Gyaltsen. *Great of Stainless Eloquence: A Biography of Nāropa (NA ro pa'i rnam thar dri med legs bshad bde chen)*. Palampur, H.P., India: Sungrab Nyamso Gyunphel Parkhang, 1972–76.

Yang Gönpa, as recorded by Chen-nga Rinchen Den. *Ornamental Notes on the Stages of the Four Yogas (rNal 'byor bzhi'i rim gyi zin bris rgyan)*. In Collected Works of Yang Gönpa, vol. 1, 279–95. Tango, Thimphu, Bhutan: Tango Monastic Community, 1982.

English

Abboud, Gerardo. *The Royal Seal of Mahamudra Volume One: A Guidebook for the Realization of Coemergence*. Boston: Snow Lion, 2014.

Adam, Martin T. "Meditation and the Concept of Insight in Kamalaśīla's *Bhāvanākramas*." Master's thesis, McGill University, 2002.

AIBS Translation Team, Robert Thurman, et al. *The Universal Vehicle Discourse Literature*. Treasury of the Buddhist Sciences. New York: American Institute of Buddhist Studies / Columbia University's Center for Buddhist Studies / Tibet House US, 2004.

Anālayo. *Early Buddhist Meditation Studies*. Barre: Barre Center for Buddhist Studies, 2017.

——. "Mindfulness in Early Buddhism." *Journal of the Centre for Buddhist Studies* 11 (2013): 147–74.

Bodhi, Bhikkhu. "What Does Mindfulness Really Mean? A Canonical Perspective." *Contemporary Buddhism* 12, no. 1 (2011): 19–39.

Boin-Webb, Sara, trans. *Abhidharmasamuccaya: The Compendium of the Higher Teaching (Philosophy)*. Fremont, CA: Asian Humanities Press, 2001.

Braitstein, Lara. *The Adamantine Songs (*Vajragīti*) by Saraha: Study, Translation, and Tibetan Critical Edition*. Treasury of the Buddhist Sciences. New York: American Institute of Buddhist Studies, 2014.

——. "The Extraordinary Path: Saraha's Adamantine Songs and the Bka' brgyud Great Seal." In *Mahāmudrā and the Bka' brgyud Tradition: Proceedings of the Eleventh Seminar of the International Association for Tibetan Studies*, edited by Roger Jackson and Matthew T. Kapstein, 55–88. Andiast, Switzerland: International Institute for Tibetan and Buddhist Studies, 2011.

Bretfeld, Sven. "The 'Great Debate' of bSam yas: Construction and Deconstruction of a Tibetan Buddhist Myth." *Asiatische Studien: Zeitschrift Der Schweizerischen Gesellschaft Für Asienkunde / Etudes Asiatiques: Revue de La Société Suisse D'études Asiatiques*, no. 1 (2004): 15–56.

Broido, Michael. "Sa-skya Paṇḍita, the White Panacea and the Hva-shang Doctrine." *JIABS* 10, no. 2 (1987): 27–68.

Brunnhölzl, Karl. *The Center of the Sunlit Sky: Madhyamaka in the Kagyü Tradition*. Nitartha Institute Series. Ithaca, NY: Snow Lion, 2004.

——. *In Praise of Dharmadhātu*. Ithaca, NY: Snow Lion, 2007.

——. *Mining for Wisdom within Delusion: Maitreya's Distinction between Phenomena and the Nature of Phenomena and Its Indian and Tibetan Commentaries*. Boston: Snow Lion, 2012.

——. *Straight from the Heart: Buddhist Pith Instructions*. Ithaca, NY: Snow Lion, 2007.

——. *When the Clouds Part: The Uttaratantra and Its Meditative Tradition as a Bridge between Sūtra and Tantra*. Boston: Snow Lion, 2014.

Buswell, Robert E., and Donald S. Lopez. *The Princeton Dictionary of Buddhism*. Princeton: Princeton University Press, 2014.

Callahan, Elizabeth M. *Mahāmudrā: The Ocean of the Definitive Meaning*. Seattle: Nitartha *international* Publications, 2001.

——. *The Profound Inner Principles*. Boston: Snow Lion, 2014.

Cha, Sangyeob. "The *Yogācārabhūmi* Meditation Doctrine of the 'Nine Stages of Mental Abiding' in East and Central Asian Buddhism." In *The Foundation for Yoga Practitioners: The Buddhist Yogācārabhūmi Treatise and Its Adaptation in India, East Asia, and Tibet*, edited by Ulrich Timme Kragh, 1166–91. Harvard Oriental Series 75. Cambridge: Harvard University Press, 2013.

Chang, C. C. *The Teachings of Tibetan Yoga*. New Hyde Park, NY: University Books, 1963.

Charrier, Christian. *Lumière de diamant: Présentation générale des quatre classes de tantras bouddhistes*. Collection Tsadra. Plazac, France: Éditions Padmakara, 2016.

Choephel, David Karma. *Jewels from the Treasury: Vasubandhu's* Verses on the Treasury of Abhidharma *and Its Commentary* Youthful Play *by the Ninth Karmapa Wangchuk Dorje*. Woodstock, NY: KTD Publications, 2012.

Cleary, Thomas. *Flower Ornament Scripture*. Boston: Shambhala, 1993.

Cüppers, Christopher. *The IXth Chapter of the Samādhirājasūtra*. Stuttgart: Franz Steiner Verlag, 1990.

Dalai Lama, His Holiness the. *Stages of Meditation*. London: Rider, 2001.

Dalai Lama, Tenzin Gyatso. *The Buddhism of Tibet.* Translated and edited by Jeffrey Hopkins. Ithaca, NY: Snow Lion, 1987.

Dalai Lama, Tenzin Gyatso and Alexander Berzin. *The Gelug/Kagyü Tradition of Mahamudra.* Ithaca, NY: Snow Lion, 1997.

Dalton, Jacob, and Sam van Schaik. "Lighting the Lamp: The Structure of the *Bsam gtan mi sgron.*" *Acta Orientalia* 64 (2003): 153–75. 2003.

——. *Tibetan Tantric Manuscripts from Dunhuang: A Descriptive Catalogue of the Stein Collection at the British Library.* Leiden: Brill, 2006.

Dewar, Tyler. *The Karmapa's Middle Way: Feast for the Fortunate.* Ithaca, NY: Snow Lion, 2008.

Dharmachakra Translation Committee. *Middle Beyond Extremes.* Ithaca, NY: Snow Lion, 2006.

——. "The Ornament of the Light of Awareness that Enters the Domain of All Buddhas." 84000: Translating the Words of the Buddha. http://read.84000.co/#UT22084-047-002/title.

——. *Ornament of Reason: The Great Commentary of Nāgārjuna's* Root of the Middle Way. Ithaca, NY: Snow Lion, 2011.

——. "The Play in Full." 84000: Translating the Words of the Buddha. http://read.84000.co/#UT22084-046-001/title.

Dölpa, Gampopa, and Sakya Paṇḍita. *Stages of the Buddha's Teachings: Three Key Texts.* Translated by Ulrike Roesler, Ken Holmes, and David P. Jackson. Library of Tibetan Classics. Somerville, MA: Wisdom Publications, 2015.

Dowman, Keith. *Masters of Mahamudra: Songs and Histories of the Eighty-Four Buddhist Siddhas.* Albany, NY: State University of New York Press, 1985.

Draszczyk, Martina. "Some Dwags po Mahāmudrā Responses to Sa skya Paṇḍita' s Critique at 'Present-Day Mahāmudrā.'" *JIABS* 29, no. 2 (2006): 375–403.

Ducher, Cécile. "bKa' brgyud Treasure and rNying ma Revealer: The Sras mkhar ma of Mar pa Lo tsā ba." *Revue d'Etudes Tibétaines* 37 (2016): 98–126.

Dudjom Rinpoche, Jikdrel Yeshe Dorje. *The Nyingma School of Tibetan Buddhism: Its Fundamentals and History.* Translated and edited by Gyurme Dorje and Matthew Kapstein. Boston: Wisdom Publications, 1991.

Eckel, Malcolm David. *Jñānagarbha on the Two Truths: An Eighth Century Handbook of Madhyamaka Philosophy.* Delhi: Motilal Banarsidass, 1992.

Engle, Artemus B. *The Bodhisattva Path to Unsurpassed Enlightenment: A Complete Translation of the Bodhisattvabhūmi.* Boulder: Snow Lion Publications, 2016.

——. *The Inner Science of Buddhist Practice.* Ithaca, NY: Snow Lion Publications. 2009.

Fremantle, Francesca, ed. and trans. "A Critical Study of the Guhyasamāja Tantra." PhD diss., University of London, 1971.

Garfield, Jay L. *The Fundamental Wisdom of the Middle Way: Nāgārjuna's Mūlamadhyamakakārikā.* New York: Oxford University Press, 1995.

Gethin, Rupert. "On Some Definitions of Mindfulness." *Contemporary Buddhism* 12, no. 1 (2011): 263–79.

Gómez, Luis. "The Direct and Gradual Approaches of Zen Master Mahāyāna: Fragments of the Teachings of Moheyan." In *Studies in Ch'an and Hua-yen*, edited by Robert M. Gimello and Peter N. Gregory, 393–434. Honolulu: University of Hawai'i Press, 1983.

Gray, David B. "Imprints of the 'Great Seal': On the expanding semantic range of the term of *mudrā* in eighth through eleventh century Indian Buddhist literature." *JIABS* 34, nos. 1–2 (2011): 421–81.

Gruber, Elmer. *From the Heart of Tibet: The Biography of Drikung Chetsang Rinpoche, the Holder of the Drikung Kagyu Lineage.* Boston: Shambhala Publications, 2010.

Guenther, Herbert V. *Ecstatic Spontaneity: Saraha's Three Cycles of Dohā.* Berkeley: Asian Humanities Press, 1993.

———. *The Life and Teaching of Nāropa.* London: Oxford University Press, 1963.

Gyamtso, Yeshe (Peter O'Hearn). *The Hundred Tertöns.* Woodstock, NY: KTD Publications, 2011.

Gyatso, Janet. "Healing Burns with Fire: The Facilitations of Experience in Tibetan Buddhism." *Journal of the American Academy of Religion* 67, no. 1 (1999): 113–47.

Harding, Sarah. *Niguma: Lady of Illusion.* Tsadra Foundation Series. Ithaca, NY: Snow Lion Publications, 2010.

Harrison, Paul M. *The Samadhi of Direct Encounter with the Buddhas of the Present: An Annotated English Translation of the Tibetan Version of the* Pratyutpanna-Buddha-Saṃmukhāvasthita Samādhi-Sūtra. Tokyo: The International Institute for Buddhist Studies, 1990.

Harvey, Peter. "Mindfulness in Theravāda *Samatha* and *Vipassanā* Meditations, and in Secular Mindfulness." In *Buddhist Foundations of Mindfulness*, edited by E. Shonin et al., 115–37. Cham: Springer, 2015.

Henning, Edward. *Kālacakra and the Tibetan Calendar.* Treasury of the Buddhist Sciences. New York: American Institute of Buddhist Studies, 2007.

Higgins, David. "On the Development of the Non-mentation (*amanasikāra*) Doctrine in Indo-Tibetan Buddhism." *JIABS* 29, no. 2 (2006): 255–303.

———. "Padma dkar po's (1527–92) Defence of Bka' Brgyud *Amanasikāra* Teachings." *JIABS* 39 (2016): 429–85.

Higgins, David and Martina Draszczyk. *Mahāmudrā and the Middle Way: Post-Classical Kagyü Discourses on Mind, Emptiness and Buddha-Nature.* 2 volumes. Wiener Studien zur Tibetologie und Buddhismuskunde 90.2. Vienna: Arbeitskreis für Tibetische und Buddhistische Studien, Universität Wien, 2016.

Holmes, Ken. *Ornament of Precious Liberation.* In *Stages of the Buddha's Teachings: Three Key Texts.* Translated by Ulrike Roesler, Ken Holmes, and David P. Jackson, 121–381. Library of Tibetan Classics. Somerville, MA: Wisdom Publications, 2015.

Hopkins, Jeffrey. *Tsong-kha-pa's Final Exposition of Wisdom.* Ithaca, NY: Snow Lion, 2008.

Jackson, David. "The *bsTan rim* ('Stages of the Doctrine') and Similar Graded Expositions of the Bodhisattva's Path." In *Tibetan Literature: Studies in Genre, Essays in Honor of Geshe Lhundrup Sopa*, edited by José I. Cabezón and Roger Jackson, 229–43. Ithaca, NY: Snow Lion Publications, 1996.

——. *Clarifying the Sage's Intent.* In *Stages of the Buddha's Teachings: Three Key Texts.* Translated by Ulrike Roesler, Ken Holmes, and David P. Jackson, 385–630. Library of Tibetan Classics. Somerville, MA: Wisdom Publications, 2015.

——. *Enlightenment by a Single Means: Tibetan Controversies on the "Self-Sufficient White Remedy"* (Dkar po Chig Thub). Beiträge zur Kultur- und Geistesgeschichte Asiens 12. Vienna: Österreichische Akademie der Wissenschaften, 1994.

——. "Sa-skya Paṇḍita the 'Polemicist': Ancient Debates and Modern Interpretations." *JIABS* 13, no. 2 (1990): 17–116.

——. "Which bKra shis rnam rgyal Wrote the Renowned Tibetan Mahāmudrā Manual?" In *Esoteric Buddhist Studies: Identity in Diversity: Proceedings of International Conference on Esoteric Buddhist Studies, Koyasan University, 5 Sept.–8 Sept. 2006*, 199–205. Koyasan: Executive Committee, ICEBS, 2011.

Jackson, Roger. "A Brief History of Mahāmudrā Studies in the West." In *Mahāmudrā and the Bka' brgyud Tradition*, edited by Roger R. Jackson and Matthew T. Kapstein, 3–54. Proceedings from the Eleventh Seminar of the International Association for Tibetan Studies, Königswinter, Germany, 2006. Andiast, Switzerland: International Institute for Tibetan and Buddhist Studies, 2011.

——. "The dGe ldan-bKa' brgyud Tradition of Mahāmudrā: How much dGe ldan? How Much bKa' brgyud?" In *Changing Minds: Contributions to the Study of Buddhism and Tibet in Honor of Jeffrey Hopkins*, edited by Guy Newland, 155–91. Ithaca, NY: Snow Lion, 2001.

——. "The Indian Mahāmudrā Canon(s): A Preliminary Sketch. *Indian International Journal of Buddhist Studies* 9 (2008): 151–84.

——. "Mahāmudrā in India and Tibet." *Oxford Research Encyclopedias.* http://religion.oxfordre.com/view/10.1093/acrefore/9780199340378.001.0001/acrefore-9780199340378-e-184.

——. "Sa skya paṇḍita's Accounts of the bSam yas Debate: History as Polemic." *JIABS* 5, no. 1 (1982): 89–99.

——. "Saraha's *Queen Dohās.*" In *Yoga in Practice*, edited by David Gordon White, 162–84. Princeton: Princeton University Press, 2012.

——. *Tantric Treasures: Three Collections of Mystical Verse from Buddhist India.* Oxford: Oxford University Press, 2004.

——."Two Bka' 'gyur Works in Mahāmudrā Canons: The Ārya-ātajñāna-nāma-mahāyāna-sūtra and the Anāvila-tantra-rāja." *JIATS* 5 (2009): 1–24.

Jinpa, Thubten, trans. "A Commentary on the Awakening Mind." *Institute of Tibetan Classics.* http://tibetanclassics.org/html-assets/Awakening%20Mind%20Commentary.pdf.

——. "Songs of Spiritual Experience: Condensed Points of the Stages of the Path." *Institute of Tibetan Classics.* http://tibetanclassics.org/html-assets/Songs%20of%20Experience.pdf.

Jitta, Yanneke Josephus. "Mipham Gyatso Rinpoche's 'Makeover' of Hwashang Moheyan." Master's thesis, Rangjung Yeshe Institute / Kathmandu University, 2015.

Kapstein, Matthew. "Dohās and Gray Texts: Reflections on a Song Attributed to Kāṇha." In *From Bhakti to Bon: Festschrift for Per Kvaerne*, edited by H. Havnevik and C. Ramble, 291–301. Oslo: Novus Forlag, 2015.

——. "An Inexhaustible Treasury of Song." In *Divine Madness*, edited by Rob Linrothe, 23–35. Chicago: Serindia, 2005.

——. "Mahāmudrā: The Quintessence of Mind and Meditation (Lobsang Lhalungpa)." *JIABS* 13, no. 1 (1990): 101–14.

——. *The Tibetan Assimilation of Buddhism: Conversion, Contestation, and Memory.* Oxford: Oxford University Press, 2000.

Kittay, David R. "Interpreting the *Vajra Rosary*: Truth and Method Meets Wisdom and Method." Ph.D. diss., Columbia University, 2011.

Kongtrul Lodrö Taye, Jamgön. *The Treasury of Knowledge: Book Eight, Part Four: Esoteric Instructions.* Translated by the Kalu Rinpoché Translation Group (Sarah Harding). Ithaca, NY: Snow Lion Publications, 2007.

——. *The Treasury of Knowledge: Book Five: Buddhist Ethics.* Translated by the Kalu Rinpoché Translation Group (Elio Guarisco and Ingrid McLeod). Ithaca, NY: Snow Lion, 1998.

——. *The Treasury of Knowledge: Book Seven and Book Eight, Parts One and Two: Foundations of Buddhist Study and Practice.* Translated by the Kalu Rinpoché Translation Group (Richard Barron). Ithaca, NY: Snow Lion, 2012.

——. *The Treasury of Knowledge: Books Nine and Ten: Journey and Goal.* Translated by the Kalu Rinpoché Translation Group (Richard Barron). Ithaca, NY: Snow Lion, 2011.

Kragh, Ulrich T. "Culture and Subculture: A Study of the Mahāmudrā Teachings of Sgam po pa." Master's thesis, University of Copenhagen, 1998.

——. "The Significant Leap from Writing to Print: Editorial Modification in the First Printed Edition of the Collected Works of Sgam po pa Bsod nams rin chen." In *JIATS* 7 (2013): 365–425.

——. *Tibetan Yoga and Mysticism: A Textual Study of the* Yogas *of Nāropa and* Mahāmudrā *Meditation in the Medieval Tradition of Dags po.* Studia Philologica Buddhica 32. Tokyo: The International Institute for Buddhist Studies, 2015.

Kyabgon, Traleg, trans. *Moonbeams of Mahāmudrā.* Victoria, Australia: Shogam Publications, 2015.

Lamrim Chenmo Translation Committee. *The Great Treatise on the Stages of the Path to Enlightenment.* Vol. 3. Ithaca, New York: Snow Lion Publications, 2002.

Lati Rinbochay. *Mind in Tibetan Buddhism.* Translated and edited by Elizabeth Napper. 3rd ed. Ithaca, NY: Snow Lion Publications, 1986.

Lhalungpa, Lobsang. *The Life of Milarepa.* New York: E.P. Dutton, 1977.

——. *Mahāmudrā: The Quintessence of Mind and Meditation.* Boston: Shambhala Publications, 1986.

Lindtner, Christian. "Atiśa's Introduction to the Two Truths, and Its Sources." *JIP* 9 (1981): 161–214.

———. *Master of Wisdom: Writings of the Buddhist Master Nāgārjuna*. Berkeley: Dharma Publishing, 1986.

Mabbett, Ian. "The Problem of the Historical Nagarjuna Revisited." *Journal of the American Oriental Society* 118, no. 3 (1998): 332–46.

Mathes, Klaus-Dieter. "bKa' brgyud Mahāmudrā: Chinese *rDzogs chen* or the Teachings of the Siddhas?" In *Tibet After Empire: Culture, Society and Religion Between 850–1000*, edited by Christoph Cüppers, Robert Mayer, and Michael Walter, 267–94. Lumbini: Lumbini International Research Institute, 2013.

———. "Blending the Sūtras with the Tantras: The Influence of Maitrīpa and his Circle on the Formation of Sūtra Mahāmudrā in the Kagyu Schools." In *Tibetan Buddhist Literature and Praxis: Studies in its Formative Period, 900–1400: Proceedings from the Tenth Seminar of the International Association for Tibetan Studies*, edited by Ronald M. Davidson and Christian K. Wedemeyer, 201–27. Leiden: Brill, 2006.

———. "Can Sūtra Mahāmudrā be Justified on the Basis of Maitrīpa's Apratiṣṭhānavāda?" In *Pramāṇakīrtiḥ: Papers Dedicated to Ernst Steinkellner on the occasion of His 70th birthday*, edited by B. Kellner, H. Krasser, H. Lasic, M.T. Much, H. Tauscher, 545–66. Wiener Studien zur Tibetologie und Buddhismuskunde 70, no. 2. Vienna: Arbeitskreis für tibetische und buddhistische Studien, 2007.

———. "The Collection of 'Indian Mahāmudrā Works' (*phyag chen rgya gzhung*) Compiled by the Seventh Karma pa Chos grags rgya mtsho." In *Mahāmudrā and the Bka'-brgyud Tradition: Proceedings of the Eleventh Seminar of the International Association for Tibetan Studies*, edited by Roger Jackson and Matthew T. Kapstein, 89–127. Andiast, Switzerland: International Institute for Tibetan and Buddhist Studies, 2011.

———. *A Direct Path to the Buddha Within: Gö Lotsāwa's Mahāmudrā Interpretation of the Ratnagotravibhāga*. Somerville, MA: Wisdom Publications, 2008.

———. *A Fine Blend of Mahāmudrā and Madhyamaka: Maitrīpa's Collection of Texts on Non-conceptual Realization* (Amanasikāra). Vienna: Verlag der Österreichischen Akademie der Wissenschaften, 2015.

———. "Maitrīpa's Amanasikārādhāra ('A Justification of Becoming Mentally Disengaged')." *Journal of the Nepal Research Centre* 13 (2009): 5–32.

Martin, Dan. "A Twelfth-century Tibetan Classic of Mahāmudrā: The Path of Ultimate Profundity: The Great Seal Instructions of Zhang." *JIABS* 15, no. 2 (1992): 243–319.

Meinert, Carmen. "The Legend of *Cig car ba* Criticism in Tibet: A List of Six *Cig car ba* Titles in the *Chos 'byung me tog snying po* of Nyang Nyi ma 'od zer (12th century)." In *Tibetan Buddhist Literature and Praxis: Studies in its Formative Period 900–1400*, edited by Ronald Davidson and Christian Wedemeyer, 31–54. Leiden: Brill, 2006.

———. "Structural Analysis of the *bSam gtan mig sgron*. A Comparison of the Fourfold Correct Practice in the *Āryāvikalpapraveśanāmadhāraṇi* and the Contents of the four Main Chapters of the *bSam gtan mig sgron*." *JIABS* 26, no. 1 (2003): 175–95.

Nalanda Translation Committee. *The Life of Marpa the Translator: Seeing Accomplishes All.* Boulder: Shambhala Publications, 1986.

———. *The Rain of Wisdom.* Boulder: Shambhala Publications, 1980.

Nyenpa, Sangyes. *Tilopa's Mahamudra Upadesha: The Gangama Instructions with Commentary.* Boston: Snow Lion, 2014.

Olendski, Andrew. "The Construction of Mindfulness." *Contemporary Buddhism* 12, no. 1 (2011): 55–70.

Padmakara Translation Group. *Introduction to the Middle Way: Chandrakīrti's 'Madhyamakāvatāra' with Commentary by Jamgön Mipham.* Boston: Shambhala Publications, 2002.

———. *Ornament of the Mahāyāna Sūtras: Asaṅga's Classic Text Received from Maitreya with a Commentary by Jamgön Mipham.* Boulder: Shambhala Publications, forthcoming.

———. *The Way of the Bodhisattva.* Boston: Shambhala Publications, 1997.

Passavanti, Marco. "The Life of Maitrīpā/Maitreyanātha from a Thirteenth-Century Tibetan Biography (MS 1095 of the Tucci Tibetan Fund)." In *Manuscripta Buddhica* 2, edited by Harunaga Isaacson and Francesco Sferra, 431–48. Naples: Universita Delgi Studi Di Napoli "L'Orientale," 2014.

———. "A Thirteenth-Century Work on the Doha Lineage of Saraha." In *Contributions to Tibetan Buddhist Literature,* edited by Orna Almogi, 435–88. Beiträge zur Zentralasienforschung 14. PIATS 2006: Tibetan Studies: Proceedings of the Eleventh Seminar of the International Association for Tibetan Studies, Königswinter 2006. Halle (Saale): International Institute for Tibetan and Buddhist Studies, 2008.

Powers, John. *Jñānagarbha's Commentary on Just the Maitreya Chapter from the Saṁdhinirmocana-Sūtra: Study, Translation and Tibetan Text.* New Delhi: Indian Council of Philosophical Research, 1998.

———. *Wisdom of Buddha: The Saṃdhinirmocana Mahāyāna Sūtra.* Berkeley: Dharma Publishing, 1995.

Pruden, Leo M. *Abhidharmakośabhāṣyam.* 4 vols. Berkeley: Asian Humanities Press, 1988–90.

Quintman, Andrew. *The Life of Milarepa.* New York: Penguin Books, 2010.

———. *The Yogin and the Madman: Reading the Biographical Corpus of Tibet's Great Saint Milarepa.* New York: Columbia University Press, 2014.

Rhoton, Jared Douglas. *A Clear Differentiation of the Three Codes: Essential Distinctions among the Individual Liberation, Great Vehicle, and Tantric Systems.* Albany: State University Press of New York, 2002.

Roberts, Peter Alan. *The Biographies of Rechungpa: The Evolution of a Tibetan Biography.* London: Routledge, 2007.

———. *Mahāmudrā and Related Instructions: Core Teachings of the Kagyü Schools.* Boston: Wisdom Publications. 2011.

———. *The Mind of Mahāmudrā.* Boston: Wisdom Publications, 2014.

Roerich, George N. *The Blue Annals.* 1949. Reprint, Delhi: Motilal Banarsidass, 1979.

Ruegg, David Seyfort. "On the Historiography and Doxography of the 'Great Debate of bSam yas.'" In *Tibetan Studies: Proceedings of the Fifth Seminar of the International Association for Tibetan Studies (Narita 1989)*, edited by Ihara Shōren et al., 237–44. Tokyo: Naritisan Shinshoji, 1992.

Schaeffer, Kurtis R. *The Culture of the Book in Tibet.* New York: Columbia University Press, 2009.

———. *Dreaming the Great Brahmin: Tibetan Traditions of the Buddhist Poet-Saint Saraha.* Oxford: Oxford University Press, 2005.

Schmidt, Erik. *Clarifying the Natural State: A Principal Guidance Manual for Mahamudra.* Hong Kong: Rangjung Yeshe Publications, 2001.

Shakabpa, Tsepon W. D. *Tibet: A Political History.* New Haven: Yale University Press, 1967.

Sharma, Parmananda. *Bhāvanākrama of Kamalaśila.* New Delhi: Aditya Prakashan, 1997.

Sherburne, Richard. *The Complete Works of Atīśa Śrī Dīpaṃkara Jñāna, Jo-bo-rje: The* Lamp for the Path *and* Commentary, *together with the Newly Translated* Twenty-five Key Texts. 2000. Reprint, Delhi: Aditya Prakashan, 2003.

Sherpa, Trungram Gyaltrul Rinpoche. "Gampopa, the Monk and the Yogi: His Life and Teachings." PhD diss., Harvard University, 2004.

Siderits, Mark and Shōryū Katsura. *Nāgārjuna's Middle Way: The Mūlamadhyamakakārikā.* Boston: Wisdom Publications, 2013.

Sørensen, Per K. "The Prolific Ascetic lCe-sgom Śes-rab rdo-rje alias lCe-sgom źig-po: Allusive but Elusive." *Journal of the Nepal Research Center* 11 (1999): 175–200.

Sørensen, Per K. and Sonam Dolma. *Rare Texts from Tibet: Seven Sources for the Ecclesiastic History of Medieval Tibet.* Lumbini International Research Institute Series. Lumbini: Lumbini International Research Institute, 2007.

Stein, Lisa and Ngawang Zangpo. *Butön's History of Buddhism in India and Its Spread to Tibet: A Treasury of Priceless Scripture.* Boston: Snow Lion Publications, 2013.

Stenzel, Julia. "From Radishes to Realization: Saraha and His Impact on the Mahāmudrā Tradition of the Tibetan Karma Kagyü School." Master's thesis. University of the West, 2008.

———. "The Mahāmudrā of Sakya Paṇḍita." *Indian International Journal of Buddhist Studies* 15 (2014): 199–228.

Sterns, Cyrus. *Luminous Lives: The Story of the Early Masters of the Lam 'Bras Tradition in Tibet.* Boston: Wisdom Publications, 2001.

Suzuki, Daisetz Teitaro. *The Laṅkāvatāra Sūtra.* Boulder: Prajñā Press, 1978.

Tamphel, Khenpo Könchok. *Introduction to Mahāmudrā: The Co-emergent Unification.* Dehra Dun: Songtsen Library, 2006.

Tatz, Mark. "The Life of the Siddha-Philosopher Maitrīgupta." *The Journal of the American Oriental Society* 107, no. 4 (1987): 695–711.

Tauscher, Helmut. "The Rnal 'byor chen po bsgom pa'i don: Manuscript of the 'Gondhla Kanjur.'" In *Text, Image and Song in Transdisciplinary Dialogue,* edited by Deborah Klimburg-Salter, Kurt Tropper, and C. Jahoda, 79–103. Leiden: Brill, 2007.

Thrangu Rinpoche, Khenchen. *Essentials of Mahamudra: Looking Directly at the Mind.* Boston: Wisdom Publications, 2004.

———. *King of Samādhi: Commentaries on the Samadhi Raja Sūtra and the Song of Lodrö Thaye.* Kathmandu: Rangjung Yeshe Publications, 1994.

———. *Moonbeams of Mahamudra: A Commentary on Tashi Namgyal's Classic Text on Meditation.* Boulder: Namo Buddha Publications, 1992.

———. *The Moonlight of Mahāmudrā: Volume III, Teachings from the Fourth Mahamudra Retreat at Big Bear.* Boulder: Namo Buddha Publications, 1995.

———. *The Moonlight of Mahāmudrā: Volume IV, Teachings from the Fourth Mahamudra Retreat at Big Bear.* Boulder: Namo Buddha Publications, 1995.

———. *A Song for the King: Saraha on Mahāmudrā Meditation.* Boston: Wisdom Publications, 2006.

———. *Songs of Nāropa: Commentary on Songs of Realization.* Boudhanath: Rangjung Yeshe Publications, 1997.

Torricelli, Fabrizio. *The Life of the Mahāsiddha Tilopa.* Dharamsala: Library of Tibetan Works and Archives, 1995.

Torricelli, Fabrizio and Āchārya Sangye T. Naga. "Chos drug and bKa'-babs bzhi Material for a Biography of the Siddha Tilopa." *East and West* 43, no. 1/4 (1993), 185–98.

Tuttle, Gary and Kurtis R. Schaeffer, eds. *The Tibetan History Reader.* New York: Columbia University Press, 2013.

van Schaik, Sam. *Approaching the Great Perfection: Simultaneous and Gradual Approaches to Dzogchen Practice in Jigme Lingpa's Longchen Nyingtig.* Boston: Wisdom Publications, 2004.

———. "The Great Perfection and the Chinese Monk: rNying-ma-pa Defences of Hwashang Mahāyāna in the Eighteenth Century." In *Buddhist Studies Review* 20, no. 2 (2003), 189–204. Updated: http://earlytibet.com/about/hashang-mahayana.

———. *Tibet: A History.* New Haven and London: Yale University Press, 2011.

———. *Tibetan Zen: Discovering a Lost Tradition: The Stories Told by the Dunhuang Cave Manuscripts.* Boston: Snow Lion, 2015.

Wallace, Vesna. *The Inner Kālacakra: A Buddhist Tantric View of the Individual.* Oxford: Oxford University Press, 2001.

———. *The* Kālacakratantra*: The Chapter on the Individual together with the* Vimalaprabhā. Treasury of the Buddhist Sciences. New York: American Institute of Buddhist Studies, 2004.

Wangdu, Pasang and Hildegard Diemberger. *dBa' bzhed: The Royal Narrative Concerning the Bringing of the Buddha's Doctrine to Tibet.* Vienna: Verlag der Österreichischen Akademie der Wissenschaften, 2000.

Willis, Jan. *Enlightened Beings: Life Stories from the Ganden Oral Tradition.* Boston: Wisdom Publications, 1995.

Yamamoto, Carl S. *Vision and Violence: Lama Zhang and the Politics of Charisma in Twelfth-Century Tibet.* Brill's Tibetan Studies Library 29. Leiden: Brill, 2012.

Index